The Limitless City

For my wife, Janis

The Limitless City

A Primer on the Urban Sprawl Debate

OLIVER GILLHAM

Aerial photographs by Alex S. MacLean

ISLAND PRESS

Washington • Covelo • London

Library of Congress Cataloging-in-Publication Data
Gillham, Oliver.
   The limitless city : a primer on the urban sprawl debate / Oliver
Gillham ; aerial photographs by Alex S. MacLean.
        p.   cm.
 Includes bibliographical references and index.
   ISBN 1-55963-833-8 (pbk. : alk. paper)
   1. Cities and towns—United States—Growth.   2. Metropolitan
areas—United States.   3. Suburbs—United States. 4. Land
subdivision—United States.   5. Regional planning—United States. I.
MacLean, Alex S. II. Title.
   HT384.U5 G55 2002
   307.76'0973—dc21

                                        2001007268
                                            CIP

Printed on recycled, acid-free paper ✿

Manufactured in the United States of America
09 08 07 06 05 04 03 02 8 7 6 5 4 3 2 1

Contents

Preface   xi

Introduction   xiii

PART I: UNDERSTANDING SPRAWL   1

Chapter 1: What Is Sprawl?   3
Characteristics and Indicators of Sprawl   3
Definition of Sprawl   8
What Makes Sprawl?   8
The Limitless City   17
Sprawl in Summary   22

Chapter 2: The Origins of Sprawl   25
Industrial Cities   25
Reform   26
The First Modern Suburbs   27
Automobiles and Roads   31
Post-War Suburban Expansion   36
Suburbanization and Cities   41
The Origins of Sprawl in Summary   45

Chapter 3: Reactions and Countertrends   47
Protesting the Highways   48
Cleaning up the Environment   52
The Importance of History   54
Resurgent Older Cities   57
Analyzing the Trends   61
Mounting Protest and Reaction   63
Reactions and Countertrends in Summary   65

PART II: THE SPRAWL DEBATE   67

Chapter 4: Outlining the Debate   69
In Defense of Sprawl   69
Why Is There Any Debate?   71
The Charges Against Sprawl   75
Pro-Development   78
Untangling the Sprawl Brawl   79

Chapter 5: Land and Habitat   83
Vanishing Landscape?   83
Natural Habitat   89
Land and Habitat in Summary   91

Chapter 6: Transportation and Energy   93
Traffic   93
Energy Consumption   105
Transportation and Energy in Summary   111

Chapter 7: Pollution and Public Health   113
Air Quality   113
Water Quality   115
Public Health   118
Pollution and Public Health Summary   121

Chapter 8: Economics and Social Equity   123
The Economics of Sprawl   123
Social Divides and Cities   132
Economics and Social Equity in Summary   142

Chapter 9: Aesthetics and Community   143
Sprawl and Aesthetics   143
Community   148
Aesthetics and Community in Summary   151

PART III: SEARCHING FOR ALTERNATIVES   153

Chapter 10: Growth Management and Smart Growth   155
Growth Management   155
What is "Smart Growth"?   156
Smart Growth Measures   158
Growth Management and Smart Growth In Summary   160

Chapter 11: Preserving Open Space   161

The Importance of Open Space   161
Open-Space Conservation Programs   164
Growth Boundaries   172
The Downside of Open-Space Conservation   175
Preserving Open Space in Summary   176

Chapter 12: Changing Development Patterns   179

Compact, Mixed-Use Developments   179
Revitalizing Older Downtowns and Inner-Ring Suburbs   186
The Density Issue   197
Changing Development Patterns in Summary   199

Chapter 13 : Viable Public Transportation   201

The Importance of Public Transportation   201
Local Public Transportation Initiatives   201
Metropolitan Transit Initiatives   202
Innovative Transit Technology   207
Barriers to Transit   208
The Land-Use Connection   209
Viable Public Transportation in Summary   210

Chapter 14: Regionalism   211

Expansion and Annexation   211
Recurrent Regionalism   212
Case Studies in Regionalism   215
Regionalism in Summary   234

PART IV: THE FUTURE AND CONCLUDING THOUGHTS   237

Chapter 15: Thinking About the Future   239

The Prospects for Change   239
Technology and Cyberspace   239
A Picture of the Future   246
Thinking About the Future in Summary   250

Chapter 16: Conclusion   251

The Suburban Pattern   251
A Willing Nation   251
Suburban Malaise   251
A Paradigm of Democracy   252
A Misuse of Resources   252

Increasing Pollution   252
Pushing for Transit   253
A Widening Gulf   253
Losing Open Space   254
Changing Growth Priorities   254
The Sprawl We Already Have   255
The Continuing Debate   256

Notes   259

Bibliography   283

Index   297

Preface

This book was already in production when terrorists turned two commercial airliners into guided missiles, destroying the World Trade Center in New York and killing thousands of people. Many Americans feel that the world has changed since that terrible tragedy. It is probable that we will not know the full extent of that change for many years. In this book you will find pictures taken before the event, and a discussion of the development of Battery Park City, which was evacuated as a result of the attack. Where possible, note has been made of the disaster.

A number of the major financial companies doing business in and around the World Trade Center have relocated across the river to New Jersey or elsewhere in the New York metropolitan area. Some may never return to Manhattan. Some of the people living in Battery Park City say that they are uncomfortable moving back. Meanwhile, discussion has emerged in the news media and on the Internet about the wisdom of building tall towers and the perils of urban concentration. It is possible that densely crowded urban communities may make better terrorist targets than the spread-out world of suburbia around them.

For millennia, cities have been planned with defense in mind. Densely concentrated, walled cities and towns were built that way partially for defense reasons. After World War II and the advent of nuclear weapons, atomic scientists counseled the wisdom of deconcentrating the nation's cities and industries, making them more difficult targets. This advice was part of the rationale used to justify the Interstate Highway Act that hastened the onset of suburbanization in America. As nuclear weapons proliferated and missiles became the delivery system, it became evident that nuclear war would mean total destruction. The shape of cities became less relevant to national defense. With the emergence of terrorism as a clear and present danger to the nation's cities, it is possible that America may return to the same defense-minded considerations that helped to drive suburbanization in the 1950's. Further suburbanization and deconcentration may be part of our response. It is impossible to know that now, and only time will tell if that is the way of the future.

This book would not have been possible without the help of many people. My wife, Janis Mones, has supported me in this endeavor in more ways than I can count. Without my agent, Deborah Grosvenor, this book might not exist at all. I also owe much to the very knowledgeable and patient Heather Boyer, the Island Press editor who worked very closely with me in developing the final shape of this project.

Many others have contributed in various ways , and I shall never be able to name them all. However, I will try to acknowledge at least a few. Specifically, I would like to thank the following people: Alex MacLean, for opening his library of superb aerial photographs to me; Paul McGinley of McGinley Hart and Associates, for providing my first education about downtown revitalization and historic preservation as well as supplying material on Newburyport; Wig Zamore of the Mystic View Task Force and Jeff Levine of the City of Somerville, for providing (occasionally differing) viewpoints and information about Assembly Square; David Dixon of Goody, Clancy and Associates and Larissa Brown of the Community Design Partnership, for persuading me to help out on the Regional Charrette for the New England Civic Initiative; David Dixon and Pat Sherman for providing information about Concord and Keene, New Hampshire; Rhett Lamb, planning director of Keene, also for providing information about Keene; and William Kuttner of Boston's Central Transportation Planning Staff for providing mode split and other transportation information for the Boston area.

I need to offer special thanks to Rebecca Barnes, formerly president of the Boston Society of Architects and now planning chief of the Boston Redevelopment Authority, for encouraging me to collaborate on writing the background literature for the Civic Initiative, for providing enlightened leadership of that same initiative (from which so many have learned so much), and for having many excellent ideas, some of which have made their way into this book. I would also like to thank Allegra Calder of the Lincoln Institute of Land Policy and Nancy Goodman of the Environmental League of Massachusetts, who provided some of the information in this project, and Jennifer Bradley of The Brookings Institution and Sara Savitt of Sprawl Watch Clearinghouse, for spending time with me and providing me with valuable information early in the process. Others who deserve recognition include Robert Stacey, formerly director of planning for Portland, Oregon, the only U.S. city with an elected regional government. I also received help from Richard Garver of the Boston Redevelopment Authority, who provided me with excellent background information and historic photographs of the redevelopment of Boston. Milone and MacBroom provided wonderful photographs of their restorative work on the Merritt Parkway. Dover/Kohl and Partners donated their terrific phased development concept for the Eastergate Mall in Chattanooga, Tennessee.

Cooper Carry and Carter Associates provided information about the Lindbergh Center in Atlanta. I don't know how I would have obtained graphic information about Boston's Urban Ring without the help of Claire Barrett and Associates.

Dom Nozzi (who also has an interesting website at http://user.gru.net/domz/index.htm) contributed an illuminating photo of Boulder's greenbelt. The Maryland Department of Planning and the Maryland Department of Natural Resources provided valuable maps of smart growth planning in Maryland. Mary Daniels, librarian for special collections at the Francis Loeb Library of the Harvard School of Design, was very helpful in obtaining some photographs. Margo Stipe of the Frank Lloyd Wright Foundation Archives was of great assistance in obtaining an image of one of Wright's perspectives of his planned Broadacre City. The Fondation Le-Corbusier provided permission for reproduction of that architect's work.

There are others, I am sure—as well as many who have helped indirectly. If I have forgotten anyone, I offer my most profound apologies.

OLIVER GILLHAM, AIA
Cambridge, Massachusetts

Introduction

The View from Thirty Thousand Feet

From a jet plane window, thirty thousand feet in the air, the intricate pattern of what many call "sprawl" can be startlingly clear. Huge expressways snake out over the land, generating a wide, loosely formed network across the world below (see Figure I.1). The system is punctuated at predetermined intervals by interchanges in cloverleaf, diamond, and other geometric forms that connect to a secondary network of arterial roadways lined with glittering commercial buildings. These, in turn, lead to a winding labyrinth of neighborhood roads, a web of capillaries connecting to the individual housing cells that make up most of the landscape below—a landscape stretching beyond the horizon.

The *Merriam-Webster Online Dictionary* defines the term *urban sprawl* as "the spreading of urban developments (as houses and shopping centers) on undeveloped land near a city."[1] Yet, as can be seen from the airplane window, the development below isn't necessarily anywhere near what one might think of as a traditional city. Every day, it looks more and more like something unto itself, spreading out ever farther into the countryside.

Even though it may be called sprawl, the whole pattern actually can seem well-ordered when viewed from above. The hierarchy of roadways is easily grasped as is the market-determined spacing of regional shopping malls. It is

Figure I.2. Remnant open spaces may be left between patches of new development. (Alex S. MacLean/Landslides)

easy for the eye to make out the leapfrog pattern of development, in which patches of farms, fields, and forests are left intact between new "pods" of subdivided and developed land (see Figure I.2). The few remaining farms and fields stand out while the checkerboard pattern fills in the last vacant squares. Both the land use separations and the various low-density patterns are obvious. From the air, the distinctions between residential, commercial, and industrial areas are easily understood while town, county, and state boundaries go unseen.

In the world below our jet plane, people are free to come and go as they choose in their own personal conveyances without depending on services with fixed schedules. If they don't like where they are, they can always move: to another subdivision, to a more rural environment, or even into one of the older cities. The suburban pattern we see is rooted in the very history and culture of the United States. It is the expression of U.S. democracy, individual rights, individual wealth, and the right to individual determination as expressed by this country's founders.

But the view from an airplane doesn't tell the whole story. Once on the ground, things can look very different (see Figure I.3). Here, one can become lost in a world of seeming sameness, where streets, stores, and houses make up places that could be anywhere in the United States—in Houston, Atlanta, San Jose, or somewhere out-

Figure I.1. When viewed from the air, the pattern of sprawl can be very clear. (Alex S. MacLean/Landslides)

Figure I.3. On the ground, things may appear less organized. (Oliver Gillham)

side Boston or Washington. Each place can seem a limitless city—a suburban continent stretching beyond the horizon. In this spread-out metropolis, it can be hard to find the features that define great urban places, such as generous public parks, walkable neighborhoods, and well-appointed civic gathering areas. While this suburban world seems to offer so much to so many, concerns increasingly arise about the environmental, economic, and social costs of this pattern of development. Meanwhile, some critics, such as James Howard Kunstler, are asking whether this pattern forms anything like a true community that contributes to the greater public good of the broader region (of which it is a part), or even to the welfare of its own future generations.[2]

On the other side of the issue, groups like the Reason Foundation argue that consumers know what they want and that it is our free markets that should ultimately define the public good.[3] Those same markets, it is argued, have given our country an unparalleled standard of living, and our suburbs are the ultimate expression of that lifestyle. If we believe that, then why should there be any change at all to the pattern that has characterized our nation's success for more than fifty years?

Just how real are all these concerns, anyway? Maybe what some call sprawl is the best city building that can exist in contemporary America. Clearly, it is extremely popular since so many people live in this relatively new form of urbanization. If the market dictates what should be built, and this is the market, then why should things be any different than they are? Maybe just a small crowd of discontented intellectuals believes this new world should be changed—and that people shouldn't be allowed

to have what they so obviously want, at a price that they can afford.

A Gathering Storm

In recent times, it has become harder and harder to believe that sprawl is simply of interest to only a small, well-lettered minority. What was once a fairly small trickle of attention has become a huge flood. With each passing day, the nation is deluged with headlines, articles, and sound bites on this issue. Search for "urban sprawl" on the Internet and you will find over three hundred thousand entries to choose from. The rhetoric has reached a fever pitch, and most of it is opposed to sprawl. This opposition supports *smart growth,* a concept variously defined that fundamentally (for most people, but not all) means changing the nation's predominant pattern of urban development so that the country can continue to grow without covering the landscape with expanding suburbs and crowded highways (see Figure I.4).

Fighting sprawl has become far more popular today than it was even two or three years ago. In 1998, there were more than 240 anti-sprawl initiatives at the ballot box, and 72 percent of those measures were approved.[4] By 1999, a Time/CNN poll showed that 57 percent of respondents nationally favored some sort control over sprawl, while state polls taken in California the same year showed that a growing percentage of voters there were concerned about sprawl.[5] Also in 1999, lawmakers introduced one thousand bills in state legislatures across the nation aimed at reining in sprawl.[6]

According to a poll conducted by Smart Growth America in September 2000, 78 percent

Figure I.4. Continuing development pressure on open space has helped fuel the debate about sprawl. (Alex S. MacLean/Landslides)

of those surveyed said they favor smart growth, while voter referendums and legislative action continue at a torrid pace. That kind of mounting opinion depicts of a great tide of anti-sprawl sentiment washing across the country. Polls and ballot box initiatives seem to shout out loud that the American people are increasingly demanding a change in the way their land is developed. One of the most extreme expressions of anti-sprawl sentiment occurred in December 2000, when the Earth Liberation Front (an ecoterrorist group) went so far as to set fire to several houses being built in a new subdivision in Suffolk County, New York. Spray painted messages on the houses read "Stop Urban Sprawl" and "If You Build It We Will Burn It."[7] While no one on either side of the sprawl debate condones such violent action, the incident does demonstrate how inflammatory the subject has become.

Bucking the rising tide of anti-sprawl sentiment were several turnabouts in the fall 2000 election results. Two major smart growth ballot initiatives went down to resounding defeat in Colorado and Arizona. In Colorado, a multimillion-dollar media blitz funded by the real estate industry and development groups warning of lost jobs, higher housing costs, and high-density communities was effective in getting a growth measure on the ballot (Amendment 24) defeated.[8] Arizona's ballot initiative suffered a similar fate. In Oregon, the state with the longest and most impressive track record for fighting sprawl, voters passed a state ballot initiative called Measure 7, which requires compensation to landowners whose property loses value as a result of zoning changes or growth boundaries.

"We're ten years behind the anti-sprawl forces," says David Bowes, executive vice president of the Cato Institute, a libertarian think tank. A wide range of other organizations— including the National Association of Home Builders, the National Association of Realtors, the Reason Public Policy Institute, the Heritage Foundation, the Cascade Policy Institute, and others—have started campaigns that they claim will debunk the smart growth movement.[9] In view of these movements, the *Wall Street Journal* recently saw fit to declare, "The sprawl debate has just begun."[10] Maybe they are right—maybe the debate has just begun—but the interesting part is that the issue has become popular enough to show up on the radar screens of the real estate and building industries, not to mention those of

conservative think tanks. Formerly, the road seemed so inevitable that it wasn't worth their while to bother with the small gathering of voices raised in opposition. Even though the anti-sprawl volume may be turned down in the current recession (as it usually is), it will almost certainly reemerge more quickly and forcefully when better times return. It has become an issue that can no longer be ignored.

Clouded Issues

As forceful as the anti-sprawl movement may have become, the issues remain as clouded as they have ever been. Although the rhetoric is impassioned, it is a fair question to ask whether any of us really understands what all the uproar is about. What exactly is sprawl anyway? The dictionary definition paints only part of the picture. Far more vivid images and descriptions can be found in books and articles on the subject. Multiple definitions of sprawl exist, given by different groups of people with different views on the subject.

It is difficult to wage a war against something that is not well understood. However it may be defined, the perception of the word *sprawl* is certainly negative, suggesting some sort of confused and unhappy wilderness. But whatever this new world is, can it really be so awful if it is so popular? After all, the expanding suburbs many people call sprawl are where the majority of our country lives and works—where most of our children are growing up. And what about the alternatives to sprawl, such as smart growth? Seventy-eight percent of the nation thinks they are for smart growth, but numerous definitions of this concept exist, too. Furthermore, the parties on either side of the debate cannot be easily identified. It isn't just real estate interests that are worried about the anti-sprawl movement. For example, Habitat for Humanity joined the fight to defeat Amendment 24 in Colorado out of concern that the measure would drive up the cost of land and make it difficult to provide affordable housing.[11]

Some scholars believe that all of this confusion may lead to a dangerous outcome. As Nicholas Retsinas, director of Harvard's Joint Center for Housing Studies, recently wrote in the *Boston Globe:* "Before we press city and town solons into vanquishing the-beast-that-is-sprawl, let us make clear what we are fighting lest we unwittingly foster a social landscape that is far worse than the current physical one of strip malls."[12]

The Purpose of This Book

The intent of this book is to try to clear up some of the confusion, to make some sense of the tangle of terminology and statistics, and to understand more clearly what it really is that we call sprawl and what, if anything, can be done about it. The book is organized into four parts, each of which examines different aspects of the sprawl question. Part I takes a look at what sprawl actually is, or what it has become, and provides a brief history of how we got to where we are. Part II sets out to determine the real impacts of sprawl on our environment, our resources, and our society. Part III examines the search for alternatives to sprawl, including the smart growth movement. Part IV ends the book with a consideration of what might happen in the future, a summary of some of the book's major points, and some concluding thoughts about the suburban debate.

This book is intended to introduce the reader to the issues surrounding sprawl so that informed and objective decisions can be made about future growth. In doing this, it tries to make an appraisal of what we call sprawl, its good and bad points, and the alternatives that are currently being advanced to change the way our nation is growing.

The Limitless City

PART I

Understanding Sprawl

Part I of this book is a quest to define and understand what constitutes sprawl. Chapter 1 provides a review of varying uses of the term, arriving at a broad contemporary definition of sprawl that will be used throughout this book. The chapter continues with an examination of the conditions that give rise to sprawl and shape its pattern, concluding with an assessment of how the rapid and continuing expansion of American suburbs has significantly changed the role of the nation's center cities.

Chapters 2 and 3 chronicle the history of sprawl in the United States. Chapter 2 tells the story of the national movement toward suburbanization from the nineteenth century to contemporary times. Chapter 3 recounts the reactions and countertrends to postwar suburbanization that emerged in the late 1950s, continuing through to the present day to form the framework for the current debate about urban sprawl.

CHAPTER 1

What Is Sprawl?

Images of urban sprawl are familiar to almost everyone. Smart growth groups often flash images of the nation's great urban centers erupting across the countryside in a devastating flow of superhighways, shopping centers, baking asphalt, and twinkling cars (see Figure 1.1). Our contemporary metropolitan areas have been widely described as a vast horizontal world of places and things that are accessible only through relentless driving.

These are the images that we read about in the work of James Howard Kunstler, Jane Holtz Kay, Andres Duany, and other well-known writers and urbanists vigorously protesting the ill effects of sprawl. Not everyone agrees, of course, that this suburban world is as negative as is often portrayed. And, as we shall see, it is a world that Americans have brought upon themselves willingly. Still, the rhetoric grows louder and more widespread each day, as more and more people decry the maze of crowded suburban expressways in which the nation has become lost. Even the supporters of the status quo no longer deny the existence of sprawl, but any consensus stops right there, because not everyone agrees about exactly what sprawl is.

Figure 1.1. The contemporary metropolis has been widely described as a vast horizontal world. (Alex S. MacLean/Landslides)

Characteristics and Indicators of Sprawl

Despite powerful imagery and deepening national concern, there is no single, clear and succinct definition of sprawl that is shared by everyone. Moreover, the idea of what constitutes sprawl has been known to change over time. The definition from the *Merriam-Webster Online Dictionary* that appears in the Introduction ("the spreading of urban developments . . . on undeveloped land near a city") actually dates from 1958.[1] The current *Encarta World English Dictionary* presents a subtly different, contemporary interpretation, stating that urban sprawl is "the expansion of an urban area into areas of countryside that surround it."[2] "Undeveloped" has become "countryside" (a word with more pastoral associations), while "city" has become "urban area" (a vaguer term that can include suburbs as well as city centers).[3] But the dictionaries aren't the last word on the subject. There are other definitions and descriptions offered by groups on both sides of the issue, and they vary from the subtle differences that can be found in dictionaries to much more extreme characterizations. The accompanying box provides a sampling of the different descriptions of what constitutes sprawl.

As can be seen from the box, descriptions of sprawl vary from simple portrayals of a transitional landscape to more suggestive characterizations of wholesale destruction of the nation's farms and forests. One thing that almost all of the definitions shown have in common is that they portray sprawl as essentially a suburban phenomenon—"beyond a city's limits," "transitional," or "on the urban fringe." It is also generally characterized as low density, favoring automobiles, and possibly "scattered," "unplanned," or "ad hoc" in its pattern.

One of the more widely accepted characterizations of sprawl (one that encompasses many of the attributes listed in the box) has been developed by Professor Reid Ewing of Florida International University, an architect of Florida's statewide growth management plan. His definition of sprawl is essentially a list of descriptors that has been used by groups working to curb sprawl (such as the Natural Resources Defense Council and the National Trust for Historic Preservation) as well as those defending the status quo (like the Reason Public Policy Institute). Ewing posits the following four forms of development as among the most widely cited characteristics of sprawl:

• Leapfrog or scattered development
• Commercial strip development
• Low density
• Large expanses of single–use development.[11]

Ewing goes on to note that one or more of these characteristics have been cited as descriptors of sprawl by a long list of widely regarded urban scholars dating back to 1957.[12] Still unsatisfied with this definition, Ewing names two additional "indicators" of sprawl, included in Florida's anti–sprawl rule, that he feels help to more accurately define the term:

• Poor accessibility
• Lack of functional (that is, public) open space.

Below, each of the characteristics and indicators cited by Ewing is explored in depth.

Leapfrog Development

Leapfrog development means exactly that: subdivisions, shopping centers, and office parks that have "leapfrogged" over intervening tracts of farmland or forest or both (see Figure 1.2). The result is a haphazard patchwork, widely spread apart and seeming to consume far more land than contiguous developments. Unless preserved or unbuildable, the remaining open tracts are usually filled in with new development as time

Figure 1.2. An example of leapfrog development. (Alex S. MacLean/Landslides)

Figure 1.3. A typical suburban commercial strip. (Alex S. MacLean/Landslides)

Figure 1.4. Typical suburban subdivision—approximate FAR 0.05 to 0.2. (Alex S. MacLean/Landslides)

progresses. Familiar to most people, this pattern characterizes many rapidly developing suburban and exurban fringe areas.

Commercial Strip Development

Commercial strip development is characterized by huge arterial roads lined with shopping centers, gas stations, fast-food restaurants, drive-thru banks, office complexes, parking lots, and many large signs (see Figure 1.3). Retail is configured in long, low boxes or small pavilions surrounded by multiple acres of surface parking. Landscaping is usually minimal so as not to interfere with parking and signage. The office complexes differ little from the shopping centers, but usually are a little taller. Sidewalks and pedestrian crosswalks are rare, and trips between different centers, on the strip are almost all by automobile. The concept of the strip is so famous that it has become an American icon, enshrined in Las Vegas and celebrated in the book *Learning from Las Vegas,* by architects Robert Venturi and Denise Scott Brown, as well as in such films as *American Graffiti.*

Low Density

In terms of density, sprawl is neither a crowded urban core nor an open countryside. It lies between the two in varying gradations. Compared to older city and town centers, the density of sprawl is very low indeed. Suburban buildings are often single-

story and widely spaced, with intervening parking lots and roadways. Sprawl is not a typical older city with solid blocks of eight- and ten-story buildings; nor is it a typical older Main Street of two- and three-story buildings. It isn't even a rural village of comfortably spaced single-family homes and stores. If present, tall buildings are often separated from one another by large areas of roadways and parking. The low-density patterns shown in Figures 1.4 are generally considered characteristic of sprawl development. Low-density and leapfrog patterns are both blamed for making sprawl both land consumptive and auto dependent.

Density can be defined several ways: by the number of people per acre or per square mile or by the number of dwelling units per acre or floor area ratio (FAR). FAR is the ratio of the number

Table 1.1. Relative Density of Top Ten Cities and Their Metro Areas—2000

	City		*Metro Area*	
	Population	Pop./mi^2	Population	Pop./mi^2
New York	8,008,278	25,925	21,199,865	2,085
Los Angeles	3,694,820	7,873	16,373,645	482
Chicago	2,896,016	12,747	9,157,540	1,321
Houston	1,953,631	3,619	4,669,571	606
Philadelphia	1,517,550	11,233	6,188,463	1,043
Phoenix	1,321,045	3,146	3,251,876	223
San Diego	1,223,400	3,776	2,813,833	669
Dallas	1,188,580	3,471	5,221,801	574
San Antonio	1,144,646	3,437	1,592,383	479
Detroit	951,270	6,858	5,456,428	831

Sources: U.S. Census Bureau, Census 2000 PHC-T-5, *Ranking Tables for Incorporated Places of 100,000 or More: 1990 and 2000,* Table 1; Census 2000 PHC-T-3, *Ranking Tables for Metropolitan Areas: 1990 and 2000; State and Metropolitan Data Book, 5th Edition (Washington, D.C.: U.S. Government Printing Office, 1998)*

Table 1.2. Selected Residential Densities

	Building Type	Dwelling Units / Acre	FAR
Rural	Single-Family, 100 Acres	0.01	0.0005
	Single-Family, 25 Acres	0.04	0.0018
Suburban	Single-Family, Acre	1	0.05
	Single-Family, Half-Acre	2	0.09
	Single-Family, Quarter-Acre	4	0.18
Urban	Townhouse	24	0.88
	3-Story Apartment	50	1.38
	6-Story Apartment	75	1.72
	12-Story Apartment	125	2.87
High-Density Urban	Townhouse	36	1.16
	3-Story Apartment	75	2.07
	6-Story Apartment	110	2.53
	12-Story Apartment	220	5.05

Note: The above data is based on an analysis of characteristic development in the Boston metropolitan region. This data is given for illustrative purposes only. Typical developments may vary significantly from the examples given depending on age of project, target market, setting, local codes, and other factors.

Figure 1.5. Farmland—approximate FAR 0.0005 to 0.002. (Alex S. MacLean/Landslides)

Figure 1.6. Typical New England village center—approximate FAR 0.2 to 1.0. (Alex S. MacLean/Landslides)

of square feet of built area to land area. Built area usually includes all floors of all buildings. Note that FAR takes account of built commercial space in an area while dwelling units and population do not. These different methods are appropriate to different scales of analysis. Population or employment per square mile is appropriate to the city and regional scale. Dwelling units and FAR are usually used for community and neighborhood scale. Table 1.1 displays the relative density of selected cities and their metropolitan areas in terms of population and population per square mile. Table 1.2 provides a comparison of selected rural, suburban, and urban residential densities in dwelling units and FAR. Figures 1.4 through 1.8 are photographs of different settings comparing approximate FAR.

Figure 1.7. Beacon Hill in Boston—approximate FAR 1.0 to 4.0. (Alex S. MacLean/Landslides)

Figure 1.8. Manhattan—approximate FAR 2.0 to 10.0+. Note: this photo was taken prior to the destruction of the World Trade Center(Alex S. MacLean/Landslides)

Single-Use Development

The low-density pattern of sprawl is often further characterized by the deliberate segregation of land uses. Housing consists predominantly of single-family homes on individual lots. While older downtowns may have a combination of stores, offices, and apartments all on one street—and sometimes on top of one another—such mixing of uses is rarely a feature of most post–World War II suburban areas. In these areas, different land uses are usually intentionally disconnected, sometimes by large distances. This separation is formalized through zoning and subdivision bylaws and the dictates of a compendium of widely used planning standards.

Poor Accessibility (or Automobile Dominance)

Low-density development combined with segregated land uses leads to what Ewing terms "poor accessibility." As he describes the situation: "Residences may be far from out-of-home activities, a state of poor residential accessibility. Or out-of-home activities may be far from one another, a state of poor destination accessibility. Both types of accessibility affect the efficiency of household travel patterns."[13]

Ewing believes that this characteristic is a good indicator of sprawl because it is measurable in terms of typical trip lengths, average trip times, vehicle miles traveled (VMT), and vehicle hours traveled (VHT)—the idea being that the longer trips and trip times become (the higher the number of VMT or VHT or both), the worse the accessibility situation becomes.

"Poor accessibility" arguably may be a somewhat judgmental term. Essentially, this indicator shows that the distances between suburban origins and destinations are relatively far, a consequence of low-density development and large expanses of single-use development. Implicit within these distances is another widely used gauge of sprawl: automobile dominance or auto dependency.[14] The longer distances between activities means that the only way to get around easily is by car. For this reason, many people list auto dependency not only as an indicator but also as a main characteristic of sprawl.[15] Compared to denser downtown environments, suburban sprawl offers relatively little transit, and often walking or biking between home and different activities can be very difficult.

Lack of Public Open Space

In ideal circumstances, the low-density residential pattern of sprawl can achieve the sought-after appearance of rustic cottages nestled in a leafy, parklike setting. It was this idyllic effect that the planners of some of the finest early suburbs tried to achieve (see Chapter 2). Yet, even in the best of situations, the parklike setting is rarely public. It belongs to individual homeowners as part of their yards and gardens. In other areas, much of the open space is taken over by paved parking areas that are also in private hands. The great malls may provide galleria-like "public" spaces, where crowds of shoppers gather, but again the malls are ultimately privately owned. Except around the school yard, public open space can be quite difficult to find in many suburban areas. This is another key indicator of sprawl: that it is, for the most part, an unbroken fabric of privately owned land divided only by public roads (see Figure 1.9).

Figure 1.9. Postwar suburbs can be an unbroken fabric divided only by public roads. (Alex S. MacLean/Landslides)

The major civic open spaces, parks, and commons that grace many older urban-core areas can be few to nonexistent in much of the nation's post-war suburban world.

A Definition of Sprawl

Having reviewed the principal characteristics and indicators of sprawl described by Ewing and accepted by many professionals in the field, it is now possible to propose a definition of sprawl that will be used throughout this book. It will be what a logician would call a connotative definition of sprawl—that is, an analytical definition by genus and difference, or by class and subclass.[16] In this kind of definition, sprawl is a type (or subclass) of urbanization (the broader class of urban development as a whole). As a subclass, sprawl has a set of distinct attributes that differentiate it from all other types of urbanization (for example, a city of crowded skyscrapers or a medieval hill town). Using the connotative method, we can translate Ewing's set of characteristics and indicators into a broad definition:

> *Sprawl (whether characterized as urban or suburban) is a form of urbanization distinguished by leapfrog patterns of development, commercial strips, low density, separated land uses, automobile dominance, and a minimum of public open space.*

This definition has no suggested connection with a nearby city center, which makes it a more accurate characterization of contemporary sprawl development patterns. (As we shall subsequently see, this form of urbanization can occur anywhere within or adjoining a metropolitan region, without any necessary connection to the core city.) The defining attributes of sprawl addressed earlier are also common to most types of late-twentieth-century suburban development. For this reason, we can add a secondary definition of sprawl:

> *Sprawl (whether characterized as urban or suburban) is the typical form of most types of late-twentieth-century suburban development.*

With this definition in hand, we can now explore the meaning of another very important term: *suburbanization*. The *Merriam-Webster Online Dictionary* defines suburbanization as "making suburban" or "giving a suburban char-

acter to."[17] Planners have sometimes used this term to describe the spreading of suburbs or suburban patterns across a region or a nation.[18] If we take this to mean specifically late-twentieth-century suburban development, then we can make the following definition:

> *Suburbanization is the spread of suburban development patterns across a region or a nation—that is, the proliferation of sprawl forms of urbanization across a region or a nation.*

The terms *sprawl* and *suburbanization* will be used interchangeably throughout this book.

What Makes Sprawl?

The aforementioned definitions of sprawl and suburbanization still do not tell the whole story. While we now have an idea of what sprawl looks like and what its principal traits are, we still don't know why it is the way it is or exactly what goes into its construction. While sprawl development owes its existence to many factors, it is important to understand four essential ingredients of suburbanization:

- Land ownership and use;
- Transportation patterns;
- Telecommunications technology; and
- Regulations and standards.

The sections that follow deal with each factor in turn.

Land Ownership and Use

Most of the land in the United States—about 70 percent—is privately held (see Figure 1.10).[19] Under American law, each parcel of land comes with a bundle of rights related to ownership, including water and air rights and the rights to sell the land, pass it along to heirs, use it, or develop it. These privately held entitlements give land value and marketability. As long as land remains privately owned—and its rights remain unencumbered—it is susceptible to being subdivided and built upon.

Land itself—along with the rights attendant to its ownership—can be bought and sold like any other commodity. Without a highly developed system of private land ownership and a viable market for land, sprawl as we know it would be virtually impossible. The concept of private land

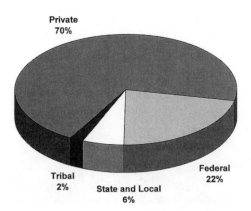

Private
70%

Tribal
2%

State and Local
6%

Federal
22%

Figure 1.10. Land ownership in the United States. *Source:* U.S. Department of Agriculture, Natural Resources Conservation Service, *1997 National Resources Inventory,* and the National Wilderness Institute.

ownership is the foundation upon which the private home is built. It wasn't always that way, however. Native Americans viewed the land as something held in common. It was the early settlers from Europe who brought the concept of individual land ownership to the United States.

With the arrival of the Europeans, land ownership quickly achieved great importance in the New World. Since then, it has remained a basic tenet of the American ethos that being a landowner is the key to being a successful, fully vested member of society. In fact, during the decades following the ratification of the U.S. Constitution, many states limited voting rights to landowners. Thus, you not only had to be a white male over age twenty-one but also had to own land to be counted as a real citizen. As Kenneth T. Jackson tells us in *The Crabgrass Frontier:*

> The idea that land ownership was a mark of status, as well as a kind of sublime insurance against ill fortune, was brought to the New World as part of the baggage of the European settlers. They established a society on the basis of the private ownership of property, and every attempt to organize settlements along other lines ultimately failed. The principle of fee-simple tenure enabled families to buy, sell, rent, and bequeath land with great ease and a minimum of interference by Government. It became . . . "the freest land system anywhere in the world."[20]

Today, the American Dream is still to own one's own home on one's own piece of land. More than two-thirds of Americans own their own homes, and many have most of their money tied up in that very investment—which is also their shelter.[21] Purchasing a home is often the biggest investment Americans will make in their lifetimes.

REAL ESTATE MARKETS

A colossal industry has been built around real estate, not only around simply buying and selling the land or its rights (or both) but also around deliberately increasing the value of the land by building on it. This is why most land gets developed: to increase its value and create wealth. Along with the basic bundle of entitlements, increasing land value is every landowner's right in America, just as making a profit is every individual's right whether that person owns land or not. The private ownership of land and the huge, almost liquid, market for it are vital to the very survival of suburban sprawl.

In 1997, the U.S. real estate industry produced revenues totaling over $240 billion.[22] That same year, related industry revenues for private construction totaled nearly $400 billion.[23] The size of the real estate and construction industries gives them significant influence in what gets built, where, and in what quantity. The real estate development industry delivers its products in response to demand—demand for houses, demand for offices, demand for shops, demand for hotel rooms, and so forth. Wheat fields in Kansas are wheat fields and not housing partly because of real estate markets. There is a smaller market for housing in the middle of rural Kansas than exists in a big metropolitan area, but there is a market for land on which to grow wheat. It is market demand that initially establishes what, where, and how much of everything gets built. The industry simply delivers the product.

But market demand is also determined to some degree by the product industry delivers. There was little demand for personal computers before the first one was invented and brought to market. Similarly, there was no recognizable market for indoor suburban shopping malls before the first one was built in Southdale, Minnesota, in 1956. When a successful formula like the indoor suburban shopping mall comes along, it can rapidly develop into a new market, exploding across the countryside. Financing feeds a growth industry, be it business or real estate. If a formula is successful and therefore profitable, it becomes easy to finance. The tendency is then to repeat the same formula many times, which partly explains the repetitiveness of suburban development. Single-family homes, shopping centers, and office parks in their current forms have been very successful models.

THE COST OF LAND

But sprawl would not have its current attributes if land were scarce and expensive. The existence of a large market for land development helps to explain U.S. patterns of urbanization overall, not just suburban sprawl. The unique pattern of sprawl can be partly attributed to the abundance and relatively low cost of land, which is necessary to allow dispersed, low-rise development to occur. Tall vertical cities like New York result, among other things, from the high cost of the land under the buildings. To justify the higher cost of the land, a developer has to build to a much higher density in Manhattan than in a typical suburban environment.

Why does land cost more in some center cities than it does in the suburbs? The higher cost can be traced to two factors: clustering and access. It is widely accepted that the monetary advantages of clustering (also known as the economies of agglomeration) are among the primary forces driving urbanization in general.[24] Businesses benefit economically by being able to shop for goods and services in a cluster. Furthermore, employees benefit from being able to shop for jobs in that same cluster and employers benefit from the large labor pool that results. The gathering of the labor pool in turn causes housing, stores, and other uses to be drawn into the resulting conurbation.

The second factor is access. Many cities originated by gathering around some major means of access to other, more distant markets in order to reduce transportation cost. Businesses originally needed to be as close as possible not only to one another, but also to a central import-export node, such as a harbor, river port, or rail station. This need reinforced clustering, which in turn drove up land cost and density. A typical result was the late-nineteenth- or early-twentieth-century U.S. manufacturing city with a high-density central business district gathered near port facilities and rail termini (see Figure 1.11).

The equation changes when access becomes much more widespread, as happened with the

Figure 1.11. Early high-density central business districts gathered near port facilities and rail termini. (Courtesy of the Francis Loeb Library, Graduate School of Design, Harvard University)

introduction of cars, trucks, and pervasive high-speed roadway networks. Widespread access means that cheap land far from any city center becomes a usable commodity for businesses and homes alike. Without a compelling need to cluster, homes and businesses will naturally begin to spread out (see Figure 1.12). As Terry Moore and Paul Thorsnes have written in *The Transportation/Land Use Connection:*

> Business firms . . . respond to land prices by spacing themselves as widely as possible. Spacing reduces competition for land which reduces its price. No other reasons (such as proximity to a port) exist to cause competition for land, and businesses reduce cost by occupying lower-priced land.[25]

What is true for businesses is also true for home owners. Reduced land cost means that

Figure 1.12. Modern suburban industrial parks are often spread out near highway interchanges. (Alex S. MacLean/Landslides)

single-family homes on relatively generous individual plots of land within commuting distance of work suddenly become an affordable commodity for many Americans. This demonstrates the very close relationship between land and transportation in defining modern patterns of human settlement. To have any worth, land must be served by some means of transportation, whether a transit stop, a highway interchange, or even just a lane or an alleyway connecting to a larger roadway system. When land is both accessible and inexpensive, building at much lower densities can be profitable. This combination is fundamental to sprawl development.

Transportation Patterns

Land and market forces alone could not establish the low-density membrane that characterizes sprawl. History and economics tell us that without a transportation system capable of serving this pattern, sprawl simply would not exist. Without automobiles and paved roadways, we would inhabit an entirely different world.

MODE CHOICE

Two major transportation factors determine development patterns: mode (or modal) choice and the physical layout or pattern of the transportation system itself (sometimes known as the transportation network). Mode choice refers to the availability of different kinds of transportation. Transportation modes consist of everything from walking to automobiles, railroads, boats, and air travel. When you travel from your home to work, what choices do you have for making the trip? Can you, for example, choose between walking, biking, driving, and riding public transportation? Sometimes a trip may involve multiple modes—for instance, driving to the train from home or taking a bus from the train to work. The transfer between each mode is called a mode change.

In the suburbs and beyond, mode choices typically are few. In many instances, the car is the only choice. When trip origins and destinations are highly dispersed over a wide area (the result of a continuum of low-density development), the private automobile is often the only adequate mode of transportation. When alternative choices are available, a discouraging number of different mode changes may be required. A traveler may have to change from bus to bus to rail and back to bus again. All things being equal, the more mode changes that are required, the greater the disincentive will be to choosing an alternative to the automobile.

Travel time and cost also affect mode decisions. Travel time may be influenced by congestion on the roadways or the number of transit stops. Cost may be affected by the cost of passage as well as by the availability of reasonably priced parking. The automobile can sometimes seem to be the least expensive mode due to the tendency to ignore both the cost of the car and the overall cost of the auto/roadway transportation system—even though that cost is actually quite substantial in both dollars and externalities (see Chapters 6 and 7).

Modal choices can vary significantly, depending on the kind of trip taken. Trips generally can be categorized as either local or long distance. Local trips (also referred to as daily trips) are less than 100 miles one way. These trips basically fall into two categories: (1)work trips or commuting (travel to and from work) and nonwork trips (errands, shopping, school, and so forth).

Local Work Trips

Commuting trips in contemporary suburbs are almost invariably beyond walking distance and mostly have been since the days of railroads and streetcars. In those cases where a major urban core or other high-density employment center is involved, bus or rail transit may be available for trip making, but a car may be needed to get to the train or bus. As suburban patterns develop farther and farther from major urban centers, the car becomes the only real mode choice for most commuter trips. More than 70 percent of all commuting trips in the nation have nothing to do with downtown; rather, they are to and from suburban and exurban destinations.[26] For this type of commuting trip, the automobile often is the only option.

Local Nonwork Trips

As with work trips, the car is usually the only choice for suburban nonwork trips because of the low density and horizontal separation of uses. This means that many basic errands are generally too far to walk, and the "trip-ends"—or origins and destinations—are too dispersed for any form of mass transit to make sense. These disparate origins and destinations do not usually lend themselves to any sort of fixed-route transit system. Bicycles might work, but because of lack of suitable roads, distance, weather, or other reasons, biking is often ruled out.

Furthermore, local trips may include a number of stops on each trip with varying numbers of people and bundles to be picked up or dropped off. This succession of stops is called trip chaining. A typical example might be a short journey where a parent takes a child to a music lesson and then drives on to drop off the dry cleaning, make a stop at a hardware outlet, and then do the grocery shopping. Interestingly, local nonwork trips are by far the largest segment of all travel. According to the U.S. Department of Transportation, nonwork trips make up more than 75 percent of total person miles traveled in the United States.[27]

Long-Distance Travel

In sheer numbers, the amount of local travel in the United States is overwhelming when compared to long-distance travel. More than 99 percent of all person trips made in the United States on all modes are local, accounting for more than 75 percent of all person miles traveled in the nation.[28] Thus, it is tempting to dismiss the contribution of long-distance travel in defining the pattern of sprawl as relatively trivial. This might be justified were it not for the issue of the central import-export node described earlier in this chapter.

In the early part of the twentieth century, long-distance passengers and freight accessed a typical city by means of one or more centrally located import-export nodes, such as a rail station or a port. This phenomenon reinforced the dense clustering of early-twentieth-century manufacturing cities. Roadways and airports have significantly changed that pattern. Cluster-

ing is still an urbanizing force, but highway interchanges and multiple regional airports have replaced rail terminals and harbors as primary import-export nodes, radically altering the geographic scale and pattern of clustering.

Today, about 83 percent of the value of all freight in the United States is shipped by truck and plane, while 97 percent of all passengers travel by air and by road when taking a long trip.[29] Ports and rail termini are still used for heavy bulk cargo, but almost all people and most valuable goods travel in planes, cars, and trucks. As suburbs have spread and air and roadway travel has increased, the center-city train depot has become increasingly less relevant. Long-distance trips are now more likely to be made from one suburban area to another, with the car being the only practical way to get to and from the airport at either end of the trip.

In the end, almost all contemporary transportation choices use the car somehow in the process. The car is often the choice for local trips, commuting, and long-distance travel (see Figure 1.13). Because automobile travel accounts for 92 percent of the total person miles traveled in the United States, the roadway system is by far the nation's foremost transportation network.[30] This means that auto-dependent development is basically self-perpetuating. Any new land development that hopes to succeed has to hook into the transportation pattern that connects everything else, which means extending the pattern of automobile dominance and limited mode choice.

THE TRANSPORTATION NETWORK

The nation's roadway network is one of the most powerful forces determining the shape of metropolitan regions across the United States. Railroad, water, and air transportation have

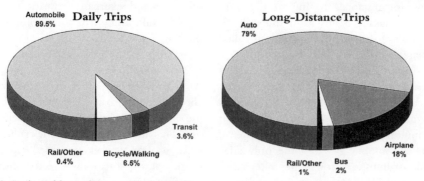

Figure 1.13. Daily and long-distance trips by mode.
Source: U.S. Department of Transportation (DOT), Bureau of Transportation Statistics, *Transportation Statistics Annual Report 1999* (Washington, D.C.: DOT, 1999).

never been able to match the access granted by roadways. Combine this omnipresent network with automobiles and trucks, and once-simple roadways are converted to a high-speed transportation system that often outmatches railroads in travel time and accessibility. Mode choice could never be so dramatically skewed toward the automobile if it were not for the universal presence of roadways. It is this vast network that has made decentralization possible on a truly gigantic scale. It also, to a very large extent, defines the look and feel of our suburban world. As James S. Russell recently observed in *Harvard Design Magazine:* "What unites suburbia is not shared public space, or a coherent architectural vision, but a vast civil-engineered network of roads."[31]

As noisy, congested, and chaotic as the nation's roadway system can appear, it actually possesses a very intricate hierarchical structure. Under ideal circumstances, all of its component roadways are designed to function together as a unified structure of greater and lesser arteries and veins—like the human circulatory system, only made to move vehicles instead of blood cells. As extensive as it is, the entire network ultimately comprises just a few distinct roadway types (see Figure 1.14). Together, this system of expressways, arterial roads, collector roads, local streets, and cul-de-sacs makes up almost the entire public environment of our suburbs.

But roads alone don't describe all of the system. All of the automobiles need someplace to park, and these parking areas define suburban sprawl as much as, if not more than, the roadway system. Garages, carports, and driveways adorn every contemporary residential subdivision, and shopping centers, malls, and office parks offer great fields of surface parking. Sometimes, these areas are landscaped but often only minimally to avoid blocking clear views of commercial signs. These areas could be designed differently (the cars could be—and sometimes are—placed underground or in structures), but surface parking is the most economical way to build parking as long as land is inexpensive enough. And, as we have seen, it is the roadway and car transportation system that has helped to make the cost of accessible land inexpensive enough to decentralize clustering patterns while at the same time leaving enough room to park most of the cars at grade.

Figure 1.14. (a) Expressway and interchange. (Alex S. MacLean/Landslides) (b) Major arterial road. (Alex S. MacLean/Landslides) (c) A typical network of arterials, collector roads, and cul-de-sacs. (Alex S. MacLean/Landslides)

Telecommunications Technology

Electronic telecommunications are rapidly transforming the world around us. As William J. Mitchell recently wrote in his foreword to Thomas Horan's *Digital Places:*

Digital telecommunications networks [will] transform urban form and function as radically as . . . mechanized transportation networks, telegraph and telephone networks and electrical grids [have] done in the past. These networks . . . loosen many of the spatial and temporal linkages that have traditionally bound human activities together in dense clusters, and they . . . allow new patterns to emerge.[32]

While Chapter 15 of this book does review current thinking on how telecommunications may affect future urban patterns, we cannot know for certain what kind of world will finally emerge from this new revolution. However, we can clearly see what electricity, telephones, and computers have already done.

ELECTRICITY

The electrical grid is as pervasive as the roadway system (in fact, it often follows it). This shared ubiquity has freed businesses and homes to locate just about anywhere and be assured of a power source to run the machinery necessary for modern living and commerce. Before the twentieth century, no such widespread infrastructure existed. The machinery that electricity runs includes much of the infrastructure of modern telecommunications, such as computers, remote telephones, modems, fax machines, printers, copiers, and the like. Without available electrical power everywhere, most of the machines of modern commerce would not exist, nor would the systems that run our homes.

Corporations could not do business in a low-density suburban environment without at least electricity and telephone. Initially, it was the telephone that greatly reduced the need for businesses to share a common location—such as a major city—in which communications are facilitated by proximity.

TELECOMMUNICATIONS AND COMPUTERS

Although telephones have been in existence since the end of the nineteenth century, the truly exponential advances in telecommunications and information systems have occurred only in the past fifty years. This technology revolution has made suburban sprawl possible on a scale that could never have been envisioned in the early twentieth century. The development of main-frame computers connected by telephone lines in the 1950s and 1960s meant that information could be readily and simultaneously shared by a network of remote facilities. Until then, major corporations had struggled to keep all of their operations under one roof to realize what economists refer to as "economies of scale of production."

Businesses realize economies of scale when the average cost of a unit of output (anything from a camshaft to a bank statement) falls as the total volume or scale of output increases. To realize these economies, businesses typically massed people and machines together under one roof. This phenomenon, together with clustering, has historically been one of the primary forces shaping urbanization by centralizing urban development.[33] For example, many service industry businesses once realized economies of scale by having everyone in one building in a big city. This meant paying a single rent check while simplifying management, information sharing, and communications. At the same time, the businesses were clustered near their customers and vendors, giving them ready access to both.

Together with roadways, cars, and airports, advances in telecommunications and computer technology have substantially changed how these forces work, allowing many companies to abandon older models and to decentralize, relocating major portions of their businesses to suburban locations or even to other parts of the country or overseas—wherever land or labor or both cost less. Many major corporations also realized that they no longer needed to have even their headquarters downtown. Now, the head office could move closer to the suburban homes of the CEO and other corporate officers, while links with customers and vendors could be handled electronically. Combined with roadways, automobiles, and airports, the growth of electronic telecommunications helps explain why more than 80 percent of the employment growth in the United States between 1980 and 1990 was in suburban and exurban locations—not downtown.[34]

WIRING THE HOME

Suburban housing owes much to telephone, radio, and television. The telephone allowed instant communication between worker and household, even if the worker was miles away, making it easier to manage business and domestic affairs in two locations. The spread of residential subdivisions far from any theater district or concert hall also has been helped considerably by radio and television. Countless channels of programming have brought entertainment right into the home. You no longer need to get in your car to go to the movies. By 2000, average daily household television viewing was approaching eight hours per day, the number of television sets was climbing toward an average of 2.5 per household, and more than 80 percent of American households owned a VCR. Between 1995 and 1998, the number of households connected to the Internet increased from less than 10 percent to more than 50 percent. Greater than 80 percent of the nation spends each evening watching television.[35] Thus, even suburban movie houses have had to transform themselves into huge multiplex entertainment centers to survive. The advent of home entertainment centers and digital TV and recording media may make further inroads into the cinema business.

THE INTERNET AND BEYOND

There is little question that modern information systems have vastly expanded the freedom of location in our society. Businesses and residences can now situate themselves practically anywhere. Employees don't even have to show up at the office to go to work anymore. The number of telecommuters (those who spend at least part of their days working from home via computer and telephone) quadrupled from 4 million to almost 16 million between 1990 and 1998.[36] By 2000, the number had jumped to nearly 24 million.[37] The fiscal 2001 appropriations bill for the U.S. Department of Transportation requires that every federal agency give at least 25 percent of its eligible workforce the option of working outside the office by fall 2001.[38]

The future of the retailing industry also may be changing as on-line retailing becomes more popular. Books, music, computers, and an ever expanding list of other items can now be ordered electronically on-line and sent via air express right to your door. The volume of "e-retailing," as it is called, increased at an annual rate of 67 percent from 1999 through the end of 2000.[39] Since then, there has been an industry shakeout, but people are still buying on-line. It is impossible to predict where all of this will ultimately lead, but these communications develop-

ments undeniably have given us more freedom than ever to choose where we live and work. It seems almost as certain that they have made decentralization increasingly easier.

Regulations and Standards

Another key factor that helps determine the final pattern of suburbanization is the battery of regulations, codes, and standards that govern development in communities across the United States. The result of a century-long interdisciplinary effort, this vast compendium of rules forms the "genetic code" of sprawl. Various parts of the compendium can be found in the subdivision regulations and zoning codes of most U.S. municipalities. Other segments can be found in the roadway manuals and standards issued by state and federal governments. Still other sections appear in the myriad privately published standard planning and design reference works for engineers, surveyors, planners, architects, and landscape architects.

These works set forth guidelines for minimum roadway widths, street patterns, parking layouts, lot grading, and many other items, right down to steps, curbing, and residential swimming pools. Although the patterns established by the genetic code can be very hard to make out from the monotony and chaos we see on the ground, they are very much a part of the suburban world around us. It is this genetic code that forms the pattern that we can see from the air, and it is this same compendium of rules, regulations, and standards that makes sprawl development in Georgia look just like sprawl development in California or New Jersey.

ZONING AND BUILDING CODES

As we have seen, the fact that land is private is fundamental to its development potential. How land gets developed—where and for what use—is largely determined by real estate markets. Even density and form are determined to some extent by market forces. But once the market for development has been established (or is on the way to becoming so), publicly regulated land use controls, or zoning, also can become a critical determinant in how land can be developed.

In most American communities where there is a market for new development, zoning controls land—and to some extent its value—by regulating both land use and density (see Chapter 2 for a brief history of zoning). Use districts are established together with height and bulk regulations, the number of units or square feet of building allowed per acre, and setbacks that buildings are required to observe from the street and from one another. Zoning can govern what landowners can build on their own land as well as clarify expectations about what can be built next door. For example, a home owner who decides to put an addition on a house may find that zoning controls the size and location of the new construction. The addition may be limited in height, square footage, how far it may extend toward the boundaries of the lot, and what its use may be. After market forces have been established, zoning can ultimately be a major factor in determining what any given development will consist of and what it will look like. Some early subdivisions were built in rural areas that had no zoning. As communities grew, zoning was often put in place with the endorsement of home owners for their own protection.

Without some sort of formal control over how land in a particular district is used, each landholder in the district is continually at risk from neighbors. If you invest in building a house, you don't know for sure that a tannery or a pulp mill won't get built next door someday. This is one reasons for controls: to provide reasonable expectations for the continued value of a given piece of land and thereby create a relatively stable marketplace. Regulations also exist to protect the public. Building a tannery or a pulp mill in the middle of a residential neighborhood can endanger public health and welfare. Crowding wooden residential structures too close together without adequate ventilation or emergency access can be both a health hazard and a fire hazard. Thus, zoning bylaws, subdivision regulations, and related codes continue to be considered necessary and effective for protecting public health and welfare.

In suburban areas, separation of land uses can be far more extreme than in older, urban-core areas. In older cities, compatible land uses are often mixed together. But, as Reid Ewing notes in his definition of sprawl shown earlier in this chapter, classic suburban zoning partitions all land uses into distinctly separate districts, which often are defined by roadways. Large arterial roadway and highway corridors, for example, are often zoned commercial or light industrial. Typically, industrial uses will be buffered from any

residential uses by roads, landscaping, and open spaces or by intervening commercial uses (or both). Commercial uses, in turn, are themselves buffered from adjoining residential uses, often by roadways and landscaped areas. While some contemporary planners may rue the extreme to which the separation of uses has been taken, it should be remembered that many people still prefer quiet residential streets with nothing but houses on them. To these people, dictating otherwise would disrupt the character of the neighborhood and threaten property values.

But the codes do not stop at simply separating uses. Frequently, they also distinguish between different varieties of the same kind of use. For example, housing is sometimes separated into multifamily and single-family detached housing or even into different kinds of single-family housing, usually based on lot size (for example, half an acre, one acre, or two acres per unit). It has been argued that such finer gradations may discriminate by segregating people by economic class, with the plots in large-lot zoning areas available only to wealthy people.

In many ways, horizontal zoning seems very rational, both from the private as well as the public perspective. Because it protects public health and welfare as well as property values, a lot of people support it. Yet, as we have seen, it is this very horizontal separation of uses—ruling out other possible outcomes—that helps to define sprawl. As Andres Duany, one of the founders of New Urbanism, writes in *Suburban Nation:*

> The problem is that one cannot easily build Charleston any more, because it is against the law. Similarly, Boston's Beacon Hill, Nantucket, Santa Fe, Carmel—all of these well-known places, many of which have become tourist destinations, exist in direct violation of current zoning ordinances. Even the classic American Main Street, with its mixed-use buildings right up against the sidewalk, is now illegal in most municipalities.[40]

Many contemporary land use codes have ruled out older, walkable cities and downtowns in favor of horizontally separated zoning districts—in other words, sprawl zoning. This is why you can't walk to a corner store; it's usually too far away. It is true that not everyone wants to live over a store, but Duany's argument is that current codes don't allow any choice in the matter.

On the other hand, lest zoning be blamed for too much, it is useful to observe that places like Nantucket and Beacon Hill have zoning bylaws and other regulations that actually work to protect their historic character and require that new development fit the existing pattern. Also note that a sprawling city like Houston, Texas, has no zoning. In theory, Houston could have built itself like Manhattan or Colonial Williamsburg, or even a medieval Italian hill town, but it did not turn out that way. Even without zoning, Houston exhibits many of the sprawl characteristics of other metropolitan areas. It is spread out and generally low density, ranking fourth in degree of sprawl (ahead of Los Angeles and Miami) out of twenty-eight metropolitan areas ranked by the Surface Transportation Policy Project.[41]

THE REQUIREMENTS OF FINANCE

To some degree, Houston makes up for its lack of zoning with other types of regulations, but market and financing factors have also helped fill the gap. As noted earlier in this chapter, markets help define real estate product and most housing, offices, and shopping malls require financing to get built. In the case of housing, much of the financing takes the form of residential mortgages. Many home mortgages are guaranteed by government agencies who, over the years, have developed their own preferences and standards for what should be built (see Chapter 2). Those standards are reflected in many contemporary zoning codes and contribute to the genetic code of suburban development written into the manuals of many design and development professionals and sometimes even into covenants contained in the deeds of various projects.

The banks and insurance companies that finance many suburban commercial and residential projects have similar standards. Their requirements can dictate the size of the project, the uses that may be included, the number of parking spaces needed, and even the materials to be used in construction. To finance, build, and sell their real estate products, developers in places like Houston have had to follow many rules established elsewhere—just as if the missing suburban zoning were in place. Figure 1.15 shows examples of typical suburban commercial developments arising from market forces, land-use regulations, and design standards.

Figure 1.15. (a) Shopping centers are a classic modern suburban retail form. Note the hallmark fast-food restaurants and banks closest to the roadway and the large expanses of surface parking. (Alex S. MacLean/Landslides) (b) Regional shopping malls are a second major suburban retail form. They are usually sited to attract regional rather than local shoppers. (Alex S. MacLean/Landslides) (b) A typical suburban office park—sometimes associated with nearby shopping centers and malls. (Alex S. MacLean/Landslides)

The Limitless City

The dictionary definition of urban sprawl presented in the Introduction implies that sprawl emanates from a nearby city. Sprawl is fundamentally suburban in origin, and a suburb, as its name would suggest, is supposed to be subordinate to a city. That meaning is encapsulated in the *Webster's New World Dictionary* definition of a suburb: "a district, especially a residential district, on the outskirts of a city."[42] In 1966, when that definition was written, it was a fairly accurate characterization of the situation. From 1920 until the mid-1960s, big industrial cities were the nation's dominant centers of population and employment, the economic engines where most Americans lived and worked.[43] In that era, suburbs resembled the dictionary definition: generally less populated outlying residential areas that served as bedroom communities for the big cities. (Los Angeles, a polycentric city almost from the beginning, was a clear exception.)

Beyond Suburbs

Since the 1960s, however, that situation has changed dramatically. At the dawn of the twenty-first century, more people live and work in suburbs than live and work in the nation's center cities. The statistics are revealing: slightly over 8 million people live within the city limits of New York City, but that is only 40 percent of the over 20 million people estimated to live in the total New York Consolidated Metropolitan Statistical Area (CMSA) defined by the U.S. Census Bureau.[44] The same is true of Boston, where almost 5.5 million people inhabit the CMSA but only 1.5 million live in the Boston urban-core area.[45]

What is true of New York and Boston is true of the nation. In 1950, nearly 60 percent of the nation's metropolitan population lived in the center city (see Table 1.3). By 1990, the balance had shifted markedly and more than 60 percent of the U.S. metropolitan population lived in suburban areas outside the center city (see Table 1.3 and Figure 1.16).[46] By now, that figure has

doubtless climbed higher.[47] Even though the year 2000 census shows population gains in cities like New York, Chicago, and Boston, it also shows that population has increased at a far more accelerated rate in suburban areas surrounding those same cities.[48] It is estimated that, if current trends continue, about four-fifths of nation's growth in the decades ahead will be in the suburbs—and that means a growth in employment as well as in population.[49]

During the 1970s, 95 percent of the nation's population growth and 66 percent of job growth were in the suburbs. During the 1980s, all of the nation's population growth was in suburban and exurban areas along with more than 80 percent of employment growth. By 1990, 62 percent of the nation's jobs were in suburban and exurban locations.[50] Suburbs are also where the money is. By 1995, the median income in our older, urban-core areas was $29,000, while in what used to be the nation's suburbs, the median income was nearly $41,000—more than 40 percent higher than in the cities.[51]

What is true of jobs, population, and income is also true of construction. As Joel Garreau has said in his book *Edge City: Life on the New Frontier:* "Americans are creating the biggest change in a hundred years in how we build cities. Every single American city . . . is growing in the fashion of Los Angeles."[52] In America today, single-family detached housing (that is, suburban housing) comprises more square feet of floor space than all other building types combined.[53] Between 1979 and 1999, new office space in the suburbs was constructed at triple the rate of that being built in U.S. central cities.[54] These simple facts demonstrate that, over the last few decades, far more construction has occurred in the nation's suburbs than in the cities.

These statistics and commentary highlight

Table 1.3. Center City and Suburban Population, 1950–2000 (In Millions)

	1950		1960		1970		1980		1990		2000	
	Pop.	%	Pop.	%	Pop.	%	Pop.	%	Pop.	%	Pop.	%
Center City	49.7	59	58	51	63.8	46	72.4	42	77.8	40	85.4	38
Suburbs	35.2	41	54.9	49	75.6	54	99.3	58	114.9	60	140.6	62
Metropolitan Total	84.9	100	112.9	100	139.4	100	171.7	100	192.7	100	226	100

Source: Alan E. Pisarski, *Commuting in America II: The Second National Report on Commuting Patterns and Trends* (Landsdowne, Va.: Eno Transportation Foundation, 1996).

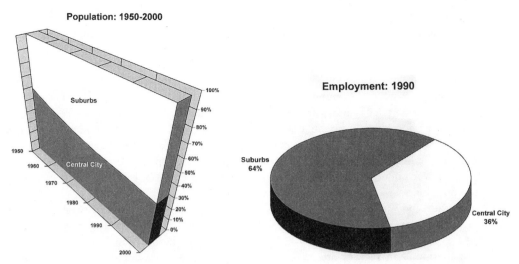

Figure 1.16. City and suburban population and employment.
Sources: Alan E. Pisarski, *Commuting in America II: The Second National Report on Commuting Patterns and Trends* (Landsdowne, Va.: Eno Transportation Foundation, 1996); and the U.S. Census Bureau.

the fact that suburbia doesn't really seem to fit its dictionary definition anymore. As Michael Pollan wrote in the *New York Times Sunday Magazine,* suburbs are no longer "sub" to any "urb":

> "Urban sprawl" might be a better term. Certainly sprawl hints at the centerlessness of it, "urban" at the fact that there's nothing in the city you can't find here. And maybe, as some have suggested, that is what [we're] looking at but can't quite see: a new kind of city, one we still don't have the words or name for.[55]

Metropolitan Nation

Suburbia has so vastly outgrown our older cities that many urban planners and economists have come to recognize that the old distinctions are not as meaningful as they once were in determining what drives the nation's economy and defines society. Cities or suburbs no longer matter as much as do "metropolitan regions." To quote Robert Yaro, executive director of New York's Regional Plan Association:

> It is now widely recognized that the nation's metropolitan regions are its basic economic units. The largest of these places are incubators of new technologies and industries and centers of American culture, communications, and media. They are the crucibles in

which the new American society of the early twenty-first century will be formed from the swelling ranks of immigrants and native-born Americans who live in them.[56]

Our once-great industrial cities have become subsumed into sprawling conurbations that cover hundreds and even thousands of square miles (see Figure 1.18).[57] Metropolitan regions like Los Angeles–Riverside–Orange County don't even have a single dominant city center. They are polycentric. Predominantly suburban in geography, population, and employment, these urbanized areas are spread out like no metropolis has ever been before. Just as Manhattan is vertical, the new metropolitan region is flattened out beyond the horizon. Where the elevator made possible the skyscraper, so the automobile has enabled a new horizontal metropolis.

The nation's metropolitan regions have grown so quickly and spread so far that they have become multijurisdictional, overspreading city, town, county, and even state borders. When communities within a metropolitan region increasingly share more in common, the political boundaries created in earlier times can become quite transparent. As Bruce Katz and Jennifer Bradley of the Brookings Institution recently wrote in an article for the *Atlantic Monthly:*

> People work in one municipality, live in another, go to church or the doctor's office or the movies in yet another, and

all these different places are somehow interdependent. Newspaper city desks have been replaced by the staffs of metro sections. Labor and housing markets are area-wide. Morning traffic reports describe pileups and traffic jams that stretch across a metropolitan area. Opera companies and baseball teams pull people from throughout a region. Air or water pollution affects an entire region, because pollutants, carbon monoxide, and runoff recognize no city or suburban or county boundaries.[58]

Most metropolitan regions are an elaborate mosaic of individual cities, towns, and villages, each with its own social, economic, and educational facilities. But, like a mosaic, each of these individual communities is part of the larger whole, set into a regional matrix of political, economic, infrastructure, and ecological systems. All regional communities share and depend upon this matrix for their well-being. Yet, even with these shared regional interests, only some cities have managed to keep up with this fact by continually annexing adjoining territory. For many older urban areas, annexation simply is not a viable option (see Chapter 14). This results in outdated jurisdictional boundaries in many areas, creating some of the allegedly more intractable problems of sprawl.

LOCAL AND REGIONAL TENSION

Older political boundaries persist in part because many localities still place great value on their independence, even though advancing suburbanization has made them an intimate part of a greater metropolitan region. Many people in the metropolitan United States still view themselves as residents of small, autonomous towns with little or no real connection to any larger region. Local determination is a proud American tradition dating back to the town meetings of colonial times, which are still the prevalent form of municipal government in places such as New England. Home rule invites local participation, offering many people a framework for a rich community life. Thus, home rule is widely perceived to be a good thing, even though it can sometimes result in haphazard municipal boundaries and fragmented political structures.

The tension between home rule and the regional nature of the nation's metropolitan areas

is one of the most compelling characteristics of sprawl, as well as an engine that helps drive its continued spread. The self-perpetuating contest between different jurisdictions for commercial tax dollars to offset residential tax expenditures produces ever more shopping centers and office and industrial parks. New commercial development creates new employment, which in turn generates demand for more housing, which drives the need for more commercial tax dollars, and so on.

Because it is a regional phenomenon, sprawl development not only leapfrogs tracts of property but can also leapfrog entire municipalities, reacting to development controls in one community by sprouting up next door, in another town or county. While one town may turn down a major store or shopping mall on the grounds of community preservation, the town next door may roll out the carpet for the same project. Similarly, a new office park may generate new taxes for one locality but result in tax-draining, new residential subdivisions and schools in an adjacent community.

In the heat of this competition, local jurisdictions are sometimes unwilling or unable to accommodate such larger, areawide needs as affordable housing, infrastructure improvements, and regional land use controls within their boundaries, thus perpetuating the spread of sprawl while ensuring the continued existence of some of its main detractions. A related, familiar issue is dwindling urban resources in the face of suburban prosperity. Even though the city may remain a key part of the regional image and economy, suburban localities are not usually willing or eager to share their revenues with other jurisdictions. Furthermore, the endless quest for new suburban commercial development often draws still more resources out of the city.

Beyond Metropolitan

In 1915, urban planner and regionalist Patrick Geddes predicted that America's northeastern cities would eventually flood over the landscape, depleting the urban cores, and that "the not very distant future will see practically one vast city-line along the Atlantic Coast for five hundred miles."[59] What may have seemed like science fiction eighty-five years ago seems a lot closer to becoming reality today. Figure 1.17 shows how

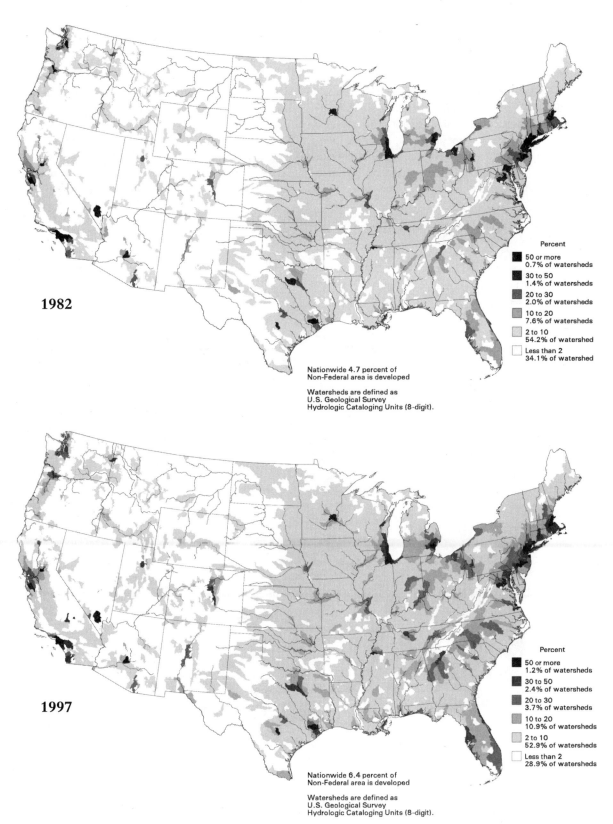

Figure 1.17. Developed land in the United States in 1982 and 1997.
Source: U.S. Department of Agriculture, Natural Resources Conservation Service, *1997 National Resources Inventory.*

rapidly urbanization spread across the nation in just fifteen years. This change is also reflected in the U.S. Census Bureau's map of metropolitan areas displayed in Figure 1.18.

Metropolitan areas are not necessarily composed entirely of urbanized area as defined by the U.S. Census Bureau (area having a density of at least one thousand people per square mile). They are essentially functionally related regions containing large population nuclei and adjacent urbanized communities "having a high degree of economic and social integration."[60] In other words, some metropolitan areas can be a patchwork of urbanized area and as yet undeveloped land. Others, such as New York, Chicago, and Philadelphia, contain more than one thousand people per square mile throughout the entire region.

The Census Bureau maps in Figure 1.18 depict America's northeastern cities as a chain of regional metropolitan areas, linked together along the Eastern Seaboard.[61] As we can see from the maps, the Northeast is not alone. The same thing has hap-

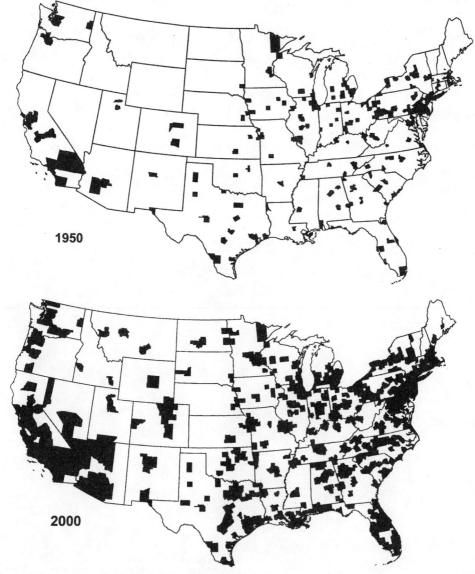

Figure 1.18. Metropolitan regions of the United States in 1950 and 2000.
Sources: U.S. Census Bureau mapping from 1999 Country Based Metropolitan Area Page Size Maps (see www.census.gov/geo/www/mapGallery/macbpage.html) and U.S. Census Bureau mapping as presented in Jean Gottman, Megapolis: The Urbanized Northeastern Seaboard of the United States (New York: The Twentieth Century Fund, 1961), 44.

pened to the nation's midwestern, southern, and West Coast cities. The Los Angeles–Riverside–Orange County metropolitan area flows south as far as Mexico and north to Santa Barbara and beyond. San Francisco–Oakland–San Jose spreads west to Sacramento-Yolo and south to Salinas. Chicago-Gary-Kenosha stretches east toward Detroit/Ann Arbor–Flint and north to Milwaukee-Racine. Seattle-Tacoma reaches out toward Salem-Portland, and so on. The nation's metropolitan regions are extending beyond their own limits to merge with other regions, perhaps to form even larger units in the future or maybe to redefine the meaning of the terms *metropolitan area,* changing anew the scale in which we view urban sprawl. Perhaps it was a vision such as this that prompted Lewis Mumford to write in 1961 that "the whole coastal strip from Maine to Florida might coalesce into an almost undifferentiated conurbation" composed of "undifferentiated urban tissue, without any relation either to an internally coherent nucleus or an external boundary of any sort."[62]

Sprawl in Summary

Urban sprawl traditionally has been viewed as a suburban phenomenon, something that happens as an urbanized area spreads into undeveloped countryside. This spreading of development can be further characterized by leapfrog patterns, commercial strips, overall low density, large areas of single-use development, and a heavy reliance on automobiles for transportation. With these characteristics, sprawl can largely be equated with what the nation has called "suburbia" since at least the 1950s.

American attitudes toward the private ownership of land combined with market forces and a large industry in real estate and construction are preconditions to sprawl, just as they have been for much of the nation's urbanization. But it is inexpensive land—made so by the proliferation of automobiles and roads—that makes the low-density pattern of sprawl so widespread. Automobiles and roads have redefined the so-called economies of agglomeration or clustering, allowing businesses and residents alike to scatter widely. At the same time, reliance on the automobile reinforces low-density, single-use development patterns by ruling out many other transportation modes, basically compelling further expansion to be equally dependent on cars and roads.

Pervasive power and communications networks aided roadways and automobiles in redefining clustering. At the same time, these networks also changed the meaning of economies of scale, freeing businesses from the need to operate under one roof and freeing employees from the need to be in a central workplace. In these ways, both power and communications networks have helped foster low-density suburban patterns.

Although land, markets, automobiles, and communications networks form the framework of sprawl development, a regulatory environment of codes and standards act together with financial practices to create the finished product. These regulations, standards, and practices largely determine the shape, size, and configuration of the land subdivisions, houses, cul-de-sacs, parking lots, and strip commercial buildings that make up our sprawling suburbs.

But our suburbs are no longer suburbs in the strict sense of the word. Cities and suburbs together create the contemporary metropolitan regions that are now the fundamental economic units of our society. Within these metropolitan regions, our suburbs are bigger in geography, population, and employment than our cities. Our metropolitan regions are dominated by what we call sprawl, as we have now defined it: *a form of urbanization distinguished by leapfrog patterns, commercial strips, low density, separated land uses, automobile dominance, and a minimum of public open space.* We have defined the spread of this pattern throughout a region as suburbanization. Through suburbanization, sprawl can extend over thousands of square miles, encompassing many different political jurisdictions left over from an era before metropolitan regions became the dominant centers of our nation. Thus, sprawl is often politically fragmented, with different cities, towns, and even counties setting their interests before those of the broader region of which they are a part. This tension between home rule and regional interests has become a defining characteristic of our sprawling metropolitan regions.

Lastly, our metropolitan regions are getting bigger and more spread out everyday, merging into one another, forming areas of urbanization that now stretch across thousands of square miles. This is what urban sprawl has become: a city without limits. How did we come to this pass? That question is addressed in Chapter 2.

CHAPTER 2

The Origins of Sprawl

To fully understand what sprawl is, it is necessary to know something of its origins and history to the present day.[1] Suburbs are not a new phenomenon. They have existed together with cities for thousands of years. In his landmark work *The City in History,* the famous urban scholar Lewis Mumford tells us that "the suburb becomes visible almost as early as the city itself." [2] Mumford notes that the first archaeological evidence of suburbs dates back to ancient Ur in Mesopotamia and that suburban villas are evident in early Egyptian paintings and funerary models.

However ancient suburbs may be, it is safe to say that modern suburban sprawl is far different in scale and character than the suburbs of antiquity. The principal differences are due mostly to vast changes in industry and technology that have taken place in just the past 150 years. We owe our contemporary version of suburbs and sprawl to the industrial revolution of the nineteenth century. It was the rapid growth and change of cities brought about by the industrial revolution that brought us the modern suburb. Factories, mills, mass production and, above all, new forms of transportation and communication have led us to where we are today.

Industrial Cities

From the mid–nineteenth century until about 1950, the industrial revolution transformed America from an agricultural economy to one based on large-scale manufacturing.[3] At the beginning of the 1800s, more Americans lived on farms than in the nation's cities. The onset of the industrial revolution brought about a great shift in population, drawing people from farms into burgeoning cities. By 1920, more Americans dwelled in cities than on farms.

The cities contained the big companies and factories as well as all the services that catered to them. In some cases, factories chose to locate in preexisting cities, such as New York, that had a central import-export node—generally a major harbor connected to a river system—as well as a labor pool already in place. Lowell, Massachusetts, on the other hand, was built from scratch at a confluence of rivers that offered both a source of power and the potential for transportation. Wherever the factories started up, people came in droves, attracted by relatively high manufacturing wages and the promise of a better life than what the farm offered. As the labor pool expanded, more factories were attracted, drawing in more people, and so on.

In mid-nineteenth-century America, factories and their workers existed in close proximity because affordable transportation to and from work (or to anywhere else for that matter) was limited to walking. Only the wealthy owned carriages, horseless or otherwise. Industry later would give birth to mass transportation, but initially, most people walked.

From its onset, the industrial revolution and the vast urban migration that it sparked radically altered the character of the city. In Lewis Mumford's words:

> Large-scale factory production transformed the industrial towns into dark hives, busily puffing, clanking and screeching, smoking for twelve and fourteen hours a day, sometimes going around the clock. . . . Extraordinary changes of scale took place in the masses of buildings and the areas they covered: vast structures were erected almost overnight. Men built in haste, and hardly had time to repent of their mistakes before they tore down their original structures and built again, just as heedlessly. The newcomers . . .

Figure 2.1. An industrial-era city in Pennsylvania. (Library of Congress, FSA-OWI Collection)

crowded into whatever was offered. It was a period of vast urban improvisation: makeshift hastily piled upon makeshift.[4]

Industry wrought terrible environmental and social chaos on the cities. Pleasant, mercantile settlements were suddenly overwhelmed by the industrial tide. Factories and rail yards were jammed together with shoddily constructed housing, ignoring the need for light and fresh air. City dwellers were deafened and choked by the roaring fumes of rail and industry both day and night. The new workers were crowded together in abysmal living conditions presenting serious fire hazards. The city became an ugly place to live (see Figure 2.1). Much of Charles Dickens's lifework was devoted to writing about the horrors of life in the industrial city. As the nineteenth century became the twentieth, social reformers such as Jacob Riis photographed the squalid living conditions of the immigrant factory workers, and as the public's attention was caught, a counterrevolution of sorts began.

Reform

The counterrevolution took two different forms. First was the reform of the cities; second was the start of the first modern suburbs. Both forces combined to create sprawl. In the cities, two things happened: (1) the advent of zoning and (2) the City Beautiful Movement.

Early Zoning

The first zoning ordinance in the United States was put into effect in New York City in 1916.

The New York code provided regulations for building size and use within given districts. During the next twenty years, 85 percent of the cities in America adopted zoning ordinances. These new codes were intended to bring light and air back to the city streets and homes and to bring some order to property values by providing assurance about what might be built next door.

One of the main innovations of zoning was the separation of land uses into "zones" or "districts." This separation meant that, in theory, factories and rail yards were confined to "industrial zones" and houses and apartments to "residential zones," the intent being to keep incompatible land uses apart so that city dwellers would no longer be forced to live next door to noxious and, in some cases, toxic factories.

As zoning has evolved, continued refinements in gradations of land use, combined with enforced low density, have caused it to be blamed for sprawl development (see Chapter 1). Jane Jacobs, in her famous work *The Death and Life of Great American Cities,* also blamed single-use zoning for disrupting the mixed-use vitality of dense cities such as New York.[5] Despite these flaws, few people dispute the improvement that zoning initially made to the cities of the industrial revolution. What is questioned is the later application of the first urban regulations to suburban development and postindustrial American cities.

The City Beautiful Movement

Another important occurrence was the City Beautiful Movement, which was sparked by the dirt, grime, and overcrowding that industry had brought to the cities. Starting in the late 1800s and fueled by the World's Columbian Exposition in Chicago in 1893, the City Beautiful Movement strove to create new civic monuments and great public open spaces in the industrial warrens of the cities. The movement and others like it succeeded admirably, giving us such great works of urban design as the monumental core of Washington, D.C., and the Charles River Reservation in Boston as well as many other well-respected works of civic architecture and park design throughout the nation. A principal thrust of the movement lay in bringing light, air, and green space back into the city. In an era of little-understood diseases, these elements were considered absolutely essential to the health and well-being of the general populace.

Greener Pastures

The same concerns about the wholesomeness of wide-open spaces, sunlight, and fresh country air were reflected in a parallel movement: the development of the first modern suburbs. Starting in the 1840s, as industrialization of the cities became pronounced, an ever more idealized view of the outdoors began to emerge. Although industry had been considered a threat to the bucolic image of the United States since Thomas Jefferson's time, the period of 1840 to 1860 produced a tremendous outpouring of literature and sentiment on the subject.[6] It was during this period, for example, that Thoreau published *Walden* and that a steady flow of publications emerged on suburban cottages and landscaping.[7] America began to yearn for homes in the healthful and wholesome countryside. This desire became a quest for a new Eden, an idyllic paradise of garden cottages far removed from the smoke and din of the industrial city.

The First Modern Suburbs

Ironically, it was one of the noisy, smoky creations of the industrial era that made modern suburbs possible: the steam locomotive. The first American exodus was carried out to greener pastures on rails of steel.

Railroad Suburbs

The communities created by the railroad during the late nineteenth and early twentieth centuries included the largely experimental suburbs of Llewellyn Park in New Jersey, Riverside outside of Chicago, and Garden City in Long Island. But it was not long before the railroad created some of the most successful suburbs in America, including Chestnut Hill and Brookline in Massachusetts, Forest Hills Gardens and Bronxville in New York, Lake Forest and Oak Park in Illinois, and the string of communities that make up Philadelphia's Main Line. Some of these early suburbs were designed by such renowned designers as Frederick Law Olmsted and Calvert Vaux, the designers of Central Park in New York City and major urban parks across the nation. As park designers first and foremost, Olmsted and Vaux visualized their new suburbs as cottages in a park. Winding streets, generous lots, compatible architecture, and sumptuous landscaping were all combined to realize the desired outcome (see Figure 2.2).

Figure 2.2. A late-nineteenth-century railroad suburb in Newton, Massachusetts. (Oliver Gillham)

These first suburbs were not built for the masses. They were, for the most part, fairly exclusive enclaves, intended only for those who could afford to live there, and the "cottages" were more like mansions. This exclusivity added a special cachet to the idea of dwelling in the suburbs right from the start. The suburbs became a place you could go when you had made enough money to get out of the city. Perhaps it was during this period that the suburban home started to become a coveted symbol of having "arrived."

Studs, Nails, and Gingerbread

But suburbs wouldn't be for the rich alone for very long. Rapid innovations in both housing construction and transportation in the late 1800s were to make suburban living an affordable option for more and more people. A revolution in wood construction allowed the first industrialized production of housing, making it possible to match the pace of expansion of the new rail transportation systems. Prior to 1840, most wooden construction consisted of post-and-beam building techniques, in which heavy timbers were joined together to form the structural frame of the house. The new method used only light framing made mostly of two-by-four studs and other light wooden members. Instead of time-consuming mortise joints, the new framing used industrially produced nails and screws to connect the framing.

Within only a few decades, the new techniques transformed home building from an ancient craft into a full-blown industry that was aided by the rapid development of common designs, pattern books, precut housing "kits," and manufactured windows, doors, and molding. For the first time, housing was almost capable of being mass-produced. The industrial revolution had given birth to the housing industry.

Streetcar Suburbs

Improvements in housing construction were soon matched by a sea change in transportation: the development of electric streetcars and subway trains (see Figure 2.3). By the 1880s, electric trolleys were beginning to replace horse-drawn streetcars in metropolitan areas across the nation. Trolleys were both faster and cheaper than the horsecars. By 1903, nearly thirty thousand miles of America's street railways were electrified, more than enough to circle the globe.

The combined effects of electric railways and light wood framing quickly transformed the American cities and their suburbs. The first rail suburbs were often generally secluded enclaves, or "pods," some distance from the city. Streetcars and subways created an entirely different pattern—part urban and part suburban. Long "ribbons," or bands, of new construction shot outward from the center city in hub and spoke fashion. The ribbons formed around the spokes of the new transit lines, with the land often developed by the transit operators themselves. The width of the band was partly controlled by walking distance from the rail line and partly by other factors, such as land acquisitions made by the transit operators. This ribbon pattern became what we now call the streetcar suburb. These suburbs included Chevy Chase in Washington, D.C.; parts of Brooklyn and the Bronx in New York; Hyde Park in Chicago; the East Bay area of San Francisco; Shaker Heights in Cleveland; Watertown, Medford, and Arlington in Massa-

chusetts; and many other "inner-ring" urban and suburban areas throughout the United States. Ironically, one place the streetcar was particularly influential was Los Angeles. The extensive streetcar network—not the automobile—first imbued L.A. with its spread-out, polycentric plan.

The electric transit lines created a vast, new territory of urbanization, tripling the size of many older, "walking" cities. Electrified transit combined with light wood-frame construction meant that the suburbs were no longer just for the rich. As Kenneth T. Jackson writes: "For the first time in the history of the world, middle-class families in the late nineteenth century could reasonably expect to buy a detached home on an accessible lot in a safe and sanitary environment."[8]

Nevertheless, the development pattern remained relatively "urban" compared to later automotive suburbs. Lot sizes were often smaller than a tenth of an acre, and much of the new housing consisted of two- and three-family homes(see Figure 2.4). Urban or not, the new streetcar suburbs were so popular and spread so rapidly that they soon evoked protests. A common complaint was that this great tide of building was washing away all traces of the rural charm that had lured the new home buyers in the first place.[9] Compact and auto-free though they were, the streetcar suburbs were greeted in much the same way that sprawl is today. Rapid transit had allowed the urbanized area surrounding the center cities to expand at what must have seemed to be a stunning rate, swallowing up the countryside in a whirlwind of pattern-book gingerbread and triple-decker homes.

Streetcar sprawl also was responsible for dividing the cities both geographically and socially. The rapid expansion of housing into the

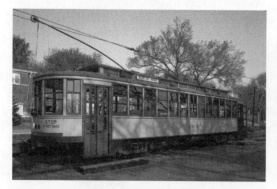

Figure 2.3. An electric streetcar in Minneapolis. (Library of Congress, HABS/HAER)

Figure 2.4. A typical streetcar suburb in the Boston area. (Alex S. MacLean/Landslides)

THE PEDESTRIAN CITY OF 1850 (2 mile radius)
  Boston Proper
  East Boston
  South Boston
  Cambridge
  Charlestown
  Roxbury
THE PERIPHERAL TOWNS IN 1850 (3 mile radius)
  Brookline
  Chelsea
  Dorchester
  Somerville
THE NEW SUBURBS IN 1900 (10 mile radius)

Figure 2.5. Expansion of suburban Boston in the streetcar era.
Source: Sam Bass Warner, *Streetcar Suburbs: The Process of Growth in Boston 1870–1900* (Cambridge, Mass.: Harvard University Press and MIT Press, 1978).

new suburbs wrought great changes to the older urban cores. Sam Bass Warner Jr., in his classic work *Streetcar Suburbs*, cataloged these changes in a case study of Boston, Massachusetts. Until about 1850, the urban core of Boston was the entire city. It was a dense, walkable, mixed-use commercial, industrial, and residential area with a radius of about two miles. This radius placed most destinations within about a half-hour walk from any point in the city—a half-hour being the maximum desirable commute time then as now. Outside the city lay surrounding towns and farmland. Within fifty years, the radius of the urbanized area had increased to ten miles, a distance accessible only by transit (see Figure 2.5). Those who could move out did. The new city

became a dense core of commercial and industrial uses surrounded by communities of middle-class commuters. The housing left in the core became increasingly the home of the working poor, and the first truly significant geographic social divisions began to emerge.[10]

Suburbs for the Motor Age

Rapid though the streetcar expansion was, it was nothing compared to what was to occur with the automobile—and what finally did take place would have happened far sooner were it not for a severe economic depression and a devastating foreign war. As early as the 1920s, with electric streetcars still in their heyday, U.S. cities began to build their first automotive suburbs. These first attempts were quite idyllic and not that different from the earlier railroad suburbs, except that the mode of access was totally changed: you reached to the new enclaves by driving your motorcar along recently paved roads leading out from the city.

Perhaps the most celebrated early auto suburb is Radburn in Fairlawn, New Jersey (see Figure 2.6). Established in 1927, Radburn became nationally famous as a "town for the motor age."[11] Its layout included separate pathways for pedestrians and cars, with streets designed for automobiles and sized according to the estimated amount of traffic. Overpasses and underpasses separated the pedestrian pathways, or "greenways," from the auto roads. Other innovations included a planned hierarchy of roads, with large arterial streets carrying the heaviest traffic outside the community, while roads through the residential neighborhood narrowed down until each reached a cul-de-sac serving a cluster of individual residences. The prevalence of the cul-de-sac and the limited use of through streets were deliberately planned to reduce neighborhood traffic. The entrances to the individual homes were turned away from the street and faced private gardens, which in turn provided

Figure 2.6. Site plan of Radburn, New Jersey—America's first planned automotive suburb.
Source: Peter Calthorpe, *The Next American Metropolis: Ecology, Community and the American Dream* (New York: Princeton Architectural Press, 1993).

access to the pedestrian greenways behind the houses. Many of Radburn's innovations later became standard features of subdivisions throughout the nation, although the common space provided by the parklike greenway system at Radburn generally is either absent or rare in the suburban communities that followed.

Radburn was quickly followed by other, similar developments. In the ten years following World War I, a boom in suburban development occurred across the United States. Between 1922 and 1929, new homes were built on the edges of every major city at the rate of 883,000 per year, more than twice that of any previous seven-year period. During the 1920s, the suburbs of America's ninety-six largest cities grew in population at double the rate of their center cities. Grosse Pointe outside Detroit and Elmwood Park outside Chicago both expanded by more than 700 percent. Nassau County, bordering New York City, tripled in population during the same period, while Los Angeles experienced torrid growth as work began on more than 3,200 sub-

divisions, yielding a total of almost 250,000 homes, nearly all of which were single-family detached houses. Most of Kansas City's Country Club District was built during the 1920s as was much of the housing along Philadelphia's Main Line. Some of these new suburbs (in such areas as the Main Line) were also served by rail or streetcar or both, but a steadily increasing number were solely dependent on the automobile. As early as 1922, almost 135,000 homes in sixty cities belonged entirely to the motorcar.

Whereas the previous streetcar suburbs had been long ribbons, the new pattern differed, allowing growth wherever there were roadways or where roadways could be built. Previously untouched land between the rail and streetcar corridors was now subdivided and sold off for new home sites. The density of development also changed. The streetcar suburbs had been quite compact due to the walking-distance requirement and the higher price of land next to the transit line. The new automotive subdivisions spread out as increasingly pervasive access decreased the cost of buildable land. Building lots rose from an average of about three thousand square feet to more than five thousand square feet while residential densities dropped from as high as twenty thousand per square mile in the older, transit suburbs to about ten thousand or fewer per square mile in the new automobile suburbs. Front porches and gingerbread disappeared as houses began to turn away from the street and toward driveways.[12]

Broadacre City

Also during the 1920s and 1930s, Frank Lloyd Wright, the great American architect, began to formulate his plans for a new kind of metropolis that were to culminate in his book *The Living City*. He called his vision "Broadacre City." Although the census of 1920 had been the first to show that a majority of Americans lived in

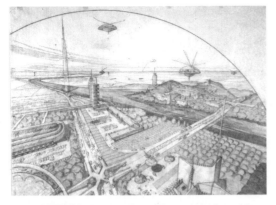

Figure 2.7. Aerial view of Broadacre City drawn by Frank Lloyd Wright (©1962, 1998, 2001 The Frank Lloyd Wright Foundation, Scottsdale, AZ)

cities, Wright could already see the cities' demise. By 1930, he would pronounce: "I believe the city, as we know it today, is to die."[13] He was referring to the dense city centers, which, as he saw it, were dominated by the machine and choked for air by huge, towering skyscrapers. In their place, Wright visualized a great horizontal city connected by the automobile and advanced telecommunications. "Natural horizontality," he wrote, "is the true line of human freedom on earth." Dense vertical cities, he wrote, are "pig-pilings" unbecoming to man.[14] Broadacre City would be rolled out across the land like a great carpet of widely scattered single-family homes, apartment houses, and office towers and shopping centers (see Figure 2.7). In Wright's vision, the houses would be interspersed with farms and forests held "in trust for future generations."

Wright strongly believed that this new city would be the ultimate expression of a democratic society. According to Wright, decentralization was the only way to guarantee individual freedom, and it was inevitable that this should come about through the nascent beginnings of the nation's highway system. He wrote: "The great highways are in the process of becoming the decentralized metropolis."[15] In the end, it would be largely as Wright envisioned. Automobiles and highways became the most formidable agents of change in bringing about all that followed. Modern suburban sprawl would simply not be possible without the automobile. The car is as essential to sprawl as it has been detrimental to the older cities. Without the car, the resultant patterns of development would have been far different. Only the automobile can support the dispersed pattern of development that characterizes sprawl.

Automobiles and Roads

When it was introduced at the end of the nineteenth century, few people seriously thought that the automobile would catch on at all, let alone become the nation's premier transportation system. It was, at first, an idle plaything of the wealthy, nothing more than an expensive toy. At the beginning, cars were quite primitive (see Figure 2.8). Although the first tinkering had started in 1860, it wasn't until 1894 that the first cars began to be marketed in small quantities, and this was in France. By 1898, there was only one automobile for every eighteen thousand Americans. By 1900, the total number of motor vehicles in the United States had climbed to only eight thousand.[16] To really grow in popularity, the car faced serious hurdles: the first was its cost, and the second was the lack of smoothly paved roads. Country roads were mostly dirt, and city streets were often paved with cobblestones.

Costs came down as more companies began to manufacture motor vehicles. Henry Ford solved the cost problem by introducing the Model T in 1908 and the moving assembly line in 1914. The assembly line made it possible to drop the cost of the Model T from $950 in 1910 to $290 in 1924. By 1925, Ford was turning out nine thousand cars per day, more each day than had existed in the entire country only a generation earlier. By 1927, there were 26 million cars in the United States, an increase of well over 3,000 percent from 1900 (see Figure 2.9). The

Figure 2.8. Motoring in an early automobile. (Fred Hultstrand Collection, North Dakota State University)

Figure 2.9. The soaring popularity of the automobile quickly transformed the American landscape. (Library of Congress, Theodor Horydczack Collection)

car was no longer a luxury item but was a necessary accouterment of the middle class.[17]

Rutted Roads and Early Highways

All of these cars produced a huge amount of pressure on the nation's roadway system. Everyone driving a car wanted and needed better roads. Industry coalitions may have wanted the same things and lobbied for them, but so did the owners of 26 million cars. Road conditions were frequently abhorrent, and the millions of car owners were the victims. In his book *The Power Broker: Robert Moses and the Fall of New York,* Robert Caro chronicles the plight of middle-class families trying to escape a hot summer's day in New York City:

> On Northern Boulevard, 160 feet of smooth macadam shrank to eighteen at the city line. The cars heading east [to the Long Island beaches] had to cram into a single file. As they crept along, the paving of the boulevard deteriorated, so that each family had to watch the cars ahead jounce, one after the other, into gaping potholes, and then wait for the jolts themselves. More and more frequently, they came to unpaved stretches in which, if there had been a recent rain, cars became mired, bringing the endless line behind them to a halt. If the earth was dry, thick clouds of dust hung over the unpaved stretches, turning dirty the gay dress Mother had worn for the occasion. . . . There was

no shade on Northern Boulevard and the children became cranky early. . . . [The New Yorkers] found the road becoming worse and worse. They would see Long Island villagers sitting on the fences and laughing at the families who, because of engine overheating or in a desperate try at a piece of grass, pulled off the road. The line of cars was so solid, the radiator of one almost touching the tailgate of the one before it, that, once out of line, it was hard for a car to get back in—and it was fun, the villagers said, to watch them try. . . . Most New Yorkers . . . didn't last to Smithtown. They turned around and slunk home, eating their picnic lunches in their cars, washing them down with bitterness and frustration. If they swam on Long Island, they swam in their cars in their sweat.[18]

If they made it to where they were going, it might not be until close to the end of the day, where they would have to turn around and repeat the whole process in reverse. With seventy-five years of hindsight, one might be tempted to blame these poor wayfarers for having bought the contraptions in the first place, but it was already far too late for that. The situation was pretty grim, and it called for action.

Parkways

The terrible circumstances on Long Island were soon remedied by the Northern and Southern State Parkway systems built in the latter part of the 1920s by Robert Moses, the master builder of much of New York's highway, bridge, and tunnel systems. These projects were not alone. Parkways were under construction all over the country. Between 1925 and 1931, New York also saw the construction of the Bronx River, the Hutchinson, the Saw Mill River, and the Cross County Parkways. Neighboring New Jersey had started a thirteen-mile expressway, Chicago had built an elevated highway, and Boston had finished two major traffic arteries north and south of the city. In California, what was to become the Pasadena Freeway was being planned as early as 1911, although it didn't open until 1940.

The new parkways were aptly named. Originally built for "pleasure vehicles" only, these roads were often an integral part of a park system

Figure 2.10. The Merritt Parkway in Connecticut today, one of the early landscaped motorways. (Matt McDermott/Milone and MacBroom Inc.)

or had parks as destinations. Moses's Northern and Southern State Parkways, for example, carried people to Jones Beach and other state parks on Long Island. The parkways were considered civic improvements and, as such, they were carefully landscaped and had picturesque bridges to provide a scenic ride. As primarily recreational roads, the parkways were not designed for commercial truck traffic; trucks are still excluded today from many parkways because the bridges are too low and the ramps too narrow and tightly wound (see Figure 2.10).

These roads were functional for the automobiles they were intended for, however. They were among the first divided highways in America to have grade-separated roadway crossings and ramped interchanges. In many cases (but not all), they were also primarily "limited access" in that they aimed to confine entrances and exits from the roadway to specific points—discouraging multiple curb cuts and driveways.

Although intended for recreation, the radial nature of the new parkway systems also provided an excellent way to get to work from houses built out in the suburbs. It was not long before the parkways came to serve primarily as commuter rather than recreational roads.

National Highways

At the federal level, there was insistent clamor for a national highway system. The Federal Roadway Acts of 1916 and 1921 provided U.S. government funding for up to two hundred thousand miles of "primary roads" to be constructed or rehabilitated by the individual states. The legislation of 1921 also created a Federal Bureau of Roads, which was charged with planning a U.S. highway network to connect all cities

of fifty thousand or more inhabitants. These were not the massive interstate highways we know today; those would come later. The first national highways were basically two- to four-lane arterial roads with traffic lights, strip retail, and multiple curb cuts, but the system was gargantuan by the standards of the day. State gasoline taxes provided revenues for construction of the national highway system, and by 1925 over $1 billion in highway construction projects was under way. Roadways and streets across the nation were being widened and paved, interchanges were being built, and traffic control systems were being installed.

Magic Motorways

By the late 1930s, America was looking beyond its rudimentary highway system to the expressways of the future. More than 5 million people visited the General Motors (GM) Pavilion at the New York World's Fair in 1939, making it the most popular exhibit within the purview of the Trylon and Perisphere. Accessed by huge serpentine ramps, the GM pavilion provided a clairvoyant image of what was to come. Designed by Norman Bel Geddes, the "Futurama" exhibit provided displays and models of what would one day be the nation's interstate highway system (see Figure 2.11). Multilane expressways with ramped access and looping interchanges were shown snaking their way across the countryside, delivering automobiles to the detached single-family homes of "the World of 1960." Commuters whisked to work along these "magic motorways" at up to 100 miles per hour.

It was indeed a brave new world of high-speed freedom of mobility. Individual Americans were about to burst free from the crowded oppression of the rail and streetcar systems. No longer would average Americans be at the mercy of schedules, routes, and service dished up by some faceless authority. They would be free to go as they pleased, when and where they pleased. It seemed a bright prospect at the end of the long tunnel of depression through with the nation was crawling.

General Motors was by no means out on a limb in proposing such a future. Europe had been experimenting with express motorways since the 1920s and Germany had already built the first sections of its world-famous autobahn by the time of the 1939 World's Fair. Americans were already riding on the first limited-access

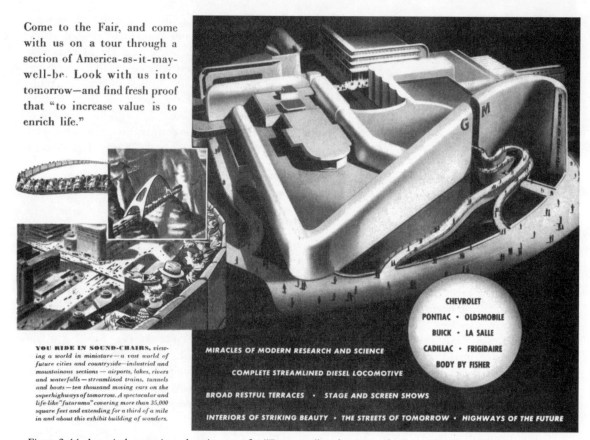

Come to the Fair, and come with us on a tour through a section of America-as-it-may-well-be. Look with us into tomorrow—and find fresh proof that "to increase value is to enrich life."

YOU RIDE IN SOUND-CHAIRS, *viewing a world in miniature—a vast world of future cities and countryside—industrial and mountainous sections — airports, lakes, rivers and waterfalls—streamlined trains, tunnels and boats—ten thousand moving cars on the superhighways of tomorrow. A spectacular and life-like "futurama" covering more than 35,000 square feet and extending for a third of a mile in and about this exhibit building of wonders.*

MIRACLES OF MODERN RESEARCH AND SCIENCE

COMPLETE STREAMLINED DIESEL LOCOMOTIVE

BROAD RESTFUL TERRACES · STAGE AND SCREEN SHOWS

INTERIORS OF STRIKING BEAUTY · THE STREETS OF TOMORROW · HIGHWAYS OF THE FUTURE

CHEVROLET
PONTIAC · OLDSMOBILE
BUICK · LA SALLE
CADILLAC · FRIGIDAIRE
BODY BY FISHER

Figure 2.11. A period magazine advertisement for "Futurama" at the General Motors Pavilion, 1939 New York World's Fair.

parkways, and a bigger and better highway system may have seemed an imminent possibility to many World's Fair visitors.

But, although road building continued throughout the depression, the construction of Futurama's magic motorways would be delayed until after World War II. That undertaking would become the largest public works project in the world—the U.S. interstate highway system as we know it today—and would have broad support from both industry and the general public.

TRUCKS

Among the industry groups supporting a national system of superhighways was the American Trucking Association. The advent of motorized trucking created transformations almost as radical as the automobile. In 1915, there were only 158,000 trucks in the nation. By 1930, the number had climbed to 3.5 million.[19] In 1995, the figure stood at more than 72 million.[20] The impacts of this transformation were sweeping.

First, an enormous shift of freight traffic from

privately owned rail systems to trucks traveling on publicly owned roads took place. In 1930, railroads carried nearly 75 percent of all intercity ton-miles of freight. By 1997, railroads carried less than a third of that figure, while trucking accounted for more than 80 percent of the total value of all freight shipped in the United States.[21] This shift did not contribute to the continued health of the nation's railroads. During the 1970s, as return on investment dipped below 2 percent while inflation zoomed into the double digits, nearly every major railroad in the Northeast declared bankruptcy, including the vast Penn Central network.[22] Only recently has rail freight traffic begun to recover, with the total volume of revenue ton-miles carried by railroads increasing about 40 percent between 1981 and 1994—still well below the peak numbers of 1930.[23] Meanwhile, the total value of domestic goods shipped by rail increased by only about 6 percent between 1993 and 1997, while the total value of goods shipped by truck went up by more than 14 percent.[24] Thus, the total value of goods shipped by truck continues to outpace rail, despite the fact that rail freight is making a comeback.

THE ROAD GANG

The trucking industry was far from alone in its support for a national system of highways. A large group of business and public sector officials joined what became known as the Road Gang, an informal but very powerful lobbying group that included automotive manufacturers, automobile clubs, oil and tire companies, highway engineers, and others.[25] By collectively seeking to advance their own interests, this group was pivotal in pushing through the legislation that finally created the interstate expressway system that we have today.

As sinister as the name "the Road Gang" may appear, the interstate highway system wasn't exactly the result of a dark conspiracy—even though General Motors did operate a subsidiary corporation for thirty years that quietly bought up streetcar lines and replaced them with buses.[26] The Road Gang was joined in supporting new highways by a swelling tide of car commuters. Suburban dwellings were developing at a furious pace throughout the country, and the parkways and highways built before the war just weren't sufficient. More and more people were spending more and more time in bad traffic—one of the things Americans complain about most. As long as building a new road system didn't hit the American public too obviously in the pocketbook, they were for it.

The Interstate Highway System

It wasn't until 1956 that Congress finally passed the Interstate Highway Act, authorizing nearly $25 billion for the construction of forty-one thousand miles of superhighways spreading across the nation. The entire system was to be completed by 1969.[27] The amount authorized would be increased substantially over succeeding years, just as the deadline would be extended and the size of the project would be expanded. The Interstate Highway Act committed the federal government to paying 90 percent of the cost of building the vast, high-speed road network, with the remainder to be paid by the individual states. Although the new highway act allowed for using general tax revenues, the majority of the money for building the system was to come from the

Highway Trust Fund, a nondivertible fund supplied by gasoline taxes. Because the tax amounted to only a marginal amount per gallon and was perceived largely as a "user fee," it proved palatable to the general public.

NATIONAL DEFENSE

The official name of the new highway system was the National System of Interstate and Defense Highways. The justification of need based on national defense was what raised the federal aid share to 90 percent.[28] Even though 80 percent of the war materials used to fight World War II had traveled by train, this argument nonetheless prevailed.[29] Mechanized warfare and the use of trucks for transport in the European Theater may have influenced the decision, along with the fact that transport in World War I had frequently been stymied by problems with rail systems. That consideration had weighed upon earlier highway legislation as well.[30]

The defense side of the Interstate Highway Act had yet another aspect. It had been debated for some years whether the new roadway system should be extended into the cities. The trucking industry (which was to foot part of the bill through taxes) was actually opposed to doing so because funds might be diverted from the rest of the system. However, the final legislation did include the cities. It also asked fewer sacrifices of the trucking industry than had previous versions that failed to pass.[31]

The urban decision hinged partly on the issue of national defense. In 1951, the *Bulletin of Atomic Scientists* had devoted an entire issue to the topic "Defense through Decentralization." Three years earlier, the National Security Resources Board had warned that concentration of industry in the cities left the national economy badly exposed in case of a nuclear attack. The idea was that splintering the large cities into dispersed settlements and scattering the industries would help to avoid total national destruction in a nuclear holocaust. Evacuation was also an issue. President Eisenhower stated that getting people out of the cities in the event of an atomic attack was one of the principal reasons for signing the highway bill. Thus, the Cold War and the atomic bomb became important factors affecting the spread of suburbanization.[32]

INTO THE CITIES

If the interstate system had not been extended into the cities, it is possible that the outcome might have been different. As it was, many cities used federal highway funds to construct extensive radial and beltway roads as part of the interstate highway system. Although this activity created massive disruptions in the cities, it also improved access between city and suburb, making it easier to commute to ever more distant outlying areas. An unforeseen side effect of the beltways was the impetus they gave to new suburban commercial development in direct competition with the urban-core areas. Combined with the radials, the beltways provided a crucial transportation network for developing large, new mixed-use centers outside the center cities that combined office parks, hotels, and shopping centers. In essence, the new highway system literally paved the way for the creation of major commuting and general travel destinations outside of downtown.

THE TRIUMPH OF THE AUTOMOBILE

To date, the construction of the U.S. highway system with all of its connecting parts, including state and local expenditures, has cost Americans somewhere in the vicinity of $4.5 trillion, making our nation's roadway system quite possibly the largest public works project in world history.[33] (By contrast, the construction of the Great Wall of China is estimated to have cost about $360 billion in today's dollars.[34]) Even so, the true cost of the U.S. highway system may be much higher still. According to some economists and planners, the cost of construction and maintenance amounts to just over 3 percent of the total cost to society of the nation's highway system.[35] If this is true, then the true cost of the U.S. highway system as it exists today could be as much as $150 trillion.

The interstate system was to form the principal circulatory system of suburbanization. The huge new freeways would become the trunk veins and arteries of a rapidly spreading membrane of development, spilling over state and regional boundaries and changing the face of the United States forever. The beltways and their radials, originally conceived to ensure access to downtown, conspired to grant the nation's suburbs independence from the center cities. The interstates became a vast trellis lying across America, rapidly overgrown by tangled vines of burgeoning development (see Figure 2.12).

Figure 2.12. Expressways have become the principal circulatory system of metropolitan America. (Alex S. MacLean/Landslides)

Postwar Suburban Expansion

As influential as they were, automobiles and highways were not the only factors leading to the vast suburban expansion that has become sprawl. Another major determinant was the housing finance system established prior to World War II.

Financing the Suburban Boom

During the Great Depression of the 1930s, a vast spectrum of programs had been undertaken to revive the economy. Among them were a number of measures aimed at stimulating the crippled housing industry, including the construction of new greenbelt towns and other direct interventions. The most influential programs, however, were "indirect" efforts aimed at housing finance. By 1933, mortgage foreclosures numbered more than a thousand per day and the home financing system was in ruins. Until then, there had been no such thing as a long-term, self-amortizing mortgage in the United States. The mortgages that did exist were generally for only up to 50 percent of a house's cost. Furthermore, these loans were available for periods of only five to ten years, and no principal was paid off during that time. Only interest payments were made, with the entire loan principal plus any remaining interest due in a balloon payment at the end of the mortgage.[36] Sometimes the mortgage could be rolled over, or renewed, for another five to ten years, thus postponing the balloon payment. However, if money was tight, renewal might not be an option.

The Federal Housing Administration

In 1934, President Franklin D. Roosevelt signed the National Housing Act into law, leading to the creation of the Federal Housing Administration (FHA). The FHA was mostly aimed at stimulating employment by reviving the housing industry, and would rely on private enterprise rather than direct government spending to achieve that objective. Thus, the FHA did not build houses or provide financing. What it did do was to insure long-term loans made by private sector banks for home buying and housing construction. The FHA did this by collecting premiums and setting up loan loss reserves. It also mandated an extension of the loan period for up to thirty years, reduced down payments to 10 percent and required that the mortgages it guaranteed be fully self-amortizing. This meant that interest charges and a portion of the principal were paid off with each loan payment, eliminating the huge balloon payments at the end of the loan. In essence, the FHA helped popularize the home mortgage as we know it today.

The FHA met its objective. Within six years of the creation of the program, new home starts rose more than 500 percent. With its focus on stimulating new construction, the new loan insurance program also gave a powerful impetus to suburban expansion. By reducing risk to the lender, the FHA caused interest rates on mortgages to fall several percentage points, for the first time in history making it cheaper to own than to rent. By 1972, the FHA had helped nearly 11 million families become proud home owners. By contrast, the same agency had provided insurance for only 1.8 million multifamily dwellings units— a fact that was overlooked as, for the first time, the single-family detached house became a real possibility for thousands of middle-class Americans.

Redlining the Cities

At the end of World War II, the work of the FHA was augmented by the passage of what came to be called the G.I. Bill. This act created a Veteran's Administration (VA) loan program aimed at helping returning veterans afford new homes. Modeled after the FHA, the VA program achieved many of the same ends. It also added further accelerant to the suburban home-building conflagration that soon consumed the nation. As Kenneth T. Jackson has written: "Not surprisingly, the middle-class suburban family with the new house and the long-term, fixed-rate, FHA-insured mortgage became a symbol, and perhaps a stereotype, of the American way of life." Jackson goes on to conclude: "Unfortunately the corollary to this achievement was the fact that FHA programs hastened the decay of inner-city neighborhoods by stripping them of much of their middle-class constituency."[37]

Although the legislation was not explicitly anti-urban, the resultant FHA/VA loan system encouraged the evacuation of the cities in several ways. To start with, FHA's loan terms generally favored single-family homes while discouraging apartment projects. The result was that, during the 1950s, FHA-insured loans for single-family housing exceeded FHA-insured loans for multi-family housing by a ratio of seven to one.[38] At the same time, FHA underwriting policies and criteria allowed an agency partiality to white, middle-class subdivisions in the suburbs. The rating systems used by the FHA to determine which types of loans it would guarantee heavily weighted the "economic stability" of the neighborhood and protection from "adverse influences." FHA's published guidelines to its underwriters specifically cautioned against densely populated neighborhoods with older properties—in other words, most urban areas throughout the country. This led to wholesale "redlining" of entire urban neighborhoods on confidential maps shared with the banking industry (see also Chapter 8).[39]

The Colonial Standard

The FHA also set minimum standards for new housing construction that essentially ruled out nonsuburban projects. These minimum requirements included lot size, setbacks, and the overall width of the house. In addition, FHA publications standardized subdivision design by setting specifications for creating "a homogeneous residential subdivision of houses that stood apart from one another on standard streets of standard widths."[40] Wide streets with homes set far back on large lots were labeled "Good," whereas traditional, pedestrian-scaled neighborhoods were labeled "Bad."[41] The FHA went even further, dictating the architectural styles of what went into the subdivisions whose financing the agency guaranteed. The agency expressed a preference for traditional styles, especially "New England colonial" architecture (see Figure 2.13).

Figure 2.13. "Colonial" homes are still popular in suburbs across America. (Oliver Gillham)

Thus, colonial revival architecture spread across the country from Maine to California and from Minnesota to Florida, regardless of any preexisting regional styles. Soon, new neighborhoods in California and Texas began to resemble similar neighborhoods in Connecticut.

Mass-Produced Housing

The effects of the FHA and VA loan guarantees were intensified by a severe postwar housing shortage because the housing industry couldn't build houses fast enough for the returning veterans. With new roadways snaking out from the city and the juggernaut of financing underwritten by the FHA and the VA, land around the cities was quickly gobbled up as productive farmland became much more valuable as sites for new housing. The process was hastened by another revolution in housing construction. Plywood, drywall, prefabricated building elements, and the use of mass production techniques all combined to accelerate the way houses were built. This new transformation in building technology was a whole order of magnitude larger than the nineteenth-century revolution in light wood framing that had preceded it.

Many of the new construction innovations were initially displayed in the first Levittown, in New York (a second was later built in Pennsylvania and a third in New Jersey). Beginning in 1946, Levitt and Sons bought four thousand acres of potato farms in this Long Island town. They proceeded to build a new city of 17,400 Cape Cod boxes and ranches, each on its own six-thousand-square-foot lot. At the height of production,

they were turning out more than thirty houses daily while crowds of hopeful people stood in line for days to buy them. Prior to 1945, the typical contractor had, on average, built fewer than five homes in an entire year.[42] In the end, eighty-two thousand people made Levittown their home. In the words of Richard Moe and Carter Wilkie: "At Levittown, the Levitts did for the suburban house what Henry Ford did for the automobile."[43] Housing was now a mass production industry just as automotive manufacturing had been earlier in the century.

With the financing in place and the highways being built, thousands upon thousands of mass-produced houses rolled out, carpeting the landscape for miles around the great cities. By 1955, new homes in suburban subdivisions amounted to more than three-quarters of all new housing built in the nation's metropolitan areas.[44] Housing starts numbered in the millions, creating the first wave of industrialized suburbanization in the United States. This wave was almost entirely residential at first. Most working fathers still went to the city for employment, returning to their suburban families in the evening. The major department stores were still downtown as were theaters and entertainment. The first suburban boom was an explosion of bedroom communities, still focused on the cities from which they had sprung. It was the television world of *Ozzie and Harriet* and *The Dick Van Dyke Show.*

Shopping Centers

That world was not to last. It was only a matter of time before department stores and jobs followed the houses to the suburbs. By the end of World War II, shopping had been working its way into the suburbs for almost two decades. Initially, these small "village" shopping centers served only local needs. This focus began to change in 1925 when Sears decided that automobiles were the future and began locating major stores in suburban locations. The first real regional shopping centers were built in the 1920s and 1930s and included such famous examples as Country Club Plaza in Kansas City, Highland Park Village in Dallas, and Suburban Square in Ardmore, Pennsylvania. Despite these early developments, by 1946 only eight full-blown suburban shopping centers had been built in the United States, and some of these (such as Suburban Square) were located near railway stations. More common were the shopping strips that began to organize along major arterial streets in the 1920s. By the 1950s, these areas had largely become the strips we know today, characterized by gas stations, fast-food chains, car dealerships, convenience stores, and other auto-oriented shopping opportunities.

By the late 1950s, full-fledged regional shopping centers began to pop up all over the nation in response to the flood of new suburban housing. A typical example was Shopper's World in Framingham, Massachusetts. Opened in 1951, Shopper's World encompassed almost ten city blocks of retail, including major department stores surrounded by a vast desert of parking. In 1956, Southdale, the first fully enclosed shopping mall, opened in Edina, Minnesota, a suburb of Minneapolis. It was to be the prototype for countless others to follow. What this meant, of course, was that people who lived in the suburbs no longer had to go downtown to find a department store. Now, several might be within a short drive from home. Soon, all of the shopping and entertainment opportunities once available only downtown became available in the suburbs. Retail developers were taking the old urban Main Street model out to the suburbs and putting it all under glass, in an indoor, climate-controlled environment. By the 1980s, nearly two-thirds of all retail trade in the nation took place in large shopping centers outside the center city.[45] By then, the building industry was at work on "super-regional" shopping malls, such as Tyson's Corner in suburban Virginia, near Washington, D.C.; Long Island's Roosevelt Field; and the largest mall in the United States, the Mall of America in Bloomington, Minnesota, a suburb of St. Paul.

Manufacturing Moves Out

The workplace was next. The advent of trucks and highways accelerated the passage of industry out of the city center and into the suburbs, essentially abetting a fundamental change in the workings of the urban economics of agglomeration and scale discussed in Chapter 1. This trend had already started at the end of the nineteenth century as factories moved out to suburban locations. Previously, factories had remained in the core, crowded near railheads and water transportation (see Figure 2.14). As the railroad network widened, junctions outside the cities

became more common, providing new location opportunities for industry. The substitution of electric power for steam or water power (see also Chapter 1) assisted rail in furthering the trend toward spread-out, single-story plants on less-expensive suburban or exurban land.

But it was the introduction of a widespread, paved roadway network and the rise of trucking that provided the final impetus toward moving industry out of the center cities, a trend that is still continuing. As early as the 1920s, large industrial concerns such as DuPont were already switching from trains to trucks in moving significant segments of their chemical products.[46] The result of this shift was that from World War II to the present, manufacturing has become increasingly an element of the urban fringe, deserting the center cities and many of the former factory workers.[47] Clearly, a system of high-speed interstate roadways was a helpful agent in moving freight from rail to trucks and in helping to move manufacturing out to the suburbs. It was natural that the trucking industry should seek to advance its own interests by supporting the highway movement.

By 1963, more than half of all industrial employment in the United States had moved to the suburbs. By 1981, almost two-thirds of all manufacturing in the nation was taking place in suburban industrial parks (see Figure 2.15). But manufacturing also was becoming less important to the nation's economy. Textile jobs that first started moving south out of New England in the 1920s eventually began to move overseas. During the 1920s, labor was cheaper and less organized in the South, but by the end of the twentieth century, labor was

Figure 2.14. During the early twentieth century, industry and commerce crowded near railheads and water transportation. (Aerial Photos International)

Figure 2.15. Today industry is spread out in suburban and exurban areas. (Alex S. MacLean/Landslides)

cheaper abroad. The garment manufacturing industry that had thrived in lower Manhattan also began moving out after World War II for similar reasons.

Textiles and garments weren't the only sectors affected, however. Steel, automotive, electronics, and other big industries were consolidating in the face of foreign competition. The nation was changing from a manufacturing economy into a service economy. During the 1970s and early 1980s alone, the United States lost 5 million industrial jobs while gaining more than 100 million jobs in the service sector—and that is but one period in a much longer trend line.[48] While the new service and information economy was well suited to the suburbs the effect of the flight of industry on older manufacturing cities was palpable. Between 1970 and 1980, Philadelphia alone lost 140,000 jobs.[49] The decentralization and emigration of industry was bad for blue-collar employment in many older cities. Such cities as Detroit, Camden, New Jersey, and Bridgeport, Connecticut are still suffering the effects of the erosion of industrial jobs that left many unemployed workers behind.

On the other side of the equation, the industrial exodus has noticeably improved urban living conditions. From the 1860s right through the 1960s, middle-class families were leaving the cities partly because of the noise, pollution, and crowded living conditions caused by manufacturing. As industries have moved out (and as antipollution laws have taken effect), the noise and pollution that once characterized the manufacturing city have significantly diminished. Pittsburgh, once famous as a steel and glass manufacturing center, was also famous for its industrial air pollution. Smoke filled the sky, visibility was poor, and soot blanketed the city. As Lewis Mumford described it:

> The poisonous pall of smoke . . . closed in everywhere . . . in Pittsburgh. In this . . . environment, black clothes were only a protective coloration, not a form of mourning. . . . The clouds of acrid dust . . . smarted the eyes, rasped the throat and lungs, lowered the general tone, even when they did not produce on contact any definite disease.[50]

It has been estimated that in the 1930s, as a result of air pollution, the citizens of Pittsburgh spent an extra $2.3 million per year in laundry costs alone.[51] Since then, the economy of the city has diversified, and manufacturing is no longer dominant. The largest employer in Pittsburgh today is not a steel company but the University of Pittsburgh Medical Center, with twenty-eight thousand employees.[52] In 1999, Pittsburgh had far fewer unhealthy air quality days than many other cities in the United States—with less than half as many unhealthy air quality days as Atlanta, Houston, and even Fresno, California.[53]

The flight of manufacturing also opened new vistas in cities. In the industrial era, factories, wharves, coal bunkers, cranes, and storage tanks crowded the waterfronts of many of the nation's cities, cutting off views and access. As industry moved out, the waterfronts opened up to the city, becoming available for a host of new opportunities, though it would take many years to realize those possibilities.

The Corporate Diaspora

The changing economy demanded huge amounts of office space. Until the 1950s, office space typically was located in large urban centers, such as Manhattan or downtown Chicago, as businesses struggled to keep their operations under one roof. From the 1950s onward, many companies began to disaggregate their operations as communications and roadway networks dramatically improved and more employees began to live in the suburbs. The fact that land was less expensive and taxes frequently less onerous also figured in the move. The outward trend was amplified as major corporate headquarters began their own exodus from the city (see Fig-

Figure 2.16. Like housing and manufacturing, many corporate headquarters have also moved to the suburbs. (Alex S. MacLean/Landslides)

ure 2.16). General Foods started the big rush when it moved its headquarters to White Plains, New York, from Manhattan in 1954. The company was soon followed by a parade of other corporate titans, including Texaco, Gulf Oil, IBM, Xerox, and many others. McDonald's made its home in suburban Oakbrook, Illinois, and AT&T went to New Jersey. AT&T alone has more than 22 million square feet of space in suburban New Jersey, more than all of the office space in downtown Seattle or St. Louis.[54]

Some of the new corporations that today dominate the U.S. economy have spent all or most of their existence in the suburbs. Computer hardware, software, and chip-making industries are typical examples. IBM relocated to the suburbs fairly early, while many of the businesses in Silicon Valley and in suburban Boston never had any presence in cities. As a result of this change in location for major office centers, by 1990 only 28 percent of national employment was in cities (the rest was suburban and exurban), whereas between 1980 and 1990, 82 percent of the increase in new workers was in the nation's suburban and exurban areas.[55]

The Final Pattern

Corporate headquarters and back-office operations were soon followed by the entities that serve them: accountants, lawyers, engineers, brokerage houses, banks, office supply houses, fitness centers, and all of the other myriad elements of the office support network followed. The combined effects of shopping centers and industrial and office parks provided the critical mass for sprawl to become free of the cities. No longer did the majority of people in the nation simply have their bedrooms in the suburbs; they also worked there, shopped there, played there, and raised their children there. No longer would the majority of workers head for the city each waking day.

Suburbanization has forever changed the character of our nation and still continues to do so. It has changed our country just as much as the industrial and urban revolutions that preceded it. Just as the industrial revolution built our great cities with their skyscrapers, the information and service economy has given us our new horizontal metropolis. While some prescient critics, such as Lewis Mumford and Jane Jacobs, were sounding alarms nearly forty years ago of what was to come, they were largely ignored as the United States continued building its new utopia. It is only now, at the dawn of the new century, after fifty years of accelerating suburbanization, that we can truly see the shape of what we have wrought and can begin to understand its impacts.

Suburbanization and Cities

Perhaps nowhere has the suburban revolution had greater effect than in the nation's pre–World War II core cities. Once the nation's premier population centers, the core cities were also America's centers of wealth, commerce, and industry. In the more than fifty years following 1950, as both wealth and employment have moved into the suburbs, many cities have been transformed into concentrations of poverty, containing more than half the people in the United States who are living below the poverty line.[56]

Draining the Cities

During the 1950s and 1960s, Levittown and similar communities across the country began to drain the cities of their white middle class. Millions upon millions of new homes were being constructed in the suburbs, all of them cheaper to own than to rent, all of them subsidized by guaranteed mortgages, all with huge new freeways unrolling like magic carpets to their doors. Between 1950 and 1990, the suburban population of the United States grew from 41 percent of the metropolitan total to more than 62 percent.[57] The worst decade for most older industrial cities was the 1970s. Of the thirty-six cities analyzed by the Fannie Mae Foundation, all of them lost population in the 1970s, with some cities losing between 20 and 30 percent of their population in that decade alone.[58] All of the 2000 census data has yet to be analyzed, but as of this writing, suburbanization is continuing, with suburban and exurban areas in such metro areas as Boston increasing in population at between two and five times the rate of the core city and its inner-ring suburbs.[59]

While the initial post–World War II residential relocations were worrisome enough when combined with an ongoing industrial exodus, the worst nightmares of downtown business interests soon came true as major corporations and the big-city retailing chains changed their focus to the suburbs. A wealth of urban real estate seemed poised to become worthless, prompting urgent calls for drastic action.

Figure 2.17. Le Corbusier's Voisin Plan for Paris. *Source:* © Artists Rights Society (ARS), New York/ADAGP, Paris/FLC.

Figure 2.18. A residential zone in Le Corbusier's Ville Contemporaine, a planned new city for 3 million people. *Source:* © Artists Rights Society (ARS), New York/ADAGP, Paris/FLC.

Urban Renewal

Not long before Frank Lloyd Wright announced the death of the city, a Swiss architect, Charles-Edouard Jeanneret, proclaimed an equally sweeping vision. Practicing in France, Jeanneret had adopted the pseudonym Le Corbusier, meaning "the crowlike one." Early on, he had joined the race to bring the industrial revolution to the field of architecture. Together with the Constructivists in Russia and the Bauhaus in Germany, Le Corbusier conspired to bring the world a new international style of architecture, which took its cue from modern industrial buildings and the newly discovered possibilities of steel, reinforced concrete, and elevators. The house was to become a machine for living. Office buildings were to become giant towers of glittering glass.

THE VOISIN PLAN FOR PARIS

Le Corbusier viewed older cities such as Paris as antiquated, dark, congested, and unsanitary. Worse, these old medieval cities were totally unsuited to the automobile. In 1925, Le Corbusier unveiled his Voisin Plan for the renewal of Paris (see Figure 2.17). Expanding upon a sketch presented three years earlier, the Voisin diorama was part of a larger exhibit in the Pavilion de l'Esprit Nouveau, which was financed in part by the Voisin automobile company. The plan pro-

posed nothing short of the demolition of almost all of the historic city of Paris north of the Seine River. In its place was to rise a huge superblock of sixty-story, glass office towers centered on a vast highway interchange. The towers were arrayed in a grid formation, with each standing eight hundred feet apart from the others. Open parkland and superhighways filled the vast voids between the towers, while titanic linear apartment buildings zigzagged across the fine grain of historic Paris (see Figure 2.18). Like Wright's Broadacre City, Le Corbusier's Voisin Plan would also prove prescient, although it would never be built atop the historic city of Paris. Instead, it was in the United States that his dream would first be realized.

A NEW VISION FOR AMERICA'S CITIES

Spurred on by the fear caused by the suburban exodus, cities all across the United States were quick to embrace the ideas of Le Corbusier and the International Style. Whereas the Voisin Plan appalled Paris, America saw it as the metropolis of the future. People were leaving in droves to escape the gloom and congestion of the industrial city for the light and air of the suburbs. Why not bring the magic of light and fresh air downtown? If the old, rat-infested neighborhoods could be wiped clean, then a sanitized, new world of gleaming buildings, freeways, and parks could be built in their place. It seemed to many that only such a bold and radical sweep could stem the tide. If the magnetic glow of the suburbs could not be dimmed, then downtown must become the suburbs, only on a far grander scale. This bold new vision was to become urban renewal.

Although urban renewal did not begin in earnest until the 1950s, it had important precursors. Even before World War II, public officials and business leaders had begun to see portents of trouble ahead for the nation's cities. The remaining threads of earlier social reform and civic improvement movements generally reinforced this view. Government and civic groups had been talking about improving slum conditions since the previous century. The Housing Act of 1937 proposed a sweeping solution for getting rid of the slums while putting people back to work. Under this act, federal tax dollars were to be used to help fund the construction of one new unit of housing for each one that was torn down, thus starting the slum clearance program. Whole blocks of older "blighted" housing were to be razed and replaced with brand-new apartment blocks.[60]

POSTWAR HOUSING ACTS

Slum clearance gained even greater appeal following World War II. The theory was that clearing the slums would also eliminate the conditions that gave rise to the slums in the first place.[61] Slum clearance became the cornerstone of the Housing Act of 1949. Under this act, city authorities with the power of eminent domain could seize and assemble whole blocks of slum or "blighted" property with federal funds and then sell the land for redevelopment. The rampage of urban renewal that followed this act razed whole sections of America's central cities to pave the way for new development. One unanticipated result was that many city blocks leveled in this manner simply lay fallow as parking lots (see Figure 2.19). In many cases, the prospect of such wholesale clearance actually accelerated the decline of the center city. People and businesses struggling to remain in the city were forced out to make way for "redevelopment" that never came. Already plagued by boarded-up storefronts and empty office buildings, these new asphalt lots only added to the

Figure 2.19. City blocks razed by urban renewal lying fallow as parking lots. (Alex S. MacLean/Landslides)

lifelessness and sense of abandonment in downtown. Many businesses and residents hastened to exit such deserted environments.

URBAN EXPRESSWAYS

The Interstate Highway Act determined that the expressway system would reach into the heart of the nation's prewar cities. Civil defense evacuation concerns aside, the automobile was a fact of contemporary life and the city had to accommodate it in order to survive in an increasingly suburban world. Nonetheless, cleaving the big roads through the cities created a lot of destruction, especially as a counterpart to what was being wrought by the housing acts. Furthermore, the new urban expressways opened the door to a whole new auto-friendly kind of downtown—one that would be far different from the dense, low-rise pattern of narrow streets that characterized many of the nation's older cities in the years immediately following World War II.

MOVING THE SUBURBS DOWNTOWN

Where redevelopment did occur, it often mimicked key elements of Le Corbusier's Voisin Plan of 1925. Dense, finely grained neighborhoods were razed in their entirety to be replaced by widely spaced apartment blocks, monolithic glass office towers, enclosed shopping malls, and futuristic expressways. The new redevelopments also borrowed another concept from Le Corbusier's city plans: single-use zoning. In Le Corbusier's Ville Contemporaine of 1922, an idealized city for 3 million people on which the Voisin Plan was based, all of the component uses were separated into distinct zones. Office towers were placed together in the center of the city without intermixed housing.[62] The housing was exiled to a district surrounding the tower zone and was further disaggregated by density. Although zoning had been in place in many American cities since before World War II, it was often overlaid upon preexisting districts made up of densely crowded mixed uses. Urban renewal allowed whole sections of cities to be razed and rebuilt according to single-use models. This was essentially suburban zoning brought downtown, only with much higher allowable densities.

Although much has been done since to reverse this pattern, the results of single-use urban renewal can still be recognized in many cities across the nation—for example, in "downtown" Los Angeles, in Dallas, and in parts of core cities in Atlanta, Chicago, Boston, and New York. Huge glass office towers dominate the skyline, sometimes unhindered by the admixture of other uses. The downtowns bustle during the day only to empty out at night. Where older residential neighborhoods have been razed, the looming sentinels of apartment slabs have replaced them. Giant freeways have been unrolled across dense urban cores, delivering the millions of automobiles and trucks that now serve both cities and suburbs alike. Starting in the 1950s and lasting into the 1980s, the nation's center cities were increasingly remodeled into denser versions of the expanding communities around them as such suburban models as the enclosed shopping mall were grafted onto the hearts of many older downtowns.

THE SHOCK OF THE NEW

Where change was wrought, particularly in the older cities, the results were often shocking. In the city of Boston alone, the West End, an entire historic neighborhood not unlike Beacon Hill, was condemned and demolished. In its place rose a Corbusian enclave of widely separated high-density apartment blocks called Charles River Park. A major intent of the project was to provide a brand-new in-town alternative to suburban living. In this spirit, the developer of the project put up a sign next to a neighboring expressway ramp that said, "If you lived here you'd be home now." Not long after the sign was put up, an unidentified graffiti artist crossed out the word *home* and replaced it with "dead"—an indication that not everyone was happy with the changes that were occurring.

Figure 2.20. Downtown Boston circa 1940, before urban renewal. (Courtesy Boston Redevelopment Authority)

By then, Boston was at work demolishing a historic but seedy commercial district called Scollay Square to create a new, modern government center replete with glass-and-concrete office towers. At the time, much of this work earned Boston high praise as a unique city combining the old with the new. Only within the last decade have increasing numbers of people come to criticize the drastic changes that were made to old Boston—particularly as what was once brand-new concrete begins to deteriorate while the great expanse of City Hall Plaza lies vacant most days of the year (see Figures 2.20 through 2.22).

In New York City, Sixth Avenue was renamed the Avenue of the Americas in the 1960s as a multiblock stretch of the midtown portion of the street was razed and replaced with modern glass-and-steel office buildings.[63] The result is a sort of "city-within-a-city" of austere towers, each standing apart from the others in a series of generous open plazas that are mostly free of active ground-floor uses.

Through urban renewal, the core of the old industrial city of Stamford, Connecticut, was almost completely erased. In its place is a new pattern of broad, automobile-oriented streets lined with multilevel parking garages, modern corporate headquarters, inward-looking atrium-style hotels, and a giant, totally enclosed shopping mall called Stamford Town Center. All of the major corporate headquarters have their own private dining facilities, so it is rare indeed to see anyone walking on the street. The few remains of the original Stamford can be difficult to find.

Figure 2.21. Downtown Boston circa 1964, with the Central Artery completed and the West End and Scollay Square removed. (Aerial Photos International)

Figure 2.22. Downtown Boston today. (Alex S. MacLean/Landslides)

Even such a city as Portland, Oregon, was not immune. Portland tore down whole blocks of historic, older buildings before changing its approach. The San Francisco Bay area altered much of its cityscape to accommodate a cluster of towering glass office buildings, together with new expressways needed to serve ever-growing numbers of cars and trucks.

The Proceeds of Urban Renewal

Some of the drastic actions of urban renewal were ultimately regarded as successful, but some, such as Boston's Charles River Park and New York's Avenue of the Americas, are regarded by many as unfortunate—even though they brought people and investment into the city and continue to do well economically today. What these projects replaced is gone forever.

However regarded, none of the grand urban renewal efforts succeeded in stemming the rampant development of the suburbs. By the 1980s,

sprawl was becoming a metropolis in its own right. Urban-core areas became superfluous as a starting medium for what was once "suburban" development as suburbs began to outpace cities in population and economic activity. One result was an increasing level of economic disparity between inner city and suburbs, and despite all of their urban renewal efforts to the contrary, cities began to suffer from a declining tax base that led to a series of financial crises in the late 1970s and early 1980s. This effect, in turn, led to a decline in city services and city educational systems, increasing the push factors that have continued to drive middle-class families into the suburbs to the present day.

The Origins of Sprawl in Summary

American suburbanization has its roots in the nation's nineteenth-century industrial revolution. Initially an urbanizing force, the industrial revolution drew people out of the countryside and into cities until, by 1920, for the first time in American history, more people lived in cities than in rural areas. Yet this remarkable urban implosion contained within it the seeds of the suburban explosion that was to follow.

Overcrowded, unhealthy conditions in industrial cities, combined with the haphazard mixing of industrial and residential uses, eventually led to the use of zoning. Zoning, in turn, separated different land uses into discrete districts—a fundamental component of modern urban and suburban development patterns. The crowded living conditions of industrial cities also caused increasing numbers of urban dwellers to idealize the same rural countryside many had left, eventually creating an impetus to seek greener pastures in newly developing suburbs.

Improvements in transportation technology brought about by the industrial revolution allowed cities to rapidly expand beyond walking distance into railroad and streetcar suburbs. The advent of automobiles and widespread roadway networks hastened this expansion. Combined with pervasive electric power and communications grids, a nationwide system of high-speed expressways and feeder roads helped create the conditions for a radical transformation in the economic forces of urbanization. These transformations, in turn, formed the framework for the dispersed, low-density development pattern that makes up the majority of today's metropolitan regions.

The rapid expansion of suburbs quickly drained the older center cities, which were the nation's dominant centers of population and commerce. The cities reacted to this mass exodus with a sweeping program of urban renewal and highway building. Urban renewal, urban highways, and other urban redevelopment from the 1950s through the 1970s significantly changed the physical pattern of the nation's older cities, remaking parts of them along the lines of their surrounding suburbs. Although this transformation may have helped preserve investment in some cities, it did little to stem the general tide of suburbanization. As suburbs continued to outpace older cities, the cities began to experience financial difficulties and declining services, which increased their disadvantage relative to the expanding and increasingly independent suburbs around them.

None of this process followed any broad plan. In 1900, few could have foreseen that the huge urban implosion caused by the industrial revolution would one day lead to an explosion of suburban development across the landscape. It has all resulted from many independent but inadvertently interlinked actions. No one had a huge interstate highway system in mind when the automobile was first introduced. Few people even thought that the automobile would prove popular. But mass production made cars affordable for all, and big roads soon followed. When the interstate highway system was being planned, few, if any, of its designers were prescient enough to realize that it would form the veins and arteries of a vast new development pattern that would quickly fill up the roads that had been planned to be free flowing for many decades after they were opened. When the FHA began insuring mortgages, it was mainly to put America back to work, not to create endless suburbs that would one day triumph over cities. Yet, the net result of all these actions has been the suburbanized nation that we know today.

Although today's sprawl is sometimes termed a "postindustrial" phenomenon, much of what constitutes suburbia can be attributed directly to the industrial revolution. Even though the industrial revolution is most often associated with the dense cities of the early twentieth century, it is that same revolution that ultimately manufactured sprawl. Without the industrial revolution, cars, highways, and mass-produced building products simply wouldn't exist. There would be no telecommunications network, computers, electricity, plumbing, or air conditioning. These are all things without which sprawl, as we know it, would not exist.

A huge transformation in society and city building in America has accompanied suburbanization. How and where the majority of Americans live and work, how they spend their leisure time, and how they travel have all changed. Suburbanization has affected how American society is organized and has changed the location of the balance of wealth and power in the United States. And all of this change has taken place— and is still taking place—at an incredibly rapid pace.

In the past 150 years, the United States has gone from a rural nation to a city-dwelling nation to a suburban nation. In the history of city building, this is a very short time. Before the industrial revolution, patterns of urban settlement had changed only gradually over many centuries. The early cities and towns that were built by the first European settlers in the New World were not that different from the cities and towns that had been built in Europe for more than a thousand years. They were walking cities with streets defined by the wandering paths of humans and animals. The industrial revolution changed all of that and, in just the last fifty years, the pattern has changed more dramatically than ever before. In Massachusetts alone, more land was developed in the last fifty-year period than had been in the three centuries that preceded it. In that same time period, the population of the state increased by only 28 percent.[64] The pattern of development has clearly been radically altered. Thus, it is not surprising that America's rapid suburbanization has been marked by sometimes bitter controversy.

CHAPTER 3

Reactions and Countertrends

As we have seen, the wave of suburban development and highway construction that followed World War II was far more massive than anything that preceded it. Predictably, it set off somewhat louder complaints than had previously been heard in the nation. In 1961, Lewis Mumford labeled the new wave of suburbia the "anti-city:"

> The absurd belief that space and rapid locomotion are the chief ingredients of a good life has been fostered by the agents of mass suburbia. That habit of low-density building is the residual bequest of the romantic movement, and by now it is one of the chief obstacles to reassembling the parts of the city and uniting them in a new pattern that shall offer much richer resources for living than either the congested and disordered central metropolis or the outlying areas reached by its expressways. The *reductio ad absurdam* of this myth is, notoriously, Los Angeles. Here, the suburban standards of open space, with free standing houses, often as few as five houses to the acre, has been maintained: likewise the private motor car, as the major means of transportation has supplanted what was only a generation or so ago an extremely efficient system of public transportation.[1]

Mumford wrote those lines more than forty years ago. Today, the same things could be said about almost any urban area in the United States. Mumford presciently understood the implications of the rapid postwar suburban boom. He was not alone—in 1962, Malvina Reynolds wrote a protesting folk song about sprawl called "Little Boxes." Subsequently popularized in a recording by the folk artist Pete Seeger, "Little Boxes" excoriated the dreary sameness of the emerging suburban explosion:

> Little boxes on the hillside,
> Little boxes made of ticky-tacky,
> Little boxes, little boxes,
> Little boxes, all the same.
> There's a green one and a pink one
> And a blue one and a yellow one
> And they're all made out of ticky-tacky
> And they all look just the same.[2]

Only a few years earlier, in 1956, William Whyte had written his famous work *The Organization Man* about life in the corporate world and "the new suburbia, the packaged villages that have become the dormitory of the new generation of organization men."[3] In 1961, a year before Malvina Reynolds's song, Jane Jacobs published her masterwork *The Death and Life of Great American Cities,* in which she wrote: "City character is blurred until every place becomes more like every other place, all adding up to Noplace."[4] All over the country, people were waking up to the fact that a decade and a half of booming construction wasn't resulting in the utopia that many had hoped for at the close of World War II. Writing again about Los Angeles, Mumford said:

> Los Angeles has now become an undifferentiated mass of houses, walled off into sectors by many-laned expressways, with ramps and viaducts that create special bottlenecks of their own. These expressways move but a fraction of the traffic per hour once carried by public transportation, at a much lower rate of speed in an environment befouled by smog, itself produced by the lethal exhausts of the technologically backward motorcars. More than a third of Los Angeles is consumed by

these grotesque transportation facilities; *two-thirds* of central Los Angeles are occupied by streets, freeways, parking facilities, garages.[5]

In fact, the expressways themselves were among the first elements of post-war suburbanization to cause real conflict and bring about serious action. By the late 1960s, the havoc these huge engineering projects had wrought upon the older cities had become a widespread concern.

Protesting the Highways

One example of the destruction caused by urban roadway construction was the Cross-Bronx Expressway, a seven-mile-long superhighway constructed in a dense residential neighborhood in New York City during the 1950s. Like many other highways in the region, its construction was overseen by New York's master builder of highways, bridges, and tunnels, Robert Moses. The engineering challenges were formidable, including blasting through rock while supporting heavily used subway lines, highways, and bridges. As Robert Caro writes in his book *The Power Broker: Robert Moses and the Fall of New York:*

> What was most significant about the Cross-Bronx Expressway was not that seven miles of brick and mortar and steel and iron had to be removed from its path but that seven miles of people had to be removed, removed from homes which in a time of terrible housing crisis in New York were simply irreplaceable.[6]

According to Moses's own calculations (which are alleged to be low), a single mile of the expressway required the demolition of 1,530 apartments housing 5,000 persons.[7] Residents of neighborhoods along the right-of-way protested desperately but could not halt the project. The Cross-Bronx was only one of thirteen expressways Moses hewed through New York, only 7 miles of a 130-mile system. Communities filled with dense residential buildings stood in the path of many of those miles.[8] Jane Jacobs, then a senior editor at *Fortune* magazine began crusading against Moses's planned Lower-Manhattan Expressway, an experience that led to her writing *The Death and Life of Great American Cities.*[9] Meanwhile, crowds began to fill the streets of New York's residential neighborhoods, burning Robert Moses in effigy. Moses defended his projects by saying, "You can draw any kind of picture you like on a clean slate . . . but when you build in an overbuilt metropolis, you have to hack your way with a meat ax."[10]

Fighting for Survival

New York and Los Angeles were not alone in having to defend or alter development decisions due to public pressure. In San Francisco, plans for a network of freeways crisscrossing the city sparked a "freeway revolt" in 1958 that caused the cancellation of seven out of ten planned highway routes (see Figure 3.1). While part of the Embarcadero Freeway was being built, cutting off the waterfront from downtown, a loud opposition formed that began to campaign immediately for its removal. Citizen groups continued their fight into the 1960s, resulting in the 1964 cancellation of the Panhandle–Golden Gate Freeway.

In Baltimore, Maryland, in the late 1960s, people rose up against a new freeway cutting through the heart of the Inner Harbor. In Portland, Oregon, most of the city's oldest surviving district, Old Town, was razed to make way for a new expressway called Harbor Drive.[11] In Boston, Massachusetts, a delicate tracery of older mercantile buildings was leveled in the late 1950s to make room for the huge, elevated, steel-and-concrete Central Artery that thundered across the waterfront and the historic North End (see Figures 3.2 and 3.3). Today, over $14 billion is being spent partly to put the roadway underground.

Citizens everywhere were up in arms about

Figure 3.1. 1948 Plan for expressways in San Francisco. (Courtesy SPUR)

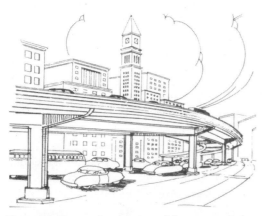

Figure 3.2. Perspective drawing of the proposed elevated Central Artery in Boston. (Courtesy Boston Redevelopment Authority)

Figure 3.3. Boston's elevated Central Artery as actually built. (Alex S. MacLean/Landslides)

the destruction being caused by the superhighways. In addition to the Central Artery, plans for Boston called for extensions of three major highways to a new "inner belt" that was forecast to displace 1,300 households with an eight-lane highway, replete with a vast double-deck bridge over the Charles River.[12] People from all walks of life joined to fight the plan. During the late 1960s, signs and posters all over Cambridge declared: "Cambridge is a city, not a highway." The uproar became so intense that, in 1970, Governor Francis Sargent declared a moratorium on all highway construction while a broad-based regional planning process was conducted. As a result of this process, much of the planned highway system was ultimately scrapped.

Meanwhile, by 1965, the freeway revolt in San Francisco had succeeded in canceling the planned construction of the remainder of the Embarcadero Freeway. The Embarcadero remained uncompleted until the vestige of the expressway was damaged by an earthquake in

1989 and later completely torn down. Because of citizen pressure, the Jones Falls Expressway in Baltimore was halted, Philadelphia shelved plans for a crosstown expressway, and a proposed highway through the Vieux-Carre in New Orleans was removed from the planned transportation system. Opposition to the Mount Hood Freeway helped touch off a revolution in regional planning in Portland, Oregon. In the 1970s, after the defeat of the planned Strathcona Highway, the city of Vancouver, British Columbia, banned all future expressways, opting instead to build an array of highly innovative mass transit facilities and high-density urban villages.[13]

Getting Results

The antihighway movement gathered strength and soon yielded results in Washington, D.C. As early as 1962, a series of bills began to make their way through Congress that would ultimately change the nature of highway planning and building in America. The Federal Highway Act of 1962 mandated that urban highways must be considered as part of a broader regional planning context in order to receive federal highway funds.[14] States responded to this mandate by setting up a series of metropolitan planning organizations (MPOs). Under federal rules, MPOs are charged with developing twenty-year transportation plans that identify all the transportation facilities that will be needed in the regional transportation system, and they are responsible for approving the transportation improvement program (TIP) for each of their respective regions. Previously, highway planning and building had been subject to no such restrictions.

Mass Transit and the Environmental Impact Statement Process

In 1964, Congress passed the Urban Mass Transit Act, authorizing federal capital grants for up to two-thirds of the capital cost of new mass transit facilities. The act authorized $375 million in 1964 to be spent over three years for this purpose. In 1966, section 4(f) of the Federal-Aid Highway Act of that year prohibited building federally funded highways in parks, wildlife refuges, and historic areas unless no other reasonable alternatives could be found. Previously, parks and older downtown areas had been some of the prime candidates for new highway corridors.

The real watershed came in 1970 with a raft of critical environmental and transportation measures that changed highway planning forever. On January 1, 1970, the National Environmental Policy Act (NEPA) became law, requiring for the first time that an environmental impact statement (EIS) be filed for all federally funded actions that would significantly affect the environment. The EIS process required that highway projects evaluate the environmental, social, and economic consequences of their planned actions together with alternatives. The Federal Highway Act of 1970 echoed the change in the national mood by adding the new requirement (beyond those established in 1962) that states consult with local officials on urban highway projects while also mandating more attention to social, economic, and environmental factors.

The Urban Mass Transit Assistance Act of 1970 established a long-term federal commitment to transit with multiyear transit-funding obligations and allocated $3 billion for a five-year period. The Federal Highway Act of 1973 authorized the substitution of new mass transit facilities for interstate highway projects, providing an 80 percent federal match to state or local funds (or both). However, transit dollars had to come from the nation's general fund rather than the Highway Trust Fund, which was financed by gas tax revenues. Nonetheless, it was a giant step that allowed cities such as Boston to substitute a series of rapid transit projects for planned highways.

The process continued with the National Mass Transportation Assistance Act of 1974, which authorized a 50 percent federal match for transit operations. The Surface Transportation Act of 1982 expanded the gasoline tax by five cents, one cent of which was to be dedicated to mass transit. This revenue was used to set up what became known as the Mass Transit Account of the Highway Trust Fund, thereby dedicating a small portion of highway revenues to public transportation.[15] Despite these events, the trend toward increased federal financing for mass transit generally slowed during the later years of the Reagan administration, and operating subsidies were actually cut as doubts began to surface about the efficacy of these projects in shifting ridership from private auto to mass transit.

ISTEA AND TEA-21

A major change came in 1991 with the passage of the Intermodal Surface Transportation Act (ISTEA), which was intended to reshape funding, intergovernmental relationships, and the highway and transit mix, increasing the flexibility of states and metropolitan areas in using federal funds to choose between transit and highway projects. Previously, states and localities could use federal transportation dollars only for the types of projects for which the federal government had designated the funds. Highway dollars could go only to highways, while transit dollars could be used only for transit. With ISTEA, more than a quarter of the $190 billion in transportation money distributed by the federal government in the 1990s was designated as "flexible" funding. States and localities could choose to spend this portion of their federal transportation dollars on almost any transportation project, from roads to transit to bikeways.

The ISTEA legislation was linked to the Clean Air Act of 1990 and the Energy Policy Act of 1992. According to Robert Dunphy of the Urban Land Institute, this produced "a remarkable triad of legislation that deals with the complex interaction between transportation, air quality and energy, and makes very subtle forays into the touchy subject of land use."[16]

The legislation produced a new focus on planning alternative approaches rather than relying on foregone conclusions. For example, under the old rules, the solution to a congested highway corridor might simply be to expand the roadway. Under the new rules, a "Major Investment Study" might be required, in which the metropolitan area and state transportation officials would be required to examine a range of solutions, including mass transit. This requirement has been thought to be at least somewhat more favorable to transit because formal consideration of nonhighway options was not previously required. ISTEA was reauthorized in 1998 and renamed the Transportation Equity Act for the 21st Century (TEA-21). TEA-21 preserves all of the reforms made by ISTEA, providing $216 billion in funding through fiscal year 2003, with $41 billion designated for transit.

Antihighway Accomplishments

Although the antihighway movement didn't stop the highways, it did spur major changes in the program. Today, there are formal requirements for integration of planning and consideration of transit in future transportation undertakings. Specific funds are now earmarked for transit, e.g., in 1997, three cents of the eighteen cents per gallon tax were earmarked for the Mass Transit Account. Overall, the current situation may augur a more balanced transportation system in our country than at any time following World War II. All of this is the outcome of long and hard-fought debates and the actions of coalitions of neighborhood groups and environmentalists that arrayed themselves against the unexpected consequences of the highway-building era.

Despite all the citizen effort and government change that has occurred, most U.S. transportation money still funds roadway projects (see Figure 3.4). During the 1960s and 1970s, while making some concessions to transit, the nation was still pouring money into roads at a much greater clip. Although $375 million was authorized over three years for transit with the Urban Mass Transit Act of 1964, the federal government spent about $12 billion on highways over the same three years.[17] When authorizing the expenditure of about $600 million per year on transit in 1970, the federal government spent nearly $5 billion on highways in the following year alone.[18] In 1995, the federal government spent about $19 billion on highways and about $6.4 billion on transit.[19] The transit share of federal dollars increased significantly in the intervening twenty-five years, but the federal government was still spending much more on roads than on transit (see Figure 3.5). By 1999, the amount spent on transit projects had declined to about $5.5 billion.[20]

Although ISTEA and TEA-21 undeniably have been major breakthroughs in how transportation projects get funded, the results have been mixed. On the positive side, federal spending on bicycle and pedestrian projects was thirty times higher in 1999 than in 1990, increasing from just over $7 million in 1990 to more than $222 million in 1999. During the same time period, federal funding for transit projects increased from $3 billion to more than $5 billion. However, while federal funding for transit increased 75 percent during that period, highway funding increased by more than 124 percent. Meanwhile, of the $50 billion in federal money given to states under the designation of "flexible" funding (for use on any type of transportation project), nearly 87 percent went to roadways. Even now, only about 19 percent of TEA-21's funds are specifically earmarked for transit, and individual states can reduce that target if they so choose. Despite these figures, the increase in absolute dollars going to transit has yielded results: total transit boardings increased by 16 percent in the late 1990s after having declined throughout the 1980s and early 1990s.[21]

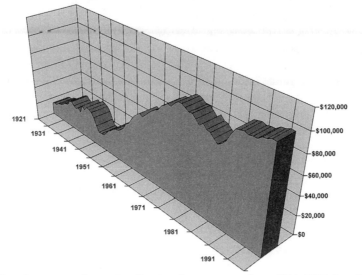

Figure 3.4. Annual roadway expenditures for all units of government, from 1921–1995 (in millions of constant 2001 dollars).
Source: U.S. Department of Transportation (DOT), Federal Highway Administration, *Highway Statistics Summary to 1995* (Washington, D.C.: DOT, 1995), www.fhwa.dot.gov/ohim/summary1995/section4.html, table HF-210.
Note: When adjusted for inflation as shown, total annual spending dips between 1973 and 1985. In current dollars, annual spending more than doubled, from $24 billion to over $50 billion, during the same period.

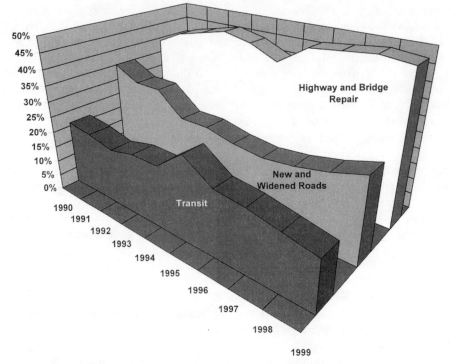

Figure 3.5. Annual roadway and transit expenditures in the 1990s (ISTEA and TEA-21).
Source: Barbara McCann, Roy Kienitz, and Bianca DeLille/Surface Transportation Policy Project, *Changing Direction: Federal Transportation Spending in the 1990s* (Washington, D.C.: Surface Transportation Policy Project, 2000), 5.

Despite the fact that about 25 percent (the largest chunk of money) of TEA-21 is for system preservation and despite the fact that states are using flexible funds for roadways, significant changes have been made in transportation funding. Until the 1970s, highways could be planned and built almost anywhere without significant public consultation or planning coordination requirements. Until 1982, no designated source of funds for mass transit existed within the Highway Trust Fund. Now, ISTEA and TEA-21 have made cross-utilization of funds between highway and transit projects more flexible than ever before. Arguably, these are improvements over the early days of the interstate highway program.

Cleaning Up the Environment

In 1962, Rachel Carson published *Silent Spring,* a book that documented how Americans were harming their natural environment. The book was immensely popular and, as a result, the environment became a mounting concern during the 1960s. Public pressure finally resulted in the passage of NEPA in 1970. NEPA and related legislation—including the Clean Air Act, the Clean Water Act, and the Endangered Species Act—have had a profound effect on urbanization in America. The Clean Air Act of 1970 made the U.S. Environmental Protection Agency (EPA) directly responsible for establishing limits on air pollutants and enforcing those limits, an act with subsequently far-reaching consequences.[22] Regulations and schedules for compliance were established for smokestack emissions from industry and tailpipe emissions from automobiles. The new law also required states to either develop implementation plans for meeting the new air quality standards or face the cutoff of federal funds. As a result of the Clean Air Act, air pollution has decreased dramatically in the United States since 1970. Aggregate emissions of the six principal pollutants tracked by the EPA have decreased by more than 30 percent.[23] Airborne lead has decreased by 98 percent, carbon monoxide by nearly 30 percent, and sulfur dioxide by 40 percent. Combined with the exodus of industry, the Clean Air Act has made many cities, such as Pittsburgh, livable again.

Figure 3.6. An industrial riverfront in Pittsburgh in the early twentieth century. (Library of Congress, Theodor Horydczack Collection)

The laws on air quality were followed by the Clean Water Act (CWA) of 1972, which set restrictions on paving wetlands while spurring the nation to clean up its waterways. Before the CWA, U.S. cities everywhere were actively using their harbors and rivers as sewers, filling them with garbage, untreated sewage, and industrial waste (see Figure 3.6). Boston Harbor and the Charles River were two of the dirtiest bodies of water in the nation. New York Harbor and the Hudson River were also seriously contaminated as were Lake Erie and the Potomac and Upper Mississippi Rivers. Water pollution was a nation-wide problem that attracted national attention when the Cuyahoga River in Cleveland became so burdened with petroleum products that it actually caught fire in 1969.

In 1972, Congress responded to public outrage over polluted waterways by enacting the CWA. The CWA committed the nation to restoring the integrity of its rivers, harbors, and lakes. Since the CWA was passed, the total population served by waste treatment facilities has increased from 140 million in 1968 to almost 190 million in 1996 while industrial pollutant loads have been significantly curtailed.[24] Through permitting and funding, the CWA, in conjunction with state programs, has doubled the number of rivers, harbors, lakes, and streams that are safe for both fishing and swimming. The Willamette River in Oregon and the Potomac River adjoining the nation's capital are two examples.[25]

With industry gone and waters restored by the CWA, the waterfronts of many older cities and towns have blossomed into parks and vibrant mixed-use projects. Urban waterfronts have become sought-after places to live and work that are unmatched by anything that can be found in the suburbs. Examples of award-winning restored urban waterfronts can be found throughout the country: Boston Harbor, the San Antonio Riverfront, the C & O Canal in Georgetown, the Baltimore Inner Harbor, Harbortown in Memphis, the Riverwalk in Charleston, and many more. In Lowell, Massachusetts, the canals once used for transportation and to power mills have been turned into a major water feature that interconnects city neighborhoods.

In Providence, Rhode Island, the Woonasquatucket River had been decked over by a highway in the 1950s. Now, the river has been uncovered and reconfigured to create a crowd-drawing waterfront attraction in the heart of the city (see Figure 3.7). The Norwalk River in Connecticut was once a dark industrial creek bounded by landfills, factories, and oil storage tanks. The river is now being transformed into a linear park like the Charles River Reservation in Boston, lined with parks, museums, an aquarium, and new mixed-use developments.

In 1973, the Endangered Species Act was passed and subsequently helped stop a number of large public works projects, including a major waterfront highway project in New York City known as Westway. Since the Endangered Species Act was passed, Americans have become increasingly aware of the fragility of the individual plants and animals and of urbanization's adverse effects on their ecosystems. More and more Americans have come to support preserving open space to protect natural communities.

Figure 3.7. Riverwalk in Providence, Rhode Island— a restored urban riverfront. (Richard Benjamin)

Many people now view open space and habitat preservation as national priorities.

Environmentalism and environmental legislation have significantly changed how people view the nation's natural resources and how projects get supported and realized. Before the 1960s, many people considered air and water pollution and suburbanization unavoidable. Now, they view fields, forests, and streams as valuable resources and polluted air and water as abnormal phenomena that must be redressed.

The Importance of History

In 1963, New York City's Pennsylvania Station—masterpiece of the renowned architects McKim, Mead, and White—came crashing to the ground (see Figure 3.8). The ninety-foot-tall Doric columns were shipped out to the Secaucus Meadows of New Jersey to lie like the shattered ruins of a petrified forest (see Figure 3.9). Penn

Figure 3.8. Penn Station in New York City before demolition. (Library of Congress, HABS/HAER)

Figure 3.9. Statuary from Penn Station in the Secaucus meadows after demolition. (Edward Hausner/ NYT Pictures)

Station was just fifty-three years old at the time of its demise. In its day, it had been one of the most innovative rail stations ever built and was certainly one of the best loved. In 1945, 109 million passengers used Penn Station annually. By the end of the 1950's passenger levels had fallen to a quarter of that number. [26] With Americans on the highway, the great railroad era had come and gone and the huge public rooms and grand carriageways of the station were considered surplus space.

The Historic Preservation Movement

In January 1963, the New York City Planning Commission handed down a zoning variance to build a new Madison Square Garden on the site of Penn Station. As much as the commission might have wished to preserve the station, they could not do so under existing laws. They could rule only on proposed uses, not existing ones. At the time, no law existed to protect historic buildings.[27] As Ada Louise Huxtable, at the time an architectural critic for the *New York Times,* wrote:

> If a giant pizza stand were proposed in an area zoned for such usage, and if studies showed acceptable traffic patterns and building densities, the pizza stand would be "in the public interest," even if the Parthenon itself stood on the chosen site. Not that Penn Station is the Parthenon, but it might as well be because we can never again afford a nine-acre structure of superbly detailed travertine any more than we could build one of solid gold. It is a monument to the lost art of magnificent construction, other values aside.[28]

Indeed, almost forty years later, the better part of a billion dollars is being spent in an effort to convert New York's central post office into a new rail gateway to America's largest city. Also designed by McKim, Meade, and White in the same era as Penn Station, the post office building stands directly across Eighth Avenue from what is now Madison Square Garden. The attempt is noble as well as costly, but the result will never replace the original Penn Station.

The demolition of Penn Station was a watershed. Major celebrities from across the country came to the aid of the old station, only to see their efforts wasted. Widely considered a national tragedy, this act of destruction turned out to be spark that kindled the bonfire of the historic preservation movement. Within two years, New York City had established a landmarks preservation law. Formerly an exclusive domain of upper-crust Americans, the historic preservation movement expanded dramatically as preservationists joined with community groups to protect endangered neighborhoods. Highway construction and urban renewal had combined to unleash a national countermovement to the drastic actions taking place in U.S. cities.

THE NATIONAL HISTORIC PRESERVATION ACT

In 1966, the federal government passed the National Historic Preservation Act. Section 106 of that act required all federal agencies to account for the impacts of federally funded projects on historic properties. That same year, section 4(f) of the National Transportation Act of 1966 went into effect, prohibiting the U.S. Department of Transportation from funding projects that damaged historic properties and public parks unless no other feasible alternative could be found. It is possible that some combination of these enactments might have saved Penn Station, as it was, the demise of Penn Station did serve to hasten the passage of preservation legislation.

What has happened in the aftermath of the Penn Station debacle has been far more encouraging for the protection of the nation's older cities and towns. The historic preservation movement in America has gained enormous strength and a far broader base. This growth, in turn, has helped foster a change in attitude among the various city, state, and federal agencies that govern the redevelopment of our cities and towns. Urban renewal has largely become a thing of the past. Before Penn Station was demolished, urban renewal could easily mean the wholesale removal of entire city districts. In the decades following the demolition, the nature of federal funding has changed and an increasing number of people have come to recognize the irreplaceable historic assets of the nation's downtowns. The emphasis has changed from "clean slate" redevelopment to more thoughtful tactics aimed at maximizing the resources of the existing built environment.

The National Register of Historic Places

Among other things, the National Historic Preservation Act of 1966 created the National Register of Historic Places, which is administered by the National Park Service. The register is the nation's official list of cultural resources deemed worthy of preservation. The National Register has become part of a national program to identify and protect our historic and archeological resources. Properties listed in the register include entire districts of cities and towns as well as sites, buildings, and structures. National Register status is a formal regulatory means of protecting historic buildings and districts throughout America. That status constitutes formal recognition of the cultural significance of a building, district, or landmark and makes it extremely difficult for any federal project to cause its removal. Register status also makes projects eligible for federal tax benefits and federal funds when such funds are available.

The National Register is supported by individual state historic preservation offices and by local historic and landmarks commissions. Only the local commissions actually have the power to prevent or delay nonfederal demolition of a historic building through designation of landmark status. Regulations for the promulgation of state historic preservation offices in each state and certification of local historic commissions were part of the National Historic Preservation Act.

The organizations and regulations created by the National Historic Preservation Act have aided in the successful restoration of a broad array of historic towns, villages, and urban districts throughout the nation that might otherwise have been lost forever. In many cases, these projects have been vital in helping to restore economic health to their communities. Examples, among many others, include Lowell, Massachusetts; Denver's Larimer Square; most of downtown Providence, Rhode Island; the Miami Beach Art Deco District; Philadelphia's Society Hill; Boston's Back Bay and the Quincy Markets; Downtown Portland, Oregon; and Pittsburgh. (See Chapter 12 for a more detailed description of typical projects.)

Figure 3.10. Battery Park City (foreground), a mixed-use waterfront development in New York City prior to the destruction of the World Trade Center. (Alex S. MacLean/Landslides)

Figure 3.11. Rowes Wharf, a mixed-use redevelopment project on Boston Harbor. (Alex S. MacLean/Landslides)

Contextualism in Architectural Design

Interest in historic buildings arguably has helped foster other trends in planning and architectural design. Beginning in the 1960s, a small group of architects, city planners, and social critics began arguing that the modern movement in architecture was creating a nation of stark towers and vacant plazas that were inferior to the richness and detail of the older neighborhoods being replaced. In this sense, this group was in harmony with the growing historical preservation movement. Historical motifs that had been thrown out in the modernist revolution were brought back and reinterpreted in a small panoply of new styles that were variously called postmodernism, historicism, and contextualism. Whereas before, context had been thought to have relatively little value, it now became extremely important and it was urged that buildings "fit in" with their existing surroundings. This trend set the stage for refreshing changes in urban redevelopment and the design of new suburbs. In urban areas, more attention was paid to existing street grids, and the character of existing buildings was used to determine the design of new city blocks. Examples of this type of thinking include the highly regarded Battery Park City complex in New York (before the World Trade Center disaster) and Rowes Wharf in Boston (see Figures 3.10 and 3.11). In the suburbs, "neotraditional" town planning has looked to widely regarded models from the past in creating such developments as Seaside

and Celebration in Florida and Kentlands in Maryland (see Chapter 12).

But architects and urban designers continue their search for new directions. In a widening movement, architects have begun to reinterpret the designs and plans of modernism, discarding the contextualism of the 1980s and early 1990s. Recently, Herbert Muschamp, the architectural critic for the *New York Times,* derided contextual works such as Battery Park City as "ersatz prewar urbanism" that close the door to art.[29] In other words, Muschamp believes that architects should be free to create novel and sculptural designs without any constraints posed by the aesthetics and patterns of surrounding older buildings and neighborhoods. Battery Park City, for example, was a conscious attempt to create an extension of the urban fabric that it adjoined. It is difficult to predict where such thinking may lead, but it is possible that historic buildings and neighborhoods will have a less significant influence on what drives the design of new parts of cities than they have had in the last twenty years.

A Counterpoint to Suburbanization

Whatever the future holds, the broadening interest in historic buildings and places that has spread across the United States, abetted by many successful historic revitalization efforts, has helped provide at least some counterpoint to the dominant theme of suburbanization. In a sense, the historic preservation movement may actually owe its success to the rapid growth of suburbia and the drastic countermeasures of urban renewal. In the decades following the destruction of Penn Station, preservation has significantly changed the meaning of downtown redevelopment, heightening public awareness of the fragility and uniqueness of the nation's urban centers.

Resurgent Older Cities

Many newer, largely suburban southern and western cities continued to grow during the decades of suburbanization as well as during the 1990s, sometimes by more than 70 percent (for example, Las Vegas, Nevada, and Plano, Texas).[30] In some cases, cities such as Houston (19.8 percent growth in the 1990s) have been able to grow partly by annexing their suburbs. Older, industrial cities often have not had this option. However, in a surprising turnabout, the past two decades have seen the return of population growth to some older cities that had been declining for many years. Between 1980 and 1990, the population of the city of Boston grew from 563,000 to 574,000 after having declined steadily since 1950.[31] Boston is not an isolated case, however. On average, the top thirty cities in the United States gained almost 3 percent in population during the 1980s.[32] New York City grew by 4 percent, and San Francisco expanded by 8 percent.[33] The 2000 census shows that this trend is continuing. New York City grew 9 percent in the 1990s, topping 8 million for the first time in its history.[34] During the same period, the city of Chicago grew by 4 percent, reversing fifty years of declining population, while San Francisco grew by more than 7 percent.[35]

Many urban planners believe that, in the past two decades, the nation's older cities have become increasingly attractive both to existing citizens and to newly arrived immigrants as places to live and work. This increasing appeal is believed to have kept some Americans from moving to the suburbs while at the same time drawing others, including new arrivals, into the cities.[36] The principal factors widely considered to have contributed to the resurgence of cities are include the following:

- Revitalization movements
- Unique resources and improving environments
- Changing homeownership options
- Immigration.

Revitalization Movements

The backlash to the highway-building program was caused in part by people who continued to treasure living in cities. Artists, writers, and other people connected to them were among the first to be attracted to older neighborhoods, such as New York's Greenwich Village, Boston's South End, San Francisco's North Beach, and Philadelphia's South Street area. The concentration of culture and creativity in these places also appealed to many other people, including young professionals who were neither artists nor writers but who shared the same preference for city living. Such people were responsible for grassroots movements that began the transformation of whole districts of older cities.

A well-known example of this phenomenon occurred in New York City in the 1960s and 1970s. As garment manufacturing gradually exited lower Manhattan, a huge collection of nineteenth-century loft buildings remained behind. Low rents and large undivided spaces attracted painters, sculptors, photographers, dancers, and many other artists, who used these commercial loft spaces as both dwelling space and work space.

The City of New York initially balked at this movement because it was unplanned, contrary to zoning (residential use of industrial buildings), and threatened to push needed manufacturing jobs out of the city. Despite the city's hesitancy, the movement exploded in the 1970s as many nonartists began moving into lofts, following the cultural scene. The city eventually relented and began to encourage the movement, so that by the 1980s SoHo (South of Houston Street) and neighboring Tribeca (the Triangle below Canal Street) had become fashionable addresses for many people. Over a twenty-year period, these old industrial buildings were recycled into new mixed-use residential and commercial neighborhoods that had never existed before in New York City, with rehabilitated loft condominiums selling for well into the millions of dollars.

The spark of grassroots reinvestment in cities was not confined to Manhattan loft buildings. Urban pioneers across the nation were hard at work from the 1960s onward, fixing up and restoring old buildings in such neighborhoods as Charlestown in Boston; Lower Downtown in Denver; Pittsburgh's North Side; Downtown Charleston, South Carolina; and College Hill in Providence, Rhode Island. Such forces are still at work in many cities, aided in the past few decades by help from city, state, and federal governments in the form of infrastructure improvements, loans, grants, and tax credits. Cincinnati experienced a 25 percent increase in people living downtown between 1990 and 1999 because of conversion of commercial buildings into apartments.[37]

Like New York, many other cities initially recoiled at this unplanned, independent movement. The basic tenets of urban renewal still held sway over city planning departments across the nation, and many older neighborhoods were considered blighted areas that would eventually have to be razed and rebuilt. It was beyond expectation that people would illegally set up house in industrial loft buildings, as they were doing in SoHo and elsewhere. Furthermore, many cities were trying to stanch the loss of industrial jobs and were not anxious to start replacing industrial facilities with residential uses.

Despite initial hesitation, most cities soon changed their outlooks and began to actively to encourage these new developments. It was in their best interest to do so, because it clearly fostered urban reinvestment, bringing new life to neighborhoods that had been in decline. Furthermore, these unplanned transformations were occurring because of unique neighborhoods, buildings, and institutions that already existed in the cities—not because of municipal government's efforts at urban renewal projects.

By forming around existing resources, grassroots movements eventually helped dismantle the prevailing thinking about "clean slate" urban redevelopment, supporting the urban revitalization and preservation movements. Yet, even though these grassroots movements would eventually have broad planning impacts, they were, at the outset, statistically very small relative to the sheer volume of suburban growth trends. Thus, many cities across the nation continued to show net population declines from the 1960s through the 1980s. Only cities able to annex their growing suburbs (such as Houston and Nashville) showed any real population growth during that period.[38]

Unique Resources and Improving Environments

Although the proliferation of suburbs drew the masses away from urban life, some cities—such as

Figure 3.12. Universities such as MIT and amenities such as the Charles River helped to keep people in Boston while the suburbs beckoned. (Alex S. MacLean/Landslides)

New York, San Francisco, Washington, D.C., and Boston—had special qualities that still beckoned many people. Park Avenue, Nob Hill, Georgetown, and Beacon Hill remained fashionable addresses even through the high out-migration years of the late 1960s. These were unique neighborhoods with reputations so solid that they were able to resist the outgoing tide.

But even neighborhoods such as these might have succumbed if it weren't for other anchors. People who chose to remain in cities mainly did so because of such fundamental considerations as employment, social connections, business ties, and civic, cultural, educational, and other resources that simply couldn't be duplicated elsewhere. These resources were inculcated in such major institutions as centers of finance, large universities, museums, and government offices. The president of the United States still lives and works in the District of Columbia. Manhattan is home to Wall Street, the United Nations, and a world-famous arts scene. Harvard, MIT, and many other major universities crowd around the city of Boston (see Figure 3.12).

The cities that possessed these kinds of unique resources could continue to act as magnets even while most of the nation was moving to new homes in the suburbs. These cities continued to attract people from different walks of life—even people who couldn't afford a fashionable address like Park Avenue or Georgetown but who still wanted to live downtown, next to the magnets that drew them there. University students and faculty, for example, often continued to live near campus despite whatever general decline might be affecting other neighborhoods in a given city. Universities also attracted people with no ties other than a general desire to share in campus cultural attractions.

Major employment centers, museums, universities, centers of government, centers of arts, music, and creativity, in-place mass transportation systems, and great civic spaces (such as Central Park in Manhattan) all helped keep people interested in living and working in cities, even as much of the white middle class picked up and left, and such problems as urban finance and crime mounted, and the quality of education and services declined. It was people like these who sparked some of the revitalization movements, staying long enough to watch conditions improve substantially over time.

As service sector employment has replaced manufacturing, enhanced quality of life combined with a downward trend in urban crime rates has helped make cities more competitive with suburbs. Smokestack industries have gone while environmental laws have helped clean up metropolitan air and urban waterfronts, markedly improving the quality of life in many cities. Falling crime rates have also helped. Cities have long had a reputation for high crime rates that has put them at a disadvantage to suburbs, a reputation that generally has been justified by crime statistics. Between 1993 and 1998, for example, the violent crime rate in urban areas was about 37 percent higher nationally than that of suburban areas. On the other hand, during that same period, violent crimes in cities fell by 36 percent.[39] That downward trend has helped make cities a more attractive choice for living. Although violent crimes also fell in suburban areas, the decline (about 26 percent) was not as significant.[40] Thus, crime has been declining more quickly in cities than in suburban areas, another factor that helps make cities more appealing than they have seemed in past years.

Changing Home Ownership Options

Another factor that has made city living attractive to more people is a change in urban real estate ownership patterns that has been brought about by the increasing popularity of cooperatives (co-ops) and condominiums (condos). Although cooperative forms of real estate ownership had been in existence in the United States at least since the nineteenth century, it wasn't until the 1960s that the condominium was introduced here. Even then, early buyers treated both co-ops and condos with some trepidation because the arrangements weren't as straightforward as fee-simple ownership of a house on its own plot of land.

But the cost of a townhouse in some crowded cities was beyond the means of many people, while apartments could be had at affordable prices. Thus, from the 1960s on, co-ops and condos became gradually more popular and an increasing number of rental apartment buildings in U.S. cities were converted to co-op or condominium ownership. The practice was quite profitable for landlords, some of whom were also interested in unwinding their residential real estate holdings in the unstable urban environment of the 1960s and 1970s. Changes to tax laws in the 1980s also helped make co-op and condo projects in some ways preferable to rental apartment construction, and many of the new residential buildings constructed since the 1980s have been condominiums or cooperatives built specifically for sale rather than for rent.

The transformation to individual ownership would never have occurred on the scale that it has, however, if the arrangement weren't also extremely popular with the buyers. Co-ops and condos made it possible for many city dwellers to own rather than rent their apartments, matching one of the great advantages of suburban living: home ownership at a price most people could afford. The same types of mortgages once available only to those buying suburban homes could now be had by someone buying an apartment in the city, along with the same tax-deductible mortgage interest. It is true that the per-square-foot price of housing generally has remained less expensive in suburban areas, but at least now there was a choice. You no longer had to move to the suburbs to achieve the American Dream. Furthermore, if city dwellers lived in a walkable city with decent public transit, they might be able to live happily without the expense of owning a car (or cars).

Moreover, condominiums and cooperatives have proven every bit as marketable upon resale as houses on individual lots. Today, it is not unusual to see a condominium in New York, Boston, or San Francisco selling for millions of dollars—a price for an individual apartment that can sometimes exceed the market value of the entire host building thirty or forty years earlier. In fact, a single penthouse apartment in a new project on New York's Columbus Circle was recently advertised for over $40 million, a price that only a few years ago could have purchased an entire apartment building in a reasonably decent neighborhood.

Where condos and co-ops have sold well, their advent has had a generally positive effect on the urban real estate tax base. In New York City, condominiums and co-ops now make up almost half of the multifamily residential tax base, and the residential share of the tax levy has steadily climbed, offsetting the decline in the total share of the tax levy of commercial uses.[41]

Apartment ownership has changed city living in many important ways. During the 1950s, more people rented than owned their apartments, leaving ownership in the hands of a relatively small number of landlords. Now, the number of property owners has greatly multiplied, and each owner is invested in what happens to the city around the property. In earlier times, if things didn't seem propitious, a tenant could always move out at the end of the lease. Now, many city dwellers have much of their savings invested in their apartments. This means they are also invested in their neighborhoods—they have become stakeholders in their communities.

Immigration

Since the 1980s, immigrants from the Caribbean, Latin America, Asia, and other parts of the world have significantly increased their presence in the nation's cities and towns. For example, New York City is experiencing the largest wave of immi-

gration in a century. Foreign-born residents of New York reached 40 percent in 1999, a figure not seen since 1910, at the peak of the last great wave of foreign immigration to the United States.[42] New York is not alone—Los Angeles, Dallas/Fort Worth, Houston, Washington, D.C., San Francisco, and Seattle have all experienced high levels of immigration.[43]

For the most part, this trend is considered positive. Some have questioned whether the economic boom of the 1990s could have been as sustained as it was without the current wave of immigration.[44] There are some dissenting voices, however. The Sierra Club (a group that is, among other things, against the proliferation of sprawl development) was forced by its membership to hold a vote on its immigration policy in 1998. Some felt that the club should have a policy of restraining immigration to the United States in order to protect the nation's environmental resources. In the end, the club voted to retain its policy of neither supporting nor condoning immigration.[45]

The evidence so far seems to suggest that immigration is helping to support urban revitalization more than it is fostering suburbanization. In many cities, new entrepreneurial immigrants are reviving abandoned commercial districts by opening shops, restaurants, and other businesses. By the end of the 1990s, largely immigrant-owned businesses made up more than 25 percent of all businesses in Houston, Miami, and parts of New York City.[46] More and more immigrant families are buying homes in city neighborhoods and voicing their concerns about schools and

Table 3.1. Population Gains and Losses—Ten Largest Cities

| City | Population | | Change, 1990 to 2000 | |
	2000	1990	Number	Percent
New York	8,008,278	7,322,564	685,714	9.4
Los Angeles	3,694,820	3,485,398	209,422	6.0
Chicago	2,896,016	2,783,726	112,290	4.0
Houston	1,953,631	1,630,553	323,078	19.8
Philadelphia	1,517,550	1,585,577	-68,027	-4.3
Phoenix	1,321,045	983,403	337,642	34.3
San Diego	1,223,400	1,110,549	112,851	10.2
Dallas	1,188,580	1,006,877	181,703	18.0
San Antonio	1,144,646	935,933	208,713	22.3
Detroit	951,270	1,027,974	-76,704	-7.5

Source: U.S. Census Bureau, *Population Change and Distribution, 1990 to 2000,* Census 2000 brief (Washington, D.C.: U.S. Census Bureau, 2001), 7.

urban policies through their emerging political leaders. All of this activity adds to the dynamic of city life and counters the trend of suburbs growing at the expense of cities (see Table 3.1).

While the cities are being invigorated by immigration, they are not in danger of becoming "ghettos" for the foreign born. Immigration is also changing the makeup of suburban areas. The Hispanic population of New York's inner suburbs increased by 50 percent between 1990 and 2000.[47] The Asian population of Boston's suburbs increased anywhere from 50 percent to 150 percent during the same period, while the Hispanic population of those same suburbs increased by 50 to 75 percent.[48] Nationally, the population of Asian origin increased between 50 and 75 percent while the number of people of Hispanic origin increased by about 60 percent.[49] According to the 2000 census, California is now officially the first state (other than Hawaii) in which non-Hispanic whites are no longer in the majority; as recently as 1970, the state was 80 percent white.[50] These data point to fact that immigration is changing the entire nation, not just its cities.

Analyzing the Trends

The causes of urban resurgence in older cities continue to be analyzed by many people sharing an interest in national development patterns. In his book *The New Geography: How the Digital Revolution Is Reshaping the American Landscape,* Joel Kotkin expresses a view shared by many urban planners and writers: "The new urbanites are not, for the most part, drawn from the typical American middle-class family . . . but two distinct groups largely outside the mainstream." These two groups are immigrants (that is, foreign-born citizens) and "childless people—aging boomers, childless couples, gays, 'empty nesters,' and singles." These groups may be out of the mainstream, but as Kotkin goes on to write:

> This is an increasingly significant portion of the population. Nearly one third of all baby boomers are single or childless or have one child, the largest such population in modern history. In contrast to most middle-class American families, these demographic groups tend to hold a far more positive view of city life.[51]

As to which group (immigrants or boomers) has had the most influence, there is some disagreement. Some would credit young, single urban professionals and boomers, as Robert Yaro, executive director of New York's Regional Plan Association, recently did in an article in the *New York Times:*

> This [resurgent population growth in the cities] is about the changing prospects of New York and big cities. These places are really safer, cleaner and more livable. The other related change is demographic. Baby boomers can live wherever they want. The kids are out of the house. They're tired of mowing the lawn. So we have this big countertrend of folks staying in the city or moving back in. That was an aberration until this decade.[52]

Yaro's statement effectively summarizes the sentiment of a wide group of people who are anxious to see some counterbalancing movement to suburbanization. We have already seen that the nation's cities have become cleaner, safer, and more livable, just as Yaro said. We have also seen how condominiums and cooperatives offer nearly the same advantages of ownership as houses in the suburbs. Anecdotal evidence, together with the evidence of increasing prices for city housing, would appear to validate the claim that baby boomers and single urban professionals are fueling at least some of the new urban population growth, but hard statistical evidence is difficult to come by. According to some demographers, baby boomers—and others like them—may account for only a small part of the increase. Quoted in the *Boston Globe,* Paul Harrington, a demographer at Northeastern University's Center for Labor Market Studies, put it this way: "There's this idea out there that people from the suburbs are moving back in. I don't think that's true at all. You really see sharp growth in the outer suburbs. I think most of the city's population growth is foreign-born persons."[53]

Supporting this claim is the fact that while New York and Boston grew by 9 percent and 3 percent respectively, the outer suburban areas in both the New York and the Boston metropolitan regions continued to outpace the cities with growth rates reaching more than 20 percent in some outer suburban areas of New Jersey and as high as 45 percent in Boston's outer suburbs.[54] It is also true that, for each of the older U.S. cities that experienced growth, there are others whose population continued to decline or remained steady. The city of Philadelphia lost more than 4 percent of its population during the 1990s, while Detroit lost 7.5 percent.[55] Yet, the fact that population is increasing rather than declining, at least in some older cities, is still positive news compared to the 1970s and 1980s, when population decline was the norm for most of the nation's older cities.

As to whether the growth is being fueled principally by immigration or by people moving back in from the suburbs, the answer to that question is complex—at least from the studies done to date. Currently available 2000 census data clearly show that the nation's cities are becoming much more diverse and that immigration is a major factor in population growth in both cities and suburbs. This supports similar findings in the 1990 census.

Where data from the 2000 census is available and has been analyzed, it seems to point toward immigration being a larger factor in urban population growth than baby boomers. For example, there was enough evidence for demographers in Chicago to conclude that the city's recent growth spurt can be largely attributed to an influx of Hispanic and Asian immigrants.[56] Analysis of 2000 census data by the City of Boston shows that its number of non-Hispanic whites declined by nearly 10 percent between 1990 and 2000. In New York, the number of non-Hispanic whites declined by 12 percent.[57] A study released in April 2000 by the Brookings Institution appears to confirm this trend nationally (see Figure 3.13). In *Racial Change in the Nation's Largest Cities,* Brookings reports that the total number of non-Hispanic whites in the nation's top one hundred cities declined from 52 percent of the population in 1990 to about 44 percent in 2000, with thirty cities losing between 10 and 20 percent of their non-Hispanic white population. The largest gain was in Hispanics and Asians. The Hispanic population increased by more than 50 percent in over sixty of the top one hundred cities.[58]

On the other hand, a recent joint study by the Fannie Mae Foundation and the Brookings Institution that examined trends in "downtown" areas within a sample of twenty-four cities found slightly different outcomes (see Table 3.2). The study defines "downtown" generally as the central business district of a city that is also usually the "oldest, most established part of a city."[59] This study found that eighteen of the twenty-four downtowns gained population during the 1990s and that, grouping all twenty-four downtowns together, there were 7.5 percent more non-Hispanic whites living downtown in 2000 than in 1990, while Hispanics and blacks increased by about 5 percent and 6 percent, respectively. Overall, the total population of the twenty-four downtowns was about 55 percent non-Hispanic white, 22 percent black, 13 percent Hispanic, 8 percent Asian, and 2 percent multiracial. The study attributes the growth in downtown areas to aging empty nesters and young professionals moving into downtown areas. Thus, both trends appear to be fostering increases in the older cities that are experiencing renewed population growth. The main contributor appears to be immigration, but non-Hispanic whites are also contributing to growth in the downtown areas of the nation's older cities.

However, those non-Hispanic whites who are

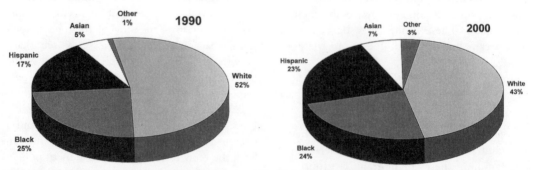

Figure 3.13. Ethnic composition of the nation's top 100 cities—1990 and 2000.
Source: Brookings Institution, *Racial Change in the Nation's Largest Cities: Evidence from the 2000 Census* (Washington, D.C.: Brookings Institution, 2001).

Table 3.2. Ethnic Composition of Selected Downtowns—1990 and 2000

City	Year	Total	Hispanic	White	Black	Asian/Other
Atlanta	1990	19,763	161	2,328	17,077	197
	2000	24,731	1,002	4,466	18,750	513
Boston	1990	75,823	4,368	57,916	3,562	9,977
	2000	79,251	5,432	57,227	3,468	13,124
Chicago	1990	27,760	1,424	20,916	4,170	1,250
	2000	42,039	2,216	27,623	6,912	5,288
Cleveland	1990	7,261	228	2,500	4,285	248
	2000	9,599	311	2,663	6,012	613
Denver	1990	2,794	230	2,217	164	183
	2000	4,230	445	3,147	229	409
Detroit	1990	5,970	92	1,687	4,133	58
	2000	6,141	124	1,290	4,518	209
Houston	1990	7,029	1,370	2,061	3,449	149
	2000	11,882	2,688	4,158	4,837	199
Philadelphia	1990	74,655	2,404	57,707	11,067	3,477
	2000	78,349	3,172	57,419	9,707	8,051
Portland, Or.	1990	9,528	429	7,611	516	972
	2000	12,902	645	9,651	831	1,775
San Diego	1990	15,417	4,504	8,086	2,139	688
	2000	17,894	4,354	9,728	2,079	1,733

Source: Rebecca Sohmer and Robert Lang, *Downtown Rebound* (Washington, D.C.: Fannie Mae Foundation and Brookings Institution, 2001).

choosing cities over suburbs are, as Kotkin, Yaro, and Fannie Mae have noted, mostly empty nesters or childless. White, middle-class families with children apparently are still put off by problems with urban schools. Schools are one of the critical push factors alleged to be driving the middle class from the nation's cities. The National Center for Education Statistics concluded in a recent report that children in urban schools are more than twice as likely to be from impoverished backgrounds than are suburban students and that "urban students and schools compared less favorably to their nonurban counterparts on many measures even after accounting for the higher concentration of low-income students in urban schools."[60]

Urban schools still present a problem for many families. However, it is possible that the influx of immigrants may help change this situation somewhat by bringing more middle-class elements into city life. At the moment, the census does not clearly describe the economic status of the wave of new immigrants. But most planners generally agree that the ultimate need is to get more middle-class families with children (of any and all ethnic backgrounds, immigrant or otherwise) living in cities. It is this economic

group that is most widely thought to be the hallmark of community stability. To some extent, this change may occur naturally, but it will largely hinge on improvements to city schools and the continued moderation of crime trends. Because schools are still a push factor, it may be that at least part of statistical puzzle can be explained by young, white urban professionals getting married and moving to the suburbs in anticipation of raising a family. This might help explain the net decease in non-Hispanic Whites in urban areas while at the same time suggesting that the trend might have been more pronounced had it not been counterbalanced by aging boomers moving back into the cities.

Mounting Protest and Reaction

The level of national protest over the rapid expansion of suburbanization that began in the early 1960s has continued to increase, reaching its most elevated state during the late 1990s. National recessions in the 1970s and early 1990s sharply reduced the pace of development, which also had the effect of briefly dampening the public debate about suburbanization. Nevertheless, various other forces continued to work to ensure that the debate would only grow louder at the next turn of the economy.

During the 1970s, an oil embargo and rising oil prices created a serious energy crisis that focused the nation's attention on the energy inefficiency of single-family detached housing and the amount of petroleum consumed by the nation's automobile transportation system. During that same period, more and more people were becoming sensitized to environmental issues. In addition to presenting energy questions, the automobile transportation system also began to raise serious air quality concerns across the nation, leading to pollution controls on automobiles as well as other key measures. By then, many communities were also aware of the phenomenon of "induced demand"—the process by which new highways stimulate new auto-dependent development, which quickly fills up the highways, leaving them more congested and the landscape more covered with development than before. Impacts to wetlands, wildlife, and other sensitive natural resources posed by urban development in general and suburbanization specifically also garnered concern. At the same time, the nation's cities experienced greater population loss during the 1970s than in any decade before or since. Rising crime rates, financial instability, and falling levels of service in the cities during the 1970s may have contributed to this spike in population loss.[61]

The 1980 census revealed that more people lived in suburbs than in cities or rural areas. During the development boom of the 1980s, many suburbanites suddenly saw nearby farms and fields sprout new homes and shopping malls. The loss of scenic landscape and farmland was added to the list of growing concerns about suburbanization. Renewed interest in cities, the historic preservation movement, and concerns about the social divides created by suburbanization further contributed to heightened levels of debate, leading to a growing number of published works on burgeoning suburban sprawl.

In 1985, Kenneth T. Jackson published his seminal work, *The Crabgrass Frontier,* which cataloged the history of suburbanization in America. A flood of books followed the peak of the development boom in the early 1990s, including such works as Joel Garreau's *Edge City* and James Howard Kunstler's *The Geography of Nowhere.* Kunstler excoriated the world of sprawl:

Eighty percent of everything ever built in America has been built in the last fifty years, and most of it is depressing, brutal, ugly, unhealthy, and spiritually degrading—the jive-plastic commuter tract home wastelands, the Potemkin village shopping plazas with their vast parking lagoons . . . the "gourmet mansardic" junk-food joints, the Orwellian office "parks" . . . the freeway loops . . . the whole destructive . . . spectacle that politicians call "growth."[62]

Clearly, the anti-sprawl rhetoric was becoming quite sharp. Meanwhile, many communities had been at work—in some cases, for a decade or more—trying to change the pattern. Starting in the late 1960s, the City of Boulder, Colorado, started to acquire outlying lands and establish development restrictions to prevent growth from spilling over into the green space surrounding the city. In 1973, the Oregon state legislature moved to require that all cities and counties in the state act to preserve forest and farmland by drawing up growth management plans together with urban growth boundaries to combat sprawl. Massachusetts tackled the problem from a different angle: rather than set limits to growth, the state tried to redirect development by reinvigorating older industrial cities such as Lowell and constructing new public transportation links. Meanwhile, Montgomery County in Maryland (outside Washington, D.C.) tried to limit the rapid development of farmland in the county through a combination of zoning measures that discouraged development in rural areas while encouraging growth in existing suburban centers served by transit lines.

The waves of rapid suburbanization during the growth periods of the 1980s and late 1990s stimulated still further national debate and renewed action. Such major environmental groups as the Natural Resources Defense Council and the Sierra Club put sprawl near the top of their national agendas as did the National Trust for Historic Preservation. Some states, including Florida, Maryland, and New Jersey, began to chart statewide growth-management plans. Architects and planners began to design and build innovative "neotraditional" communities at higher densities and oriented toward transit and walking. In 1993, several of these diverse movements coalesced into the Congress for the

New Urbanism, which advocates "the reconfiguration of sprawling suburbs into communities of real neighborhoods and diverse districts, the conservation of national environments, and the preservation of our built legacy," together with "the restructuring of public policy and development practices to support the restoration of existing urban centers and towns within coherent metropolitan regions."[63]

A major recession in the early 1990s briefly attenuated the gathering momentum of what could now be called an anti-sprawl movement in the United States. Environmental organizations, along with architects, planners, writers, and a growing number of public administrators, politicians, and citizen groups, had begun to form the outlines of a coalition. With the renewal of rapid growth in the late 1990s, some of these groups began to mount state ballot initiatives across the nation while also developing a growing body of anti-sprawl literature and acting locally to try to limit or modify growth patterns. Polls revealed that their message was getting through—more and more people were opposed to sprawl.

For many decades, protests about sprawl went largely ignored by the real estate and building industries and the marketplace at large. Demand remained strong for suburban housing, office space, and retail and industrial uses; most state and local governments continued to support suburban growth through the provision of infrastructure and services, including schools, roads, water, and sewer. In the past five years, however, as more citizen initiatives have been mounted and as more states have started taking action to manage growth, building and real estate industry groups have begun to take serious notice of the movement and to react with literature and media campaigns of their own. This reaction was largely responsible for the defeat of anti-sprawl initiatives in Colorado and Arizona in fall 2000. Worried that anti-sprawl initiatives would drive up the cost of land and make housing expensive to build, affordable housing groups joined in defeating those initiatives.

Real estate and building industry organizations and affordable housing advocates have been joined by conservative and free-market institutions that believe that managing growth means more government and government interference with constitutional property rights. Furthermore, they argue, suburbanization has emerged largely from market forces and has been an extremely successful pattern that has given Americans a very democratic and very high standard of living. Any proposed solutions, they believe, should focus on removing restraints from the marketplace. Roadway use should be priced according to market demand, and government provision of infrastructure should be privatized. Each of the groups in the debate has important points to make.

Reactions and Countertrends in Summary

Countertrends to suburbanization have brought a lot of change to America. Highways are now thought about in terms of broader transportation needs. Environmental goals and standards also affect how we think about new development. Environmental processes with the force of law are required for most major projects, public or private. New regard for historic resources has helped preserve and enhance many buildings and neighborhoods that would have been torn down in the decades following World War II. Interest in historic neighborhoods and buildings helped to foster contextualism in architecture and urban design, spurring such movements as New Urbanism.

Meanwhile, many U.S. cities continue to possess unique features that, in combination with clear improvements to quality of life, have helped make them more competitive with suburbs. Together with renewed immigration, these improvements have helped foster some of the first population increases to be seen in cities in several decades. Population increases together with increased interest in cities have caused housing prices in many cities to escalate dramatically in the past decade, causing concern about whether continued success may actually hurt cities in the future.

Despite the significance of the countertrends outlined in this chapter, and despite the important changes they have wrought, their emergence has not stopped suburbanization in America, although the pace of suburbanization may have slowed somewhat in the last decade. Slowing or not, growth in the nation's outer suburbs is still continuing at a torrid rate, and the percentage of non-Hispanic whites in the nation's major cities continues to decline, even though empty nesters and young professionals continue to move into many downtown areas of cities.

What these countertrends have done is suggest to some groups that suburbanization might actually have an end. They have reminded many people that cities can be as good (some think even better) places to live than suburbia, and they have started movements such as the Congress for the New Urbanism, showing that suburbs don't have to be built the way they have been for most of the past fifty years. Interest in the environment, reinforced by environmental laws, has caused many to rethink contemporary patterns of suburbanization and to question whether the suburbs being built today are a sustainable way to continue into the future. In response to increasing criticism, proliferating ballot initiatives and growing government action, industry, and free-market groups have begun to respond with counterpoints of their own. This exchange of views forms the current debate that is raging in the United States over urban sprawl. This debate is reviewed in detail in the chapters that form Part II of this book.

PART II

The Sprawl Debate

Part II of this book is an examination of the national debate about sprawl. Chapter 4 provides a broad outline of the sprawl debate, first reviewing some of the positive things that suburbanization has accomplished in the United States, then summarizing some of the basic positions and different groups involved in the discussion, and finally concluding with a summary of some of the current charges and countercharges being exchanged.

Chapters 5 through 8 provide more detailed assessments of the major categories of impacts associated with sprawl. Chapter 5 deals with impacts to the environment in the categories of land consumption and wildlife habitat. Chapter 6 treats the subjects of transportation and energy. Chapter 7 evaluates impacts to air quality, water quality, and public health. Chapter 8 analyzes the economic and social equity aspects of sprawl, beginning with a discussion of the costs of sprawling development patterns in terms of infrastructure and duplication of resources and services and continuing with an examination of the social divisions arising from sprawl and the issue of competition between cities and suburbs. Finally, Chapter 9 examines the aesthetic issues posed by sprawl and the claim that suburbanization is in part responsible for a loss of community in America. Each chapter presents a summary analysis of the charges that have been brought against suburbanization along with (where information is available) what is being said in defense of sprawl by those supporting the status quo.

CHAPTER 4

Outlining the Debate

Much of the rhetoric in the sprawl debate has been negative. The word sprawl itself has negative connotations. Yet it is difficult to find evidence that suburbanization was born of anything other than good intentions. In fact, suburbanization has actually brought the nation many benefits.

In Defense of Sprawl

As the review of history in earlier chapters shows, the pattern of suburbanization has allowed the nation to respond quickly to the needs of rapidly expanding metropolitan populations over the last half century. Between 1950 and 2000, the nation's metropolitan areas grew by over 141 million people, an increase of more than 166 percent (see Figure 4.1).[1] The configuration of the expansion could have been different, but the pattern that has resulted fulfills many of the key goals that America's founding fathers and their successors set out for a democratic society—including the freedom to hold land, to live and travel wherever one pleases, to accumulate wealth, and to participate in a democratic government at both the local and the national level. In many ways, suburbanization is a celebration of individual freedom and wealth. It is also the way the majority of Americans eagerly choose to live. According to a 1999 poll conducted by the National Association of Home Builders (NAHB), more than 83 percent of those surveyed said they would prefer to live in a detached single-family home in an outlying suburb.[2]

If the suburbs don't suit all residents, then the country and the city still provide completely viable alternatives to sprawl for many people. These days, if you should choose to live in a city, you can even own your own home—just as you can in the suburbs or in rural areas. For a long time, the cities were one of the few choices for many people looking to support a family without living on a farm. Today, cities are but one of many options. The expanding suburbs have granted mass access to entirely new places to live and work that simply didn't exist fifty years ago. Thus, it can be argued that the profusion of sprawl has actually provided more people in the United States with freedom of choice about where to live and work than at any time in history.

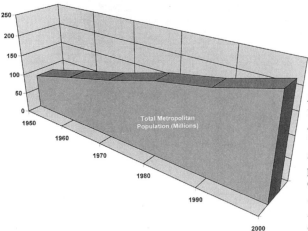

Figure 4.1. Total U.S. metropolitan population— 1950–2000.
Sources: Alan Pisarski, Commuting in America II: The Second National Report on Commuting Patterns and Trends (Landsdowne, Va.: Eno Transportation Foundation, 1996), 18; and U.S. Census Bureau, Statistical Abstract of the United States: 2000 (Washington, D.C: 2000), 910.
Note: Metropolitan territory as defined in each census year.

A Nation of Landowners

The radical expansion of suburbia not only has granted us more personal choice but also has made it possible for more Americans to own their own homes and build individual wealth than at any time previously. Today, more than two-thirds of American households own their own home, as opposed to less than half in 1920 (see Figure 4.2).[3] In early-twentieth-century cities, the best many people could do was live in a house or an apartment that was owned by a landlord to whom they paid rent. Today, inexpensive land and generous home mortgage terms have made home ownership a reality for millions of Americans. The rate of home ownership in the United States is more than double that of Switzerland and is up to 60 percent higher than in countries like Germany, Austria, France, Sweden, and Japan.[4]

It took the automobile to make land inexpensive enough to build single-family detached homes in numbers sufficient enough to house the huge population increases of the past fifty years. It also took mass-production construction methods and easy financing terms. The kind of credit available today just didn't exist in the first decades of the twentieth century. The suburban movement has made the American Dream possible for more Americans than ever before.

Maximum Mobility

Not only has owning a home become easier, but owning an automobile has also become much more affordable. With the proliferation of the automobile, fewer Americans are at the mercy of transit companies and their schedules. Owning an automobile means people can live basically anywhere within driving distance of where they need to be. They can come and go as they please, independent of anyone's schedule but their own. Since 1950, the number of privately owned automobiles has increased from about 40 million to over 131 million, while vehicle miles traveled by those autos have increased from about 365 billion miles per year to nearly 1.6 trillion miles per year.[5]

The combination of home ownership and car ownership fulfilled the basic requirements of the American Dream. Citizens could own their own homes on their own pieces of land while being free to travel anywhere at any time in their automobiles on a well-maintained, heavily funded road system. Automobiles and roads created the gold standard of freedom of mobility for a democratic society. In fact, car ownership is even more popular than home ownership: whereas 67 percent of the households in this country own their own home, nearly 90 percent own one or more cars (see Figure 4.3).[6]

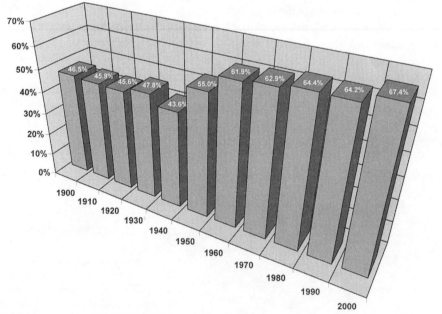

Figure 4.2. U.S. homeownership: 1900–2000.
Source: U.S. Census Bureau, *Housing Vacancies and Homeownership Annual Statistics: 2000,*
www.census.gov/hhes/www/housing/hvs/annual00/ann00ind.html; and *Historical Census of Housing Tables,*
www.census.gov/hhes/www/housing/census/historic/owner.html.

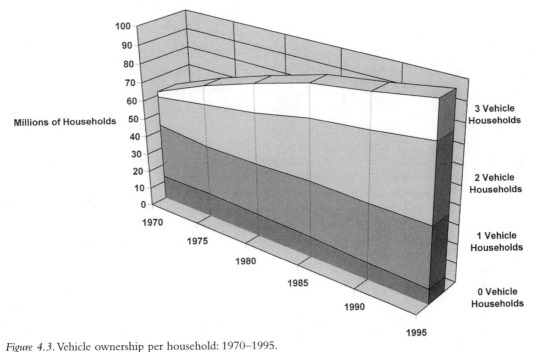

Figure 4.3. Vehicle ownership per household: 1970–1995.
Source: U.S. Department of Transportation (DOT), Bureau of Transportation Statistics, *1995 Nationwide Personal Transportation Survey* (Washington, D.C.: DOT, 1995), 6.

It can be argued that suburbanization has given the nation's citizens more freedom of choice and a better average standard of living than ever before in history. Houses on individual lots with their own gardens in safe neighborhoods with good schools are more accessible to more Americans today than at any time in the past. Wherever the denizens of suburbia roam, they are offered a cornucopia of shopping and leisure activities. Americans can work and live practically wherever they wish while being at liberty to pick up and move at any time because of the freedom provided by the real estate market.

Why Is There Any Debate?

Given how well Americans are living, it seems little wonder that some people are asking why there is any debate at all. Maybe all the talk about the harm sprawl is causing our society and our environment is simply unfounded—the inflammatory rhetoric of a disenchanted minority of environmentalists and urban intellectuals who find sprawl aesthetically displeasing. Believing themselves the arbiters of good taste but not believing that aesthetics is grounds enough for change, they have set out to redirect the course of American urbanization for environmental and

social reasons. That would be a worrisome indictment indeed.

Certainly, parts of James Howard Kunstler's *The Geography of Nowhere* dwell on the aesthetic horrors of sprawl, as do the writings of many others, including Lewis Mumford and Jane Holtz Kay. Moreover, some of the proposed solutions to sprawl appear to address aesthetic considerations more than purely social or environmental concerns. Some neotraditional townships, such as Seaside and Celebration in Florida, seem to underscore this point. It can be argued that both of these communities are actually car-centric communities, with a considerable amount of detached housing, that when carefully analyzed are not that much different from other suburban developments (see Figure 4.4).

Another possibility is that a significant portion of the debate is attributable to simple grass-roots self-interest. The polls tell us that most people still want to live in a single-family house on its own plot of land. They also want to send their children to suburban schools and to shop in suburban malls with plenty of parking. The problem is that no one wants to have any more of this suburban world built around them, that they are tired of watching neighboring open fields or wood lots turn into brand-new subdivisions and

Figure 4.4. Detached housing in Celebration, Florida. Celebration is as car-dependent as many traditional suburbs, but cars park in back, not in front. (Alex S. MacLean/Landslides)

houses, own an SUV, owe their good fortunes to the growth economy, and would be entirely outraged if there were not ample roads, stores, restaurants, and parking wherever they went. They wish everybody else would get off the highway so that they can have the road to themselves.[7]

If this is the case, it hardly seems fair to deny to other Americans what many Americans already have. That kind of thinking doesn't seem a reasonable social foundation for changing an entire pattern of urbanization, especially one that has managed to give so much to so many.

shopping malls that add up to more traffic on the roadways. As Gregg Easterbrook recently wrote in an article for the *New Republic:*

> Many of the people who now grouse about sprawl themselves live in spacious

Parties to the Debate

From looking at the history of suburbanization presented in the previous chapters, it should be evident that popular self-interest combined with

Table 4.1. Viewpoints in the Sprawl Debate

	VIEWPOINTS	
	Anti-Sprawl	*Pro-Development*
Sample Issues	No growth to managed growth	Status quo to free markets
Land and open space	Sprawl consumes valuable, limited land resources, including farmland.	There is more than enough land and farmland left to develop.
Endangered habitat	Sprawl fragments habitats, threatening endangered species.	Wildlife is increasing, not decreasing, in suburban areas.
Traffic congestion	Auto-dependent sprawl causes traffic congestion.	Traffic congestion is an urban, not a suburban, problem.
Energy consumption	Auto-dependent sprawl consumes unsustainable amounts of energy.	Auto technology is changing, and oil reserves remain adequate.
Air pollution	Increased auto travel caused by sprawl is contributing to global warming and air pollution.	Global warming is still basically unproven. Air pollution is an urban, not a suburban, problem.
Water pollution	Sprawl destroys wetlands and contributes to water pollution from increased runoff.	Environmental restrictions increase housing costs and are unfair to landowners.
Public health	In addition to polluting air and water, sprawl contributes to obesity and increased stress levels.	Risks to public health are considered unproven.
Community	Suburbia is destroying community life and character in America.	Suburbs allow plenty of opportunities for community involvement.
Aesthetics	Sprawl is devastating America's treasured landscapes.	More people want to live in suburbia than want to live in cities.
Economic	Sprawl costs more than compact development.	Cities are more expensive than suburbs.
Social divides	Sprawl geographically divides races and classes.	Suburbs are becoming more diverse. Opportunities are now equal.
Cities	Sprawl has drained the cities, leaving them problem ridden.	Cities are responsible for their own problems.

Table 4.2. Sample Organizations and Goals

Group	Sample Organizations	Goals
Environmental groups	Sierra Club, Natural Resources Defense Council, Environmental Law Institute, Conservation Fund, 1,000 Friends Groups	Protect the environment and preserve natural resources
Industry groups	National Association of Home Builders, National Association of Industrial and Office Properties, National Association of Realtors	Support a good business climate for the real estate and building industries
Inner-city advocates	Center-city mayors, downtown business leaders, urban community-based organizations, Council for Urban Economic Development	Foster redevelopment and economic growth in center city areas
Housing advocates	Habitat for Humanity, state and local affordable housing groups	Promote the development of affordable housing
State governments	State planning and environmental offices (Maryland, New Jersey, Oregon and some other states)	Promote economic development, reduce infrastructure costs, satisfy development, citizen, and environmental groups
Urban planners and architects	American Planning Association, American Institute of Architects	Foster better planning and design solutions in the context of continuing growth
Conservative policy institutions	Reason Public Policy Institute, Cato Institute, Heritage Foundation, Cascade Public Policy Institute	Reduce government control, recognize property rights, and promote free market policies.
Liberal policy institutions	Brookings Institution, Fannie Mae Foundation, Northeast-Midwest Institute	Promote policies that will redress social and economic inequities and rebuild cities and metro regions
Land policy institutions	Urban Land Institute, Lincoln Institute for Land Policy	Promote responsible use of land and urban resources and balanced development
Transit advocates	American Public Transit Association, Surface Transportation Policy Project, many state and local transit agencies	Promote transit use and shift commuters and other travelers from cars to transit
Historic preservation groups	National Trust for Historic Preservation, American Farmland Trust	Preserve historic buildings, neighborhoods, landscapes, and farmland

agitation by a small group of aesthetes would not account for the complexity and depth of the current debate. In fact, a wide spectrum of groups is involved in the discussion—from organizations that want to stop growth altogether to those who think there should be no restraints whatsoever on individual property rights and market forces. Although different groups may be characterized as belonging to different sides of the debate, they may have different goals, sometimes on both sides of the discussion. At the same time, many other groups are somewhere in the middle on many of the issues—either trying to find a way to balance growth and the impacts of growth or trying to further a specific agenda within the context of the debate.

Table 4.1 provides a summary of some of the different viewpoints involved in the debate, and Table 4.2 provides a listing of example organizations that might be characterized as belonging to the typical groups listed in Table 4.1 along with their key goals and issues. Clearly, these tables are simplified versions of the actual situation, but they serve to provide an outline sketch of the debate. Further detail on actual positions can be found on the Web sites of the organizations listed in Table 4.2.

There is a broad spectrum of opinion not only across example organizations shown within each group but also within the membership of the various organizations. Furthermore, there are organizations—such as the Thoreau Institute, an environmental group that firmly believes in free-market solutions—that don't fit comfortably within any of the groups shown in the tables. The goals and positions listed in the tables are derived from organization literature or positions expressed through the news media.

Anti-Sprawl Groups

Anti-sprawl sentiment is shared by a very loose coalition of groups with different primary goals. Inner-city advocacy groups probably have the longest track record, dating back to the 1950s and before, of working to direct new growth into cities. Center-city mayors, business leaders, and other groups generally hold that sprawl has negatively affected the nation's core cities and continues to drain them of vitality and economic health.

In recent years, environmental groups have become very strong anti-sprawl advocates. Their main issues are environmental protection and scarce natural resources. Some of these groups, such as the Natural Resources Defense Council and the Sierra Club, have produced well-researched literature that they believe demonstrates that suburbanization wastes resources and causes harm to the environment.

Historic preservation groups, such as the National Trust for Historic Preservation, have also come out with strong anti-sprawl positions. The National Trust is interested in preserving such rural heritage resources as scenic farmland and historic battlefield sites as well as in preserving historic downtown neighborhoods and buildings through revitalization. Their position is that continuing suburbanization destroys farmland and rural heritage resources while undermining historic neighborhoods and Main Streets.

Transit advocates are interested in promoting transit use and in shifting commuters and other travelers from cars to transit. Transit supporters believe that suburban development is inherently auto dependent and antithetical to increased transit use. Transit groups oppose sprawl and support higher-density nodal development patterns that they believe are more amenable to walking and transit use. Many urban planners and architects are anti-sprawl because they share parts of the agendas of inner-city, environmental, transit, and historic preservation groups. Architects also

want to keep building, so for that reason some of them side with building industry groups.

Some land policy institutions, such as the Urban Land Institute, tend to occupy more middle ground positions. They generally support continued growth, but they also support the need for planning and the need to address urban resources. State governments may tend to find themselves even more in the middle, trying to satisfy the sometimes conflicting demands of various constituency groups. Some states—such as Maryland, Oregon, and New Jersey—have come to believe that continuing suburbanization imposes greater costs on state government and state land resources than managed growth alternatives. Because of this belief, these states have developed programs aimed at curtailing or modifying sprawl development patterns (see Part III).

Liberal or liberal-center policy organizations, such as the Brookings Institution's Center on Urban and Metropolitan Policy, tend to promote actions aimed at redressing social and economic inequities while rebuilding cities and metropolitan regions. These groups may oppose suburbanization because they believe it promotes social and economic inequities and wastes urban resources.

Pro-Development Groups

Industry organizations like the NAHB clearly state that they believe Americans should continue to be given what surveys show they obviously want: more suburban housing. The NAHB believes that the majority of growth will continue to occur in the suburbs. Similar groups, such as the National Association of Industrial and Office Properties, which counts suburban office and industrial park owners and developers in its membership, also believe that further suburban commercial development should and will occur. These groups tend to oppose government controls that may raise land prices, make housing and commercial development more expensive, and inhibit consumer choice. The literature produced by these groups also recognizes that some change to existing patterns of development may be necessary.

The National Association of Realtors (NAR) similarly opposes regulations that would limit suburban development and possibly drive up land and housing costs. The NAR is joined by a number of conservative and libertarian policy institutions, such as the Reason Public Policy Institute and the Heritage Foundation, who support free-market solutions, individual property rights, and promoting home rule over big government. These groups believe that suburbanization and automobile dominance are the result of free-market choices and should be allowed to continue without government regulation. Industry groups and conservative policy institutions both believe that suburbanization has brought Americans more good than ill.

Housing advocacy groups generally are neutral on the issue of sprawl. Their primary mission is to build more affordable housing and promote actions that will lead to getting such housing built. However, housing advocacy groups such as Habitat for Humanity have recently joined forces with the NAR and other pro-development groups in fighting anti-sprawl initiatives in such states as Colorado. This is because they have come to believe that measures to stop sprawl may drive up land costs and make it harder to build affordable housing.

The Charges against Sprawl

Whatever benefits suburbanization may have brought to America, anti-sprawl groups have leveled many very significant charges against it. Some of those charges are briefly highlighted in Table 4.1. This section expands on a few of those highlights, further outlining some of the principal charges being made against sprawl.

Losing Land and Habitat

One of the most prominent concerns about sprawl (shared by self-interested suburbanites as well as inner-city advocates, environmentalists, preservation groups, and state and federal governments) is the rate at which the nation's landscape is vanishing due to the spread of sprawl.[8] The Natural Resources Defense Council (NRDC) says that the United States is losing about 365 acres of open land to sprawl development each hour.[9] The American Farmland Trust (AFT) claims that we are losing about 400,000 acres of prime farmland to suburban development each year—nearly 46 acres every hour.[10] At this rate of loss, the issue is no longer simply one of disappearing scenic resources and open

space; the AFT is asking whether there will be enough farmland left to feed the country.

But farmland isn't the only issue that has been raised about the nation's vanishing landscape. The loss of natural habitat and endangered species are also serious concerns. According to the National Wildlife Federation and the NRDC, open-space loss is threatening some of the most imperiled wildlife species in our country, including the Pacific salmon and the Florida panther.[11]

Stuck in Traffic and Running Out of Gas

Even those who don't care about land or wildlife hate being stuck in traffic (see Figure 4.5). The endless driving has become a burden for many people. From work to home, to shopping, to day care center, to school, to children's activities . . . and on and on. As we saw in Chapter 1, sprawl is a monomodal pattern that relies almost exclusively on the automobile.

Environmental groups, transit advocates, the federal government, and independent transportation analysis groups, such as the Texas Transportation Institute, all present statistics showing that the highways are becoming more congested every year (see Chapter 6). Between 1980 and 1997, total annual vehicle miles traveled (VMT) in the nation increased by 68 percent.[12] Between 1982 and 1996, the average annual delay experienced by individual drivers increased by 150 percent.[13] The amount of travel categorized as severely congested rose by 67 percent during the same period.[14]

All those vehicle miles also add up to a lot of petroleum—and the total U.S. consumption of

Figure 4.5. Between 1982 and 1996, the average annual delay experienced by drivers increased by 150 percent. (Alex S. MacLean/Landslides)

petroleum (the majority of which is consumed by cars and trucks; see Chapter 6) is predicted to continue rising. The U.S. Department of Energy forecasts that transportation energy consumption will increase by 40 percent by 2020, with almost two-thirds of the oil needed to satisfy that demand coming from outside the United States.[15] How long can this go on?

Choking on Air and Ruining Health

According to both environmental and public health groups, all of that slow-moving traffic contributes heavily to air pollution, which (because of all the traffic) is predicted to start increasing again over the next five years despite having fallen since 1970 because of the requirements of the Clean Air Act.[16] Exhaust from cars produces unhealthy air pollutants (such as oxides of nitrogen) as well as greenhouse gases (such as carbon dioxide) that contribute to global warming.

Toxic air pollutants and particulate matter from tailpipe emissions contribute to public health problems. Meanwhile, the Centers for Disease Control and Prevention believe the increase of driving and the decrease in walking are also contributing to obesity and poor health. At the same time, more than 3 million people are injured or killed in automotive accidents each year (see Chapter 7). It also is claimed that sprawl is degrading water quality (including drinking water) and eliminating wetland habitat.

Costing Too Much and Dividing Society

In the past ten years, state and local governments have become concerned that they can't go on building new roads, schools, sewers, and water lines forever while leaving the old ones to deteriorate. According to Maryland governor Parris Glendening: "Every new classroom costs $90,000. Every new mile of new sewer costs roughly $200,000. And every single lane-mile of new road costs at least $4 million."[17] Growing communities throughout the nation are searching desperately for ways to pay the public cost of all this new development. Raising taxes on residential property has sparked tax revolts in many states: Proposition 13 in California and Proposition 2-1/2 in Massachusetts are but two examples. Passed in the late 1970s and early 1980s, both were successful referenda that capped the

Figure 4.6. New office and industrial parks help pay taxes but can cost towns more money in the end. (Alex S. MacLean/Landslides)

real estate taxes that municipalities could levy in those states. Many suburban towns try to avoid significant increases in residential property taxes by attracting more commercial development to help foot the bill for money-losing residential subdivisions (see Figure 4.6).

Critics of sprawl say that this continuous chase for new tax dollars often results in more auto-oriented sprawl development covering the landscape (in Chapters 1 and 8). Meanwhile, all of the new sprawl is said to be subsidized by mortgage interest deductions and taxes, which build more roads.

SOCIAL DIVIDES

Not only does it cost too much, but inner city advocates, liberal policy institutions, and others accuse sprawl of also making the economic and racial divisions in our country more pronounced than ever before. We have already seen in Part I what suburbanization has done to the nation's cities. "White flight" was a catch phrase of the 1960s and 1970s that referred to the migration of the white middle class out of the center city and into the suburbs, seeking better schools and safer neighborhoods. According to the 2000 census, that phenomenon is still occurring (see Chapters 1 and 8). On the threshold of the new century, the poor people in our country live mostly in the cities and in the older, inner-ring suburbs, whereas the majority of the white middle class has moved ever outward.

In 2000, 86 percent of all Black Americans lived in metropolitan areas—nearly two-thirds in the center cities. Meanwhile, less than one-third of all whites living in metropolitan areas dwelled

Figure 4.7. Investment in the suburbs has been paralleled by disinvestment in urban communities. (Alex S. MacLean/Landslides)

in center cities.[18] Moreover, throughout the nation's metropolitan areas, nearly 55 percent of the nation's citizens living in poverty dwelled in the inner city in 1998.[19] Inner-city advocates and liberal policy institutions claim these facts show that our older cities and downtowns must have suffered greatly. Many of the residents who could afford to pay for the services the cities must provide have moved out—leaving the cities cash poor. The once-miraculous infrastructure of the great cities has similarly been left unmaintained, huge investments left to waste due to lack of funds (see Figure 4.7).

Despoiling the Landscape and Losing Community

Environmental groups, preservationists, architects, planners, and many others have accused sprawl of ruining scenic landscapes—by replacing farms and forests with tract houses and trading picturesque village centers for strip malls—and radically altering the character of rural communities. The evidence for these changes is widespread and is documented in the works of James Howard Kunstler and others. Furthermore, some groups assert that sprawl is reducing the sense of community in America. People are participating less in community services and social events because of a fragmented culture of individual homes on individual lots connected only by the automobile. In his book *Bowling Alone: The Collapse and Revival of American Community,* Robert Putnam blames sprawl for as much as 10 percent of the decline in American "civic engagement and social capital"—key ingredients in America's "social con-

nectedness and community involvement" (see Chapter 9).[20]

Only a Partial List

The paragraphs above are but a brief summary of the principal accusations being made about suburbanization by anti-sprawl groups in the newspapers, on television, in magazines, in books, and on the Internet. No one has to go very far to encounter some of these charges somewhere in the nation's media supply. Quite possibly, they are part of the reason that polls taken each year have shown increasingly greater proportions of the U.S. population opposed to the proliferation of sprawl (57 percent in 1999 and 78 percent in 2000).[21]

Pro-Development

Disputing the claims made against sprawl are such well-respected professionals and academicians as Peter Gordon and Harry Richardson of the University of Southern California, Samuel Staley of the Reason Public Policy Institute, Steven Hayward of the Pacific Research Institute for Public Policy, and Randal O'Toole of the Thoreau Institute. These people and others like them believe the environmental, social, and economic impacts attributed to sprawl to be largely unfounded or ultimately solvable by removing public sector interference and letting private markets do their work unencumbered.

Room to Grow

According to the Sierra Club, more than 20 million acres of rural land were lost to sprawl between 1970 and 1990 alone.[22] That seems like a lot, but then, how much is it? Dr. Samuel Staley of the Reason Public Policy Institute (RPPI) says that only 5 percent of the nation's land has actually been developed.[23] Moreover, Steven Hayward of the Heritage Foundation asserts that it takes nearly fifteen years to develop just 1 percent of the nation's land.[24] Concerning loss of farmland, the NAHB says, "Cancel the crisis: farmland is not disappearing." According to them, the amount of land used today for growing crops (cropland) in the United States is virtually the same as it was fifty years ago: 461 million acres in 1992 versus 451 million acres in

Figure 4.8. According to the National Association of Home Builders, the amount of cropland in the United States is virtually the same as it was fifty years ago. (Alex S. MacLean/Landslides)

Figure 4.9. The health effects of air pollution may be worse in urban areas. (Alex S. MacLean/Landslides)

1945 (see Figure 4.8).[25] Actually, that is *more* cropland than there was in 1945. Regarding habitat, the Heritage Foundation asserts that some species are actually increasing in the suburbs. Who's right here? The question turns a bit on the use of statistics as well what land is being used and what rate.

Traffic and Energy as Urban Problems

The Heritage Foundation references statistics that show that traffic congestion, VMT, fuel waste, and travel times all increase substantially in dense urban areas and decline in less dense, more suburban environments.[26] In other words, our real traffic and energy problems are caused by bottlenecks in the older cities and not by what we call suburbs or sprawl. Furthermore, RPPI and the Thoreau Institute both assert that the marketplace will reduce fuel consumption through higher prices and a market-driven switch to fuel-efficient auto technology, such as occurred in the 1970s.[27] Again, who's right here?

Pollution and Health

Both the Heritage Foundation and RPPI note that, along with traffic congestion, air pollution is worse in urban areas than in suburban areas (see Figure 4.9).[28] Furthermore, Dr. Samuel Staley of RPPI writes that data from the U.S. Environmental Protection Agency (EPA) indicate that air quality deteriorates as residential density increases.[29] Common sense would suggest that all of the driving that living in sprawl demands should be contributing massively to air pollution and the buildup of greenhouse gasses, but it's also true that air quality and traffic congestion are generally worse in dense, urban areas. That means that the health effects of air pollution may also be worse in urban areas. Once again, it is important to fully understand what is attributed to sprawl.

Exaggerated Costs and Social Divides

What about the cost issue? RPPI says that the cost of development studies produced by such groups as the American Farmland Trust exaggerate the costs of sprawl and that many of the costs are actually recovered through on-site improvements made by developers.[30] This is true in some cases, and there are some complications in making a case that sprawl really costs more than other, more compact forms of development on a cost of infrastructure basis alone (see Chapter 8). Furthermore, the Heritage Foundation points to studies that show that increasing density can actually act to increase infrastructure costs after a certain point.[31] That is also true, and we review some of these assertions in Chapter 8. But it is also true that the issue has other important aspects that aren't covered in the purely local infrastructure equation—such as the regional allocation and provision of new infrastructure, schools, and other services. For example, does it make sense to build new infrastructure to serve new suburban development within a metropolitan region while existing schools, roads, and utilities decay elsewhere in the same region?

CITIES AND SOCIAL DIVIDES

What about the nation's declining cities and social divides? Ronald Utt of the Heritage Foundation contends that in the past fifty years, there was actually a net population gain of over 1 million people in the nation's top twenty cities and that, for the same top twenty metro areas, the cities lost only one person for every five that the suburbs gained.[32] Meanwhile, U.S. Census Bureau data show that suburban areas are becoming increasingly diverse (see Chapters 1 and 8).

Moreover, RPPI blames urban decline on the cities themselves, citing a multitude of push factors, such as poor schools, crime, and high taxes.[33] These push factors are what is keeping middle-income families and households from locating in the cities. And, according to RPPI, this is a problem the cities should solve for themselves. There is little question that RPPI is right about the push factors—they are precisely the concerns a lot of families with children have about living in the city—but is this strictly a municipal problem or does it have broader regional implications?

What about social divides? It can be effectively argued that we would be just as segregated a society as we are today even without sprawl. After all, segregation predated the suburban explosion by many years, and the cities themselves are still quite segregated, with enclaves of white wealth that are distinctly separated from well-defined ghettos of minorities and concentrations of severe poverty. The 2000 census data confirm this pattern. Some of the nation's major cities, such as New York and Chicago, were among the top ten most segregated areas in the nation in 2000.[34] Furthermore, more minorities are moving to the suburbs all the time—an encouraging development and one that has also been confirmed by the 2000 census.[35]

Community and Aesthetics

While some groups may decry what is happening to America's landscape, the NAHB has surveys that show that the vast majority of Americans still prefer a detached home in the suburbs to other types of housing.[36] As far as loss of community is concerned, Randal O'Toole of the Thoreau Institute asserts that this is basically a myth and that sociologists, such as Herbert Gans, have found plenty of evidence of community spirit and community participation in the suburbs.[37]

Untangling the Sprawl Brawl

The above is a rough summary of some of the issues under contention together with some of the questions they raise, but it is clear from even this brief look that the debate is far from simple. Many accusations and counteraccusations exist across many different categories, without any clear-cut answers. Opinions vary widely about the benefits and problems of sprawl as well as the severity of its impacts, and the issue continues to be clouded by conflicting public opinion.

Public Opinion

Public opinion polls taken by different groups also give evidence of widely shared opposing notions: first, that just about everyone wants to live in a single-family home on its own lot, and second, that few people want more sprawl. The NAHB poll numbers not only indicate a clear preference for detached single-family homes in the suburbs but also show that 78 percent of those surveyed were opposed to transit-friendly sprawl containment measures, such as building higher-density housing of any kind in their neighborhoods.[38] On the other hand, the *Time*/CNN poll conducted within the same twelve months showed that nearly 60 percent of the nation favored some kind of control over sprawl.[39] These widely divergent desires make it difficult to find a consensus policy for dealing with the impacts of suburbanization.

These surveys show that most people want to have their own homes on their own lots and that they don't want any further growth of any kind in the surrounding neighborhood. In other words, once inside the door, most people would like to be able to close it behind them so that their area doesn't get anymore crowded than it already is. This could be considered an anti-growth viewpoint. In their recent publication *A Guide to Smart Growth*, the Heritage Foundation suggests that this is precisely what is going on. In his article "The

Suburbanization of America" in this guide, Steven Hayward argues that the nation is undergoing a change in social outlook as "the nexus between general growth and our personal well-being . . . [is] broken."[40] America's outlook, he contends, has changed to the point where economic growth is no longer seen as generally beneficial when compared with the bad traffic and vanishing open space that it engenders. While Hayward views this as an unprecedented point in U.S. history, it is also possible that it simply reflects the current U.S. economic cycle.

A Cyclical Issue

Some evidence exists that sprawl is mostly a quality of life issue for the majority of the voting public and, as such, that it is only prominent on the national radar screen during good economic times, while tending to go into stealth mode during recessions. A 1999 New York Times article by Todd Purdum quoted both Republican and Democratic political consultants who expressed the opinion that sprawl is essentially a "quality of life issue" and that "if you're worried about your basic material well-being, you don't have so much time to be worried about your quality of life."[41]

Sprawl first registered as a serious issue in the prosperous periods of the 1950s and 1960s. It resurfaced in the 1980s but became briefly dormant during the recession of the early 1990s. Now, it has surfaced again. Two fundamental reasons exist for this ebb and surge. First, the majority of the voting middle class is likely to be a lot less worried about sprawl when they are mostly worried about their jobs. After all, growth and construction create jobs. Second, it is during prosperous times that the real booms in new construction occur, which cause the protests. It is only when someone starts to build in the open field next door that people become concerned. The booms also bring more traffic along with economic activity, and that slows everybody down and gets them irritated. Traffic has been observed to smooth out when the economy takes a dive.

The cyclical nature of the issue makes it even harder to reach a consensus. Plans and constraints put in place in the boom periods are just as likely to be abandoned during the bust periods. People feel fundamentally different about sprawl and act differently depending what time it is on the economic clock.

Taking a Longer View: Sustainability

The intensity of the current debate and the propensity of the issue to change with the economic seasons suggest the need to take a longer view of sprawl development. One way is to look at the issue through the lens of sustainability. Although the benefits of suburbanization may have been substantial, what are some of the consequences of continuing this pattern for future generations? Is sprawl a sustainable way of doing things?

Sustainability, like sprawl, is a popular term with many different definitions. The United Nations World Commission on Environment and Development (also known as the Bruntland Commission) was among the first to popularize the term sustainable development in the 1980s. In the commission's final report, entitled Our Common Future, sustainable development was defined as development that allows people "to meet the needs of the present without compromising the ability of future generations to meet their own needs." The President's Council on Sustainable Development adopted this definition in 1993.[42] This is a pretty broad definition, however. A somewhat more precise definition of sustainability was once given by William Ruckleshaus, a two-time head of the EPA:

> Sustainability is the doctrine that economic growth and development must take place, and be maintained over time, within the limits set by ecology in the broadest sense—by the interrelations of human beings and their works, and the biosphere. . . . It follows that environmental protection and economic development are complementary rather than antagonistic processes.[43]

Thus, we may consider sustainability or sustainable development to mean development that limits impacts to the natural environment and our society such that it preserves existing resources of both as required to sustain future generations. Naturally, this poses other fairly fuzzy questions, such as exactly how much of what is required to sustain how many of whom living at what level, and so forth. It is not within the scope of this book to define such thresholds, but at least at a summary level, we can try in the following chapters to better understand the impacts of sprawl on the environment and on society as they have so far been identified, to weigh counterarguments, and to provide some assessment of the scope of the problem from a sustainability point of view.

CHAPTER 5

Land and Habitat

This chapter examines the impacts of suburbanization on land resources and wildlife habitat. The first section deals with land resources in general, which include undeveloped open land of all types and farmland—two areas that have been the subject of continuing debate. The second section examines another aspect of open land: the fact that it provides a habitat for a wide range of biological communities of plants and animals that exist in interdependent ecosystems.

Vanishing Landscape?

The United States has a tradition as a "frontier country" with an inexhaustible supply of land. Daniel Boone was looking for what he called "elbow room" when he crossed into the wilds of Kentucky, abandoning land to the east he had only recently settled. In many ways, Boone—pioneer, rugged individual, and property owner—is an archetypal American citizen. When faced with the demands of an increasingly populous community, Boone went over the hill to find a new and unspoiled environment to settle, leaving the settled world behind him to solve its own problems. Although things may be changing in some parts of the United States, this attitude prevails in the nation, and many people still consider America a country with a lot of room in which to grow. But after more than fifty years of suburbanization, many wonder whether that attitude is still legitimate.

The rate at which the nation's land supply is being consumed has raised alarm in the press and in the literature put out by government agencies and environmental and land-use groups. According to a July 2001 article in *National Geographic,* seventy million Americans lived in the 13,000 square-miles comprising the nation's urbanized areas in 1950. Today about three times as many people live in a total metropolitan area that is

more than fifty times as large.[1] To emphasize this point, *National Geographic* presents a nighttime satellite image of the United States that is similar to Figure 5.1. In that image, U.S. metropolitan areas appear as "galaxies of light across the United States [that] illuminate the scope of sprawl."[2]

National Geographic is not alone. Looking at individual metro areas, *Time* reports that Atlanta is the fastest-spreading human settlement in history consuming over 500 acres of farmland every week.[3] *Time* also notes that Kansas City has spread 70 percent in five years, while its population increased only 5 percent.[4] *The New York Times* reports that "bands of suburbs have started to merge with each other along Southern transportation corridors, in some cases forming almost unbroken chains of medium-density areas hundreds of miles long—from Atlanta to Raleigh along Interstate I-85, or from Washington to Norfolk."[5]

The Environmental Protection Agency (EPA) has called urban sprawl "a bona fide threat to New England's environmental and economic future," noting that development there is consuming over 1,200 acres of new land each week.[6] The Natural Resources Defense Council points out that the City of Chicago contains only 6 per-

Figure 5.1. Nighttime lights across the United States as seen from outer space. (NOAA/DMSP)

83

cent of the land area of its metropolitan region and about one third of the region's population, while accounting for only 38 percent of the region's employment.[7] According to the Urban Land Institute, the City of St. Louis contains less than 20 percent of the regional population and 10 percent of regional employment.[8] How far can suburbanization spread before it seriously threatens the nation's land resources?

How Much Land Is Left for Development?

The answer to this question depends on whom you talk to and how you look at the problem. Official records show that there is still a lot of undeveloped land in the United States, even with all the thousands of acres of sprawl that have carpeted the countryside over the last fifty years. It may seem hard to believe after looking at the maps in Chapter 1 and the satellite photo presented in Figure 5.1, but this is what the records indicate. Almost no one is predicting that the nation will run out of land anytime soon. Exactly how much land will be consumed, however, is a matter of some dispute.

RATES OF LAND LOSS

The Reason Public Policy Institute (RPPI) and the Heritage Foundation both state that only 5 percent of the land in the United States is developed and that 75 percent of the population lives on only 3.5 percent of the nation's land.[9] The National Association of Home Builders (NAHB) goes even further, claiming that "built-up and urban land" together make up just 3 percent of the 1.9 billion acres contained in the forty-eight contiguous states. RPPI's figures appear to be derived from U.S. census data, but the NAHB gives no source for its figures. A somewhat more indifferent source, the U.S. Department of Agriculture (USDA) *1997 National Resources Inventory*, lists the total land area of the United States at about 1.9 billion acres, with about 5.2 percent of the land showing as developed (see Figure 5.2).[10] The USDA database includes the forty-eight contiguous states plus Hawaii and Puerto Rico but does not include Alaska.

According to the USDA's Natural Resources Conservation Service, we are losing land to development at an average rate of nearly 2 million acres per year.[11] Of the roughly 1.9 billion acres contained in the United States (excluding water areas), more than 35 percent is either publicly owned or already developed. That leaves about 1.2 billion acres remaining. If we were to make a very broad assumption (based on data available from the USDA) that about 15–20 percent of the remainder may be undevelopable due to topography, wetlands, climate, and other factors, that leaves about 1 billion acres of developable, privately held land in the United States.[12] If the rate of development were to con-

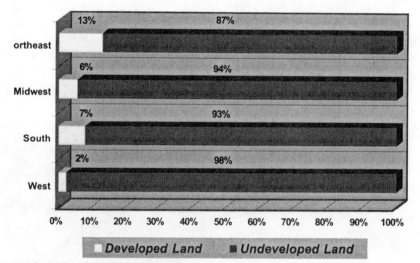

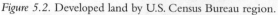

Figure 5.2. Developed land by U.S. Census Bureau region.
Source: U.S. Department of Agriculture, Natural Resources Conservation Service, *1997 National Resources Inventory* (Washington, D.C.: U.S. Department of Agriculture, 2000), table 1, www.nhq.ncrs.usda.gov/NRI/1997/summaryreport/original/table1.html.

tinue at 2 million acres per year, that would leave us about five hundred years until the entire country was built out—seemingly a long time. Even so, Steven Hayward of the Heritage Foundation contests the accuracy of the USDA figure and claims that the real rate of land development (based on information from the U.S. Geological Survey) is actually much lower, at about 1.3 million acres per year. At this rate, he writes, it would take fifteen years to develop just 1 percent of the nation's remaining land supply. However, Hayward's 1 percent figure refers to the total land area of the contiguous United States, including developed, public, and undevelopable land. It would actually take only about eight years to develop 1 percent of the hypothetical 1 billion acres described above, but that is still nearly eight hundred years to reach full build-out.[13]

SENSITIVITY TO ASSUMPTIONS

The above analysis is, of course, quite simplistic and very loose, but it is an example of the kind of published thinking available on relative to land supply. Naturally, the number of years it takes to develop all of the contiguous United States can be altered significantly by changes in the rate of development and other assumptions that make up the example. The difference in assumed consumption rates above easily demonstrates this point. Furthermore, we have already seen, for example, that in Massachusetts alone more land has been developed in the past fifty years than in the three centuries prior to 1950.[14]

But even if the USDA's rate were doubled, it would still be more years than the United States has been in existence before the land is used up—and that could still leave nearly half of the nation's land undeveloped (as long as public land remains undeveloped and if assumptions about undevelopable land are correct). Over those lengths of time, conditions may become so radically altered as to void any speculative growth scenario. After all, it has taken only about 150 years for the nation to move from small walking cities to the vastness of contemporary metropolitan areas. In that same period of time, the United States has gone through an industrial revolution and on to an information economy, while also growing from obscurity to world power. The next 150 years may hold equally dramatic transformations, and sprawl, as we know it, may evolve into something altogether different

or may simply become irrelevant. Thus, for all practical purposes, RPPI and the NAHB may be right—the United States is not going to run out of developable land per se anytime soon—at least from the point of view of the total supply available.

The Open Space Next Door

One problem with sweeping, simplistic calculations like the ones made above is that they tend to shift the focus away from the real problems, such as the ones felt by most of the people in the *Time*/CNN, Smart Growth America, and other polls, who favor some sort of control over development. These people are concerned about the loss of open land happening today right next door, not in some part of the country that won't be developed for a hundred years.

RPPI may be correct in stating that more than 75 percent of the nation's population lives on 3 percent of its land area-but that may be the problem. The most precious open land is the undeveloped property remaining within the 3 to 5 percent of the nation's acreage where all the growth is occurring, in and around the nation's metropolitan areas. It is the privately owned land right next door to where three-quarters of the nation lives that is the issue at hand—be it forest, farmland, or just an open field.

If, as Steven Hayward has argued, Americans are reaching the point where they no longer see growth as beneficial when compared with vanishing open space, it is not rural land far from any settlement that is the issue at hand; rather, it is the development of land next to where the majority of Americans live, the land in and around the 5 percent that is already developed. This is where the next 1 percent of development will occur, and when it does, it will mean that the developed area next to where most people live will increase by 20 percent or more in the next fifteen years and potentially double in area (from 5 percent to 10 percent) within the next seventy-five years. And this conclusion is reached using the Heritage Foundation's lower rate of development. At 2 million acres per year, the amount of developed land in the nation would double within approximately fifty years.

Those rates are also only the average rates of development throughout the nation. In some areas of the country, the rate may be much faster. For example, in Massachusetts the rate of devel-

Table 5.1. Hypothetical Development Rates and Projections for Selected States (Acres)

	1997			2050		
	Total Developable Land	Developed Land	Percent Developed	Annual Development Rate	Developed Land	Percent Developed
California	47,558,600	5,456,100	11	138,960	12,820,980	27
Connecticut	2,874,900	873,900	30	12,680	1,545,940	54
Delaware	1,216,400	225,500	19	7,020	597,560	49
Georgia	33,111,800	3,957,300	12	210,640	15,121,220	46
Maryland	5,737,400	1,235,700	22	44,460	3,592,080	63
Massachusetts	4,653,500	1,034,000	22	56,300	4,017,900	86
Michigan	26,014,200	2,725,300	10	110,160	8,563,780	33
North Carolina	26,430,700	2,416,700	9	156,300	10,700,600	40
Florida	24,371,100	5,185,000	21	189,060	15,205,180	62
New Jersey	3,822,000	1,778,200	47	56,640	3,822,000	100

Source: U.S. Department of Agriculture, Natural Resources Conservation Service, *1997 National Resources Inventory,* and the National Wilderness Institute.

Notes: Total developable land is the area of the state net of water and public lands. Protected lands, conservation lands, wetlands, and other nondevelopable lands have not been excluded, potentially reducing the amount of developable land further than shown.

opment is estimated by the USDA to be 56,300 acres per year. At that rate, 86 percent of the developable land in the state could be built on by the year 2050. By that same year, at current rates of development for each state, all of the developable land in New Jersey will be built out and developable land in Florida will be more than 60 percent built out. Table 5.1 displays hypothetical estimates for these states and several others based on current rates of development and other data available from the USDA.[15]

It is important to note that the developable land area estimates in Table 5.1 are quite simplistic and do not exclude private protected lands, wetlands, or other land that may be undevelopable for physical or environmental reasons. Water bodies and public lands are excluded, but the amount of developable land could quite possibly be less than is shown. Also, the rates of growth shown are purely hypothetical projections of current rates. Even though developable land supplies may be less (potentially hastening build-out), other factors may slow the pace of development. As the supply of developable land decreases, land costs will most likely go up. Rising land costs and increasing regulation are likely to slow development rates in the states shown.

Nonetheless, the figures make the point. The question is not how long it will take to fill up all

of the land in the United States, but more important, what happens when the next 2 or 3 percent of the nation's land gets developed? That is when the open land enjoyed by the majority of the population becomes endangered. By open land, what is generally meant is land that is either (1) publicly owned park or forestlands, (2) undeveloped privately owned open land (field or forest), or (3) open privately owned farmland. Because the public parks and forestlands are already held in common, it is usually the fate of the privately owned, developable land that concerns most people.

Despite the rapid pace of development, the nation can probably consider itself fortunate that about 27 percent of the land in the United States is held in common by federal, state, and local government (3 percent is tribal land, and the remaining 70 percent is private).[16] This means that the 27 percent is basically "public" and is, in theory, less likely to be sold off and developed someday. It is also supposed to be available to all U.S. citizens as a common resource, even though some of it may be leased for forestry, mining, or other "harvesting" activities. Those harvesting activities can, of course, be fairly extreme, and these public lands are not immune to development—they can, in principle, be sold or leased.

Even with this abundance of public land, 70 percent of all the land in the United States

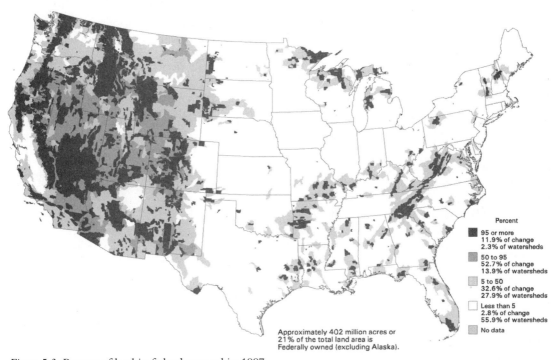

Percent

95 or more
11.9% of change
2.3% of watersheds

50 to 95
52.7% of change
13.9% of watersheds

5 to 50
32.6% of change
27.9% of watersheds

Less than 5
2.8% of change
55.9% of watersheds

No data

Approximately 402 million acres or
21% of the total land area is
Federally owned (excluding Alaska).

Figure 5.3. Percent of land in federal ownership, 1997.
Source: U.S. Department of Agriculture, Natural Resources Conservation Service, *1997 National Resources Inventory* (Washington, D.C.: 2000).

remains privately owned. Most of the land we see around us every day is in private hands. This is particularly true east of the Rocky Mountains. Most of the great tracts of federal land are in the West (see Figures 5.3 and 5.4). Almost all of the land east of the Rockies is privately held, and that is where more than three-quarters of U.S. residents live and work. Many more live in and around metropolitan areas in the West, which also contain relatively little public land. Thus, the open

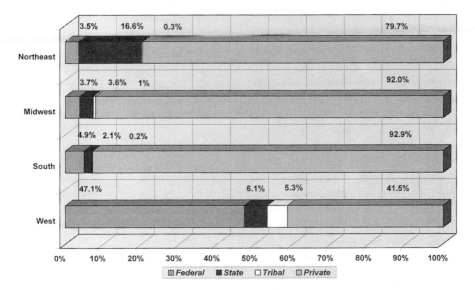

Figure 5.4. Private and public lands by U.S. Census Bureau region.
Sources: U.S. Department of Agriculture, Natural Resources Conservation Service, *1997 National Resources Inventory* (Washington, D.C.: DOA, 2000), table 1, www.nhq.ncrs.usda.gov/NRI/1997/summaryreport/original/table1.html; and National Wilderness Institute.
Note: Excludes Alaska, Hawaii, Puerto Rico, and the District of Columbia.

spaces and vistas of farmlands, meadows, and trees that are precious to many Americans are likely to be on private land, and the open land that the majority of Americans care about is likely to be next door to the 3 to 5 percent of the nation's land area on which they live.

Farmland

Of the roughly 70 percent of the nation's land that is privately held, not all of it is available for development. Increasingly stringent environmental regulations have made some kinds of land more difficult to develop than others. This is particularly true of wetlands, for example, which are protected under both federal and state laws. On the whole, however, the physical features of the landscape generally act only to add to or detract from the cost of the land or the cost of developing the land. California, Arizona, and Nevada have proven that sprawl can take place almost anywhere, even in the most rugged and barren of terrain. Notwithstanding this fact, cleared, well-drained, flat land is much preferred if it can be obtained inexpensively enough. In most places, this means either farmland or former farmland. After farmland becomes too expensive or simply unavailable in a given region, development will move to less desirable terrain.

The general preference for agricultural acreage has led some to raise the alarm about vanishing farmland. Here again, different statistics are quoted to support varying points of view. The Natural Resources Defense Council (NRDC) states that "prime farmland" is disappearing at the rate of four hundred thousand acres per year, or nearly forty-six acres per hour.[17] That seems an alarming figure. On the other hand, as noted in Chapter 4, the NAHB states that there was actually more "cropland" in the United States in 1992 than in 1945. Again, these are different figures describing different types of land. The USDA defines cropland as a land use category "that includes areas used for the production of adapted crops for harvest." "Prime farmland," on the other hand, is defined as "land that has the best combination of physical and chemical characteristics for producing . . . crops and is also available for these uses."[18] Prime farmland is the best land for growing crops, but may include land that is not currently being used for crops. "Cropland" is land that is being used for crops, but may not be the best

land. Prime farmland is therefore the most important category concerning producing food.

PRIME FARMLAND LOSS

According to the USDA, the United States has about 1.3 billion acres of "farmland," including cropland, pastureland, rangeland, and forestland.[19] However, only about 25 percent of that figure, or about 330 million acres, was classified as "prime farmland" in 1997.[20] The USDA's research indicates that the United States lost 8.8 million acres of prime farmland to development between 1982 and 1997. That translates to an average rate of about 587,000 acres per year. This figure is higher than the NRDC's estimate, but even at this rate we would not run out of prime farmland for more than 560 years. Again, this is too long a time frame to speculate reasonably relying upon historical trends.

On the other hand, during the next fifty years, the population of the United States is expected to grow by nearly 45 percent.[21] This would seem to indicate a need for more prime farmland rather than less—unless production methods improve dramatically or we start importing more food. In fact, production methods have improved dramatically over the years. According to the USDA, each acre of American cropland produces nearly three times the amount that was produced on the same acre in 1935.[22] This has allowed the amount of land actually being used for crops to remain fairly constant over almost fifty years even though the population has increased by nearly two-thirds.[23] Gains in production techniques have largely offset increasing demand to the extent that the United States is still producing enough food to continue exporting it despite population gains, and the U.S. government still has programs in place to counter the effects of overproduction. These considerations have led the USDA to conclude that "losing farmland to urban uses does not threaten total cropland or the level of agricultural production which should be sufficient to meet food and fiber demand into the next century."[24]

Although the loss of farmland doesn't appear to be an immediate threat to the nation's food supply, it may be a serious local issue and one that affects particular segments of the food market. For example, the American Farmland Trust (AFT) lists California's Central Valley as one of the nation's top twenty most endangered farm-

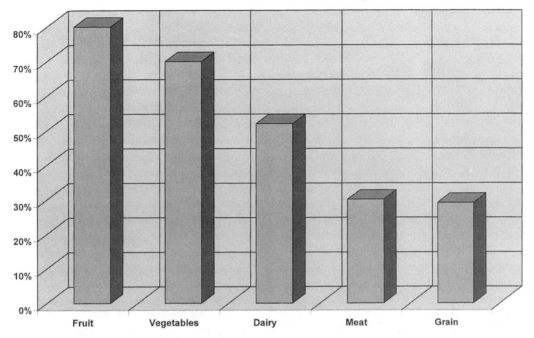

Figure 5.5. Percentage of total U.S. food production in threatened areas.
Source: Ann A. Sorenson, Richard P. Greene, and Karen Russ, *Farming on the Edge* (DeKalb, Ill.: American Farmland Trust, 1997).

land areas.[25] California produces a significant amount of the nation's fruit and vegetables. The fact that this area is affected by development pressures may eventually cause some problems in the availability or quality of certain types of produce grown in the United States. The AFT also notes that many of the areas producing specialty crops in the United States are also near expanding urbanized areas. These areas produce 80 per cent of the nation's fruit, about 70 percent of its vegetables, and slightly more than 50 percent of its dairy products (see Figure 5.5).[26] The proximity of these areas to rapid-growth areas makes them highly susceptible to replacement by sprawl development. Thus, according to the AFT, it is not so much a question of total farmland loss as it is which farmland is being lost and where. The solution to this issue should be to inventory the land and consider implementing farmland preservation measures for specific areas across the country. The AFT has already completed a significant amount of this inventory work, and their publication *Farming on the Edge* lists 127 specific areas of prime and "unique" farmland (farmland used for the production of specific high-value food and fiber crops) as currently endangered by urbanization.

Loss of farmland around expanding metro-politan areas not only threatens prime and unique farmland but also diminishes scenic resources and open space available to nearby metropolitan residents. Frank Lloyd Wright never envisioned his Broadacre City to consist of unbroken low-density development. In his plans, drawings, models, and writing, fields and farms are intentionally an integral part of the fabric of his imaginary city. Broadacre City was to be built in harmony with prevailing patterns of "tillage and forestation," and "deep feeling for the beauty of terrain" was to be "fundamental in the new city." The residents of his city were to dwell amid "native abundance."[27] Farmland and forest are open spaces that are enjoyed by many, providing needed relief to otherwise unbroken vistas of suburbia. When close to a metropolitan area, prime and unique farmland can also be a source of fresh, seasonal produce that would otherwise be unavailable—part of Wright's "native abundance."

Natural Habitat

Jane Shaw argues in *A Guide to Smart Growth* that suburban development actually provides a habitat that is more conducive to biodiversity than the farmland it replaces. That may be true, to some extent; some environmentalists view farmland as a "monoculture" with little biodiversity.[28] Furthermore, she notes that in New York State, deer populations have increased 610 percent in suburban areas while increasing by 240 percent in the state overall.[29] Beavers and geese, she goes on to note, are also becoming more prolific in the suburbs as are fox, black bears, turkeys, geese, red-tailed hawks, coyotes, and other animals. Joel Garreau and other authors have noted the same phenomenon.[30]

Those animals are increasing as their natural habitats are reduced and they find themselves able to adapt to the new suburban milieu. But, for all the animals and plants that can adapt, there are many others that cannot acclimatize to new conditions, either because of the elimination of their habitats or because of fragmentation. For example, damage done to water resources (such as wetlands, ponds, streams, and rivers) also negatively affects the plant and animal communities they support. Studies have found that as the amount of paved or impervious area in a given watershed exceeds 30 percent (not an atypical level for suburban development), many species disappear as the watershed becomes significantly

degraded.[31] Watersheds are one form of wildlife habitat, and wetlands are another. According to the U.S. Fish and Wildlife Service (USFW), spreading suburbanization is the cause of the largest amount of wetland loss (51 percent of wetlands lost) followed by agriculture (26 percent of wetlands lost) (see Figure 5.6).[32] According to the EPA, wetland loss from agriculture is declining due to the fall in profitability of converting wetlands to agricultural use.[33] Wetlands cover only about 5 percent of U.S. land area, but they include 50 percent of the animals and 33 percent of the plant species listed in the United States as endangered or threatened.[34] These are wetlands that also act as filters to enhance water quality and that serve as flood storage for runoff.

In her book *Planning for Biodiversity,* Sheila Peck notes that expanding suburban sprawl also fragments wildlife habitat, disturbing migration and breeding patterns, even when it does not result in the complete elimination of a given ecosystem. Fragmented ecosystems increase the danger to imperiled wildlife. Certain categories of species are especially vulnerable to habitat fragmentation, and rare and specialized species may be unable to compete with others that are

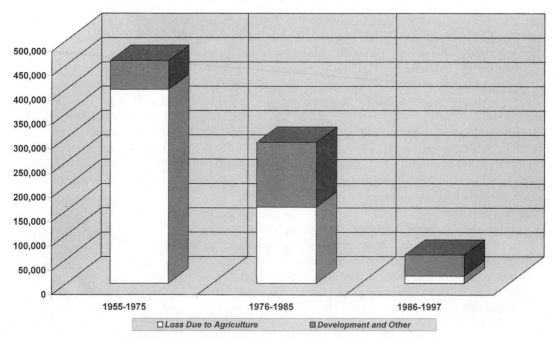

Figure 5.6. Annual U.S. wetland loss and principal causes.
Sources: U.S. Environmental Protection Agency (EPA), Office of Water, *National Water Quality Inventory: 1996 Report to Congress* (Washington, D.C.: EPA, 1996); and Thomas E. Dahl; *Status and Trends of Wetlands in the Coterminus United States 1986 to 1997* (Washington, D.C.: U.S. Fish and Wildlife Service, 2000).

better adapted to change. Populations within habitat remnants become smaller and prone to extinction as food supplies and mates dwindle and competition increases.[35] Many rare and specialized species require large, contiguous undisturbed open spaces to survive, and they become threatened by barriers that reduce or fragment their rangelands.[36]

Peck explains that fragmentation also increases "edge" habitat relative to "interior" habitat. Edge habitat generally has a more severe microclimate (more sunlight, heat, wind, temperature change, and so forth) than does interior habitat and benefits species adapted to those harsher conditions. Edge habitats are also susceptible to more impacts from adjacent uses. In areas undergoing suburbanization, these impacts may include trampling, erosion, noise, light, pollutants, and traffic. Increasing edge habitat relative to interior habitat also exposes more of the total reserve to the introduction of new species, including both plants and animals that may eventually replace existing species.[37]

The shrinking, isolated patches of edge habitat left behind by scattered development are suited only to more abundant generalist species, such as deer, skunks, beavers, raccoons, rabbits, coyotes, and some of the other species cited by Jane Shaw. The animal and plant species that are entering the suburban landscape are those that are able to adapt to the changed circumstances and are able to survive in relatively harsh edge habitats. Those that cannot change will be gradually diminished, increasingly facing the possibility of extinction. In fact, the increase in adaptable species may actually hasten the decline of other remaining species. The new suburban environment ultimately permits for a smaller range of animal and plant types over a widening area.

Urbanization not only replaces farmland, it also replaces forest. Jane Shaw notes the dramatic regrowth of eastern forests during the twentieth century, stating that between 1880 and 1991, forestlands in New England increased to between 35 and 86 percent of land cover, depending on the state.[38] This is basically true. During the nineteenth and twentieth centuries, many farms abandoned the rocky soil of New England for better soil in the Midwest and the West. New England forests continued to be clear-cut into the twentieth century to provide lumber for building, pulp for paper, charcoal for iron furnaces, and potash for fertilizer, among other things. Many of these demands have greatly diminished in the latter part of the century, allowing New England to become reforested and many plant and animal communities to become reestablished. Expanding suburban development has now begun to replace regrowth forestland, disrupting reestablished forest habitats. In Massachusetts alone, it is estimated that 15 percent of the larger animal and plant species are endangered by the fragmentation of habitat caused by increasing suburbanization.[39]

Land and Habitat in Summary

Existing development comprises only about 5 percent of the total landscape of the contiguous United States. At current levels and rates, it would appear that, broadly analyzed, there is land available to sustain sprawl patterns of development for the foreseeable future. However, this type of analysis masks what is happening at local levels, which is what concerns the more than 75% of the U.S. population that happens to reside within that same 5 percent of developed land area. At current rates of development, 5 percent could grow to 10 percent in fifty to seventy-five years. When that happens, the developed portion of the nation's metropolitan areas will double. Some states may be entirely built-out, a situation that may not be tolerable to many people and may adversely affect growth and attitudes about growth in the nation, which, in turn, will adversely affect the ability to sustain the expansion of suburban development. Meanwhile, specialized agricultural land adjoining urbanizing areas will be increasingly diminished, reducing sources of vegetables and fruit and other specialized agriculture while also diminishing scenic resources and regional open space.

Finally, the spread of suburban sprawl may be suitable habitat for certain adaptable, generalist species, but wetland and other habitat loss combined with mounting fragmentation and expanding edge habitats means that many endangered specialized species and rare biological communities may suffer substantially reduced populations and eventual extinction. Furthermore, in areas of recently reestablished forest growth, such as in New England, suburbanization threatens to disrupt habitats that only now are recovering from clear-cutting and agricultural use.

CHAPTER 6

Transportation and Energy

This chapter explores the effects of suburbanization on transportation—particularly vehicular traffic on the nation's roadways—and consequent impacts to energy consumption. The first section examines traffic congestion and looks at potential nontransit solutions, comparing these with transit. The second section deals with energy consumption and the question of future fuel supply.

Traffic

Some of the most widespread and bitter complaints about sprawl have to do with increased traffic congestion. According to the Heritage Foundation, surveys have shown that 79 percent of those polled identified traffic congestion as one of the worst aspects of suburbanization, worse even than crime.[1] Surveys by Smart Growth America found similar results, with respondents ranking traffic congestion and crime as the most important issues facing their communities.[2] Everyone can relate to the time squandered while stuck on the highway. The average American spends about 440 hours per year behind the wheel of a car—the equivalent of about fifty-five workdays.[3] One estimate of the economic cost of time wasted stuck in traffic in just thirty-nine of the nation's major metropolitan areas is close to $34 billion annually.[4] In their book *The Transportation/Land Use Connection,* Terry Moore and Paul Thorsnes put the national cost much higher, at nearly $139 billion annually.[5] Other estimates place the cost at anywhere from $43 billion to $168 billion per year.[6]

Approximately 91 percent of all the person miles traveled in the United States are in privately owned automobiles. Trains, bikes, walking, airplanes, and other forms of transportation make up the remaining 9 percent.[7] Because the U.S. transportation system is so one-sided, it seems almost guaranteed to become overwhelmed as growth continues. New roadways open up ever more land for new development. When that land fills up with office parks, tract houses, and shopping malls, the roadways also fill up, leading to another cycle of road building followed by more development. Many people complain that such induced demand is an endless cycle. Worse, the hours spent driving and stuck in traffic arguably use increasing amounts of energy and generate more air pollution.

A Suburban or an Urban Problem?

Both the Reason Public Policy Institute (RPPI) and the Heritage Foundation argue that traffic congestion is mostly an urban and not a suburban phenomenon. Wendell Cox of the Heritage Foundation reports data from the Texas Transportation Institute (TTI) that shows clearly that both vehicle miles traveled (VMT) and traffic congestion increase with population density, which means that the amount of traffic and the amount of traffic congestion are both increased in urban areas (see Figure 6.1).[8] Dr. Samuel Staley of RPPI cites data that concur with this assertion while offering a hypothetical case in which regional planners double the density of a small urban center. In that scenario, Staley argues, some (perhaps 30 percent) of new commuter trips may be diverted to transit, but the community will still have to deal with 70 percent additional auto trips—creating congestion.[9] It is an interesting case but is somewhat misleading in that it ignores the fact that the population might otherwise have spread out, creating new suburban communities around the center that are mostly dependent on cars for travel. In that case, auto trips and would still go up but any diversion to transit would be minimal. Thus, congestion at the center could be even worse without the higher density.

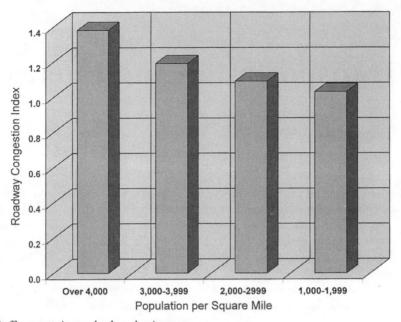

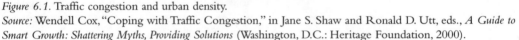

Figure 6.1. Traffic congestion and urban density.
Source: Wendell Cox, "Coping with Traffic Congestion," in Jane S. Shaw and Ronald D. Utt, eds., *A Guide to Smart Growth: Shattering Myths, Providing Solutions* (Washington, D.C.: Heritage Foundation, 2000).

However, both Cox and Staley are correct in asserting that congestion and VMT generally increase with density. The nation's cities and built-up suburban areas are where some of the early freeways were built, in what were very constrained environments to begin with—especially in cities that were built for walking and transit, not for cars. As traffic has increased, roadway capacity has remained fixed. Expanding highways in these areas is difficult and can be extremely costly (for example, Boston's Central Artery/Tunnel project, also known as the Big Dig, now projected to cost more than $14 billion).[10]

Moreover, these highways might not need to be expanded if it weren't for the huge expansion in suburban development that has occurred since they were built. It is the background increase in widespread auto-dependent suburban development that has led directly to traffic congestion in cities, combined with a shift in freight traffic to trucks and a shift in economic focus from cities to metropolitan regions served by roadways, automobiles, and trucks. People living or working (or both) in the suburbs who have destinations in, near, or on the other side of a city often have to travel into or through the city on the regional highway system because there are few

practical alternatives to the automobile for originating or terminating in the dispersed, low-density suburbs that make up most of the nation's metropolitan areas. The number of VMT is higher in cities because traffic traveling on regional roadway networks becomes more concentrated in urban areas; as the roadway network becomes finer and the sheer number of vehicles goes up, so do VMT and congestion. Arguably, cities would not be faced with such a predicament if they were not set within a spreading carpet of monomodal suburban development.

Heavy Traffic Ahead

Given the nation's heavy dependence on automobiles, and the ingrained land use patterns that support that bias, it might seem that there is little that can be done to effect any shift from cars to transit. It is a serious challenge, but the future may force significant changes upon the system.

If trends continue, the number of vehicles and the total VMT in the United States will continue to increase—even faster than the U.S. population is growing. Between 1969 and 1995, the total number of household vehicles in the nation grew by 143 percent whereas the total population increased by only 23 percent.[11]. During the

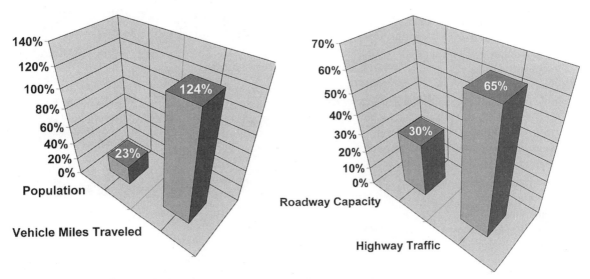

Figure 6.2. Population, vehicle miles traveled, roadway capacity, and highway traffic.
Sources: U.S. Department of Transportation (DOT), Bureau of Transportation Statistics, *1995 Nationwide Personal Transportation Survey* (Washington, D.C.: DOT, 1995); and Rober T. Dunphy et al., *Moving Beyond Gridlock: Traffic and Development* (Washington, D.C.: Urban Land Institute, 1997).

same period, total VMT increased by more than 120 percent.[12] Yet, between 1983 and 1993, although highway traffic increased by 65 percent, highway capacity increased by only 30 percent (see Figure 6.2).[13] Thus, the number of cars on the road and the amount of VMT both continue to increase while road building lags behind, meaning that capacity will fall short and congestion will increase. Between 1982 and 1999, traffic congestion increased in all sixty-eight of the metropolitan areas included in a survey by TTI.[14] The number of metropolitan areas in the study that were experiencing unacceptable congestion levels rose from ten in 1982 to thirty-nine in the late 1990s, with the average level of congestion rising by 25 percent.[15] Meanwhile, the average annual delay experienced by individual drivers increased more than threefold between 1982 and 1999, wasting almost 7 billion gallons of gasoline.[16] The amount of travel categorized as severely congested rose by 67 percent during the same period.[17]

Roads everywhere are becoming more congested mainly because a tremendous amount of the development of the past twenty years occurred in the suburban corridors of freeways completed during the 1970s, but there has been little major expansion of these facilities to accommodate the new growth.[18] Meanwhile, the transit systems that have been built are oriented mostly to downtown areas, where growth in travel has been modest amid already high congestion levels.[19]

Increasing Roadway Supply

One solution to the increasing congestion might be simply to create more roadway capacity. In fact, many metropolitan areas are already pursuing this approach. Wendell Cox of the Heritage Foundation believes that this should primarily be done everywhere. Cox recommends building new roads to serve suburbanizing areas while at the same time expanding existing roads. He argues that urban areas that have expanded roadways have experienced relatively less congestion than those that have not.[20] This may be true in the short term, but the longer term may bring the same congestion as more land is developed in response to expanded roadway capacity. The phenomenon of induced demand remains widely recognized by most professional transportation planners and traffic engineers, although it is occasionally contested.

In *The Vanishing Automobile and Other Urban Myths,* Randal O'Toole dismisses induced demand as fiction, citing a TTI study that showed little correlation between cities that built new roads and increasing congestion.[21] O'Toole's position is that if new roads increase demand, then all the cities that built new roads should show more congestion—yet they don't. This line of reasoning misses the basic point that new roadway capacity eventually attracts new land development, which eventually brings back the old congestion levels, requiring still more capacity. This doesn't happen overnight, and it doesn't mean congestion levels immediately increase as a result of road building. Often, congestion decreases for a period of time before rebounding. Induced demand simply suggests that road building alone isn't a permanent solution to the congestion problem.

O'Toole also cites TTI's *1999 Annual Mobility Report,* which says, "Additional roadway reduces the growth in travel delay experienced by motorists."[22] However, the next paragraph of this study goes on to state, "The 15-year period and the limited set of factors used in this study do not, however, allow a comprehensive assessment of the effect of additional roadway capacity."[23] Furthermore, TTI says in their *2001 Mobility Report* that "analysis shows that it would be almost impossible to attempt to maintain a constant congestion level with road construction only" and that "congestion may also increase over time due to the new development that occurs or is encouraged by the new transportation facilities."[24] In other words, TTI is saying that congestion may very well increase due to induced demand.

Increasing roadway capacity can also be quite expensive. In 1999, TTI estimated that we would need to build between four and five thousand lane miles of new roadways each year in just sixty-eight of the U.S. metropolitan areas to keep up with demand.[25] At anywhere from $4 million to $80 million per lane mile, that can add up to a lot of money as well as asphalt, not to mention loss of open space.[26] The *2001 Mobility Report* gives similar figures. In this report, TTI goes on to state: "Over the past 2 decades, only about 50 percent of the needed mileage was actually added. This means that it would require at least twice the level of current-day road expansion funding to attempt this road construction strategy."[27]

Doubling the $75 billion or so that is currently spent each year on building and maintaining roads seems unlikely, given other budget priorities. Meanwhile, rising gasoline costs have made raising fuel taxes politically even more unpalatable than they would otherwise be. Also,

Figure 6.3. Expanding congested freeways in developed areas can involve costly land takings and environmental-impact mitigation. (Alex S. MacLean/Landslides)

adding roadway capacity these days is a lot more difficult than it once was. Although some freeway corridors have adequate room to expand, many others do not. In urban and suburban areas, where Cox contends that much of the congestion exists, right-of-way considerations are far more serious than they were when the original freeways were built.[28] This is because the development that followed the freeways has also hemmed them in (see Figure 6.3). Much of the land around the highway system has been built up, making for potentially prohibitive acquisition costs and lengthy court battles.

O'Toole notes that tunneling and double decking are other options for expanding capacity.[29] While tunneling has become less expensive in some situations (nonurban or with favorable soil conditions), it still presents very serious cost premiums in most instances. The Big Dig, Boston's Central Artery/Tunnel project, is an oft-cited example of excessive cost; nearly half of that project is in a tunnel.

Double decking highways is another option. Elevated structures are usually less expensive than tunnels, but the structures and foundations they require still represent a cost premium over at-grade roads. Furthermore, elevated structures have been proven to have a blighting influence on surrounding communities, which is why they have been, or are being, torn down in many areas of the country.

It is useful to note that adding more lanes to a given highway or double decking it doesn't just mean making the highway a bit wider or taller; it can also mean reconstructing all of the highway's bridges, interchanges, and connecting roads. Modifying interchanges and their connectors can require a huge amount of costly real estate.

REVERSIBLE LANES

One way to increase capacity without widening roads is with reversible lanes, lanes that change direction depending on peak flow. Flow direction can be controlled with signals, pavement markings and signs, or movable barriers. Without barriers, reversible lanes can sometimes lead to motorist confusion and accidents when they are used for general traffic. Movable barriers or "zipper lanes" are sometimes considered a safer method of lane management.

In zipper lanes, a large machine is used to move a zipperlike chain of concrete barriers, adding highway lanes in one direction while subtracting them in another, responding to the changing direction of peak flow at different times of the day. This type of system is currently being used in Massachusetts on a portion of Boston's Southeast Expressway—in this case, the reversible lanes are reserved for car pools and buses and are not available to general traffic. Although reversible lanes can work well, they work only in situations where peak flow is mostly in one direction at a given time of day along a particular section of roadway. In the suburbs, however, where most U.S. commuting takes place, peak flows are often bidirectional. Beltways are typical examples of this phenomenon.

BYPASS ROADS

Bypass roads (often these are new beltways) are another roadway supply solution. These are new roads created in greenfield areas that bypass existing congestion points to allow for the smooth movement of through traffic. The problem with bypass roads is the same as with any new roadway or roadway expansion: induced demand. Bypassing congestion with a new road in a rural or lightly settled area will attract new development, eventually causing congestion on the bypass. Route I-495, Boston's outermost beltway, was built in part to allow interstate traffic to bypass Route 128, a previously built beltway closer to the city that had been filled up by ensuing suburban development. I-495 worked effectively in this role for a number of years. Now, it too has become congested because of the development it has attracted.

ROADWAY EXPANSION, FUNDING, AND PERMITTING

A common problem with all roadway supply solutions is that funding requirements and environmental permits are far more complex than they were forty years ago, generally necessitating a study of alternatives that may include transit options as well as a no-build scenario. Furthermore, fewer people are in favor of highway solutions these days because they believe that more highways only mean more sprawl right next door. In fact, many citizens oppose new highways. In Pasadena, California, citizen opposition has led to a series of lawsuits that have put off the proposed Route 710 highway to the year 2020 or beyond. This highway was first conceived in 1949. All of these considerations seem to point to a lot more congestion in our future.

Tim Lomax, coauthor of TTI's *Mobility Report* series, recognized these facts when he testified before Congress in March 2001:

> It will be difficult for most big cities to address their mobility needs by only constructing more roads. This is partly a funding issue—transportation spending should probably double in larger cities if there is an interest in reducing congestion. It is also, however, an issue of project approval. It is difficult to imagine many urban street and freeway corridors with an extra 4, 6 or 8 lanes, but it is entirely possible that that is what will be required if the goal is to significantly reduce congestion by adding roads. . . . Transit improvements, better operations, adjusted work hours, telecommuting and a range of other efficiency options . . . are absolutely vital components of an overall solution.[30]

Managing Demand

Because of the problems associated with creating more roads, many people believe the answer lies in managing roadway demand through congestion pricing and other measures (see Table 6.1). Part of this approach focuses on such pricing techniques as (1) simply pricing driving higher so that fewer people drive, (2) time-sensitive "congestion pricing"—using pricing to shift traffic to periods when more roadway capacity is available—or (3) using pricing to increase vehicle

Table 6.1. Sample Transportation Demand-Management Measures

Program	Typical Measures	Advantages	Disadvantages
General Pricing Measures	• Raising fuel taxes • Higher registration fees • Parking taxes/fees	• Raises driving expense • Covers unpaid costs • Encourages car pooling • Reduces fuel consumption • Encourages transit use	• Hard on low-wage earners • Political acceptability • Not peak sensitive
Employer Programs	• Van pooling • Car pooling • Reduce parking subsidy (cash in trade) • Shift work schedules • Encourage working at home	• Reduces number of cars on roads • Peak sensitive • Can be equitable to most wage earners	• Nonemployees may re-congest highways • Employer costs • Not applicable to all types of jobs
Congestion Pricing	• Variable tolls • Variable parking fees	• Peak sensitive • Raises driving expense in peak periods • Tolls/fees can be used to recover some costs • Encourages car pooling • Encourages transit use	• May cause diversions to free local roads • Hard on low-wage earners • Political acceptability • Problem of spreading peak demand
Lane Management and Pricing	• Priced lanes • Reversible HOV lanes • Exclusive HOV lanes	• Can use existing lanes • Higher throughput with HOV • Potential time advantagefor HOV • Can be used with congestion pricing • Can be peak sensitive • HOV use can reduce number of cars on roads	• Highway safety issues with reversible lanes • Low usage rates on HOV lanes can lead to lower occupancy requirements • Potential conversion to general traffic lanes

Note: There can be some overlap between the boundaries of demand and capacity or supply management. For example, HOV lanes can be considered both a supply solution and a demand-management tool, especially with differential pricing. Shifting trips out of cars and into HOVs reduces vehicle demand for roadway space but does not necessarily reduce total trip demand. If HOVs are considered a form of transit they can also be thought of a supply-side measure—adding capacity to absorb trip demand priced off the roadway.

occupancies (thereby getting more people through on the same amount of pavement).

GENERAL PRICING MEASURES

Raising fuel taxes, auto registration fees, and parking fees are other ways to make driving more costly, discouraging price-sensitive drivers and sending them to other modes. Raising fuel taxes won't necessarily reduce congestion because the response may be more fuel-efficient cars that offset the impact of the increased taxes.

However, increasing fuel efficiency may have beneficial impacts on fuel consumption and air pollution—and might more accurately reflect the true cost of driving. Again, raising fuel taxes can be politically difficult when gas prices are increasing. As Terry Moore and Paul Thorsnes have written in *The Transportation/Land Use Connection:* "An efficient tax—one that accounted for all the costs of highway trips not now paid for by highway users—might more than double the price of a gallon of gasoline."[31]

Raising registration fees can reduce driving and encourage car pooling by raising the cost of owning a car. Raising parking fees would have similar effects. In fact, many people choose transit or car pooling to commute to downtown areas, where parking fees are typically high. In suburban areas, parking is usually free and under private control, and there is little incentive to charge for parking in a competitive environment in which parking is generally free. A parking tax of some kind is the most likely way to implement this kind of charge.[32]

EMPLOYER PROGRAMS

One method for reducing peak demand is to require major employers to implement transportation demand management (TDM) programs, such as shifting work schedules, encouraging van and car pooling, and reducing (or offering cash in trade for) parking subsidies. In the Los Angeles area, for example, the South Coast Air Quality Management District requires all businesses with more than 250 employees to have TDM programs and monitor their effectiveness.[33] The problem is that drivers other than commuters in the program can take advantage of the capacity freed up by the employers' TDM efforts, thereby recongesting the roadways.

CONGESTION PRICING

Congestion pricing—assessing higher tolls or user fees during peak commuting hours for single-occupant vehicles (SOVs)—is another TDM strategy. Variable tolls have been in put in place on toll roads in California, Texas, and in some other states since the mid-1990s, when the Federal Highway Administration began funding several pilot projects across the country. Variable tolls are also scheduled to take effect in 2001 on the New Jersey Turnpike. One project widely hailed when it was first built was California's SR-91 in Orange County. The road consists of a ten-mile stretch of express lanes on the Riverside Freeway that was privately built to reduce congestion on adjacent public highway lanes. SR-91 charges a variable toll depending on the time of day—much higher at peak commuting hours than at other periods of the day. Tolls for car pools, van pools, and buses are reduced during peak hours. The project was initially successful but became mired in controversy as tolls kept rising and the neighboring public highway lanes became highly congested, prompting a move to

expand their capacity. Meanwhile, voters in California turned down a proposal to build an eighty-five-mile toll road in Northern California as public sentiment for toll roads has waned in that state.[34]

Congestion pricing remains popular among economists, such as Terry Moore and Paul Thorsnes, and free-market advocates, such as Randal O'Toole and Samuel Staley. Yet, congestion pricing has several drawbacks. First, as tolls rise, traffic may divert to other free roads, as happened in California and in other places with toll roads, simply relocating the congestion. Where the free roads are local streets instead of highways, there are likely to be community impacts as well. This suggests a need to price all roads in a given area to make the system work. While this is technically feasible with current transponder and other technology, it may not be politically acceptable. Public sentiment for pricing solutions can evaporate quickly, as it has in California, making such strategies politically unpalatable.

O'Toole writes that, in places like the Northeast, "people are used to toll roads," and introducing congestion pricing "should not be a problem there."[35] In Massachusetts, public referenda are held every several years demanding the removal of existing tolls on priced roadways, tunnels, and bridges. In New Jersey, the winner of the recent Republican gubernatorial primary campaigned on a platform that included removing the tollbooths on the Garden State Parkway.[36] Pricing roads is an extremely difficult political proposition. It was public pressure, after all, that led governments to regulate the fares of private transit companies down to the point where many companies were forced into bankruptcy. Public pressure keeps U.S. road tolls relatively low, just as it keeps transit fares artificially low. These types of problems have led Moore and Thorsnes to conclude: "Most of the evidence is that regional government cannot adopt fees to control highway congestion."[37]

The second drawback to congestion pricing is its practice of moving people out of the peak commuting hours into time periods with less traffic. The problem is that, as people spread out their trips to avoid peak congestion, they will simply be moving congestion into wider time slots as the overall volume continues to increase. Today, commuting trips on the highway are actually a minority, even in rush hour. Work trips represent only about one-third of the rush hour trips on the nation's highways (see Figure 6.4).[38] Furthermore, rush hours now spread over greater lengths of time. As noncommute driving increases as a share of total driving trips, peak travel hours are becoming increasingly less discernible. The morning peak traffic period now extends over a three-hour span, from 6:00 a.m. to 9:00 a.m., and the evening peak is spread over a similar period, from 4:00 p.m. to 7:00 p.m. Together, these periods already consume six hours of the day. In some places, the peaks last even longer. In the Denver area, afternoon rush hour now lasts from 2:30 p.m. to 7:30 p.m.[39]

Even so, there are actually more trips on the nation's highways between the peak periods than during them, although they are spread over a slightly longer period. Looking at the numbers, only 37 percent of all highway trips and less than half of all work trips take place during the peak six hours. The rest are distributed throughout the day.[40] There just isn't as much peak demand to spread out as there might be, and there is likely to be even less in the future as traffic continues to grow and spread more evenly throughout the day.

Third, congestion pricing and increasing the price of driving in general raise questions of economic discrimination: when the tolls, gas taxes, registration fees, and parking costs all go up, only the affluent will still be able to travel by car at the hours they choose. Those who can least afford it will be pushed off the road, and they may not be in any position to choose traveling at some off-peak time period. In a country where the majority of the urban pattern is monomodal, there are few, if any, other practical options for getting around. That makes it even harder for those who can least afford it to find work or even shop for food.

HIGH-OCCUPANCY VEHICLE LANES

Another way to manage demand is to try to push more people through each highway lane. This means more people riding in each car or people traveling in car pools, vans, and buses—high-occupancy vehicles (HOVs). The use of buses (transit) can make this type of measure partially a supply-side solution. HOV lanes are sometimes used in combination with congestion pricing. The pricing idea works by issuing toll discounts to car pools and van pools, particularly during peak hour, high-toll periods. These discounts have some effect, but they work better

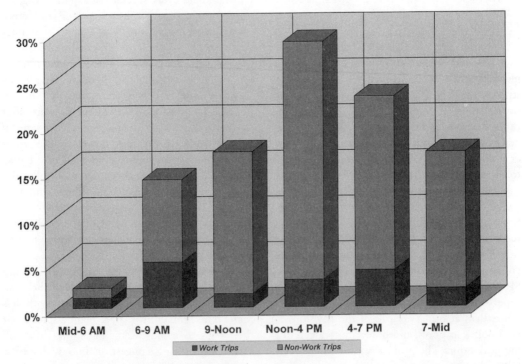

Figure 6.4. Work and nonwork trips by time of day.
Source: U.S. Department of Transportation (DOT), Bureau of Transportation Statistics, *1995 Nationwide Personal Transportation Survey* (Washington, D.C.: DOT, 1995), 14.

when the HOVs aren't stuck in traffic along with everyone else.

Time advantage for HOVs, including buses and limousines as well as car and van pools, can be gained by giving these vehicles an exclusive right-of-way separate from the single-driver cars. One common way to do this is by designating or adding exclusive HOV lanes to the highways. These are usually lanes reserved for buses, vans, and cars with three occupants or more. In some cases, such solutions have been quite successful. In the Lincoln Tunnel in New York City, an exclusive HOV lane moves more than 30,000 people per hour compared to about 3,200 people per hour maximum for a typical general-travel lane. But that is a rare case, one in which the lane is almost exclusively used by buses that are filled to capacity and traveling bumper to bumper.

Elsewhere, in places such as Hartford, Connecticut, and Boston, Massachusetts, experience with these lanes has varied. Relatively low usage in the HOV lanes while general-purpose lanes remain congested has led to political pressure to open these lanes to more types of traffic. As a result, some states now require only the driver and one passenger. The general worry is that the exclusivity of the lane will eventually be done away with altogether and the extra lanes given over to general traffic, unless they can prove themselves successful.

Despite these concerns, HOV lanes have the potential to significantly help resolve congestion problems if they are maintained as real HOV lanes, if there is a potential to combine them with congestion pricing, and if the services that use them can make a good fit with the land uses they serve. Furthermore, buses using HOV lanes can use local roads to pick up and drop off passengers at both ends of the trip, making them potentially more amenable to dispersed suburban patterns.

High Technology

Other capacity solutions under study include changes in driving technology. The most talked about development in this arena is something called Intelligent Transportation Systems (ITS). Originally, this field was referred to as IVHS (Intelligent Vehicle Highway Systems), but the name has been expanded to be more inclusive and to invite transit into the program. In the system's most advanced state, drivers would get up in the morning and consult their computers for the best way to get to work, take a trip, or go shopping. Through the magic of real-time reporting, the computer would know where all the bottlenecks were throughout the country and recommend the best route to the intended destination—whether by car, transit, rail, boat, or airplane. However, because almost 90 percent of daily trips and 80 percent of long-distance trips in the United States are made by car, the emphasis remains inevitably on the nation's roadway system.[41]

SMART CARS

Onboard navigating systems are already being installed in many vehicles being brought to market, some of which will tell you where the roadway bottlenecks are and direct you to an alternate route. This may work up to a point—that is, until the alternate routes become jammed with all of the people being directed off the highway. In a sense, this just relocates the problem rather than solving it, but it may result in some overall capacity improvement by using more of the total roadway system at a given time.

SMART ROADS

The ultimate "congestion killer" in the ITS program has been the idea of making the roads themselves smart along with the vehicles by embedding technology in the roadways that would essentially take over the driving of the car. This is an idea that has been around for at least fifty years, but with advances in electronics, it has recently been considered by some a distinct possibility in the near future. Lately, however, discussion of this scenario has waned, and ITS literature appears to be doing its best to avoid a "futurist" image by confining itself to the many advances in traffic surveillance, control, and information systems that are already available, improvements that might actually become part of the roadway system fairly soon.

In the original ultimate scenario, the idea was that cars and trucks would be put on autopilot the minute they entered a given expressway. Vehicles would then be controlled by computer, using either a cable in the pavement or wireless technology. In theory, this system could guide both cars and trucks at speeds up to sixty miles per hour while traveling within five feet of one another, dramatically improving throughput per lane. While this may be possible, its implementation is likely to be some distance in the future and may not come cheaply. Much would need to be done to the highways, cars, and trucks to prepare them for this system, because access to the smart highways would have to be limited solely to vehicles sharing the required technology. Although the potential for human error may be removed from the smart highway, it remains unclear how this system would respond to sudden mechanical failures, such as blown tires, seized engines, or unexpected physical obstructions caused by fallen debris, animals in the roadway, or even snow and ice. Heated pavement, high-security fencing, and blanket monitoring may take care of some of these problems, but what about failure of the control systems? The safety measures and redundancy required would be enormous—and these are just the issues presented by limited-access highways.

The fact is that the nation's expressways carry only about 23 percent of all the highway vehicle miles traveled in the United States.[42]

Arterials, collector roads, and local streets make up the rest. Wiring the whole system to make it smart presents far more serious challenges. The larger network includes all the roads and streets with intersections, curb cuts, driveways, loading zones, and parking spaces. Most likely, simply too many random variables need to be overcome in controlling such an extensive system—but it is this very system to which all expressway trips connect. This means that the broader network may remain uncontrolled, subject to all manner of random events, such as left-hand turns, parking cars, double-parked delivery trucks, pedestrians, and cyclists.

Thus, the potential for congestion remains high on these roads, and because the expressways ultimately connect to this network, the same potential also remains on the expressways, no matter how well controlled the limited-access highways may become. This is because traffic entering the local roadway network from the freeway system is currently "metered" by congestion on the freeway. If the volume delivered to the local streets from the freeways goes up (due to flow improvements on smart highways), then the local streets become the new "meter" slowing the traffic back onto the freeways. As with smart navigation systems, smart highways may simply end up relocating congestion from the expressway to the local street system.

Doing Nothing

While it seems to be generally agreed that our roadways are filling up, what to do about it is clearly a matter of debate and many solutions have serious drawbacks. Because of this complexity, some people take a fatalistic "do-nothing" approach to the problem. In their smart growth manifesto entitled *Growing to Greatness* (written in part by Anthony Downs, a senior fellow of the Brookings Institution), the National Association of Industrial and Office Properties (NAIOP) makes the following commentary:

> In reality, Americans should get used to traffic congestion. It is not going to get much better unless a great many of us change our fundamental values and behavior—if then. So we should try to make encountering congestion as palatable as possible. We should equip ourselves with comfortable vehicles, including air conditioning, stereo radios, telephones, compact disk or tape players, perhaps even fax machines, and commute with people we like. Then we can regard the time we spend stuck in traffic with equanimity as part of our business or leisure lives.[43]

That seems a pretty depressing commentary on where we are going. In such a vision of the future, we are always in the car, it is both home and work, and we live forever on the highway, never getting anywhere (see Figure 6.5). Yet, it seems, this picture may not be far from the truth. Although the evidence is mostly anecdotal, a recent *New York Times* article observed that more and more people are doing just what NAIOP recommends.

> Commuter time is no longer just for driving. . . . As the comforts of home and the efficiency of the office creep into the automobile, it is becoming increasingly attractive as a work space. People can use cell phones and e-mail from their cars to take advantage of lost time in traffic.[44]

Such amenities as CD players, air-conditioning, laptop computers, telephones, and palm pilots are changing people's tolerance for traffic delays and stretching their work commute time budgets

Figure 6.5. As the commute grows longer, more people are using their cars as offices, yet driving can involve complex decisions. Meanwhile, freight shipments are also stuck in traffic. (Alex S. MacLean/Landslides)

way beyond the standard, rule-of-thumb thirty minutes. As the *New York Times* goes on to state:

> Many transportation experts have long relied on an imprecise traffic principle called the "level of intolerability," which essentially holds that when traffic gets too unbearable, a certain number of frustrated drivers will give up and use mass transit, preventing permanent gridlock. But this phenomenon has been disrupted . . because people are tolerating traffic better.[45]

In the Denver area, as rush hours grow ever longer, drivers have found that the traffic moves just enough to fan the coals of a barbecue in the back of a pickup truck, leading some hungry innovators to hold tailgate parties in the middle of traffic.[46] None of this seems to bode well for reducing congestion anytime soon. Worse, there is also some impact to safety in such circumstances. Traffic consultants to the insurance industry believe that more crashes can be expected from distracted drivers, and some localities have passed laws banning phone use while driving.[47] Bumper stickers have been appearing for several years urging people to drive first and talk on the phone later. In June 2001, New York became the first state to actually ban completely the use of handheld cellular telephones in cars.[48]

Being able to work, listen to music, or even barbecue during commuting or other travel may help calm the impatience that leads to road rage, but it can still mean less time spent with family as work spills over into ever longer commutes, and it means less leisure time for other nonwork, nonsedentary pursuits that most people need to maintain their emotional and mental well-being.

LATE SHIPMENTS AND STUCK AMBULANCES

Although automobile drivers may be making the best of a bad situation, that certainly doesn't solve the other problems that traffic congestion brings. Private automobiles aren't the only ones affected by congestion. With the majority of the nation's freight—including parcel, postal, and courier service—traveling on the same congested roads, most of the raw materials and manufactured goods required by our "just-in-time" economy will be stuck in traffic along with everyone else. However, those shipments won't be doing any useful work on the cell phone; they will just be sitting there, unused.[49] The same goes for all the deliveries from Internet sales.

Roads also hold emergency vehicles on their way to accidents, fires, and hospitals. They'll be stuck in traffic, too—a situation that has serious repercussions in the longer time it takes these vehicles to get to accidents or burning buildings, to provide emergency service to someone at home or in an office, or to get someone to an operating room. This is not to mention police response times to crime reports. All of these circumstances could mean loss of life and property that might have been prevented if roads were clear.

LIMITS TO PATIENCE

Undoubtedly, there is some limit to the amount of time people are willing to spend in traffic to get to work, run an errand, travel for leisure. At some point, the amount of delay will render the objective of any trip infeasible. Otherwise, in the most extreme of circumstances, one might be forced to choose between having a home on a plot of land or simply a well-equipped recreational vehicle that is always on the road somewhere.

The national sentiment about road building could change, of course, and people might start to welcome more highway construction as congestion worsens, but as NAIOP's *Growing to Greatness* says: "Building more roads cannot relieve the resulting congestion unless we turn every metropolitan area into a single giant cement slab."[50] And, as we have already seen, not only are major expansions of existing highway capacity very costly and difficult, but they may not solve the problem. In fact, they may make matters worse when the principal of induced demand is considered. The ultimate result of roadway expansion may simply be to create even more congestion.

Transit Solutions

Despite hurdles, it may be that some form of ITS in combination with demand management measures will end up squeezing some additional capacity from our roadways. But how much capacity and for what cost? Some of the ITS solutions will be quite expensive, as will be creating more physical capacity on the roadway system, and there is no guarantee that, even if they work at the outset, any of these measures will do more than simply put off the problem a few more years. At some point, we have to ask ourselves whether the inevitably diminishing returns are worth the cost and effort. We can go on trying to make the system work, even while it is bogging down, or we can do something different now.

To many people, the only real practical alternative to building more roads is investing in mass transit, with rail the preferred solution. Rail transit is generally less ambiguous than buses or car pools in that it is almost always set in an exclusive right-of-way, even when set alongside or in the middle of a roadway, so it is not prone to the same delays experienced by buses or car pools traveling in general traffic (see Figure 6.6). It can also move large volumes of people very effectively. Existing U.S. heavy rail transit systems have been observed to move up to 50,000 passengers per hour and U.S. light rail transit up to 10,000 passengers per hour in contrast to a general lane of traffic on a freeway, which can carry up to 3,200 passengers per hour. Some European light rail systems are reported to carry up to 20,000 passengers per hour.[51]

These relative capacity comparisons are sometimes disputed. For example, in *The Vanishing Automobile and Other Urban Myths,* Randal O'Toole asserts that freeways produce about six times the number of daily passenger miles per lane mile of freeway than light rail produces in passengers per route mile of rail line. These types of calculations can be misleading, however, in that they introduce additional factors such as distance into the comparison, which are usually not considered relevant in measuring capacity. The standard capacity measure is the number of passengers past a single point in an hour, in one direction on a single track or lane of freeway as shown in the previous paragraph.[52]

The problem (as stated earlier) is that high-capacity transit systems are best suited to downtown-oriented travel, and downtown trips represent only a small portion of the total market. Buses, vans, and jitneys running on HOV lanes may allow somewhat more flexibility in terms of being able to get off the exclusive lane and use local streets to pick up and drop off at dispersed destinations within the roadway network. Those systems can carry anywhere from 1,500 to more than 30,000 passengers per hour (recall the example of Lincoln Tunnel). Approximately 5,000 to 10,000 passengers per hour is the general midrange of observed busway applications—similar in capacity to U.S. light rail systems.[53] Nonetheless, even these solutions work best when serving higher densities than what are typical of the suburban pattern comprising the majority of U.S. metropolitan areas.

The inability of high-capacity transit to serve the spread-out pattern of much of the nation's metropolitan areas has led some people to doubt its prospects. For example, the Heritage Foundation claims that transit projects are expensive to build and have little impact on existing congestion, with more than 99 percent of *new* travel in major U.S. metropolitan areas using automobiles.[54] Despite increasing transit use numbers in 2000, many feel the same way. For example, Moore and Thorsnes appear to concur, stating, "Rail is not cost-effective by any conventional analysis in most metropolitan areas."[55] It is not

Figure 6.6. Typical light rail systems can move ten thousand people per hour per direction. (Oliver Gillham)

cost-effective primarily because of the prevailing dispersed patterns of the nation's metropolitan areas. On the other hand, if congestion pricing or pricing all driving and parking higher is part of the answer, then where will all of the people being priced off the roads go? Some other transportation option, other than roads and cars, must exist to meet the demand, or pricing solutions may not make any sense.

The same is true of "doing nothing" to roadway capacity. Both highways and local streets will fill up, as they reportedly have done in cities such as Taipei (before rail transit), turning a simple crosstown trip into a three-hour endeavor.[56] Some form of alternative transportation ultimately has to be a part of the solution to congestion.

Any final solution to the problem of traffic congestion in the suburbanized world (as we shall see in Part III) must eventually reach beyond the field of transportation and begin to grapple with questions of land use and density. If these questions can be effectively addressed, then rail and other forms of high-capacity transit can become viable options for a larger share of metropolitan area trips.

Energy Consumption

The automotive traffic in the United States consumes a large amount of energy. The U.S. Department of Transportation (DOT) estimates that U.S. transportation consumed nearly 25 quadrillion British thermal units of energy in 1997, with highway vehicles accounting for 80 percent of total energy use and 84 percent of total transportation petroleum use.[57] Put another way, the Federal Highway Department estimates that highway vehicles consumed more than 132 billion gallons of gasoline in 1999.[58]

Cars, Trucks, and Petroleum

With 80 percent of the nation's transportation energy budget being spent by cars and trucks and 84 percent of that energy coming from petroleum, it is little wonder that transportation accounts for nearly two-thirds of the nation's petroleum consumption.[59] In 1995, the United States was reported to have used more than half the total oil used by all of the twenty-six countries belonging to the Organization for Economic Cooperation and Development put together. The U.S. consumption was almost six times that of the next highest consuming country in the group (Japan) and was almost thirty times that of the average consumption of any other country in the group.[60] The United States consumes more than one-third of the world's transportation energy, even though the nation accounts for less than 5 percent of the world's population and about 25 percent of the planet's combined gross product (see Figure 6.7).[61]

Moreover, highway fuel demand climbed steadily while net imports of oil exceeded total

Millions of Metric Tons of Oil Equivalent

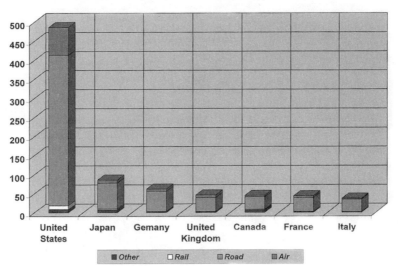

Figure 6.7. Total annual transportation energy demand for the United States and selected countries in the 1990s. *Source:* U.S. Department of Transportation (DOT), Bureau of Transportation Statistics, *Transportation Statistics Annual Report 1995* (Washington, D.C.: DOT, 1995), 75–76.

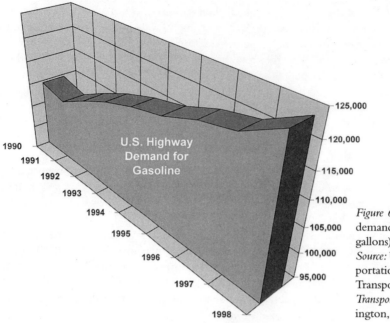

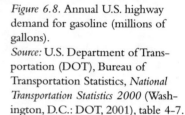

Figure 6.8. Annual U.S. highway demand for gasoline (millions of gallons).
Source: U.S. Department of Transportation (DOT), Bureau of Transportation Statistics, *National Transportation Statistics 2000* (Washington, D.C.: DOT, 2001), table 4-7.

domestic oil production (see figure 6.8).[62] Although oil prices during the 1990s tended to be historically low, encouraging these trends, they escalated considerably during 2000, bringing back new headlines not seen since the early 1980s. According to the Energy Information Administration of the U.S. Department of Energy (DOE), transportation energy consumption is forecast to grow at an annual rate of 1.7 percent between now and 2020, leading to a

total projected increase of about 40 percent. During that same time period, the percentage of imported petroleum products is expected to grow to 64 percent, from about 52 percent in 1998.[63] In 1980, only about 37 percent of U.S. petroleum was imported (see Figure 6.9).[64] These statistics have led DOT to state:

> Serious energy and environmental issues are associated with transportation. The

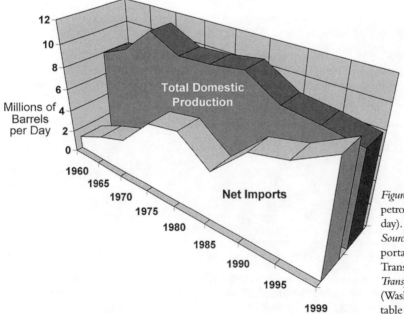

Figure 6.9. Domestic versus imported petroleum (millions of barrels per day).
Source: U.S. Department of Transportation (DOT), Bureau of Transportation Statistics, *National Transportation Statistics Report 2000* (Washington, D.C.: DOT, 2001), table 4-7.

current abundance of petroleum cannot be assured in the future. Over half the petroleum used in the United States must now be imported. Most U.S. imports are from suppliers who have been reliable, but political instability in any of the major producer regions could disrupt world supplies, leading to steep price increases, as has occurred several times since the early 1970. Economic damage could be serious. . . .The lack of significant alternatives leaves transportation particularly vulnerable should a disruption occur in the supply system.[65]

Concerned about fuel supply, the Bush administration recently announced a policy of increasing the supply of fossil fuels—dismissing as 1970s-era thinking the idea that "we could simply conserve or ration our way out" of what the administration has now termed an energy crisis.[66] Instead, the administration is pushing to find new domestic sources of oil and gas, including in the protected Arctic National Wildlife Refuge and near the Grand Teton and Yellowstone National Parks in Wyoming.[67] Other domestic possibilities that have been discussed in the past include the Great Lakes, Georges Bank off the coast of New England and other parts of the nation's coastline. Clearly, further oil and gas exploration for diminishing resources now has the potential to disrupt some of the nation's most sensitive environmental areas.

How Much Oil Is Left?

But how much oil is left, even if we drill in the nation's wildlife reserves? In their book *Sustainability and Cities: Overcoming Automobile Dependence,* Peter Newman and Jeffrey Kenworthy argue that supplies are limited. Newman and Kenworthy cite a three-volume 1995 study of the world's oil reserves by Colin Campbell and Jean Laherrere, oil geologists with more than forty years each of experience in the oil industry and currently associated with Petroconsultants in Geneva. Their study states that between 1950 and 2050, 80 percent of the world's oil will have been consumed.[68] According to Newman and Kenworthy, this means that we are "about halfway through the global oil well."[69] Figure 6.10 shows historical and projected world oil production based on supply.

These projections were confirmed in a subsequent 1998 article in *Scientific American* written by Campbell and Laherrere, in which the authors estimate world production to 1998 to have been about 800 billion barrels. Noting that 80 percent of the world's oil flows from fields found before 1973, and that during the 1990s total annual discoveries each year amounted to only a third of the oil extracted in each year, they believe that world reserves as estimated by the oil industry and the U.S. Geological Survey are inflated. There are, according to the authors, only about 1,000 billion barrels remaining to be pro-

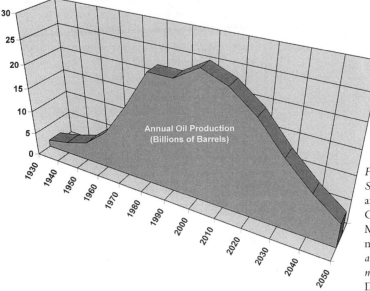

Figure 6.10. Global oil production. *Source:* Based on Colin J. Campbell and Jean H. Laherrere, "The End of Cheap Oil," *Scientific American,* March 1998. See also Peter Newman and Jeffrey Kenworthy, *Sustainability and Cities: Overcoming Automobile Dependence* (Washington, D.C.: Island Press, 1999), 51.

duced. In their words: "There is only so much crude oil in the world, and the industry has found about 90 percent of it."[70] Campbell and Laherrere predict that world oil production will peak by or before 2010 and then begin to decline. The authors point out that even studies by others who have posited reserves 50 to 100 percent higher than their estimates predict that oil production will peak between 2015 and 2020—only a five- to ten-year margin of difference. Furthermore, as Campbell and Laherrere state in their article, "from an economic perspective, when the world runs completely out of oil is . . . not relevant: what matters is when production begins to taper off. Beyond that point, prices will rise unless demand declines commensurately."[71]

Because the U.S. transportation system relies on cheap, abundant oil, it isn't too hard to imagine the impacts that will ensue. Suburbanization has depended on relatively inexpensive transportation to serve its spread-out development pattern. That transportation system is what made the land inexpensive enough to support the pattern in the fist place. What will happen when the cost of that transportation system begins to escalate beyond the economic levels required to support suburban development patterns? Future patterns may change to accommodate the situation, but what already exists may become economically unviable unless changes are made to motor vehicle technology or transportation options or both.

Worse, some power plants also run on oil, and many homes are heated with oil or gas. Oil has many uses beyond transportation. Products made from oil and gas petrochemicals include plastics, soaps and detergents, solvents, drugs, fertilizers, pesticides, explosives, synthetic fibers and rubbers, paints, epoxy resins, and flooring and insulating materials. Petrochemicals are found in everything from aspirin to polyester clothes, from cars to airplanes.[72] When oil and gas prices go up, so will the cost of many other things besides transportation.

Moreover, rising gasoline prices make it much harder to raise fuel taxes or implement pricing measures aimed at relieving roadway congestion without incurring substantial negative public reaction. Yet, despite these facts, U.S. oil consumption is predicted to continue rising into 2020 and beyond, even as global production is declining.

Sprawl, Density, and Energy Consumption

While curbing sprawl won't do much for the vast fields of auto-dependent development we already have, it will help reduce future fuel consumption. It is true that our nation has huge investments, both public and private, tied up in suburbanization. These range from the individual homes owned by millions of Americans to the giant interstate highway system, which belongs to the whole country. To the extent that our nation continues to grow while this framework still exists, vehicle mileage and petroleum consumption will continue to increase.

On the other hand, anything that can be done to change the prevailing pattern of development may help reduce the relative amount of future petroleum consumption. Studies have shown that gasoline consumption does decrease as development density increases. For example, in one instance it has been shown that residents on the exurban fringe of Denver consumed gasoline at twelve times the rate of people living in Manhattan.[73] Although this may be an extreme case, other studies back up the general theory, including studies conducted by the Natural Resources Defense Council (NRDC) that confirm that higher density means less auto use.[74] The NRDC's studies show that as residential density doubles, auto use may drop by as much as 40 percent. Conversely, studies from the United Kingdom have shown that auto use per person rises sharply as density falls below eight persons per acre. Research conducted for Portland, Oregon, shows that housing density and employment density are among the significant variables affecting transit demand.[75]

All of this seems to be common sense. After all, as we have already seen in Chapter 1, transit can work reasonably well as a mode choice only on a specified route with compatible levels of employment or residential density. We know that, almost by definition, mass transit cannot work well in a thinly populated environment with widely dispersed origins and destinations. Furthermore, local auto trips can be reduced only if an alternative travel mode is feasible—for example, walking or transit, both of which imply an order of density greater than that of the typical subdivision.

In their book *Sustainability and Cities,* Newman and Kenworthy provide an exhaustive comparison of gasoline consumption and density variables in major cities around the world (see Table 6.2 for selected highlights). In their comparison, dense

Table 6.2. Transportation Energy Use and Population Density for Selected Cities

Continent	City	Transportation Energy Use per Capita BTU (000s)	Population Density Pop./Mi^2
North America	Houston	67,890	3,000
	Los Angeles	58,926	7,400
	Chicago	53,195	12,300
	New York	48,935	23,700
Europe	Frankfurt	36,297	15,772
	Stockholm	25,419	23,710
	Paris	22,977	25,003
Asia	Tokyo	17,292	34,130
	Seoul	9,114	77,258
	Manila	6,953	96,288

Source: Peter Newman and Jeffrey Kenworthy, *Sustainability and Cities: Overcoming Auto Dependence* (Washington, D.C.: Island Press, 1999), 70, 94–95. 1990 population density for American cities from the U.S. Census Bureau; other cities from Newman and Kenworthy. *Note:* Population densities shown in this table are for cities, not metropolitan areas. Metropolitan areas are typically less dense.

cities, such as New York, Chicago, and Boston, are shown to be 10 to 15 percent below the national urban average in gasoline consumption per capita, whereas less dense cities, such as Houston and San Diego, are 10 to 15 percent above the national average. According to Newman and Kenworthy, metropolitan Houston has about half the population density of metropolitan New York.[76] Internationally, European cities are, on average, more than three times as dense as American cities while averaging 50 percent less gasoline consumption than their American counterparts.[77]

Figure 6.11 shows the relationship between energy use and density in global cities in 1990. As can be seen from the chart, private transportation energy use (that is, primarily gasoline and diesel fuel consumption) declines as population density increases and walking, transit, and bicycles are able to claim some mode share from automobiles. Thus, according to Newman and Kenworthy, trading in sprawl development patterns for greater density should help slow the increase in energy consumption. This is because slanting the pattern toward higher density should encourage more walking, cycling, and transit and rail use, decreasing automobile use and, hence, gasoline consumption (see Table 6.3). While this hypothe-

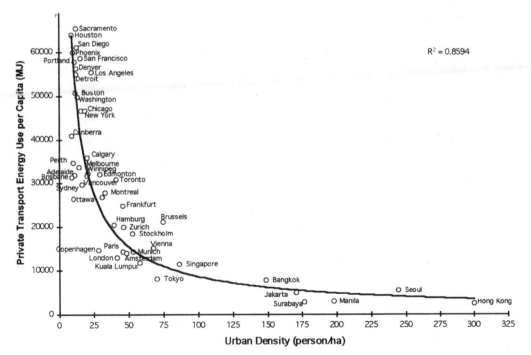

Figure 6.11. Transport energy use and urban density.
Source: Peter Newman and Jeffrey Kenworthy, *Sustainability and Cities: Overcoming Automobile Dependence* (Washington, D.C.: Island Press, 1999.

Table 6.3. Transportation Modes and Population Density for Selected Cities

Continent	City	Work Trips on Transit (%)	Work Trips by Walking and Cycling (%)	Population Density (Pop./Mi²)
North America	Houston	4	3	3,000
	Los Angeles	7	4	7,400
	Chicago	15	5	12,300
	New York	27	7	23,700
Europe	Frankfurt	42	9	15,772
	Stockholm	55	14	23,710
	Paris	36	15	25,003
Asia	Tokyo	49	22	34,130
	Seoul	60	20	77,258
	Manila	54	18	96,288

Source: Peter Newman and Jeffrey Kenworthy, *Sustainability and Cities: Overcoming Auto Dependence* (Washington, D.C.: Island Press, 1999), 82–83. 1990 population densities from the U.S. Census Bureau for American cities. All other data from Newman and Kenworthy. All numbers are rounded.

sis is sometimes contested, Newman and Kenworthy's case remains strong when typical counterarguments are examined in detail.[78]

Transportation aside, residential and commercial energy consumption accounts for about 5 to 6 percent of U.S. petroleum use, and detached houses and scattered buildings are known to be less efficient in overall energy use than attached buildings and multifamily dwellings.[79] At the end of the 1980s, single-family detached homes accounted for more than half of all the residential and commercial floor space in the United States.[80] Clearly, moving toward more compact development patterns could yield significant results in this area as well.

Vehicle Technology

Ultimately, changes in vehicle technology may help achieve some reduction in the use of oil products in transportation, but such changes may have to be pursued more aggressively than currently planned if petroleum consumption is to be reduced significantly before oil production begins to decline in the next several decades. Recent introductions of hybrid fuel and electric vehicles, such as the Toyota Prius and the Honda Insight, are reported to achieve between fifty and sixty miles per gallon—double to triple the average fuel consumption of cars on the road today.[81]

Another technology, the fuel cell, is a bit further off. In the best case, a car using this technology will be propelled by electricity from a

fuel cell fed by a hydrogen-air mixture that leaves only water vapor as a by-product. Most likely, the first fuel cell systems will operate on gasoline and use a device called a fuel reformer to convert gasoline to the hydrogen mixture used by the cell. These would produce more than just water vapor, but it is claimed that emissions from this type of system would still be less than those produced by current fuel combustion processes.

However, the DOE forecast of 40 percent additional petroleum consumption by 2020 already assumes some reduction in fuel consumption due to the introduction of alternative fuel and hybrid technology vehicles. Under a more aggressive "high technology" scenario (also modeled by DOE), total fuel consumption predicted for 2020 might be reduced by as much as 15 percent or more, but the DOE did not consider this a likely enough outcome to include it in their "reference" case.[82]

Relative Energy Efficiency of Cars and Transit

Whatever form of energy is used, private automobile transportation remains highly energy inefficient. Newman and Kenworthy analyzed energy use by transportation mode in forty-six cities around the world (see Table 6.4). The resulting data showed that the energy efficiency of car travel (in terms of energy consumed per passenger-mile of travel) is significantly less than

Table 6.4. Energy Efficiency of Selected Transportation Modes

Cities	BTUs/Passenger Mile		
	Car	Bus	All Rail
United States	5,338	3,822	1,122
Australian	4,732	2,487	1,699
Canadian	5,232	2,442	773
European	3,973	2,002	743
Wealthy Asian	4,595	1,274	243
Developing Asian	3,215	1,122	364

Source: Peter Newman and Jeffrey Kenworthy, *Sustainability and Cities: Overcoming Auto Dependence* (Washington, D.C.: Island Press, 1999), 76.

most types of transit (including bus) and even worse when compared to rail transit. Rail transit was found to be by far the most energy-efficient form of motorized transportation across the globe, with rail systems in European cities seven times more energy efficient than car travel in U.S. cities.[83]

Transportation and Energy in Summary

Traffic congestion and energy consumption are interlinked and are both heavily affected by suburban sprawl development patterns. The increasing traffic congestion the nation is experiencing is a direct result of an unbalanced transportation system that is heavily skewed toward automobiles and trucks. That transportation system is tied to a dispersed, low-density land use pattern that is simply not amenable to alternative forms of transportation. The more of it that is built, the more extreme the congestion situation will become. Adding roadway capacity simply results in further suburban development, which in turn congests the roadways. Demand and pricing management solutions cannot work effectively without some alternative transportation mode to which roadway trips can be shifted. All congestion solutions point to the need for planned coordination of land use and transportation.

Increasing energy consumption is also tied to suburbanized development patterns and to traffic congestion. The continuing spread of auto-dependent development means that VMT will

only increase over time, meaning ever-rising consumption of petroleum. While new vehicle technology may eventually reduce petroleum demand, this is not likely to happen before dwindling supplies of easily recoverable oil begin to significantly increase energy prices, causing potentially serious economic dislocations. Petroleum also has other uses in our society, including the production of plastics and other industrial materials.

Whatever the nation may do in the future, the reality is that the suburban development that has already been built will not simply go away. The national investment in suburbanization is heavy, and a lot more of continues to be built. This means that current levels of auto trips (along with consequent congestion and fuel consumption problems) aren't likely to be reduced anytime soon. In fact, as we have seen, fuel consumption will likely increase during the next twenty years. Furthermore, the nation is already so committed to the automobile transportation system that it will be very difficult to trade it all in rapidly for something radically different.

The final solution to oil consumption will not be reduction of car trips alone but, rather, making cars that consume less, or different kinds of, fuel. But many questions remain as to when and over how long a period of time the changeover will take place. In the meantime, anything that can be done now to change development policies so as to reduce auto use can only help in the long run. Not only will curtailing sprawl development help lessen the severity of national energy consumption problems, it can also help the United States move toward balancing its transportation system and forestalling roadway congestion and economic gridlock.

Even if improvements to automobile technology eventually bring high-mileage, zero-emission vehicles, that action alone will not rid the nation of the other impacts that auto dependence has on our environment. The roadways, parking lots, garages, and service stations necessary to support the system would all still be there, along with the driveways and the by-products of the road construction, auto manufacturing, and disposal processes.

CHAPTER 7

Pollution and Public Health

The automobiles, trucks, roads, and parking lots that serve suburban development patterns have impacts other than traffic congestion and energy consumption. Among these are the contribution they make to air pollution, degradation of water quality, and effects on public health.

Air Quality

The petroleum used by all of the automobiles and trucks that are required to serve the nation's suburbanized metropolitan areas becomes transformed into the air pollution and smog that plague those same metropolitan areas. The contaminants cars and trucks release into the atmosphere include greenhouse gases and other major pollutants that affect both the environment and public health.

Sprawl and Emissions

The U.S. transportation system (which is composed primarily of cars and trucks) releases nearly 450 million tons of carbon into the atmosphere each year. That is nearly a third of all annual U.S. carbon emissions.[1] The United States contributes more than a third of the annual world total of carbon dioxide emissions—a major greenhouse gas (see Figure 7.1). If global warming is a reality, and there is mounting evidence that it is, then the U.S. transportation system alone is making a significant contribution to the greenhouse gases responsible for this trend. And, the U.S. contribution is forecast to increase by more than 1 percent per year.

The consequences of this warming trend ultimately may cause serious damage to our nation and the world. Global warming may result in

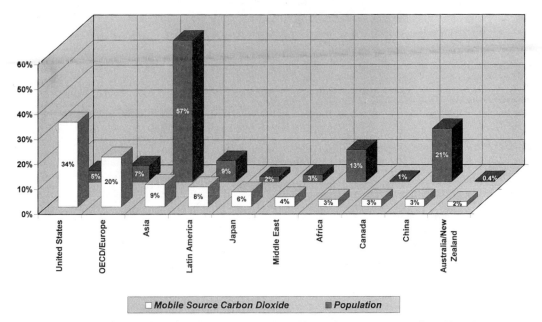

Figure 7.1. Mobile source carbon dioxide emissions and world population—percent of world totals.
Source: U.S. Department of Transportation (DOT), Bureau of Transportation Statistics, *Transportation Statistics Annual Report 1996* (Washington, D.C.: DOT, 1996), 224; and U.S. Census Bureau, Report WP/98, *World Population Profile: 1998* (Washington, D.C.: U.S. Census Bureau, 1999), table A-4.

polar ice melt, which in turn may cause rising sea levels and untold damage to coastal communities, cities, ports, urban infrastructure, wetlands, and beaches. Global warming could potentially disrupt climate and rainfall patterns worldwide, including major changes to regional ecosystems and the farms, forests, fisheries, and societies that depend on them. Species extinctions, agricultural damage, and an increasing incidence of cancer are among the potential results of global warming.

For example, the current range of the sugar maple covers an area of about twenty states in the East and the Midwest. The sugar maple has long been an important part of the countryside, forest ecosystems, and agricultural economies of many of these states. If warming trends continue, the range of the sugar maple is forecast to shift northward into Canada, with the only U.S. presence remaining in northern Maine.[2] This is but one species of tree, and clearly, many other plant and animal communities will be affected as well. In June 2001, the National Academy of Sciences released a report commissioned by the U.S. president that reaffirmed the connection between human activity and global warming.[3]

Carbon dioxide isn't the only gas cars contribute to the environment. Automobiles, trucks, and buses also produce about 60 million tons of poisonous carbon monoxide each year, more than 60 percent of the annual U.S. production of that pollutant. In addition, highway vehicles emit some 7 million tons of carcinogenic volatile organic compounds (VOCs)—about 26 percent of the U.S. annual total—and 32 percent (or about 8 million tons) of the U.S. total of poisonous oxides of nitrogen each year.[4] Furthermore, diesel engines in cars, trucks, and buses emit significant amounts of soot and other fine particulates (known as particulate matter and classified as PM-10 and PM-2.5).

Even though it is estimated that automobile emissions in most of the six major pollutant categories (carbon monoxide, lead, nitrogen oxides, ozone, particulate matter, and sulfur dioxide) have been reduced in varying amounts (e.g., carbon monoxide by 29 percent and lead by 98 percent) from what they were in 1970, one category, oxides of nitrogen, actually has increased by 17 percent.[5] This is in part due to diesel trucks and continuing increases in vehicle miles traveled (VMT) on the nation's highways. In fact, the U.S. Environmental Protection Agency's (EPA's) Office of Transporta-

tion and Air Quality states that, although cars today are capable of emitting 90 percent less air toxics (carcinogenic VOCs and particulate matter) on a per-mile basis than in 1970, growth in VMT will offset progress in reducing air toxics by early this century, causing air pollution from highway vehicles to actually increase within the next twenty years.[6] This projection is based, among other things, on the continued growth of auto-dependent sprawl, which will inevitably increase the number of VMT nationally.

As discussed in Chapter 6, an alternative to sprawl is to increase density. A clear correlation exists between increased density and lowered fuel consumption, and lowered fuel consumption should basically translate into decreased air pollution overall.

Counterarguments

The Reason Public Policy Institute (RPPI), the Heritage Foundation, and others object to the argument that suburban sprawl is responsible for increased air pollution. They argue that both traffic congestion and air pollution are higher in dense urban areas than in less densely populated suburbs. We have already seen in Chapter 6 the statistics cited by both groups that show that increased density in a given area also means increased auto trips and traffic congestion in that same area, because not everyone is diverted to alternative modes.[7] Density in itself is not responsible for the increased congestion. It is the monomodal pattern of suburban sprawl that surrounds cities that essentially is responsible for the traffic entering the cities.

Nonetheless, the greater congestion actually occurs mostly in denser areas, and greater congestion almost invariably means higher local air pollution loads because more emissions are generated by slow-moving, start-stop traffic than by freely moving cars and trucks. This leads RPPI, the Heritage Foundation, and the Thoreau Institute to make the observation that the greatest air pollution problems in the United States are in the cities, not in the suburbs, implying that higher density actually makes air pollution worse rather than better.[8]

This argument may be true locally but certainly not regionally. Mobile source air pollution problems (that is, pollution problems generated by cars and trucks) ultimately are caused by the existence of auto-dependent development outside the cities. If the auto-dependent development weren't there, many of the auto trips wouldn't be either. Regional trips would shift to other modes, such as walking and transit. The cities would also be less congested with automotive vehicles, which should mean better air (because, as RPPI, the Heritage Foundation, and others contend, cars make more pollution when standing in traffic than they do when they are moving). Furthermore, elimination of sprawl outside the cities would also eliminate a vast majority of the auto trips outside the cities. The correct way to view air pollution is not on a city versus suburban basis but to look at the region as whole, including both dense urban areas and the suburbanized areas that make up most of the geography, population, and employment of U.S. metropolitan areas. We have already seen in Chapter 1 that metropolitan areas—not cities or suburbs—are the nation's fundamental economic units, and they work together as a system.

Water Quality

What happens to the land also affects the water that is part of everyday life. Much of our natural surroundings consist of harbors, rivers, watersheds, and wetlands (see Figure 7.2). A lot has been done in the past thirty years to improve the quality of these critical water resources, enough for the *EPA Journal* to declare: "Gross pollution of the nation's rivers, lakes and coastal waters by sewage and industrial wastes is largely a thing of the past."[9] The number of the nation's water bodies meeting Clean Water Act standards has almost doubled since 1972, climbing from 36 to 63 percent. This means they are suitable for recreation and for the protection and propaga-

Figure 7.2. Tidal wetland near Cape Cod. (Alex S. MacLean/Landslides)

tion of aquatic life. Almost all U.S. sewage is now treated before discharge, with nearly 98 percent of all municipal wastewater plants providing secondary or more stringent treatment.[10] Nonetheless, water pollution remains a serious national problem.

Nonpoint Source Pollution

One of the principal stumbling blocks to further environmental clean-up is water contamination from nonpoint source pollution (or runoff)—rainfall or snowmelt moving over and through the ground as opposed to emanating from a "point source," such as a sewer. Runoff water can carry pollutants coming from widespread surfaces and contributed to by a wide variety of sources, including agriculture, urbanized areas, logging operations, and construction sites. According to the EPA, runoff pollution "remains the nation's largest source of water quality problems." Pollution from runoff is the main reason that about 40 percent of U.S. rivers, lakes, and estuaries fail to meet water quality standards.[11]

AGRICULTURAL RUNOFF

The largest contributor of nonpoint source pollutants to our rivers and lakes is agricultural runoff, which degrades about 60 percent of impaired river miles and 50 percent of impaired lake acreage.[12] Runoff from agriculture includes large amounts of silt as well as toxic pesticides and "nutrients" from fertilizers and animal manure. These outflows can cause pollution as well as massive algal blooms and fish kills.

Ultimately, agricultural runoff is a predicament that calls for changes in farming practices, not in development patterns. Farms can help protect watersheds from runoff pollutants through such best management practices as improving pesticide and nutrient control, improving irrigation systems, reducing erosion, fencing livestock away from streams, proper siting and maintenance of animal feeding operations, and making use of natural predators in pest control to reduce pesticide use. Setbacks from lakes and creeks and planting of waterside shrubs and other vegetation can also help trap sediment and slow flow while providing shade and wildlife habitat.[13] In some cases, best management practices such as these have reduced siltation by 50 percent or more and nutrients by more than 80 percent.[14]

Table 7.1. Population and Density of the Top Ten Metro Areas and Their Cities

Metro Area	Population	Area (Mi²)	Density (Pop./Mi²)	City	Population	Area (Mi²)	Density (Pop./Mi²)
New York/ N. Jersey/LI	21,199,865	10,166	2,085	New York	8,008,278	309	25,925
Los Angeles/ Riverside/ Orange Co.	16,373,645	33,966	482	Los Angeles	3,694,820	469	7,873
Chicago/Gary/ Kenosha	9,157,540	6,931	1,321	Chicago	2,896,016	227	12,747
Washington/ Baltimore	7,608,070	9,578	794	Washington	572,059	61	9,317
San Francisco/ Oakland/San Jose	7,039,362	7,369	955	San Francisco	776,733	47	16,632
Philadelphia/ Wilmington/ Atl. City	6,188,463	5,936	1,043	Philadelphia	1,517,550	135	11,233
Boston/ Worcester/ Lawrence	5,819,100	6,450	902	Boston	589,141	48	12,172
Detroit/Ann Arbor/Flint	5,456,428	6,566	831	Detroit	951,270	139	6,858
Dallas/ Fort Worth	5,221,801	9,105	574	Dallas	1,188,580	342	3,471
Houston/ Galveston/ Brazoria	4,669,571	7,707	606	Houston	1,953,631	540	3,619
Average Density			959				10,985

Note: 2000 population data used. Source: U.S. Census Bureau, *Census 2000 PHC-T-3, Ranking Tables for Metropolitan Areas: 1990 and 2000,* table 1; www.census.gov/main/www/cen2000.html.

THE SUBURBAN CONTRIBUTION

In 1998, runoff from urbanized areas ranked third as a major polluter of the nation's rivers and lakes, and it was the second largest source of impairment to U.S. estuaries.[15] While urbanized areas include both cities and suburbs, low-density suburban areas cover most of the territory in the nation's metropolitan areas, as can be seen in Table 7.1. The average density of the nation's top ten metro areas is just under 1,000 persons per square mile, which is basically a light suburban density when compared with such cities as New York City (25,925), Boston (12,172), Washington, D.C. (9,317), and even Los Angeles (7,837).[16]

Table 7.2 shows the relative rankings of the five leading sources of water quality impairment

attributable to human activity. Suburban runoff problems are caused chiefly by the proliferation of impervious surfaces, such as roads, parking lots, and buildings (see Figure 7.3). Suburban lawns and gardens are also contributing factors. The increase in the effects produced by impervious surfaces may be gradual at first, but the consequences are often dramatic. Much of the rain falling on undeveloped land is absorbed into soil, groundcover, and vegetation. By contrast, when rain falls on a developed area, a disproportionate amount becomes surface runoff. As a result, a fully developed watershed can generate fifteen to twenty times more runoff than an undeveloped area, increasing flood hazard.[17]

This increase in volume is coupled with an increase in pollutants. Suburban lawns and gar-

Table 7.2. Leading Sources of Water Quality Impairment

Rank	Rivers	Lakes	Estuaries
1	Agriculture	Agriculture	Municipal point sources
2	Hydromodification	Hydromodification	Urban runoff
3	Urban runoff	Urban runoff	Atmospheric deposition

Source: U.S. Environmental Protection Agency (EPA), Office of Water, *National Water Quality Inventory: 1998 Report to Congress* (Washington, D.C.: EPA, 1998), 62, 88, 108.

Figure 7.3. Suburban runoff problems are caused chiefly by impervious surfaces such as parking lots. (Alex S. MacLean/Landslides)

dens produce many of the same sediments, pesticides, and fertilizers found in agricultural runoff as well as bacteria from pet waste and animals killed on roads. At the same time, the parking lots, roadways, and other impervious surfaces contribute heavy metals, hydrocarbons, and VOCs. In regions with cold winters, roadways and parking lots require a lot of salt, which is also released into the watershed.

Drinking Water

Most of the water quality issues discussed above have to do with impacts to water bodies that render them unable to support recreation or aquatic life. Pollution also affects watersheds used to supply drinking water. Contaminants produced by encroaching suburban development can affect these watersheds as well. For example, the city of Cambridge, Massachusetts, drew much of its drinking water from a once-rural reservoir. During the 1950s, Route 128, a suburban beltway, was built next to the reservoir. Since then, the reservoir has become surrounded by suburban development, including housing, hotels, and office parks. Over time, the sodium (from salt) content of Cambridge's drinking water became nearly equal to that of mayon-

naise. Since then, the city has acted at some expense to correct the problem by putting in a new filtration plant, and pursuing an aggressive watershed management program. Problems like this one are growing more common. The city of New York has an elaborate reservoir system, planned many years ago, that stretches into the Catskill Mountains far from the city. Nonetheless, New York has had to campaign to halt encroaching development from contaminating its water supply system.

Meanwhile, the nation is running out of places to drill new wells for water. Suburbanization combined with continued widespread use of on-site septic systems continues to threaten water supply in areas across the country. In Massachusetts, for example, the Ipswich River runs dry in the summer because of nearby wells draining off its source. Similar problems are occurring in other river basins in the region.[18] Water demand in Atlanta, Georgia, is projected to outstrip its supply by 2020.[19] In California and other parts of the West, the demand for water fueled by suburbanization has been draining off major rivers and lakes for years. The mighty Colorado River is reduced to a mere trickle that evaporates in the desert before it reaches the Gulf of California. In Texas, drilling for water has replaced drilling for oil as a moneymaking enterprise because every major urban area in the state has become desperate for more water to meet the needs of unbridled expansion. The Rio Grande, a primary water source for counties along the Mexican border, has diminished so much that it recently failed for the first time in fifty years to reach the Gulf of Mexico.[20]

Even in areas with plentiful rain, potable water resources can dry up because sprawl development replaces wetlands and forests while paving over natural recharge areas with impermeable parking areas, roads, and buildings. Rainwater falling on impermeable surfaces becomes storm water runoff that is fed directly into sewers and streams, where it enters the ocean rather than naturally filtering into underground aquifers. Remember that the developed areas generate fifteen to twenty times the runoff of a field or woodlot, and most of that is water that would have gone to recharge the local aquifers. Because of this, some groups have alleged that our nation is literally throwing its drinking water away.

Solutions exist, however. There are ways to improve the permeability of parking lots. Street widths and parking ratios can be reduced, meaning less paved area. Storm water runoff can be channeled into "bio-retention" areas, such as filtering swales and wetlands that can be used to recapture some of the water. Shifting more trips to transit and walking also reduces the need for parking and roadway surface area.[21] These solutions also suggest a general development approach that would reduce and consolidate built and paved areas while leaving more open fields, wetlands, and woods to act as natural filters and groundwater recharge areas.

Public Health

In recent years, discussion about the affects of sprawl development on public health has become more common, not only because of air and water pollution but also because of all the constant driving. Driving everywhere means that people living in suburbia walk less and, without other exercise, are becoming prone to obesity and poor health. While some scholars tend to dismiss this notion as having little to do with the pattern of suburbanization, many health professionals are taking the idea quite seriously.[22] Among those deeply concerned about the issue are the Centers for Disease Control and Prevention (CDC), which is operated by the U.S. Department of Health and Human Services.

Inactivity Patterns

In a recent working paper entitled *How Land Use and Transportation Systems Impact Public Health*, the CDC stated that "improper diet and inactivity patterns were the root causes of some 300,000 deaths in the United States in 1990, second only to tobacco."[23] The CDC is worried by physical activity levels in the United States, citing that only 30 to 40 percent of Americans engage in regular exercise and that 30 percent are totally inactive.[24] The CDC considers regular forms of physical activity, including walking and biking, to have significant health benefits, a view that has caused the CDC to focus on interventions designed to change lifestyles and reduce deaths caused by inactivity. They believe that the best way to accomplish this is to make changes in the built environment in which people live, work, and play—such changes are thought to be more effective than structured activities like aerobics classes.

In their working paper, the CDC notes that automobile travel accounts for 86 percent of all person trips in the United States whereas walking accounts for only 5 percent. They attribute this largely to the design of the suburban environment, which is configured to favor auto trips and discourages walking and biking through separated land uses and long cul-de-sacs. Worried about safety, people are more inclined to drive their children rather than let them bike or walk through suburban traffic. The CDC concludes that their research supports the hypothesis that higher densities, mixed land uses, a balance between housing and jobs, and pedestrian-friendly street design will all help promote increased walking and biking and, hence, better public health. In summary, the CDC study states:

> A detailed assessment of the interface between land use, transportation, and human behavior suggests that nonmotorized improvements in areas that possess both a concentration and heterogeneity of uses could maximize the likelihood to walk more and drive less. Strategies that increase human powered travel and offset sedentariness would seem to hold potential health benefits.[25]

Traffic Injuries and Fatalities

There are, of course, other public health issues associated with suburbanization and too much driving, including an increased risk of accidents and air toxics. In 1999, there were more than 41,000 traffic fatalities in the United States and nearly 3.2 million automotive injuries.[26] The number of traffic fatalities in 1999 was approximately equal to the population of a small U.S.

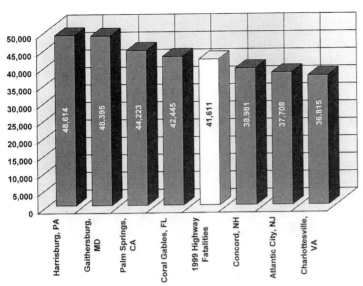

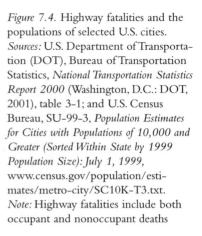

Figure 7.4. Highway fatalities and the populations of selected U.S. cities. *Sources:* U.S. Department of Transportation (DOT), Bureau of Transportation Statistics, *National Transportation Statistics Report 2000* (Washington, D.C.: DOT, 2001), table 3-1; and U.S. Census Bureau, SU-99-3, *Population Estimates for Cities with Populations of 10,000 and Greater (Sorted Within State by 1999 Population Size): July 1, 1999,* www.census.gov/population/estimates/metro-city/SC10K-T3.txt. *Note:* Highway fatalities include both occupant and nonoccupant deaths

Figure 7.5. U.S. highway fatalities compared with all other modes.
Source: U.S. Department of Transportation (DOT), Bureau of Transportation Statistics, *National Transportation Statistics Report 2000* (Washington, D.C.: DOT, 2001), tables 2-4 and 3-1.

city—such as Charlottesville, Virginia; Concord, New Hampshire; or Wilkes-Barre, Pennsylvania (see Figure 7.4).[27] By contrast, there were only about 2,800 fatalities and 95,000 injuries from all other transportation modes combined, including aviation and recreational boating (see Figure 7.5). According to the U.S. Department of Transportation, motor vehicle crashes accounted for about half of all U.S. accident-related deaths annually and 60 percent of years of life lost from all accidents before age 65.[28]

Highways, cars, and trucks accounted for 95 percent of the nation's transportation fatalities and 97 percent of the injuries.[29] To provide another yardstick for comparison, the number of highway fatalities in 1999 is equal to about 72 percent of the total number of U.S. service personnel killed in the Vietnam War between 1961 and 1975 and is nearly three times the number of U.S. service personnel killed in Vietnam in 1968, the year of the Tet Offensive and the year with the highest number of U.S. war casualties (see Figure 7.6).[30]

Comparing total trips and fatalities, whereas highways were responsible for about 86 percent of all person trips, they accounted for 94 percent of the nation's transportation fatalities. Transit, on the other hand, accounted for nearly 4 percent of all person trips yet less than 1 percent of all transportation fatalities and 2 percent of injuries. These figures may appear differently when passenger miles are used instead of total trips, but total trips are a better measure than passenger miles across modes that have different average trip lengths.[31] Table 7.3 compares fatalities and injuries for transit and private vehicle modes by total trips taken for 1995 (the year for which all comparable data are readily available). Another way to look at the issue is in terms of occupant-only fatalities (see Table 7.4). This measure excludes fatalities outside of the vehicle such as pedestrian deaths, grade-crossing accidents, suicides and losses from rail industry occupational illness. Occupant-only fatalities arguably provide a more accurate assessment of the risk to a passenger faced with alternative mode choices.[32] As can be seen from Table 7.4, relative occupant fatalities for auto significantly exceed all other modes, even when compared on a per-passenger-mile basis (the number of passengers times the number of miles traveled).

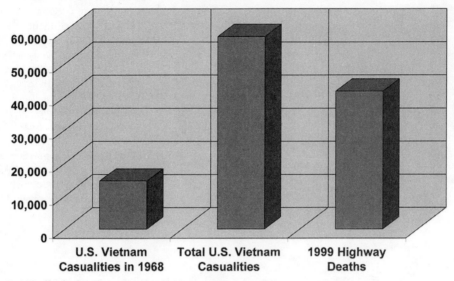

Figure 7.6. Traffic fatalities compared with Vietnam War casualties.
Sources: U.S. Department of Transportation (DOT), Bureau of Transportation Statistics, *National Transportation Statistics Report 2000* (Washington, D.C.: DOT, 2001), tables 2-4 and 3-1; and American War Library, http://members.aol.com/warlibrary/vwc18.htm.

Table 7.3. Fatalities and Injuries for Highway and Transit—1995

	Total Trips (millions)	Fatalities	Fatalities/ Million Trips	Injuries	Injuries/ Million Trips
Auto	339,935	41,817	0.12	3,465,000	10.19
Transit	13,663	274	0.02	57,196	4.19

Source: U.S. Department of Transportation (DOT), Bureau of Transportation Statistics, *Transportation Statistics Annual Report 1999* (Washington, D.C.: DOT, 1999).
Note: Auto figures include motorcycles, pick-ups, vans, and SUVs but exclude heavy trucks. Transit includes rail and bus transit but excludes long-distance and commuter rail. Includes both occupant and nonoccupant fatalities and injuries.

Table 7.4. Occupant Fatalities by Transportation Mode—1995

	Passenger Miles Traveled (billions)	Total Occupant Fatalities	Occupant Fatalities per Billion Passenger Miles Traveled
Auto	3,633.00	35,106	9.66
Transit	151.20	126	0.83
Rail	12.60	13	1.03
Airplane	403.20	168	0.42

Note: Excludes nonoccupant fatalities, such as pedestrians, cyclists, grade-crossing accidents, suicides, and rail occupational illness deaths that may be included in Table 7.3. Auto figures include motorcycles, pick-ups, vans, and SUVs but exclude heavy trucks. Transit includes rail and bus transit but excludes long-distance and commuter rail. Rail includes long-distance and commuter rail.
Source: U.S. Department of Transportation (DOT), Bureau of Transportation Statistics, *Transportation Statistics Annual Report 1997* (Washington, D.C.: DOT, 1997) (for rail passenger fatalities, see page 66).

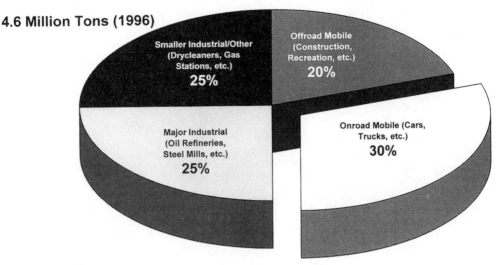

4.6 Million Tons (1996)

Smaller Industrial/Other
(Drycleaners, Gas
Stations, etc.)
25%

Offroad Mobile
(Construction,
Recreation, etc.)
20%

Major Industrial
(Oil Refineries,
Steel Mills, etc.)
25%

Onroad Mobile (Cars,
Trucks, etc.)
30%

Figure 7.7. Toxic air pollution sources.
Source: U.S. Environmental Protection Agency (EPA), Office of Air Quality Planning and Standards, *National Air Quality and Emissions Trends Report, 1999* (Research Triangle Park, NC: EPA, 2001), 82.

Toxic Air Pollutants

The cars and trucks that serve the suburbanized world also produce toxic air pollutants that constitute health hazards of their own. In 1996, the United States released close to 5 million tons of toxic pollutants into the air, nearly one-third of which was generated by cars and trucks (see Figure 7.7).[33] These mobile sources produce such carcinogenic compounds as benzene as well as formaldehyde, toluene, acetaldehyde, xylene, 1,3–butadiene, sulfur compounds, and particulate matter (PM-10 and PM-2.5). Particulate matter can be seriously damaging to lung tissue. Some of these particulates (PM-2.5) are so fine that they can enter the bloodstream through the lungs while carrying carbon, metals, and other ingredients. The Harvard School of Public Health and the American Cancer Society both have found strong links between high levels of small particles and a rise in death rates.[34] Noncancer effects of some of the toxic compounds created by auto emissions can include reproductive and neurological problems. The EPA estimates that cars and trucks account for about half of all cancers attributed to outdoor air sources of toxics.[35]

Pollution and Public Health in Summary

Increasing energy consumption from rising VMT means more air pollution from cars and trucks in the years ahead, despite the progress that has been made toward cleaner vehicles. The cause of the pollution is the same as the cause of the VMT: low-density, spread-out, auto-dependent development patterns. While some may argue that cities have more traffic congestion and air pollution, cities are only a part of a greater auto-dependent suburban metropolitan region, which dominates in area, population, and employment. The congestion and air pollution cities suffer is caused by the prevailing transportation and development patterns of the metropolitan regions that surround them. The ultimate solution is to find regional growth solutions that create a more balanced transportation system over time.

The solution to the air pollution problem, like the solution to oil consumption, will ultimately be making cars that consume less fuel or a different kind of fuel and that therefore do not pollute or that at least pollute a lot less. This will not solve some of the public health or water pollution problems, however. As metropolitan areas continue to expand geographically along with roads and parking lots, they increasingly affect their water supplies. If nothing is done to change how new suburbs are built, increasing runoff from urbanized areas may begin to reverse the progress that has been made in cleaning up the nation's water bodies. Furthermore, drinking water resources are threatened by the same continued outward expansion of urbanized area.

Overreliance on cars for travel also creates serious public health problems, from lack of adequate exercise to the huge number of traffic fatalities and injuries suffered by the nation to the cancers and other illnesses caused by the toxic compounds produced by tailpipe emissions. Working toward a more balanced transportation system, which contains more walkable environments, can help ease these problems as well.

CHAPTER 8

Economics and Social Equity

The term *sustainability* refers just as much to social and economic resources as it does to those of the natural environment. Suburbanization appears to be using limited natural resources in a nonsustainable fashion, and many argue that it also is doing the same with the nation's man-made capital. This chapter reviews the effects of suburbanization on two aspects of the national fabric: economics and social equity.

The Economics of Sprawl

As is the case with environmental costs, there is considerable debate about whether we spend more dollars to build sprawl than we do to build "more compact" development alternatives modeled on older cities and towns. The question has several aspects. Among the most frequently discussed issues are the following:

• The comparative capital infrastructure cost of sprawl
• The hidden subsidies in sprawl
• The cost of inefficient growth patterns
• The tax question and the commercial development problem.

Infrastructure Costs

A fair amount of analysis has been performed on the relative capital infrastructure costs of sprawl versus "compact development." In their book *Once There Were Greenfields: How Urban Sprawl Is Undermining America's Environment, Economy, and Social Fabric,* Kaid Benfield and Donald Chen provide a comprehensive review of previous studies on the subject, while claiming that their cited research efforts are "overwhelmingly consistent in their conclusion that sprawl is a more costly form of development than compact alternatives."[1]

The majority of studies that Benfield and

Chen present tend to agree that the cost of infrastructure—including roadways, sidewalks, water, and sewer—are higher on a per-unit basis in spread-out suburban areas because more roads and longer runs of pipe are required to serve those patterns. In denser communities, reduced roadway lengths and shorter runs of pipe can be amortized over more units in a smaller area. This seems like common sense, and the authors cite a series of reports from across the country that support this theory, including work by the Real Estate Research Corporation, the American Farmland Trust, and the States of Florida and New Jersey. The Florida study, conducted by James Duncan and Associates in the late 1980s, calculated the cost of providing roadways, utilities, schools, emergency services, and public parks to urban development patterns of varying density across Florida. The study concluded that the cost of providing these services on a per-dwelling-unit basis to "scattered" areas was, on average, about twice as expensive as providing those same services to "compact" downtown areas.[2]

The most recent study cited by Benfield and Chen was conducted by Robert Burchell of Rutgers University for the State of New Jersey. It assessed the relative costs of providing schools, roads, water, and sewer facilities under two different future forecast scenarios: an existing trends extended scenario of continuing suburbanization versus a planned scenario that directed new growth to existing urban and suburban centers (see Table 8.1). The study found that the planned scenario saved nearly $2 billion, or about 9 percent, over the trends extended case.[3] This study has since been updated and now predicts that planned growth will save more than $2 billion in roadway and sewer costs alone and will reduce fiscal deficits attributable to growth by $160 million annually by 2020.[4]

Another recent study was done for the Salt

123

123

Table 8.1. Projected Costs of Trend Versus Planned Development in New Jersey (Billions of $)

	Trend (Suburban)	Plan (Managed Growth)	Savings	Percent Savings
Roads	3.72	2.86	0.86	23
Water/Sewer	7.54	6.28	1.26	17
Total	11.26	9.14	2.12	19
Net Annual Fiscal Impact	(0.418)	(0.257)	0.161	39

Source: Robert Burchell et al., *The Costs and Benefits of Alternative Growth Patterns: The Impact Assessment of the New Jersey State Plan* (Trenton: New Jersey Office of State Planning, 2000).

Lake City region of Utah by the Envision Utah planning effort of the Coalition for Utah's Future, with Calthorpe Associates as the principal consultant. The planning effort is documented in the book *The Regional City,* written by Peter Calthorpe and William Fulton. According to the authors, Envison Utah developed four alternative growth scenarios for the future of the Salt Lake City region (see Table 8.2). Two were based on traditional postwar development patterns, and two were based on more compact, walkable forms of development. All were targeted to accommodate the next 1 million in population growth expected in the region. Each scenario was characterized by increasing levels of density. Scenario A (the least dense) required 409 square miles of new development, whereas Scenario D (the most dense) required only 85 square miles to meet the same population goal. According to Calthorpe and Fulton, the most dramatic difference that emerged in the analysis of the alternative was in infrastructure costs (roadways, transit systems, utilities, and water and sewer systems). The costs ranged from nearly $38 billion for Scenario A down to $22 billion for Scenario C (126 square miles), showing a distinct trend of diminishing infrastructure costs as den-

sity increases. At this point, a curious thing happens. Scenario D (the most dense), at $23 billion, is actually more expensive than Scenario C. The trend starts to go up instead of down, which Calthorpe and Fulton attribute to increased spending on transit in Scenario D.[5]

As the authors themselves note, this case points out that the relationship is not linear—that is, it is not a straight line to go from farmland to Manhattan in terms of cost per unit of infrastructure. This is because new infrastructure, such as transit systems, that may not be relevant as less-dense scenarios begin to enter the mix. In fact, this phenomenon is a criticism that has been raised by such skeptics as Peter Gordon and Harry Richardson of the University of Southern California, who state: "The economic and resource efficiency of compact development has never been adequately demonstrated."[6] They point to studies by Richard Peiser and Helen Ladd showing that infrastructure cost savings from compact development are very small or nonexistent and that public service costs actually can increase with higher density.[7] Randal O'Toole extends this theme in his book *The Vanishing Automobile and Other Urban Myths: How Smart Growth Will Harm American Cities,* pointing

Table 8.2. Envision Utah Planning Scenarios

	Projected Population Growth	Percent Multifamily Housing	New Urbanized Area (Mi^2)	Farmland Urbanized (Mi^2)	Infrastructure Costs (Billions of $)	Infrastructure Costs/Dwelling Unit ($)
Scenario A	1,000,000	11	409	174	37.6	99,048
Scenario B	1,000,000	16	325	143	29.8	78,404
Scenario C	1,000,000	32	126	65	22.1	58,291
Scenario D	1,000,000	45	85	43	23	60,590

Source: Calthorpe Associates et al., *Envision Utah: Producing A Vision for the Future of the Greater Wasatch Area* (Salt Lake City: Envision Utah, 2000).

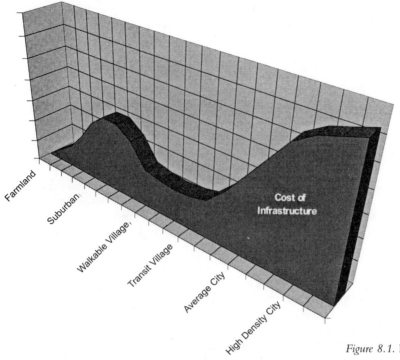

Farmland

Suburban

Walkable Village

Transit Village

Average City

High Density City

Cost of Infrastructure

Figure 8.1. Hypothetical infrastructure cost curve.

out that urban revitalization can cost more than new suburban development if old infrastructure has to be dug up and replaced with new.[8]

As a counterpoint to Gordon and Richardson's criticism, Reid Ewing's article, entitled "Is Los Angeles-Style Sprawl Desirable?" takes up the issue, elaborating on Ladd's theory, which notes that in higher-density situations, there may be a savings on the total units of output required but the cost of a given unit of output may become higher. In other words, denser development may require fewer total miles of roadway, but the cost of a mile of urban roadway may be much higher than a mile of suburban road because of added cost of such features as traffic lights, increased-capacity storm sewers, pavement, catch basins, curbing, increased street lighting, landscaping, and so forth.[9] This agrees, to some extent, with O'Toole's observations on the subject. As urban areas grow denser, we might also have to add the cost of rail transit, grade-separated roads, bridge structures, and multiple layers of underground utilities to a typical mile of roadway—not to mention replacement of aging infrastructure. These considerations lead Ewing to conclude that:

> Within the normal range of urban-suburban densities, per capita infrastructure

costs almost certainly fall as densities rise. However, at the density extremes, there could be some surprises. At very low densities the use of septic systems, open drainage, and rural street cross-sections may cause the cost function to turn downward. At very high densities, the special needs of high-rise structures may cause the cost function to turn upward.[10]

Ewing suggests that the infrastructure cost equation could assume something like the hypothetical shape shown in Figure 8.1. This seems to make sense, especially based on the fact that other studies, such as Envision Utah, seem to confirm this hypothesis. It would appear that there may be some as yet unidentified level of density lying somewhere between typical postwar sprawl and dense high-rise urban environments that is optimal in terms of infrastructure costs. The problem is that the boundaries of this optimal zone have not yet been clearly demarcated.

What to Count?

There is also the concern that the studies reviewed by Benfield and Chen, Gordon and Richardson, Reid Ewing, and others may not be accounting for all of the relevant capital infrastructure cost factors over a wide range of densities. The 2001 *New Jersey State Development and Redevelopment Plan* (the result of a multiyear state planning effort begun in 1985) is based on a very comprehensive analysis of the impacts of alternative growth patterns. The plan's "Impact Assessment" analyzes in detail the potential fiscal effects of a range of growth scenarios, which vary from continuing suburbanization to managed growth directing more development to existing urban areas.[11] But even in that analysis, the elements included in the study are not necessarily the same as those included in other studies. This makes the whole exercise somewhat hazy when trying to compare a wide range of different studies, as Benfield and Chen freely admit.[12]

Developing a national study using universal criteria and counting exactly the same elements would, indeed, be quite difficult to do and would require a major effort even to agree on what should and should not be included in the calculations. While no immediately obvious and clear answer to the question of density and infrastructure costs seems to exist, the studies done to date, as different as they may be, all seem to point consistently to the fact that there is some level of density that is generally more cost efficient in terms of infrastructure than are typical postwar suburban development patterns—and that beyond that point of density, infrastructure costs may begin to trend upward again.

Hidden Subsidies

Regardless of the fact that infrastructure may cost more in spread-out suburban patterns of development, developers still find it economical to build this way, creating single-family houses that historically have been affordable to much of America's middle class. This is because the land is still relatively cheap and, in many cases, developers pay only for the cost of on-site infrastructure while municipalities, counties, and states pay the bill for new water, sewer, and roadway networks to link each new development into the regional system as well as for the schools, fire, police stations, waste transfer stations, and other public facilities (including reservoirs and treatment plants) necessary to support new development. Expansion of facilities needed to handle the higher loads generated by new development is also paid for by the public. Ultimately, these pub-

licly funded elements are underwritten by existing home owners as well as newcomers through taxes and use-rate charges. Arguably, this is somewhat unfair to existing home owners, who face higher rates to pay for the expansion of services to serve the newcomers. However, the costs are also being spread over an increasing larger population in the community, which can somewhat offset the impact to existing home owners.

Nonetheless, the resulting distribution can be inequitable. In one typical example, *U.S. News and World Report* relates that the cost of providing a sewer hookup in the center-city neighborhoods of Tallahassee, Florida, is less than $5,000, whereas the cost of a remote suburban connection in the same metro area is more than $11,000, yet all households in the region pay an even $6,000, with downtown essentially subsidizing the suburbs.[13] In the book *Metropolitics: A Regional Agenda for Community and Stability,* Myron Orfield reports that, in the metropolitan area surrounding Minneapolis and St. Paul, regional sewer funds go primarily to pay the costs of newly developing suburbs, yet both capital costs and operations are financed on a uniform regional basis, with all users paying the same fee. The result is that, on average, the central cities and inner suburbs of the region "pay over $6 million more in fees each year than they incur in costs."[14]

In the nation's older cities, downtowns, and inner-ring suburbs, the infrastructure—including the street system, utilities, water and sewer, and sometimes even public transportation—is already in place. In the urban renewal days, whole neighborhoods were eradicated and all new streets and utilities were put in place—in those cases, brand-new infrastructure was sometimes part of the total development cost. Contemporary revitalization efforts are less likely to make such sweeping changes.

Redeveloping a brownfield or another type of urban site doesn't necessarily require all new infrastructure to support it. True, sometimes existing infrastructure in the district may have to be replaced because it is obsolete, but that is an ongoing problem in any community that has been developed for any length of time. It is a problem that today's new suburbs also will have to eventually face. In fact, building ever-expanding networks of new water, sewer, and roadways while deferring maintenance in older areas only makes that future task more daunting.

Table 8.3. Cost of Car Ownership in Selected Metro Areas

Metro Area	Annual Household Expenditures on Transportation	Percent of Total Household Expenditures
Houston	$8,840	22.1
Miami	$6,684	19.0
Philadelphia	$6,904	18.1
Cleveland	$6,384	17.5
Los Angeles	$7,224	17.4
Portland, Or.	$6,848	16.8
San Diego	$6,319	15.8
Washington, D.C.	$7,207	15.4
Boston	$5,788	15.2
Chicago	$5,436	14.9
New York	$5,956	14.5

Note: 98 percent of household transportation expenditure is for the ownership and operation of automobiles. *Source:* Surface Transportation Policy Project/Barbara McCann et al., "Driven to Spend: Sprawl and Household Transportation Expenses," *Progress*, vol. 11, no. 1 (January–February 2001).

This is the point of development plans in such states as Maryland and New Jersey. The cost savings in New Jersey are to be realized partly through directing development to areas with the existing infrastructure to support new development. The same type of strategy is being used in Maryland. Also, urban areas tend to be denser, more efficient mixed-use communities, where the cost of development can be more easily shared with intensive high-density commercial uses as infrastructure charges are spread over a greater number of residents and businesses per acre than in suburban environments.

To the extent that state and federal funds are used to build the roads that new suburban development needs to exist, these roads are paid for by everyone in the state plus by some share of federal gasoline taxes and other fees paid by everyone in the nation. These facilities are often used in common with a much larger district, thus raising the question of how these costs should be equitably shared across the broader region. For example, Orfield notes that of the approximately $1.1 billion spent in metropolitan highway construction in the Twin Cities area, 75 percent funded new roadways in rapidly developing suburban areas.[15]

It can be argued that the interstate highway system and all of its connecting roadways are actually a huge subsidy to suburbanization across the entire nation. The acres of single-family housing, the shopping malls, and the industrial and office parks wouldn't be possible without the continental, high-speed roadway network that has been built by federal and state governments. Ostensibly, that network was created primarily for transportation and national defense purposes, not to serve land development. Yet, developers of suburban projects have benefited enormously from those projects without paying their prorated share of the total cost. Those projects are paid for by the residents of the entire country through fuel and other taxes. In this sense, the developers are receiving a subsidy in the form of an access improvement for which they have not paid their full share. In a true user-fee situation, the developers might be required to pay back their share of the benefit out of the proceeds of the land development-reducing gas taxes and other road-use fees.

In contrast to roadways, transit projects that serve cities have received relatively little funding, yet many people view them as subsidized. As discussed in earlier chapters, almost all of the travel in the United States is by car. The fact that everyone is on the highway can make transit spending seem an unnecessary waste of money. This leads to a public perception that transit is "subsidized" while people driving cars pay their own way—in other words, that cars are a cheap necessity, whereas transit is an expensive drain. The fact is that roads and cars cost the nation far more than any transit system ever has. According to some estimates, the average family spends about $6,000 per year on cars, excluding parking charges and tax bills for road maintenance and so forth (see Table 8.3).[16]

Estimates by the Surface Transportation Policy Project (STPP) place the costs of household spending on automobile transportation even higher—nearly $9,000 per year in metro areas such as Houston, or about 22 percent of the average annual household budget in that metro area.[17] Automobile travel is not free. American households are said to spend more money on their cars than for any other expense category except housing—even more than health care, education, food, or clothing (see Figure 8.2).[18]

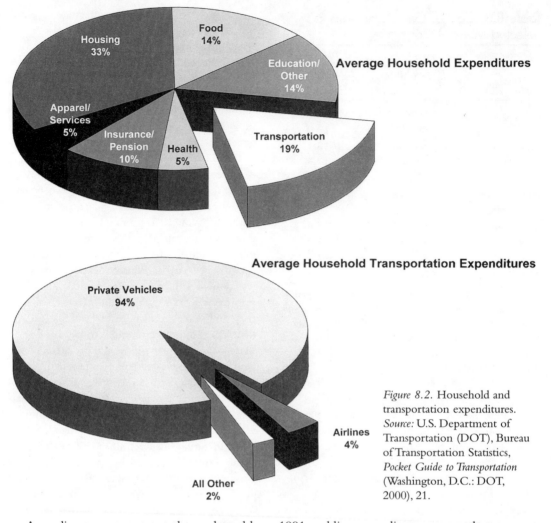

Average Household Expenditures

Average Household Transportation Expenditures

Figure 8.2. Household and transportation expenditures. *Source:* U.S. Department of Transportation (DOT), Bureau of Transportation Statistics, *Pocket Guide to Transportation* (Washington, D.C.: DOT, 2000), 21.

According to one recent study conducted by the Conservation Law Foundation, the government subsidy for drive-alone commuting is more than 40 percent higher than it is for rail commuting.[19] Furthermore, between 1980 and 1996 alone, the federal government spent more than $303 billion on transportation, with only 11 percent of that amount going to transit—and that with all of the legislation that has been passed to increase the transit share of total transportation spending.[20] Moreover, as discussed in Chapter 3, the allocated funds for transit for the next three years under the Transportation Equity Act for the 21st Century are less than 19 percent of the total amount funded. Although this is more than it has been, roads are still getting a vastly greater share of federal funds than transit is.

Gordon and Richardson argue that roads actually pay their way while transit does not. In their paper "Are Compact Cities a Desirable Planning Goal?" the authors estimate that in 1991 public expenditures on roadways were $66.5 billion while revenues were $53.8 billion—an 81 percent recovery of costs. For the same year, they estimate that public expenditures on transit were $20.8 billion while revenues were $8.8 billion—a 42 percent recovery.[21] What is missing in this analysis is a view of the transportation system as a whole rather than as discrete parts. The money spent on transit succeeded in keeping nearly 5.4 million cars off congested roads in peak commuting hours by giving commuters an alternative to the highway, thus avoiding the cost of adding the roadway capacity needed to serve those cars and the cost of lost hours from additional congestion.[22]

Furthermore, other sources report smaller figures for roadway recovery costs. In their book *The Transportation/Land Use Connection,* Terry Moore and Paul Thorsnes report that fuel and vehicle taxes recapture only about 60–65 percent

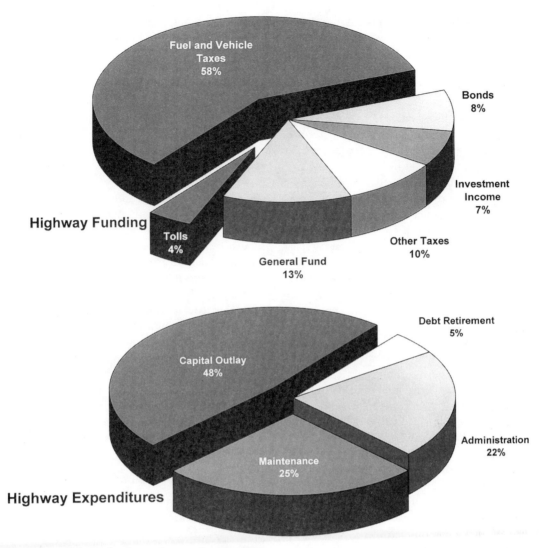

Highway Funding

Fuel and Vehicle Taxes 58%

Bonds 8%

Investment Income 7%

Other Taxes 10%

General Fund 13%

Tolls 4%

Highway Expenditures

Capital Outlay 48%

Debt Retirement 5%

Administration 22%

Maintenance 25%

Figure 8.3. Highway funding and expenditures—1998.
Source: U.S. Department of Transportation (DOT), Federal Highway Administration, *Our Nation's Highways: Selected Facts and Figures* (Washington, D.C.: DOT, 1998), 31.

of the cost of providing highway infrastructure; a significant share comes from general fund and other tax revenues (see Figure 8.3).[23] None of these figures accounts for the costs of roadway externalities (environmental, social, and health impacts). These costs have been estimated by Jane Holtz Kay to run an additional $3,000 to $5,000 per household on top of the $6,200 per household that the STPP estimates is spent annually on car ownership and driving.[24] Divided by an average 1.78 motor vehicles per household, that works out to about $5,700 per motor vehicle. Multiplied by about 192 million registered vehicles, it adds up to a significant number: more than $1 trillion annually.[25]

Some of these costs are recaptured by insurance payments and property and general taxes that drivers as a group pay along with everyone else, but a substantial chunk of these costs aren't paid by drivers at all. Those unpaid costs arguably constitute a subsidy to the users of the system. Moore and Thorsnes estimate that drivers as a group fail to pay about $200 billion of the total annual social cost of running the nation's roadway system.[26] *U.S. News and World Report* estimates that it would require a gas tax of $6.60 per gallon to fully pay for the cost that car travel imposes on the economy.[27]

Despite these types of figures, such well-respected authorities as Anthony Downs also argue that the relative ridership of transit doesn't justify its cost. In a recent article in *Planning* magazine, Downs notes that transit receives 25 percent of all public funding (federal as well as state and local) while accommodating somewhere in the vicinity of 2 percent of all person trips.[28] Some sources estimate that the average transit share is higher—at perhaps 4 percent of total trips—depending on what is counted as transit and that transit's share of commuting trips is definitely higher, at more than 5 percent.[29]

Missing from this analysis is the cost of buying, operating, and maintaining the vehicles that use the highways. Transit costs typically include vehicle-related expenses. If we look at a typical year for which data is available, we can see how this plays out. In 1995, for example, federal, state, and local governments spent a little over $92 billion to build, operate, and maintain the nation's highway system.[30] In the same year, these governments plus fare-paying passengers spent a total of about $24 billion on the nation's transit systems.[31] This figure is somewhat less than 25 percent of the combined total of roads and transit, and it does not include expenditures on water or air transportation. However, the $24 billion does include farebox revenue (user fees paid for transit use). A major difference is that the transit figure includes the cost of the rolling stock (or vehicles), while the roadway number does not.

Adding the cost of buying, operating, and maintaining the rolling stock for the highways changes the equation considerably. Using an average annual cost per vehicle of about $3,500 (excluding external costs) multiplied by about 192 million private vehicles in 1995 (excluding publicly owned vehicles as well as freight trucks, farm vehicles, buses, and so forth) yields a total vehicle capital and operations cost of about $667 billion, which, when added to the $92 billion annual cost of the highways, brings the total cost of running the roadway system to about $810 billion in 1995.[32] If trailer trucks are added in, the total cost rises to more than $900 billion.[33] At $24 billion, the cost of transit approaches 3 percent of the total cost of transit and roads combined. Thus, in the context of the transportation system as a whole, the nation is spending about 3 percent of the combined public-private, highway-transit budget to support a transit share of between 2 and 5 percent of total system trips.

It is true that much of the highway vehicle costs are privately paid for by the users of the system, but owning and maintaining a car is not a matter of choice for anyone who lives and works in the suburbs. There, the cost of transportation is the cost of the car. Given the high price of vehicle ownership already paid by private individuals, it is not surprising that there can be public opposition to raising fuel taxes and roadway user fees to cover the full cost of the roadway transportation system.

Another issue traditionally raised is that of tax-deductible mortgage interest. This deduction has long been a factor in making home ownership preferable to renting. During the postwar suburban boom, it was certainly a factor in the growth of suburban homes; urban housing was almost exclusively rental during the 1950s and 1960s. It has been estimated that this tax policy costs the federal treasury between $50 billion and $60 billion annually.[34] The advent of the condominium has leveled the playing field somewhat. Now, someone purchasing a condominium in the city can get the same favorable tax treatment as someone buying in the suburbs, although many people living in cities still rent their homes, and, unlike mortgage interest, there is no federal tax deduction for residential rent.

Inefficient Growth Patterns

Another very serious issue may be the regional cost of the inefficient growth patterns inherent in sprawl development. As documented in Chapter 4, the rapid suburbanization in states such as Maryland has caused enormous fiscal strains. New public facilities, such as schools, roads, and sewers, are needed to keep pace with rapid development where little but farms and forests existed before. Yet, this pattern of rushing to build new facilities to keep pace with new, unplanned development can be extremely wasteful. In Montgomery County, Maryland, seventy new schools were built to accommodate newly developing areas while, at the same time, the total countywide school population dropped by ten thousand and sixty-eight schools were abandoned elsewhere in the county.[35]

These expenditures for public facilities are not required to meet the needs of population growth within the metropolitan region; they are needed to meet the *displacement* of population from one part of the region to another. This means that, regionally, superfluous funds are being spent needlessly on new schools and infra-structure when adequate facilities to serve regional population growth already exist. Arguably, on a regional basis, these types of expenditures are fiscally irresponsible. This is part of the point of planning programs in both Mary-land and New Jersey: to redirect growth to areas that already have infrastructure to support new development, thereby creating public savings overall.

The rest of the nation differs little from Maryland or New Jersey. In the nine counties surrounding Philadelphia, ninety-four thousand homes were built between 1993 and 1999, while the population expanded by only six thousand people.[36] As we saw in Chapter 1, since 1950 the center cities of our nation's metropolitan regions (particularly those in the Northeast and Mid-west) have generally lost population steadily while the suburbs have gained. By 1990, subur-ban growth stood at 62 percent nationally, while central cities were still losing up to 3 million people per year to the suburbs.[37] In 2000, some cities began to regain population but not nearly equal to the rate at which suburban areas are continuing to develop.[38]

Had the population remained stable in the center cities over the past fifty years, a significant amount of the suburban public expenditures for roads, sewers, drinking water, and schools might not have occurred. This type of displaced growth can have a negative effect on regional economies as federal, state, and local tax dollars are spent to duplicate facilities already existing in the region. Center-city areas are forced to repair and main-tain aging infrastructure with a dwindling pool of resources to cover the cost while suburbs scramble to come up with the cash to pay for the new roads, schools, and sewers needed to support an explosion of new families. Moreover, all of these new facilities will have to be repaired and maintained, just like those that already exist in the cities.

All of this means more taxes for everyone—more taxes in the city, because of the smaller pool of taxpayers sharing the burdens, and more taxes in the suburbs, because of the redundant new facilities being built. In response to steady increases in taxes, "tax rebellions" have occurred in many states as electorates and state legislatures limited the ability of municipalities to raise taxes. Proposition 13 in California and Proposition 2-$\frac{1}{2}$ in Massachusetts are typical examples in which public referenda succeeded in capping tax growth rates in both states.

Chasing Commercial Tax Revenues

In both urban and suburban areas, residential development is almost always a municipal money loser. More public money is spent on education and other services needed to support residential neighborhoods than comes back from them in revenue—a state of affairs that has been well documented in many studies of the cost of community services such as those conducted by the American Farmland Trust as well as in books like Joel Garreau's *Edge City: Life on the New Frontier.*[39] The situation is made more acute by the limitations on taxing power placed on municipalities by the state legislatures and the electorate. As a result, many communities seek new revenues by attracting commercial develop-ment into their jurisdictions. This is true of cen-ter cities as well as of suburban communities. As Randal O'Toole notes in *The Vanishing Automo-bile and Other Urban Myths:*

> If both existing and new residential areas cost more than they pay in taxes, then who makes up the difference? The answer is commercial and other non-residential uses. This is because tax rates on commercial and residential areas tend to be about the same, yet the com-mercial areas do not add to the local school services, which normally makes up the largest share of the local tax bill.[40]

SHORT-TERM GAINS AND LONG-TERM COSTS

Because commercial development can help pay the school bill, it has become a sought-after prize in many communities. In the longer term, how-ever, the same treasured commercial development can also lead to higher costs. Commercial projects create jobs, new jobs create a demand for new housing nearby, and new housing requires more subsidy from the community in which the new commercial complex is to be located. This leads some communities to seek even more commer-cial investment to pay off the costs of all of the new housing the last round of commercial devel-opment attracted.[41] Some communities actually promise incentives, such as new roads or tax breaks, to attract the commercial development. This approach further erodes any tax gains that might be realized in the development.

COMPETING COMMUNITIES

When considered at the regional level, the problem is compounded because revenue gains from commercial building in one community can result in a residential explosion in a neighboring jurisdiction that causes new deficits with no offsetting commercial tax gain. It is also important to look at where the new commercial development is coming from. In some cases, it is not regional growth but regional displacement as corporate headquarters and other businesses leave center-city locations for suburban sites in the same metropolitan area. The center city loses a source of tax revenue, a source of employment, and, possibly, tax paying middle-class workers who may move with the company, while new burdens are added to the strains of growth in the suburbs (including roads and sewer to handle new office buildings and infrastructure and schools for new families).[42]

Retail development can produce results similar to those of office development. The prospect of a huge volume of tax revenues from a new regional mall may tempt a community to literally give away the store. Once it is built, the new mall may generate new tax revenues and employment, but it may entail boarding up Main Street as stores go out of business, meaning a loss of revenue elsewhere. Like office development, a new mall in one community can have regional impacts on adjoining communities as downtown stores close their doors for miles around. In some cases, even older suburban malls may be put out of business by newer malls, damaging the tax base of surrounding communities. Just as with new suburban housing, new commercial development can be a lose-lose situation for both the center city and the suburbs.

Regional Abandonment

The pattern of suburbs robbing the cities of their office buildings and workers is fiscally unsound for any metropolitan region. A battle has been waged in New York City for decades in which major corporations and entire stock exchanges have threatened to move to New Jersey unless special breaks can be offered by New York. Meanwhile, the sites in suburbs are offering their own incentives, which will ultimately cost them money as well as effort. In reality, the suburbs stand to benefit little, because they will have to scramble to subsidize the secondary residential development that the corporate relocations will bring. The wealth that will be realized will be short-term, with the ultimate result being higher long-term costs. At the same time, the city tax base will suffer erosion and more middle-class city dwellers will have a reason to move to the suburbs. The only real gains to be made by this type of regional shuffling generally fall to the companies who are moving and the real estate and construction industries that serve them.

Yet, as inefficient as this pattern of development is at the regional level, and as detrimental as it has been to the cities, the fact remains that considerable investment in suburbanization has already occurred over the past fifty years and these investments will have to be maintained or even the newest suburbs will eventually experience the same phenomenon of deterioration experienced by the cities and their older suburbs. Minnesota state representative Myron Orfield, Bruce Katz of the Brookings Institution, and many others argue that what is ultimately required is a regionally balanced approach to the future, in which communities look at the region as a whole rather than exclusively to their own immediate self-interests (see Chapter 14).

Social Divides and Cities

One of the most worrisome allegations about suburbanization is that it divides racial and economic classes along geographic lines. It is often charged that the suburbs of today are overwhelmingly white and middle-class, leaving diversity and poverty to the older city centers.

A Segregated Metropolis

In each of the country's metropolitan areas, almost 64 percent of each region's black people live inside the central city, while more than 72 percent of whites live outside (see Figure 8.4).[43] Throughout the nation's metropolitan areas, almost 55 percent of the nation's citizens living in poverty dwelt in the inner city in 1998.[44] In 1960, that number was less than one-third.[45] Nearly 87 percent of the population of the United States living outside of U.S. Census Bureau–defined poverty areas were white, while

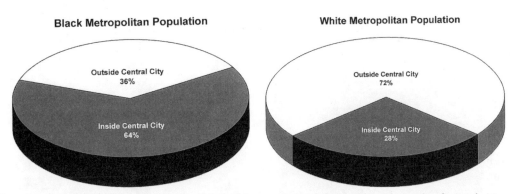

Black Metropolitan Population

Outside Central City
36%

Inside Central City
64%

White Metropolitan Population

Outside Central City
72%

Inside Central City
28%

Figure 8.4. Percentage of metropolitan black and white population living inside and outside of central cities. Source: U.S. Census Bureau, *Black Population in the United States: March 1999 (Update): Detailed Tables and Documentation for PD20-530 (PPL-130),* (Washington, D.C.: U.S. Census Bureau, 2000), table 16, www.census.gov/population/www/socdemo/race/black99tabs.html.

only 7 percent were black.[46] The average income of families living in U.S. poverty areas in 1989 was about 67 percent of those living outside such areas.[47] Data analyzed from the 2000 census indicate that, despite a trend toward increasing numbers of African Americans moving to the suburbs, the United States remains a highly segregated country. The average white person in metropolitan America lives in a neighborhood that is nearly 83 percent white and only 7 percent black, while a typical metropolitan black individual lives in a neighborhood that is only 33 percent white and 54 percent black.[48] Our current development pattern is largely the outcome of past public policies, which reflected the social attitudes of their times.

Race, Class, Cars, and Mortgages

Before the first modern suburbs, rich and poor, black and white, dwelled in relative proximity to one another. The different races and classes may have resided in different parts of any given city or town, but most were within walking distance of all the others—or just a few stops away on the trolley or subway line. For hundreds of years, the chances of different races and classes encountering one another on the street, in the marketplace, or even at home were much higher than they have become in our new, suburbanized world.

STREETCAR EXODUS

The first significant changes to this pattern occurred with the development of railroads, subways, and electric streetcars. Streetcars and subways in particular led to the first mass exodus of

middle-class families from the inner core of the city.[49] This flight was largely an economic separation, at least in places like the Northeast. Middle-class families moved outward along the streetcar and rail lines while those who could not afford to move stayed in the city next to the industries where they worked. In northeastern and midwestern cities, the remaining working-class families were composed of a broad array of people. Adjoining neighborhoods contained newly arrived immigrants from different parts of the world as well as African Americans and European Americans who had been in the United States for many generations. Even then, in the heyday of mass transit and the first inner-ring suburbs, different classes and races frequently encountered one another on trolleys or in subway cars.

CARS AND MORTGAGES

The real change came with the advent of the automobile and the housing policies of the depression. The automobile quickly led to auto-only suburbs, where owning a car was an essential ingredient of life, shutting out all those who could not afford one. Today, nearly 90 percent of households in America own a car, yet only 70 percent of all African American households do (see Figure 8.5). Viewed another way, African Americans comprise less than 12 percent of all U.S. households, but they account for 35 percent of American households without a vehicle.[50] The automobile made it possible for new suburbs to be built much farther away from the older cities and from poverty-stricken neighborhoods than ever before.

But, as we saw in Chapter 2, it took more

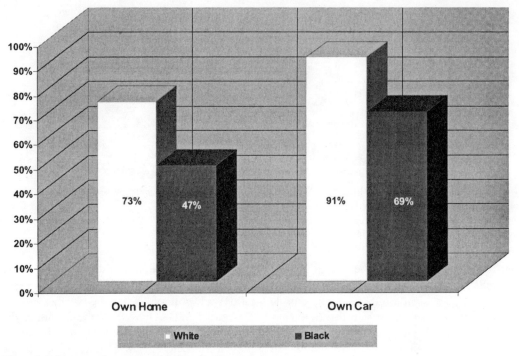

Figure 8.5. Home and car ownership by ethnic group.
Sources: U.S. Department of Housing and Urban Development (HUD), Office of Policy Development and Research, *Issue Brief No. III, Homeownership: Progress and Work Remaining* (Washington, D.C.: HUD, 2000) 8; and Alan E. Pisarski, *Commuting in America II: The Second National Report on Commuting Patterns and Trends* (Landsdowne, Va.: Eno Transportation Foundation, 1996) 36.

than just the automobile to start the suburban avalanche. Another key component of the American Dream is owning one's home. The loan mechanisms developed during the depression with the founding of the Federal Housing Administration (the FHA) helped many Americans purchase their own homes for the first time, but these same policies were also fundamental to the spread of the suburban world that we know today, along with its housing ownership patterns. While more than 73 percent of non–Hispanic white Americans owned a home in 1999, only about 47 percent of African Americans could make the same claim.[51] To some extent, this is the result of earlier policies.

Although FHA loans were a godsend to many people, almost all of these people were white and middle-class at the beginning. This is because, in making loans and promoting the pattern of sprawl that we have today, the FHA also fostered the segregationist policies of the climate in which it was created. In the end, the policies of the FHA not only favored suburbs over cities but also favored white Americans over black Americans. This fact has been well

documented in Kenneth Jackson's book *Crabgrass Frontier: The Suburbanization of the United States:*

> Reflecting the racist tradition of the United States, the Federal Housing Administration was extraordinarily concerned with "inharmonious racial or nationality groups." It feared that an entire area could lose its investment value if rigid white-black separation was not maintained. Bluntly warning, "If a neighborhood is to retain stability, it is necessary that properties shall continue to be occupied by the same social and racial classes," the Underwriting Manual openly recommended "subdivision regulations and suitable restrictive covenants" that would be "superior to any mortgage." Such covenants, which were legal provisions written into property deeds, were a common method of prohibiting black occupancy.[52]

The FHA went even further than simply making these recommendations. The agency produced meticulous documents mapping the present and probable future locations of African American families. In FHA maps of Brooklyn produced in 1939, the existence of a single non-white family in any given block was enough to register the entire city block as African American. Similar maps of Washington, D.C., diagrammed the extent of the black population and the percentage of nonwhite dwelling units. In 1948, an assistant commissioner of the FHA was to record that the FHA "has never insured a housing project of mixed occupancy [because] such projects would in a short period of time become all-Negro."[53]

Policies such as these fed fuel to the suburban lending practices of the FHA. Cities are inherently mixed places, where different kinds of people live in relatively close proximity to one another. The presence of African Americans automatically ruled out mortgage insurance for large portions of the city. Loan examiners were directed to refer to the FHA's Residential Security Maps "to segregate for rejection many of the applications involving locations not suitable for amortized mortgages."[54] Favoring all-white, middle-class suburbs over inner-city locations was therefore a natural consequence of such practices.

The effects were dramatic. In metropolitan St. Louis alone, samples show that 91 percent of new homes insured by the FHA during the 1930s were in suburban locations and that 50 percent of the buyers getting the loans had lived in the city immediately before their purchase of their new homes. A comparison of FHA loan activities between 1934 and 1960 in ten selected urban and suburban U.S. counties shows that the suburban counties received about $600 per capita in loans while the urban counties received less than one-tenth of that amount (see Table 8.4). According to Kenneth Jackson, the FHA "exhorted segregation and enshrined it as public policy." In the South, segregation was already enshrined as public policy, but the FHA was applying that same policy to the whole nation. It wasn't until 1966 that the FHA shifted its policy and began to make much more mortgage insurance available to inner-city communities. By

Table 8.4. FHA Mortgage Activities for Ten Selected Counties, 1934–1960

Jurisdiction	Cumulative Number of Home Mortgages 1934–1960	Cumulative Amount of Home Mortgages 1934–1960	Per Capita Amount of Home Mortgages as of January 1961
St. Louis County, Mo.	62,772	$558,913,633	$794
Fairfax County, Va.	14,687	$190,718,799	$730
Nassau County, N.Y.	87,183	$781,378,559	$601
Montgomery County, Md.	14,702	$159,246,550	$467
Prince George's County, Md.	15,043	$144,481,817	$404
St. Louis City	12,166	$94,173,422	$126
District of Columbia	8,038	$66,144,612	$87
Kings County (Brooklyn), N.Y.	15,438	$140,330,137	$53
Hudson County, N.J.	1,056	$7,263,320	$12
Bronx County, N.Y.	1,641	$14,279,243	$10

Source: Kenneth T. Jackson, *Crabgrass Frontier: The Suburbanization of the United States* (New York: Oxford University Press, 1985), 211.

then, much of the current pattern had already been established.[55]

Public Housing

The white suburban bias of the FHA was exacerbated by U.S. public housing polices. The United States Housing Act of 1937 brought the federal government into the business of funding the construction of public housing for the first time. The program was put in place with the best of intentions: to provide a decent home for every American family. Like other well-intentioned programs, it had unexpected consequences. The public housing that resulted tended to concentrate the poor in the inner cities.

The 1937 legislation created the U.S. Housing Authority, which was to fund public housing projects through duly constituted municipal housing agencies. As modified in 1949, the legislation required that each community decide for itself whether it wanted housing assistance from the federal government. If it did, the municipality would then form its own housing agency, after which the federal government could provide funds to the local agency, which was then responsible for acquiring land and getting the housing developed. The net result of this policy was that mostly urban areas formed the agencies and applied for funds, whereas suburban jurisdictions generally refrained from doing so. At the same time, the municipalities could locate the housing wherever they chose within their boundaries, often reinforcing segregation by tearing down poor neighborhoods and replacing them with high-density housing "projects."

Instead of eliminating the slums they replaced, this concentration of public housing actually caused surrounding neighborhoods to deteriorate further and faster. Displaced families from the buildings being cleared moved into adjacent neighborhoods, and the insensitive design of the new housing projects further encouraged crime and vandalism. The "projects" became some of the most dangerous places to live in the city, destabilizing what had previously been established, socially cohesive black neighborhoods.[56] Because of the continuing desperate need for shelter, people still added their names to thousands of others on the waiting lists for public housing. Yet, as the "projects" infected ever-wider areas around them, more and more people who had the means left the city for the suburbs.

The result of such policies has been the isolation of poverty-stricken racial groups in the urban parts of today's metropolitan areas. As John Powell of the University of Minnesota writes:

> Segregation and concentrated poverty found within metropolitan areas is not self-induced, but is the predictable result of a concentrated effort to isolate poor minorities. That such segregation and concentrated poverty exist and are worsening, despite the healthy national economy, cannot be denied. . . . Of those living in concentrated poverty, more than half are black.[57]

School Desegregation

In the end, the housing policies of the era were inadvertently abetted by civil rights policies aimed at desegregating the nation's school system and providing equal education to minority children. The school busing programs were developed specifically to meet these goals. Although these programs were absolutely necessary and were carried out with the best of intentions, they also had some unanticipated results. Even more white, middle-class families left the city so their children could go to school in independent suburban municipalities where busing wasn't an issue and where they could have more of a voice in determining the education of their children. Housing policies changed as a result of the Fair Housing Act of 1968, and some middle-class African Americans began moving to suburban areas.[58] Still, only those (black or white) who had the money to move could do so. Others had no choice but to stay where they were while those with means who remained in the city began to take their children out of the public school system. As a result, entire center-city school systems began to deteriorate along with an eroding city tax base. Education became yet another reason to move out of the city.

The Resulting Settlement Pattern

The settlement pattern that we see today is a major problem of sprawl development, and it perpetuates one of the most precipitous and persistent calamities in our nation's history: the racial and economic segregation of our society. Regional sprawl separates new job opportunities from those who remain in the central cities, creating what has been termed a "spatial mismatch" between jobs and employees.[59] The highways that provide access to jobs and employment in the suburbs are actually a barrier to those who can't afford residences near their places of employment.

The suburbs accounted for 100 percent of overall metropolitan area employment expansion during the 1980s in such regions as Chicago, Cleveland, Dayton, Detroit, Greensboro, and Louisville.[60] In the Twin Cities area, the suburbs accounted for 90 percent of regional employment growth over the same period.[61] But it is very difficult to get to suburban jobs without a car, and the hardships of getting there by transit can be daunting, if not impossible. In the New York area, a region with extensive mass transit systems, housekeeping, restaurant, and childcare workers can find themselves spending up to four hours on buses commuting between suburban jobs that would take them less than thirty minutes to reach by car—it's either that or spend hard-earned money on expensive cab fare.[62] In San Jose, California, full-time workers actually use the bus as a place to sleep. They ride the bus all night long because they have no other option. In Silicon Valley, people making $50,000 a year are seeking the services of homeless shelters because they can't afford to live even in a local trailer park and commuting is impossible.[63]

According to M. David Lee, professor of urban planning and design at Harvard University, a simple spell of bad weather is enough to throw a serious monkey wrench into the workings of a typical contemporary metropolitan area. For example, when it snows in Boston these days, it's likely to mean a spate of absenteeism in the office—not because people can't get to work but because the schools are either closed or are opening late and parents have to stay home to take care of the kids. The reason school is delayed or cancelled is that the teachers can't get to work on time because they live too far away. They simply can't afford to live in the communities in which they teach.[64]

Suburban Diversity and Segregation

Despite these discriminatory housing and transportation hurdles, some positive trends have surfaced since the 1960s. In the past thirty years,

middle-class African American families have been moving to the suburbs at an ever-increasing pace. Only about 1 percent of the African American population had a median income equal to that of white people in 1950.[65] By the 1990s, however, more 30 percent of black Americans were middle-class in income and lived in the suburbs.[66] This is an impressive change. Noting trends in the New York area as well as in Houston, Dallas, Atlanta, and Los Angeles, the *New York Times* recently made the following assessment:

> The new ethnic diversity marks a sharp contrast to the immediate postwar era, when these suburbs were bastions of homogeneity. From 1950 to 1970, a period of intense suburban development, 95 percent of suburbanites were white. "The people you want for neighbors are here," noted an advertisement for one Long Island development in the 1960's.
>
> The demographic shift started in the 1970's when African-Americans began moving in large numbers to the suburbs. In the next two decades, middle-class American-born Hispanics and Asians as well as upwardly mobile recent immigrants surged in, particularly to the older, closer-in suburbs.
>
> The immigrants have moved to suburbia, rather than to the cities, for many of the same reasons that others before them did: cheaper land, more open space, better schools and business opportunities.[67]

Even so, integration has not necessarily been the result; instead, now there are suburban enclaves that are almost all black.[68] For example, in Atlanta, African Americans have moved to the suburbs in such substantial numbers that, of all of the nation's metropolitan areas, only Washington, D.C., outnumbers Atlanta in black suburban population. Yet black and white populations remain largely segregated, living in different areas of the suburbs (see Figure 8.6).[69] An analysis of the 2000 census data by the Lewis Mumford Center of the State University of New York at Albany recently concluded:

> Despite a substantial shift of minorities from cities to suburbs, these groups

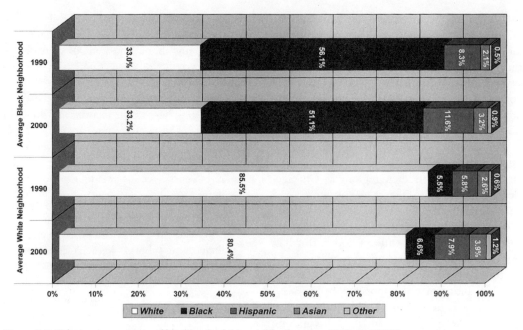

Figure 8.6. Ethnic composition of black and white neighborhoods—1990 and 2000.
Source: Lewis Mumford Center for Comparative Urban and Regional Research at the State University of New York (SUNY) at Albany, *Ethnic Diversity Grows, Neighborhood Integration is at a Standstill* (Albany: SUNY, 2001).

have not gained access to largely white neighborhoods. Residential segregation, particularly among blacks and whites, remains high in cities and suburbs around the country.[70]

This situation is an unfortunate legacy of past trends, but it could be argued that it is in some ways a better outcome than if African Americans had remained totally concentrated in the inner city. Yet, the pattern remains so segregated both in cities and suburbs, as the 2000 census data show, that the benefits of black suburban migration can still be questioned, especially in view of what has happened to the urban-core areas.

Poverty Remains in the City

Although the movement of minorities into the suburbs may be positive news, there is also a downside. Some urban scholars argue that the movement of the black middle class to suburbia only adds to the erosion of resources in the urban core as low-income blacks are left behind—creating both racial and economic geographic segregation.[71] As middle-class minority groups move out to the suburbs, just like the

middle-class whites before them, the poor are remaining behind in the cities. If this is, in fact, what is happening, its continuation would bode ill for center cities. This issue is a top concern among many urban scholars and was recently articulated in a roundtable forum in *Harvard* magazine, in which M. David Lee summarized the problem as follows:

> I think that the city has to be a viable choice for people too. It really distresses me that in order for African Americans or Latinos to find reasonable schools and safe streets, they've got to move out and be a tiny minority in a neighborhood somewhere else. I want them to have that option in the city itself.[72]

There is a pervasive worry that the poor are being left behind as the middle class leaves because the cities are unable to offer the safety, level of services, and quality of education that can be found in the suburbs. This worry persists despite the anecdotal evidence that more middle-class whites are actually moving back to the city, as crime rates in urban areas have dropped, and as 2000 census statistics indicate that the population has risen in some urban areas.

Suburban Poverty

U.S. Census Bureau data show no increase in the number of people living in poverty in the central city compared to outside of it for all metropolitan areas in the United States between 1989 and 1998.[73] This would seem to indicate that the number of poor people in the city is not increasing at any precipitous rate relative to the suburbs. On the other hand, poverty inside U.S. metropolitan areas but outside the central cities (that is, in the suburbs) actually increased by about 2.5 million people between 1989 and 1998. This trend is supported by other sources that contend that problems once regarded as "urban," such as unemployment and crime, are now spreading to the suburbs. Yet, as noted previously, this isn't happening to all suburbs uniformly. The difference is again geographic—the suburban areas experiencing negative change are not the newer, exurban communities; they are the so-called inner-ring suburbs, the older suburbs closer to the central city.[74]

The continuous rise of new, exurban housing and employment centers has resulted in the decline of many older, inner-ring suburbs. Typically built in the early phases of suburban development, these suburbs tend to be areas with older housing stock, antiquated commercial facilities, and strong ties to the original urban core. Some of the housing in these areas may have been built inexpensively to begin with. Clearly, this is not true of some older suburban areas, such as Chestnut Hill outside of Boston, Bronxville in New York, or the Main Line in Philadelphia, but in general, the prevailing trend in the suburbs is from higher-income occupancy to lower-income occupancy as housing stock ages.[75]

In a study of 554 suburbs in twenty-four urbanized areas in the United States, University of Virginia professors William Lucy and David Phillips found that 405 of the suburbs actually declined in income between 1960 and 1990 while nearly half of those 405 suburbs were declining in both income and population faster than their neighboring central city.[76] Almost all of the declining suburbs are older, inner-ring suburbs, and their decline has been taking place while the great outward push has continued unabated, building more new, all-middle-class suburbs and exurbs in an ever-expanding periphery zone.

These trends imply that the poverty and racial isolation that have become characteristic of the inner cities is now spreading to the inner suburbs, while the majority of the white middle class moves ever farther away. Although the 2000 census data show that the population of some formerly declining cities is now rising, that appears to be largely due to immigration rather than people moving back in from the suburbs, as we have see in Chapter 3. If it weren't for immigration by Hispanic and Asian minorities, the population of Boston and other cities, such as Chicago, might have dwindled further in the last ten years. Even if some of the nation's cities are recovering, the evidence from Lucy and Phillips's analysis of inner-ring suburbs would seem to indicate that new segments of the nation's urban settlements are declining while the geographic divisions between different races and between the rich and the poor become ever wider.

Growing Cities and Expanding Boundaries

In his article "The Relationship of Cities and Suburbs," Dr. Ronald Utt disputes the notion that the nation's urban-core areas are losing population to expanding outer suburbs. He presents data that show that eight of the nation's top twenty cities actually grew in population between 1950 and 1998, creating a net population gain of about 1.1 million people for all twenty cities combined (see Table 8.5).[77] This information seems to be confirmed by a recent analysis of 2000 census data by the *New York Times,* which states that the nation's largest cities "grew nearly twice as fast in the 1990's as in the 1980's."[78] However, the *Times* also notes that this growth was uneven, favoring such as cities Las Vegas, Charlotte, and Columbus over such cities as St. Louis, Cleveland, Philadelphia, and Detroit.

What is missing in these analyses is the element of expanding city boundaries. Some cities, particularly those in the West and Southwest, have been able to expand their boundaries over time by annexing neighboring suburbs. As a consequence, these cities now include a significant amount of growing suburban territory within their limits. In his book *Cities Without Suburbs,* David Rusk calls these municipalities "elastic cities" (see Chapter 14 for a detailed explanation of this concept). By contrast, many other cities are unable to annex any additional

Table 8.5. Population Changes from 1950 to 1998 in the Top 20 U.S. Cities in 1970

1970 Rank	City	Population Increase (Decrease)
1	New York	(472,000)
2	Chicago	(819,000)
3	Los Angeles	1,628,000
4	Philadelphia	(636,000)
5	Detroit	(880,000)
6	Houston	1,191,000
7	Baltimore	(304,000)
8	Dallas	642,000
9	Washington, D.C.	(279,000)
10	Cleveland	(419,000)
11	Indianapolis	314,000
12	Milwaukee	(59,000)
13	San Francisco	(29,000)
14	San Diego	887,000
15	San Antonio	706,000
16	Boston	(246,000)
17	Memphis	208,000
18	St. Louis	(518,000)
19	New Orleans	(104,000)
20	Columbus	294,000
Net Gain		1,105,000

Source: Ronald D. Utt, "The Relationship of Cities and Suburbs," in Jane S. Shaw and Ronald D. Utt, eds., *A Guide to Smart Growth: Shattering Myths, Providing Solutions* (Washington, D.C.: Heritage Foundation, 2000), 78.

territory and are confined to jurisdictional limits imposed (for the most part) before the postwar suburban expansion.[79] These tend to be older cities, such as New York, Boston, Philadelphia, and Detroit. Population counts of these cities do not include their suburbs, whereas population counts of cities such as Houston and Columbus, Ohio, do.

Table 8.6 compares the same cities cited by Dr. Utt according to their ability to annex territory. As can be seen from the table, most of the cities experiencing population growth expanded their territory to include their burgeoning suburbs in their population count. Thus, these figures do not reveal what the real urban/suburban split in population growth was for each of these cities. What is being shown is quite likely to be suburban growth or growth as a result of annexation of suburban area. An exception is Los Angeles, which grew significantly in population

and density while growing only modestly in area. Table 8.7 compares relative density of the twenty cities shown in Table 8.5, from this table we can see that most of the cities that are shown as growing, are growing at suburban densities. The 2000 census has changed things a bit. As noted earlier, some of the inelastic cities on the list have actually shown some modest growth for the first time in decades. However, the core areas of many of the nation's cities, such as Philadelphia, Detroit, Cleveland, Hartford and Pittsburgh have continued to decline in population in the last decade.

Push Factors

Dr. Samuel Staley suggests that middle-class people are leaving the city because of push factors, which include poorly functioning schools, high tax rates, deteriorating housing stock, and crime.[80] According to Dr. Staley, middle-income households are the most sensitive to these push factors because they have the wealth and the income to relocate. The ones who stay behind do not. As Dr. Staley says of the middle class: "Rather than fight city hall, they simply move to a friendlier one and help build a new community."[81] This could be cited as an example of the Daniel Boone phenomenon discussed in Chapter 5.

Yet, according to Dr. Staley, the problems of the cities have been caused by the cities themselves, by years of bad city government policy that has placed "enormous artificial costs" on urban economies. The solution is to deregulate central cities, eliminate barriers to business investment, and lower taxes.[82]

It is true that schools, crime, and housing are major concerns that a lot of families with children have about living in the city—and schools are often at the top of the list. But the problems of the inner cities are historically the result of policies that popularized suburbanization; mortgage policies, public housing policies, highway policies, and even infrastructure development and pricing have all combined with fragmented political jurisdictions to place increasing social and economic costs on the older cities of the nation's metropolitan regions while gracing the suburbs with new roads, schools, and sewers. In the end, it is the nation's metropolitan regions that are now its principal economic units. These regions include both cities and suburbs, and the

Table 8.6. Top 20 U.S. Cities in 1970—Changes in Population and Geographic Area

City	Population Increase (Decrease)	Area 1950 (Mi²)	Area 1990 (Mi²)	Change in Area (Mi²)	Percent Change in Area
New York	(472,000)	315	309	(6)	(2)
Chicago	(819,000)	208	227	20	9
Los Angeles	1,628,000	451	469	18	4
Philadelphia	(636,000)	127	135	8	6
Detroit	(880,000)	140	139	(1)	(1)
Houston	1,191,000	160	540	380	237
Baltimore	(304,000)	79	81	2	3
Dallas	642,000	112	342	230	206
Washington, D.C.	(279,000)	61	61	0	0
Cleveland	(419,000)	75	77	2	3
Indianapolis	314,000	55	362	307	555
Milwaukee	(59,000)	50	96	46	92
San Francisco	(29,000)	45	47	2	5
San Diego	887,000	99	324	225	226
San Antonio	706,000	70	333	264	379
Boston	(246,000)	48	48	1	1
Memphis	208,000	104	256	152	146
St. Louis	(518,000)	61	62	1	1
New Orleans	(104,000)	199	181	(19)	(9)
Columbus	294,000	39	191	152	385

Sources: Ronald D. Utt, "The Relationship of Cities and Suburbs," in Jane S. Shaw and Ronald D. Utt, eds., *A Guide to Smart Growth: Shattering Myths, Providing Solutions* (Washington, D.C.: Heritage Foundation, 2000), 78; and Campbell Gibson, *Population of the 100 Largest Cities and Other Urban Places in the United States: 1790 to 1990,* Population Division Working Paper No. 27 (Washington, D.C.: U.S. Census Bureau, 1998), www.census.gov/population/www/documentation/twps0027.html#cities.
Note: Numbers may not add up due to rounding.

Table 8.7. Top 20 U.S. Cities in 1970—Relative Density in 1950 and 1990

City	Population Increase (Decrease)	Density 1950 (Pop./Mi²)	Density 1990 (Pop./Mi²)
New York	(472,000)	25,046	23,075
Chicago	(819,000)	17,450	12,252
Los Angeles	1,628,000	4,370	7,427
Philadelphia	(636,000)	16,286	11,736
Detroit	(880,000)	13,249	7,411
Houston	1,191,000	3,726	3,020
Baltimore	(304,000)	12,067	9,109
Dallas	642,000	3,879	2,941
Washington, D.C.	(279,000)	13,065	9,884
Cleveland	(419,000)	12,197	6,566
Indianapolis	314,000	7,739	2,022
Milwaukee	(59,000)	12,748	6,536
San Francisco	(29,000)	17,385	15,502
San Diego	887,000	3,364	3,428
San Antonio	706,000	5,877	2,811
Boston	(246,000)	16,767	11,865
Memphis	208,000	3,800	2,384
St. Louis	(518,000)	14,046	6,408
New Orleans	(104,000)	2,861	2,752
Columbus	294,000	9,541	3,315

Sources: Ronald D. Utt, "The Relationship of Cities and Suburbs," in Jane S. Shaw and Ronald D. Utt, eds. *A Guide to Smart Growth: Shattering Myths, Providing Solutions* (Washington, D.C.: Heritage Foundation, 2000), 78; and Campbell Gibson, *Population of the 100 Largest Cities and Other Urban Places in the United States: 1790 to 1990,* Population Division Working Paper No. 27 (Washington, D.C.: U.S. Census Bureau, 1998), www.census.gov/population/www/documentation/twps0027.html#cities.

economic and social health of the greater region is ultimately a reflection of the health of its individual parts.

A Persistent Pattern of Desertion

The rapid proliferation of new development and desertion of the old is a trend that has persisted for some time in America and that, without intervention, is likely to continue. Furthermore, it can be argued that the geographic division of race and class is a characteristic of that same pattern. In this case, it involves abandonment not only of older urban resources but also of the people who live there—shutting them out of new job opportunities in the rapidly expanding fringe. This is in keeping with a widely held American view that the future rightfully belongs to those willing and able to capture it for themselves, justifiably leaving behind those who are unable to fully compete.

Economics and Social Equity in Summary

Suburbanization costs the nation economically and socially. Although the relative costs of building infrastructure in compact versus spread-out communities can be debated, there evidence that an unfair portion of the cost of building roads and sewers falls on existing, older communities within metropolitan regions as suburban expansion continues. In the Twin Cities and other metro areas, cities and older, inner-ring suburbs may be essentially subsidizing the infrastructural cost of building new exurban communities while suffering a simultaneous loss of tax revenues and declining services. Moreover, the relocation of population from established centers to new suburban communities is resulting in the duplication of utilities, roads, and schools as urban schools and infrastructure become under-utilized. This type of unsustainable growth pattern has led such states as New Jersey and Maryland to implement state growth plans that direct new development to established urban and suburban centers.

The continued spread of suburbanization is also exacerbating the nation's social divisions, leaving poverty behind in older cities and inner-ring suburbs while economic growth continues to expand outward toward ever-new frontiers. Meanwhile, the increasing decentralization of employment centers and the monomodal access pattern are making it increasingly difficult for job-hungry people in cities and inner-ring suburbs to gain access to employment growth in the suburbs. Middle-class African Americans are moving to the suburbs, possibly diminishing the resources available to core cities. At the same time, even as the suburbs have been opened up to African Americans since the late 1960s, the patterns of segregation by neighborhood have not appreciably improved.

CHAPTER 9

Aesthetics and Community

Suburbanization has been accused of diminishing the aesthetic value of the nation's countryside and the visual character of its communities. At the same time, some researchers and writers believe that the suburbs have created an environment that is less conducive to community involvement than the rural towns or the dense cities that preceded suburbanization. This chapter examines these issues.

Sprawl and Aesthetics

Many scholars who set out to define sprawl generally shy away from using aesthetics as a determining factor—other than to remark, as Kenneth Jackson and others have done, on the bland, architectural similarity of our new metropolis.[1] Yet, aesthetic appearance has a lot to do with the prevailing negative image of contemporary sprawl (see Figure 9.1). The word itself implies something ugly, and certainly writers such as James Howard Kunstler have written many pages attesting to this fact. Consider this passage from Kunstler's book *The Geography of Nowhere: The Rise and Decline of American's Manmade Landscape* in which he describes the nation's highway strip commercial areas as:

Figure 9.1. Aesthetic appearance is an important part of sprawl's negative image. (Oliver Gillham)

boulevards so horrible that every trace of human aspiration seems to have been expelled, except the impetus to sell. It has made commerce itself appear to be [an] obscene . . . commercial highway . . . assaulted by a chaos of gigantic, lurid plastic signs, golden arches, red-and-white-striped revolving chicken buckets, cinder-block carpet warehouses, discount marts, asphalt deserts, and a horizon slashed by utility poles.[2]

On the other side of the debate, there are writers like Randal O'Toole. He states that

a large part of the criticism of the suburbs is simply an aesthetic judgment: suburbs are ugly, older cities are beautiful. This judgment is based on a nineteenth century idea of what a city should be. . . . In the end, beauty is in the eye of the beholder. . . . Government planners should not try to force a few architects' ideas of beauty on everyone else.[3]

More Than Just a Pretty Face

In truth, aesthetics is a tricky subject, and as O'Toole has said, what looks good to one person may be ugly to another. That gives ample cause for worry that discussing the aesthetics of the landscape is venturing into vague territory with shifting ground. However, it is also true that aesthetics has value. Looks are important to many people. In America, a lot of money is spent to address the aesthetic concerns of everyday life by people who care about how they look and how their homes and gardens look. Today, Americans spend untold millions of dollars not just on their appearance but also on travel to places they find aesthetically pleasing, such as Europe, Yosemite National Park, and Colonial Williamsburg.

143

Maybe part of the problem is that *aesthetics* is too narrow a word for what is actually being discussed. What looks "nice" is more than just a pretty face—it is actually a whole grab bag of things that make up what is important to us about who we are, where we want to be, and in what landscape. It is appearance, cultural significance, and history. It is many of the things that most people like about themselves and their world, and it is an important part of the way people would like the world and themselves to be. Together, these different images and concerns create what might be termed our "cultural landscape."

Figure 9.2. The pastoral ideal: an iconic American barn and field. (Oliver Gillham)

Our Cultural Landscape

Our cultural landscape is our idealization of what we, our friends, and the world around us should look like based on our cultural training—what we were brought up to believe from watching television, going to school, sitting in the movies, reading books and magazines, listening to advertisements, and discussing matters with friends, teachers, and family. Our cultural landscape extends to the places we occupy and visit, whether those places are open countryside, a simple village, or the big city.

The Pastoral Image

Many Americans believe that one of the nicest places on earth is an open countryside replete with barns and meadows. This bucolic image has been an extremely strong force in shaping American history. As Leo Marx says in the beginning of his inquiry *The Machine in the Garden:*

> The pastoral ideal has been used to define the meaning of America ever since the age of discovery, and it has not yet lost its hold upon the native imagination. . . . It was embodied in the various utopian schemes for making America the site of a new beginning for Western society.[4]

The pastoral ideal still resonates with us today (see Figure 9.2). It has been well evidenced, for example, in an advertisement by one of the insurance companies supporting public television. In it, we see an early-morning meadow with mist rising, a red barn in the distance, as a man and his four-year-old son amble through the ankle-high grass, heading toward a split-rail

fence. A disembodied yet comforting voice says, "Have you heard from the quiet company?" This ad is aimed at every American of childbearing age. The insurance company wouldn't use the image if it didn't sell the product somehow. We can all see that this is a place that we would like to be, safe and secure in the serene world of "the quiet company" holding our toddler's hand as we cross the dewy meadow, breathing the sweet morning air, so filled with promise. It is a place anyone would think of as "pretty." It is also a place that has a lot of psychological and cultural meaning for us. It is the "country," the heart of America. It is the place Americans hoped to move to when they left the city for the suburbs. It is the place everyone would like to have next door.

The Village

As powerful as the pastoral ideal is, it isn't the only theme that has meaning for us. At Disney World in Florida, there is a place called "Main Street" U.S.A. It is an idealized replica of the small-town America of bygone days. Kunstler describes it very well in his book *The Geography of Nowhere:*

> It is a well-proportioned street full of good relationships between its components, and blessedly free of cars. The two-and three-story buildings are architecturally unified, but individually various—out of an era when rooflines were interesting, when windows meant something more than holes in a wall, and when building ornament relied on pattern rather than symbolistic doodads. . . . The buildings along the street are designed to a five-eights scale, the

Figure 9.3. Main Street America: Stockbridge, Massachusetts—home of Norman Rockwell and the subject of many of his paintings. (Oliver Gillham)

Figure 9.4. New York, New York Casino in Las Vegas—homage to the iconic American city. (*About Guide to Las Vegas for Visitors,* http://govegas.about.com.)

toylike appearance supposedly adding to their charm.[5]

This is America's Main Street—a place we all think of as part of our heritage (see Figure 9.3), a place many people visit at Disney World because the real ones are increasingly difficult to find. A lot of people would like to have one of these within a short drive of home, as long as the parking was as convenient as it is at the shopping center. Main Street is another American icon, a place most of us think is as "right" or "fitting," as Colonial Williamsburg, or a town green from a 1950s New England Calendar, or Bedford Falls in the famous Christmas movie *It's a Wonderful Life.*

THE CITY

We can find other images on postage stamps and in Las Vegas. A couple of years ago, the U.S. Postal Service issued a stamp with an image of Art Deco skyscrapers reaching into the heavens. It was supposed to be a celebration of the American city. In Las Vegas, a huge new casino has been built to resemble a miniature version of the New York City skyline, replete with its own set of 1930s-era skyscrapers (see Figure 9.4). These artifacts are portrayals of our collective images of the American city or of what the American city should be—not the nineteenth-century city that O'Toole has spoken of but a mid-twentieth-century city, a place of tall, Art Deco buildings. It is also a place of intense action and excitement, where something is happening all the time. This is why this image has been transplanted to Las Vegas, and it is also why we see ads on television of people surfing down Wall Street, roaring around in cars with rap music blasting. If you don't like the quiet places or the small towns, this is the other place you can be: the iconic American city. In imitation of this icon, many cities across America—even Los Angeles and Houston—have made great efforts and spent millions of dollars to build tall office towers downtown to at least give themselves a skyline, an image of being a city in the twentieth-century sense. It is possible that this trend may change in the wake of the World Trade Center tragedy, but that remains to be seen.

IMAGE AND REALITY

These images of the country, of the small town and the big city, represent our ideals of what the world around us should be like. They are not the reality of any one of these places. In these archetypal realms, there is no cow manure or pesticide. There are no boarded-up storefronts, and no parking meters, dog droppings, crime, or noise. Furthermore, none of these images is of the place where most Americans live: the suburbs.

Strangely, these images are also of the very places we are taking apart to make more suburbs, and that is a part of the problem. We are erasing the original places that make up the images of our United States. This may be part of the reason at least some people are discontented. Families move to the suburbs expecting them to be like "the country," but they aren't. They're full of other houses, shopping malls, and highways. In fact, new suburban growth is often developing whatever iconic countryside remains nearby. That same suburban growth is simultaneously draining older cities and replacing them with modern landscapes that lack the cultural significance of the past. Meanwhile, village Main Streets are boarded up because most people are shopping at the mall. The historic icons that make up our cultural heritage are being replaced by something that no one understands in the same way.

THE IMAGELESS METROPOLIS

The only prevalent iconic image we have of our new metropolis is that of the previously described strip. Although it has been the subject of much social and aesthetic criticism, the strip is generally not an icon as sacred to the nation as those of city, country, and Main Street. In written commentary, the strip image is either disparaged or romanticized, depending on the era portrayed (that is, it is either Denny's or diners). In addition to the strip, there are a few lesser images of what we consider to be the suburbs, mostly older and residential in character. If we have a treasured image of residential suburbs, it is the world of *Mr. Blandings Builds His Dream House*—white colonial revival houses built before 1950, graced with spreading shade trees. There may even be a hint of an older downtown nearby and some open fields on the other side of the neighborhood. It is quiet, leafy, residential, and lived-in, but it's not what we usually think of as sprawl. No, sprawl is something new and garish. It is an image of Jiffy-Lube and Dunkin' Donuts, not the silver diners of yesteryear. It is a treeless plane of new houses that all look more or less alike. It is a desert of parking with little sticks of vegetation.

Maybe part of the problem is the very newness of this all-too-new world. It lacks what the architect Robert Stern has called "the patina of age."[6] Time might seem an odd thing to attach as a defining characteristic of sprawl, but it is indeed a potent visual determinant. Almost all photographs intended to portray sprawl are photographs of relatively new developments. Because landscaping is usually sparse and trees are no more than matchsticks at the outset, all of the new homes seem to stand in a wilderness of roadways, driveways, and garages. Commercial buildings appear to arise from bare expanses of asphalt.

Stark visions such as these, contrasted with the softer appearance of many older downtowns or long gone rural areas, can conjure up a fright-

Figure 9.5. A newly finished subdivision can appear quite stark. (Alex S. MacLean/Landslides)

ening specter in the public consciousness. There is little doubt that Jane Holtz Kay intended to invoke very similar images when she titled her recent book *Asphalt Nation,* a classic work that decries the desecration of America by the automobile.[7] Other examples are articles that have appeared in *Time,* the *New York Times,* and *National Geographic* that show endless brand-new tract houses, devoid of landscape.[8] There are practically no trees anywhere, and the garages and driveways are the most prominent features together with a disturbing sameness of the architecture (see Figure 9.5). With these and other, similar images in mind, it can be argued that much of the perception of sprawl has to do with its newness, which in turn owes much to the fact that most of the sprawl world is less than fifty years old.

AGING GRACEFULLY

Forty years ago the same types of barren, sterile pictures were being shown of new communities in Long Island, New York, and elsewhere. But if you go back to visit now, you may find quite a difference. A ride on the eastern section of the Long Island Expressway in the late 1990s (prior to a planned expansion) revealed that time had softened many of the hard edges of this huge roadway. Trees and other landscaping have matured along the service roads, creating an almost parklike setting around what used to be a desolate, rough-edged world of speeding cars and trucks. People today worry that a planned project to expand the expressway will take away its old-growth parkway character, restoring the titanic road to its former harsh brutality.

A trip into an older post-war suburban residential development can yield similar surprises. Great trees have grown up in the front yards of many of the once-identical houses, arching over once-desolate streetscapes (see Figure 9.6). The houses themselves have changed over time, giving many of them the varied hues of individuality. A series of recent articles about the first Levittown, in New York, provides further testimony to the softening effects of age.[9] Levittown, N.Y. was once decried as one of the worst examples of sprawl in the United States. Small, identical cottages were stamped out across a desert devoid of any landscape. But they provided affordable housing for many. A visitor returning to Levittown at the start of the new century finds that the landscaping has matured and various additions and improvements have so altered the houses that they now bear little resemblance to one another. As Paul Goldberger, architectural critic for the *New York Times,* wrote on the eve of Levittown's fiftieth anniversary:

> Now it is a struggle to find a house that looks even remotely like the original . . . . The Levittown houses have been embellished with new windows, shutters, porticos, verandas, bay windows, brick fronts, carports or extra rooms tacked onto the sides. . . . Paradoxically, this place that was once dismissed as the ultimate in suburban conformity has now metamorphosed into the most eclectic of suburbs, a place in which personal expression seems an essential part of the experience of home ownership.[10]

Goldberger goes on to observe how the matchstick saplings planted fifty years ago have now become a generous canopy of shade trees. What was once a wilderness of sameness is now

Figure 9.6. As landscape matures and houses take on individual character, the appearance of suburbia softens. (Alex S. MacLean/Landslides)

a collection of individual streets that can be identified by recognizable landmarks, such as individually unique houses and distinctive plantings.

FUTURE HISTORIC DISTRICTS

Such transformations make considering the time factor important. Much of what America dislikes about sprawl is the barren newness of it all. In thirty years, some of the new subdivisions may begin to age gracefully. They may, in fact become more like the "cottages in a park" envisioned by Olmsted and other noteworthy designers of earlier American suburbs. In fifty or a hundred years, many of these subdivisions may come to be neighborhoods as treasured as the suburbs of the nineteenth century are today. There is even an outside chance that they may someday become iconic images in themselves, possibly even protected by historic district designations.

SUBURBAN BEAUTIFUL

In the end, aesthetics is a critical issue. What we may offhandedly dismiss as "just aesthetics" is all about our image of ourselves and what surrounds us. It is a fundamental part of what we call our quality of life. Aesthetics is also one of the reasons that neotraditional development has been so successful, having brought the nation a small cornucopia of iconic images packaged in whole new towns, such as Seaside and Celebration in Florida and Kentlands in Maryland. They are new suburban developments that hark back to cultural images of small-town America. They include many features missing in traditional suburbia, such as front porches, streets you can walk on, and places you can walk to, perhaps a corner store or a village green. But a lot of the change is aesthetic, as Andres Duany and company emphatically state in their book *Suburban Nation: The Rise of Sprawl and the Decline of the American Dream,* and it is largely the aesthetic qualities of these new developments that garners the positive response.

Indeed, many of the remedies proposed for sprawl are aesthetic. Inspiring before-and-after illustrations have been created for many commercial and residential settings that show how good urban design can transform typical sprawl situations in to something more desirable (see Figure 9.7). Commercial areas are often the focus of these visual essays because of the large expanses of treeless parking. A common theme in these exercises in aesthetic improvement is substantially improved landscaping combined

Before	After

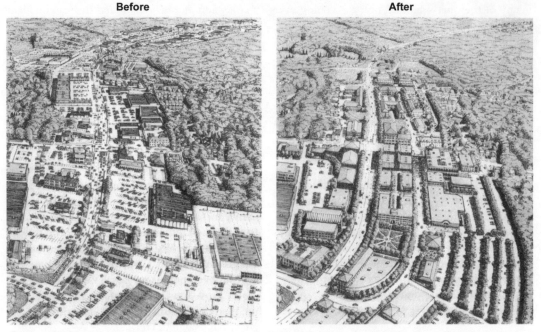

Figure 9.7. Although the commercial area shown is denser and functionally altered in the "after" version, much of the change is also aesthetic. Buildings are moved up to the edge of the street, and parking is placed behind, in structures, or underground. Substantial landscaping has also been added.
Source: Regional Plan Association/Dudson Associates, 1991.

with pushing the buildings up to the street line and placing parking in the back.

Although most of this sounds straightforward (and it is), it can be difficult to achieve in the real world. For example, most retailers prefer having the parking out front, and they don't like trees obscuring their signage. Not too long ago, the owner of a large shopping center in the middle of a heavily developed strip in Falmouth, Massachusetts, ordered all the big, mature shade trees in his parking lot cut down so that shoppers could once more see his stores and their billboard-scaled signs. These trees, which had taken years to mature, were gone in an instant, eliminated to make the mall compete better with the other strip retailing that had grown up around it while the trees were becoming a stately (if somewhat obscuring) grove.

Another consideration, of course, is money. It costs a lot to invest in and maintain good landscaping, so it is usually one of the first items to go when the budget gets tight. The buildings have to be there to function as stores, and the parking has to be there so that people can shop there. Trees and bushes are pretty far down the ladder. If such concerns as budget and visibility could be overcome, whether through education or regulation, the visual environment of many suburbs could be

improved. However, improving the visual environment won't do much to address the other impacts of suburbanization, such as traffic congestion, air and water pollution, energy and land consumption, and social ills.

Community

Many critics of sprawl have mourned the loss of community in the suburbanized world. As James Howard Kunstler has written:

> Community, as it once existed in the form of places worth caring about, supported by local economies, has been extirpated by an insidious corporate colonialism that doesn't care about the places from which it extracts its profits or the people subject to its operations. Without the underpinnings of genuine community and its institutions, family life has predictably disintegrated, because family alone cannot bear all the burdens and perform all the functions of itself and the community.[11]

That is, perhaps, an extreme point of view, and it even sounds a little bit socialist (for example, "corporate colonialism"). But Kunstler does have a point. Much of New Jersey looks similar to parts of Georgia or California, with the same stores, the same kinds of houses and streets, the same fast-food restaurants, the same everything. Sometimes, it seems there is little left in the public realm that clearly distinguishes one community from another, at least in the suburbs.

On the other hand, there is more to community life than looks and shopping choices. In many cities and towns across America, citizens volunteer countless hours of their time on planning boards, town committees, and volunteer fire departments, at the hospital, in schools, and in other venues to help what they believe is their community—be it a small town, a suburban area, or part of a city. America has traditionally offered and continues to offer the possibility of rewarding community involvement for many people regardless of changes that have occurred to development patterns.

Furthermore, not everyone agrees that suburbanization has diminished America's sense of community. Writing about Levittown (the third one, which was built in New Jersey) in 1967, Herbert Gans, a noted sociologist who now teaches at Columbia University, said:

> The critics have argued that . . . [the suburban lifestyle] and the absence of urban stimuli create depression, boredom, loneliness, and ultimately mental illness. The findings from Levittown suggest just the opposite—that suburban life has produced more family cohesion and a significant boost in morale through the reduction of boredom and loneliness.[12]

Gans added that the critics of suburbia "approach the community with a 'tourist' perspective. The tourist wants visual interest, cultural diversity . . . [and] esthetic pleasure. . . . The resident, on the other hand, wants a comfortable, convenient, and socially satisfying place to live."[13] Basically, Gans argues that there is a fairly strong sense of community in suburbia—at least there was in Levittown, New Jersey in 1967.

Community, like aesthetics, is a difficult concept to pin down. Suburbs may or may not have it, depending on who's doing the evaluation, but it has also been argued that cities also lack a sense of community. Big cities in particular can be some of the loneliest places to live, especially for people from small-town environments or

from other cultures. The folkways, mores, and intimate relationships established in smaller communities can become lost in the vast populations and mixing of different cultures that can be found in large American cities. On the other hand, in some ethnically cohesive urban neighborhoods—places like the North End in Boston or South Philadelphia—some people have found a very strong sense of community identity.

Despite the haziness of the issue, loss of community remains one of the key concerns that many people share about suburbanization. A large part of people's senses of community has to do with the image they share of their communities. Image is a very strong part of what makes up "community character." Many individual parts combine to create the image of a community, which may include treasured open spaces and walking trails, open fields, views, older buildings and neighborhoods, town greens, village squares, and "main streets." As these things become replaced by new development, or as village centers become abandoned for new strip malls outside of town, the image—or "character"—of the community becomes changed. William Whyte, one of the original experts on what makes community, once said that the first 5 percent of change in a landscape or a townscape—the first new house or strip mall or the first abandoned storefront—is the most damaging to a community's image.[14] As more housing is built and more strip malls collect outside of town, and as traffic steadily rises, a community's sense of definition can become lost as one township begins to blend into the next, with nothing left to distinguish where one community ends and another begins.

These sentiments are supported by surveys indicating that most people reject the typical suburban subdivision as a model for promoting a sense of community. Studies done by Rutgers University in suburbanizing townships in New Jersey showed that the lowest preference ratings were for classic "cookie cutter" subdivisions, while there was a clear preference for pedestrian-oriented, mixed-use, human-scale "downtown" areas with "village-style" housing on narrow lots with front porches and traditional rooflines.[15]

Other studies have shown similar results. A study of neighborhoods in Columbus, Ohio, revealed that residents of mixed-use neighborhoods felt a much greater sense of community than those who lived in single-use residential communities.[16] In theory, the mixing of uses in a pedestrian environment should foster more everyday face-to-face and verbal contact between people who live in a given community—as long as the residents feel safe and unthreatened by one another. In a single-use suburban community, where driving is required for basic errands, face-to-face contact is inhibited by the insulating effect of the car. Contact is more often between cars signaling intent to turn or park or trying to communicate some other message through gesturing and the use of the horn. It isn't easy to be polite when driving, because the means of communication are limited.

Robert Putnam, author of *Bowling Alone: The Collapse and Revival of American Community,* is among those who believe that the suburbs have led to a loss of community in America. Putnam believes that, since the 1960s, there has been a steady decline in what he calls America's "social capital." According to Putnam: "Social capital refers to connections among individuals—social networks and the norms of reciprocity and trustworthiness that arise from them."[17] It is characterized by "civic engagement": involvement and interest in civic and community affairs.

Throughout the pages of *Bowling Alone,* Putnam points to a series of indicators that show declines in civic engagement and social capital. These include declines in presidential voting and in political activity in general as well as declines in local community participation, such as serving on town committees, local organizations, and clubs. Average membership in national, chapter-based associations, the PTA, and national professional associations has also dropped as have charitable giving, basic socializing, and the general level of mutual trust. On average, Putnam finds, national involvement in political and community events has declined about 25 percent since 1973.[18] During the same period, the number of Americans attending club meetings has declined by 58 percent, family dinners have declined 33 percent, and just having friends over has declined by 45 percent.[19]

Putnam ascribes the decline in civic engagement and social capital to a variety of factors, including generational change, electronic entertainment, and the pressures of two-career families, but he also attributes at least 10 percent of the decline to suburbanization.[20] Putnam notes that residents of the nation's largest suburbanized metropolitan areas "report 10-15 percent fewer group memberships, attend 10-15 percent fewer club meetings . . . and are 30-40 percent less likely to serve as officers or committee members of local organizations or to attend public meetings on local affairs."[21] Noting that the nation's metropolitan areas are predominantly suburban, Putnam concludes: "Living in a large metropolitan agglomeration somehow weakens civic engagement and social capital."[22] Furthermore, Putnam notes that civic engagement rose significantly during the first two-thirds of the twentieth century, when the nation was urbanizing, and then declined precipitously as the nation has become increasingly suburban.

If this is the case, then what has happened to the community-rich suburbs of the 1960s described by Herbert Gans? According to Putnam, the postwar wave of suburbanization initially produced a "frontier-like enthusiasm for civic engagement."[23] These were suburbs like Park Forest, Illinois, which William Whyte referred to in his book *The Organization Man* as a "hotbed of participation."[24] This is what Herbert Gans found in Levittown, New Jersey in 1967.

Putnam believes that, as suburbanization continued, things have changed. As metropolitan areas expanded, the suburbs became fragmented into homogeneous enclaves "segregated by race, class, education, life stage, and so on" that, instead of bonding, have become increasingly less interactive.[25] The homogeneity of these communities reduces the local conflicts that draw residents and neighbors into public contact. For Putnam, this phenomenon is exemplified by the proliferation of gated communities that exclude Girl Scouts selling cookies and have community association representatives who enforce landscape maintenance standards, thus minimizing contact between neighbors. Putnam also believes that the increasing amount of time spent driving alone has reduced the available time and inclination for civic engagement. As he summarizes the situation, contemporary suburban life in a large metropolitan area means more time spent alone in the car with less time for friends and neighbors, increased social segregation, and a lack of community "boundedness" as cars, work, shopping, and errands spread people's daily lives across community boundaries and into an ill-defined metropolitan region. If Putnam is right, then suburbanization may be responsible—at least in part—for a decline of community in America.

Aesthetics and Community in Summary

Suburbanization has created a cultural landscape that confuses many Americans. It is not the rural ideal to which many have aspired; nor is it the intimate venue of the small town nor the active swirl of the big city. It is a seeming continuum of sameness in which it is difficult to tell Atlanta apart from Houston or Chicago. Yet, there may be some hope that as this new suburban world begins to acquire "the patina of age," the different neighborhoods of the suburban world may someday become imbued with their own special character, as the original Levittown has—at least to some degree. Meanwhile, it seems likely that the expanding fringe will always be a victim of its own stark newness and sameness.

There is also the question of community. Some believe the vast sameness of the suburban world, combined with its autocentric, spread-out, single-use nature, has diminished the sense of community that is available at least in the small town if not the big city. This problem may be partially cured as our suburbs age and acquire character. However, if Robert Putnam is correct, the segregated homogeneity of suburbs, combined with too much time spent driving alone and the loss of community boundaries in a sub-urbanized metropolitan world, is a contributing factor to a continuing decline of civic engage-ment and social activity in the nation.

PART III

Searching for Alternatives

Part III of this book concentrates on the current search for alternatives to the pattern of suburbanization that has dominated the last fifty years of urban development in the United States. Many groups have begun to seek out alternative paths for future growth as they accept that (1) the environmental, social, and fiscal costs outweigh the benefits of suburbanization, (2) suburbanization is ultimately not a sustainable form of development, and (3) the nation simply cannot cease to develop. New directions in planned growth in the past two decades include growth management, new urbanism, regionalism, and smart growth. In recent years, the term *smart growth* has become an umbrella concept endorsed by a range of diverse groups seeking a way to plan for continued growth. But each of these diverse groups has seemingly different definitions of smart growth, making the term ambiguous.

This section of the book is divided into four chapters. Chapter 10 looks at growth management and smart growth, reviews some of the different definitions of smart growth, and proposes working definition for this book. Chapter 10 also identifies a range of planning measures common to some of the more widely accepted interpretations of smart growth. The chapters that follow examine different groups of those planning measures. Chapter 11 looks at techniques for preserving the land and the environment, including programs for open space conservation and limiting the outward expansion of suburban growth. Chapter 12 considers ideas for changing development patterns, including compact developments and channeling new development into the nation's existing cities and towns. Chapter 13 examines possibilities for balancing the transportation system. Finally, Chapter 14 reviews regional approaches to planned growth across metropolitan areas.

CHAPTER 10

Growth Management
and Smart Growth

Growth Management

Although the concept originated in the late 1960s, *growth management* is a term that was popularized during the 1970s and 1980s and that is still widely used today, sometimes interchangeably with *smart growth*. This is because many of the growth-management techniques developed in the past three decades have become instruments in the toolbox of today's smart growth movement.

The original emphasis of growth management was on preserving environmental resources by setting limits on new development. Early examples include the communities of Ramapo, New York; Petaluma, California; and Boulder, Colorado. All three communities experienced rapid growth during the 1960s. In 1969, Ramapo (a northern suburb of New York City) adopted an ordinance that would permit new residential development only as public facilities (for example, water and sewer) were built to support it. This kind of regulation is sometimes called an "adequate public facilities ordinance." As a result of the ordinance, Ramapo housing construction dropped by two-thirds. During the 1970s, both Petaluma (north of San Francisco) and Boulder (northwest of Denver) adopted rigorous growth limits. Petaluma voted to limit development to five hundred new units per year, and Boulder limited new housing growth to 1.5 percent per year, or about 450 units annually. Restrictions in both Petaluma and Ramapo survived court challenges. These types of annual limits—often implemented through an annual cap on building permits—continue to be used today in various U.S. communities, including Edgartown, Massachusetts, on Martha's Vineyard.[1]

Since the 1970s, growth management has evolved into a more broadly focused planning and governmental approach aimed at supporting and coordinating the development process. In other words, it has come to be viewed as a positive framework for directing development in communities rather than as a method for simply restricting growth. Briefly summarized, growth management as it is understood today attempts to use planning, policy, and regulatory techniques to influence the allocation of new development across a designated area. The boundaries of that area could be a local jurisdiction, a metropolitan region, or an entire state. The goals of growth management are to accommodate new development while preserving community character and environmental and open space resources and limiting new infrastructure investments.[2] To accomplish these goals, communities have developed an array of tools, including annual building limits, boundaries mapping geographical limits to urban growth, innovative zoning techniques, land conservation programs, and adequate public facilities ordinances.

The concept of growth management and the techniques that can be used are best illustrated through an actual example. The Maryland–National Capital Park and Planning Commission (M-NCPPC) began implementing what are now recognized as growth-management policies as far back as the 1950s. The M-NCPPC oversees planning in Montgomery and Prince George's Counties in suburban Washington, D.C. In their 1957 two-county master plan, the M-NCPPC adopted a "wedges and corridors" approach, focusing new development along transportation corridors while preserving "wedges" of open space (farmland and forest) in between. In the following decades, the M-NCPPC developed other elements of what

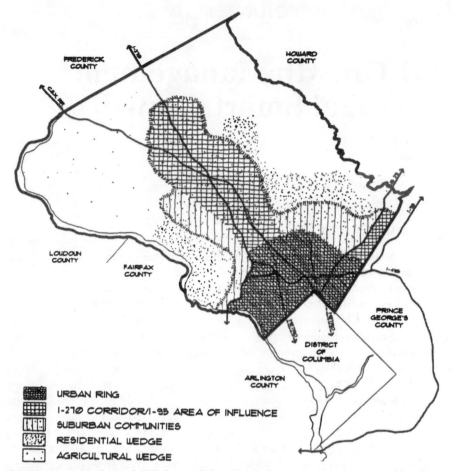

URBAN RING

I-270 CORRIDOR/I-95 AREA OF INFLUENCE

SUBURBAN COMMUNITIES

RESIDENTIAL WEDGE

AGRICULTURAL WEDGE

Figure 10.1. Montgomery County's "Wedges and Corridors" plan is considered a successful early example of growth-management planning.
Source: Douglas R. Porter, *Managing Growth in America's Communities* (Washington, D.C.: Island Press, 1997)

eventually became a full-fledged growth-management strategy for Montgomery County, aimed at conserving open space and new infrastructure investment while directing growth to specified areas within the county (see Figure 10.1). For instance, more than twenty years ago, the northern third of Montgomery County was targeted for agricultural preservation. Agricultural zoning and transferable development rights (see Chapter 11) have been used to preserve more than forty thousand acres of farmland while incentives have been put in place to encourage high-density development around rail transit stations.

Meanwhile, an adequate public facilities ordinance steers development toward existing infrastructure while an inclusionary housing program requires each new housing project of more than fifty dwellings to include a set percentage of low- and moderate-income units.[3]

The measures taken in Montgomery County together with others like them in communities around the nation—including Portland, Oregon; Boulder, Colorado; and the states of Maryland and Florida—make up a kit of tools for managing and directing growth so as to avoid the unplanned, haphazard, and sometimes undesirable effects of uncontrolled suburbanization (sprawl). Since the 1990s, the aims and techniques of growth management have largely become a part of what is now called smart growth.

What Is Smart Growth?

Broadly defined, smart growth is managed growth that attempts to fulfill the need to provide for growth (both economic and in population) while at the same time limiting the undesirable impacts of that growth. The population of the United States is forecast to grow by 45 percent over the next fifty years, and it is widely hoped that smart growth will help the nation meet the needs of that expansion without the kinds of negative impacts that have accompanied widespread suburbanization.[4]

A Big Umbrella

Since the term was coined, smart growth has received support from a variety of groups across the nation. Organizations endorsing smart growth range from the Sierra Club and the Natural Resources Defense Council (NRDC) to various state governments, the U.S. Environmental Protection Agency, the Urban Land Institute, the National Association of Home Builders (NAHB), and the National Association of Industrial and Office Properties (NAIOP). However, as Anthony Downs of the Brookings Institution recently noted in an article for *Planning* magazine, the term *smart growth* may be widely supported but the appearance of broad-based backing can be deceiving: "Under the umbrella of this appealing term, groups with very different goals are trying to create the appearance of a united front. But in reality, that umbrella is being pulled apart."[5]

The appearance of wide endorsement may have partly to do with the nature of the term itself. As NAIOP has eloquently stated, smart growth is "a term no one can object to, since who could possibly favor its alternative: dumb growth?"[6] People as widely different in their relative points of view as Steven Hayward of the Pacific Research Institute for Public Policy and Anthony Downs of the Brookings Institution also have said exactly the same thing.[7] No one wants to be an advocate of "dumb" growth," but what is "smart" about smart growth can be a lot of different things to different people.

The quotations in the accompanying box provide a sampling of some of the differing interpretations of the term *smart growth*. Reading the quotes, one can begin to get a sense of what Anthony Downs means about the umbrella being pulled apart. Depending on who is speaking, the meaning of smart growth can vary from advocating much stronger regional government to simply maintaining the status quo. For example, as we have seen in Chapter 4, both NAIOP and the NAHB are industry groups with vested interests in suburbanization as it has existed for the past fifty years. NAIOP members are in the business of suburban office and industrial parks, while the NAHB represents the nation's home builders. It is therefore not unexpected that their definitions of smart growth would tend to reaffirm the status quo.

Yet, for many people, particularly those who are not affiliated with any particular interest group, smart growth means making least some

---

Characterizations of Smart Growth

Sprawl Watch Clearinghouse: Smart growth is "calling for an end to sprawl and a new vision of urban/suburban collaboration and regional growth management."[8]

Natural Resources Defense Council: Smart growth solutions are "those that reinvigorate our cities, bring new development that is compact, walkable, and transit-oriented, and preserve the best of our landscape for future generations."[9]

Urban Land Institute: "Smart growth does not seek to stop or limit growth, but rather to accommodate it in a way that enhances the economy, protects the environment and preserves or improves a community's quality of life."[10]

Governor Parris Glendening of Maryland: Smart growth is "not no growth or even slow growth. Rather, the goal is sensible growth that balances our need for jobs and economic development with our desire to save our natural environment."[11]

National Association of Industrial and Office Properties: "Smart growth promotes economic prosperity and enhances the quality of life through measures that respect the importance of freedom of choice, flexible land uses, and natural resource management."[12]

National Association of Home Builders: Smart growth is "understanding that suburban job growth and the strong desire to live in single-family homes will continue to encourage growth in suburbia."[13]

modification to the way things are currently done. There has to be change if the continuing demand for economic growth is to be reconciled with trying to contain the resulting sprawl. Even the NAHB and NAIOP recognize this point to some degree in their literature. Furthermore, many people across the United States are making serious efforts to bring the different groups under the umbrella together so that something can actually get done and growth can continue with fewer impacts and less public outcry. This is partly why some of the definitions presented in the accompanying box place strong emphasis on economic development as well as housing.

Defining Smart Growth

None of the different meanings of smart growth offered in the accompanying box constitutes a "definition" of the term in the ordinary sense of the word. That is, none of them is a crisp statement of exactly what smart growth means. However, one doesn't have to wander very far to find one. Among the wealth of scholarly material on the subject, Microsoft's *Encarta World English Dictionary* has one of the best concise definitions of smart growth. *Encarta* lists the term *smart growth* as a noun that means "sensible growth" or "economic growth that consciously seeks to avoid wastefulness and damage to the environment and communities."[14] This definition is not dissimilar to one offered by the Northeast-Midwest Institute and posted on the Smart Growth Network's Web site. There, smart growth is defined as "a view that metropolitan growth patterns can and should serve the environment, the economy, and the community equally."[15] Both of these offerings fit comfortably with the characterization given by Governor Glendening, whose administration is highly regarded as having developed an innovative approach to managing growth in Maryland.

We have seen in Part II that sprawl is arguably wasteful in a number of categories, and finding a way to provide for "economic growth that consciously seeks to avoid wastefulness" as *Encarta* suggests—or even one that is simply less wasteful than current patterns—would be a laudable goal. Even so, the dictionary's definition might arguably be a bit broad. It doesn't give a lot of detail; nor does it spell out what might be involved in achieving such an outcome. But we don't have to search much farther for that, either.

Returning once more to the box, one characterization does give a sense of what is really implied by smart growth. This definition is the one borrowed from the Web site of the NRDC. The NRDC's definition actually is a succinct list of recommended actions that might help achieve the outcome described by the *Encarta*'s definition. Following the NRD's prescription (reinvigorate our cities; bring new development that is compact, walkable, and transit oriented; and preserve the best of our landscape for future generations) would significantly reduce the wastefulness of current development patterns and change the future of growth in the nation. Similar prescriptions can be found on the Sierra Club's Web site and on the Web sites and in the literature of many groups that have taken up the question of smart growth.[16]

Smart Growth Measures

The NRDC's characterization of smart growth can be expanded into a list of discrete measures. In his article "What Does Smart Growth Really Mean?" Anthony Downs lists as many as fourteen potential smart growth elements, but, for the purposes of this book, it is possible to reduce that list to seven commonly discussed measures.[17] Reviewing the growing number of Web sites and publications on the subject, it is likely that one or more of the following seven elements will be found listed as part of most recommended smart growth programs:

1. Open space conservation
2. Boundaries limiting the outward extension of growth
3. Compact, mixed-use developments, amenable to walking and transit
4. Revitalization of older downtowns, inner-ring suburbs, and rundown commercial areas
5. Viable public transit to reduce auto dependence and support alternative development patterns
6. Regional planning coordination (particularly of transportation and land use)
7. Equitable sharing of fiscal resources and financing burdens, including affordable housing across metropolitan regions.

In theory, this list allows for growth but in a directed and balanced manner, with each of these measures helping to support the others.

Table 10.1 provides a summary of sample techniques associated with the smart-growth elements listed above. Conserving land is at the top of the list for many communities. This measure helps preserve community character, provide shared public open space, and protect vulnerable natural habitats. Growth boundaries also help preserve open space, including farmlands and forests, while encouraging more compact development. Compact communities help preserve open space by using less land. Revitalizing older downtowns and suburbs helps promote an economically healthy region by recycling vital urban resources, using existing infrastructure, and relieving development pressure on surrounding lands. Building viable transit options helps relieve congested roads and preserve open space from roadway expansion and follow-on development while supporting compact developments and revitalized downtown areas. With mixed-use and walkable environments, these communities also can reduce car dependence and support mass transit.

Regional coordination of land use and transportation planning can help make transit work effectively by emphasizing existing downtown areas and compact developments connected to transit systems instead of depending solely on roadways for transportation. Finally, equitable regional sharing of fiscal resources, financial burdens (such as infrastructure and education), and regional promotion of affordable housing can help to nurture a healthy regional economy, in which people can afford to live near where they work, while reducing regional inequities.

At least, in theory, that is how these measures should work together. In reality, it is quite difficult to achieve the political consensus necessary to implement all of the measures on the list, and only a few locations (such as Portland, Oregon) have managed to actually act on a significant number of them. Even then, they are challenged repeatedly with lawsuits and ballot initiatives. The fragmented political environment of most metropolitan areas can make regional planning a difficult proposition. Yet, while some of the measures listed above can be enacted locally and independently from one another, others argue the need for a coordinated regional planning effort, and even regional governance, to be effective.

Table 10.1. Smart Growth Measures and Sample Techniques

Smart Growth Measure	Sample Techniques
Open space conservation	• Regulatory controls (environmental restrictions, zoning controls, transfer of development rights, etc.) • Easements and deed restrictions • Tax incentives • Land acquisition
Growth boundaries	• Local urban growth boundaries • Regional urban growth boundaries
Compact developments	• Traditional neighborhood developments • Transit-oriented developments • Transit villages
Revitalization of older areas	• Downtown and Main Street redevelopment programs • Brownfield redevelopment • Greyfield redevelopment
Public transit	• Local transit programs • Regional transit programs
Regional planning coordination	• Regional governments • Regional authorities • Regional infrastructure service districts • State planning initiatives
Equitable sharing of resources/burdens	• Regional revenue sharing • Regional affordable housing programs

Regional Versus Local

Not every community wants to be part of a regional effort aimed at managing growth. As we have seen, multiple, discrete jurisdictions are a hallmark of the nation's sprawling metro areas, and many communities believe strongly in local self-determination and oppose regionalism—despite the fact that sprawling suburbanization rarely respects local governmental boundaries. Even so, some of the measures on the list—such as urban growth boundaries, public transit, fiscal resource sharing, affordable housing, and even some types of urban revitalization—can raise broad, complex regional issues that are beyond local resolution. For example, urban-growth boundaries can be put in place locally, as they have been in a number of municipalities, but the tendency for sprawl development to simply leapfrog into the community next door can severely weaken the effects of such undertakings. Similarly, even though many municipalities, large and small, take care of their own roads and even have their own transit systems, transportation is often more of a regional issue than a local one, affecting multiple communities across a given metropolitan area.

Because sprawl is mostly a regional phenomenon, and because some of the issues raised by sprawl are most critical at the regional level, many communities may find that they must begin to think more broadly to achieve any real change. This means thinking regionally rather than locally about such questions as growth boundaries and transportation as well as land use and, ultimately, the general distribution of fiscal resources.

Growth Management and Smart Growth in Summary

Smart growth is a term that has grown out of growth-management initiatives undertaken across the country from the late 1960s into the 1980s. The unbridled growth of the 1990s brought new urgency to the issues posed by suburbanization, and a wide array of groups has banded together under the burgeoning smart growth movement, which has built upon the growth-management techniques from earlier decades. Yet, smart growth remains a wide umbrella, and different groups carry different agendas within the movement. However, some basic principles are exemplified by various smart growth movements in states across the country. These are summarized in the list of seven elements presented earlier in this chapter.

As we shall see in the chapters that follow, this list of smart growth measures offers an impressive array of promising ways to change the pattern of urban development in the United States. Many U.S. communities have used one or more of these tools to try to change the way they grow. There is much that can be achieved simply through local determination and home rule, two elements that are fundamental to the history of this country. Yet, it also seems clear that when used in isolated instances on a city, town, and county basis, these tools may not yield the widespread results that many are seeking. By themselves, these tools will not put an end to sprawl as we know it, and some of them, such as public transportation, really require a broader approach to the problem, one that takes in a whole metropolitan region rather than just discrete individual jurisdictions.

CHAPTER 11

Preserving Open Space

The Importance of Open Space

Loss of open space is among the topmost concerns expressed in ballot measures and polls about land and development conducted across the nation. There were more than 240 ballot measures nationwide in 1998 aimed at protecting open space, and 72 percent of them passed.[1] A poll conducted in fall 2000 by Smart Growth America showed that 83 percent of those surveyed favored preserving zones of green space for framing and forest that would be off-limits to developers.[2] At that same time, there were another 209 ballot measures nationally that aimed conserving land. Of these, 179 passed (about 86 percent), resulting in $7.5 billion in funding for preserving land.[3]

A National Association of Realtors (NAR) poll of one thousand voting Americans conducted in March 2001 showed that more than 88 percent of those canvased supported preserving farmland, forests, fields, and other natural areas. The same poll showed that 74 percent of those surveyed supported local government purchase of open space.[4] Public support for open space preservation has continued to mount across America as metropolitan regions have spread out into formerly rural areas while filling in remaining patches of farmland, field, and forest in already suburbanized areas.

Although public pressure may be a prime motivator in preserving land, communities usually choose to do so in order to satisfy differing goals among the following categories:

• Environmental considerations
• Community needs
• Economic benefits.

Environmental Considerations

A key motivation for preserving land is to protect and nurture environmental resources. In the past forty years, communities across the nation have become increasingly aware of the critical role that environment plays in sustaining human habitation and maintaining a desirable quality of life. In many cases, preserving the environment can mean setting aside undeveloped land either to protect wildlife or plant habitats and rare ecosystems or because of its role in the watershed or other factors.

Wetlands, estuarine, and riparian systems are typical examples of valuable environmental lands that harbor a rich diversity of species while serving as flood storage and natural filtration for storm runoff from adjacent developed areas. Forests and fields act as recharge areas for aquifers that feed streams, rivers, and reservoirs. Many states and local communities have land conservation programs in watersheds leading to reservoirs. To address mounting concern about preserving biodiversity and natural ecological systems, major projects are being undertaken across the country. For example, millions of dollars are being spent to restore part of the Florida Everglades after decades of draining and filling. There also has been extensive discussion about modifying the system of dams on rivers in the Pacific Northwest. As more is understood about rivers and wetlands, it has been theorized that much of the damage caused by flooding of the Mississippi River in the past decade could have been avoided if flood-storing natural wetlands systems had been left in place.

HABITAT CONSERVATION

Building in certain rare wildlife habitats could endanger the survival of some species. Some special habitats are preserved because they are needed to support migratory birds or butterflies. In some cases, large tracts of forestland (interior habitat) may be required to support ecosystems that cannot survive in suburbanized fringe areas. In other situations, vulnerable biological communities or special ecosystems may be the target of conservation efforts. The coastal sage scrub in California is an example of such a vulnerable community; up to 90 percent of its historic distribution has been eliminated by development.[5]

Rare or endemic biological communities also may be planning targets. Rare communities are easily threatened because they exist in very few locations, whereas endemic communities exist in a particular region but no other place in the world. The Monarch butterfly winters in only two areas in North America: in Mexico and along the coast of California. Thus, the Monarch's winter habitat is endemic to those areas. Old-growth forests are an example of a rare community in the United States. They take centuries to develop, and a national history of widespread logging has left only a few places where such forests still exist. Many biological communities in such states as California, Hawaii, and Florida are considered endemic because they have evolved to suit a specific limited climactic zone and their dispersal is largely restricted to one particular geographic area.[6] The Florida Everglades is one example.

Habitat-conservation planning can require protecting a network of interconnected open spaces—rather than simply isolated pockets of land—to support a threatened species or biological community. If carefully planned, such a network can sometimes exist within the fragmentation of habitat caused by suburban development. Examples of this type of habitat conservation planning exist in Boulder, Colorado, and in the state of Washington. In Boulder, a network of conservation areas has been established to protect the black-tailed prairie dog, a species that was almost extinguished during the 1970s. In Washington State, a series of separate conservation areas have been planned to support the northern spotted owl. Although they are not physically connected, the conservation areas are all planned to be within the dispersal range of juvenile spotted owls.[7]

WATER RESOURCES PROTECTION

Recharge areas, wetlands, lakes, estuary systems, and riparian systems such as streams and rivers are among the most important resources needed to sustain the environment and ensure the continued health of the nation's communities (see Figure 11.1). The objectives of protecting water resources and habitat often overlap with community and economic needs. Recharge areas can be some of

Figure 11.1. Wetlands, ponds, streams, and rivers are among the most important resources needed to sustain the environment and support human communities. (Oliver Gillham)

the most endangered habitats as well as the most necessary for providing healthy drinking water.

A prominent example is the Long Island Pine Barrens. The Pine Barrens lie along the top of the terminal glacial moraine that forms Long Island. The pitch pine and scrub oak barrens form a rare ecological community of plants and animals while at the same time serving as the main recharge area for much of Long Island's drinking water. After decades of encroachment by suburbanization, a one-hundred-thousand-acre area of the Pine Barrens was put under state and local management, including a fifty-two-thousand-acre core preservation area, in which no new development is permitted, and a forty-eight-thousand-acre compatible growth area, in which limited, environmentally compatible development is allowed. State and local entities are in the process of acquiring land in the core area.[8]

Wetlands have been the subject of federal and state protection regulations for several decades, and there are continuing efforts across the nation aimed at protecting estuaries, rivers, lakes, ponds, and streams. The City of New York is engaged in an aggressive effort to protect the upstate watershed system that provides city drinking water. Efforts in the Florida Everglades have water resources goals as well as habitat preservation, community, and economic objectives.

Community Needs

Open space fulfills a variety of community needs. Among the most important are preserving local character and way of life (sometimes including the local economy) as well as providing needed common-use green space accessible to the whole community.

Figure 11.2. Preserving farmland can mean preserving scenic views and a way of life. (Oliver Gillham)

COMMUNITY CHARACTER AND WAY OF LIFE

Open space can be a critical part of the visual character of a settlement. Special views and vistas across open lands are a vital part of the image of many communities, large and small. How the land is used also has a lot to do with a community's makeup and way of life. If the community is rural, then preserving character may also mean preserving farm and forestry uses (see Figure 11.2). Preserving community character and way of life is much of what preserving land in rural New England and Pennsylvania is about, and it can also be vital to tourism (an economic consideration addressed later in this chapter).

Open space can be private or public and can be farmland, forest, parkland, or wetlands. Conserving open land for community character preservation may mean saving land in its present use, preserving important views across land, or maintaining an historic landscape. Usually, the issue is preserving the character of privately held land that might otherwise be developed for housing, commercial, or industrial use. If the main goal is to preserve the land in its current use, to maintain specific views, or just to keep the land looking the way it is, then acquiring property outright isn't absolutely necessary. Growth limits and regulatory techniques (such as zoning), tax incentives, and purchase of easements or deeded covenants on the land are other methods (addressed later in this chapter).

COMMON-USE GREEN SPACE

Another reason for conserving land is to provide expanses of green space accessible to the whole community. This is different than preserving the visual character of a parcel of land or simply maintaining it in the same use. Making land accessible means allowing the land to be used by the public—turning private land into public open space. Of course, conserving such lands and allowing public access can also serve community character purposes, but public access and use are often the main objectives. Preserving farmland or other open spaces that remain privately held and inaccessible doesn't solve the need for shared green space, which can be a common ground for the entire community to use and enjoy. Publicly accessible open space is as vital to a community as is visual character; some might say even more so. In the NAR poll cited earlier in this chapter, the highest percentage of respondents felt that open space that was accessible to the public was the most important, with playgrounds, playing fields, neighborhood parks, and walking trails at the top of the list.[9]

One of the major complaints about contemporary suburbia is the lack of functional public open space. Most of the open space in the suburbanized world has been divvied up among the myriad private lawns of the individual property owners. Typically, very little green space remains to be used for public gathering and recreation. Golf courses are usually private, and special purpose and public parks can sometimes be few and far between and not within walking distance. The nearest public open spaces are often remnant landscape areas, such as drainage swales and highway ramp slopes and buffer zones. Sprawling metropolitan areas require various levels of public open space. At the local level, neighborhood parks and fields are treasured spaces in many communities. At the regional level, larger tracts are needed, such as state and county parks, beaches, and forests used as common ground by many communities. These spaces provide wide, green tracts of relief to an otherwise unbroken field of development.

Economic Benefits

Preserving open space can also have important economic benefits. In her article "The Economics of Preserving Open Space," Elizabeth Brabec argues that open space preservation produces significant economic benefits in most communities.[10] Those benefits are realized by the community as a whole, by individual landowners, and by developers. Brabec cites reports by real estate firms and governors' committees that highlight open space as the "key element in the quality of life that brought rapid economic growth and multi-billion dollar tourism" to their regions.[11]

As far back as the 1860s, Frederick Law Olmsted demonstrated the tax benefits that accrued to the City of New York from increased value of land surrounding Central Park, which was then under construction. Since the park was completed, the value of nearby residential property has continued to increase significantly relative to other residential real estate in the city. The same is true of parks and green space in communities across the nation. Studies in Boulder, Colorado, found that the aggregate value of property in one neighborhood near a greenbelt acquisition rose sufficiently to generate an additional $500,000 per year in increased tax revenue—enough to pay off the $1.5 million cost of the acquisition in just three years.[12] Brabec lists a series of other communities in California and elsewhere that have similarly benefited.

Not only does the community benefit fiscally, but individual landowners and developers can also benefit from increasing land values next to preserved open space. Brabec reports that a study in Salem, Oregon, showed that urban land next to exclusively zoned agricultural land was worth $1,200 more per acre than similar land one thousand feet from the greenbelt. Brabec cites similar studies in Seattle, Boulder, Dayton (Ohio), and Worcester (Massachusetts).[13]

Tourism is another important benefit. Preserving a community's character can add significantly to its tourism attraction or simply insure that a community continues to attract tourists. Open space is often a key part of a community's character; also, it can offer recreational opportunities—such as biking, hiking, and general sightseeing—that are important to generating tourism income.

For example, October is usually the busiest month for the rental car industry at Boston's Logan International Airport. This is when millions of visitors descend on New England to view the autumn colors in the hills and mountains of Massachusetts, Vermont, and New Hampshire. These tourists bring millions of dollars into New England's economy each year, and they come primarily to see New England's fields, farmlands, forests, and rural villages. Brabec notes that observing and photographing wildlife and enjoying nature and natural scenery are activities shared by over 130 million Americans, who spend more than $14 billion per year on such activities nationwide.[14]

Preserving open space can bring economic benefits while also protecting a way of life. The farmlands of New England are one example of this phenomenon; Pennsylvania provides another. Safeguarding a farming community such as exists in predominantly Amish Lancaster County, Pennsylvania, can entail preserving the economics that support that way of life. This could mean preserving farmland that might otherwise get developed if left to the marketplace alone. In a sense, this is both an economic and a community character issue. The presence of the Amish is also a tourist draw, attracting about $500 million in tourist income annually. In this case, preserving the land means preserving a way of life and a part of America's cultural heritage while also maintaining a healthy tourist economy.[15]

Open-Space Conservation Programs

Open-space conservation has a long and honored tradition in the United States, and as the polls show, it is often amenable to broad community consensus, depending on cost and other issues. Open-space conservation programs are carried out at many different levels: by federal or state government, by a local community or by an individual or group within that community, or by local or national private nonprofit groups. Open space can be preserved by several methods, including outright purchase of private land or purchase of development rights or property easements, transferable development rights (TDRs), or through such land-use controls as zoning or wetlands regulations enforced by local conservation commissions and backed up by state and federal regulations; state-designated areas of critical environmental concern, in which development may be strictly regulated or even prohibited (as in the Long Island Pine Barrens); or state growth and land conservation plans such as those in Oregon and Maryland (see Chapter 14).

The method to be used usually depends on the goals to be achieved and the scale of the undertaking. For example, is the goal community preservation or common-use (publicly accessible) green space? Different techniques may apply. If it is common-use green space, then what scale? Is the subject local fields and woodlands or a regional park or forest? Different levels of action (local, county, state or federal, or private nonprofit) may apply. Table 11.1 presents

Table 11.1. Selected Open Space Conservation Techniques

Category	Technique	Summary	Environment	Community	Economic	Scale/Other
	OPEN SPACE MEASURES			GOALS		
Regulatory	Downzoning	Increases residential lot size (3 to 5 acres/unit common)	Usually little effect without other measures	Does not preserve open lands or allow community access/common use	Local property benefits within zone	Usually local
	Cluster zoning	Requires common open space set aside and may reduce lot size	Can be used to protect some habitat/water resource areas	Can be used to protect community character (e.g. open space, views, farmland, etc.) and may allow access/common use	Property, local economy, and tourism potentials	Usually local but can be required regionally
	Agricultural zoning	Agricultural/forestry use only—usually 25 acres/unit and higher	When land is kept in forest use	Often used to protect community character and way of life—not used for common access/use	Local economy preservation and tourism potentials	Can be used locally or regionally
	Transfer of development rights	Land development rights purchased for use on another site	Can be used to protect habitat, water, and other resources	Can be used to protect community character and way of life (e.g., farming community)—not usually used for common access/use	Local economy preservation, allows some gain from protected land, directs development to targeted areas	Usually countywide or regional
	Environmental restrictions	Restricts development in or near environmentally sensitive areas such as wetlands	Usually affects specific habitats or resources (wetlands, watersheds, endangered species, etc.)	Can protect some aspects of community character (wetlands, forestlands, prairie, etc.)—usually no public access	Potential property benefits to abutters, tourism potentials	Can be local, regional, state, and/or federal
Easements and Deed Restrictions	Purchase or donation of development rights	Land remains with owner, but future development restricted or prohibited	Can be used to protect habitat, water, and other resources	Can be used to protect community character and way of life (e.g., farming community)—not for public access/common use	Potential property benefits to abutters and others in community, tourism potentials	Programs can be local, regional, state, or federal; can be done by government or local or national land trusts and/or conservancy organizations
	Use-restriction purchase or donation	Land remains with owner, but change of use restricted or prohibited	When land is to be kept in natural state	Can be used to protect community character and way of life (e.g., farming community)—not for public access/common use	Local economy preservation, potential property benefits in community, tourism potentials	Often local or regional but can be state or even federal; government, trusts, or conservancies
	Public-access easement purchase or donation	Land remains with owner, but public access granted to all or part of land	Not usually for environmental purposes	Can be used to protect community character and provide public access/common use	Potential economic benefits accrue to whole community	Programs can be local, regional, state, or federal; can be done by government or local or national land trusts and/or conservancy organizations
	Environmental/Other restrictions or donations	Land remains with owner, but covenants protect habitat or other resources	Usually for specific environmental purposes	Can protect some aspects of community character (wetlands, forestlands, prairie, etc.)—usually no public access	Potential benefits from watershed/water resources protection, potential tourism benefits	Programs can be local, regional, state, or federal; can be done by government or local or national land trusts and/or conservancy organizations
Tax Incentives	Use credits	Tax credits or lower tax rate for land kept in farm or forest use	May be environmental benefits in forest use	Can help to protect rural community character and way of life	Preservation of local economy, potential tourism benefits	Usually state or federal
	Donation credits	Tax deduction for donation of property or rights	May be environmental benefits in forest use	Can help to protect rural community character and way of life	Benefit to local property owners, potential tourism benefits	State and federal
Acquisition	Eminent domain land taking or negotiated sale of land in fee with all rights	Land transferred to public domain, trust, or conservancy organization	Can protect habitat, water resources, and endangered species	Very effective in protecting community character and in providing common use green space	Community-wide economic benefits, including tourism	Federal, state, regional, municipal or private trust, or conservancy organization

selected open space conservation techniques together with the goals and scales to which they are best suited and the likely level of action. Different techniques and their applicability are discussed below.

Regulatory Controls

Regulatory controls can be used to control the use of private land but not to transfer it directly into public hands—at least not without just compensation. The extent to which government can regulate land without having to compensate the owner in certain circumstances is still being worked out in the courts and at the ballot box. Court cases have tended to uphold the zoning powers of localities in most instances, and some control mechanisms actually include compensation for landowners.

FEDERAL, STATE, AND LOCAL

At the federal level, section 404 of the Clean Water Act controls the discharge of dredged and fill material into waters of the United States, including wetlands. Waters of the United States are generally those that cross state jurisdictions or that may be affected by interstate commerce. Because this includes tributaries to those waters as well as waters that contain fish that may be sold into interstate commerce, the interpretation can be fairly broad. Section 404 requires developers to file for a permit with the Army Corps of Engineers. Thus, the federal government can control the alteration of the land to some degree as well as the way it is developed. In certain instances, permits may be denied, preventing (at least temporarily) development of some wetlands areas. However, most wetlands regulations are enforced at the local level through conservation commissions backed up by state law and regulations.

States may control development with various regulations that require permits from developers. The Long Island Pine Barrens in New York is one example in which the state has prohibited development in a given area but has backed up the regulation with a program of gradual land acquisition. In Massachusetts, the state holds permitting control over all tidelands and filled tidelands and essentially can dictate terms within the guidelines of its own regulations. Massachusetts also can designate areas of critical environmental concern, in which the extent of development is

regulated. There are also state sanitary codes that regulate the distance between septic systems, wells, and wetlands. These codes also affect development patterns.

The power a state may have over land use varies from state to state. States can influence or even mandate local consistency with state plans (as has been done in Oregon and Maryland), but on average most land-rights use regulation is given over to localities, towns, counties, and cities. Local regulatory controls include zoning and subdivision regulations as well as local environmental rules, public health ordinances, and other regulations. Zoning and subdivision regulations can be used in a variety of ways to preserve open space. The land remains privately held, but the amount and spacing of development can be controlled as can the use.

Zoning can require substantial public input to promulgate and, once put in place, can be very difficult to change. Once established, unless there is substantial public objection at the outset, zoning regulations tend to become inculcated in many communities. People buy houses in certain zoning districts based in part on what they expect may someday be built (or torn down and rebuilt) in the neighborhood. In other cases (farmland, for example), people may have expectations about what they may be able to build on their land and what the land is worth according to how it may be developed. They may be opposed to zoning changes that reduce the amount of development that can be built on their land.

DOWNZONING

One zoning technique used by many local governments is known as downzoning, the process of decreasing the amount of development that can be built upon a given number of acres of land (or, conversely, increasing the amount of land required to build a set amount of development). For example, using the case of a single-family house, downzoning might mean changing the amount of land required to build the house from, say, half an acre to three acres. The notion is that this will keep the houses farther apart, with more land and trees between them. Demanding minimum setbacks or landscaped "buffer zones" between buildings and lot lines can further refine this technique.

Downzoning has enjoyed widespread popularity in the United States, and many communities have used it in an effort to preserve community character. It is often advocated by existing home owners in areas that are becoming suburbanized in the hope of retaining some semblance of the low-density, open environment that they bought into or grew up in. Longtime landholders of large parcels hoping to maximize the development potential of the land may object at times, but within a certain range, the prices commanded by larger lots can sometimes outweigh or equal the reduction in the total number of lots.

However, whether the land is subdivided into three-acre lots or half-acre lots, the total site is still carved up into individually owned parcels of land. Downzoning alone does not imply any shared open space. Thus, at least in small increments like three-acre lots, it usually is not useful for creating significant open space, nor is it usually a successful technique for preserving endangered habitat, nor does it yield any public access land.

Mostly used as a method for preserving community character, downzoning is not always effective in meeting this goal. The total number of units in the neighborhood will still increase if large tracts of undeveloped land (for example, twenty-five acres or more) are subdivided into three-acre lots. There will be more traffic, and because dwellings are quite spread out, the district will be heavily car-dependent. Furthermore, the views and vistas provided by fields and farmland will vanish behind the hedges and landscaping of the new houses. A typical example of this outcome is Long Island's fashionable Hamptons

district, where the hedgerows of sumptuous new houses have walled off the long vistas of sea and countryside once afforded by farmlands. The views and character of the community that first attracted people there are rapidly disappearing, leaving a heavily built-up seashore and the promise of nearby wealth and society as the region's main attractions.

Although downzoning may not adequately preserve community character, it may protect and even enhance property values, which may be good for the existing owners but bad for anyone trying to buy into the neighborhood. Thus, downzoning often can be purposefully exclusionary. Even so, the technique remains widely used.

CLUSTERING

Clustering (or open-space development design) is another technique used to preserving open space. It can be used in conjunction with downzoning or independently from it. Simple downzoning without any cluster or open space provisions usually results in a standard subdivision with larger lots and no contiguous common open space. Clustering, on the other hand, can be used to set aside land to remain in existing use (such as farmland or forest), to be reserved for public use, or to protect vulnerable habitats, or in some combination of the foregoing. Thus, clustering can be used for community character preservation, common-use open space, or protection of habitat or water resources (see Figure 11.3).

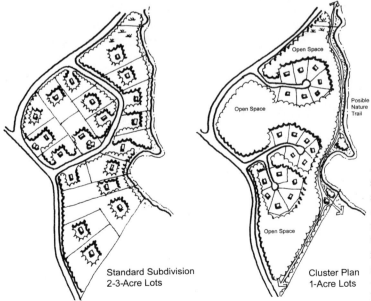

Standard Subdivision
2-3-Acre Lots

Open Space

Open Space

Open Space

Posible Nature Trail

Cluster Plan
1-Acre Lots

Figure 11.3. Comparison of a standard subdivision and a cluster subdivision on the same site. The cluster plan leaves the majority of the site as protected open space that can be held in trust. Adapted from Randall Arendt et al., *Rural by Design: Maintaining Small Town Character* (Chicago: American Planning Association, 1994)

Essentially, a cluster subdivision concentrates development on a particular part of a given property, leaving the rest open. The result may be the same number of units as—or even more units than—might be built under a downzoning scheme, but clustering schemes can leave more undivided open space than downzoning alone can usually achieve. The open space that results may be private but still held in common by all of the dwellings in the subdivision (for example, a homeowners association), or it may be private with public easements or given over to the public realm or a private nonprofit organization. There also can be restrictive covenants that protect habitats or existing uses within the open space. In some cases, for example, the open land in an open-space design is held by a home owner's association or a land trust and leased to a farmer for use as farmland.[16]

Clustering can require a combination of zoning and subdivision regulations to make it work properly. Zoning may be used to reduce the required lot size per dwelling unit in the cluster as well as setback requirements, while the subdivision regulations may set narrower road widths and grades and alternative lot configurations. For example, if a cluster option is available under zoning in a three-acre residential district, the zoning would probably allow individual lot sizes and setbacks to be reduced so that the same or a similar number of lots could be developed as would be allowed under a non-cluster design while a percentage of the land is set aside undivided. Or, zoning and subdivision regulations can be tailored to require that most or all subdivisions in a district be open space development designs. This has been done in such places as South Berwick, Maine, and Isle of Wight County, Virginia. According to Randall Arendt, author of *Rural by Design: Maintaining Small Town Character*, Isle of Wight County has designated 80 percent of county land as a rural preservation district. Within the district, new subdivision development is prohibited from consuming more than 50 percent of any parcel.[17]

Of course, even at just 50 percent of a given site, clustering still means that at least part of the land is getting developed. The parcel in question is not being preserved in whole as it might be if other options, such as acquisition of the property or its development rights, were pursued. On a project-specific basis, without other measures, the cluster pattern also does relatively little to alter the prevailing pattern of separated land uses, auto dependence, and limitless surrounding development. Even so, cluster or open space development design can be a marked improvement over the standard subdivision, and (if properly designed) it can be an excellent compromise method of preserving open space while allowing for growth.

AGRICULTURAL ZONING

One fairly common technique for preserving farmland or forest is agricultural zoning. The land remains in private ownership and zoned for farming or forestry use, so this technique is not useful for adding to a community's publicly accessible green space, but it may protect biological communities, depending on how forestry uses are managed. The main purpose of agricultural zoning is to preserve working farmland, forestland, rural economy, and community character. Since the 1970s, communities in Oregon have used "existing-use" zoning to keep land in agriculture. In Oregon, the use of agricultural zones property basically is limited to farming, forestry, and related activities. Other types of uses, such as nonfarm residential uses, are prohibited or strictly limited.

Agricultural zoning is sometimes combined with ultra-low-density zoning, which is actually a type of downzoning but is far more restrictive than the usual two or three acres per unit. Agricultural low-density zoning can require twenty-five to forty acres per unit or more, in addition to promoting or requiring agricultural use within the district. In some cases, ultra-low-density zoning is sometimes used in place of existing use or strictly agricultural use zoning. This kind of very low density zoning makes it difficult to use the land in a district for anything other than farming or forestry.

A corollary of the extreme low-density zoning is that the potential development value of the land may be reduced. Significant value is often derived from the land's potential to be subdivided and sold off into multiple-home sites. Historically, this strategy has usually yielded more dollars per acre than selling one very large lot with a single unit. This factor also helps keep the land in farm or forest. By reducing the number of units that can be built on a given plot of land below a certain point, the land then has relatively little value for any use other than farming or forestry.

Nonetheless, in some areas, residential home

owners seeking large lots of twenty-five acres or more (or developers with such a market in mind) have been known to simply convert large tracts of farmland land to vary large lot residential use. Generally, such situations have been rare, but they are reported to be increasing in some areas of the country, such as Oregon, where people have begun to purchase smaller farm properties (under forty acres) and use them as second homes—or "martini ranches," as they are sometimes called.[18] This phenomenon has caused Oregon to examine the possibility of stricter rules for farm use.

Usually, the issue is that such restrictive zoning can be quite unfair to the existing landowner, who may be a farmer counting on selling his land for retirement or to send his children to college. In fact, this kind of treatment has led to court battles in which landowners claim that their land has actually been "taken" by the local community without fair compensation. For this reason, some localities have tried to work indirect forms of compensation into the zoning mix.

TRANSFER OF DEVELOPMENT RIGHTS

One way to try to compensate property owners for restrictive zoning is through the use of instruments called transferable development rights, or TDRs. TDRs allow the sale or transfer of valuable land-development rights between one landowner and another. The TDR technique requires identification of "sending areas," in which a property owner may sell development rights, and "receiving areas," to which development rights may be transferred. Using this technique, a locality or region may grant additional development density above what is zoned in the receiving areas (usually targeted development zones) if the developer first purchases a TDR from a landowner in a sending area (often an agricultural district in the same locality or region). After the transfer is made, a deed restriction is placed on the seller's land limiting or prohibiting future development. Thus, a farmer's land can still have development value—just for development on a different piece of land in another area. TDRs have been widely used by individual municipalities, but problems can arise in accepting higher density in one part of a community in order to preserve the open character of another part—there simply may not be an acceptable place to put the higher density.

Because of the density problem, not all local-

ities are willing to accept such a bargain. For this reason, TDRs can sometimes work better on a county or a regional basis, where the potential for special target areas is increased. For example, Montgomery and Calvert Counties in Maryland have both used TDRs quite effectively in preserving farmland. In Montgomery County, TDRs have been used to direct growth to priority development areas, including specially designated nodes surrounding Washington-Area Metro stops. Their program combines downzoning (for example, from three acres to twenty-five acres) with TDRs within agricultural reserve areas. The TDR credits are based on the original, higher zoning, meaning that an owner of one hundred acres may choose between selling twenty TDR credits or developing four houses on individual twenty-five-acre lots. The market for development rights is guaranteed by a publicly funded TDR bank, which can buy and sell TDRs in the absence of private demand. So far, the program has preserved about thirty-two thousand acres of agricultural land in Montgomery County.[19]

In addition to protecting farmland, TDRs can be used to protect woodlands and open fields as well as views, historic neighborhoods and buildings, and other key community character elements. They also can help protect fragile habitats and water resources. This technique is being used in the Long Island Pine Barrens and in the New Jersey Pine Barrens (a rare ecological area similar to the Long Island Pine Barrens). In Long Island, TDRs are being used to purchase development rights in the designated nondevelopment zone for use in designated receiving areas in three participating municipalities. A Pine Barrens Credit Clearinghouse was established to ensure a market for the TDRs. The New Jersey Pinelands operates a similar program with a Pinelands Development Credit Bank, which is empowered to track and facilitate transfers and to buy and sell credits directly when necessary.[20]

ENVIRONMENTAL RESTRICTIONS

Most states have wetlands restrictions that are enforced by local jurisdictions through their conservation commissions. Wetlands regulations are generally established at the state level but can sometimes be modified locally. Usually, these regulations require development setbacks from wetlands or special permission to build in wetlands, usually only if the wetlands are replaced in kind elsewhere. Wetlands regulations may also govern alteration of vegetation (for example, tree cutting) within a set distance (often, one hundred to two hundred feet) from the edge of the wetland. What constitutes the border of a wetland may vary. The federal government uses soil types (hydric soils) whereas some states use characteristic vegetation. In many cases, such permissions can be difficult to get, and in some communities any disturbance of local wetlands may be prohibited. This measure helps to protect wetland biological communities, including estuarine and riparian environments. Wetlands also support richly diverse plant and animal habitats while acting as groundwater filters and absorbing and storing storm runoff.

Wetlands regulations also help retain community character by preserving the open space around wetlands, but they may do little for providing accessible community open space, because the land often remains private and the environment is fragile. Federal and state wetlands regulations can also come into play, as described earlier. Other environmental restrictions may include state-established areas of special or critical environmental concern. In these areas, special development restrictions may apply to preserve targeted scenic resources and biological communities. Other environmental regulations that may help preserve open space include state and federal regulations governing endangered species, which may prevent development in certain areas, as well as the environmental impact assessment process required of most federal and federally funded projects and at the state level for private projects meeting certain size, type, and impact criteria. Approval of environmental filings may set conditions that require open space set-asides.

Easements and Deed Restrictions

Another option for conserving land is through the purchase of deed restrictions (also referred to as covenants or easements). Here, a buyer (a town, state, land trust, conservation organization, or other group) makes a deal to have a permanent easement or binding covenant put upon the deed to a given piece of land in exchange for a negotiated payment to the owner or for consideration in the form of tax deductions or both. Any one of the bundle of rights running with a given piece of land may be separated from the

rest and sold, donated, or otherwise encumbered. Thus, easements can take many forms.

An effective community preservation measure involves the sale or donation of a property's development rights—prohibiting subdivision and development of the property in perpetuity. Use rights also may be affected with covenants requiring, for example, that the land remain in its current state. Easements and covenants can be used to meet the goal of community character preservation by ensuring that certain key properties within a community will remain the way they are. Easements also can be used to grant public access to all or part of a property as well as for other purposes, such as protection of natural habitat or protection of water resources. The land can still be sold to another owner, but the deed restrictions usually remain in perpetuity unless negotiated otherwise or unless a property owner can make a deal to repurchase the relinquished rights.

Because of the lesser cost of this strategy when compared with outright acquisition, this approach has become popular throughout the United States and is being used by localities as well as states and private conservation organizations. In many cases, private land trusts are either the purchasing agents or the end recipients of the development rights. Approximately 1,200 land trusts have been formed across the nation to hold donated or purchased land and easements for conservation purposes.[21] Many of these trusts are local or regional organizations that confine their activities to a single state. Such national and international groups as The Nature Conservancy, the Trust for Public Land, and the Conservation Fund are larger trust organizations that are also in the business of acquiring and maintaining conservation easements.

Acquiring development rights does not require the often-difficult political and community process hurdles posed by modifying zoning regulations. Yet, because it usually works on a case-by-case basis, the technique does not necessarily ensure the preservation of a whole district the way zoning changes or long-term purchase programs can.

Tax Incentives

In certain states (Massachusetts, Oregon, and others), tax credits are given for keeping land in farm or forest—that is, certified owners of working farmland or forestland pay less annual property tax than owners of land used for other purposes. If and when the land is converted, additional taxes may be assessed covering the difference between the lower rate and the normal residential or commercial rate paid for each of the years that the lower farm use tax was paid. This can make the penalties for conversion substantial.[22] However, there is always the chance that at some point alternative development will become attractive enough for a landowner to disregard both credits and penalties or that a landowner may refuse to take the credits in the first place in order to avoid any penalties for conversion in the future. Furthermore, this type of technique is useful mainly to sustain rural economies and to preserve community character—not for common green space, because the land remains privately held.

Other types of tax incentives also can work to meet land-conservation goals. Such incentives usually involve donation of easements or restrictions upon a piece of property. For example, property owners may choose either to donate the development rights to their land to a land trust or a conservation organization (as discussed above) or to encumber the land (free of charge) with a conservation easement, protecting a particular habitat, or an easement granting public access to all or part of a property. Some or all of these types of actions can qualify for tax-deductible, status depending on the exact nature of the transaction and the parties involved.

Acquisition

To provide public access and full public control over open space for recreation and preservation, outright purchase of land is sometimes the chosen route, either by government or by private conservation organizations, such as the Audubon Society, The Nature Conservancy, or the Trust for Public Land. Although more expensive than simply purchasing development rights or easements, these types of programs have greater potential for conserving large expanses of natural habitat that can be both protected where necessary and open in many areas for enjoyment by the expanding population of the nation's metropolitan regions.

For example, the huge expanses of federally held lands in the western United States hold great promise for the future as public green space and protected wilderness. The federal government owns nearly 21 percent of the land in the contiguous United States, and most of that (more than 90 percent) is west of the Mississippi (see Chapter 5).[23] However, if these lands are not managed properly or if they are widely opened to mining, energy exploration, and poor forestry techniques, their future as protected wilderness and public green space may be questionable, placing greater pressure on the need to provide for such spaces in a rapidly developing nation.

In the eastern United States, which has relatively few such federal properties, some ambitious acquisition exercises have already been required to protect the scarce remaining open land resources from succumbing to suburbanization. Cape Cod National Seashore is one outstanding example as are the long-term programs of land acquisition in Vermont and in the Adirondack region of New York. Yet, the political will for these expenditures is variable, and big state-bond issues for acquiring and preserving land have been known to fail dramatically as have smaller, local measures. In fact, the same NAR poll that showed an 80 percent support level for preserving open space also revealed that only 53 percent of those polled would actually support raising taxes to save land.[24] However, this is still a majority, if only barely. In Massachusetts, passage of the Community Preservation Act has allowed communities to vote up to a 3 percent surcharge on existing real estate tax bills to receive state matching funds for open space preservation. As of November 2001, 52 percent of communities that have moved on the act have voted in favor of the surcharge. The City of Boston voted it down.

Land trusts and private conservation organizations have made tremendous progress toward conserving land in America. Land trusts have protected more than 5 million acres of land in the United States, and they protect more every day.[25] The Nature Conservancy has protected another 12 million acres of land.[26] The National Audubon Society and other organizations protect other lands.

Despite these remarkable contributions, private organizations do not have the powers of government when it comes to preserving land. In June 2001, a combined bid by The Nature Conservancy, the Audubon Society, the Trust for Public Land, and other groups to buy nine thousand acres of cranberry farms in southeastern

Massachusetts was rejected by the landowner, who intends to build 3,500 units of housing on the land.[27] In the 1980s, faced with the prospect of development on a 334-acre island in Waquoit Bay on Cape Cod, the Commonwealth of Massachusetts stepped in and acquired the island by eminent domain (the right of government to take private land for public use at a just price). As with many such cases, the final price of the island was established in a court settlement after the taking. The result was that a sizable parcel of land, including rare natural habitats, in an area of critical environmental concern was permanently preserved and made available to the public on a managed basis.

Growth Boundaries

Another way to preserve open space is to limit the outward expansion of growth and preserve surrounding land to create a greenbelt around a community. This is often achieved through the use of an urban growth boundary (UGB). The UGB is an idea gaining in popularity in the United States, especially in association with downtown or core-city revitalization. The basic idea behind the UGB is to adopt a mapped cordon line around an urban area (whether a village, a town, or a city) officially separating it from surrounding open lands, farms, forests, watersheds, parks, and so forth. Urban services (including water, sewer, and schools) are usually prevented from extending beyond the boundary. Doing this in effect creates a greenbelt around the city or town. Development and growth are encouraged in the urbanized area contained within the boundary and are discouraged outside the boundary, in the greenbelt. UGBs are usually adopted for significant periods of time (fifteen to twenty years or longer) to frustrate short-term land speculation around the outside edge of the boundary while encouraging long-term investment within the cordon. UGBs are usually drawn to accommodate forecast growth within the planning period. In communities such as Portland, Oregon, processes have also been implemented for redrawing the boundary to accommodate future expansion beyond the planning period.

Growth-Boundary Goals

Broadly speaking, the aim of the UGB is usually to establish a development pattern that consists

Figure 11.4. San Giminiano in Tuscany, a dense medieval village surrounded by farmland. (Oliver Gillham)

of relatively dense urban islands surrounded by green space. This idea owes much to the "greenbelt town concept" developed by planner Ebenezer Howard at the end of the 1800s—a vision of self-contained towns with distinct boundaries surrounded by farm, forest, and field (see Chapter 12). The greenbelt concept evokes images of New England villages of yore or the hill towns of Tuscany, where dense, medieval villages can still be found surrounded by farmland (see Figure 11.4). Of course, even in Tuscany this pattern has been disrupted, as development has been allowed to crop up outside of these older villages—sometimes through "abusivo," or illegal, disregard of planning laws. But in Tuscany, as elsewhere in Europe, the compact pattern is generally far better preserved than it is in the United States.

Local and County Growth Boundaries

UGBs can be implemented on a local or a regional basis. Local UGBs can be established by an individual municipality by drawing the UGB on land within the municipality's incorporated boundaries. Such an action makes sense only if the incorporated land of the municipality exceeds its primary developed area by some significant margin—for example, a city or township that includes farmland and other undeveloped land as well as other towns or villages within its borders.

A typical example might be Southampton, on New York's Long Island, a township that includes not only the village of Southampton proper but also the communities of Watermill, Quogue, Westhampton Beach, and Bridgehampton as well as undeveloped agricultural land, fields, and forests. Another example is Gaithersburg, Maryland, a city that includes Gaithersburg and such communities as Montgomery Village, Washington Grove, and Kentlands plus some quantities of undeveloped land. In such cases, the municipality could choose to implement one or more UGBs that would act to limit development to prescribed areas around specific villages or town centers.

Large cities that are able to gain control of adjoining lands and towns through annexation are also in a position to consider this type of UGB measure. Houston, Texas, and Albuquerque, New Mexico, are typical of a number of southern and western cities that are continuing to grow through annexation and that could potentially implement UGB type measures as part of that process.

CONCORD AND KEENE, NEW HAMPSHIRE

Despite the advantages that larger cities with annexation powers may have, it is often smaller communities with no options for annexation that have chosen to go the UGB route. Two examples are Concord and Keene in New Hampshire, both of which have established planning programs with UGBs or UGB proxies.

Concord, a city of about thirty-seven thousand, is the state capital of New Hampshire. Concord's UGB has been in place for about a decade, yet it has not yielded the hoped-for results. Although the UGB is tied to both zoning and an urban-services district, development has been allowed to overflow beyond the UGB without any real effort at containment by Concord. On-site wells and septic services are used to circumvent the service district, and zoning has proven ineffective. In the city's current planning to control sprawl, the UGB is viewed as largely irrelevant; the city and its planning consultants have decided to place the emphasis on supporting and developing the city's five village centers.[28]

In Keene, a city of about twenty-three thousand, there is no formal UGB, but the city has made it a matter of policy to contain development within the limits of four state roads that

form the boundaries of Keene's downtown. While the boundary is not regulatory, it has served as a very effective policy deterrent to zoning proposals that would extend commercial zoning beyond the limits of downtown. As a result, Keene is said to have successfully contained sprawl within its own political borders.[29] However, results have been mixed in that new sprawl development has leapfrogged outside of Keene and is flourishing in adjoining municipalities that have no such policies.

Keene's leapfrog experience indicates that UGBs are generally more effective when they cover more than a single municipality. Thus, county-level UGBs have sometimes been viewed as offering a better solution for containing sprawl and directing growth toward existing centers, particularly if county government is relatively strong in a given region (not the case in New Hampshire). Counties typically cover a greater land area than most cities or towns and usually include multiple municipalities within their boundaries.

BOULDER, COLORADO

Boulder, Colorado, is an example of a combined city and county UGB. The city of Boulder is located twenty-seven miles northwest of Denver, at the base of the Rocky Mountains in Boulder County. With ninety-six thousand people, Boulder has a burgeoning high-tech economy augmented by the University of Colorado. There is no strong, effective regional government in the Denver metropolitan area, and as a result, there is little direction to the continuously expanding suburbanization of the Front Range district around Boulder.

Boulder's population more than doubled during the 1950s and 1960s, causing the city to undertake a number of growth-management measures (see Chapter 10). In 1967, the city of Boulder was the first city in the United States to pass a sales tax dedicated to preserving open space, which it used to begin acquiring greenbelt land in the Boulder Valley. In 1970, the city began a joint planning effort with the county that culminated in the Boulder Valley Comprehensive Plan (BVCP) of 1978. The BVCP curtailed the expansion of the city into the surrounding plains by defining a limited city service district. "Urban" services, such as water and sewer systems, could not be extended to proposed developments outside the boundaries of

Figure 11.5. The greenbelt surrounding Boulder, Colorado. (Dom Nozzi)

also controls sprawl by creating a greenbelt of rural land uses around the city comprising some twenty-seven thousand acres (more than twice the size of the city itself) that is jointly controlled by the city and the county through an intergovernmental agreement. Boulder's service area UGB creates a defined urban-rural edge to the city while linking land use and infrastructure planning to provide for rational extension of city services. Rural lands are preserved while development is focused within the city.

The current version of the BVCP was adopted in 1996 by four bodies: the City of Boulder Planning Board, the city council, the county planning commission, and the board of county commissioners. The plan designates what areas within the land surrounding Boulder may be developed over the next fifteen years while also reaffirming the huge rural-preservation area set-aside (see Figure 11.6). Boulder seems to have clung closely to its goals over the years; the boundaries of its service area have remained virtually unchanged since they were initiated in 1978.[30]

the district. Land outside the service district boundary is kept at rural densities and remains under county jurisdiction, creating, in effect, an urban growth boundary and greenbelt around the city (see Figure 11.5).

The 1978 BVCP boundary protects Boulder against development outside the city limits that would put demands on city services without contributing taxes to finance those services. It

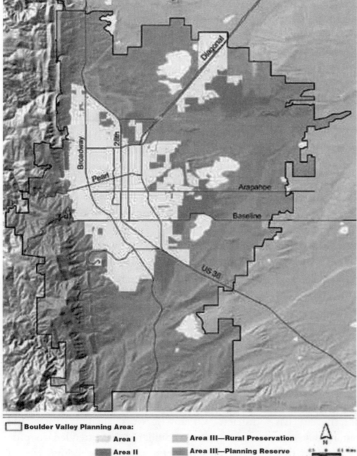

Boulder Valley Planning Area:
- Area I
- Area II
- Area III—Rural Preservation
- Area III—Planning Reserve

Figure 11.6. Map of the greenbelt surrounding Boulder, Colorado.
Source: City of Boulder, Colorado.

LANCASTER COUNTY, PENNSYLVANIA

Another example of local and county UGB initiatives is Lancaster County, Pennsylvania, a county at the heart of the Pennsylvania Dutch country, which contains some of the nation's most scenic and productive farmland. About 30 percent of the county's farmers belong to the Plain Sect community—Amish, Mennonite, and Brethren. Development pressures in Lancaster County have risen steadily over the past forty years. Between 1970 and 1990 alone, county population increased by 32 percent, or about 102,000 people. Counties have relatively little real power over land use in Pennsylvania. Planning and zoning authority generally resides in the cities and townships, of which Lancaster County has forty-one. However, the counties can engage in comprehensive planning and can make nonbinding recommendations.

In 1993, a growth-management proposal drafted by the county as part of a new comprehensive plan had broad enough consensus to become adopted as official policy. The plan called for the creation of "urban and village growth boundaries." County staff had made population estimates for a twenty-year period for each of the cities, towns, and villages and had drawn possible growth boundaries for each community based on estimated land use needs. It was up to the localities to accept the plan, and many of them did. By 1999, twenty-two urban and twelve village growth boundaries had been implemented by amending local comprehensive plans and by coordinating local zoning ordinances and public sewer and water districts—and this despite a survey completed two years earlier that indicated results had so far been uneven.[31] Between 1994 and 1997, about 75 percent of all new residential units were built within the UGBs, while 61 percent of the land developed was outside the boundaries. Part of the unevenness may have had to do with the fact that some communities were still adopting the plan. These programs can take many years to bear fruit, and if local communities continue to adopt the UGB approach, it could still be a success in Lancaster County.

Meanwhile, Lancaster has not been relying solely upon the UGB program to achieve results. The UGB was combined with a land-conservation initiative aimed at purchasing the development rights of farmland in the county. To date, that program has succeeded in preserving 261 farms and over more than twenty-three thousand acres of farmland.[32] Also, thirty-nine of the forty-one towns have used an aggressive program of agricultural large-lot zoning (usually one dwelling unit per twenty-five acres), which prevents easy subdivision of certain large tracts of land into small-lot subdivisions. This demonstrates the value of pursuing more than one approach to smart growth.

Accomplishments of Local and County UGBs

Clearly, local or local and county UGBs can be very helpful in managing growth within a discrete area. If properly designed, this technique can encourage compact development patterns with more outlying land remaining as open space, farmland, or forest. At the same time, this UGB technique can be used to direct growth to desired areas, such as older commercial areas within the district, with existing infrastructure. Boulder seems to be accomplishing both of these aims, resulting in a quite remarkable greenbelt around the city.

Furthermore, by limiting the amount of developable land, a UGB may result in increased land prices within the development cordon, which will influence developers to build at higher densities than they would normally. At some point, depending on the economics of land price and potential revenue stream, this could even lead a given developer to consider parking structures rather than surface parking. Taking up less land with parking is considered by many growth management experts to be better for walking and transit use as well as for aesthetics. This outcome can be further encouraged through the use of zoning controls mandating density and parking design. The local nature of the Boulder type of UGB can mean that it is more flexible and easier to regulate and change than a regional alternative, because only local legislative action is required. Because the UGB is implemented at a local level, it may also be easier for local citizens to become directly involved and invested in the UGB process.

The Downside of Open-Space Conservation

Although land conservation may be popular, it can have several disadvantages. First, while conserving open space can have a positive effect on land values, higher land prices may drive the cost of housing up, making it both more difficult for first-time buyers to access the housing market and more difficult to build affordable housing. Critics of the UGB approach often raise this as an issue. The UGB can restrict the land available for development, effectively driving up market prices. What is true of the UGB is true (although to a lesser degree) of land conservation in general. Taking land off the market restricts the total amount of land available for development in a given region, potentially driving up land prices. Thus, conservation programs need to be coordinated with affordable housing initiatives so that they work for the community as a whole.

Second, when aggressive conservation programs are enacted locally, higher land prices and more restrictions may simply drive development into adjoining communities. People seeking less expensive housing and businesses seeking lower overhead simply may vote with their feet. Both of these effects may be occurring in the Boulder area. According to some sources, housing prices in Boulder County are some 13 percent higher than in nearby Denver and 24 percent higher than in Fort Collins.[33] Boulder is addressing this disparity by making affordable housing a top agenda item in its current planning initiatives. However, this won't solve Boulder's other problem: the leapfrogging of sprawl outside of Boulder's greenbelt—not only in other parts of Boulder County but also along the rest of the Front Range. By way of example, the population of the nearby town of Superior soared from 255 in 1990 to 3,377 in 1996.[34] Such issues raise the question of regional urban growth boundaries, such as those that have been used effectively in Oregon. (This type of boundary is discussed in Chapter 14.)

On the positive side, if the land acquired for conservation provides for public access and recreation, then it can be available to the whole community, rich and poor alike, to use as a common resource, enhancing everyone's quality of life. For example, although condominiums facing the Boston Public Garden may sell at prices only the very wealthy can afford, the garden itself is a welcome oasis available to the whole Boston region. The same can be said of Central Park in New York or of the publicly accessible lands in Boulder's greenbelt (see Figure 11.7).

Figure 11.7. Setting aside the land for Central Park created substantial benefits for Manhattan and the whole New York Metropolitan region. (Alex S. MacLean/Landslides)

Preserving Open Space in Summary

Open space has become an increasingly important concern in many metropolitan areas across the United States as development has continued to spread outward, making open countryside ever more distant. Open land preservation is therefore at the top of many communities' lists of smart growth measures. The principal goals of land conservation programs include preserving community, providing for public open space, and preserving the environment. The two main methods of preserving open land have been implementing open space conservation programs and setting limits on outward urban expansion. Open-space conservation programs can be achieved through a variety of means, including regulatory controls and the purchase of land or development rights. Growth boundaries can be put in place at local, county, or regional levels.

Despite laudable goals and widespread popularity, land preservation programs may have unwanted consequences. Moving to larger land requirements per unit can raise housing costs, even while preserving existing agricultural uses. Taking land out of development can do the same thing. Community preservation shouldn't mean preserving the appearance of a community at the expense of pricing out the people who live there. Clearly, land preservation programs need to be coupled with plans to provide affordable housing to insure a healthy mix of income levels. This is an issue in almost every community that is wrestling with these types of measures. Though difficult to solve, it is important, because a community is the people that live there at least as much, if not more, than it is how it looks.

Although impacts to housing cost cannot be ignored, public open space remains a vitally important part of any community and any metropolitan region—for all of the people who live there. We have only to think once again of the example of Central Park. What would Manhattan be like today if no one had thought to put aside the large expanse of land required for Central Park? The nation's rapidly expanding metropolitan areas are in the same position now. These regions are far more spread out than Manhattan, encompassing thousands of square miles of suburban development, but this simply means that, to have the same effect, the tracts of land to be preserved will need to be concomitantly larger. They will need to become Central Parks on a regional scale to have the impact required to offset the vast horizontal expanse of current development patterns. At the same time, communities and regions may have to work together to offset the impacts to housing cost that necessary land preservation programs may entail.

CHAPTER 12

Changing Development Patterns

Another way to ensure more open space in the nation's future is to build on less of the land, thus preserving more field, forest, and farmland. This means making changes to the pattern of development that has characterized suburbanization since World War II. In particular, it means considering two of the smart growth measures discussed in Chapter 10:

- Compact mixed-use developments amenable to walking and transit
- Revitalization of older downtowns, inner-ring suburbs, and rundown commercial areas.

Compact developments would, in theory, build on less of the land where new development on greenfield sites is deemed necessary (that is, on undeveloped land in open countryside). Revitalization of older urban and suburban areas could reduce pressure on open land completely by directing new growth to abandoned or underused sites in already urbanized areas with existing infrastructure, including brownfield and greyfield sites. (Brownfield sites are urban sites that have been previously built on but that are currently unused or underused, such as abandoned industrial properties. Greyfield sites are suburban sites that have been previously built on but that are similarly abandoned or underused, such as older shopping malls or surplus airfields.) Finally, directing future development into these new molds can help reduce automobile dependence if viable mass transit is made an integral part of these alternative building patterns (see Chapter 13).

Compact, Mixed-Use Developments

Building on less land while emphasizing transportation choice are two of the fundamental ideas behind compact, mixed-use developments. This does not necessarily mean building fewer units or less interior square feet per unit but,

rather, building a similar amount on much less land while leaving the remainder open. The ultimate vision is intimately linked with the greenbelt concept discussed in Chapter 11, a vision of discrete villages, towns, and cities that are clearly demarcated and surrounded by green space.

Ebenezer Howard's Garden Cities

Compact development is not a new idea. It dates back to ancient walled cities and towns surrounded by field and forest. But our contemporary ideas about compact development owe more to the early twentieth century and the work of Ebenezer Howard, the inspirational planner of England's greenbelt towns. In his famous book *Garden Cities of Tomorrow,* Ebenezer Howard set forth a vision of a decentralized alternative to the big, sprawling industrial cities of the late nineteenth century. Rejecting the emerging suburbs as a poor compromise, Howard proposed to replace the uncontrolled expansion of the industrial cities with a series of basically self-sufficient cities of about six thousand acres and thirty thousand people each (see Figure 12.1). Each new city would contain its own employment centers, residential neighborhoods, and shopping districts together with an ample supply of parks and other public open space. In the words of Lewis Mumford:

> Against the purposeless mass congestion of the big metropolis, with its slums, its industrial pollution, and its lengthening journeys to work, Howard opposed a more organic kind of city: a city limited from the beginning in numbers and in density of habitation, limited in area, organized to carry on all the essential functions of an urban community, business, industry, adminis-

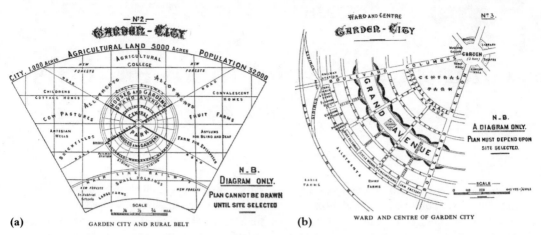

Figure 12.1. (a) Ebenezer Howard's Garden City and greenbelt. (b) Sector of Ebenezer Howard's Garden City. (Courtesy of the Town and Country Planning Association.)

tration, education; equipped too with a sufficient number of public parks and private gardens to guard health and keep the environment sweet. To achieve and express the reunion of city and country, Howard surrounded his new city with a permanent agricultural greenbelt.[1]

Although Howard's work had wide influence, inspiring many planned communities that followed—especially in the United Kingdom—his vision of the discrete city, contained by a green wall of farmland, was quickly eclipsed in the United States by the automobile-driven suburban revolution. And even though some of Howard's planning ideas became incorporated in the American suburb, they have been quite watered down. Although the occasional greenbelt can be found in the nation's metropolitan areas, it is hard indeed to find anything like the true, self-contained greenbelt town that Ebenezer Howard envisioned.

However watered down Howard's town planning vision may have become in the United States, the greenbelt town concept has never been forgotten. In his book *Toward New Towns for America,* Clarence Stein (the visionary behind Radburn, New Jersey) proposed a series of "regional towns" for the nation based on Howard's ideas. Another brief resurgence of the greenbelt community concept occurred in the new town planning ideas of the 1960s and 1970s, and fragments of Howard's vision can be found in the communities of Columbia, Maryland, and Reston, Virginia, which date from that

era. Within the last ten years, the works of Ebenezer Howard have emerged from history once again, this time with redoubled support, in the works of the New Urbanist movement.

Compact Developments and New Urbanism

In contemporary times, almost any conversation about new compact developments is likely to turn into a discussion of New Urbanism. This is because many of the widely cited examples of these new communities are also considered to be New Urbanist projects. Like smart growth, New Urbanism can mean different things to different people. For some, the term *New Urbanism* means postmodern or neotraditional new developments, such as Seaside and Celebration in Florida (see Figure 12.2). For others, *New Urbanism* is a broader, more encompassing term that applies to whole metropolitan regions while embracing most of the goals and measures of smart growth. As Peter Calthorpe and William Fulton have written in their book *The Regional City:* "New Urbanism is best known (and often stereotyped) for its work at the neighborhood and town scale. . . . Too often, New Urbanism is misinterpreted simply as a conservative movement to recapture the past while ignoring the issues of our time."[2] New Urbanism is, or at least has become, something far broader and more complex than that, supported by a wide array of different professions and interest groups.

The New Urbanist movement started in the 1980s with a small group of architects who were interested in developing more compact, livable

Figure 12.2. Seaside in Walton County, Florida, planned by Duany/Plater-Zyberk—the first neotraditional town plan. (Alex S. MacLean/Landslides)

communities. That group has developed into today's two-thousand-member organization known as the Congress for the New Urbanism (CNU). The CNU describes its mission as follows:

> Based on development patterns used prior to World War II, the New Urbanism seeks to reintegrate the components of modern life—housing, workplace, shopping and recreation—into compact, pedestrian-friendly neighborhoods linked by transit and set in a larger regional open-space framework.[3]

In following this prescription, the CNU has helped many communities recognize the barriers to alternative development presented by their existing zoning and subdivision regulations. Planners and architects within this movement have proposed rules for creating anew compact, "traditional," mixed-use neighborhoods and "towns" at moderate densities that lend themselves to walking and transit while leaving surrounding green space intact. In these respects and others, they follow the tradition of Ebenezer Howard. Pioneering efforts of the movement have included the aforementioned Seaside in Florida (planned in 1982) and Kentlands in Maryland (planned in 1988). Other communities include Windsor and Celebration in Florida. A few of the new "sustainable" projects include Civano, outside of Tucson, and Prairie Crossings, outside of Chicago.

Architects Andres Duany, Elizabeth Plater-Zyberk, and Peter Calthorpe are three of the founders and leading lights of the New Urbanist movement. Much of their thinking and some of their projects can be found in *New Urbanism,*

edited by Peter Katz, and *Suburban Nation,* written by Duany and Plater-Zyberk with Jeff Speck. *The Next American Metropolis* by Peter Calthorpe and *The Regional City* by Peter Calthorpe and William Fulton provide insightful information about the intentions of this rapidly spreading movement as does *The Charter for the New Urbanism,* published by the CNU. Although the movement's intentions are sweeping, questions have been raised from time to time about how much actual change has been accomplished by CNU when the built projects are reviewed, mostly because many early New Urbanist plans and projects were designed for greenfield sites. Possibly in response to such criticism, the New Urbanist emphasis has changed in recent years toward infill development in existing urbanized areas. Thus, the New Urbanist movement now encompasses both compact developments on greenfield sites and infill development on urban brownfield sites. To quote CNU: "The leading proponents of New Urbanism believe that infill development should be given priority over new development in order to revitalize city centers and limit sprawl."[4] In actuality, both paradigms are pertinent to effecting a change in post–World War II patterns of suburbanization.

Traditional Neighborhood Developments and Transit-Oriented Developments

The New Urbanists introduced two basic concepts to describe aspects of their compact planned communities: traditional neighborhood developments and transit-oriented developments.

TRADITIONAL NEIGHBORHOOD DEVELOPMENTS

Traditional neighborhood developments (TNDs) typically are new projects, usually on greenfield sites, that are more compact than the usual contemporary subdivision and emphasize walking rather than car dependence, mixed use (where possible), narrower roads, and common greens and squares. Architecture is an important element of these projects. Most strive to create a "traditional" village neighborhood flavor by designing in pre–World War II housing styles, relegating the garage to the back of the lot, restoring street-focused front porches, and placing neohistorical houses on small lots, such as

Figure 12.3. Kentlands in Gaithersburg, Maryland, planned by Duany/Plater-Zyberk. (Alex S. MacLean/Landslides)

those found in older village centers and street-car suburbs. TND developments generally frown upon the cul-de-sac because it inhibits social contact while creating obstacles for the free flow of pedestrians and traffic. TNDs are the trade-mark of the works of Duany and Plater-Zyberk and their followers. Typical examples of this work are Seaside and Windsor in Florida and Kentlands in Maryland (see Figure 12.3). Celebration, a new community near Disney World developed by Disney with Cooper, Robertson as planners and Robert A. M. Stern as architect, also follows the TND mold (see Figure 12.4).

Despite their innovations, TND communities have been accused of simply promoting a new kind of sprawl or even of putting "a smiley face on sprawl." Several reasons are usually given for this criticism. First, TNDs generally are not infill developments (thus, they consume open land, even if they theoretically are using less of it); second, TNDs usually are not purposefully set

Figure 12.4. Celebration, a new community near Disney World in Florida by Cooper, Robertson & Partners with Robert A. M. Stern. (Alex S. MacLean/Landslides)

within a regional planning framework; third, their target markets tend to be the same socioeconomic groups that buy other suburban homes (few provide any affordable housing); and fourth, although they are more walkable than other sub-urban developments, they are still connected to the automobile as the primary transport system outside the community.

Also, despite the goals of the movement, few of these new communities have managed to set aside significant greenbelt open space around them. Kentlands, for example, fills up almost its entire site, which is bordered by arterial roads, a shopping center, and other suburban communities. Furthermore, the built examples of these developments are mostly residential and have yet to achieve a full mix of different uses. Finally, despite narrower streets, it is not clear that total paved surface area and runoff have been reduced relative to standard postwar subdivisions because, in Kentlands and in other developments, a secondary alleyway system is used to provide car access to the backs of building lots. It is important to note that some of these issues have little to do with the planners and designers of the projects in question. Developers, banks, and local regulations place many requirements on these developments, some of which may conflict with the planning goals of the project.

Despite these concerns, these innovative TND developments so far have provided a refreshing change from the classical sprawl development that pervades so much of the nation's countryside. They intentionally bring back the elements of traditional towns that many people favor and that have been lost in the modern subdivision. Uses are mixed to the extent possible, promoting walking and cycling, while the design guidelines of the roadway system have also been overhauled—excessive roadway widths are narrowed, and a greater emphasis is placed on such urban design considerations as pedestrian scale. People have at last been offered a real choice in suburban living, as Duany and company have said in their book, *Suburban Nation*. Ideally, however, the innovative zoning used to create these communities should be combined with land conservation measures if the true greenbelt town vision is to be achieved.

TRANSIT-ORIENTED DEVELOPMENTS

The concept of transit-oriented developments (TODs) has been largely pioneered by Peter

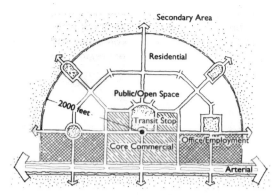

Figure 12.5. Diagram of typical transit-oriented district.
Source: Peter Calthorpe, *The Next American Metropolis: Ecology, Community and the American Dream* (New York: Princeton Architectural Press, 1993).

Calthorpe. TODs are functionally much different from TNDs in that they are focused specifically on transit and are meant to function within a regional framework. A diagrammatic TOD has a mixed-use core and is circumscribed by an average walking distance of two thousand feet to the transit station, which is usually at the heart of the planned community (see Figure 12.5). Most major streets and pathways are oriented to provide access to the local transit station, which forms the center of a higher-density, mixed-use nucleus within the TOD. In this respect, TODs are not so different from some of the older railroad suburbs, such as Forest Hills Gardens in New York, which is similarly organized, or parts of the Main Line in Philadelphia.

Like the earlier railroad and streetcar suburbs, TODs are by their nature located either on the trunk line of a regional transit system or on a feeder bus line providing no more than a ten-minute ride from the transit trunk line.[5] Thus, they are usually geared toward fitting a regional strategy of similar planned transit nodes—either new, on greenfield sites, or as infill projects—into existing urban and suburban areas. The majority of Calthorpe's planned TODs have been for infill sites in existing neighborhoods, and his clearly stated priority is that existing infill areas and planned-growth zones should be built first before considering new towns. But, in his book *The Next American Metropolis,* Calthorpe sets forth criteria for creating freestanding new TOD towns: "This type of site should be planned as a 'satellite' New Town, with a strong jobs/housing balance and a greenbelt separation between existing communities."[6] This description provides a fairly accurate match to Ebenezer Howard's Garden City concept.

Calthorpe's efforts in Oregon included planning for a freestanding TOD called Orenco Station, which is located on a greenfield site in Portland's "Silicon Forest" (see Figure 12.6).

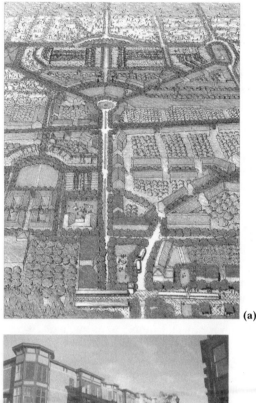

(a)

(b)

Figure 12.6. (a) Early perspective drawing of Orenco Station. (b) Orenco Station town center and multiplex housing as built.
Sources: Peter Calthorpe and William Fulton, *The Regional City* (Washington, D.C.: Island Press, 2001); Metro, *Getting There: Metro's Regional Plan in Brief* (Portland, Oreg.: Metro, 1999).

Located directly on Portland's Westside MAX line, much of the 190-acre Orenco Station project has been built out by other architects, mostly in conformance with the initial Calthorpe plan. The project has won awards from groups as diverse as 1,000 Friends of Oregon, the National Association of Home Builders, and the U.S. Department of Transportation. The project includes a wide variety of housing types, from loft apartments over retail to town homes to single-family homes on small lots. The town center, located near the MAX station, includes twenty-five thousand square feet of retail space and thirty thousand square feet of office space.[7] Missing, however, is the greenbelt part of the concept. The development seems to extend to its site boundaries, abutting other suburban neighborhoods. Also, the transit center is located several blocks from the town center, deviating from Calthorpe's ideal diagram.

Transit Villages

Although not necessarily a New Urbanist idea, transit villages are quite similar to TODs, and sometimes the terms are used interchangeably. The main differences are that, with some notable exceptions, transit villages are generally more ad hoc in nature and almost all of them are located on rail rather than bus lines. These villages have not generally been planned to conform to a prototype replete with detailed physical design guidelines, as have Calthorpe's TODs. These villages also may be higher in density than most TOD examples.[8] Whereas Calthorpe recommends residential densities of between 7 and 15 dwelling units per acre, transit villages can have recommended densities ranging from 12 to 60 dwelling units per acre. This doesn't necessarily mean high-rise development, however. It is estimated that Howard's garden cities were built to average densities of 12 units per acre. Row houses have a typical density of about 36 units per acre, while mid-rise apartments can reach 160 units per acre.[9]

In most other respects, the transit village concept is very close to the TOD idea. In their book *Transit Villages in the 21st Century*, Michael Bernick and Robert Cervero describe a typical transit village:

> At its core, the transit village is a compact, mixed-use community, centered

around the transit station that, by design, invites residents, workers, and shoppers to drive their cars less and ride mass transit more. The transit village extends roughly a quarter mile from a transit station, a distance that can be covered in about 5 minutes by foot. The centerpiece of the transit village is the transit station itself and the civic and public spaces that surround it. The transit station is what connects village residents and workers to the rest of the region.[10]

The quarter-mile distance is slightly more than half the radius recommended by Calthorpe, but it is a standard planning factor for transit station walking distance. Otherwise, the description given for the transit village is quite similar not only to the TOD but also to many early railroad suburbs, such as Scarsdale, New York, and Shaker Heights near Cleveland.

Bernick and Cervero point to the series of satellite cities built around Stockholm, Sweden, starting in 1950 as some of the earliest and best post–World War II examples of totally planned transit villages. It is claimed that these transit-oriented planned communities have helped make Stockholm a "transit metropolis." Rather than spread out on roadway networks, Stockholm elected to build a series of outlying Ebenezer Howard–like new towns of between forty thousand and one hundred thousand people each. Each new town includes residential, retail, and office space, and each is clearly focused on the Tunnelbana regional rail system. About half the residents of the Stockholm metropolitan area live in these new towns. On average, for all of the new towns, about two-thirds of all daily work trips are by transit, walking, or bicycle, with about 55 percent of all work trips on transit. For the Stockholm region, the total mode split to transit is just over 40 percent. That compares to about a 6 percent mode share for transit in U.S. metropolitan areas.[11]

Closer to home, Vancouver in British Columbia provides another good example of transit village development. Following a decision to halt major roadway building in the 1970s, Vancouver built a light-rail transit system called Skytrain that was completed in the late 1986. The eighteen-mile line has undergone three expansions since it opened and now carries more than forty

Figure 12.7. Skytrain spurred the development of a series of transit village or nodes in the Vancouver, British Columbia, metro area. (Peter Newman and Jeffrey Kenworthy, *Sustainability and Cities: Overcoming Automobile Dependence* [Washington, D.C.: Island Press, 1999])

million passengers per year. A new twelve-mile line is currently under construction.

Since the original line was built, land around many of the stations has been rezoned for higher-density, mixed-use development. The result has been the development of a series of successful transit villages, including New Westminster, Metrotown, and others. New Westminster, about fourteen miles from downtown Vancouver, clusters high- and low-rise residential, office, and retail development around a public market adjacent to the rail station. Metrotown, about nine miles out, is a similar mixed-use node that emphasizes walking and bicycling to the central Skytrain station (see Figure 12.7).[12]

Bernick and Cervero mention the San Francisco Bay area and the Washington, D.C., metro area as two places where examples of U.S. transit villages can be found. One example in the Bay Area is Pleasant Hill, in Contra Costa County, on the east side of San Francisco Bay. When the Pleasant Hill BART (Bay Area Rapid Transit) station opened during the early 1970s, it was located in the middle of a typical expanse of postwar suburban development. Things remained largely unchanged for nearly a decade, until BART and representatives of the county and local communities began an aggressive effort to transform the area around the station into a higher-density, mixed-use complex of office buildings, multifamily housing, and retail. Although much remains to be completed, the vision of higher-density, mixed-use development around the Pleasant Hill station had come a considerable distance by the 1990s, with more than

1,800 units of multifamily housing, nearly a million square feet of office space, a 250-room hotel, and a four-hundred-thousand-square-foot retail and entertainment center. Problems remain, with some large parcels sitting empty and a large arterial road hindering pedestrian access from some parts of the site, but the plan is still being built out, and it is hoped that these problems can be overcome.[13]

Washington, D.C. has also had some success in developing higher-density, mixed-use centers around transit stations, including Ballston and Rosslyn in Virginia and Bethesda, Silver Spring, and other centers along the Washington Metro's Red Line in Maryland. Bethesda is actually a multimodal interchange, where a series of bus lines join together in a subterranean plaza above a Washington Metropolitan Area Transit Authority (WMATA) Metrorail station. Above this is an active pedestrian plaza surrounded by medium- to high-density, mixed-use development (see Figure 12.8). WMATA and Montgomery County worked diligently together to make this project happen. When Metrorail arrived in 1984, Montgomery County rezoned the metro station district to FAR 6 from FAR 4 in exchange for developer contributions to public open space and other amenities while developing transit-

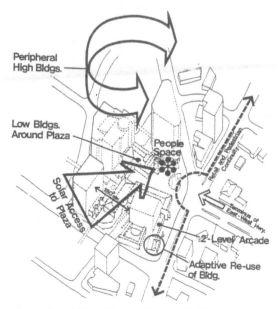

Figure 12.8. Urban Design diagram for Bethesda Center by the Maryland National Capital Park and Planning Commission.
Source: Douglas R. Porter, *Managing Growth in America's Communities* (Washington, D.C.: Island Press, 1997).

supportive urban design guidelines for the project. As Bernick and Cervero relate: "These initiatives paid-off handsomely, giving rise to one of the most pleasant, pedestrian-friendly suburban transit nodes in the country."[14] More than 7 million square feet of office space, 2.3 million square feet of retail and restaurant space, five thousand housing units, a hotel and convention center, and thirty-nine thousand jobs are contained within an area of less than square mile surrounding the station.[15]

These are a few of many examples of transit villages completed, under construction, or planned across the nation. Others include a series of transit-based developments in Los Angeles County and San Diego as well as a series of efforts in the New York metropolitan area. New Jersey also has been working to encourage growth around transit stations and in 1994 published guidelines for communities to use in planning for mixed-use development around these stations.[16]

Regional and Local Implications

Compact development can be planned either locally or regionally. TNDs can be achieved in any community willing to alter its zoning bylaws and subdivision regulations to accept this type of project. TODs and transit village developments can be implemented locally, as long as there is an existing transit system on which to focus development. If not, then there may be a need for a regional or state component to the planning effort, in which a local community becomes a party to a wider effort to implement or restore transit service throughout all or part of a given metropolitan region. TODs and transit villages in Vancouver, San Francisco, Portland, Los Angeles, San Diego, and Washington have all been part of wider metropolitan transportation efforts. Skytrain was the impetus for developing Vancouver's transit villages. In San Francisco, the regional BART and commuter rail systems have provided the framework for TOD and transit village planning in the Bay Area. Similarly, in the nation's capital, Metrorail transit and regional commuter rail systems have formed the basis for developing mixed-use nodes in outlying suburban areas of Maryland and Virginia.

Compact Developments in Summary

Compact communities, whether developed on greenfield sites or as new nodes in existing urban and suburban areas, offer an opportunity to conserve open space while at the same time promoting walking and transit use and a sense of community and place. These types of developments hold great promise in achieving both goals. Compact developments can and have been implemented locally. But where broader transit and open-space issues are concerned, placing these developments in a regional planning setting may be highly desirable.

Obstacles to these types of projects continue to be outmoded zoning bylaws together with development and financing standards. Community opposition to increased density for a variety of reasons (for example, real estate values and traffic congestion) also can pose a formidable stumbling block to implementing these endeavors. Education and a continuing supply of successful built examples are needed to promote these types of projects.

Revitalizing Older Downtowns and Inner-Ring Suburbs

Compact infill developments such as those described above are clearly linked to continuing efforts at revitalizing the nation's downtown and older suburban areas. Urban transit villages and infill TODs are urban revitalization projects in and of themselves. Arguably, creating incentives for new development in existing urban and suburban centers, thereby reducing the demand for outward expansion, could be one of the keys to preserving more open space and reducing other impacts of suburbanization, such as traffic congestion and air pollution.

Many of the nation's older cities, towns, and suburbs still possess the characteristics that kept people living there by choice, even while others were leaving. These places frequently offer good mass transit and rail systems as well as a wealth of older architecture in a living environment that just can't be matched in modern suburbia—environments that even new, neotraditional suburbs can't match. Furthermore, older cities are home to an increasingly rich mixture of diverse groups, and most of their downtowns offer shops, museums, parks, and theaters, all within walking distance. They also offer special, treasured features that simply don't exist anywhere else. The Washington Mall can't be found in suburbia, nor can Savannah's famous public squares, San Francisco's Presidio, Baltimore's Inner Har-

Figure 12.9. Charles River basin and Esplanade in Boston, Massachusetts. (Alex S. MacLean/Landslides)

bor, or Boston's Charles River Reservation (see Figure 12.9).

In the past decade, a number of older American cities actually have seen a rebound in population after years of steady declines, although the resurgence may be due more to foreign immigration than to suburbanites moving back in.[17] Whatever the reason for the change in population trends, a new respect exists across the country for the historic character and cultural quality of older downtown areas. If these tendencies can be nurtured, these older urban centers may represent the nation's best prospect for creating compact, walkable, mixed-use, transit-friendly communities. On many urban sites, such required development infrastructure as streets, water, sewer, major utilities, and transit systems are already in place, unlike most at greenfield sites.

The major opportunities presented by older cities, towns, and suburbs generally fall into three categories:

- Downtown and Main Street
- Brownfield sites
- Greyfield sites.

Downtown and Main Street

Revitalizing downtown is certainly not a new idea. It has been around for a long time, in various incarnations.[18] For nearly the past twenty-five years, the commercial areas of many of the nation's older cities and towns have been the target of intensive efforts aimed at restoration and revitalization of existing built resources. These efforts include whole districts of large cities as well as smaller urban areas and village Main Streets.

CITY DISTRICTS

In many urban areas, the flight of industry abandoned entire districts of completely reusable industrial buildings, many of which would be too costly to build today. During the 1950s and 1960s, many cities simply demolished many of these buildings to make way for development that sometimes never arrived. Meanwhile, in other cities, grassroots movements were quietly transforming whole neighborhoods, such as Lower Manhattan's garment manufacturing district, into new residential and mixed-use communities (see Chapter 3). When the results of those efforts became apparent, the idea caught on rapidly across the nation, often becoming inculcated into formal planning programs.

In Denver, a twenty-five-block area of railroad-era warehouses and commercial buildings known as Lower Downtown is undergoing a planned transformation similar to the metamorphosis of New York's SoHo. After falling into decline and going through a "blitzkrieg of demolitions" during the 1970s, Denver's Lower Downtown district was rezoned during the 1980s with preservation and adaptive reuse in mind.[19] Since then (with the help of involved citizen and business groups, creative developers, historic preservation groups, and a proactive city government), the district has been transformed into a lively mixed-use, residential district. Vacancy rates have fallen from 40 percent to just 10 percent as $75 million in private investment has poured into this area now known as LoDo.[20] In downtown Denver today, $1 billion in residential construction is under way. And between 1995 and 1998, 1,334 apartments were being built or converted, much of it sparked by the adaptive reuse of historic loft buildings in Lower Downtown and nearby historic Larimer Square.[21]

This same model has been successfully followed in many other U.S. cities, including Boston, Seattle, Birmingham, and the Twin Cities. In Boston, starting in the 1960s and 1970s, private developers began to rehabilitate many of the older wharf and industrial buildings along the waterfront, transforming them into residential, restaurant, and office use. As a result, the waterfront has become a vibrant upscale, mixed-use district that still retains the masonry and heavy timber character of the old mercantile and industrial waterfront. Since then, multiple blocks of underused and vacant industrial loft

Figure 12.10. Rehabilitated mill buildings along the Merrimack River in Lowell, Massachusetts. (Alex S. MacLean/Landslides)

buildings in Boston's Leather Manufacturing and Fort Point Channel Districts near South Station have been transformed into a mix of residential, office, and retail uses. This process is continuing in other parts of the city.

Recently in Cincinnati, Ohio, ten older loft buildings were successfully converted to residential use, with five more buildings undergoing renovation and two more in development.[22] These trends have caused Cincinnati's downtown residential population to rise rapidly, exceeding projections by nearly 40 percent.[23] Industrial mill buildings also have been the targets of reuse efforts in many cities. In Lowell, Massachusetts, with the help of proactive state and city governments, thousands of square feet of former industrial mill buildings have been recycled into office, residential, and museum use (see Figure 12.10). In North Adams, Massachusetts, a huge former mill complex has been recycled into a highly successful museum of contemporary art, which has become a catalyst for regional revitalization.

Although these older multistory industrial buildings generally are not suited to modern manufacturing, they provide flexible space that is amenable to any number of alternate uses, including housing, office, and high-tech uses. Some are even being recycled into server space for Internet operations. They also make ideal incubator space for new start-up companies. Furthermore, these spaces sometimes even possess their own sources of power, such as water-driven turbines. In many U.S. cities, these older industrial buildings are being transformed into vibrant neighborhoods, where people can walk to take care of most daily errands.

SMALL CITIES

Like some of the nation's core cities, many smaller urban centers in metropolitan areas have been neglected and allowed to decay as suburbanization has gradually surrounded them. Auto-friendly commercial strip shopping centers, office parks, and shopping malls have sprung up outside of town while the older downtown shopping streets fill with vacant storefronts. Even as some of these centers continue to decline, there have been some exciting accomplishments in such places as Newburyport, Massachusetts, and South Norwalk, Connecticut. In these communities and many others, downtown buildings have been restored and rehabilitated for new uses, including new shops, offices, restaurants, and housing. Local streets have been rebuilt with new landscaping, paving, and lighting, bringing these older commercial cores back to life as vibrant mixed-use centers that are compact, walkable, and amenable to mass transit.

Newburyport is an early example of fixing up downtown instead of tearing it down. A historic seaport village north of Boston, Newburyport comprises one of the best collections of early nineteenth-century Federal-style architecture in New England. By the 1960s, Newburyport had fallen on hard times. The city's downtown and waterfront were falling apart, and nearly half of the older buildings had been demolished to make way for a planned suburban-style shopping center.

This widespread destruction provoked a heated debate in the community. As a result, the political landscape changed and the Newburyport Redevelopment Authority changed direction, turning from demolition toward saving what remained of its downtown (see Figure 12.11). The Newburyport Redevelopment Authority got its downtown listed on the National Register of Historic Places in 1971 and began qualifying for historic preservation grants and tax credits in addition to the urban renewal funds that were now directed toward saving the city instead of erasing it. It was an elaborate and groundbreaking public-private enterprise. Public funds were used to create historic brick-paved streetscapes and pedestrian plazas with period lighting and sumptuous landscaping. This public investment leveraged millions of private dollars that restored Newburyport's historic buildings. The result is stunning even today, decades later.

South Norwalk, Connecticut, is another good example of bringing Main Street back to

Figure 12.11. (a) Abandoned historic buildings in Newburyport, Massachusetts, before renovation. (Paul McGinley) (b) Renovated downtown Newburyport. (Phokion Karas)

Figure 12.12. (a) Streetscape improvements in Norwalk, Connecticut. (Oliver Gillham)(b) Renovated buildings in Norwalk, Connecticut. (Oliver Gillham)

life. South Norwalk is an older industrial center near Long Island Sound. By the late 1970s, surrounding Fairfield County had become fully suburbanized and many of the industries and stores that comprised downtown South Norwalk had moved out. An earlier urban renewal plan had cleared several blocks of the commercial district, and what remained was an assortment of disheveled and abandoned buildings. However, underneath the grime and decay was a handsome collection of 1870s commercial buildings, including a few rare remaining examples of cast iron architecture in Connecticut.

Like Newburyport, the Norwalk Redevelopment Agency decided to stand their previous thinking on its head and try to restore rundown commercial and industrial buildings that were driving people away. They placed a two-block area of the city on the National Register of Historic Places and went on to use many of the same formulas that had worked in Newburyport, putting in place a matrix of public improvements to serve as the formwork for private rehabilitation of South Norwalk's historic buildings. Then they went even further. They converted a former lock works (an industrial

brownfield site) into an aquarium and created a state heritage park along the waterfront, recycling an old landfill (another brownfield site) into a river edge park. From a threatening, abandoned environment, South Norwalk has been transformed into a lively retail and restaurant district supported by an aquarium and a cluster of cultural attractions that have become major regional draws (see Figure 12.12).

VILLAGE MAIN STREETS

Many smaller towns and older villages have fallen prey to the same forces that have challenged the nation's cities, both large and small. The book *Changing Places* by Richard Moe (president of the National Trust for Historic Preservation) and Carter Wilkie presents a series of encouraging case studies, including those of Chippewa Falls, Wisconsin, and Franklin, Tennessee.

Chippewa Falls fell victim to the same exodus of manufacturing and competition from suburban retail that has hurt many older downtowns. The town joined the State of Wisconsin's Main Street program in 1988, a local self-help effort guided by state and national expertise from sources such as the National Trust's Main Street Center. The Main Street Center has assisted in many local efforts, providing technical assistance that has attracted investments totaling more than $15 billion spread over 1,600 communities nationwide.[24] Chippewa Falls used the program's expertise to help launch a grassroots campaign, pulling downtown businesses and property owners together to form a local business improvement district, which raised funds to manage and improve the downtown district. Together with public funds from local, state, and federal sources and loan funds from local banks and investors, Chippewa Falls has made real progress. By 1996, Chippewa Falls Main Street had attracted eight-nine new businesses and 621 new jobs downtown. More than a hundred buildings had been renovated, and 95 percent of storefronts were occupied. Nearly three hundred people now live downtown, with one hundred of these living in apartments above stores and offices, making for pedestrian traffic day and night on Main Street.[25]

Franklin, Tennessee, is a historic rural town about fifteen miles outside Nashville. Since 1980, the population of Franklin has doubled due to rapid suburbanization spreading out from Nashville. Yet Franklin has managed to preserve the historic quality of its downtown district while remaining competitive with nearby suburban retail centers, by using the influx of money from suburbanization to fix up its downtown rather than allow investment go to new strip malls and development outside of downtown. It has done this by working hard and getting an early start. Franklin started revitalizing its ailing downtown during the late 1970s, just as the wave of suburbanization was moving outward toward the town. Local citizens sought advice from the National Trust for Historic Preservation's Main Street Center in the 1980s and soon afterward formed the Downtown Franklin Association. The association worked hard to attract public and private funds to restore downtown streetscape and building facades. As Moe and Wilkie have written: "The result is one of the most appealing Main Streets in the South."[26] Because of these efforts, Franklin is unique in an area of increasing suburban sprawl and country and western theme parks. Like those of Chippewa Falls, Franklin's first floors are now well leased with retail and many upper floors have been converted to residential use. The quality of the downtown environment is unique enough in its region that it actually draws spillover customers from a huge shopping mall nearby.[27]

Brownfield Sites

Perhaps the greatest promise for the future of many of the nation's older manufacturing cities is the multitude of brownfield sites that they har-

bor. These are former industrial areas or other underutilized or abandoned sites that can present large tracts of promising development lands. Such properties often come with low levels of contamination, which can create obstacles to development. But, as former industrial sites, many brownfields are also supported by their own infrastructure, alleviating the need to extend new sewer, water, utility, and communications lines as is required for a greenfield site—open forest or farmland outside of town. The flight of industry not only created innovative reuse opportunities for many former industrial mill and loft buildings but also opened up large multi-acre brownfield sites in many cities, often on waterfronts with sweeping vistas and parkland potentials. These opportunities continue to unfold in industrial cities across the nation.

Although the waterfront sites are some of the most spectacular, they are far from being the only brownfield opportunities. Such former industrial sites as abandoned rail yards and factories cut large swaths through many cities, and opening these areas for new development can hold great promise for transforming whole sections of cities. Because of this potential, many states and municipalities have taken a proactive approach to cleaning up these sites so that they can become new development opportunities.

In 1997, the federal government announced the National Brownfields Partnership, which committed the federal government to make $300 million in investments and provide $165 million in loan guarantees to communities with brownfield sites, principally through the U.S. Environmental Protection Agency (EPA) and the Department of Housing and Urban Development (HUD).[28] That same year, new tax legislation was passed that provided an incentive for brownfield redevelopment. With the tax incentive, environmental cleanup costs for brownfield properties became fully deductible in the year in which they are incurred, rather than having to be capitalized over many years, making it easier for development groups to bear the up-front costs of site cleanup. Since its inception, the brownfields program has provided more than $162 million in grants, which are claimed to have leveraged $2.9 billion in development.[29] The EPA lists a number of achievements under this program.

In one example, the City of Astoria, Oregon received a $200,000 EPA Brownfields Pilot grant for converting Astoria's Plywood Mill into a mixed-use project. Located adjacent to downtown Astoria's historic area, the former industrial property combined EPA funds with assistance from local and state sources to transform the mill into a vibrant waterfront project. The site will soon house a public promenade, shops, and residential housing.[30]

In another example, a $400,000 grant provided by EPA's Brownfields Initiative has helped to start things moving on a 238-acre tract in Pittsburgh known as Nine Mile Run. Acquired by the city in the 1990s, the Nine Mile Run site had for years been used to store the waste products of the LTV Steel Corporation. Following assessments, $6.1 million of public infrastructure funds have so far been secured, and $600,000 has been spent on predevelopment costs. Total private investment in the site is forecast to exceed $200 million, resulting in 713 new housing units, approximately one hundred thousand square feet of new neighborhood commercial retail space, and 80 acres of parkland. By project completion, more than $240 million of new housing stock and $10 million in new retail construction is projected.[31]

In Massachusetts, the EPA provided $500,000 in revolving loan funds to the Mystic Valley Development Commission (MVDC) to help spark the development of the Telecom City project on a blighted industrial site bordering the Malden River, a former industrial creek. Telecom City is unique in that the project lies within the jurisdiction of three cities: Malden, Medford, and Everett. All three are older, blue-collar streetcar suburbs of the city of Boston that were also major industrial centers. The three cities jointly formed the MVDC and cooperated in raising approximately $70 million in funding commitments to acquire and develop the eighty properties comprising the site, the largest of which was a former General Electric manufacturing plant. The MVDC is now moving ahead with plans to develop nearly 2 million square feet of state-of-the-art telecommunications research and development space along with substantial waterfront park improvements on the two-hundred-acre river-edge site. When completed, the complex will be accessible to two rail transit stations on the MBTA's Orange Line—a commuter rail station as well as a planned future circumferential transit link.[32]

Not far from Telecom City is another unique

Figure 12.13. Existing Assembly Square site. (Courtesy Mystic View Task Force)

brownfield site in Somerville, Massachusetts, another traditionally blue-collar streetcar suburb of Boston. Known locally as Assembly Square, this site comprises 144 acres on the Mystic River, another former industrial water body cut off from the neighboring community by industrial and transportation uses (see Figure 12.13). As the Mystic View Task Force (MVTF; a local advocacy group) has stated: "Most residents do not even realize that we have a waterfront [in Somerville]."[33] The site was formerly home to a Ford Assembly plant that closed in the late 1950s. During the early 1980s, the plant and its surrounding property was developed into a regional shopping mall and movie theater complex dubbed Assembly Square. Although the mall closed down in the 1990s, a K-Mart and the movie theater complex remain on the site along with a Home Depot, a Circuit City store, and surface parking to support those uses.

As of 2002, the city is in negotiations with a developer who wants to add an Ikea store to the site, combined with a mix of hotel, office, and restaurant development (see Figure 12.14). The Mystic View Task Force (MVTF) believes that this plan would only serve to expand auto-dependent, suburban-style, "big-box" retail development in the area. Surprisingly, the MVTF has opposed the low-density nature of these plans, and instead has called for a vision of a much higher-density, mixed-use project to take advantage of the site's proximity to existing transit and commuter rail facilities, as well as a planned future circumferential transit called the Urban Ring (see Figure 12.15). The MVTF believes that the city's suburban-style project will generate considerable automobile traffic, whereas its own mixed-use plan will include substantial

Figure 12.14. Current proposal for Assembly Square site. (Courtesy Mystic View Task Force)

Figure 12.15. Mystic View Task Force proposal for Assembly Square site. (Courtesy Mystic View Task Force)

amounts of office and residential development, encouraging higher walking and transit mode shares. At the same time, the higher-density plan would build on less of the site, leaving more land for waterfront park space.

The result has been a confrontation over the vision for this waterfront brownfield site. Each group had important points to make. The City of Somerville has a developer who wants to build as soon as possible, and the city desperately needs the near-term tax revenue to pay for many needs, including schools, police, firefighting, and capital projects. The development plan endorsed by the city would also result in near-term river-edge park improvements, though it remains unclear how the infrastructure and park improvements envisioned in the MVTF plan would be financed. Despite these concerns, the MVTF maintains that the city is "giving away the store" on Somerville's only waterfront site, that it could someday be a high-density transit village that will ultimately yield far greater benefits.

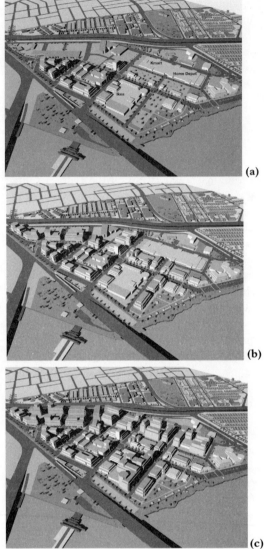

Figure 12.16. (a) Assembly Square Proposed City Plan Phase I. (b) Assembly Square Proposed City Plan Phase II. (c) Assembly Square Proposed City Plan Phase III. (Courtesy City of Somerville)

The problem is that the MVTF's vision will take a long time to plan and build, delaying any benefits into the future while accruing substantial near-term costs. In an attempt to compromise, the city hired a concultant to develop a phased plan, where the Ikea and the office, hotel and restaurant uses would be built first, and joined over time by increasing amounts of mixed-use development (see Figure 12.16). The MVTF so far does not believe this plan is realistic, and the debtate continues.

The Assembly Square site underscores some of the problems of redeveloping brownfields sites when a long-term vision with an uncertain out-come conflicts with a plan for a real project that can help meet critical short-term needs. Even urban brownfield sites with good transit access can be candidates for successful, auto-oriented, suburban formulas. Few people are likely to come by transit to shop at Home Depot or Ikea, but those are the projects that are ready to start making money for the city immediately.[34]

Meanwhile, the City of Somerville recently announced that it is evaluating alternative proposals for a major mixed-use development on a site adjacent to Assembly Square called "Yard-21." This project would include high-density housing, office, and cultural uses similar to those recommended by the MVTF for Assembly Square. It is not presently clear how this new turn of events will affect the ongoing public discussion, but it is hoped that this project will develop common ground between the city and the MVTF.

Whatever the final outcome, public debates like this one are healthy, and they showcase the emerging importance of these formerly under-valued and overlooked urban sites. Brownfield sites like Assembly Square and Telecom City represent tremendous opportunities for creating high-density, mixed-use development nodes on large industrial sites in inner-ring suburbs connected to transit. In fact, not far from Assembly Square, in the city of Cambridge, another inner-ring streetcar suburb of Boston, plans have just been announced for a $1 billion mixed-use development on a former rail yard adjacent to the MBTA's green line and the proposed Urban Ring with up to five thousand units of housing. This project will continue the mixed-use rede-velopment of the formerly industrial part of East Cambridge and the Charles River that has been unfolding for the past thirty years.

Greyfield Sites

We have already seen how Main Streets are being brought back to life in downtowns across the nation and how brownfield development sites are being treated in the older streetcar suburbs of Boston. Similar opportunities exist in parts of early post–World War II automotive suburbs. These sites are sometimes called suburban greyfields.[35] Some greyfield sites may be older suburban commercial centers, such as suburban office parks, shopping centers, and indoor shopping malls, that are at least thirty to forty years old and are either vacant, underutilized, or targeted for "repositioning." Other greyfield sites include such surplus institutional properties as state hospitals, decommissioned airfields, or abandoned racetracks.

Greyfields are frequently located near major regional transportation corridors, and they comprise relatively large land holdings in an other-wise finely subdivided environment. As such, they represent prime opportunities for redevelopment as higher-density, mixed-use centers amenable to walking and transit. These opportunities some-times have more appeal because some older sub-urbs already have the advantages of walkable neighborhoods, interesting architecture, and access to mass transit. Higher-density develop-ments next to mass transit in these locations can help revive some of these older areas while at the same time aiding in curtailing sprawl.

Examples of these types of projects include

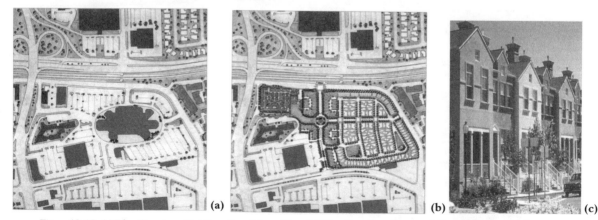

Figure 12.17. (a) The Crossings, Existing Conditions Plan. (b) The Crossings, Proposed Development. (c) The Crossings, typical housing.
Source: Peter Calthorpe and William Fulton, *The Regional City* (Washington, D.C.: Island Press, 2001).

The Crossings in Mountainview, California, and the Eastgate Mall in Chattanooga, Tennessee. The Crossings, a project by Peter Calthorpe, is a relatively small former shopping mall site of about twenty acres (see Figure 12.17). The mall became surplus partly because of overbuilding (that is, loss of market share to newer competition) and partly because of changing retail economies (possibly shifts to discount outlets, big-box retail, and so forth). The site is adjacent to a CalTrain commuter station, which connects The Crossings to the rest of the region. The former mall was converted to mixed-use development with a mix of housing types, ranging from small-lot bungalows to high-density townhouses and multistory apartments. The highest-density housing is located near the train station and has ground-floor retail. Clearly, the development of this greyfield site could also qualify as a transit village or a TOD.[36]

The Eastgate Mall in Chattanooga, Tennessee is a project by Dover, Kohl and Partners of Miami, Florida (see Figure 12.18). Their plan is the outcome of an extensive public involvement process that included the property owners, city representatives, and the public at large. The plan

is for a large indoor mall that was built in the 1960s along with its expansive parking areas. The scope of the project includes conversion of the mall itself into a series of mixed-use buildings, mixed-use infill development of the parking areas, and new development connecting to surrounding neighborhoods and a nearby office park. The project is already under construction with a planned build-out of several decades.[37]

Other projects around the country include a very large infill development covering the 4,700-acre Stapleton Airport site in suburban Denver, which was closed when the new Denver International Airport was opened in 1995. This site is planned to be a walkable, mixed-use community with up to twelve thousand units (10 million square feet) of housing.[38]

The availability of such sites, however, does not guarantee that they will be developed in a way that offers an alternative to traditional suburban development. Following the closure of the 4,255-acre Pease Air Force Base outside Portsmouth, New Hampshire, in 1991, a significant part of the base has been very successfully redeveloped for office and commercial use. How-

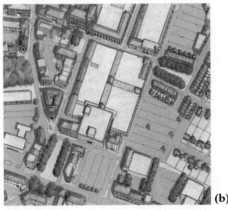

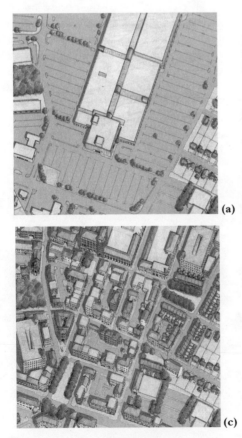

Figure 12.18. (a) Eastgate Mall, existing conditions. (b) Eastgate Mall, Phase I. (c) Eastgate Mall, Long-Term Plan.
Source: Dover Kohl & Partners.

ever, this has largely been done along the lines of traditional suburban office park development. The closure of the 1,450-acre South Weymouth Naval Air Station outside Boston has produced several plans. One called for a substantial suburban-style commercial development, including a super-regional mall and entertainment center. That element of the plan was subsequently dropped, and a new, mixed-use office, residential, and retail "Urban Village" plan with rail connections is currently under consideration.[39]

The Strains of Economic Transition

The revitalization opportunities afforded by the flight of industry have not come without cost. Though less of an issue at greyfield sites, urban brownfield sites come at the expense of the manufacturing jobs that built a lot of the nation's cities. This has left many people unemployed, sometimes resulting in charges that our older cities are being converted into historical "theme parks" primarily oriented to tourism and services. During the 1970s, Lowell, Massachusetts, became the first city in America to become a national historical park based on its industrial heritage. At the time, the city was in ruins, abandoned by the textile industries that had brought it to life and victim of the rapid suburbanization occurring around it. The historical park (built and operated by the National Park Service) rehabilitated a series of mill buildings and workers' dormitories to create a living museum of American industrial history. This project now brings millions of visitors every year to Lowell. Arguably, the city is relying upon what might be called a historical theme park to draw in tourism dollars and jobs to replace those lost with the manufacturing industries. Many cities have tried to follow this same model with varying degrees of success.

But, in the process, Lowell has become far more than a theme park. The national park project has helped spark the revitalization of the city as a whole, drawing in millions of dollars in investment in new and rehabilitated office space, housing, and retail while also creating many new jobs. The thousands of square feet of rehabilitated mill buildings would probably not have happened without the park. The issue remains that the textile manufacturing jobs are gone, but they are not likely to return, and the jobs that are replacing them are service industry and high-

technology jobs that can require education and/or new sets of skills.

Underlying these problems is the fact that the nation as a whole is undergoing a fundamental national economic change from a manufacturing economy to a service and information economy. Outmoded industrial spaces are being recycled for uses that make sense in today's business markets—and this can be a serious struggle. To quote the Mystic Valley Development Commission regarding Telecom City, their main aim is to "reposition an abandoned manufacturing-based economy into a new global technology-based economy."[40]

At Assembly Square, the City of Somerville is also trying to compete in a changing economy, but it initially took an alternative approach, replacing abandoned industrial facilities with retail service and consumer uses that are also viable in today's marketplace. Those opposed to the city's initial plan have a different view, wanting to see high-density housing, office, and research and development uses that also make current economic sense but may take longer to develop. Cities are not changing into theme parks; they are struggling to reinvent themselves to respond to current economic conditions—the same conditions that are shaping the principal business activities and use patterns of the suburbanized world that surrounds them.

The Gentrification Problem

The struggle of cities to meet changing economic conditions and attract new investment has provoked continuing concern over "gentrification": the displacement of lower-income city dwellers linked to older manufacturing economies by higher-income professionals working in the service and information industries. In many cities, this ongoing change combined with condo and co-op conversions has driven up urban real estate prices while reducing the inventory of rental units—causing justifiable worries over the vanishing availability of a ready supply of affordable housing. New housing being built is targeted to higher-income professionals. These concerns have prompted some cities to place limits and restrictions on condominium conversions. Where restrictions have been attempted, they have sometimes caused the market price for preexisting condominiums to spike even higher due to limited supply while controlled housing suffers from serious disinvestment. On the other hand, when controls have been lifted, as they have been in some states, both rents and real estate prices can escalate dramatically as reinvestment improves the neighborhood, increasing desirability and demand.

The result is that rising housing cost in comeback cities across the nation is pricing a lot of longtime city residents out of the market. New York City, San Francisco, and Boston are typical examples. Affordable housing remains a crisis in many areas, where urban real estate prices and rents have soared in the very areas that were once the only places many people could afford to live. In some cases, this has led to relocations to older inner-ring suburbs or to former satellite manufacturing cities, where prices can be lower. In New England, poorer people leaving successful cities such as Boston are resettling in less-well-off satellite industrial cities, such as New Bedford, Fall River, and Brockton, prompting some city governments to consider demolishing part of their public housing to avoid becoming regional magnets for the poor.[41]

In an effort to solve this problem, some cities (including Cambridge, Massachusetts; Rockville, Maryland; and Anaheim, California) have adopted inclusionary housing programs, requiring new housing projects to include a certain percentage of affordable units, sometimes in exchange for density bonuses.[42] Other cities, such as Boston, have chosen linkage programs, requiring developers (often of commercial space) to contribute to affordable housing funds or actually to build affordable housing (sometimes on a separate site) as a condition of development approval. Still others offer low-cost financing or other incentives to build affordable units.

Although affordable housing is indeed a serious issue demanding action, it is not, strictly speaking, a city issue alone. Affordable housing also is needed in suburban locations, within reasonable travel distance of suburban employment opportunities. This is particularly true because the majority of the job generation in the nation continues to occur in the suburbs. In fact, many industrial jobs are now in the suburbs rather than in the city.

Furthermore, urban displacements caused by rising real estate and rental prices will be inevitable if cities are to reverse their decline and become home to increasing numbers of middle-

and upper-income families. Given the simultaneous needs of both city and suburb, it can be argued that gentrification and affordable housing are really regional issues that need to be addressed at the metropolitan level rather than placing the entire burden on cities in general or on certain cities in a region. The trend toward middle- and upper-middle-class families moving back into the city is continuing in some areas, and many would argue that it should be nurtured. This requires a balanced approach that looks at the housing problem on a regional basis and finds a way to balance housing and job locations.

Push Factors

Even cities with resurgent populations and renewed investment still have many problems. These problems are the push factors that cause many middle-class families to seek out the suburbs. New York's South Bronx and Boston's Roxbury are cases in point, where abandoned housing, neighborhood disinvestment, and crime are still major issues. Moreover, for every city that has a rising population and gentrification issues, there are many more, such as St. Louis, Buffalo, and Birmingham, that are still losing residents at significant rates. Between 1990 and 2000, St. Louis lost more than 12 percent of its population, while Buffalo lost nearly 11 percent and Birmingham nearly 9 percent.[43]

Some smaller cities across the nation also are in serious trouble. These are America's small industrial cities of under two hundred thousand, in which manufacturing has largely vanished. Left behind is a constellation of ragged and timeworn industrial centers, many with still-dwindling center-city populations. These places include Camden, New Jersey; New Bedford, Massachusetts; Bridgeport, Connecticut; Gary, Indiana; and Syracuse, New York—to name but a few. Yet, some—such as Lowell, Massachusetts; Norwalk, Connecticut; and Providence, Rhode Island—have undergone a resurgence fueled by both public and private investment as have other small cities and towns that have worked hard to fix up their downtowns and Main Streets.

Even in successful cities, crime and education remain deterrents to middle-class families considering moving back. Falling urban crime rates over the last five years have helped diminish this problem, but crime remains a serious problem in many cities. Education is an equally, if not more serious, issue. Until middle-class households feel they can send their children safely to a school in the city with the expectation of a good education, those people who do not have access to alternative education will continue to elect the suburbs over the city. To a certain extent, this situation may cure itself if revitalization continues in the city. If more information and service jobs are created in the cities, if office space continues to be built and leased, and if urban residential real estate goes up in value, the city tax base will increase and, ideally, more money will go toward urban education. Obviously, a lot of assumptions are involved in this scenario, and many cities are still on shaky ground while some have not recovered at all. An alternative approach for some cities may be to seek additional funding for urban school systems from the broader metropolitan area (see Chapter 14).

Whatever is accomplished in the nation's older urbanized areas won't do much to shift people out of cars and into transit if no regional public transportation system is available nearby. Moreover, without some sort of regional framework guiding the revitalization of older urban areas, there is no guarantee that the town or city next door won't put up some huge suburban office park or shopping mall that will simply put downtown right out of business. Nor is there any guarantee that fixing up downtown will result in less green space being divided up for housing lots. Thus, fixing up our older urban areas may be an important regional question as well as a local one, even though local efforts and concern are clearly the most immediate and vital to most downtown revitalization initiatives.

The Density Issue

In the beginning of his book *The Vanishing Automobile and Other Urban Myths,* Randal O'Toole provides an account of a struggle over density in his own community of Oak Grove, an inner-ring suburb of Portland, Oregon. Metro, the regional government of Portland (see Chapter 14), had designated Oak Grove as a "town center" in its draft 2040 plan. As part of the plan, Metro wanted to rezone part of the community for higher-density, mixed-use development and introduce a series of bikeways and pedestrian ways to make it more amenable to transit use— in essence, to lay the groundwork for recreating

Oak Grove as a transit village. O'Toole provides an instructive account of the bitter battle that followed between the regional planners and a community that liked things just the way they were. Oak Grove was eventually dropped from the list as a proposed town center.[44]

As promising as compact developments, transit villages, brownfields, and greyfields may be for meeting the goals of conserving land and environmental resources, revitalizing cities, and promoting transit, many proposed projects have encountered strong local resistance. To begin with, *compact* is a word that has sometimes been applied to avoid having to use the term *higher-density.* There are good reasons for this. As the Oak Grove experience shows, few existing suburban communities react well to the idea of increasing "density" in the neighborhood. Many people perceive this as a threat to their property values and their way of life. According to polls by the National Association of Realtors, nearly three-quarters of the respondents said they wouldn't even consider buying a home that is closer to other houses and located on a smaller lot.[45] Americans still value having some land between themselves and their neighbors.

Furthermore, many people think of density as referring to the big city rather than to a small town, even though many older villages (such as Nantucket and Edgartown in Massachusetts, Williamsburg in Virginia, and Georgetown in Washington, D.C.) are quite dense when compared with modern subdivisions and shopping centers (see Figure 12.19). Despite prevailing attitudes, some of the new traditional communities appear to be successful in overcoming some of these biases by selling themselves as a new model of development, one that emphasizes

Figure 12.19. Edgartown, Massachusetts, on Martha's Vineyard-denser than most modern subdivisions, yet a sought-after place to live. (Alex S. MacLean/Landslides)

community over individual home lots. The new emphasis on community is one of the most positive aspects of this new trend, as long as it can be sold.

Even so, many localities doubtless will hold to the individualism of the current pattern, a pattern reinforced by fears about real estate values and traffic congestion. These considerations can make it difficult to find an unobjectionable location for new compact developments in many localities, especially where density remains an issue and large lot sizes are considered a hallmark of value. However, in rapidly developing areas, the concern for preserving open space and farmland may outweigh such worries and, with the proper persuasion, some people may eventually come to realize that this type of pattern (as opposed to downzoning) will yield the best results.

This debate is going on in many communities in the nation today. Martha's Vineyard is one such place. There, the pace of development has been torrid, prompting building permit caps and other measures to slow the process. It has also caused some of the small towns that make up the island to actively consider replacing large-lot zoning with some sort of TND mechanism to preserve at least some of the character of the island that originally attracted so many people there.

Despite such discussions and the possibility of a change in the wind, there is a fairly solid history of community opposition to higher-density projects, even when focused around transit and even when in dense urban areas. For example, the Atlantic Center TOD project in Brooklyn, New York, fell victim to community opposition over concerns about impacts related to density.[46] Recent proposals for increasing density near rail and transit stations in Fairfax County, Virginia (outside of Washington) have met with extensive controversy.[47] Similarly, the increased density that resulted in the transit villages around the Silver Spring and Bethesda Metrorail stations in Maryland also sparked local community opposition.[49] In Cambridge, Massachusetts, proposals for mixed office and multifamily housing development in a former industrial area near a major rail and bus transit station have met with opposition from neighboring communities concerned about increased traffic congestion. On the other side, as documented earlier in this chapter, a proposal to redevelop a former auto

assembly plant site in nearby Somerville has met with objections from the community partly because the project's density isn't high enough.

Assembly Square aside, people in the inner suburbs often are just as anxious as those in the outer suburbs to retain the character of their communities. What happened in Oak Grove is a testament to this. Not only are higher densities perceived as potentially a drag on housing values, but the appearance of high-rise buildings (for example, six stories) in the middle of a low-rise community can have other impacts that are often equally as important to the residents of the community.

Thus, the composition and design of these projects become extremely important features. Greater density can be achieved with low-rise buildings in contextual harmony with what already exists in the neighborhood. Even this can be difficult if it means rezoning a community for smaller lot sizes. However, if objections to density can be overcome, there is relatively little question that these types of projects could have important advantages regionally by potentially shifting regional trips to transit, shifting local trips to walking, and satisfying what might otherwise be a demand for more exurban sprawl development.

Density is not an issue for suburbs alone—as the Atlantic Center project in Brooklyn has shown. Even the tallest and most crowded of cities can regard more concentrated development with trepidation. In Manhattan, a towering mixed-use project planned for Columbus Circle has been delayed for more than a decade over objections about its size and scale. Another project proposed for rail yards adjacent to the Hudson River on the Upper West Side has been stalled just as long due to density concerns, including congestion on local transit lines. In South Boston, development of a multiblock brownfield section of formerly industrial waterfront has also been delayed over similar discussions and for a similar length of time. During the 1980s, San Francisco went through a major change in its zoning code to limit high-rise development. The situation is the same in many other cities.

Yet increasing density, in some form, is generally the direction of growth needed by cities and inner suburbs if they are to absorb the increased share of regional development that will be required to curtail further sprawl development. This factor is an important roadblock in redirecting development into the cities. Part of the solution lies in the piecemeal nature of the problem. In many cases, the cities and suburbs are as dense as they want to grow only in certain prime areas, yet there are many brownfield and greyfield sites in less desirable areas of both the cities and their inner suburbs that could absorb more density, probably without much objection. They are just not in the right market area to attract current interest. Thus, how, where, and in what form new growth takes place in the cities and in the inner suburbs will be keys to the general success of any effort made in that direction.

Changing Development Patterns in Summary

Compact developments, revitalization of the nation's older urban areas, and viable public transit are all linked. Shifting development patterns from spread-out, low-density configurations to compact, walkable, mixed-use centers helps to conserve land. At the same time, when compact communities are planned as TODs or transit villages, they also create a pattern that is more amenable to transit use.

Revitalization of downtown and older suburban areas, particularly large urban brownfield sites and suburban greyfield sites, also reduces pressure on open land resources in metropolitan areas. At the same time, many of these sites possess existing roadway, water, sewer, and other infrastructure, reducing the need to build redundant systems to support expanding suburbanization. Development of these sites improves the image and quality of metropolitan centers while at the same time helping regional economies make the transition from an outmoded manufacturing base to emerging information and service markets.

Brownfield and greyfield development also can be amenable to increased transit use. Many of these sites are in urban and suburban districts that already have good transit systems as well as high transit and walk mode shares. Targeting an increased share of regional development to these areas takes advantage of these factors, reducing pressure both on greenfield sites and on congested roadways by potentially increasing transit use. However, no net gain in transit use can be realized without viable public transit in place at the start.

CHAPTER 13

Viable Public Transportation

The Importance of Public Transportation

Even though public transportation may appear as a simple line item on the list of smart growth measures in Chapter 10, it is a very large and complex issue that is linked to many others. Some might say that public transportation is an even bigger and more encompassing question than smart growth itself—for many of the other items on the list won't have as much impact as they might without some basic national change in the way America uses its transportation system. For example, compact, walkable communities and even fixing up our cities and towns won't do much to mitigate the major impacts of suburbanization without viable public transportation systems that can serve in place of at least some automobile trips.

Public transportation is usually considered to be mass transit: a network of public passenger vehicles running on designated routes at set times for established fares.[1] These systems typically operate at local or metropolitan levels. National-level transportation systems (air, road, rail, and water) are usually considered separately, although they may link into local and regional systems and can also be determinants of urban form.

Local Public Transportation Initiatives

Within limits, public transportation systems put in place locally can have very reasonable positive effects. This is even more of a possibility today than in the past, with the advent of ISTEA and TEA-21, since more power has been given to localities to choose transportation options than previously.[2] Many communities in the United States already have regional transportation agencies or local transit districts that cover a given municipality or a discrete part of a larger rural or

metropolitan region. For the most part, these are bus systems running on local streets and highways.

Brockton Area Transit

A good example is the Brockton Area Transit Authority, known as BAT. BAT covers the area around the older, industrial city of Brockton, Massachusetts, and provides connections to Boston's regional transit and commuter rail systems (see Figure 13.1). BAT operates about seventeen bus routes running on a "pulse" system, which means that all routes converge within a fifteen-minute period at a central downtown "pulse point" or bus transfer station, where passengers can transfer between buses for any destination within the BAT operating area. After a brief layover during which passengers alight, board, and change routes, all buses then depart on their routes in a single "pulse." The City of Norwalk, Connecticut, operates a similar system as do other communities elsewhere in the nation.

Most local public transportation systems cross local boundaries somewhere, and all local systems work far better when they have a regional

Figure 13.1. Brockton Area Transit Intermodal Center in Brockton, Massachusetts, by Gillham, Gander & Chin Associates, Inc. (Jerry Howard/Landscape Photography)

network into which they connect. This is because many daily trips are regional rather than local. BAT is no exception. Regional express bus service run by another operator has traditionally been available to commuters at BAT's main pulse point, and until 1999, one of the BAT-run routes connected to the terminus of one of Boston's rapid rail transit lines. In 1998, to provide fully intermodal connections to Boston's regional rail transportation system, BAT moved their pulse point adjacent to a new rail station that is part of an extension of the Boston region's commuter rail network. The BAT system has an average weekday ridership of more than twelve thousand passengers, keeping up to eleven thousand vehicle trips off the local roads.[3]

Hop Shuttle Service

Since the advent of ISTEA, a number of communities have implemented effective and innovative local networks that connect to regional transit systems. Boulder, Colorado, used ISTEA funds to start the Hop Shuttle Service—a frequent shuttle service using eight midsized buses running on clean-burning propane and operating on ten-minute headways throughout the day. The service operates on a two-way loop and is aimed at providing viable transit for employees, students, residents, and visitors to get around Boulder's congested core. The service provides an alternative to the car for shopping, lunch trips, errands, and meetings. It is also intended to connect transit riders to the regional Denver Metro Transit System. By 1996 (after about four years of operation), the system was reportedly operating close to capacity at 4,300 passengers per day, well beyond initial estimates of 2,000 passengers per day, and replacing more than 3,900 potential vehicle trips. Average daily ridership in October of 2000 was around 3,000 passengers per day.[4]

Shuttle Bug

Another innovative project is the Shuttle Bug Reverse Commute Project in Deerfield and Northbrook, Illinois. This project provides shuttle service using a series of fifteen-passenger minibuses operating on six routes between a commuter rail station and a suburban business center in the Lake-Cook Road corridor approximately twenty-five miles northwest of downtown Chicago. The project promotes reverse commuting from downtown Chicago to suburban employment destinations while reducing traffic congestion.[5]

Local and Regional

Local projects like these provide viable local public transportation that feeds into and augments broader regional systems. But even with innovative local public transit systems that have good regional connections like those described above, getting a significant number of people out of their cars and onto buses and trains is still a very tall order—and, in fact, this may be a national issue as much as it is a regional or local one. The many bold public transportation initiatives undertaken across the country have accomplished a great deal, and transit ridership nationally is on the increase, but the nation's transportation system still remains heavily slanted toward the automobile.

Metropolitan Transit Initiatives

Regional transit initiatives have a long and continuing history in the United States. Boston and New York started building public transportation systems in the nineteenth century as did many other U.S. cities. Some cities, such as Los Angeles and San Diego, abandoned their light rail systems in the middle of the twentieth century only to revive transit later on. San Francisco still has its famous cable cars, but in 1964, the Bay Area embarked on a much larger project, the Bay Area Rapid Transit system (BART), which generally has been a tremendous success. Washington, D.C., has perhaps the most outstanding showcase metro system in the nation, planned in the 1950s and completed mostly during the 1970s (though it is still being extended). Such cities as Atlanta, Los Angeles, San Diego, Seattle, St. Louis, Portland (Oregon), Buffalo, and many others have made huge investments in rail transit systems. Philadelphia went to great expense to through-connect the entire regional commuter rail system, making it possible to travel throughout the Philadelphia region (including the airport) by rail with, at most, only one in-station transfer downtown.

To better understand the national experience with transit systems, two case studies are presented here: (1) San Diego, a relatively newly revived system (since 1970) in a western automotive city that has experienced explosive expansion since 1950, and (2) Boston, a system started more than a hundred years ago but one that is still growing in an historic eastern city that has experienced multiple waves of suburbanization.

San Diego

The San Diego Metropolitan Area grew rapidly following World War II, from five hundred thousand in 1950 to more than 2.8 million by 2000. During the 1950s and 1960s, the San Diego area aggressively pursued freeway planning and building, resulting in a region currently served by four interstate highways as well as an extensive network of state and local roads. The result was rapid suburbanization of the metropolitan area, particularly areas such as Mission Valley, which

attracted a significant amount of strip commercial development. Previously, during the late 1940s, an extensive streetcar system serving San Diego was dismantled and replaced with buses. Rapid suburban population growth, dependent on roads and highways, eventually led to severe traffic congestion. By 1991, San Diego led the nation in the rate of increasing traffic congestion in metropolitan areas.[6]

Planning for revitalizing light rail transit began in 1975 with the creation of the Metropolitan Transit Development Board (MTDB). In 1978, the MTDB purchased a 108-mile, defunct railroad for a proposed new light rail transit (LRT) line to be called the San Diego Trolley (see Figure 13.2). In a unique turn of events, the MTDB decided not to seek federal funding for the first segment of its new project. Acquisition of the rail line, together with strong construction

Figure 13.2. Map of the San Diego Trolley System.
Source: San Diego Association of Governments, Metropolitan Transit System.

management by the MTDB, allowed the first line to be constructed for the relatively low price of $7.3 million per mile. The line was successful, with ridership quickly climbing to thirty thousand passengers per day by the mid-1980s, a level not initially expected until 1995. More than 40 percent of riders have a car that they could use for the trip.[7]

During the 1980s, San Diego voters narrowly approved a sales tax increase of 0.5 percent for twenty years to pay for transportation improvements, with one-third of the resources going to transit. With the sales tax in place, the trolley was gradually expanded using bonding augmented by federal aid. Today, the system covers approximately forty-eight miles and has two major extensions planned.[8] More than 93,000 passengers ride the trolley on an average weekday, out of a total of 328,000 riding the entire metropolitan transit system. Without transit, many of those trips would be by automobile. Fare box recovery (the amount of operating costs covered by fares) for the entire transit system was 50 percent, up from 30 percent in 1976, before the trolley opened. Farebox recovery on the trolley itself is reported to be even higher—as much as 66 percent in 1995. In 1976, annual transit ridership was 34 million and steadily declining. By 2001, annual ridership for the total transit system was more than 90 million, with 35 million riding the trolley.[9]

Despite these impressive ridership numbers and above-average fare box recovery figures, total transit commute ridership in the San Diego metropolitan area remains in the 3 to 4 percent range, although 15 to 20 percent of peak period work trips to downtown are by transit.[10] This continuing imbalance may have been partly why the City of San Diego adopted transit-oriented development (TOD) and design guidelines during the 1990s. The guidelines were implemented through revisions to the zoning code, street design standards, and the city's general plan. The guidelines focus on creating higher-density TOD nodes along the city's principal transit corridors. Since the guidelines were implemented in the early 1990s, regional transit ridership has increased by about 28 percent, although this upturn may be due principally to regional economic and population changes and to new and expanded trolley services. It is probably too soon to gauge the effects of the TOD guidelines.

Boston

The Boston transit system started as a railroad and streetcar network during the mid–nineteenth century. By 1897, Boston was home to the first subway tunnel in America, which was dug to relieve streetcar congestion on Tremont Street. During the next four decades, Boston's transit system underwent significant expansion, with new elevated and underground electric rapid rail transit lines extended throughout Boston and its inner suburbs. Most of these lines were privately built by the Boston Elevated Railway Company. During the same period, the Boston region was also served by an extensive network of private commuter railways, including such companies as the Old Colony Railroad and the Boston and Albany Railroad. In 1947, the Boston Elevated Railway was taken over by the Metropolitan Transportation Authority (later the Massachusetts Bay Transportation Authority, or MBTA) and has been publicly run ever since. By the 1950s, the regional focus had largely turned to building new highways. Many regional railway companies began to close down or curtail passenger service as patrons were increasingly lost to automobiles and buses.

THE BOSTON TRANSPORTATION PLANNING REVIEW

During the late 1960s, the citizens of Massachusetts called for a moratorium on new highways in the Boston area (see Chapter 3). Many Boston area residents felt that the highway projects were destroying their city and their countryside. Furthermore, some began to lament the decline of rail services as local scholars and community activists noted that the big new roads just weren't solving the problem of ever-increasing traffic congestion.

In a bold gambit that later became a model for cities such as Toronto in Ontario, Canada, Massachusetts initiated what was to become the Boston Transportation Planning Review (BTPR). Concluded in the early 1970s, the BTPR was responsible for transforming the region's highway plan into a more balanced transportation system. Proposed highways and their federal funding allotments were traded in for new mass transit links, including extensions of two transit lines.

Nonetheless, even with ample federal funding available, ultimate plans were thwarted by local opposition. Planned transit links to subur-

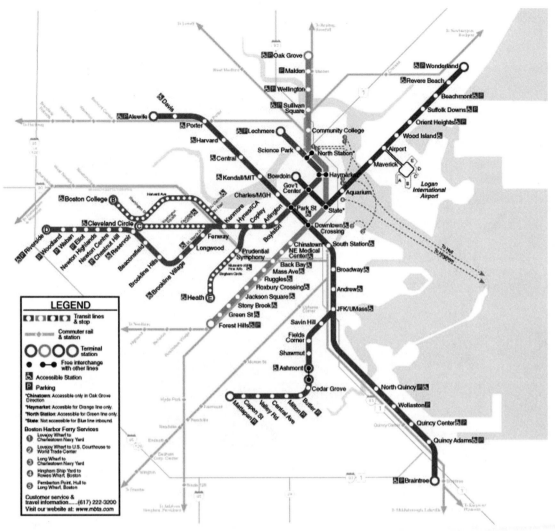

Figure 13.3. Map of the Boston transit system (the MBTA).
Source: Massachusetts Bay Transportation Authority.

ban communities along Boston's beltway (Route 128) were halted far short of their proposed termination points. Some of those limitations have since been remedied with the revitalization of Boston's commuter rail system. Many of these older passenger rail links, shut down during the 1950s and 1960s, were started up again, extending the passenger rail network out to the Interstate 495 region (Boston's outermost beltway) and beyond (see Figure 13.3). This system is still being extended but not without significant local opposition in some suburban areas.

RESULTS

As a result of these sweeping efforts combined with a long tradition of transit use by 1990 more than 14 percent of the Boston metropolitan region were commuting to work using some form of transit while about 76 percent were driving their cars.[11] This is better than the national metropolitan average of just over 6 percent transit use for commuting and far better than San Diego's 3 to 4 percent transit-commute rate.[12] Furthermore, 20 percent of commuters in Boston and its innermost suburbs use transit to get to work while nearly 25 percent walk to work.[13] The MBTA region has a daily transit and commuter rail ridership of more than 1.1 million, with a total fare box recovery of about 34 percent (less than the national average).[14] Two planned transit projects—the Urban Ring and the North/South Rail Link—may help improve Boston's transit share in the future.

Figure 13.4. Map of the proposed Urban Ring Corridor. *Source:* Massachusetts Bay Transportation Authority.

THE URBAN RING

The Urban Ring is a projected circumferential transit corridor that will be completed over fifteen years and will link Boston's older inner-ring communities and its radial rapid transit and commuter rail lines (see Figure 13.4). The Urban Ring will roughly follow the path once intended for an inner-belt highway. The ring as currently proposed will use a combination of rail and bus transit to connect through Boston and the former streetcar suburbs of Brookline, Cambridge, Chelsea, Everett, Medford, and Somerville, as well as link directly to Logan Airport.

Along its path, the ring will transect a series of major brownfield sites slated for future mixed-use development, including Assembly Square, Telecom City, East Cambridge, Chelsea, and the South Boston Waterfront. The line also will connect through the Dudley Square neighborhood revitalization district in Roxbury and Boston's Longwood Medical Area, home to the majority of the region's teaching hospitals. This link between transit and land-use initiatives will create significant high-density transit village opportunities in Boston's inner-ring suburbs that will be connected to existing regional activity centers, such as the Medical Area and Logan Airport. The ring and its associated brownfield sites target development toward communities that already have significant transit commute mode shares (the 20 percent transit commute snare described above and 15 percent of all daily trips), high walking mode share (25 percent of commute trips and 31 percent of all daily trips), low car ownership (0.8 cars per household versus the regional average of 1.37), and high potential for employment growth (nearly double that of the region as a whole). The ring also will eliminate a significant impediment to transit use in its proposed corridor: the radial nature of the region's transit system means that those people living or working in the circumferential corridor have to make nearly twice as many interline transfers to reach their destinations when compared with average regional transit trips.[15]

The North/South Rail Link

The North/South Rail Link is a long-term project targeted on the Boston region's commuter rail system. Currently, this network radiates across the region from two stub-end rail termini: North Station and South Station in downtown Boston. Making connections between the two requires a long walk or cab ride or a trip on the subway with at least one change of lines. This situation makes it a real effort to travel from the North Shore to the South Shore by commuter rail. A car is a much more likely choice, even though it usually means negotiating very heavy traffic, either though downtown Boston or around the Route 128 beltway.

Boston's Central Artery/Tunnel project has been designed to accommodate a planned rail tunnel alignment that will be constructed at some point in the future. This rail tunnel would connect the rail systems at North and South Stations, allowing through-rail connections across the Boston region to the I-495 outer beltway and beyond. This would be similar to what was accomplished in Philadelphia during the 1980s and to what is already in place in many European cities. The German S-Bahn systems (formerly stub-end rail systems as in Boston) are through-connected in Munich, Frankfurt, and other cities. The Paris RER system is similar. The opportunity for crossregional rail travel, if combined with land-use planning encouraging transit village development at regional nodes, could potentially increase the shift to transit modes.

Innovative Transit Technology

Projects such as the Urban Ring and many others could benefit from the use of innovative transit technologies from abroad. LRT systems are preferred over buses by many transit advocates because of the higher-service levels they offer and the higher volumes they can carry, and because they usually travel on an exclusive right-of-way. However, innovative bus technologies exist that fold some of the key aspects of LRT into bus transit. Three examples are the Spurbus system in Essen, Germany, the O-Bahn in Adelaide, Australia, and the express bus system used in Curituba, Brazil.

Spurbus and O-Bahn

Essen's Spurbus is essentially a high-capacity dual-mode bus that operates as a normal self-propelled bus on local streets and as an electric trolley on shared LRT guideways (see Figure 13.5). This technology allows great flexibility for creating, expanding, and changing transit route systems without adding expensive transit infrastructure, and for creating lines where portions of the route must travel in mixed traffic on local streets before rejoining an exclusive right-of-way or guideway. This type of bus can also operate as both local feeder and distributor (picking up and dropping off passengers on local streets) and as a line-haul service (along an express trunk line), eliminating the need for line or mode transfers.

The long, articulated buses (a flexible joint is provided in the middle to allow turning on tight corners) carry more people than a typical bus (sixty or more seats versus forty), and they allow level platform boarding at LRT stops and curb boarding at street stops. Buses can be routed along neighborhood loops to pick up passengers and then mount an exclusive guideway for line-haul service to an employment center, demounting the guideway to provide loop distribution at the employment center, whether a downtown area or an office park. These characteristics make this type of technology well suited to many different environments, including lower-density suburban settings. Similar technology also is used in Adelaide, Australia, where it is called O-Bahn and is configured to create multiple loop routes serving Adelaide's northeast suburbs that all feed into a seven-and-one-half-mile exclusive line-haul guideway, with buses running to downtown on five-minute headways and traveling at more than sixty miles per hour. The Adelaide O-Bahn carries more than 7 million passengers per year and is capable of moving up to eighteen thousand people per hour in each direction. Adelaide Metro claims that the O-Bahn is 50 percent

Figure 13.5. Spurbus vehicles on a shared light rail guideway in Essen, Germany. (Oliver Gillham)

Figure 13.6. O-Bahn bus and guideway in Adelaide, Australia. (Adelaide Metro)

cheaper to operate than equivalent rail systems while providing more flexible service (see Figure 13.6).[16]

Curituba, Brazil

Curituba provides both regular and articulated buses running in express-lane medians of regional arterial roads. High-platform bus technology allows level boarding at all stops, eliminating steps and boarding problems for people with disabilities, people with baggage, and parents with small children in carriages (see Figure 13.7). Steps slow boarding times and are part of what give buses a reputation for low service levels. In addition, wireless technology coordinates the opening of bus doors with doors on the transit station, allowing for climate controlled bus stations and in-station fare collection, speeding bus boarding and alighting. Like the O-Bahn, the Curituba system can be configured to pick up at street level as well as at transit plat-

*Figure 13.*7. Curituba bus and shelter in Manhattan demonstration project. (Oliver Gillham)

forms, allowing it to operate as both feeder and rapid line-haul service.[17]

Both Curituba and O-Bahn mix bus and LRT features to create systems that could work effectively to capture greater suburban transit shares through flexible loop service on local streets while also providing the high level of rapid line-haul service on exclusive rights-of-way that is one of the hallmarks of LRT service.

Barriers to Transit

Despite large investments made in transit, as well as the promise of innovative transit technologies, America's metropolitan areas continue to have much higher auto travel rates than transit travel rates. In fact, in such cities as Atlanta and St. Louis, where major expenditures have been made on new transit systems, total transit use rates actually declined relative to auto share between 1980 and 1990.[18] New York City alone accounts for 37 percent of all transit commuters in the United States.[19] But even in New York, about 68 percent of all weekday trips in the metropolitan region are made by car, which is still a majority, even though it is considerably lower than the rest of the nation, where about 86 percent or more of commuting trips are made by automobile.[20]

This continuing imbalance is largely due to the suburbanization that has occurred during the past fifty years combined with the huge, parallel road-building projects of the interstate era. It is not just lack of transit service that promotes the national imbalance; it is also because only automobiles can effectively serve today's predominantly suburban metropolitan areas. Even though investments in innovative technology might help remedy this problem to some degree, studies across the nation have come to dim conclusions about the future of transit in the suburban environment. One recent study in New England concluded that

> congestion problems in the suburbs go much deeper than a simple lack of transit service. The style of suburban development seen in the postwar period entails reliance on automobiles. Low densities and many-to-many trip patterns make conventional transit services infeasible.[21]

The fact that almost everyone drives to get to

work, as well as to do practically everything else, also is a strong influence on the national attitude toward transportation. Most people view capital expenditures for roadways and roadway repair as essential to the national transportation system, which they are, given the nation's heavy dependence on cars and trucks. Yet, few people seem to see roadways and cars as "subsidized" in the same way that rail and mass transit are perceived to be, even though the total amount of money Americans spend each year on owning and operating their cars is nearly $800 billion, whereas the total annual cost of operating America's transit systems is about 2 percent of that figure.[22]

The money spent on cars is perceived as essential and not much different than money spent on clothes. Like clothes, the car is both a necessity and an important part of most people's identity—it belongs to them, it is under their control, and it is a statement about who they are. With a car, individuals can come and go as they please. The traffic may get bad, but they are always free to seek another route, and their personal privacy "bubble" (complete with music, air-conditioning, and a phone) doesn't have to be shared with anyone else. In this way, the car is a lot like the single-family house on its own insular lot, which is also viewed as a personal choice that is individually owned. Furthermore, money spent on roads comes largely from gas taxes and user fees. Many of these are considered largely innocuous or just "facts of life," like mortgage payments and insurance.

The relatively small amount of money Americans spend on operating transit just isn't seen the same way. Not only are there extra "roads" to be built and maintained in the form of tracks, but there also are stations and vehicles. And, unlike your garage or your car, neither the stations nor the vehicles belong directly to you. Although they are actually common property, they are perceived as being owned by the operating agency. Since most people drive and don't use transit much, they also see the trains and buses as being provided for "others." Funds for transit come from gas and other taxes, including sales and income tax. The gas taxes that go to transit don't go to the roads, even though it is the people driving cars on roads who are paying the fuel taxes.

These perceptions form a major obstacle to funding transit systems. Most people, even many planning professionals, do not view the nation's transportation system as an integrated whole—and perhaps it isn't. But it needs to be thought of that way in order to make appropriate plans for the future. Both roads and rails are needed to make the nation's metropolitan areas work effectively. For example, transit is needed to carry the massive high-volume, peak-hour radial loads that are characteristic of many of the nation's metropolitan areas. This is what the Atlanta Metropolitan Planning Commission, for example, decided when it recommended building a transit system for Atlanta in the early 1960s.[23] The nation's transit systems helps keep millions of commuter trips off congested roads every day.[24]

The Land-Use Connection

The problem of increasing roadway congestion would be a clear invitation for creating more rail and transit alternatives to take the pressure off the roadway system if the problem were simply suburb-to-downtown commutation (where mode share for transit climbs to more than 11 percent—more than double the national average).[25] However, the big numbers on the roadways are in the suburbs—with suburb-to-suburb commuting making up nearly 60 percent of all commuting growth between 1980 and 1990—and the suburbs are the hardest of places to make transit work effectively, even for the one-third of peak-hour auto trips that are actually work related.[26] As stated Chapter 6, the majority of travel in the nation (about 80 percent) has nothing to do with commutation, and the fact that the origins and destinations of the trips are so dispersed makes it difficult indeed to find a good way to make rail or even bus transit work effectively.[27] In fact, a 1998 study of suburban transit conducted by the Boston Metropolitan Planning Organization stated that "an increase in [suburban] public transportation service, absent major changes in land use and parking policy, would likely have little or no effect on suburban congestion."[28]

A major problem is that metropolitan transportation systems are inherently regional. For these systems to work most effectively, urbanization and transportation should be coordinated regionally. If pressure on the highways is to be relieved, transit provides a good alternative, but it can only work if development is planned in a way that makes it amenable to walking and transit access. Just as transportation systems need to be looked at as a whole, land use and transportation also need to work together.

Viable Public Transportation in Summary

Viable public transportation is a critical ingredient to changing development patterns. Reducing auto dependency is part of the solution to reducing spread-out development patterns, including large surface parking areas and high-capacity roadways. Without viable transit, development has little alternative but to adopt an auto-dependent suburban pattern. The nation has a good history of building new transit as well as adding onto and reviving existing systems. Even so, transit use across the nation remains diminutive compared to auto use. Barriers to transit include a general tendency to regard transit as a separate part of the nation's transportation network, when, in actuality, it should be viewed as an integral component of the whole system. Transit is fundamental to reducing roadway congestion in metropolitan areas. Congestion pricing and similar demand management strategies won't be effective if there is no place to shift the demand.

To rely upon the expectation that roadways can always be expanded at reasonable cost to serve new growth is considered unrealistic by most planners. At some point, the roads will be completely filled, despite whatever management and Intelligent Transportation System measures

may be taken. When that happens, they won't work well for anyone—for commuters, for people running errands, or for the nation's goods and services traveling on the roadways. Some portion of the travel demand has to be shifted to transit, rail, and just plain walking.

However, for transit to work most effectively and to shoulder ever-greater shares of regional trips requires land use patterns that are amenable to transit use. Thus, plans for how land will get developed and plans for what kind of transportation system will serve that development need to be coordinated in some fashion. In most situations across the United States, land development is controlled and permitted locally whereas transportation is handled regionally. Sometimes, regional transportation agencies are there first, as when the interstates were built, with unplanned-for development following. In other cases, localities permit development until the state or county road-building agency has to catch up because of mounting congestion. The answer is almost always new road capacity, because development hasn't been planned for anything else and regional agencies, except in notable instances, haven't proposed anything else. This has been changing in some parts of the country, such as Oregon, Maryland, and Georgia, where the state or regional agencies or both are trying to take a more proactive role in coordinating land use and transportation to the benefit of the metropolitan region as a whole. These regional efforts are the subject of Chapter 14.

CHAPTER 14

Regionalism

The land-use, transportation, and growth management issues raised in the previous chapters all converge on the issue of regional thinking, planning, and governance. To prevent the leapfrogging of suburbanization across local community borders, growth boundaries need to be considered over a whole metropolitan area. Municipal tax competition between localities can lead to an office park in one community, bringing unwanted growth and fiscal strains to the town next door. Regional transportation decisions can work most effectively when made in conjunction with regional land use decisions. Meanwhile, new suburbs are still being built while older suburbs are allowed to decline. All of these problems seem to indicate a need for some type of regional solution that transcends the local boundaries of any given town or city.

Expansion and Annexation

The fact that the nation's basic economic units are its metropolitan areas is the outcome of an expansion process that has been going on for more than one hundred years. During the mid–twentieth century, the nation's city centers that were its main economic units, and now those city centers have grown into today's vast metropolitan areas.

Annexation and Consolidation

As the nation's cities have grown, many of them have engaged in a continuous struggle over how to manage their rapidly increasing areas. To address problems brought about by rapid expansion, New York City chose to annex a large part of its surrounding region in 1898.[1] In doing so, New York followed the lead of many other cities, including Boston, Philadelphia, and St. Louis. Annexation (adding unincorporated land to the city) and consolidation (absorbing adjacent municipalities) was a common method of handling urban growth throughout the nineteenth century.

As Kenneth Jackson has pointed out in his book *The Crabgrass Frontier*, without annexation, many large cities would have been surrounded by independent suburbs before the Civil War. Instead, between 1850 and 1910, New York City increased its territory by nearly 1,400 percent while Philadelphia became sixty-five times larger than it was sixty years earlier. Annexation and consolidation have not gone out of fashion. In fact, annexation remains a time-honored technique available to some cities in the nation that has been used to counteract some of the negative effects of sprawl development.[2]

Elastic Cities

The twelve largest U.S. cities that showed population gains between 1950 and 1980 were those that expanded their geographical areas.[3] Houston, Texas, for example, grew by nearly 350 percent in area between 1950 and 1980.[4] But the metropolitan areas of many cities like New York (cities that shared net population losses in the same period) have long since outgrown their nineteenth-century boundaries, and annexing adjacent communities is no longer a viable option for them. Boston's annexation and consolidation stopped at Brookline, a wealthy suburb that saw no advantage in annexation, and this is the view generally held by the suburbs of many older urban areas today.

According to David Rusk, author of *Cities Without Suburbs*, those cities that are capable of annexation and are still growing are among the most successful in the nation. Rusk calls these "elastic cities," in that they are able to change their physical shape to accommodate growth. According to Rusk, nearly all metro areas were growing in population in 1990, but many cities, such as Detroit and Cleveland, were shrinking while the rest of their metro areas continued to grow.[5] Meanwhile, such cities as Houston, San Antonio, and San Diego, were able to grow in population and area, making them elastic cities.

Rusk goes on to point out that these elastic cities have managed to save themselves from some of the more dire fiscal problems of suburbanization by acquiring their suburban tax base. This means they are free to pool downtown and suburban taxes to provide equal service to both—including education. They also circumvent (to some degree) the problem of tax-base competition between suburban and urban communities, which has plagued the Northeast. Downtown and the suburbs are part of the same jurisdiction. Rusk compares twelve metropolitan areas across the United States and demonstrates that elastic cities are typically less segregated than nonelastic cities in terms of both race and economic class.[6] Rusk further asserts that elastic cities are also less dense, creating more opportunities for infill development.[7]

Elasticity and Suburbanization

It is clear from reviewing Rusk's well-documented study that annexation can do a lot to erase some of the more poignant impacts of suburbanization discussed in Part II of this book. However, when we come to the question of density, it is also apparent that annexation alone doesn't seem to be doing much to change the rapidly spreading, auto-dependent, low-density *pattern* of development that is so characteristic of sprawl. In elastic cities such as Houston, land and energy are still being consumed at a nonsustainable pace while community character, air quality, and water quality suffer. The city limits simply are spreading out to encompass the growth of sprawl development. Annexation could be used to curtail sprawl and create a more compact pattern by annexing enough land to create a zoned greenbelt around the city, but this is not typically being done.

Furthermore, annexation simply is not an option for many cities. Some state laws do not even provide for annexation, and many cities are surrounded by incorporated communities that are opposed to annexation. Some metropolitan areas, including New York, Boston, Chicago, and Washington, D.C., include parts of different states, making the question of annexation moot.

Thus, metropolitan areas like these are forced to look to other methods if they wish to pursue a regional approach to solving their problems.

Recurrent Regionalism

Regionalism, or metropolitanism (as it is sometimes also called), has recurred from time to time as a possible solution to the urban ills caused by the rapid explosion of American metropolitan areas. There was considerable debate about regionalism in the 1920s, during the first automotive suburban boom. Then, the debate focused on how regions should be controlled—by dominant central cities or by dispersed settlements. That era saw the birth of the Regional Planning Association of America (RPAA), of which Lewis Mumford was a founding member. The RPAA served as a forum for much of this debate until its demise in the late 1930s.

Prior to the present day, the most recent episode of regionalism occurred during the 1960s and 1970s, when it became the subject of significant research, academic discourse, and policy innovation. That period was at the end of the first major postwar suburban building boom. Following a rash of city-county consolidations in that era, regionalism then waned again, foundering perhaps on the political realities of the times in combination with a downturn in the economy.

Contemporary Regionalism

During the past few years, regionalism has once again come into fashion. In some respects, this may be due to the cycle of growth and change, because development has mushroomed during the 1990s, resulting in increased concern about the effects of sprawl. The recognition that our nation's metropolitan areas have reached a whole new level in transcending their boundaries has lent renewed urgency to the subject.

Where annexation and consolidation are no longer viable, other alternatives are being examined. These include the organization of powerful new metropolitan governments, the creation of new regional services districts, the formation of special regional tax districts and various state-level initiatives. Regional initiatives can include all of the smart growth measures listed in Chapter 10. However, where regional strategies are being attempted, they tend to be organized around one or more of the following concepts:

- Regional-growth control, including boundaries limiting the outward extension of growth
- Regional coordination of transportation and land use
- Regional sharing of fiscal resources (tax-base sharing).

Regional-Growth Control

Local and county efforts at urban-growth control, though potentially quite effective in a small area, don't necessarily solve broader regional sprawl problems. Low-density development can simply continue on to other, less restrictive communities in the same metropolitan region. The question of housing expense may be solved in part by accompanying a defined urban growth boundary (UGB) with a strong affordable housing program, but this is not always achievable, because of funding limitations and local opposition to affordable housing next door. There is no guarantee that any grouping of local-level UGBs within a given metropolitan area will either act to stem sprawl or result in any kind of rational pattern for future development of the region as a whole. Some communities may elect to put in place a UGB whereas others won't. Without any mandatory coordination between municipalities, growth-management efforts in one community may simply be canceled out by unrestrained growth next door.

Adopting a regional approach to the UGB can help solve some of these problems. A regional UGB can cover an entire metropolitan area, including multiple cities, towns, and counties. If properly planned and administered, such a technique can be used to manage and direct growth on a regional basis, effectively limiting sprawl. Because the land both within and outside of the UGB crosses community borders, the chances for local plans canceling each other out with leapfrog development are greatly reduced.

On the other hand, a regional UGB cannot be implemented or administered by existing local government unless a group of localities agrees to work together in a formal process. Even that usually requires the cooperation of a broader regional entity, such as the state in which the localities exist. By definition, a regional-growth control program is broader than any one city or town and is likely to include multiple counties. Because it is aimed at containing sprawl on a regional basis, the program ultimately must be implemented and administered at the regional level either by state government or by a specially created regional governmental entity. Thus, although such a UGB may be more effective on a regional basis, it clearly implies a greater order of complexity and an ambitious governmental agenda that may be very difficult to accomplish in some parts of the nation. But, as we shall see, it can be done.

Regional Coordination of Transportation and Land Use

Ultimately, the primary transportation burden will continue to fall upon the nation's roadway system in serving the existing land uses that make up the majority of the nation's urbanized areas.[8] But it is widely recognized that congestion is a very serious issue and that something needs to be done to keep this primary system from seizing up entirely. It also is considered unlikely by many planners that roadway-capacity measures alone will be able to fulfill this need. Ultimately, more transit is needed to bring balance to the system and to protect the nation's huge investment in its roadway network.

If transit is to work, we now understand that a change in land-use patterns is needed. Compact developments are a start, but what is needed even more are regionally coordinated land-use and transportation programs, programs that make use of existing urban resources to the maximum extent possible. Portland, Oregon, is one of the few metropolitan areas where this is being done. There, it is being made possible through their regional government, Metro—the only elected metropolitan government in the country. As the Oak Grove case shows, even in Portland coordinating transportation and land use is not necessarily an easy thing to accomplish.

Atlanta, Georgia, has recently begun an undertaking of its own through its newly formed Georgia Regional Transportation Authority (GRTA), a state-chartered authority that has the power to build or veto roads and transit systems in the Atlanta metropolitan area. GRTA also has the power to veto major development projects in the Atlanta area by denying permits to tie into the roadway system.[9] But

Portland and Atlanta are more the exception than the rule. For the rest of the nation, though both highway and transit systems are regional infrastructures, they are not usually integrated with each other or with planning for the land uses they serve.

In most metropolitan areas, there simply is no formal regional structure with any significant powers linking expansion of transit or highway systems to land use planning for their areas. Metropolitan planning organizations (MPOs) were originally established with planning coordination in mind—and they do provide valuable and needed transportation planning and coordination functions—but the MPOs typically have no real power over how land gets developed. That power remains with localities. The result is that planning for most rail extensions and highway improvements are not formally coordinated with regional and local land-use planning in any enforceable way.

In the future, things may change slightly. It is possible that coordination between land use and transportation agencies may happen more frequently with new federal mandates for transportation planning, such as ISTEA and TEA-21, in which state agencies will be required to assess alternative modes when considering improvements to a given transportation corridor. Ultimately, it will be up to states and regional governments to initiate formal coordination between land use and transportation and to create the mechanisms necessary to implement it.

Land-use and transportation must be coordinated at a regional level if there is to be any alternative to auto-dependent sprawl development. Land-use plans must be tailored to transit for transit to be effective and vice versa. Without some kind of "top-down" regional action on this issue, there will be no truly significant change to post–World War II sprawl-development patterns. Furthermore, without any counterbalancing transit initiatives, it is quite possible that the roadway system that has served the nation's growth will no longer be able to keep up, even after significant capacity improvements have been made.

Regional Tax-Base Sharing

The fiscal measure of tax-revenue sharing is, among other things, intended to promote greater equity of resources between both suburban and urban districts. For example, tax-revenue sharing can be used to improve education in urban areas, a necessary ingredient to making downtowns more attractive and leveling the playing field between city and suburb. Such measures can also be used to relieve the pressured competition between municipalities to attract commercial projects to offset losses on residential properties. As Minnesota state legislator Myron Orfield argues in the book *Metropolitics:*

> The link between basic local services and local property wealth fosters socioeconomic polarization and sprawling, inefficient land use. . . Basic public services such as police and firefighters, local infrastructure, parks and (particularly) local schools should be equal throughout the metropolitan area. People of moderate means should not have inferior public services because they cannot afford to live in property-rich communities.[10]

Yet, as Orfield goes on to note: "In almost every part of the United States, wherever social needs are growing, the tax base is uncertain or declining; wherever tax base is solid, social needs are stable or declining."[11] In other words, there is a mismatch between social needs and property tax base resources across most U.S. metropolitan regions. Orfield argues that this situation is made worse by intrametropolitan competition for a commercial tax base to offset social costs and reduce or contain residential property tax rates. Regional tax sharing can be used to even out social inequities and reduce the need for tax-base competition.

This type of regional measure is clearly a controversial issue. Not everyone shares Orfield's point of view. Many taxpayers believe they should get back what they invest in their own communities. As a rule, those in wealthy communities are paying more money, based on the valuation of their property. Why should their taxes, or the taxes of upscale commercial development that they are able to attract to their community, go to serve someone else in another part of the region? This point of view might hold that those in communities of modest means get the services they can afford. If individuals in those communities want better services, then they can always work to improve themselves and move to a community that provides those serv-

Table 14.1. Sample Regional Programs

State(s)	Metro Area(s)	Sample Programs	Scope	Functions/Goals
Georgia	Atlanta	Georgia Regional Transportation Authority (GRTA)	Regional—Atlanta metro area	Coordinates transportation and land use, works toward increasing transit use and achieving compliance with federal clean air act requirements
	Atlanta	Metropolitan Atlanta Rapid Transit Authority (MARTA)	Regional—Atlanta metro area	Provides regional public-transportation services, encourages joint-development opportunities
Maryland, District of Columbia, and Virginia	Washington/Baltimore metro area	Maryland Smart Growth and Neighborhood Preservation Program	Statewide in Maryland	State program aimed at directing growth to existing developed areas, preserving open space, rural areas, and environmental resources, reducing infrastructure costs, relieving transportation congestion, and improving air quality
	Washington/Baltimore metro area	Maryland Mass Transit Administration	Regional/multistate	Provides light rail, bus, and subway service in Baltimore metro area and commuter rail service in greater Washington/Baltimore metro area
	Washington metro area	Washington Area Metropolitan Transit Authority (WMATA)	Regional/multistate	Provides regional public transportation, helps to promote joint development at transit stations
Minnesota	Minneapolis/St. Paul (Twin Cities) metro area	Metropolitan Council	Regional—Twin Cities	Oversees regional sewer, transit, land planning, and tax-revenue sharing
		Metropolitan Urban Service Area (MUSA)	Regional—Twin Cities	Coordinates growth and infrastructure, sets planned limits to growth
		Regional tax-base revenue sharing	Regional—Twin Cities	Distributes commercial property tax base across the region, reduces fiscal disparities, reduces municipal competition for commercial tax base
Oregon	Oregon cities and counties	Oregon Land Conservation and Development Commission (LCDC)	Statewide	Requires cities and counties to draw up growth-management plans and urban growth boundaries—reviews regional planning efforts for compliance with state goals
	Portland metro area	Metro	Regional—Portland metro area	Directly elected regional government—oversees planning for the metro area, sets growth limits, oversees growth boundary, coordinates land-use and transportation planning
		Urban Growth Boundary (UGB)	Regional—Portland metro area	Establishes mapped limit to urbanization within a 3-county, 24-city metro region
		Tri-County Metropolitan Transportation District of Oregon (Tri-Met)	Regional—Portland metro area	Provides regional light rail and bus service throughout 3-county metro area
New York, New Jersey, and Connecticut	New York metro area	Regional Plan Association	Regional/multistate	Regional civic organization that promotes regional planning objectives, draws up periodic regional plans
		Port Authority of New York and New Jersey	Regional/multistate	Bi-state regional authority overseeing New York metro area seaport, airports, and Trans-Hudson transportation facilities
		Metropolitan Transportation Authority	Regional/multistate	Provides regional rail and bus service, including commuter rail service extending through New Jersey and into Connecticut

ices. America's traditional ethos of individual rights, self-determination, and private-property ownership tends to support this viewpoint.

On the other hand, Americans also have a strong tradition of community service and reaching out to help others within their communities. The problem is that the local community usually ends at the town boundaries, where local control and local determination also end. Regional tax-base sharing takes funds out of local control and directs it to other communities. This can seem very unfair unless a wider perspective is taken and the economic health of the local community is viewed in a broader regional context.

Case Studies in Regionalism

Throughout the nation, only a small number of metropolitan areas have formally established regional entities to carry out any of the above measures. Portland, Oregon, is among the most widely cited, having adopted the most ambitious

regional agenda in the nation, but there are other initiatives that have been undertaken or are underway throughout the United States (see Table 14.1). These include both metropolitan-area undertakings as well as state-level programs. In addition to Portland, the efforts of Minneapolis/St. Paul, Maryland, Atlanta, and the Regional Plan Association of the New York metropolitan region are worthy of special mention because of what they have tried (or are trying) to do and how they have fared. The case studies presented here are intended not for direct comparisons but to give an idea of how different kinds of programs can work in different settings.

Portland, Oregon

Portland is generally considered to be the national model for regionalism in the United States. Like Boulder in Colorado, Portland has an urban growth boundary based on an urban service district, in this case, the Portland Metropolitan Services District (see Figure 14.1). Unlike

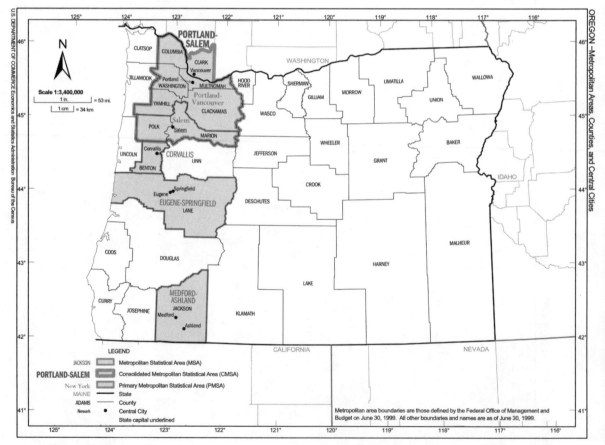

Figure 14.1. Census map of Oregon showing the Portland metropolitan area.
Source: U.S. Census Bureau.

Boulder, Portland's UGB encompasses an entire metropolitan region nearly equal in population to the Denver metro area (which includes Boulder), and administration and enforcement of the district are handled differently. Portland's UGB is administered by a directly elected regional government called Metro, which serves 1.3 million residents and twenty-four cities in the Portland area. Metro is the result of a multidecade planning and political process that dates back to the 1970s.

Although Metro has chalked up many remarkable achievements, its existence remains threatened even today, with recurring ballot initiatives that would effectively curtail its powers. Until recently, Metro has managed to survive these assaults, but in fall 2000 Oregon voters passed a ballot initiative called Measure 7. Measure 7 requires payment to property owners if their land loses value due to growth boundaries or other land-use regulations. Supporters of Oregon's planning programs consider this measure nothing less than a "hydrogen bomb" directed at all the work that has been done to date.[12] As of this writing, Measure 7 was overturned in county court and is now being appealed in the Oregon State Supreme Court.

METRO

In 1973, reacting to the suburban sprawl that was rapidly consuming neighboring California, the Oregon state legislature made it mandatory for cities, towns, and counties in the Portland region to join together in the Columbia Regional Association of Governments (CRAG). At the same time, the state legislature created a Land Conservation and Development Commission (LCDC), whose mandate was to preserve forest and farmland resources by encouraging orderly development adjacent to existing communities. The LCDC in turn required all cities and counties in Oregon to draw up growth management plans together with UGBs to combat sprawl. These moves, like others that followed them, did not go unchallenged. For example, there was a statewide ballot measure to abolish all councils of government (including CRAG) that nearly won in 1976. Despite this, Oregon continued to pursue the regional approach. In another narrow victory in 1978, voters agreed to create Metro, a directly elected regional government for the Portland

area that is the only one of its kind in the United States. Metro includes three counties and twenty-four municipalities in the Portland area. It is governed by an executive officer that is elected at large and a thirteen-member council that is directly elected from council districts in the region.

PORTLAND'S REGIONAL UGB

Following its creation, Metro took up where CRAG had left off in drawing up a UGB for the Portland region (see Figure 14.2). Oregon was not the first place in the nation to have growth boundaries. Lexington, Kentucky, has had one since 1958 to preserve the bluegrass countryside, but the scale of Oregon's undertaking has been extraordinary.[13] There, growth boundaries around every incorporated municipality have preserved 25 million acres of forest and farmland across the state, an area nearly five times the size of Massachusetts.[14] The first UGB drawn for Portland in 1978 contained an area of 234,000 acres, or 365 square miles. It was projected to be enough land to accommodate development for twenty years.[15]

Although the UGB is based to some degree on Metro's service district, its shape and enforcement are largely determined by other factors. The power to define the UGB is derived from state legislation and zoning. Metro has the responsibility for drawing the boundary and for any modifications that may be made to it. The boundary is drawn in part to preserve the best agricultural land. Metro is also charged with requiring consistency of local comprehensive plans with regional planning goals. This requirement is enforced through review powers granted to Metro. Thus, local cities and towns, which retain actual zoning powers, are obliged to implement the boundary using those powers through the consistency requirement. Existing-use agricultural zoning is one of the main tools used to enforce the boundary. This zoning is based partly on agricultural soils (which also affect how the boundary is drawn). Zoning mandates that in areas having those soils, things must essentially stay as they are. In other words, a property owner has the right to build what's there now and not much else. In effect, this strategy guarantees an agricultural and forest greenbelt outside the UGB.[16]

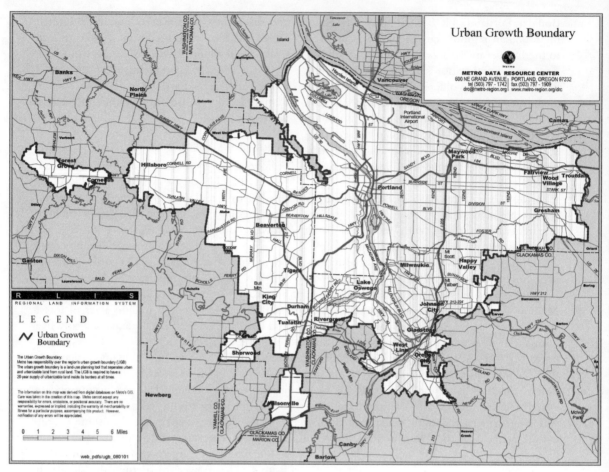

Figure 14.2. Map of Portland's urban growth boundary.
Source: Portland Metro.

Success of the UGB

The UGB program in Oregon appears to be quite successful in meeting its original objectives. Between 1979 and 2000, only about six thousand acres have been added to the UGB—slightly more than a 2 percent increase in overall territory.[17] Nearly 90 percent of the state's population growth during the 1980s occurred inside UGB limits. In Portland, it is estimated that 95 percent of population growth occurred within the UGB.[18] Furthermore, between 1979 and 1997, the average size of a residential lot shrank from 13,000 square feet to 7,400 square feet.[19] Although this trend clearly is moving in the intended direction, build-out within Portland's UGB is also said to be occurring at only 70 percent of planned density.[20] That fact, combined with rapid development during the 1990s and a projected 65 percent population increase by 2040, has created considerable pressure for expansion of the UGB.[21]

In a 1993 referendum, voters opted for restricting development to the existing growth boundary. The policy preference that won the referendum called for retaining the existing UGB and concentrating on infill development and higher density near transit stations. Even so, development pressures later in the decade caused Metro to set aside nineteen thousand acres outside the UGB as a thirty-year reserve for future development.

Housing Costs

Population increase and development pressure have raised concerns about rising housing costs in the Portland metro area given the restrictions on the amount of land available for growth. Some groups strongly believe that readily available, inexpensive land is an essential ingredient for providing moderately priced housing. This may be true when the housing is produced in the mold of the typical subdivision of single-family homes.

There is a countervailing theory that the price of housing could be kept down by simply increasing the number of units per acre (for example, density or compactness) as land cost goes up. This is part of the UGB's intent: to promote higher density and to conserve land. Although construction costs can also rise with increasing density, this general premise should hold true at moderate levels of compactness (single-family homes on smaller lots and townhouses, for example). As we have already seen, the UGB appears to have resulted in a marked downsizing of lot size, which was one of its goals. Furthermore, Portland has not left housing patterns to market forces alone. The Metropolitan Portland Housing Rule requires that 50 percent or more of new housing developments be built in attached single-family or multifamily structures.[22]

Density theories and housing requirements aside, the fact remains that housing prices have gone up considerably for the region, but this does not entirely resolve the debate. Studies to date have shown that the median price of housing in the Portland region more than doubled from $64,000 in 1989 to almost $140,000 in 1996, an increase of about 25 percent per year over an eight-year period.[23] This is clearly a substantial upsurge for any region. On the other hand, as dramatic as that escalation has been, the resultant median price of housing in the Portland area was actually about 8 percent below the average median price for the western part of the United States in 2001 (see Table 14.2).[24] Moreover, hous-

ing price escalation appears to be moderating, having increased only slightly more than 2 percent in 2000, which is about half of the 4 percent national average.[25] Thus, it has been argued that Portland simply is catching up to the rest of the nation.

Furthermore, it is not entirely clear that housing prices went up during the 1990s simply because of limits on developable land. The economic picture in the region was also improving during the same period. During the past decade, Portland has continued its transition from forestry and farm products to newer industries, with high-tech companies investing $13 billion in new plants in the region and with Intel alone adding one thousand jobs in 1999.[26] The high-tech boom has been so successful that part of the Portland region is now known as the "Silicon Forest."[27] Good jobs and an attractive environment naturally have drawn more people to the area. Portland was growing at the rate of fifty thousand new residents per year in 1996, a number sure to put pressure on housing prices regardless of boundaries.[28]

Nor is Portland alone in the nation in experiencing higher housing costs due to economic growth. Other prospering U.S. metropolitan areas that have no growth boundaries have also experienced rapid run-ups in housing price. In the Boston region, where housing prices are nearly double those of Portland, housing prices increased by nearly 14 percent in 2000.[29] Prices in parts of California increased by more than 20 percent in 2000.[30] In the most expensive home

Table 14.2. Comparative Housing Costs in 2000–2001 (in thousands)

Region/Metro Area	*QUARTER*					
	I	*II*	*III*	*IV*	*I★*	*% Change*
United States	133.5	138.0	142.7	139.3	139.7	4.6
U.S. Western Region	175.7	183.9	183.9	186.3	183.5	4.4
Las Vegas	134.3	135.7	139.8	139.5	142.7	6.3
Los Angeles	202.0	210.5	220.4	225.8	225.2	11.5
Phoenix	130.9	134.4	136.7	134.9	135.5	3.5
Portland	166.7	173.1	170.8	169.5	170.3	2.2
Sacramento	133.0	142.6	150.4	151.9	163.4	22.9
Salt Lake City	137.7	140.9	145.6	140.9	144.0	4.6
San Diego	251.4	269.9	272.5	279.5	284.7	13.2
San Francisco	418.6	465.4	452.3	470.2	483.3	15.5
Seattle	226.1	233.9	228.6	234.7	235.7	4.2

Source: National Association of Realtors, *Metropolitan Area Prices, First Quarter 2001,* www.onerealtorplace.com/Research.nsf/Pages/MetroPrice?OpenDocument.
★First quarter in 2001.

market in the nation, the San Francisco Bay area, where median home prices are nearly triple those of Portland, costs were increasing at more than 15 percent in 2000.[31] In addition to experiencing economic growth, these areas offer special attractions for many people. In fact, it can be argued that part of the increase in housing prices in the Portland area is due to the increased appeal of the region to both companies and individuals. Part of the region's magnetism can be attributed to the regional planning measures undertaken since the 1970s (including the UGB) that have preserved the amount of green space in the region.[32]

Another way of looking at the issue is income and housing value disparity. In many metropolitan areas that have no growth boundaries, there are pronounced disparities in income and housing value between city and suburb. This gap is widely perceived to be one of the major problems generated by sprawl. In Portland, disparities in income level and housing value between central city and suburban areas are said to be about half of those in many other urban areas.[33] Thus, it could be interpreted that Portland's growth management actions have helped to even out income levels and housing costs throughout the region. Portland's efforts essentially have redirected middle- and upper-income home buyers from the outer suburbs back to the center city and inner suburbs.

TRANSPORTATION INITIATIVES

Portland's efforts at growth management have not been limited to the UGB. During the mid-1970s, Portland vetoed a series of highway projects, including a planned Mount Hood Freeway. The city tore up the six-lane Harbor Drive expressway and replaced it with a waterfront park. They made investments in downtown Portland and its historic buildings while placing a cap on downtown parking spaces and creating a downtown transit mall. Meanwhile, Portlanders used federal funds to build a fifteen-mile light rail line during the 1980s. Within fifteen years after opening, the new light rail and bus lines carried nearly one-third of all commuters to downtown. As a result, downtown's workforce has grown by 67 percent while adding half a million square feet of retail space since 1972.[34]

During the 1990s, Portland put into place the Transportation Planning Rule (TPR), which advocates a direct approach to integrating land use and transportation. Adopted in 1991, the TPR requires local governments to amend their local land-use ordinances to encourage higher-density, mixed-use development near transit lines. The TPR was modified in 1995, and suggested examples were issued as guidelines.[35] Subsequently, Portland has adopted the 2040 Regional Framework Plan and the Metro 2040 Growth Concept Plan (see Figure 14.3). These plans expand the UGB only slightly while turning attention to the land use–transportation connection. The new plan calls for encouraging the development of regional town centers around light rail stops, thereby maintaining jobs and services in better balance while reducing auto trips. Although controversy over the plan has arisen (as witness Oak Grove), there have also been successes, such as the new development at Orenco Station. In a continuing endorsement of transit in the region, voters in Portland also approved a $472 million bond issue to fund a new $900 million light rail line.[36]

RESULTS

Although Portland's measures been successful in many ways, so far they have not proven to be a "silver bullet" for sprawl. Specifically, whereas total employment in downtown Portland has gone up, the city's share of regional jobs has trended downward. In 1972, the city held 90 percent of the region's best office space and 70 percent of its jobs. By the 1990s, those shares had dropped to 61 percent and 14 percent, respectively.[37] Meanwhile, even though transit use to and from downtown is relatively high, with up to 35 percent of peak-hour work trips using transit downtown, transit use in the region as a whole actually dropped between 1980 and 1990 with the transit share of the daily regionwide commute standing at a little more than 5 percent of the total in 1990.[38] The automobile remains by far the preferred mode of transportation, with about 87 percent of the total trips in the Portland region.[39] The problem is that sprawl has continued inside the UGB. As mentioned earlier, Metro has only achieved 70 percent of density projected for development within the UGB, even though average lot size has decreased. Additionally, many of the new high-tech jobs are in suburban areas.

Another issue has to do with equity to property owners. The value of land can change radically from one side of the boundary to the other.

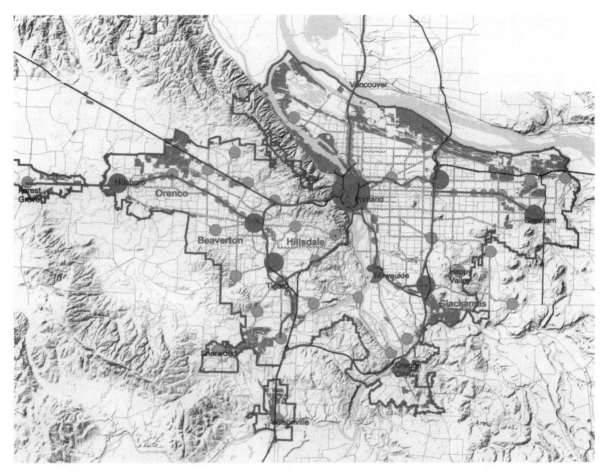

Figure 14.3. Map of Portland's 2040 Regional Growth Concept.
Source: Peter Calthorpe and William Fulton, *The Regional City* (Washington, D.C.: Island Press, 2001).

When land is moved inside the boundary (as it is when the boundary is occasionally adjusted), the value of land can increase tenfold, from $15,000 an acre to $150,000. As Mike Burton, the executive officer of Metro, was recently quoted in the *New York Times:* "We make instant millionaires out of some people."[40] This type of property value disparity may be a contributing factor to the public sentiment behind the passage of Ballot Measure 7 in fall 2000.

On the other hand, Portland has made some bold and positive forward steps. The Metro regional system is still evolving to address new issues as they become evident. The 2040 Plans hold forth particular promise for directing and containing sprawl while shifting a greater share of the region's transportation burden to transit. Making a real effort to integrate land use and transportation at the scale of Portland's TPR and the 2040 Plans is something that is rare in the United States. Portland's approach to met-

ropolitan government and land-use controls is equally rare—though they have not fully succeeded in stopping sprawl, what they have achieved is remarkable. One can only imagine what might have occurred had nothing been done.

AN EVOLVING PROCESS

Programs such as Portland's can take a very long time to leaf out, and no one can know all of the exact consequences before setting out on an untried course of action. Because of this, Portland has been cautious. Portlanders didn't seek to stop growth or even to radically alter it. They sought only to manage it, reducing lot sizes, encouraging slightly greater density, establishing boundaries, and creating alternative transportation modes. If anything, they seem to be moving gradually toward increased control in response to the pattern that has developed. They are fine-tuning their program to improve the regional results. The

Portland program is still evolving and will continue to do so, provided it isn't disassembled first.

Minneapolis/St. Paul

Minneapolis/St. Paul is another oft-cited example of regionalism, with a metropolitan agenda dating back to the 1960s (see Figure 14.4). Like Portland, the Twin Cities region has a metropolitan government that oversees an urban service district, and it also has a form of UGB based on the services district, which is called the Metropolitan Urban Services Area, or MUSA.[41] But the Twin Cities' track record on containing sprawl with these tools is far more mixed than Portland's. The main achievement for which

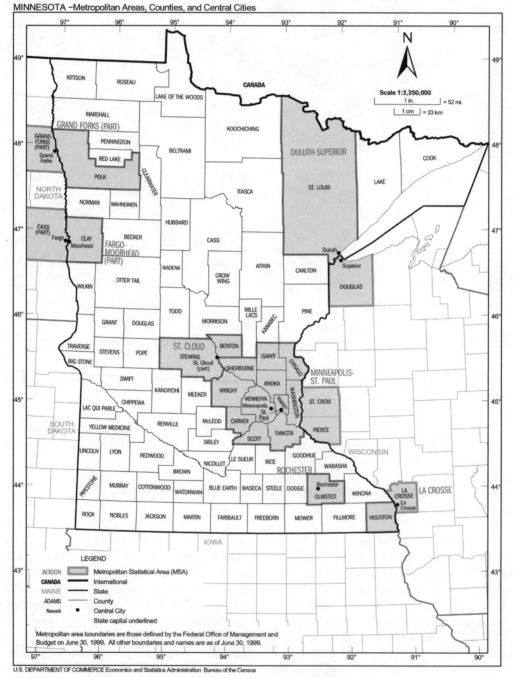

Figure 14.4. Census map of Minnesota showing the Twin Cities metropolitan area.
Source: U.S. Census Bureau.

Minneapolis/St. Paul is usually cited is regional tax-base revenue sharing.

The Metropolitan Council

In 1967, the Minnesota State Legislature created the Minneapolis/St. Paul Metropolitan Council (the Met Council). The council was established as a planning agency with sixteen members. Despite similarities, the model is quite different from Portland's Metro in that the council is appointed by the governor rather than directly elected. This means that the council is not directly accountable to the people—as Metro is in Portland. Instead, the Met Council essentially is directed by the executive branch, with the amount of gubernatorial control depending on the cycle of appointments.

For its first twenty-seven years, the council had no direct powers over other regional agencies. It had supervisory power over the Metropolitan Waste Control Commission and the Metropolitan Transit Commission in the service district, and review powers over set budget thresholds of capital projects carried out by the Metropolitan Airports Commission (more than $5 million at Minneapolis/St. Paul International Airport and more than $2 million at other regional airports). In 1994, the state legislature passed the Metropolitan Reorganization Act, which placed all regional sewer, transit, and land planning under the operational authority of the Met Council, transforming the council from a planning agency with a $40 million annual budget to a $600 million per year regional government overseeing regional sewers and transit, with continuing supervisory responsibility over the $300 million per year Metropolitan Airports Commission.[42] Although these responsibilities were late in arriving, the council had from the beginning the responsibility for developing a comprehensive plan to guide regional growth.

Tax-Base Revenue Sharing

Starting in 1971, 40 percent of the tax revenue from new industrial and commercial development in all jurisdictions in the seven-county region has gone into a common fund. These "growth-sharing" revenues were then dispensed annually as payments to each jurisdiction, based on the inverse of each locality's industrial and commercial tax revenue capacity. The Met Council has been the agency responsible for collecting and dispensing the growth-sharing revenues.[43]

Although growth sharing is reported to have had some mixed results in the Minneapolis/St. Paul area, on balance the results appear positive. Distribution of the fund has reduced tax-base disparities between regional localities from a fifty-to-one ratio to a twelve-to-one ratio.[44] This would seem to indicate that the revenue benefits from growth have been evened out across the region, at least to some degree, allowing inner suburbs and central city areas to provide better services than they would otherwise have been able to do.

On the other hand, in his book *Metropolitics,* Myron Orfield contends that disparities still remain higher than they might be. Furthermore, there have been some unanticipated inequities. Some poorer city centers with a high commercial tax base, relatively low-valued homes, and high social costs actually have ended up as contributors to the system while some wealthier suburban communities with highly valued homes and little commercial tax base receive money from the system. Additionally, competition for commercial tax base remains intense between different districts, even though 40 percent of the revenue is shared.[45]

Despite these issues, the program is considered to have had generally positive effects. Public service and property tax-rate differences have been lessened across the region, which mitigates the tendency for people to abandon high-tax–low-service city centers and older suburbs for low-tax–high-service suburbs on the fringe. In theory, this should act to limit tendencies toward sprawl. Furthermore, between 1960 and 1990, regional income disparities increased less in the Minneapolis/St. Paul region than in twenty-three other U.S. metropolitan regions studied by urban scholars William H. Lucy and David L. Phillips.[46]

Other Measures

Following its inception, the Met Council drafted a regionwide plan for guiding regional growth and moved to broaden the distribution of affordable housing throughout the region. Between 1971 and 1983, the suburban share of subsidized housing rose from 10 percent to 41 percent. Meanwhile, the council oversaw a policy of sewer-connection pricing that rose in proportion to distance from the central treatment plant—a policy that, in theory, encourages more compact development.[47] Despite this promising start, these bold policies and programs were dismantled during the 1980s. The subsidized housing program dried up along with the federal funds that fueled it, and the Minnesota state legislature regionalized the capital and operating costs of the sewer system, eliminating the differential charges for hookups. As a result, any operative obstacles to continued sprawl were largely removed, resulting in the expected forms of suburban development, even as extensive reinvestments were being made in the city centers.

RECENT HISTORY

During the 1990s, in response to continued and increasing problems generated by suburban sprawl, a series of metropolitan governance reform measures were introduced in the state legislature that would have restored the affordable-housing program and the marginal pricing of sewer connections as well as modified the tax-base sharing system, all of which were designed to contain development and reinforce the older suburbs and city-center areas. Legislation was also introduced that would have changed the

Met Council from an appointed body to an elected body. These measures either failed to pass the legislature or were subsequently vetoed by the former governor of Minnesota Arne Carlson.[48] However, according to Orfield, these legislative endeavors have helped to build a city–inner suburb coalition that could help passage of similar legislation in the future.

Maryland

Maryland has a planning context that offers some significant differences when compared with either Portland or the Twin Cities. With nearly 5.3 million people in 2000, Maryland is about 8 percent more populous than Minnesota and 55 percent more populous than Oregon. Yet, at 12,297 square miles, Maryland has only 13 percent of the land area of Oregon and 14 percent of the land area of Minnesota. Maryland also contains a substantial portion of the Washington–Baltimore Consolidated Metropolitan Statistical Area (CMSA) that is shared with Virginia and the District of Columbia (see Figure 14.5).

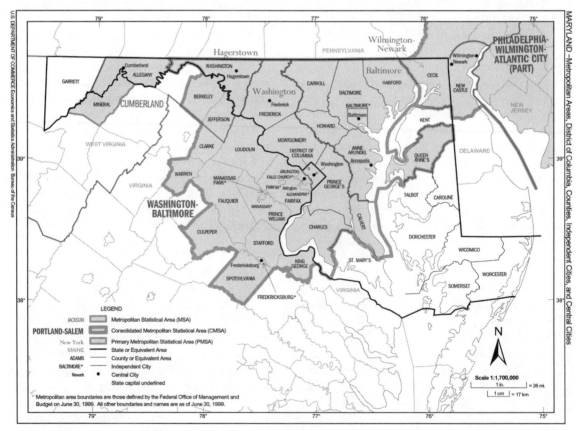

Figure 14.5. Census map of Maryland showing the Baltimore-Washington metropolitan area.
Source: U.S. Census Bureau.

The Washington–Baltimore CMSA comprised 7.6 million people in 2000.[49]

Maryland has had a number of aggressive growth-management efforts at the county level since the 1950s (see Chapter 10). Despite these efforts, suburbanization has continued to mushroom throughout the state while city centers such as Baltimore have steadily lost population. During the 1990s, the situation became dire enough that Maryland felt it was necessary to begin thinking about a statewide growth-management plan. Maryland's situation as a small state with a relatively large population in a shared metropolitan area led them to choose state government as the appropriate institution for crafting and implementing a regional-growth strategy.

Maryland's Smart Growth and Neighborhood Preservation Program was passed by Maryland's General Assembly in 1997, making it more recent than those of Portland and Minneapolis/St. Paul. Baltimore is Maryland's largest city. Maryland has strong county governments that handle many local functions in the state. Prior to initiating its smart growth program, Maryland had a tradition of providing substantial funding assistance to its localities for roads, public transportation, public school construction, and sewer and water projects. That tradition put the state in a good position to assume a certain measure of regional control over development.

The legislation passed in 1997 included five specific programs that are collectively referred to as the Smart Growth Initiatives. Together, these five programs are aimed at directing state resources to revitalizing older developed areas, preserving resource and open space lands, and discouraging "the continuation of sprawling development into . . . rural areas."[50] The five programs of the smart growth legislative package include the following:

- Priority funding areas
- Rural legacy
- Brownfields
- Live near your work
- Job creation tax credit.

PRIORITY FUNDING AREAS

This element of the legislation is considered central to the whole initiative. It establishes a policy for using state funds to steer development to targeted economic development zones called priority funding areas (PFAs). Projects in PFAs receive state funding before any other areas in the state. State funds include monies for roadway, water and sewer, and school construction and reconstruction as well as other monies, such as development loans and grants.

Under the legislation, Maryland counties are required to designate PFAs within their jurisdictions according to guidelines issued by the state.

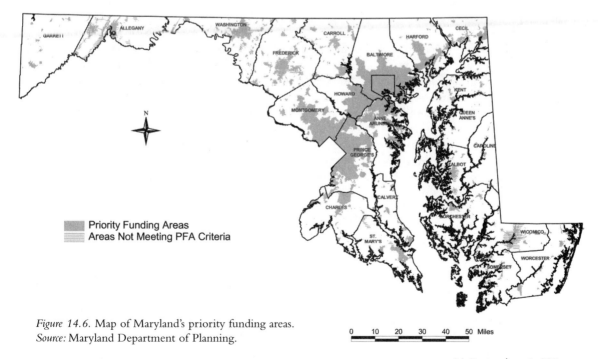

Priority Funding Areas
Areas Not Meeting PFA Criteria

0   10   20   30   40   50 Miles

Figure 14.6. Map of Maryland's priority funding areas.
Source: Maryland Department of Planning.

These guidelines cover intended use, density, and existing infrastructure. According to criteria issued by the state planning office, areas that would qualify include the developed areas inside the Washington, D.C., and Baltimore beltways, cities, and towns targeted for economic development as well as areas already designated as enterprise zones, neighborhood revitalization areas, heritage areas, and existing industrial land. Areas principally used for employment also qualify as long as they are within a designated growth area and have an existing or a planned sewer system. Designated growth areas are districts specifically identified in county comprehensive plans through statements or maps in the plan.[51] Vacant residentially zoned land in existing communities can receive PFA designation only if located within a designated growth area with existing water or sewer service (or both) and planned at a minimum density of two units per acre.[52]

Counties also may designate greenfield areas for new residential communities as long as they meet state guidelines for density and water and sewer service. These sites also have to be within designated growth areas with planned sewer service and planned at a minimum density of 3.5 units per acre.[53] As of this writing, PFAs have been designated and mapped for all Maryland counties and the City of Baltimore (see Figure 14.6). These maps now serve as the basis for reviewing requests for state infrastructure funding.[54]

RURAL LEGACY

The Rural Legacy Program is a land-conservation initiative directed toward community preservation, public access, and habitat conservation goals. This program targets state conservation funds to the purchase of conservation easements on large contiguous tracts of farmland and forestland as well as natural habitats that are subject to development pressure. It also uses fee purchase for open space intended for public access. For fiscal years 1998 through 2002, Maryland has authorized the funding of the Rural Legacy Program with $71 million from a combination of general obligation bonds, real estate transfer tax revenue, and funds from existing open space programs. If funding is continued at this level, it is projected that the state could protect up to 240,000 acres of resource lands by the year 2011. To oversee the process, the legislation created a Rural Legacy Board, which will be responsible for reviewing applications from local governments and land trusts for the designation of Rural Legacy Areas. The state has already produced a map of proposed legacy areas.

BROWNFIELDS

The brownfields law limits liability for developers revitalizing unused or abandoned properties that are thought to be contaminated. The law also includes an incentive program that provides grants and low-interest loans to fund brownfields redevelopment.

LIVE NEAR YOUR WORK

This program encourages Maryland's employees to buy homes near their workplaces. This initiative is intended stabilize the neighborhoods near major downtown employers by stimulating home ownership in targeted communities. The program provides a minimum of $3,000 to home buyers moving to these designated neighborhoods. The local government designates program areas with the state's concurrence and administers the program within its jurisdiction. To join the program, an employee must purchase a home in a designated program area and live there for at least three years.

JOB CREATION TAX CREDIT

According to the Maryland Office of Planning, small businesses comprise 80 percent of the state's employers and generate the majority of new job growth. Tax credits are provided to business owners who create at least twenty-five jobs in PFAs. The intent of the program is to foster small-business development and create new jobs in areas with existing available labor pools.

RECENT INITIATIVES

In 2001, Maryland initiated several new smart growth efforts. Of special note are the Green-Print Program and expanded transit funding. GreenPrint is a $145 million land-acquisition program aimed at protecting the state's remaining network of ecologically valuable lands (see Figure 14.7). According to the state's Department of Natural Resources, this network is characterized as a two-million-acre system of "green hubs" (large habitat areas hundreds of acres across) connected by linear corridors called green links. Both the hubs and their links are targets of this program. The State of Maryland also passed legislation adding $500 million to the

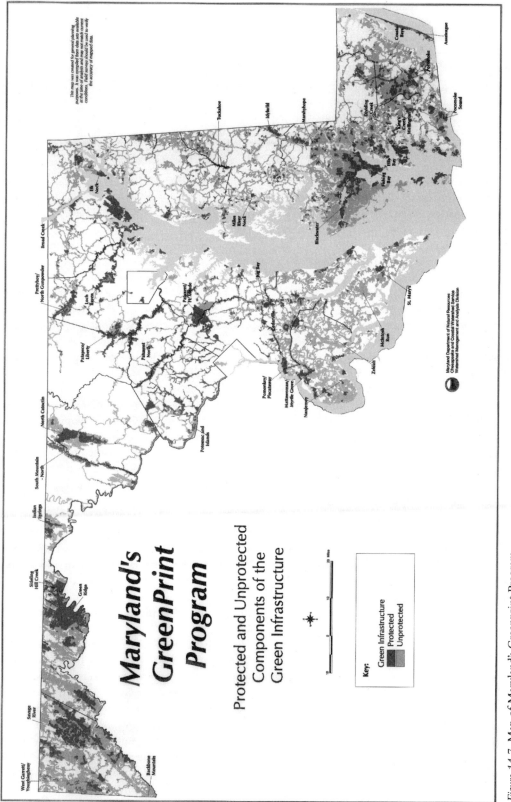

Figure 14.7. Map of Maryland's Greenprint Program.
Source: Maryland Department of Natural Resources.

state's capital funding of transportation. Major initiatives include expanding transit and commuter rail links, with a statewide goal of eventually doubling mass-transit ridership.[55]

MARYLAND IN SUMMARY

Maryland's program has been in effect for only about four years, in contrast to those of Minnesota and Oregon, which have been in place since the 1970s. Thus, it is a little early to make judgments on the program's outcome. It is only within the past year or so that the PFA designations have been finalized. However, the program clearly is a unique effort that differs in significant ways from that of either Portland or the Twin Cities. First, it is a statewide program in a state with considerably different population, area, and metropolitan characteristics than either of the previous two cases. Second, Maryland takes a somewhat different approach to growth management, using an array of mechanisms to contain suburbanization and concentrate new growth in areas that are already developed and have—or are planned to have—infrastructure in place.

The PFA, brownfields, live near your work, job creation tax credit, and expanded-transit programs all act to direct and encourage growth in existing developed districts while the Rural Legacy and GreenPrint Programs are acting to protect open land. At the same time, the PFAs are not growth boundaries. In this sense, they may succeed in avoiding some of the problems that Portland has had with its UGB (such as making instant millionaires by simply moving an invisible line). Instead, the emphasis is on public infrastructure and services. Presumably, anyone can subdivide their land (in accordance with local bylaws), but if they aren't in a PFA they may have to wait a long time before roads, water, and sewer are provided at public expense. To some degree, the PFA strategy could be circumvented without some parallel prohibition of on-site wells and septic systems. However, local communities may be hesitant to permit such development outside of their designated PFAs since they may not receive the state funding for school and road construction that they may later need to support such projects.

On a different note, the recommended densities for existing and new development are relatively low. In the case of existing development, this is probably intended to help infill development fit in with existing suburban patterns

without generating too much controversy. On the other hand, it isn't the kind of density required to build a TOD or transit village node within an existing community (7 to 15 units per acre or higher). The 3.5-unit-per-acre requirement for new development is also low. This actually is a lower density than the original Levittown in Long Island, New York—17,500 homes on four thousand acres, which breaks down to more than 4 units per acre built on six-thousand-square-foot lots.[56] Again, this type of density may be the best that currently can be negotiated within the state.

Atlanta

Atlanta's regional program is unique in that it is directed specifically to one area: the coordination of transportation and land use within the Atlanta metropolitan area. Atlanta and Georgia also present different situations than any of the previous case studies. At about fifty-nine thousand square miles in physical size, Georgia is about 60 percent the size of Oregon but nearly five times the size of Maryland. With more than 8 million people, Georgia has a much larger population than any of the previous three states. About 50 percent of Georgia's population lives in the Atlanta metropolitan area, which is contained (at least as of 2000) completely within the state of Georgia (see Figure 14.8).[57]

As noted in Chapter 5, Atlanta has a reputation for being one of the most rapidly suburbanizing regions in the nation, with new development in the region covering about fifty acres of open space and forestland each day.[58] Between 1990 and 1996, the population of the region increased about 16 percent while the amount of developed land increased by 47 percent—three times faster than the population growth.[59] At about 1,400 people per square mile, Atlanta is one of the least dense metropolitan areas in the nation. In contrast, Los Angeles has about 5,400 people per square mile. Residents of Atlanta drive about thirty-five miles per day, more than any other U.S. metropolitan area.[60] Road building (other than highways and interstates) is largely done by the counties, and with the population growth of the suburbs nearly one hundred times greater than that of the city, and with few regulatory barriers, the counties have built hundreds of miles of roads to accommodate their rapid growth.[61] Even with the Metropolitan

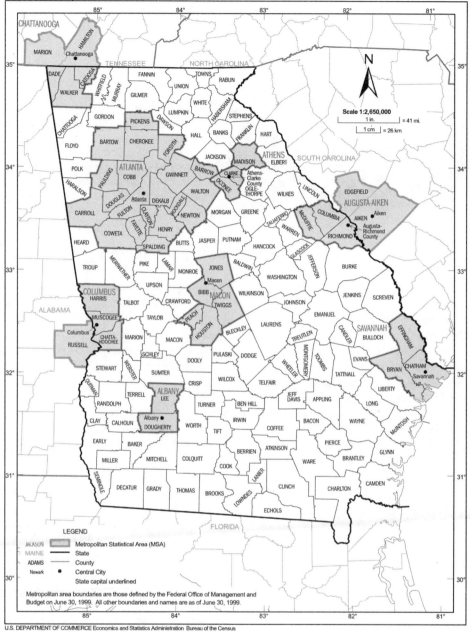

Figure 14.8. Census map of Georgia showing the Atlanta metropolitan region.
Source: U.S. Census Bureau.

Atlanta Rapid Transit Authority (MARTA) rail transit system and a network of bus lines, Atlanta's transit commute share was slightly below 5 percent in 1990 (see Figure 14.9).[62]

During the late 1990s, Atlanta's situation reached a crisis point when federal funds for new highway projects were cut off because of the region's failure to meet air quality standards mandated by the Clean Air Act. In 1999, the state settled a lawsuit filed by environmental groups

challenging sixty-one roadway projects in the thirteen-county Atlanta metropolitan region. Under the terms of that settlement, only seventeen of those projects could move forward until the region adopted a transportation plan meeting air quality standards.[63]

These pressures, plus national publicity about Atlanta's problems with traffic congestion and air pollution, led Georgia state government to create the Georgia Regional Transportation

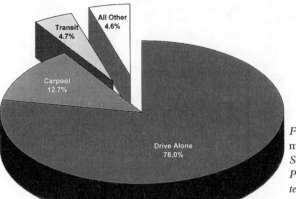

Figure 14.9. Commuting Shares in the Atlanta metropolitan region.
Source: U.S. Census Bureau, *Journey to Work and Place of Work: 1990 Census-Travel to Work Characteristics for the 50 Largest Metropolitan Areas by Population in the United States: 1990,*, www.census. gov/population/socdemo/journey/msa50.txt.

Authority (GRTA) in 1999. The legislature granted GRTA fairly broad regional powers in dealing with the crisis, which allow the GRTA to use a "carrot and stick" approach in dealing with local governments and development projects. The carrot is that the GRTA is empowered to issue up to $2 billion in bonds to assist local governments in financing mass transit and other measures to combat air pollution. The stick is that GRTA approval is required for local land transportation plans and for major development undertakings, such as large subdivisions or commercial projects that can affect the metropolitan transportation system. However, local governments can override a GRTA project veto with a three-quarters "supermajority." The fifteen GRTA board members also act as the Governor's Development Council, on which they are charged with ensuring that local governments meet state land use planning requirements.[64]

Since its formation, GRTA's top priority was to bring the region's transportation plan into federal compliance. Working with the Atlanta Regional Commission, the GRTA helped win federal approval of the region's three-year transportation improvement program (TIP) in July 2000, meaning that the Atlanta region once again qualifies for federal transportation funds following a two-year hiatus. The TIP includes nearly $2 billion in transportation spending, with the majority of funds dedicated to public transportation, HOV lanes, and bicycle and pedestrian improvements.

In addition to the TIP, GRTA has been at work expanding bus service in the region, conducting transportation needs assessments, and

working with the State Department of Transportation and the Georgia Rail Passenger Authority to start commuter rail service in the Atlanta region. Other than these projects, there seems to be relatively little news about an agency that was given sweeping powers to bring land use and transportation together to curtail suburbanization and improve air quality in one of the nation's most sprawling metropolitan areas.

However, GRTA has been in existence for just two years and has had an executive director and staff for less time than that. It can take time for a new agency to produce results, particularly in a region as overcome with sprawl as Atlanta. The hope is that, as time progresses, GRTA may help the region see more projects like the Lindbergh Center, a fifty-one-acre, transit-oriented project spearheaded by MARTA in Atlanta's Buckhead region (see Figure 14.10). The project is projected to include nearly 3 million square feet of office space and about 950 apart-

Figure 14.10. The Lindbergh Center in metropolitan Atlanta, a planned high-density transit village served by heavy rail transit (MARTA). (Carter Associates/Cooper Carry Inc.)

ments and condominiums together with more than 300,000 square feet of retail and a 190-room hotel, all to be developed above and around MARTA's Lindbergh rapid transit station. The project is to be built on land leased from MARTA. BellSouth, a major communications company, will become the anchor tenant. This project combines walkable streets with transit access and could be a model for similar land use–transit projects if and when GRTA moves beyond transportation and begins to fulfill its anticipated role as a bridge between land use and transportation planning in the region.[65]

New York and the Regional Plan Association

The New York metropolitan area is unique in America. With New York City at its center and its population of more than 8 million people, the New York CMSA encompasses more than 21 million people in an area of over 10,000 square miles in parts of four states: New York, New Jersey, Connecticut, and Pennsylvania (see Figure 14.11). Thus, the New York CMSA includes nearly as many people as all of the previously discussed states combined, in a region slightly smaller in area than the state of Maryland.

Metropolitan Areas of the United States and Puerto Rico : 1999

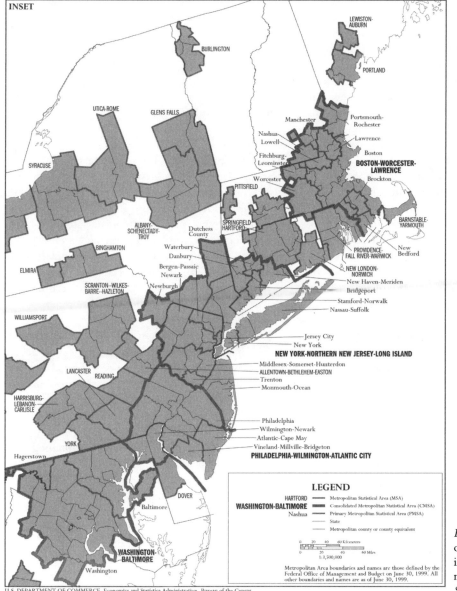

Figure 14.11. Census map of the Northeast Corridor, including the New York metropolitan area.
Source: U.S. Census Bureau.

U.S. DEPARTMENT OF COMMERCE, Economics and Statistics Administration, Bureau of the Census

The New York urbanized area has been expanding rapidly for more than a century. New York City had annexed as much territory as it could by 1900, but the urbanized area of the city continued to overflow its boundaries. The greatest expansion in area came after World War II as the city's suburbs exploded across Long Island to the east, New Jersey and Pennsylvania to the west and south, and parts of Connecticut and upstate New York to the north. Outward expansion of urbanization is continuing in the region today.

The New York metro area has no regional government or even any formal regional coordinating mechanism. In fact, the different counties, municipalities, and states are often at odds with one another on a wide variety of topics, including transportation, ports, territory, finances, and competition for businesses and governance, among others. Nonetheless, the New York metro area also has a history of forming joint institutions to deal with regional issues. The Port Authority of New York and New Jersey is a bi-state authority responsible for the region's major seaports and airports as well bridges, tunnels, and transit systems connecting New York and New Jersey. The Palisades Interstate Park Commission manages a bi-state park running along the west bank of the Hudson River. The Metro-North commuter rail system operates in New York, New Jersey, and Connecticut. Its parent agency, the Metropolitan Transportation Authority, crosses jurisdictional lines throughout the region. The New York Metropolitan Planning Council (the Metropolitan Planning Organization for part of the region) includes the directors of key New Jersey transportation agencies as nonvoting members and representatives of surrounding New York counties as voting members.

The Regional Plan Association

There is also a network of regional civic groups that attempts to guide coordinate the policies and investments of the diverse special purpose agencies and authorities that operate throughout the region. The Regional Plan Association (RPA) stands out among these organizations in promoting long-range comprehensive planning for the region. The RPA has its origins in the 1920s, publishing its first "Regional Plan for New York and Its Environs" in 1929. The RPA is an independent, private, nonprofit membership organization with some 1,200 members,

including approximately 100 of the region's major employers. About half of the association's operating budget comes from member contributions, with the rest coming from foundations and government grants and contracts. The RPA's board consists of business leaders, university presidents, civic leaders, and former mayors and governors.[66] Although the metropolitan area covered by the RPA is similar to the census-defined CMSA, it is not identical. The RPA's area of influence includes additional counties in upstate New York and Connecticut but does not include any of the state of Pennsylvania.[67]

The RPA has no legal powers or official status, relying instead on the influence of its membership, the persistence of its staff, and the quality of its work to achieve its ends. As a result, the RPA claims that many of its recommendations have been implemented over the years, although some of this credit is also due to the association's coalition partnerships. Coalition building and alliances have also been key to the RPA's achievements in the region.

The Three Regional Plans

During its history, the RPA has created three regional plans for the New York metropolitan area. The first regional plan, which coincided with the RPA's formation in 1929, recommended a growth pattern of concentrated sub-urban subcenters combined with an extensive program of infrastructure improvements—including new railway networks, parks, parkways, bridges, tunnels, and highways—to accommodate a projected doubling of the region's population by 1965.

Because of the RPA's work, the New York region had plans in place to move forward quickly with public works projects funded by New Deal programs when the Great Depression arrived in the 1930s. Robert Moses built many of the plan's proposed parkways, highways, tunnels, and bridges during the 1930s and 1940s. As a consequence, the New York region contained more than 60 percent of the nation's limited-access highway lane miles as recently as 1965.[68] However, most of the railway projects did not get built, and the proposed pattern of concentrated subcenters never materialized.

The RPA's second regional plan was initiated in response to the increasing decentralization and deconcentration of the New York region brought about by suburbanization. It was aimed

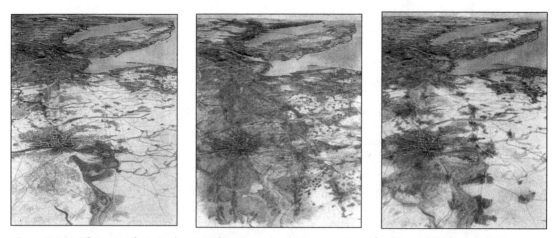

Figure 14.12. Three aerial views showing alternative development patterns for New Jersey from *A Region at Risk* by the Regional Plan Association. (Regional Plan Association)

at controlling suburban sprawl, expanding the regional open space system, and revitalizing the regional rail network. A key aspect of the second plan was the proposed creation of a system of transit-oriented satellite employment centers organized around the rail network. These were planned as a counterpoint to spreading, auto-dependent, low-density development. In essence, the second plan reconstituted in altered form some of the key elements of the first plan that were bypassed in the national rush to suburbanization. As a result of this effort, the RPA claims that approximately half of the region's employment base remains in New York City and in concentrated satellite centers, such as Stamford, Connecticut.[69] Nonetheless, during the 1970s and 1980s, suburbanization continued throughout the region, with substantial employment and residential growth occurring outside of the region's centers. The RPA estimates that in the twenty-five years leading up to 1996, the region grew in population by just 13 percent while it grew in urbanized area by more than 60 percent.

The RPA started work on its third regional plan *(A Region at Risk)* in 1989 and completed it in 1996 (see Figure 14.12). The third plan calls for a $75 billion investment in regional infrastructure, the environment, education, and cities to lay a foundation for the region's competitiveness in a future global economy. Major elements of the plan call for expansion of the regional rail network, creation of an extensive greenbelt network of open spaces and natural resource systems around the region, and economic development focused on New York City and an expanded system of regional centers. In essence, the third plan reiterates and expands upon major themes of the first and second plans: revitalized rail, concentrated centers, and expanded open space systems.

The third plan also made recommendations about local governance. For example, it recommended the creation of a new regional transportation authority to manage the regional rail, bridge, and tunnel system, and a tri-state infrastructure bank to finance these systems. The plan also recommended that the states making up the region embark upon smart growth initiatives along the lines of the Maryland program while encouraging the formation of groups, such as the Long Island Pine Barrens Commission, to manage growth and conserve open space in the region's sensitive environmental areas. In addition, the plan recommended that the states assume the cost of primary and secondary education and that the eight hundred independent municipal governments in the region examine the possibility of shared service districts.

RESULTS

Over the years, the RPA's results have been mixed, but the association remains highly persistent in pursuing their goals. This persistence has sometimes paid off handsomely, even after long periods of time. One example is the purchase of the Sterling Forest, a seventeen-thousand-acre natural area split between New York and New Jersey. This tract was finally acquired during the 1990s after being recommended in the RPA's first regional plan sixty-five years previously.[70] When confronted with the failure of the rail and regional centers elements of the first plan, the RPA has stuck to its guns, bringing these important concepts back with each subsequent plan and achieving some additional measure of success each time.

As far as the third plan goes, the RPA is again meeting with mixed results. So far, no action has been taken on the regional transportation governance recommendations. But as regards smart growth, New Jersey has responded with a new state development plan that has similar goals to that of Maryland's—directing development to existing centers and conserving open space. New Jersey has also enacted a school finance reform plan in which the state supplies additional funds to urban schools while setting statewide educational achievement standards. New York City is proceeding with an innovative program to protect its upstate watershed by negotiating new land use regulations and conservation easements in upstate communities in exchange for city financing of local economic development, and a substantial portion of Long Island's one hundred thousand acres of the Pine Barrens aquifer zone is now protected by the Long Island Central Pine Barrens Commission.

There is little question that the RPA's comprehensive long-range planning and its consistency and persistence in its recommendations have been a significant boon to the region. By building and aligning itself with major coalitions and by doing quality work, it has managed to achieve some significant results. Without the RPA, there would be no significant and consistent entity engaged in pursuing an agenda of regional improvement. The RPA shows that it is possible to achieve regional results without a formally empowered regional government or even a formal planning agency that covers the full extent of the region.

Regionalism in Summary

The expansion of metropolitan areas over the past fifty years has made them into the nation's primary economic and social units. This same expansion has created local and regional tensions that call for metrowide solutions to the twenty-first-century problems of spreading urbanization. Major debates are occurring over urban-growth control, coordination of land-use planning and regional transportation systems, and

regional fiscal disparities and social and economic burdens.

Different metro areas have attempted to deal with regional problems in different ways. Some metro areas have been able to address these problems by simply expanding and incorporating their mushrooming suburbs into their municipal boundaries. Others have instituted metropolitan governments, as in Portland and the Twin Cities. Atlanta is trying to address a specific sector of issues (regional land use and transportation) with a regional authority. Still other regions, such as Maryland and New Jersey, have adopted statewide plans to deal with their expanding suburbs. Finally, in New York, where the metropolitan region spreads over multiple states and more than eight hundred municipalities, the charge is being led by a nongovernmental civic institution.

Each solution is appropriate to its place and is not applicable in every situation. Metro governments like Portland's could be a model for some cities in some states but certainly not for all. Portland has made significant progress in trying to manage its growth, and it is often hailed as a national model for smart growth. But even in Portland, there are problems, and growth is spilling over into neighboring Washington State—beyond Metro's control. The Twin Cities have had arguably less success with regional government than Portland. Some people, including Myron Orfield, contend that this is partly because the Met Council is appointed and not elected. However, the Twin Cities do have a nationally recognized tax base revenue sharing program. Georgia is progressing with GRTA, but it is too soon to tell what this effort may eventually yield. One accomplishment by GRTA has been the reinstatement of Georgia's federal transportation funds. New York has a regional civic institution that has been in place for over seventy years and has been a very positive influence in shaping a very complex region.

Maryland appears to have a very innovative state program that is becoming a model for other states, especially those that are small in area, large in population, and have metro areas that overlap with other states. New Jersey has a similar plan in place, and other states could be candidates for this type of solution. In the end, most metropolitan solutions, even in those areas that are spread over several states, will end up requiring state action to get going.

Portland would not have Metro or its UGB were it not for state legislation that started during the 1970s. The efforts at regional government in the Twin Cities have mostly been played out in the Minnesota state legislature. It took the State of Georgia to create GRTA. The Port Authority of New York and New Jersey exists because of state legislation in two states. State governments typically are in control of regional transportation funds, and state legislatures are the source of land use control laws. State governments ultimately sign agreements with other states in multistate metro areas. In the quest for metropolitan solutions, state government has generally been the place to start.

PART IV

The Future and Concluding Thoughts

This final part contains a discussion of possible future trends and a concluding chapter. Chapter 15 speculates about the prospects of suburbanization given current trends derived from the 2000 census and recent writings by scholars on the subject. Included in the chapter is a brief overview of some of the contemporary discussion about the role of information technology in shaping future urbanization patterns.

Chapter 16 provides a brief general summary of some of the points raised in the book and some concluding thoughts on the continuing debate about sprawl.

CHAPTER 15

Thinking About the Future

The Prospects for Change

Having reviewed the history of suburbanization, the debate about its merits, and what different groups are doing to effect change, a serious question remains about whether any fundamental change is likely to occur in the future. In fact, there is continuing debate about whether there should even be any change. Without the intervention of some crisis event, the nation may simply continue to build more of the same suburban pattern. This is the tyranny of easy development decisions, those that follow the path of least resistance.

However, strong sentiments for change are in the wind, stronger, perhaps, than at any previous time. These sentiments may become muted by international events and a change in the nation's economic fortune, but history suggests that the voices favoring change will only become louder when better times return. This emerging tide of popular opinion may eventually become the force that is necessary to effect change. Industry groups are listening to the polls, and their positions increasingly show a willingness to accommodate some modification to past patterns.

There is also a question about the amount and extent of the suburban pattern that can exist without literally suffocating itself. Calling for vast new roadway expenditures may bring only diminishing returns. There are limits to how big roadways can become and still provide reasonable local and regional service. Three or four left-hand turn lanes may be nearing the maximum, and you can't grade separate everything. There also are coming technological and economic changes that we can't yet see but that we know are in our future, just as they are firmly established in our past.

Technology and Cyberspace

The continuing information technology revolution is one of the most prominent topics of future change. Some scholars believe that continuing advances in computer technology and communications may someday change our world more profoundly than the automobile has.[1] The nation is only just beginning to understand the implications of living and working practically anywhere. For example, May 25, 2001, was the last day of face-to-face trading on the Pacific Stock Exchange. The exchange is moving to cyberspace to join the more cost-efficient and profitable electronic marketplace.[2] More events like this are taking place every day. The question is, what effect is future technology likely to have on the nation's metropolitan patterns?

Limitless Expansion?

Today, companies can "virtually" exist wherever they want. According to the *New York Times,* such corporations as General Electric and British Airways have set up supermarket-sized phone banks in call centers located as far away as Bangalore, India. Dell Computer bases its technical support calls there. High-capacity phone lines and employees who speak American English can make calls to these centers indistinguishable from calls to similar centers in the United States.[3] But a business doesn't have to go as far as India to reduce overhead. Any company can reduce land and rental costs simply by moving ever farther from established urban-core areas—which employment figures show they are doing. As Andrew Gillespie of the University of Newcastle recently said in a Lincoln Institute of Land Policy roundtable on the subject of technology and urban development:

Telephone call centers are . . . one of the most radical innovations in the service sector. . . . They also have a strong deconcentration effect within metropolitan regions. . . . These huge centers with thousands of people at desks just don't fit within the central city fabric. These companies are on a tight schedule so they build where they can do it quickly and cheaply, which is almost invariably out in the suburbs in business parks where people have to use their cars to get to work.[4]

A recent television advertisement for a computer information services company provides a case in point. Loosely summarized, the ad shows a junior executive and his boss getting out of a rental car on a desert roadway. The boss wants to know why his employee has brought him way out into this wilderness. The junior executive replies, "$1 per square foot." The boss wants to know what good that is in the middle of nowhere. The junior executive asks in return, "How did we get here?" He points to the road and his cell phone and says: "Airport, roadway, Internet!" "Genius!" says the boss, after a momentary pause.

Anecdotes like this would suggest that the tendency toward outward expansion is likely to continue. Certainly, telecommunications and computers have made it far easier for businesses to locate just about anywhere. Cost will be a frequent factor, meaning that, given more or less fixed building expenses, cheap land will be important, potentially leading to ever-more exurban locations. As Robert Atkinson of the Progressive Policy Institute stated at the same Lincoln Institute roundtable:

> If . . . we had to vote on the question of how technology will affect urban development patterns—that is, toward deconcentration and decentralization versus increased "localization" imperatives—I would cast my vote right away for deconcentration and decentralization. I think that's what the new economy and the IT revolution are all about.[5]

Among other things, Atkinson was a project director at the Congressional Office of Technology Assessment, where he directed the publication of *The Technological Reshaping of Metropolitan America,* a report on the impact of the information technology revolution on America's urban areas.

There is also the possibility that as technology improves, leading to face-to-face conversations via computer, more people may end up spending part or all of their workdays in the same place they live, diminishing the importance of the work commute in transportation. The advent of the Internet in retailing also has implications. Books, groceries, and even automobiles can be ordered on-line, reducing the need to travel for shopping errands. More educational and leisure activities may happen at home using computers and the Internet, and the entertainment possibilities are only just being broached.

But what can all this mean for where we choose to live? Again, the first guess is that the preferred option may be suburban. Atkinson believes that the offices where people work are more likely to be located in anonymous buildings in suburban office parks, which means the people that work there will be living in the suburbs as well.[6] There, the commuting distance will be shorter, and employees will still have a house surrounded by some green space and privacy. As Atkinson says, deconcentration offers "lower costs for single-family homes and . . . the increasing ability of Americans to own homes, and both avoid the disamenities of core urban areas, such as poor government services, high costs, a decrepit built environment and traffic congestion."[7]

Suburban life may be further improved by having shopping, work, and digital entertainment all brought right into the home. Listening to the symphony may be a better experience at home, with enhanced sound and visuals and more comfort than can be had at a live performance. Ordering over the Internet can minimize tiresome errands and commutes involving the car. It is possible that all this would help reduce suburban roadway congestion while simultaneously reducing fuel consumption and air pollution. If the trend catches on, Internet shopping and telecommuting may even have the potential to reduce development pressures for new commercial retail and office space.

Virtual Work

Telecommuting could reduce the number of square feet required for office space if (and it's a big if) such concepts as "hoteling" become popular. Hoteling is a practice in which people share office space on an as-needed basis rather than having a dedicated space provided for each employee. Widely touted a decade ago, hoteling largely failed to catch on in the following years, leading many to lose interest in the idea.

However, improvements in technology, combined with tight labor markets, corporate cost cutting, and increasing roadway congestion, may be making telecommuting more attractive. Between 1980 and 1990, the number of people working at home in the United States increased by 56 percent, reversing a multidecade downward trend.[8] A recent study conducted by the *Boston Globe* shows that, although only 16 percent of the nation's employers currently allow telecommuting, the number of Americans working from home at least one day per week increased fivefold during the 1990s.[9] Other sources report higher figures. The *New York Times* relates that telecommuting increased nearly sixfold during the 1990s, jumping from about 4 million telecommuters in 1990 to almost 24 million in 2000 (see Figure 15.1).[10]

In the area of back-office operations, telecommuting has begun to catch on with some major financial institutions. According to the *Boston Globe,* Putnam Investments, a large mutual fund house in New England, is beginning to farm out some of its back-office paperwork to individual contractors working at home. In 2001, Putnam hired four hundred employees in Vermont and Maine to work at home, hundreds of miles from company headquarters in the Boston area. Each employee is supplied with a powerful computer that is connected to a high-speed data transmission line. These new telecommuting employees perform such tasks as recording deposits into customer accounts, transferring money between accounts, and checking the accuracy of customer transactions. These out-of-state employees are joining five hundred in-state telecommuters already on Putnam's staff. Other companies across the nation are also adopting at-home programs. Airline travel companies are employing reservation staff working from home, and the medical industry is hiring telecommuters for medical dictation and transcription.[11]

Of note is that Putnam's new hiring program is in exurban locations and that all of those interviewed for the *Boston Globe* article lived in rural settings, which they stated was part of the attraction of being in a telecommuting job. So far, no one seems to be touting city living as being one of the allures of telecommuting. If this is part of a trend, it does not bode well for the nation's urban areas. In fact, it suggests an impetus toward exurbia, the rapidly growing fringe of sprawl. However, a recent survey conducted by the

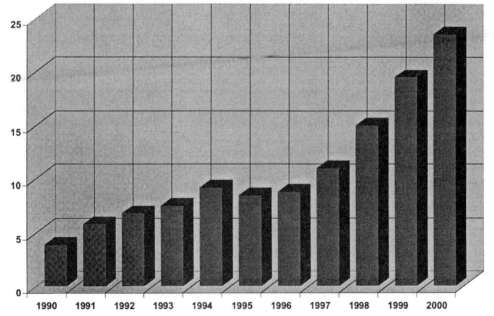

Figure 15.1. Telecommuting in the Uniter States. The number of people working at least part of the week at home (in millions).
Source: Jonathan D. Glater, "Telecommuting's Big Experiment," *New York Times,* May 9, 2001.

International Telework Association and Council shows that telecommuters tend to be more urban than rural, although the survey does not appear to distinguish between the "city" and "suburban" components of the "urban" category.[12]

Ordering In

On-line shopping, if it really becomes popular, could reduce the need for retail square footage in the suburbs. So far, "e-retail" sales climbed from $5.2 billion in the fourth quarter of 1999 to nearly $8.7 billion in the fourth quarter of 2000, an increase of about 67 percent, before dropping to about $7 billion in the first quarter of 2001. As a percentage of total retail sales, e-retail remains quite small, having climbed from only 0.63 percent of total retail sales in 1999 to just over 1 percent in 2000. This may be a very small slice of the total pie, but it is an increase in market share of nearly 60 percent in just one year.[13] If market share were to keep increasing at similar rates, it hypothetically could reach 50 percent in less than ten years. Such a rapid increase may not be likely, however, because total share declined from about 1 percent in the fourth quarter of 2000 to just over 0.9 percent in the first quarter of 2001. Furthermore, many e-retail start-ups went out of business in 2000 and 2001. The problem is that e-retail has only been tracked by the U.S. Commerce Department since 1999, which is too short a time frame on which to base any serious projections. But, in the long run, industry watchers believe that e-retail may capture a significant share of the market.[14]

If such a shift were to occur, the role of some suburban icons, such as big-box stores and strip mall outlets with all their staff, could become questionable when they could be replaced by warehouses full of automated systems that simply send out bulk items in response to an Internet order. Or, maybe the warehouse would have a dual role, still acting as a store for those who want to see their merchandise before they buy or who simply want to save shipping costs. Either way, there may be fewer shopping outlets. This ultimately will depend on the success or failure of the e-retail business over time, but Thomas Horan, author of *Digital Places: Building Our City of Bits,* believes that many subregional malls from the 1960s and 1970s may well be casualties of e-retailing.[15]

If Thomas Horan is right and on-line shopping were to gain enough market share in the long term to put some stores out of business, then there may be less pressure on the land. Furthermore, the Internet can also grant smaller independent stores in cities access to much broader international markets, which could help keep them afloat and maybe even take away some business from the large, market-controlling retail chains. This could be good news for cities. Meanwhile, excess commercial and office properties could become prime sites for transit- and pedestrian-friendly higher-density, mixed-use developments.

On the other hand, if e-retail is the way of the future, then the roadways will have to work for everyone to receive the goods they order in a timely fashion. This means solutions need to be found for increasingly congested roadways. As Thomas Horan says:

> The impact on the transportation system as you move to just-in-time delivery systems is certainly an area that was not predicted in traditional highway design. The disproportionate number of trucks vis-à-vis cars is something that many states are just beginning to grapple with. . . . The hundreds of fed-ex trucks running around in small suburban areas are beginning to have an impact on traffic flows. Recently some in the delivery business have called for changes in the physical design of streets, and their ideas are not in the pedestrian-friendly direction.[16]

Part of the solution may be the shifting of some shopping and work trips to cyberspace, but the effectiveness of such a shift may ultimately depend on the type of land use pattern that e-commerce eventually fosters.

There are still many trips people can't eliminate. Children will still have to get to music lessons and soccer matches, office workers will still have to go to some meetings, everyone will have to see the doctor, and the plumber will still need to get to your house to fix the sink. There are also shopping trips consumers may wish to make themselves. While toilet paper and dishwashing detergent can easily be ordered on-line, many people may still want to go to the market to choose their own fresh produce. Similarly, it is usually customary to test out a new car (or another similar item) before purchasing it. Or, you might get tired of your own cooking and Internet delivery options and want just to go out to dinner.

Isolation and Community of Place

Working at home, watching the symphony on digital TV, and having everything delivered can mean a lot of isolation. Most of the experiences of shopping, working, and education involve social interaction. It is uncertain to what degree that element can be removed from everyday life without suffering ill consequences of some kind. People living and working in isolation may crave relief in the form of getting out, doing errands, and interacting with other people. For these reasons, the indoor shopping mall seems less likely to disappear, and some form of the workplace seems likely to remain.

SEARCHING FOR COMMUNITY IN THE DIGITAL AGE

Social interaction and other considerations may persuade some people to opt for the city or small town environment, where personal contact can be had simply by walking out the door. This may be particularly true if more and more work, education, and entertainment are happening at home. Suddenly, the isolation may become palpable. Whereas now the suburban home on its island of land provides refuge from the teeming workplace, it may be that the crowded city will someday provide refuge from the isolation of the home based virtual workplace. The basic unreality of what is available over the Internet or through interactive television may cause people to treasure real encounters with people, art, culture, and food all the more. The people who are moving back into the cities are moving there partly for those very reasons. Compact, walkable communities may hold appeal to the same people who are searching for some sense of community in a world of increasing isolation.

In his book *The New Geography: How the Digital Revolution Is Reshaping the American Landscape,* Joel Kotkin argues that cities will still matter in the future, remarking that "informational industries can conduct their business electronically and at great distance, yet the essential nature of many of these linchpins of urban commerce remains dependent on the sorts of individuals who prefer to live in cities."[17]

Kotkin believes that at least some of the nation's cities will recapture their preindustrial role as centers of commerce and information and that those working at home will choose to do so in an urban setting, where they have access to the sort of privileged information that comes only through close personal networking in an urban environment. Thomas Horan echoes some of these thoughts in his book *Digital Places,* in which he asserts that "real life is still the best high-bandwidth experience" and that "digital settings cannot fully replace the traditional sensory experience of place."[18] In fact, Horan argues that the "communities of interest" represented by the Internet must intersect successfully with "communities of place" represented by streets, cafés, public places, and public interactions of the communities in which we live.[19] Horan sees the home workplace as existing primarily in urban lofts and townhouses.

Some of those participating in the Lincoln Institute of Land Policy roundtable on technology and urban development mentioned earlier seemed to agree that at least certain cities still have a future in a digital world. The innovative "knowledge" part of the economy still needs teamwork and people working in close proximity to one another. They point to knowledge industries and investment centered in such places as Silicon Valley, Boston, New York, and Los Angeles, and to the need for companies to attract and retain skilled talent, which requires them to be in attractive settings that offer amenities as well as labor markets where households with two skilled workers can both do well.[20]

LONG-TERM TRENDS

Militating against these theories are long-term trends toward the acceptance of increasing isolation in our society. One hundred years ago, even on relatively isolated farms, more people lived in large, extended families than do so today. Middle-class families, be they rural or urban, typically had servants or other employees associated with the household to take care of everyday chores. More human labor was required in the workplace as well—which meant interaction with more people during the day—just to get the most mundane of tasks accomplished. In the teeming industrial cities, daily travel tended to be on crowded transit systems and elbow-to-elbow sidewalks. At home, city dwellers lived in apartments and townhouses. Neighbors were right on

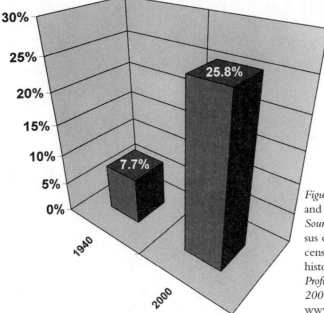

Figure 15.2. Single-person households 1940 and 2000.

Source: U.S. Census Bureau, Historical Census of Housing Tables: Living Alone, www.census.gov/hhes/www/housing/census/historic/livalone.html, and Table DP-1, *Profile of General Demographic Characteristics: 2000,* www.census.gov/Press-Release/www/2001/2khus.pdf.

the other side of the wall or even overhead or below or down the hall. Before radio and television, entertainment involved going out on the town somewhere, amid of other people, or just sitting on the front porch or the front stoop.

Given these considerations, there may well have been a lot more human interaction throughout the course of a typical day a century ago than exists today. Now, typical workers may spend most of the day interacting with their computers. The commute is performed in relative isolation in their personal vehicles. Home is a single-family house on its own plot of land, minimizing unnecessary contact with the neighbors. Upon returning home, entertainment may consist of television, a video, or more computer time. Household chores are mostly automated and don't require servants. Families are smaller, and single households are increasingly common.

Even just twenty-five years ago, the nation's level of social interaction arguably was higher than it is today. Robert Putnam, in his book *Bowling Alone: The Collapse and Revival of American Community* presents a convincing array of statistics showing that civic engagement in America has been steadily declining since the 1960s while isolation has increased (see Chapter 9). His statistics are supported by data from the U.S. Census Bureau that show that between 1940 and 2000 the number of people living alone in the United States increased from less than 8 percent of all households to more than 25 percent (see Figure

15.2).[21] Between 1960 and 1998, the average size of the U.S. household declined from 3.33 persons to 2.67 persons.[22] Putnam ascribes about 10 percent of the decline in American community to suburbanization and 25 percent to electronic media, with the majority (50 percent) attributable to generational change—that is, a baby boom generation that is simply not as involved in community affairs and social relations as their parents were. To some degree, Putnam believes, this is because the current generation grew up with and continues to depend upon electronic media (see Figure 15.3). Putnam also notes that the "Gen X" children of the boomers are even less socially engaged than their parents and that "as a result, the biggest generational losses in engagement still lie ahead."[23] This pattern is also coincident with the rise of electronic play stations, personal CD players, computers and computer games, and the Internet.

People in America have come a long way in terms of coping with being more isolated than they could be a century ago or even sixty or twenty-five years ago. Who knows what may happen in the century ahead? Internet chat rooms and dating are already becoming commonplace, cell phones are replacing the need for direct contact, and e-mail is replacing some telephone contact. Even Horan, who is relatively optimistic about personal contact, has said, "Our electronic experiences appear to be flourishing while our communities of place seem to be

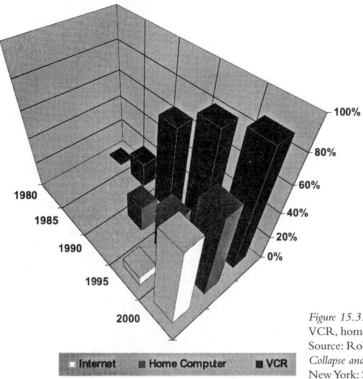

Figure 15.3. Percentage of households with VCR, home computer, and Internet. Source: Robert D. Putnam, *Bowling Alone: The Collapse and Revival of American Community* New York: Simon & Schuster, 2000), 223.

Internet   Home Computer   VCR

withering on the vine."[24] Will the next generation be even more isolated than the current one and think of it as normal?

In his book *The Vanishing Automobile and Other Urban Myths,* Randal O'Toole argues that "in today's jet-speed, internet economy, people have a far greater sense of community than ever before."[25] Possibly what O'Toole says is true, but contact increasingly is not face-to-face. Does that make a difference? In the 1920s, E. M. Forster wrote a short story called "The Machine Stops."[26] In Forster's imagined future world, people live in individual cells, bodies atrophied, connected to one another only by machine. There is no face-to-face contact. Communications, lectures, food, music, and entertainment are all delivered via "the machine" to each individual cell. Is this the future of the suburban dwelling or the urban condominium? If so, it is a daunting prospect.

Increasing Choice and Increasing Deconcentration?

The reality of the situation is that we simply can't know exactly how rapidly changing technology will affect our lives in the future. But it's a reasonable guess that technology is likely to increase our choices about how and where we choose to live, just as it has in the past. Living in the city and telecommuting to some remote location may be a serious possibility for some in the future. Furthermore, if square-footage requirements for office buildings drop (because there are fewer people working in them), then having corporate headquarters in the city may become more affordable to some corporations—although the lower cost of more exurban locations is likely to be a more significant consideration for many others, especially when technology levels the playing field. On the other hand, if what Kotkin says is true and informational industries really do rely on people who like to live in cities, then that would bode well for at least some urban-core areas.

In the end, new computer and communications technology will offer advantages to both city and suburban living and working conditions. Although this is good news in some ways, it also means that it may be risky to wait to see what will happen and leave the future totally up to advances in electronics. There is too much at stake to hope that information technology alone will solve our problems. Even Kotkin believes that some cities, such as Detroit and St. Louis, may never rebound, because they lack the amenities of such cities as New York, San Francisco, and Boston, and there are only so many "new urbanites" to go around.[27] As Kotkin remarks in *The New Geography:*

> The more technology frees us from the tyranny of place and past affiliation, the greater the need for individual places to make themselves more attractive. Surveys of high-technology firms find that among factors that drove their decision to of where to locate, a "quality of life" that would make the area attractive to skilled workers was far more important than any traditional factors such as taxes, regulation, or land costs.[28]

If what Kotkin says is true, it would imply that cities and their regions need to take initiative now to create the kind of "quality of life" that will enable them to compete in the future. This may mean, among other things, preserving open space, finding ways to relieve traffic congestion, improving the vitality and attractiveness of downtown, improving local education and skill levels to fit modern economic needs, and working to redress social and economic inequities while improving access to employment across the region.

Whether urban or suburban, those in our society who are not trained in the skills necessary to participate in this new information economy will be left behind, increasing the difficult social and economic divides that characterize our metropolitan areas today. Areas that remain so divided will continue to suffer from a poor image and may be less attractive to the businesses and employees that are the backbone of the new economy. Furthermore, if education in the cities is not addressed, the "new urbanites" may end up moving to the suburbs when they decide to have families—even from those cities that manage to retain their attraction.

The concluding thoughts of the Lincoln Institute of Land Policy's roundtable on technology and urban development are of interest in this regard. Caesar McDowell of the Massachusetts Institute of Technology made the following remarks:

> We will not see technology bring any sizable change in the equity issues in this country—and thereby very little will change in the spatial form of that portion of the urban environment that poor people inhabit—unless one of two things happens. First, we can formulate policies that try to make up for the failures inherent in the market. Second, we can foster opportunities in poor communities to use the deregulated telecommunications market to build new forms of economic cooperatives that can serve to build new economic institutions at the community level.[29]

In a similar vein, Elizabeth Burns of Arizona State University stated:

> As a geographer, it is my opinion that existing spatial inequalities in urban development will be reinforced by the diffusion of new information technologies, because these innovations are not sufficient to reverse long-standing spatial patterns of public and private investment. . . . The wider impacts of new communications technologies are likely to reinforce not only present urban deconcentration but also the current advantages of favored locations.[30]

A Picture of the Future

Even as uncertain as the future may be, it is possible to make some educated guesses as to what the future may hold and how the various anti-sprawl measures and movements are likely to fare.

Continuing Suburbanization

Reviewing current 2000 census trends and the thoughts of such experts as the members of the Lincoln Institute roundtable, it seems likely that suburbanization will continue in most of the nation's metropolitan areas, possibly abetted by the information technology revolution. However, new suburban growth may take on some modified form. The National Association of Home Builders (NAHB) forecasts that about 18 million new housing units will be built between now and 2010 (see Table 15.1). Of those, about 12 million will be single-family homes.[31] This number is just slightly less than the 12.2 million housing units of all types that exist in the state of California today.[32] Most of these units will be built in and around the nation's metropolitan areas. It therefore is not surprising that the

Table 15.1. Housing Supply and Demand—1971–2010 (Average per Year in 1,000's of Units)

	1971-1980	1981-1990	1991-2000	2000-2010
Demand				
Change in Households	1,578	1,281	1,137	1,255
Change in Vacancies	151	219	184	223
Net Removals	333	214	343	344
TOTAL DEMAND	2,062	1,714	1,664	1,822
Supply				
New Single-Family	1,111	979	1,108	1,203
New Multifamily	602	491	257	343
Mobile homes	349	244	298	276
TOTAL SUPPLY	2,062	1,714	1,663	1,822

Source: National Association of Home Builders (NAHB), *The Next Decade for Housing* (Washington, D.C.: NAHB, 2001), 9.

NAHB believes that the "clash" between market preferences and "incumbent residents" will force consideration of new housing configurations in the nation. According to the NAHB:

> The preponderance of home buyers will prefer detached homes in the suburbs, but growth controls and shortages of developable land in major metropolitan areas will encourage higher-density development as well as home building in the cities, in "exurbia," and in satellite cities at the fringes.[33]

The NAHB seems to be suggesting that the new single-family homes that will be built may be denser and that more home building will occur in the cities. But they also believe that the potential for further increased share of homes being built in central cities is limited. Their forecast that the greatest demand in what is now "exurbia" (that is, on the fringe of today's newest suburbs) and that there will be parallel shifts in new homes and economic activity to "satellite cities having concentrations of offices and services that once existed only at the metropolitan core."[34] This means that the spread of suburbanization will continue. One question is what form the so-called "satellite cities" will take. Will they be these be the auto-oriented "edge cities" that Joel Garreau has documented, or will they be more like Orenco Station? In regions that already have older, industrial-era satellite cities, can development be pushed in their direction? The answers to these questions can be left to market forces alone, or the nation's metropolitan areas can choose to shape their future.

Open Space

The level of concern over open space has become high enough and continuing development pressure great enough that it seems likely that more people will eventually favor spending more money on land conservation—through either donations or tax dollars or through both. That trend is proving to be the case in Massachusetts, where a slim majority of communities have so far voted to raise taxes so that they can qualify for state matching funds to preserve open space. Such local or state-local initiatives can be very beneficial in creating common open space, preserving habitat, or simply keeping farm and forestland in its current use. However, regional and state level actions will also be needed to create the areawide greenway, greenbelt, and habitat systems that give metro areas the qualities that attract residents and businesses alike. Boulder's city-county greenbelt is one direction some communities may pursue in the future. Portland provides a regional model of a similar program. Maryland's Rural Legacy and GreenPrint programs are examples of statewide programs that may become more widespread in the decades ahead.

One consequence of taking large segments of land off the market may be increasing land prices. This may help encourage more compact development on remaining land tracts in a given district, but higher land prices may also can be bad for creating affordable housing. Open space and growth control have to be coupled with plans for affordable housing to work for the whole community. Massachusetts gives localities the choice to use their vote for increased taxes and state matching funds for either open space or affordable housing or both.

Furthermore, just increasing density is not enough to insure that development happens in a manner consistent with community preservation goals. Otherwise, the result may be a spread-out densification of the landscape in general (in other words, endless tracts of tightly packed homes with no major focal open space, no transit, and no place to walk). This may happen in some places; in others, it may not.

Battling Congestion

Increasing suburbanization means increasing roadway congestion if new exurban development follows the pattern laid out by existing interstates and other limited access highways. Although it is possible that e-commerce may someday reduce some pressure on the roadway system by trading in trips for e-business transactions, the extent to which this may happen and when it may occur is not at all clear. Even if there is significant movement in this direction, delivery services may fill some part of the roadway capacity vacated by automobiles. Any capacity that is vacated will be an encouragement to added trips and continued auto-dependent development, eventually returning the roadway system to capacity conditions.

As capacity becomes a severe issue, it seems a reasonable guess that intelligent vehicles and highway systems alone won't solve the problem. Congestion pricing and other similar demand management measures may be a possibility, but there are likely to be severe political obstacles to increasing the cost of highway travel, especially if energy prices are also increasing. Beyond these measures, a given region can opt to go the balanced transportation system route by adding more transit capacity, try to build more highway lanes, do a little of both, or just do nothing. If nothing is done, businesses may choose to leave the region for other, less congested areas—possibly solving the problem that way.

Drivers are learning to cope with congestion and more time spent on the highway as information technology makes the car into a work-place. Safety concerns may place limits on this trend as states, such as New York, pass laws on how communications devices may be used while driving. There are also limits to travel time elasticity as the time resources consumed by the journey begin to exceed the value of the journey's purpose. We can see this from the experience of other countries. In São Paulo, Brazil, busy executives have taken to using helicopters to commute to work, attend meetings, run errands, and even go to church—mostly to dodge the hopelessly congested ground traffic.[35] The prospect of the same thing happening in the United States is thought provoking.

Before major traffic flows start taking to the skies, most metropolitan areas will probably opt to make some attempt at balance, just as some have already been doing, trying to implement transit solutions where feasible while continuing to build some additional roadway capacity in key areas (such as bridges, tunnels, and arterial roads), as well as working on intelligent highways and pricing measures where politically possible. Localities and businesses may also do their part through local transit connections and ride sharing programs. Although these efforts probably ease congestion somewhat, in the absence of any regional plan, it is not likely that any of these measures will occur in a fully coordinated fashion with land use. There may be some attempts at coordinated efforts in different states and metropolitan areas—and they may yield results—but they likely will be sporadic. The most urgent attempts at some kind of coordination are likely to come in urban areas that (like Atlanta) fall under threat of losing federal funds because of noncompliance with the Clean Air Act. Environmental regulations may provide an impetus in this regard, as long as they are not modified to allow exceptions.

As discussed in Chapter 3, federal policy has already been modified to allow more flexibility in choosing how to spend local transportation funds. Ultimately, the responsibility for coordinating transportation and land use must come from state government along with the metropolitan planning organizations. Localities can help in this process by managing local growth and directing transit-friendly development toward existing transit lines, but they have to agree regionally on where new transit corridors will be. It will be up to state and local coalitions of voters and institutions to pursue these initiatives.

Compact Communities

Where suburbanization continues to occur, it seems likely that the pattern will be changed to some degree. The NAHB and other building groups have stated that, in the future, housing configurations will have to change and become more compact. New development guidelines have already worked their way into such reference works as *Architectural Graphic Standards* and are sure to begin appearing in other professional reference works as well. Limited land availability and rising land costs will also have an effect on increasing the number of dwelling units per acre, as the NAHB has recognized in its recent ten-year forecast of housing trends.[36] Developments are likely to have smaller lot sizes. Measures aimed at walkable, transit-friendly, mixed-use village or town centers may also be included as municipalities change zoning bylaws to encourage these trends. Many new developments will probably be exurban, as the NAHB suggests. Some may be transit friendly, although transit service is most likely to consist of bus and not light rail (primarily because of cost and routing considerations), although bus systems may connect to HOV lanes on nearby expressways. Yet, as the NAHB and other groups (including the Urban Land Institute) recognize, development will occur in the inner suburbs and core cities as well.

Cities and Infill Development

Based on the 2000 census and the predictions of Kotkin, Horan, and others, some hope exists that the worst is over for at least some of the nation's cities, but there is little possibility that these older centers will ever regain their preeminent national status. The role of the city has been irreversibly changed: in many areas, the center city has become simply an island of greater concentration in a mostly suburban metropolitan region. Cities differ widely in how they are adapting to this new role; some are seeing success, while others are not. How cities adapt is important, because although they may be diminished in stature, they remain a vital part of the region in which they are located. If the center city fails, the metropolitan region as a whole suffers, potentially becoming less competitive at attracting and keeping both residents and businesses.

The analysis of 2000 census data by the Fannie Mae Foundation and reports on downtown real estate trends suggest that the trend toward city living will probably continue in the downtown areas of many cities, not just New York and San Francisco (see Table 15.2).[37] Developers in such cities as Atlanta, Los Angeles, Cincinnati, and St. Louis are also hard at work building new market-rate housing in downtown areas.

In Los Angeles, a $100 million, three-block, market-rate housing project is being developed by G. H. Palmer Associates, and in Atlanta, Post Properties, a huge developer of suburban projects, has already completed seven mixed-use and residential projects within city limits—the most recent of which are right next to downtown.[38] Post has also developed projects in downtown Dallas and in other cities and is now looking at downtown areas in other parts of the nation.

Table 15.2. Selected Downtown Population Change—1990 to 2000

	NET CHANGE BETWEEN 1990 AND 2000		
	Downtown	City	MSA
Atlanta	4,968	22,457	1,152,248
Baltimore	1,470	(84,860)	170,822
Boston	3,428	14,858	179,122
Chicago	14,279	112,290	861,910
Cleveland	2,338	(27,213)	48,802
Denver	1,436	87,026	486,302
Detroit	171	(76,704)	174,897
Houston	4,853	323,078	855,621
Los Angeles	1,975	209,422	656,174
Memphis	1,388	39,763	128,308
Philadelphia	3,694	(68,027)	178,756
Portland, Or.	3,374	91,802	402,557
San Diego	2,477	112,851	315,817
Seattle	6,619	47,115	381,460
St. Louis	(1,598)	(48,496)	111,082

Source: Rebecca R. Sohmer and Robert E. Lang, *Downtown Rebound* (Washington, D.C.: Fannie Mae Foundation and Brookings Institution, 2000), 3.

Note: MSA refers to the Metropolitan Statistical Area surrounding the city. The MSA may be smaller than the Consolidated Metropolitan Statistical Area, or CMSA, used elsewhere in this book.

Some of these new in-town projects across the nation are rental properties; others are condominiums. Condominiums continue to do well in many cities, with condominium home ownership offering tax and loan advantages that once could be found only in the suburbs. As long as waterfronts and loft districts continue to be deindustrialized and as long as crime rates do not rise alarmingly, many people may continue to choose city living.

Foreign immigration also is adding vitality and population to the nation's city centers. In combination with middle-class professionals choosing the city over the suburbs, new immigration bodes well for the health cities where these trends are active. But making cities a viable alternative to suburban living for the nation's middle-class families is going to be a challenge. Education is clearly a major issue as is affordable housing. These issues need to be addressed locally and at the regional and state levels if the trend toward city living is to continue successfully.

Brownfield and greyfield sites in cities and inner suburbs remain major opportunities to be exploited mainly by municipalities with help from state and federal governments in cleaning up contaminated sites and connecting these sites to viable transit systems. Involved citizen groups, such as the Mystic View Task Force in Boston, can have a pronounced effect on the direction these projects take.

Mending Social Divisions

The 2000 census data suggest that the trend toward middle-class minority families moving to the suburbs will continue. This is good in that suburban areas will become less homogeneous overall, potentially weakening the division of regional interest along racial lines. Prince George's County, Maryland, a suburb of Washington, D.C., is now 63 percent black and middle-class.[39] However, to the extent that this migration is confined only to enclaves within inner-ring suburbs, that future outcome will be far less likely. Whereas the black population of Prince George's County grew by 36 percent in the past decade, the white population declined by 31 percent.[40]

Furthermore, the issue of economic segregation remains a serious threat if the poor remain behind. Minority, middle-class professionals

remaining in the cities along with the movement of some middle-class whites back into the cities may help mitigate this tendency. Moving forward on an agenda of better urban education, more urban housing, redeveloping brownfield sites, and providing better transit as well as increasing such civic amenities as parks and waterfronts can help make cities common ground for all groups.

Thinking About Future in Summary

Overall, it seems fair to say that there will be mostly mixed results in achieving smart growth goals for the future. This may not be the most dramatic of predictions, but it is probably what will actually occur. The extent to which goals are met is likely to vary significantly across the nation and across each region. But in the absence of major interventions at the state level led by coalitions of interest groups, the tendency toward expanding suburbanization will continue. According to the experts and a look at past trends, the information technology revolution is likely to abet this trend rather than act as a countervailing force.

Suburban trends may be modified—with more preservation of open space, with more revitalization of some inner cities and their brownfield sites, and with some changes to the pattern of suburban developments, perhaps along the lines laid out by the Congress for the New Urbanism. Additional transit will be built, but there is little question that the nation's transportation system will remain predominantly auto dependent, with more and more information technology occurring in vehicles as congestion grows and with some expansion of highways and the addition of HOV lanes. Ultimately, as the number of vehicle miles traveled continues to increase, air pollution and energy consumption also may go up. Eventually, these problems may largely be solved through large-scale introduction of hybrid vehicles, fuel cells, and other alternative technologies. In the interim, in response to air quality concerns, more metropolitan areas may follow Atlanta's path and begin trying to nudge development toward higher-density, mixed-use nodes that can work successfully with HOV lanes and new transit lines.

CHAPTER 16

Conclusion

After some examination of different definitions of the term, we have determined that *sprawl* is a pattern of urbanization that is spread out and that is relatively low in density when compared with the nation's older cities and towns. It is characterized by automotive dependence, widely separated land uses, patches of undeveloped land, and strip commercial areas with large amounts of surface parking. All of these characteristics are contributing factors to "sprawl:" a pattern of urbanization that gives the appearance of spreading out awkwardly or "sprawling" across the landscape. When all of its attributes are put together, the term *sprawl* (albeit in a pejorative sense) can be applied to the majority of the post–World War II pattern of suburbanization that is characteristic of much of today's metropolitan landscape.

The Suburban Pattern

Suburbanization essentially has been made possible by the automobile transportation system in combination with modern telecommunications and information networks. These systems have allowed the economic forces of agglomeration and economy of scale to operate across a much larger geographic area than was possible before the twentieth century. The ability of these forces to span entire regions vastly increased the amount of land viable for urban development, reducing land prices overall and giving rise to a spread-out, low-density pattern of urbanization. Once established, the suburban pattern has been perpetuated through market forces, land control laws, planning and design standards, and financing requirements, among other things. During the past fifty years, this pattern has covered more land more quickly than any previous form of urbanization. Today, the nation's metropolitan areas are predominantly suburban in both population and area,

and they are spreading out to join one another across the United States.

A Willing Nation

Reviewing history, we see that suburbanization clearly is something the nation has brought upon itself willingly—its people enchanted by the automobile and eager to escape the cramped industrial city. In the process, major financing and infrastructure building programs were put in place to help white, middle-class Americans go where they wanted to go, to find a house on its own plot of land with a garden and a place to park the family cars. When they got there, shopping, entertainment, and finally their jobs followed them, leaving the older cities weakened.

There is no conspiracy, nor is there any single decision or turn of the path that brought us here. On the other hand, there *are* vested interests that have evolved in tandem with the huge investments made in suburbanization. The real estate, construction, automotive, and oil industries and all of those they employ are but a few of the myriad entities with deep involvements in existing development patterns. There are also the millions upon millions of home owners and other property holders who have investments (sometimes all of a life's savings) tied up in their suburban homes. In short, it is most of America.

Suburban Malaise

The current malaise is hardly new. People in the United States were unhappy with big cities in the early part of the twentieth century, and they were unhappy with the first tendrils of sprawl caused by streetcars in the nineteenth century. But the level of unhappiness that exists today is what causes change—just as it caused the huge exodus from the cities seventy-five years ago. In a sense, it is only logical that Americans should find fault with where they are today, having come this far down the road. It is only natural that a nation should begin to treasure what it has lost in abandoning the cities and that its people should change their minds about what should be built in the future. But the logic of such a process doesn't mean that we, as a nation, should be complacent, either. Problems clearly exist, and if left alone, they will only get worse.

A Paradigm of Democracy

It is certainly true that suburbanization has given the nation many positive things. More people own their own homes now than ever before in our country—nearly 68 percent according to the National Association of Realtors.[1] People have tremendous freedom of choice today over where and how they choose to live their lives, possibly much more so than at any time in the history of the United States. The automobile also has granted vast freedom of movement to the nation. People can come and go as they please, according to their own schedules, to as many destinations as they choose, in a climate-controlled environment without having to change trains or buses to get there. Automobiles also let us roam farther and faster than ever before. All residents of the suburban metropolis have their own lots of land with light, clean air, and green space that they can tend to as they wish. If you become dissatisfied with where you are, you can almost always sell your house, buy another, and move—such is the general liquidity of the real estate market. These are all positive factors, and they translate into a very high standard of living.

Despite the truly wonderful things that suburbanization has granted the nation, some very serious problems still exist, many of which we have reviewed in this book. The most basic issue is that suburbanization, as it exists today, arguably is not a sustainable pattern of existence. Contemporary patterns of development consume worrisome quantities of open space, fuel, money, and environmental and social resources.

A Misuse of Resources

The fuel situation is a serious problem. Transportation energy use is projected to increase by 40 percent by 2020 while the proportion of imported petroleum products is expected to grow to almost two-thirds of total consumption.

The U.S. Department of Energy (DOE) has gone on record stating that this situation is politically and economically risky. Importing an ever-increasing percentage of our oil virtually guarantees continued international friction. To make matters worse, creditable projections indicate that world production of oil will start declining within the next twenty years, limiting availability and driving up prices. Although the DOE's forecasts claim to take a reasonable accounting of changes in vehicle technology that will reduce fuel consumption, the amount of driving continues to increase and new technology is not projected to phase in quickly enough to change the projected scenario. Many of the initiatives required to accomplish the needed reduction must come from federal and state governments. Some states, such as Arizona, have already acted by offering incentives for the purchase of hybrid cars. Massachusetts is considering similar legislation. But consumers must also do their part in their choices of vehicles and transportation modes. Increasing fuel prices from falling production eventually may help in making these decisions.

Increasing Pollution

The corollary of mounting fuel consumption is the continuing and expanding release of greenhouse gases, such as carbon dioxide. Increasingly powerful El Niño events are potentially worrisome indicators of what may be to come. The United Nations Intergovernmental Panel on Climate Change has made three assessments of global warming since 1990. Each has made increasingly conclusive links between human activity and climate change that could cause serious harm to agriculture, ecosystems, and coastal areas. In June 2001, the National Academy of Sciences released a report commissioned by the president of the United States that reaffirmed the connection between human activity and global warming.[2]

Although catalytic converters and changes in fuel have greatly reduced air pollution from tailpipe emissions since the 1970s, pollution from vehicles is projected to increase in the years ahead because of increased driving. Toxic pollutants from tailpipe emissions will have increasingly ill effects on public health. In the very long term, if these problems are to be solved, it may prove more expedient to change the auto industry than to change the nation's development patterns. This would mean accelerating and broadening the move to alternative automotive technology. Federal and state actions are needed to accomplish this. Some states, such as California, have already taken action along these lines as have others previously mentioned. Consumer choice is also a factor.

But it would be unwise to place all hopes on a single strategy. Nor will cleaner, more fuel-efficient automobiles eliminate all adverse effects of suburbanization. We must also consider changing how we live—making it easier to walk and use mass transit instead of our cars, reducing total vehicle miles traveled. We need to consider doing this not only because of energy and air considerations, but also because the parking areas and roadways required by the automotive transportation system continue to pollute rivers, harbors, reservoirs, and watersheds across the country. Furthermore, alternative automotive technology alone won't solve the problem of the nation's unbalanced transportation system.

Pushing for Transit

Positive transportation changes may lie ahead. In New York, the Regional Plan Association continues to push for cross-regional links, and a new light rail system is starting up along the Hudson River in New Jersey. Portland recently opened its new Westside MAX line, and Boston is pursuing both cross-regional and circumferential transit links. At the same time, promising new technologies that blend bus and light rail may help to meet suburban transit needs. Finally, between 1996 and 2000, transit ridership in the United States increased by 16 percent after declining for many years.[3]

Despite these positive events, serious barriers remain to increased transit use in the United States. Foremost among these are long-term national and state policies of treating highways and transit as basically separate systems. This tendency is characterized by analyses that suggest that the nation spends much more on transit (25 percent) than is warranted by what it carries in terms of national trips (2 to 4 percent). As we have seen in previous chapters, the percentages are about equal when total expenditures are considered. In reality, roadways and transit are two necessary parts of a larger system, and they need to be dealt with as such, with a goal of balancing the system as a whole. In Europe, highways and transit have been treated that way for fifty years or more and funded accordingly. ISTEA and TEA-21 are positive federal moves in this direction in providing greater funding choice. Action is now needed at the state and metropolitan level, where transportation funds are actually spent. This action can be achieved only by persistent coalitions promoting new transit projects. In Boston, the Urban Ring and the North/South Rail Link exist as possible projects only because of the citizen, institutional, and government coalitions that support them. In other metro areas, similar coalitions support comparable projects.

A Widening Gulf

Perhaps one of the worst problems created by suburbanization on a national scale is the misuse of social and economic resources. Whole segments of the population and networks of infrastructure have been left behind by outward expansion. As new roads, sewers, and schools have been built in the suburbs, those already existing in the cities have been allowed to languish. At the same time, as new service and information jobs have been created in the suburbs, an exodus of manufacturing jobs has left the cities with unemployment, poverty, and financial difficulties.

These factors have contributed to a widening gulf between races and economic classes that has become intrinsic to many of the nation's spreading metropolitan areas. Although racial and economic segregation continues in the cities, the amplified geographic and jurisdictional social divides created by suburbanization threaten to actually drive races and classes farther apart rather than bringing them together—even after decades of social, political, and economic reform. With poor minorities and white, middle-class groups dominating different geographic areas and jurisdictions of metropolitan America, things may become increasingly polarized, as each group perceives its interests to be increasingly different from the others'.

The geographic and jurisdictional division of social and economic classes has led to a similar division of interests in almost every metropolitan area in the United States. Few people—regardless of ethnic background or economic status—are willing to see themselves as part of a greater metropolitan region with common interests nearly so much as they insist on the priorities of their own local communities. The problem only worsens when race and class further divide a region's communities. On the positive side, Myron Orfield's report on activities in the Twin Cities suggests that inner cities and working-class inner suburbs can learn to work together to mount powerful metropolitan coalitions that can act in concert at the state level.

Losing Open Space

Even though there is plenty of land to go around—with only about 5 percent of the nation actually developed—there is relatively little open space, forest, or farmland left inside the metropolitan areas, where most of the country lives, and what is left is rapidly vanishing. That open acreage is the very land that arguably is the most precious to the greatest number of people, and its demise may eventually tip the national mood against growth in general. If such an outcome is to be avoided, more open space needs to be preserved close to where people live and work—in places where people can enjoy it on a daily or weekly basis—fulfilling the role that parks and public waterfronts in denser cities play, but on a much larger scale. And if community character is to be preserved—the semi-rural feel that many communities prefer—then farmland, fields, and forests also will have to be preserved as will the habitats that support the plant and animal life that many people appreciate. Local, state, federal, and private actions all can help in conserving open space; widely acclaimed efforts are already under way at each of these levels, but more statewide efforts, such as those being undertaken in Maryland and elsewhere, are needed to promote a coordinated regional approach.

Changing Growth Priorities

Reinvesting in our cities, towns, and inner suburbs offers a chance to solve some of the most serious problems brought about by suburbanization. First, it offers a chance to narrow the increasing social rift by eliminating some of the most poignant aspects of the geographic and jurisdictional division of interests that exists across many metropolitan areas. Attracting more middle-class families into the cities and keeping

them there will almost certainly help achieve a better balance of economic classes across the greater metropolitan regions, increasing common interests.

Second, concentrating development efforts first and foremost on existing city and town centers and brownfield sites avoids redundant infrastructure expenditures while helping to contain sprawl, preserve green space, alter dispersed land use patterns, and maximize the potential for the use of existing and potential future transit systems. Following such an agenda will require linking regional economic development and transportation programs in an integrated fashion. If this were to be done, decisions could be made in advance—planning for transit-amenable development while giving developers assurance that planned transit improvements will be built. To build transit-amenable development, developers must be sure that the transit line will be built, and to make the transit investment, the public sector needs assurance that development will happen in a way that guarantees maximum transit use.

The federal government has already made funds available through various agencies to help fund investment in brownfield sites. ISTEA and TEA-21 have enabled more power to go to localities and metropolitan planning organizations in making decisions about transit funds to support economic development priorities. In many cases, the states still retain most of the power in making decisions about transportation funding. Critical initiatives can be and have been made at the metropolitan and local level in making investments in downtown areas, but many of these actions often require complementary action from the state when it comes to tapping statewide economic development, environmental cleanup, and transportation funds.

Environmental and Social Benefits

Concentrating development in older urban centers while making future suburban development more compact can have important environmental and social benefits. Pursuing this agenda can mean leaving more farmland, forest, and wildlife habitats untouched. It can also mean building less total pavement and roof area, limiting runoff, encouraging recharge, and saving drinking water resources. Shifting trips to walking and transit will be better for fuel consumption and will limit air pollution.

Meanwhile, this same approach can increase the fiscal resources of the older cities, enabling them to provide better services (such as transportation and education), attracting more middle-class residents while creating new employment opportunities for city dwellers. Doing this also raises the possibility of restoring more of the nation's historical and cultural resources, including the irreplaceable stock of older buildings that make up many of the nation's city centers. These are all desirable ends, and they all can be pursued simultaneously by means of grassroots coalitions working through existing institutions at local, state, and national levels. These institutions include government entities, ranging from local planning and community development offices to state development and transportation agencies, as well as private nonprofit organizations running the gamut from local development corporations to the National Trust's Main Street program.

Smart Growth and Regionalism

Transit villages and transit-oriented developments (TODs) clearly have a role in such plans as far as new and infill developments are concerned. Changing planning and design guidelines to encourage mixed uses, walking, transit, and compactness will all help to remake sprawl. To a large extent, these initiatives can be pursued locally. But without broader regional cooperation, such an approach may yield only piecemeal results. There are different routes such efforts can take. Annexation, a path still being followed by some cities, could be used to promote regional smart growth solutions, but typically this has not been the case. So far, regionalism on a comprehensive, governmental scale without annexation has been successful only in Portland, and it currently is under assault even there.

Although following Portland's path may be possible for some metro areas, this approach simply is not applicable everywhere. Metro government in New York, Boston, or Washington would require cooperation and legislation from multiple states and districts. Federal cooperation might also be required. Western and southern cities with metro areas generally contained within a single state may lend themselves better to a Portland type of approach—particularly if they do not have the fragmented jurisdic-

tional problems of many of the older eastern and midwestern cities. Some metro areas, such as New York and Boston, have had limited success with ad hoc regional transportation authorities.

In other cases, the state has stepped in to fill the regional void. Maryland is a good model for states and metro areas throughout the nation. States such as New Jersey are following Maryland's lead. Florida also has pursued growth management programs. Furthermore, metropolitan governments, where they do exist, are in place only because of state enabling legislation. If the pattern of growth in the nation is to change, it probably will have to start at the state level. States control transportation funding and land use legislation. In the past several years, most ballot initiatives and legislative action have been at the state level.

Recently, the United States Conference of Mayors began an initiative backed by the nation's cities and their adjacent counties to pressure state and federal governments to invest more resources in metropolitan areas. As part of this campaign, the mayors released a major study in July 2001 that highlights the vital national and international economic role played by the nation's metropolitan areas, including both cities and suburbs. According to the *New York Times,* the study notes that U.S. metro areas are responsible for nearly 85 percent of the nation's economic output and that, if the New York metropolitan area were a country, it would rank fourteenth in the world, ahead of Australia, the Netherlands, Russia, and Taiwan.[4]

The Sprawl We Already Have

Whatever plans we make as a nation, we simply can't discard the vast amount of auto-dependent suburban development that has already been built. Far too much investment has been made there to abandon even the outmoded inner-ring parts of this pattern. The huge suburban landscapes that dominate the nation's metropolitan regions need to be maintained and allowed to age gracefully. The main issues are how to slow the outward expansion process, how to modify the suburbs we have to make at least parts of them a bit more transit and pedestrian friendly so that the roadway system that serves them can continue to function, and how to preserve what remains of the open space that is so important to so many. Most likely, these modifications will take place on greyfield sites of abandoned malls and on similar sites as well as in the "edge city" parts of suburbs, if they are offered transit connections and an opportunity to mature and rebuild along denser lines. These modifications can happen only if surrounding localities agree to increased density in defined areas—a proposition that generates substantial controversy in many communities.

The Continuing Debate

As much as anything else, sprawl (or suburbanization) is part of one of the oldest debates in American history. Suburbanization has done much to provide individual wealth and freedom to an unprecedented number of people in America, providing for the common good of many in the process. But some would argue that the intense focus on individual property and wealth accumulation that has accompanied the American Dream has put our common future at risk. In this argument, the suburban pattern that has characterized the majority of U.S. city building in the last half of the twentieth century is clearly unsustainable and has exacerbated social and economic divisions in our society. Following this line of thinking, if we are to avoid a fairly pessimistic future in which the nation's metropolitan areas disintegrate from their own expansion combined with widening social and economic rifts, we may all have to begin to think more about the common good and less about our own individual plots of land.

On the other side of the debate are those who believe that sustainability and social and economic divides are not the critical issues that they are being made out to be by environmental and other groups. What has historically been responsible for the success of the United States is its capitalist system combined with a democratic government that guarantees certain individual freedoms and rights, including the rights associated with the individual ownership of property. The common benefits that our system has produced are largely due to the freedoms we have allowed in the marketplace, in contrast to the failed "command and control" economies of the eastern bloc countries of Europe and some nations in the third world. Many on this side of the debate believe that solutions to the problems we do have should be generated at the local level

and that the hand of big government will produce only the sort of failures experienced in the urban renewal and highway-building eras. In this view, whatever ills the cities may be suffering are mostly of their own making and are best solved by eliminating municipal constraints on the marketplace.

In the middle are all of those who own homes in the suburbs and just want a good place to raise their families and an opportunity to find a good job. Also mostly in the middle are many of the businesses that have a stake in building more of our contemporary metropolis: home builders, commercial builders, roadway contractors, oil companies, car manufacturers and dealers, retailers, restaurant owners, real estate professionals, architects, engineers, and many, many others. Most of these people simply want to stay in business doing what they know how to do. Suburbanization is an enormous part of the nation's economy, and few people want to introduce serious economic disruptions or stop the growth that characterizes a healthy economy.

But as we have clearly seen in this book, there are serious problems with our existing patterns of suburbanization in terms of environmental degradation, public health, wasted resources, clogged transportation, and social and economic divisions. These problems do have solutions, some of them through the marketplace and others through government action. Some of the solutions will not be easy and will require extensive further public debate—as they should. If compromises can be found, the industries that have an interest in suburbanization can make a transition to modified patterns of development. They are already moving in this direction. The work that developers like Post Properties and others are doing in cities such as Atlanta shows that this can be done. Roads will continue to get built, and certainly they will need to be kept up—there is a huge amount of work to be done in continuing maintenance alone. Many roadway structures (retaining walls, bridges, tunnels, ramps, viaducts, and so forth) are more than forty years old and are beginning to show their age. New transit systems can employ many building trades as well. But density, education, and affordable housing issues remain some of the most intractable problems to solve. If they can't be solved, many social and economic divisions that characterize cities and suburbs will continue and solutions to traffic congestion will remain elusive, while open space will continue to disappear and environmental problems to proliferate.

Ultimately, because all of these issues cross so many jurisdictional lines, most of the debate and the work to achieve consensus is going to have to be carried out at the state level, as it has been in Maryland, Minnesota, New Jersey, Oregon, Florida, Massachusetts, and many other states. The coalitions that form—whether industry, grassroots, urban, housing, environmental, or other—will end up doing their work through the state legislatures and through state ballot referenda. This is where the debate will be most evident, as it was in Colorado in fall 2000.

This is not the first time America has been in such a position. The industrial revolution fostered serious urban ills, many of which were addressed by improvements to cities and by suburbanization. But now, suburbanization has created problems of its own, and it is time to move forward to solve those problems. Doubtless, new problems will be created in the process, but things are arguably better today than during the industrial revolution, and it is possible that things may be better in the future as the debate continues and actions are taken to improve the common good.

Notes

Introduction

1. *Merriam-Webster Online Dictionary,* www.m-w.com.
2. James Howard Kunstler, *The Geography of Nowhere: The Rise and Decline of America's Manmade Landscape* (New York: Simon & Schuster, 1993), chap. 10. See also James Howard Kunstler, *Home from Nowhere: Remaking Our Everyday World for the 21st Century* (New York: Simon & Schuster, 1996), 17, 106.
3. Christopher Conte, "The Boys of Sprawl," *Governing* (May 2000): 27–33.
4. Richard Lacayo with Wendy Cole, Dan Cray, Daniel Levy, Todd Murphy, and Timothy Roche, "The Brawl Over Sprawl," *Time,* March 22, 1999, 45.
5. Ibid., 45–48.
6. Haya El Nasser, "A Comprehensive Look at Sprawl in America," *USA Today,* February 22, 2001.
7. Dan Barry and Al Baker, "Getting the Message from 'Eco-Terrorists,'" *New York Times,* January 8, 2001.
8. Peter Grant, "The Sprawl Debate Has Only Just Begun," *Wall Street Journal,* November 8, 2000.
9. Conte, "The Boys of Sprawl," 27–33.
10. Grant, "The Sprawl Debate Has Just Begun."
11. Richard A. Oppel Jr., "Efforts to Restrict Sprawl Find New Resistance from Advocates for Affordable Housing," *New York Times,* December 26, 2000.
12. Nicholas Retsinas, "Before We Take On Sprawl, Let's Understand What We're Fighting," *Boston Globe,* January 29, 2000.

Chapter 1: What is Sprawl?

1. *Merriam-Webster Online Dictionary,* www.m-w.com.
2. *Encarta World English Dictionary,* www.encarta. msn.com.
3. The U.S. Census Bureau defines an "urbanized area" as basically an area with at least one thousand persons per square mile. That translates to somewhat less than two persons per acre—a fairly low residential density for many suburban areas. See the U.S. Census Bureau, *Urban and Rural Definitions,* www.census.gov/population/census-data/urdef.txt.
4. Jane S. Shaw and Ronald D. Utt, eds., *A Guide to Smart Growth: Shattering Myths, Providing Solutions*

(Washington, D.C.: The Heritage Foundation-Jane, 2000), 2.
5. Samuel R. Staley, *Policy Study No. 251—The Sprawling of America: In Defense of the Dynamic City* (Los Angeles: Reason Public Policy Institute, 1999), 9.
6. Jay Wickersham, *The State of Our Environment* (Boston: Commonwealth of Massachusetts, Executive Office of Environmental Affairs, 2000), 24.
7. National Trust for Historic Preservation, Rural Heritage Program Web site: www.ruralheritage.org/sprawl.html.
8. U.S. Environmental Protection Agency (EPA), New England, *The State of the New England Environment, 1998* (Boston: EPA, 1998), chapter on sprawl, as posted on their Web site: www.epa.gov/region01/ra/soe98/soe98.html.
9. Sierra Club Web site: www.sierraclub.org/sprawl.
10. Natural Resources Defense Council Web site: www.nrdc.org/cities/default.asp.
11. Reid Ewing, "Is Los Angeles-Style Sprawl Desirable?" *Journal of the American Planning Association,* vol. 63, no. 1 (Winter 1997): 2–4.
12. Ewing provides a table listing seventeen urban planners, theorists, and authors, starting with William Whyte and including Anthony Downs, Constance Beaumont, Richard Moe, and others. Ewing, "Is Los Angeles-Style Sprawl Desirable?," 3.
13. Ibid., 4.
14. For example, Anthony Downs as cited in Kenneth A. Small, "Urban Sprawl: A Non-Diagnosis of Real Problems," *Metropolitan Development Patterns 2000 Annual Roundtable* (Cambridge, Mass.: Lincoln Institute of Land Policy, 2000), 27.
15. For example, see the previous note and also Susan M. Wachter, "Cities and Regions: Findings from the 1999 State of the Cities Report," in *Metropolitan Development Patterns 2000 Annual Roundtable* (Cambridge, Mass.: Lincoln Institute of Land Policy, 2000), 22.
16. See Irving M. Copi, *Introduction to Logic* (New York: MacMillan, 1968), 89–114.
17. *Merriam-Webster Online Dictionary,* www.m-w.com.
18. See Kenneth T. Jackson, "Suburbanization," in *The Reader's Companion to American History,* ed. Eric Froner and John A. Garraty (Boston: Houghton Mifflin, 1991), 1040–1043; see also Kenneth T.

Jackson, *Crabgrass Frontier: The Suburbanization of the United States* (New York: Oxford University Press, 1985).

19. U.S. Department of Agriculture (USDA), Natural Resources Conservation Service (NRCS), *Land Ownership, 1992,* www.nhq.nrcs.usda.gov/cgi-bin/kmusser/mapgif.pl?mapid=2788. The figure excludes Alaska. Including Alaska and excluding nonland acreage, this figure falls to about 60 percent. See National Wilderness Institute, *State by State Government Land Ownership* (1995), www.nwi.org.

20. Jackson, *Crabgrass Frontier,* 53.

21. U.S. Census Bureau, *Housing Vacancy Survey: First Quarter 2001,* Table 5. *Homeownership Rates for the United States: 1965 to 2001,* www.census.gov/hhes/www/housing/hvs/q101tab5.html.

22. U.S. Census Bureau, *1997 Economic Census* (Washington, D.C.: U.S. Census Bureau, 2000), Table 1.

23. U.S. Department of Commerce, *U.S. Industry and Trade Outlook 2000* (Washington, D.C.: U.S. Department of Commerce, 2000), 6-2.

24. Terry Moore and Paul Thorsnes, *The Transportation/Land Use Connection: A Framework for Practical Policy* (Chicago: American Planning Association, 1994), 9.

25. Ibid., 20.

26. Alan E. Pisarski, *Commuting in America II: The Second National Report on Commuting Patterns and Trends* (Lansdowne, Va.: Eno Transportation Foundation, 1996), 72.

27. U.S. Department of Transportation (DOT), Bureau of Transportation Statistics (BTS), *1995 Nationwide Personal Transportation Survey* (Washington, D.C.: DOT, 1995), 11. See also Jane Holtz Kay, *Asphalt Nation: How the Automobile Took Over America and How We Can Take It Back* (New York: Crown, 1997), 21.

28. U.S. Department of Transportation (DOT), Bureau of Transportation Statistics, *Transportation Statistics Annual Report, 1999* (Washington, D.C.: DOT, 1999), 36.

29. Ibid., 37, 46.

30. Ibid., 37.

31. James S. Russell, "Privatized Lives," *Harvard Design Magazine,* no. 12 (Fall 2000): 24.

32. William J. Mitchell, "The Electronic Agora," foreword in Thomas A. Horan, *Digital Places: Building Our City of Bits* (Washington, D.C.: Urban Land Institute, 2000), xi.

33. Moore and Thorsnes, *The Transportation/Land Use Connection,* 10 and following.

34. Pisarski, *Commuting in America II,* 25.

35. Robert Putnam, *Bowling Alone: The Collapse and Revival of American Community* (New York: Simon & Schuster, 2000), 222–23, 228.

36. Horan, *Digital Places,* 33.

37. Jonathan Glazer, "Telecommuting's Big Experiment," *New York Times,* May 9, 2001.

38. Glazer, "Telecommuting's Big Experiment."

39. U.S. Commerce Department, "Retail E-Commerce Sales in First Quarter 2001," *U.S. Commerce Department News,* May 16, 2001, www.census.gov/mrts/www/current.html.

40. Andres Duany, Elizabeth Plater-Zyberk, and Jeff Speck, *Suburban Nation: The Rise of Sprawl and the Decline of the American Dream* (New York: North Point Press, 2000), xi.

41. See Barbara McCann et al./Surface Transportation Policy Project/Center for Neighborhood Technology, *Driven to Spend: The Impact of Sprawl on Household Transportation Expenses* (Washington, D.C.: 2001), chap. 3, fig. H, www.transact.org/reports/driven/.default.htm. See also Haya El Nasser, "A Comprehensive Look at Sprawl in America," *USA Today,* February 22, 2001. *USA Today* used a different ranking methodology in which the Houston-Galveston-Brazoria region ranks number 234 in a range of scores from 26 to 536.

42. *Webster's New World Dictionary, College Edition* (New York: The World Publishing Co., 1966), 1455.

43. Sometime between 1960 and 1970, depending on sources and definitions used. See U.S. Census Bureau/Campbell Gibson and Emily Lennon, *Historical Census Statistics on the Foreign Born Population of the United States, 1850–1990,* (Washington, D.C.: U.S. Census Bureau, 1999). See also U.S. Census Bureau, *Selected Historical Census Data: Urban and Rural Definitions and Data,* www.census.gov/population/www/censusdata/ur-def.html. See also Pisarski, *Commuting in America II,* 18–19.

44. The New York CMSA includes parts of New York, New Jersey, and Pennsylvania. CMSA data from U.S. Census Bureau, Census 2000 PHC-T-3 Tanking Tables for Metropolitan Areas, Table 1, www.census.gov/population/cen2000/phc-t3/tab01.pdf. Additional New York City data from U.S. Census Bureau, *Table 22: Population of the 100 Largest Urban Places: 1990,* www.census.gov/population/documentation/twps0027/tab22.txt. Released June 1998. New York City data for 2000 from Susan Sachs, "New York City Tops 8 Million for First Time," *New York Times,* March 16, 2000.

45. See previous note and the Boston Metropolitan Area Planning Council Area Web site (May 1999): www.mapc.org.

46. Pisarski, *Commuting in America II,* 18; and David Rusk, *Cities Without Suburbs* (Washington, D.C.: Woodrow Wilson Center, 1995), 5 and following.

47. When this book was being written, the 2000

census data were only just being made available. Where possible, the latest 2000 census data has been used. In many cases, only projections based on 1990 data have been available.

48. See, for example, David W. Chen, "Outer Suburbs Outpace City in Population Growth," *New York Times,* March 16, 2001; and Cindy Rodriguez, "City, State Take on New Cast," *Boston Globe,* March 22, 2001.

49. F. Kaid Benfield, Matthew D. Raimi, and Donald D. T. Chen, *Once There Were Greenfields: How Urban Sprawl Is Undermining America's Environment, Economy, and Social Fabric* (Washington, D.C.: Natural Resources Defense Council, 1999), 6.

50. Pisarski, *Commuting in America II,* 25–26.

51. U.S. Census Bureau, "March 1996 Current Population Survey: Income 1995—Table A: Comparison of Summary Measures of Income by Selected Characteristics: 1994 and 1995," www.census.gov/hhes/income/income95/in95sum.html.

52. Joel Garreau, *Edge City: Life on the New Frontier* (New York: Doubleday, 1991), 3.

53. U.S. Department of Energy, Energy Information Administration, *Buildings and Energy in the 1980's* (Washington, D.C.: U.S. Department of Energy, 1995), 3.

54. Robert E. Lang, *Office Sprawl: The Evolving Geography of Business* (Washington, DC: The Brookings Institution, 2000), 3.

55. Michael Pollan, "The Triumph of Burbopolis," *New York Times Magazine,* April 9, 2000 54–55.

56. Robert D. Yaro, "Growing and Governing Smart: A Case Study of the New York Region" in Bruce Katz, ed., *Reflections on Regionalism* (Washington, D.C.: Brookings Institution Press, 2000), 43.

57. See also Robert Fishman's foreword in Peter Calthorpe and William Fulton, *The Regional City* (Washington, D.C.: Island Press, 2001), xv.

58. Bruce Katz and Jennifer Bradley, "Divided We Sprawl," *Atlantic Monthly,* December 1999, 26–42.

59. Patrick Geddes, *Cities in Evolution* (London: Williams & Norgate, 1915), 48–49. See also Richard Moe and Carter Wilkie, *Changing Places: Rebuilding Community in the Age of Sprawl* (New York: Henry Holt, 1997), 47.

60. U.S. Census Bureau, *Urban and Rural Definitions,* www.census.gov/population/censusdata/urdef.txt, and *About Metropolitan Areas,* www.census.gov/population/www/estimates/aboutmetro.html.

61. See U.S. Census Bureau map gallery, www.census.gov/geo/www/mapGallery/ma_1999.pdf.

62. Lewis Mumford, *The City in History: Its Origins, Its Transformations, Its Prospects* (New York: Harcourt, Brace and World, Inc., 1961), 540–41.

Chapter 2: The Origins of Sprawl

1. For a detailed treatment of the history of suburbanization, see Kenneth T. Jackson, *Crabgrass Frontier: The Suburbanization of the United States* (New York: Oxford University Press, 1985).

2. Lewis Mumford, *The City in History: Its Origins, Its Transformations, Its Prospects* (New York: Harcourt, Brace and World, Inc., 1961), 483 and following.

3. The exact dates are debatable. The industrial revolution is generally agreed to have started in the mid–eighteenth century in England and have spread to America by the mid–nineteenth century. The first American railroad began operation in 1830.

4. Mumford, *The City in History,* 446–49.

5. Jane Jacobs, *The Death and Life of Great American Cities* (New York: Vintage Books, 1961), 235 and following.

6. Leo Marx, *The Machine in the Garden: Technology and the Pastoral Ideal in America* (New York: Oxford University Press, 1964), 26.

7. For example, Catherine Beecher's *Treatise on Domestic Economy* (Boston: T. H. Webb & Co., 1843), which offers plans for two-story cottage dwellings, and Andrew Jackson Downing's *The Architecture of Country Houses* (New York: Appleton & Co., 1850).

8. Jackson, *Crabgrass Frontier,* 136. "Sanitary" refers to the extension of sewer lines as well as to the changeover from horse to electric traction power.

9. Ibid., 136.

10. Sam Bass Warner Jr., *Streetcar Suburbs: The Process of Growth in Boston 1870–1900* (Cambridge, Mass.: Harvard University Press and MIT Press, 1978), 2 and following.

11. Mumford, *The City in History,* plate 51. See also Richard Moe and Carter Wilkie, *Changing Places: Rebuilding Community in the Age of Sprawl* (New York: Henry Holt, 1997), 42–43.

12. All statistical data in the previous two paragraphs comes from Jackson, *Crabgrass Frontier,* 175–85.

13. Frank Lloyd Wright, *Modern Architecture, Being the Kahn Lectures for 1930* (Princeton, N.J.: Princeton University Press, 1931), 101.

14. Frank Lloyd Wright, *The Living City* (New York: Horizon, 1958), 22.

15. As quoted in Moe and Wilkie, *Changing Places,* 45.

16. Jackson, *Crabgrass Frontier,* 157.

17. Ibid., 161.

18. Robert A. Caro, *The Power Broker: Robert Moses and the Fall of New York* (New York: Knopf, 1974), 153–54.

19. Jackson, *Crabgrass Frontier,* 184.

20. Federal Highway Administration (FHWA),

Bureau of Highway Statistics, *State Motor Vehicle Registrations by Years, 1900–1995,* www.fhwa.dot.gov/ohim/summary95/section2.html.

21. Association of American Railroads, *Railroads: A Historical Perspective,* http://www.aar.org/comm/statfact.nsf/5406ac733125e6c7852564d000737b60?OpenView., as of November, 2000. See also U.S. Department of Transportation (DOT)/Bureau of Transportation Statistics, *Transportation Statistics Annual Report, 1999* (Washington, D.C.: DOT, 2000), 46. The value includes parcel and postal services also formerly carried by rail.

22. Association of American Railroads, *Railroads: A Historical Perspective,* 3.

23. Ibid., 6.

24. U.S. Department of Transportation (DOT), Bureau of Transportation Statistics, *Transportation Statistics Annual Report, 1999* (Washington, D.C.: DOT, 2000), 44.

25. James J. Flink, The Automobile Age, rev. ed. (Cambridge, Mass.: MIT Press, 1998), 371.

26. Starting in 1926, General Motors joined with Firestone, Standard Oil, and Mack Truck to create a subsidiary corporation called National City Lines, which bought up nearly bankrupt streetcar systems and converted them to bus networks. By 1950, the company had converted one hundred such systems across the nation, including the famed "Red Cars" of the Los Angeles streetcar network, an event featured in the movie *Roger Rabbit.* See (among others) Jane Holtz Kay, *Asphalt Nation: How the Automobile Took Over America and How We Can Take It Back* (New York: Crown, 1997), 213 and following. It should be noted that even before National City Lines, streetcar systems were experiencing serious operating losses due, in part, to low fare structures forced upon them by public regulation.

27. Judy Davis et al., "Consequences of Development of the Interstate Highway System for Transit," *Transit Cooperative Research Program Research Results Digest* no. 21 (August 1997): 4.

28. Flink, *The Automobile Age,* 371.

29. Ibid., 371.

30. Moe and Wilkie, *Changing Places,* 59.

31. Flink, *The Automobile Age,* 372.

32. Jackson, *Crabgrass Frontier,* 249. See also Moe and Wilkie, *Changing Places,* 62.

33. Cost to 1995. Data interpreted from U.S. Department of Transportation, Federal Highway Administration, *Highway Statistics to 1995, Funding for All Highways, All Units of Government, 1921–1995,* Table HF-210, www.fhwa.dot.gov/ohim/Summary95/section4.html, as of September 2000; figures escalated to 2000 dollars.

34. Estimated cost of the largest portion of the wall, which was constructed during the Ming Dynasty.

See Vince Raus, *Secrets of the Great Wall* (Bethesda, Md.: Discovery Communications, Inc., 2000), www.discovery.com.

35. Terry Moore and Paul Thorsnes, *The Transportation/Land Use Connection: A Framework for Practical Policy* (Chicago: American Planning Association, 1994), 48.

36. Flink, *The Automobile Age,* 196–97. See also Moe and Wilkie, *Changing Places,* 48.

37. Statistical data and quotations from Jackson, *Crabgrass Frontier,* 206.

38. Jackson, *Crabgrass Frontier,* 206.

39. Moe and Wilkie, *Changing Places,* 48.

40. Ibid., 49.

41. Ibid., 49, as quoted by Moe and Wilkie from the Federal Housing Administration's 1938 bulletin "Planning Profitable Neighborhoods."

42. Jackson, *Crabgrass Frontier,* 232.

43. Moe and Wilkie, *Changing Places,* 55.

44. Jackson, *Crabgrass Frontier,* 233.

45. Ibid., 259.

46. U.S. Department of Transportation, Bureau of Transportation Statistics, *Transportation Statistics Annual Report, 1999,* 184.

47. Warner, *Streetcar Suburbs,* ix.

48. Moe and Wilkie, *Changing Places,* 69.

49. Jackson, *Crabgrass Frontier,* 267.

50. Mumford, *The City in History,* 471.

51. Ibid., 472.

52. Louis Uchitelle, "Rebuilt City Starts to Feel the Effects of the Slowdown," *New York Times,* April 9, 2001.

53. U.S. Environmental Protection Agency, Office of Air and Radiation, *Air Trends—Number of Unhealthy Days by City 1999,* www.epa.gov/airtrends.

54. Joel Garreau, *Edge City: Life on the New Frontier* (New York: Doubleday, 1991), 27. See also Robert T. Dunphy et al., *Moving Beyond Gridlock: Traffic and Development* (Washington, D.C.: Urban Land Institute, 1997), 97.

55. Alan E. Pisarski, *Commuting in America II: The Second National Report on Commuting Patterns and Trends* (Lansdowne, Va.: Eno Transportation Foundation, 1996), 25.

56. Joseph Dalaker, U.S. Census Bureau, *Current Population Reports, Series P60-207, Poverty in the United States: 1998* (Washington, D.C.: U.S. Census Bureau, 1999), table 2. See also Chapter 8 of this book.

57. Pisarski, *Commuting in America II,* 19.

58. Patrick A. Simmons and Robert E. Lang, "The Urban Turnaround: A Decade by Decade Report Card on Postwar Population Change in Older Industrial Cities," *Fannie Mae Foundation Census Note 01* (Washington, D.C.: Fannie Mae Foundation, 2001), 4–6.

59. See Metropolitan Area Planning Council (MAPC), MAPC Metro Data Center, Census 2000 (April 2000), www.mapc.org.

60. Moe and Wilkie, *Changing Places*, 51.

61. Ibid., 57.

62. See Willy Boesiger, ed., *Le Corbusier* (New York: Praeger, 1972), 14.

63. While what happened on Sixth Avenue may not have been strictly an urban renewal project, it conformed to many of the same planning notions and innovations in zoning that controlled many contemporaneous urban renewal projects.

64. Jay Wickersham, *The State of Our Environment* (Boston: Commonwealth of Massachusetts, Executive Office of Environmental Affairs, 2000), 24.

Chapter 3: Reactions and Countertrends

1. Lewis Mumford, *The City in History: Its Origins, Its Transformations, Its Prospects* (New York: Harcourt, Brace and World, Inc., 1961), 510.

2. Malvina Reynolds, "Little Boxes," © Schroeder Music Co., 1962.

3. William H. Whyte Jr., *The Organization Man* (New York: Doubleday, 1956), chap. 1.

4. Jane Jacobs, *The Death and Life of Great American Cities* (New York: Vintage Books, 1961), 338.

5. Mumford, *The City in History*, 510.

6. Robert A. Caro, *The Power Broker: Robert Moses and the Fall of New York* (New York: Knopf, 1974), 848.

7. Ibid., 850.

8. Ibid., 843.

9. Jane Holtz Kay, *Asphalt Nation: How the Automobile Took Over America and How We Can Take It Back* (New York: Crown, 1997), 249.

10. Caro, *The Power Broker*, 848–49.

11. Richard Moe and Carter Wilkie, *Changing Places: Rebuilding Community in the Age of Sprawl* (New York: Henry Holt, 1997), 213.

12. Kay, *Asphalt Nation*, 259.

13. Peter Newman and Jeffrey Kenworthy, *Sustainability and Cities: Overcoming Automobile Dependence* (Washington, D.C.: Island Press, 1999), 17 and following.

14. Judy Davis et al., "Consequences of Development of the Interstate Highway System for Transit," *Transit Cooperative Research Program Research Results Digest* (August 1997): 4.

15. Richard F. Weingraf, *The Federal Highway Administration at 100*, www.tfhrc.gov/pubrds/fall93/p93au1.htm. See also Federal Highway Administration, *Highway Trust Fund Primer* (Washington, D.C.: Federal Highway Administration, 1998), 3–4.

16. Robert T. Dunphy et al., *Moving Beyond Gridlock: Traffic and Development* (Washington, D.C.: Urban Land Institute, 1997), 19.

17. U.S. Department of Transportation, Federal Highway Administration, *Highway Statistics Summary to 1995* (Washington, D.C., U.S. Department of Transportation, 1997), Table HF-210.

18. Ibid.

19. Ibid., and Barbara McCann, Roy Kienitz, and Bianca DeLille, *Changing Direction: Federal Transportation Spending in the 1990's* (Washington, D.C.: Surface Transportation Policy Project, 2000), 13.

20. McCann et al., *Changing Direction*, 13.

21. Ibid., 12–17.

22. U.S. Environmental Protection Agency, History Office, *Taking to the Air*, http://www.epa.gov/history/publications/formative5.htm.

23. These are carbon monoxide, lead, nitrogen dioxide, ozone (formed by volatile organic compounds and oxides of nitrogen), particulate matter, and sulfur dioxide. See U.S. Environmental Protection Agency (EPA), *Latest Findings on National Air Quality: 1999 Status and Trends* (Washington, D.C.: EPA, 2000), 2, 5.

24. U.S. Environmental Protection Agency (EPA), Office of Wastewater Management/Tetra Tech, Inc. with Andrew Stoddard and Associates, *Progress in Water Quality: An Evaluation of the National Investment in Municipal Wastewater Treatment* (Washington, D.C.: EPA, 2000), 3.

25. U.S. Environmental Protection Agency (EPA), *Water Pollution Control: 25 Years of Progress and Challenges for the New Millennium* (Washington, D.C.: EPA, 1998), 1–7.

26. William D. Middleton, *Manhattan Gateway: New York's Pennsylvania Station* (Waukesha, WI: Kalmbach Publishing Company, 1996), 113 and 127.

27. Ada Louise Huxtable, *Will They Ever Finish Bruckner Boulevard?* (New York: Collier Books, 1970), 44.

28. Ibid., 44–45.

29. Herbert Muschamp, "Critic's Notebook: Fireworks or Fallbacks for a New River City," *New York Times*, March 5, 2001.

30. Edward Glaeser and Jesse Shapiro, "City Growth and the 2000 Census: Which Places Grew and Why," in *The Brookings Institution Survey Series: Census 2000* (Washington, D.C.: Brookings Institution Press, 2001), 2–4.

31. That is the area within the city limits as opposed to the broader region.

32. Kathy McCabe and James Franklin, "Cities Undergo Renewed Pressure." *The Boston Globe*, June 27, 1999.

33. Campbell Gibson, *Population of the 100 Largest Cities and Other Urban Places in the United States: 1790 to 1990* (Washington, D.C.: U.S. Census Bureau, 1998), tables 18–21.

34. U.S. Census Bureau, *Population Change and Distribution: Census 2000 Brief* (Washington, D.C.: U.S. Census Bureau, 2001), 7. See also Susan Sachs, "New York City Tops 8 Million for First Time," *New York Times,* March 16, 2001

35. Pam Belluck, "Chicago Reverses 50 Years of Declining Population," *New York Times,* March 15, 2001. See also U.S. Census Bureau, Census 2000 PHC-T-5, *Ranking Tables for Incorporated Places of 100,000 or More: 1990 and 2000,* table 1, www.census.gov/population/cen2000/phc-t5/tab01.pdf.

36. See Robert Yaro as quoted by Susan Sachs in "New York City Tops 8 Million for the First Time," *New York Times,* March 16, 2001.

37. John Eckberg, "More People Calling Cincinnati's Downtown Home," *New York Times,* July 30, 2000.

38. See David Rusk, *Cities Without Suburbs* (Washington, D.C.: Woodrow Wilson Center, 1995), 14–17.

39. Detis T. Duhart et al., *Urban, Suburban and Rural Victimization, 1993–98* (Washington, D.C.: U.S. Department of Justice, Bureau of Justice Statistics, 2000), 3.

40. Data derived from Duhart et al., *Urban, Suburban and Rural Victimization,* 3.

41. City of New York, Department of Finance, *Annual Report on the New York City Property Tax: Fiscal Year 2000* (New York: City of New York, 2000), 2, 4, 9–21.

42. Bruce Lambert, "40 percent in New York City Are Foreign Born, Study Finds," *New York Times,* July 24, 2000.

43. Steven A. Holmes, "Immigration Is Fueling Cities' Strong Growth, Data Show," *New York Times,* January 1, 1998.

44. Michael Janofsky, "Phoenix Counts Its Many Challenges," *New York Times,* April 11, 2001.

45. See the Sierra Club Web site: www.sierraclub.org/population/faq.asp.

46. Joel Kotkin, *The New Geography: How the Digital Revolution Is Reshaping the American Landscape* (New York: Random House, 2000), 18.

47. Sachs, "New York City Tops 8 Million for the First Time."

48. Metropolitan Area Planning Council, *Race and Ethnicity in the Metropolitan Area,* www.mapc.org.

49. U.S. Census Bureau, *Census 2000 PHC-T-1, Population by Race and Hispanic or Latino Origin for the United States: 1990 and 2000,* table 4, www.census.gov/population/cen2000.

50. U.S. Census Bureau, *Population by Race and Hispanic or Latino Origin for the United States, Regions, Divisions, States, Puerto Rico and Places of 100,000 or More Population* (Washington, D.C.: U.S. Census Bureau, 2001), table 2, www.census.gov/population/cen2000/phc-t6/tab02.pdf, April 2, 2001. See

also Todd S. Purdum, "Shift in the Mix Alters the Face of California," *New York Times,* July 4, 2000.

51. Kotkin, *The New Geography,* 17 and following.

52. As quoted in Sachs, "New York City Tops 8 Million for First Time."

53. As quoted in Stephanie Ebbert, "For Second Time in Two Decades, A City on the Rise," *Boston Globe,* March 22, 2001.

54. See Janny Scott, "Hispanics and Asians Fuel New Jersey's Population Growth, Countryside Yields to Suburban Sprawl," *New York Times,* March 9, 2001; and Cindy Rodriguez, "City, State Take on New Cast," *Boston Globe,* March 22, 2001.

55. U.S. Census Bureau, *Population Change and Distribution: Census 2000 Brief* (Washington, D.C.: U.S. Census Bureau, 2001), 7.

56. Belluck, "Chicago Reverses 50 Years of Declining Population."

57. See Liming Liu et al., *Boston's Population—2000* (Boston: Boston Redevelopment Authority, 2001), 2; and Sachs, "New York City Tops 8 Million for First Time."

58. Brookings Institution, *Racial Change in the Nation's Largest Cities: Evidence from the 2000 Census,* (Washington, D.C.: Brookings Institution Press, 2001), figs. 1, 2, and 3, www.brook.edu/es/urban/census/citygrowth.htm.

59. Rebecca Sohmer and Robert Lang, *Downtown Rebound* (Washington, D.C.: Fannie Mae Foundation and Brookings Institution, 2001), 2, www.fanniemaefoundation.org/key_topics.shtm.

60. Laura Lippmann et al., *Urban Schools: The Challenge of Location and Poverty* (Washington, D.C.: National Center for Education Statistics, 1995), executive summary. See also http://nces.ed.gov/index.html.

61. See Patrick A. Simmons and Robert E. Lang, "The Urban Turnaround: A Decade by Decade Report Card on Postwar Population Change in Older Industrial Cities," in *Fannie Mae Census Note 01* (Washington, D.C.: Fannie Mae Foundation, 2001), 4.

62. James Howard Kunstler, *The Geography of Nowhere: The Rise and Decline of America's Manmade Landscape* (New York: Simon & Schuster, 1993), 10.

63. Congress for the New Urbanism, *About the Congress for the New Urbanism,* www.cnu.org/aboutcnu/index.cfm.

Chapter 4: Outlining the Debate

1. Alan E. Pisarski, *Commuting in America II: The Second National Report on Commuting Patterns and Trends* (Lansdowne, Va.: Eno Transportation Foundation, 1996), 18; and U.S. Census Bureau, *Profiles of General Demographic Characteristics 2000* (Washington, D.C.: U.S. Census Bureau, 2001), 4,

www.census.gov/Press-Release/www/2001/2khus.pdf.

2. National Association of Home Builders (NAHB), *Smart Growth: Building Better Places to Live, Work and Play* (Washington, D.C.: NAHB, 1999), 16.

3. U.S. Census Bureau, *Historical Census of Housing Tables: Homeownership,* www.census.gov/hhes/www/housing/census/historic/owner.html, as revised December 3, 1999. See also U.S. Department of Commerce News/Robert R. Callis and Linda B. Cavanaugh, *Housing Vacancies and Homeownership Second Quarter 2000,* www.census.gov/hhes/www/hvs.html, as revised on July 26, 2000.

4. Kenneth T. Jackson, "Suburbanization," in *The Reader's Companion to American History,* ed. Eric Froner and John A. Garraty (Boston: Houghton, Mifflin, 1991), 1040–1043.

5. Federal Highway Administration (FHWA), Office of Policy Information, *Highway Statistics 1999* (Washington, D.C.: FHWA, 2000), tables VM-1 and MV-1, www.fhwa.dot.gov/ohim/hs99/mvinter.htm; and Federal Highway Administration (FHWA), Office of Policy Information, *Highway Statistics Summary to 1995* (Washington, D.C.: FHWA, 1996), tables MV-200 and VM-201A, www.fhwa.dot.gov/ohim/summary95/index.html.

6. Pisarski, *Commuting in America II,* 36; and U.S. Department of Transportation, Bureau of Transportation Statistics, *1995 Nationwide Personal Transportation Survey,* 6, www-cta.ornl.gov/npts/1995/Doc/NPTS_Booklet.pdf.

7. Gregg Easterbrook, "Suburban Myth: The Case for Sprawl," *New Republic,* March 15, 1999, 18–21.

8. For the federal government, see U.S. Department of Agriculture, Natural Resources Conservation Service, *A Geography of Hope* (Washington, D.C.: U.S. Department of Agriculture, 1997); and U.S. Environmental Protection Agency (EPA), Region One, *Opening Remarks, Smart Growth Strategies for New England Conference,* February 2, 1999, John DeVillars, regional administrator, EPA, New England, at www.epa.gov/region01.

9. As cited on the Natural Resources Defense Council Web site, June 19, 2001: www.nrdc.org/cities/smartGrowth/default.asp.

10. American Farmland Trust as cited in F. Kaid Benfield, Matthew D. Raimi, and Donald D. T. Chen, *Once There Were Greenfields: How Urban Sprawl Is Undermining America's Environment, Economy, and Social Fabric* (Washington, D.C.: Natural Resources Defense Council, 1999), 64.

11. National Wildlife Federation Web site: www.nwf.org/smartgrowth/wildlife.html; and Benfield et al., *Once There Were Greenfields,* 68–72.

12. U.S. Department of Transportation (DOT), Bureau of Transportation Statistics, *Transportation Statistics Annual Report, 1999* (Washington, D.C.: DOT, 1999), summary.

13. Ibid., 54–56.

14. Ibid.

15. U.S. Department of Energy (DOE), Energy Information Administration, *Annual Energy Outlook 2000* (Washington, D.C.: DOE, 1999), 5, 82, 96, 100, 101.

16. Jay Wickersham, *The State of Our Environment* (Boston: Commonwealth of Massachusetts, Executive Office of Environmental Affairs, 2000), 93.

17. Benfield et al., *Once There Were Greenfields,* 91.

18. U.S. Census Bureau, *Profiles of General Demographic Characteristics 2000,* www2.census.gov/census_2000/datasets/demographic_profile/0_National_Summary/2khus.pdf, as of June 20, 2001.

19. Joseph Dalaker, *Current Population Reports, Series P60-207, Poverty in the United States: 1998* (Washington, D.C.: U.S. Census Bureau, 1999), table 2.

20. Robert D. Putnam, *Bowling Alone: The Collapse and Revival of American Community* (New York: Simon & Schuster, 2000), 278, 283.

21. See the Introduction to this book.

22. Sierra Club, *Sprawl: The Dark Side of the American Dream,* www.sierraclub.org/sprawl/report98.

23. Samuel R. Staley et al., *The Sprawling of America: In Defense of the Dynamic City,* Policy Study No. 251 (Los Angeles: Reason Public Policy Institute, 1999), 1, 10.

24. Steven Hayward, "The Suburbanization of America," in Jane S. Shaw and Ronald D. Utt, eds., *A Guide to Smart Growth: Shattering Myths, Providing Solutions,* (Washington, D.C.: Heritage Foundation, 2000), 9.

25. National Association of Home Builders, *NAHB's Smart Growth Report* (Washington, D.C.: NAHB, 2000), 8–9.

26. Wendell Cox, "Coping with Traffic Congestion" in Shaw and Utt, eds., *A Guide to Smart Growth,* 39 and following.

27. Kenneth Greene, *Defending Automobility: A Critical Examination of the Environmental and Social Costs of Auto Use,* Reason Public Policy Institute Policy Study No. 198 (Los Angeles: Reason Public Policy Institute, 1995), www.rppi.org/environment/ps198.html; and Randal O'Toole, *The Vanishing Automobile and Other Myths: How Smart Growth Will Harm American Cities* (Brandon, Or.: Thoreau Institute, 2001), 329.

28. Wendell Cox, "Coping with Traffic Congestion," in Shaw and Utt, eds., *A Guide to Smart Growth,* 39 and following; and Staley, *The Sprawling of America,* 2 and following.

29. Staley, *The Sprawling of America,* 2.

30. Ibid., 2, 27, and following.

31. Hayward, "The Suburbanization of America," 12–13.

32. Ronald D. Utt, "The Relationship of Cities and

Suburbs," in Shaw and Utt, eds., *A Guide to Smart Growth,* 78–79.

33. Staley, *The Sprawling of America,* 2.

34. Eric Schmitt, "Analysis of the Census Finds Segregation Along with Diversity," *New York Times,* April 4, 2001.

35. Schmitt, "Analysis of the Census Finds Segregation Along With Diversity."

36. National Association of Home Builders, *NAHB's Smart Growth Report* (Washington, D.C.: NAHB, 2000), 16.

37. O'Toole, *The Vanishing Automobile and Other Myths,* 24.

38. National Association of Home Builders, *NAHB's Smart Growth Report,* 14–16.

39. Richard Lacayo with Wendy Cole, Dan Cray, Daniel Levy, Todd Murphy, and Timothy Roche, "The Brawl Over Sprawl," *Time,* March 22, 1999, 48.

40. Hayward, "The Suburbanization of America," 15–16.

41. Mark Mellman, Democratic pollster, as quoted by Todd S. Purdum in "Suburban Sprawl Takes Its Place on the Political Landscape," *New York Times,* February 6, 1999.

42. President's Council on Sustainable Development, *Sustainable Communities Task Force Report* (Washington, D.C.: U.S. Government Printing Office, 1997), Executive Summary.

43. William D. Ruckelshaus, *Scientific American,* September 1989.

Chapter 5: Land and Habitat

1. John Mitchell, "Urban Sprawl," *National Geographic,* Vol. 200, No.1, July, 2001, 48 and ff. and U.S. Census Bureau, Statistical Abstract of the United States: 2000 (Washington, DC: 2001), pp.31 and 227, www.census.gov/prod/2001pubs/statab/sec06.pdf

2. Mitchell, "Urban Sprawl," 56

3. Richard Lacayo with Wendy Cole, Dan Cray, Daniel Levy, Todd Murphy and Timothy Roche, "The Brawl Over Sprawl," *Time Magazine,* Vol. 153, no. 11, March 22, 1999.

4. Ibid., 47

5. David Firestone, "The New-Look Suburbs: Denser or More Far-Flung," *The New York Times,* April 17, 2001

6. Peter J. Howe, "EPA Takes on Sprawl in Region," *The Boston Globe,* February 2, 1999 and John DeVillars, Regional Administrator, EPA–New England *Regional Administrator's Speech, Opening Remarks, Smart Growth Strategies for New England Conference,* February 2, 1999, www.epa.gov/region01/ra/sprawl/speech_19990202.html

7. Kaid Benfield, Matthew Raimi and Donald Chen *Once There Were Greenfields: How Urban Sprawl is Undermining America's Environment, Economy*

and Social Fabric (Washington, DC: National Resources Defense Council, 1999), 23

8. The Urban Land Institute/Robert T. Dunphy et al, *Moving Beyond Gridlock* (Washington, DC: 1997), 96

9. Samuel R. Staley, *The Sprawling of America: In Defense of the Dynamic City,* Policy Study No. 251 (Los Angeles: Reason Public Policy Institute, 1999), 1, 10–11. See also Steven Hayward, "The Suburbanization of America," in Jane S. Shaw and Ronald D. Utt, eds., *A Guide to Smart Growth: Shattering Myths, Providing Solutions* (Washington, DC: Heritage Foundation, 2000), 9.

10. U.S. Department of Agriculture, National Resources Conservation Service, *1997 National Resources Inventory,* table 1, www.nhq.nrcs.usda.gov/NRI/1997/summary_report.

11. U.S. Department of Agriculture, Natural Resources Conservation Service, *State Rankings by Acreage and Rate of Non-Federal Land Developed,* www.nhq.nrcs.usda.gov/CCS/devtable.html. Note that the rate of developed land increased from 1.4 million acres per year in the ten-year period 1982 to 1992 to 3.2 million acres per year in the five-year period 1992–1997. An average number has been used for the entire fifteen-year period.

12. U.S. Department of Agriculture, Natural Resources Conservation Service, *Land Capability by Class, by State, 1992,* www.nhq.nrcs.usda.gov/cgi-bin/kmusser/mapgif.pl?mapid=2771.

13. Hayward, "The Suburbanization of America," 9.

14. Jay Wickersham, *The State of Our Environment* (Boston: Commonwealth of Massachusetts, Executive Office of Environmental Affairs, 2000), 24.

15. Land areas of states exclusive of water areas. Estimates derived from U.S. Department of Agriculture, Natural Resources Conservation Service, *Summary Report: 1997 National Resources Inventory, Revised December 2000,* table 1, www.nhq.nrcs.usda.gov/NRI/1997/summary_report/original/table1.html; and U.S. Department of Agriculture, Natural Resources Conservation Service, *State Rankings by Acreage and Rate of Non-Federal Land Developed,* www.nhq.nrcs.usda.gov/CCS/devtable.html.

16. U.S. Department of Agriculture, Natural Resources Conservation Service, *Land Ownership, 1992,* www.nhq.nrcs.usda.gov/cgi-bin/kmusser/mapgif.pl?mapid=2788.

17. Benfield et al., *Once There Were Greenfields,* 64.

18. U.S. Department of Agriculture, Natural Resources Conservation Service, *1997 National Resources Inventory,* Glossary.

19. U.S. Department of Agriculture, Natural Resources Conservation Service, *1997 National Resources Inventory.*

20. Ibid.

21. U.S. Census Bureau, *National Population Projec-*

tions, I. Summary Files, www.census.gov/population/projections/nation/summary/np-t1.txt.

22. U.S. Department of Agriculture, Natural Resources Conservation Service, *A Geography of Hope* (Washington, D.C.: U.S. Department of Agriculture, 1997), 7.

23. U.S. Census Bureau, *United States Summary of Population and Housing Counts* (Washington, D.C.: U.S. Census Bureau, 1990), table 16.

24. As quoted in Staley, *The Sprawling of America,* 23.

25. A. Ann Sorenson, Richard P. Greene, and Karen Russ, *Farming on the Edge* (DeKalb, Ill.: American Farmland Trust, 1997), chap. 4, www.farmland-info.org/cae/foe2/foetoc.html.

26. Sorenson et al., *Farming on the Edge,* chap. 3.

27. Frank Lloyd Wright, *The Living City* (New York: Horizon, 1958), 123–24.

28. Jane S. Shaw, "Nature in the Suburbs," in Shaw and Utt, eds., *A Guide to Smart Growth,* 30.

29. Ibid., 31.

30. Joel Garreau, *Edge City: Life on the New Frontier* (New York: Doubleday, 1991), 56–57.

31. Benfield et al., *Once There Were Greenfields,* 82.

32. Thomas E. Dahl, *Status and Trends of Wetlands in the Coterminous United States 1986 to 1997* (Washington, D.C.: U.S. Fish and Wildlife Service, 2000), 11. Includes both urban and rural development categories because the U.S. Fish and Wildlife Service defines rural development as including scattered suburban development and highways.

33. U.S. Environmental Protection Agency (EPA), *National Water Quality Inventory: 1998 Report to Congress* (Washington, D.C.: EPA, 1998), 147.

34. Reed F. Noss, Edward T. LaRoe III, and J. Michael Scott, *Endangered Ecosystems of the United States: A Preliminary Assessment of Loss and Degradation,* http://biology.usgs.gov/pubs/ecosys.htm. See also U.S. Environmental Protection Agency, *National Water Quality Inventory: 1998 Report to Congress,* 143.

35. Sheila Peck, *Planning for Biodiversity: Issues and Examples* (Washington, D.C.: Island Press, 1998), 69–70.

36. Ibid., 72–73.

37. Ibid., 70–71.

38. Shaw, "Nature in the Suburbs," 32.

39. Wickersham, *The State of Our Environment,* 101 and following.

Chapter 6: Transportation and Energy

1. Wendell Cox, "Coping with Traffic Congestion," in Jane S. Shaw and Ronald D. Utt, eds., *A Guide to Smart Growth: Shattering Myths, Providing Solutions,* (Washington, D.C.: Heritage Foundation, 2000), 39.

2. Donald Chen, *Greetings from Smart Growth America* (Washington, D.C.: Smart Growth America, 2000), 7.

3. U.S. Department of Transportation (DOT), Bureau of Transportation Statistics, *1995 Nationwide Personal Transportation Survey* (Washington, D.C.: DOT, 1995), 22. See also F. Kaid Benfield, Matthew D. Raimi, and Donald D. T. Chen, *Once There Were Greenfields: How Urban Sprawl Is Undermining America's Environment, Economy, and Social Fabric,* (Washington, D.C.: Natural Resources Defense Council, 1999), 36.

4. Benfield et al., *Once There Were Greenfields,* 36.

5. Terry Moore and Paul Thorsnes, *The Transportation/Land Use Connection: A Framework for Practical Policy* (Chicago: American Planning Association, 1994), 48.

6. Jane Holtz Kay, *Asphalt Nation: How the Automobile Took Over America and How We Can Take It Back* (New York: Crown, 1997), 121.

7. U.S. Department of Transportation, *1995 Nationwide Personal Transportation Survey,* 17.

8. Cox, "Coping with Traffic Congestion," 40–43.

9. Samuel R. Staley, *The Sprawling of America: In Defense of the Dynamic City,* Policy Study No. 251 (Los Angeles: Reason Public Policy Institute, 1999), www.rppi.org/ps251.html.

10. It could be said that the Big Dig is an extreme case, but it is actually a good example of the kinds of costs that may have to be incurred in some areas to expand the capacity of the highway system. The reason for the project is not simply to bury an unsightly highway. It would never have been funded if it were. It is mainly a major interstate highway capacity enhancement that arguably couldn't have been done any other way. With this project, I-93 is expanded from six to ten lanes, while I-90 gets a four-lane underwater tunnel extension to Logan Airport. A huge, partly underground interchange is necessary to connect the two as well as a bridge and three surface interchanges elsewhere in the project. In all, the project has about 161 lane miles of highway, only half of which are actually underground. A major part of what is driving the cost so high is an extremely lengthy list of environmental commitments brought about by environmental legislation from the 1970s on—for example, $80 million for a single park replacement. All information from the project website: www.bigdig.com.

11. U.S. Department of Transportation, *1995 Nationwide Personal Transportation Survey,* 3.

12. Benfield et al., *Once There Were Greenfields,* 31.

13. Robert T. Dunphy et al., *Moving Beyond Gridlock: Traffic and Development* (Washington, D.C.: Urban Land Institute, 1997), 54.

14. Texas Transportation Institute (TTI), *Urban Roadway Congestion Annual Report,* as referenced in

U.S. Department of Transportation (DOT), Bureau of Transportation Statistics, *Transportation Statistics Annual Report, 1999* (Washington, D.C.: DOT, 1999), 54–56; see also TTI, *2001 Urban Mobility Report* (College Station, Tx.: TTI, 2001), table A-5.

15. U.S. Department of Transportation, Bureau of Transportation Statistics, *Transportation Statistics Annual Report, 1999*, 54–56.

16. Ibid., 54–56; see also Texas Transportation Institute, *2001 Urban Mobility Report*, table A-7.

17. U.S. Department of Transportation, Bureau of Transportation Statistics, *Transportation Statistics Annual Report, 1999*, 54–56.

18. Dunphy et al., *Moving Beyond Gridlock*, 4–5.

19. Ibid.

20. Cox, "Coping with Traffic Congestion," 39–60.

21. Randal O'Toole, *The Vanishing Automobile and Other Myths: How Smart Growth Will Harm American Cities* (Brandon, Oreg.: Thoreau Institute, 2001), 398–99.

22. Ibid., 398–99; David Schrank and Tim Lomax, *1999 Urban Mobility Report: Information for Urban America* (College Station: Texas Transportation Institute, 1999), iv–11.

23. Schrank and Lomax, *1999 Urban Mobility Study*, iv–11.

24. Texas Transportation Institute (TTI), *2001 Urban Mobility Report*, "How Much More Road Construction Would Be Needed?" and "How Should We Address the Mobility Problem?" at TTI's 2001 Urban Mobility Study Web site: http://mobility.tamu.edu/

25. David Schrank with Tim Lomax, *1999 Annual Mobility Report* (College Station: Texas Transportation Institute, 2000), table 9.

26. Low-end figure from Benfield et al., *Once There Were Greenfields*, 91. High-end figure calculated from information available on Boston's Central Artery/Tunnel project Web site: www.bigdig.com.

27. Texas Transportation Institute, *2001 Urban Mobility Study*, "How Much More Road Construction Would Be Needed?" at http://mobility.tamu.edu/

28. Cox, "Coping with Traffic Congestion," 40–45.

29. O'Toole, *The Vanishing Automobile and Other Urban Myths*, 497.

30. Dr. Tim Lomax, testimony before U.S. House of Representatives, Subcommittee on Highways and Transit, March 21, 2001, www.house.gov/transportation.

31. Moore and Thorsnes, *The Transportation/Land Use Connection*, 115.

32. Ibid., 74.

33. Ibid., 75. See also the South Coast Air Quality Management District Web site: www.aqmd.gov.

34. Virginia Ellis, "California Toll Road Projects Lose Momentum," *Los Angeles Times,* February 8, 2000. See also the ETTM Web site for other articles on this subject: www.ettm.com.

35. O'Toole, *The Vanishing Automobile and Other Urban Myths,* 495.

36. David Halbfinger, "Schundler Wins G.O.P. Primary in New Jersey Governor's Race," *New York Times,* June 27, 2001.

37. Moore and Thorsnes, *The Transportation/Land Use Connection,* 58.

38. U.S. Department of Transportation (DOT), Bureau of Transportation Statistics, *1995 Nationwide Personal Transportation Survey* (Washington, D.C.: DOT, 1995), 14.

39. Chryss Cada, "For Colorado Gridlock, Rocky Roads Ahead," *Boston Globe,* May 6, 2001.

40. Federal highway statistics as cited in National Association of Industrial and Office Properties (NAIOP) with Anthony Downs, *Growing to Greatness: A Growth Management Manual* (Herndon, Va.: NAIOP, 1999), 95. See also Bureau of Transportation Statistics, *1995 Nationwide Personal Transportation Survey,* 14.

41. U.S. Department of Transportation, Bureau of Transportation Statistics, *Transportation Statistics Annual Report, 1999,* 37.

42. Ibid., 56.

43. National Association of Industrial and Office Properties/Downs, *Growing to Greatness,* 97.

44. Corey Kilgannon, "Road Warriors with Laptops," *New York Times,* August 15, 2000.

45. Ibid.

46. Chryss Cada, "For Colorado Gridlock, Rocky Roads Ahead," *Boston Globe,* May 6, 2001.

47. Kilgannon, "Road Warriors with Laptops."

48. James McKinley Jr., "New York Votes to Ban Phones Held by Drivers," *New York Times,* June 26, 2001.

49. U.S. Department of Transportation, Bureau of Transportation Statistics, *Transportation Statistics Annual Report, 1999,* 46.

50. National Association of Industrial and Office Properties/Downs, *Growing to Greatness,* 97.

51. U.S. Department of Transportation, Federal Transit Administration, *Characteristics of Urban Transportation Systems—Revised Edition September, 1992,* chaps. 2 and 4, www.fta.dot.gov/library/reference/CUTS/; and Transportation Cooperative Research Program (TCRP)/Kittelson and Associates, Inc, Texas Transportation Institute, Transport Consulting Ltd., *Transit Capacity and Quality of Service Manual,* TCRP Web Document No. 6 (Washington, D.C.: TRCP, 1999), 1-1 and following, http://nationalacademies.org/trb/publications/tcrp/tcrp_webdoc_6-a.pdf. Assumes 1.6 persons per car on the freeway per Bureau of Transportation Statistics, *1995 Nationwide Personal Transportation Survey,* 24.

52. TCRP/Kittelson et al., *Transit Capacity and Quality of Service Manual,* 3-2.

53. Ibid.

54. Cox, "Coping with Traffic Congestion," 48.

55. Moore and Thorsnes, *The Transportation/Land Use Connection,* 72.

56. Interview with Matthew A. Coogan, independent transportation consultant, formerly deputy secretary of transportation for Massachusetts, October 3, 1995.

57. U.S. Department of Transportation (DOT), Bureau of Transportation Statistics, *Transportation Statistics Annual Report, 1999* (Washington, D.C.: DOT, 1999), 104, www.bts.gov/transtu/tsar/tsar1999/chap05.pdf.

58. U.S. Department of Transportation (DOT), Federal Highway Administration, Office of Highway Policy Information, *Highway Statistics 1999* (Washington, D.C.: DOT, 2000), table MF-21, www.fhwa.dot.gov/ohim/hs99/tables/mf21.pdf.

59. U.S. Department of Energy (DOE), Energy Information Administration, *Annual Energy Outlook 2000* (Washington, D.C.: DOE, 1999), 231. See also Bureau of Transportation Statistics, *Transportation Statistics Annual Report, 1999,* 104.

60. Foregoing statistics quoted in this paragraph are from U.S. Department of Transportation (DOT), Bureau of Transportation Statistics, *Transportation Statistics Annual Report, 1995* (Washington, D.C.: DOT, 1995), 75–76.

61. Benfield et al., *Once There Were Greenfields,* 50.

62. U.S. Department of Transportation, Bureau of Transportation Statistics, *Transportation Statistics Annual Report, 1999,* 106–10.

63. U.S. Department of Energy, Energy Information Administration, *Annual Energy Outlook 2000,* 5, 82, 96, 100, 101.

64. U.S. Department of Transportation, Bureau of Transportation Statistics, *Transportation Statistics Annual Report, 1999,* 110.

65. Ibid., 104.

66. Joseph Kahn, "Cheney Promotes Increasing Supply As Energy Policy," *New York Times,* May 1, 2001.

67. Michael Kranish, "Cheney Faces Decision on Wyoming Drilling," *Boston Globe,* May 6, 2001.

68. Peter Newman and Jeffrey Kenworthy, *Sustainability and Cities: Overcoming Automobile Dependence* (Washington, D.C.: Island Press, 1999), 49–51.

69. Ibid., 49–51.

70. Colin J. Campbell and Jean H. Laherrere, "The End of Cheap Oil," *Scientific American,* March 1998, 78–83.

71. Ibid., 78.

72. Encyclopedia Britannica, "Petrochemical," www.britannica.com/eb/article?eu=60998&tocid=0.

73. Benfield et al., *Once There Were Greenfields,* 60.

74. Ibid., 37–38.

75. Ibid.

76. Newman and Kenworthy, *Sustainability and Cities,* 94–95.

77. Ibid., 70–71.

78. In *The Vanishing Automobile and Other Urban Myths,* 262 and following, Randal O'Toole makes a case for the idea that energy use is lower and transit use is higher in Europe not because of density but mostly because Europeans can't afford driving, and that (as the European standard of living goes up) transit share is declining as more Europeans opt for autos. This may be partly true, but it can also be argued that the higher cost of auto ownership in Europe (for example, fuel taxes, tolls, and so forth) actually reflects that the costs imposed by the externalities of auto ownership combined with better transit options and walkable cities have been effective in keeping transit ridership and walking shares higher than in the United States over time. In fact, whereas Germany owns about as many cars per capita as the United States, the vehicles they own see only about two-thirds of the annual vehicle miles traveled of U.S. autos, and they have less than a third as many miles of roadway per capita as the United States though Germany is about eight times as densely populated on average (see Federal Highway Administration, *Highway Statistics 1998,* sec. 6, Special Studies and Metric Tables, www.fhwa.dot.gov/ohim/hs98/special.htm. Meanwhile, in *Sustainability and Cities* (Chapter 3), Newman and Kenworthy present data that show that European transit and walking modes shares are on average much higher than in the United States and that their cities are more compact, making a very strong case that European transit trends are tied to density as well as price, contradicting O'Toole's argument.

79. U.S. Department of Energy, Energy Information Administration, *Annual Energy Outlook 2000,* 82.

80. U.S. Department of Energy (DOE), Energy Information Administration, *Buildings and Energy in the 1980's* (Washington, D.C.: DOE, 1995), 3.

81. Royal Ford, "Toyota Prius Gives Fuel to Gas-Electric Idea," *Boston Sunday Globe,* November 12, 2000. See also U.S. Department of Transportation, Bureau of Transportation Statistics, *Transportation Statistics Annual Report, 1999,* 106.

82. U.S. Department of Energy, Energy Information Administration, *Annual Energy Outlook 2000,* 231–32.

83. Newman and Kenworthy, *Sustainability and Cities,* 75–76. In *The Vanishing Automobile and Other Urban Myths,* 329–30, Randal O'Toole disputes these findings using data attributed to the U.S. Department of Energy (DOE), but the DOE clearly states that, according to their own analysis, "Mass transit (buses and rail) are the least energy

intensive of all modes." See U.S. DOE, Energy Information Administration, *Measuring Energy Efficiency in the United States' Economy: A Beginning* (Washington, D.C.: DOE, 1995), chap. 5, www.eia.doe.gov/emeu/efficiency/ee_report_ht ml.htm. O'Toole also adds construction energy expended to build a typical transit line to transit energy cost. It would be interesting to add in the total energy cost of building the U.S. interstate system and all its connecting roads to the energy cost per passenger mile analyses used by O'Toole. O'Toole and the DOE do not include European data in their respective surveys, whereas Newman and Kenworthy do.

Chapter 7: Pollution and Public Health

1. F. Kaid Benfield, Matthew D. Raimi, and Donald D.T. Chen, *Once There Were Greenfields: How Urban Sprawl Is Undermining America's Environment, Economy, and Social Fabric* (Washington, D.C.: Natural Resources Defense Council, 1999), 51.

2. Jay Wickersham, *The State of Our Environment* (Boston: Commonwealth of Massachusetts, Executive Office of Environmental Affairs, 2000), 91.

3. Katharine Seelye and Andrew Revkin, "Panel Tells Bush Global Warming Is Getting Worse," *New York Times,* June 7, 2001.

4. Benfield et al., *Once There Were Greenfields,* 55.

5. U.S. Environmental Protection Agency (EPA), Office of Air Quality Planning and Standards, *Latest Findings on National Air Quality: 1999 Status and Trends* (Research Triangle Park, N.C.: EPA, 2000), 2.

6. U.S. Environmental Protection Agency, Office of Transportation and Air Quality, Air Toxics from Motor Vehicles, *Fact Sheet OMS-2, EPA-400-F-92-004, August 1994*. See also Benfield et al., *Once There Were Greenfields,* 58–59.

7. Samuel R. Staley, *The Sprawling of America: In Defense of the Dynamic City,* Policy Study No. 251 (Los Angeles: Reason Public Policy Institute, 1999), 38–39; and Wendell Cox, "Coping with Traffic Congestion," in Jane S. Shaw and Ronald D. Utt, eds., *A Guide to Smart Growth: Shattering Myths, Providing Solutions* (Washington, D.C.: Heritage Foundation, 2000), 39–43.

8. Staley, *The Sprawling of America,* 38–39; Cox, "Coping with Traffic Congestion," 43–46; and Randal O'Toole, *The Vanishing Automobile and Other Urban Myths: How Smart Growth Will Harm American Cities* (Brandon, Or.: Thoreau Institute, 2001), 272–73.

9. Robert Griffin Jr., science writer for *EPA Journal,* as quoted in Benfield et al., *Once There Were Greenfields,* 78.

10. Statistics from U.S. Environmental Protection Agency (EPA), Office of Waste Water Management, *Water Pollution Control: 25 Years of Progress and Challenges for the New Millennium* (Washington, D.C.: EPA, 1998), 6, www.epa.gov/owm/25prog.pdf. Definition from U.S. Environmental Protection Agency (EPA), Office of Water, *The Quality of Our Nation's Waters: A Summary of the National Water Quality Inventory: 1998 Report to Congress* (Washington, D.C.: EPA, 2000), 4, www.epa.gov/305b/98report/98brochure.pdf.

11. U.S. Environmental Protection Agency, Office of Wetlands, Oceans and Watersheds, *Nonpoint Source Pollution: The Nation's Largest Water Quality Problem,* EPA841-F-96-004A, www.epa.gov/OWOW/NPS/facts/point1.htm.

12. U.S. Environmental Protection Agency (EPA), *The Quality of Our Nation's Water: 1996* (Washington, D.C.: EPA, 1996), 13. See also U.S. Environmental Protection Agency, Office of Wetlands, Oceans and Watersheds, *Nonpoint Source Pollution.*

13. U.S. Department of Agriculture, Natural Resources Conservation Service, *A Geography of Hope* (Washington, D.C.: U.S. Department of Agriculture, 1997), 20.

14. U.S. Environmental Protection Agency (EPA), *National Water Quality Inventory,* 69.

15. Ibid., 62, 88, 108. See also U.S. Environmental Protection Agency (EPA), *The Quality of Our Nation's Water: 1996* (Washington, D.C.: EPA, 1996); and U.S. Environmental Protection Agency (EPA), *The Quality of Our Nation's Water: 1994* (Washington, D.C.: EPA, 1994).

16. U.S. Census Bureau, *Density Using Land Area for States, Counties Metropolitan Areas and Counties,* tables 2 and 3, www.census.gov/population/www/censusdata/density.html; and *Census 2000 PHC-T-5. Ranking Tables for Incorporated Places of 100,000 or More: 1990 and 2000,* http://blue.census.gov/population/cen2000/phc-t5/tab02.pdf; and *Census 2000 PHC-T-3. Ranking Tables for Metropolitan Areas: 1990 and 2000, Table 3: Metropolitan Areas Ranked by Population: 2000,* http://blue.census.gov/population/cen2000/phc-t3/tab03.pdf.

17. Center for Watershed Protection, *The Impacts of Urbanization,* www.cwp.org.

18. Richard Higgins, "H20 Aplenty, But . . . ," *Boston Sunday Globe,* May 14, 2000.

19. David Firestone, "Booming Atlanta Saps Water As Drought Wilts Georgia," *New York Times,* June 15, 2000.

20. Jim Yardley, "For Texas Now, Water, Not Oil, Is Liquid Gold," *New York Times,* April 16, 2001.

21. See the Center for Watershed Protection Web site for the following publications: *Better Site Design, Eight Tools for Watershed Protection,* and *Impacts of Urbanization:* www.cwp.org.

22. Steven Hayward of the Heritage Foundation dis-

misses the issue in "The Suburbanization of America," 3.

23. Centers for Disease Control and Prevention (CDC)/ Lawrence Frank, Peter Engleke, Thomas Schmid, and Richard Killingsworth, *How Land Use and Transportation Systems Affect Public Health: A Literature Review of the Relationship Between Physical Activity and Built Form* (Atlanta: CDC, 2001), 11, www.cdc.gov/nccdphp/dnpa/pdf/aces-working paper1.pdf.

24. Centers for Disease Control and Prevention/ Frank, Engleke, Schmid, and Killingsworth, *How Land Use and Transportation Systems Affect Public Health*, 11.

25. Ibid., 115.

26. U.S. Department of Transportation (DOT), Bureau of Transportation Statistics, *National Transportation Statistics 2000* (Washington, D.C.: DOT, 2001), tables 2-17, 3-1, and 3-2, www.bts.gov/ btsprod/nts. Excludes bus fatalities and injuries.

27. U.S. Census Bureau, *Population Estimates for Cities with Populations of 10,000 and Greater,* July 1, 1999, www.census.gov/population/estimates/ metro-city/SC10K-T3.txt.

28. U.S. Department of Transportation, Bureau of Transportation Statistics, *Transportation Statistics Annual Report 1997* (Washington, DC: DOT, 1997), 54–55.

29. Bureau of Transportation Statistics, *Transportation Statistics Annual Report, 1999,* table 4-1 and *National Transportation Statistics Report 2000* (Washington, DC: DOT, 2001), Tables 3-1 and 2-4.

30. *Vietnam War Casualties by Branch of Service,* http:// members.aol.com/WarLibrary.

31. Figures from U.S. Department of Transportation, Bureau of Transportation Statistics, *National Transportation Statistics 2000,* tables 2-17, 3-1, and 3-2; and U.S. Department of Transportation, Bureau of Transportation Statistics, *Transportation Statistics Annual Report, 1999,* table 2-2. Note: In *The Vanishing Automobile and Other Urban Myths,* 370–72, Randal O'Toole shows figures that compare fatalities and injuries between modes on the basis of passenger miles. The resulting figures imply that auto and transit are comparable in safety, with transit showing a higher injury rate, but O'Toole separates out trucks (including pick-ups and SUVs) and motorcycles from the mix, potentially distorting the results. Also, transit and auto are not directly comparable on the basis of passenger miles since the average auto trip is at least twice the distance of the average transit trip (hence, more miles generated per trip). This also can create distortions in the results. An analysis made on the basis of total trips taken by mode yields a more accurate comparison.

32. For example, according to the Bureau of Transportation Statistics, there were over 600 rail-related deaths in 1995, but rail passenger deaths averaged about 13 per year between 1990 and 1995 (U.S. Department of Transportation, Bureau of Transportation Statistics, *Transportation Statistics Annual Report 1997* (Washington, DC: DOT, 1997), 57, 59 and 66). Most rail losses were non-passengers.

33. U.S. Environmental Protection Agency (EPA), Office of Air Quality Planning and Standards, *Latest Findings on National Air Quality: 1999 Status and Trends* (Research Park Triangle, N.C.: EPA, 2000), 20.

34. Andrew C. Revkin, "Tiny Bits of Soot Tied to Illnesses," *New York Times,* April 21, 2001.

35. U.S. Environmental Protection Agency (EPA), Office of Transportation and Air Quality, *Air Toxics from Motor Vehicles,* EPA Fact Sheet OMS-2, EPA 400-F-92-004, www.epa.gov/otaq/02-toxic.htm.

Chapter 8: Economics and Social Equity

1. F. Kaid Benfield, Matthew D. Raimi, and Donald D.T. Chen, *Once There Were Greenfields: How Urban Sprawl Is Undermining America's Environment, Economy, and Social Fabric* (Washington, D.C.: Natural Resources Defense Council, 1999), 94.

2. Ibid., 94–106.

3. Ibid., 101.

4. Robert Burchell, William Dolphin, and Catherine Galley, *The Costs and Benefits of Alternative Growth Patterns: The Impact Assessment of the New Jersey State Plan* (Trenton, N.J.: New Jersey Office of State Planning, 2000), 12, 182, 229.

5. All of the information for Utah comes from Peter Calthorpe and William Fulton, *The Regional City* (Washington, D.C.: Island Press, 2001), 130–33.

6. Peter Gordon and Harry Richardson, "Are Compact Cities a Desirable Planning Goal?" *Journal of the American Planning Association,* Vol. 63, No.1, Winter 1997. Available at http://smartgrowth. org/library/apa_pointcounterpoint/apa_sprawl. html.

7. Ibid., 5.

8. O'Toole, *The Vanishing Automobile and Other Urban Myths,* 279.

9. Reid Ewing, "Is Los Angeles–Style Sprawl Desirable?" *Journal of the American Planning Association,* vol. 63, no.1, 1997. Available at www.smart-growth.org/library/apa_pointcounterpoint/apa_compact_ewing.html.

10. Ibid., 12.

11. Burchell, Dolphin, and Galley, *The Costs and Benefits of Alternative Growth Patterns.*

12. "There are gaps in the literature and some differences in the order of magnitude of the results." Benfield et al., *Once There Were Greenfields,* 94.

13. Phillip J. Longman, "Who Pays for Sprawl: Hid-

den Subsidies Fuel the Growth of the Suburban Fringe," *U.S. New and World Report,* April 27, 1998, 22.

14. Myron Orfield, *Metropolitics: A Regional Agenda for Community and Stability* (Washington, D.C.: Brookings Institution, 1998), 71.

15. Orfield, *Metropolitics,* 69.

16. Jane Holtz Kay, *Asphalt Nation: How the Automobile Took Over America and How We Can Take It Back* (New York: Crown, 1997), 120. See also Robert Bullard, Glenn S. Johnson, and Angel Torres, *Sprawl City: Race Politics, and Planning in Atlanta* (Washington, D.C.: Island Press, 2000), 40; and Surface Transportation Policy Project (STPP)/Barbara McCann, "Driven to Spend: Sprawl and Household Transportation Expenses," *Progress,* vol. 11, no. 1 (January-February 2001): 3 and following.

17. Surface Transportation Policy Project/McCann, "Driven to Spend," 3 and following.

18. Ibid., 3.

19. Stephen H. Burrington, *Road Kill: How Solo Driving Runs Down the Economy* (Boston: Conservation Law Foundation, 1994), 29.

20. U.S. Department of Transportation, Bureau of Transportation Statistics, *1999 National Transportation Statistics,* table 2-27a, "Federal Transportation Expenditures by Mode, Fiscal Year," www.bts.gov/btsprod/nts.

21. Gordon and Richardson, "Are Compact Cities a Desirable Planning Goal?," 2 (html version).

22. Alan E. Pisarski, *Commuting in America II: The Second National Report on Commuting Patterns and Trends* (Lansdowne, Va.: Eno Transportation Foundation, 1996), 49. Approximately 5,890,155 commuters used transit for commuting in 1990; this figure translates roughly to 1.09 persons per car on average, also according to Pisarski, 61.

23. Terry Moore and Paul Thorsnes, *The Transportation/Land Use Connection: A Framework for Practical Policy* (Chicago: American Planning Association, 1994), 33.

24. Kay, *Asphalt Nation,* 120. Average household cost of car ownership from Surface Transportation Policy Project/McCann, "Driven to Spend," 3.

25. U.S. Department of Transportation (DOT), Federal Highway Administration, *Highway Statistics 1999* (Washington, D.C.: DOT, 2000), table MV-1; and U.S. Department of Transportation (DOT), Federal Highway Administration, *Highway Statistics 1995* (Washington, D.C.: DOT, 1996), table MV-1, www.fhwa.dot.gov/ohim/hs99/tables/mv1.pdf and www.fhwa.dot.gov/ohim/1995/mv1.pdf. 1995 data used. Excludes motorcycles, publicly owned vehicles, buses, and freight and farm trucks but includes pick-ups, sport/utilities, and vans.

26. Moore and Thorsnes, *The Transportation/Land Use Connection,* 48.

27. Longman, "Who Pays for Sprawl?"

28. Anthony Downs, "What Does Smart Growth Really Mean?" *Planning,* vol. 67, no. 4 (April 2001): 22.

29. See U.S. Department of Transportation, Bureau of Transportation Statistics, *1995 Nationwide Personal Transportation Survey,* 17 (about 2 percent); Pisarski, *Commuting in America II,* 63 (5.12 percent); and U.S. Department of Transportation, Bureau of Transportation Statistics, *Transportation Statistics Annual Report 1999,* table 2-2 (3.6 percent).

30. U.S. Department of Transportation, Bureau of Transportation Statistics, *Funding for Highways, All Units of Government, 1921–1995,* table HF-210.

31. U.S. Department of Transportation (DOT), Federal Transportation Administration, *National Transit Summaries and Trends, 1998* (Washington, D.C.: DOT, 1998), 13, 26, 33, www.ntdprogram.com/NTD/NTST.nsf/NTST/1998/$File/98NTST.pdf.

32. Average household vehicle cost estimated from Surface Transportation Policy Project/McCann, "Driven to Spend," ($6,200) divided by 1.78 vehicles average per household (Bureau of Transportation Statistics, *1995 Nationwide Personal Transportation Survey,* 8) yields $3,483 annual cost per vehicle multiplied by 191.6 million private vehicles.

33. Truck cost estimated at $107,000 per year per truck from American Trucking Association Web site: Truckline Information Center, www.truckline.com/infocenter/position_papers/cashcow.html.

34. David Bollier, *How Smart Growth Can Stop Sprawl: A Fledgling Citizen Movement Expands* (Washington, D.C.: Sprawl Watch Clearinghouse, Essential Books, 1998), 13.

35. Benfield et al., *Once There Were Greenfields,* 94.

36. Bob Fernandez, "Home, Population Data Show Flight to Suburbia," *Philadelphia Enquirer,* June 15, 2000.

37. Pisarski, *Commuting in America II,* 19.

38. See Chapter 1.

39. American Farmland Trust, *Fact Sheet: Cost of Community Services Studies* (Washington, D.C.: American Farmland Trust, 2000); Joel Garreau, *Edge City: Life on the New Frontier* (New York: Doubleday, 1991), 465.

40. O'Toole, *The Vanishing Automobile and Other Urban Myths,* 517.

41. Myron Orfield, *Metropolitics: A Regional Agenda for Community and Stability* (Washington, D.C.: Brookings Institution, 1998), 62. See also Bollier, *How Smart Growth Can Stop Sprawl,* 12–13; and Benfield et al., *Once There Were Greenfields,* 112–15.

42. Orfield, *Metropolitics,* 62–63.

43. U.S. Census Bureau, *Black Population in the United States: March, 1999 (Update): Detailed Tables and*

Documentation for P20-530 (PPL-130), (Washington, D.C.: U.S. Census Bureau, 2000), table 16, www.census.gov/population/www/socdemo/race/black99tabs.html.

44. Joseph Dalaker, *Current Population Reports, Series P60-207, Poverty in the United States: 1998* (Washington, D.C.: U.S. Census Bureau, 1999), table 2.

45. Benfield et al., *Once There Were Greenfields,* 123.

46. Leatha Lamison-White, *U.S. Census Bureau Statistical Brief, Poverty Areas* (Washington, D.C.: U.S. Census Bureau, 2000), 1.

47. Ibid.

48. Lewis Mumford Center for Comparative Urban and Regional Research at the State University of New York (SUNY) at Albany, *Ethnic Diversity Grows, Neighborhood Integration Is at a Standstill* (Albany: SUNY, 2001), 1, www.albany.edu/mumford/census.

49. Sam Bass Warner Jr., *Streetcar Suburbs: The Process of Growth in Boston 1870–1900,* (Cambridge, Mass.: Harvard University Press and MIT Press, 1978), 3.

50. U.S. Department of Transportation, Bureau of Transportation Statistics, *1995 Nationwide Personal Transportation Survey,* 7.

51. U.S. Department of Housing and Urban Development (HUD), Office of Policy Development and Research, *Issue Brief No. III—Homeownership: Progress and Work Remaining,* Washington, D.C.: HUD, 2000), 8.

52. Kenneth T. Jackson, *Crabgrass Frontier: The Suburbanization of the United States* (New York: Oxford University Press, 1985), 208.

53. Ibid., 208-209

54. Ibid., 208.

55. Ibid., 211–13.

56. John A. Powell, "Addressing Regional Dilemmas for Minority Communities," in Bruce Katz, ed., *Reflections on Regionalism* (Washington, D.C.: Brookings Institution Press, 2000), 225.

57. Ibid., 233–24.

58. Ibid., 227.

59. Orfield, *Metropolitics,* 66 and following. See also Bullard, Johnson, and Torres, "Dismantling Transportation Apartheid," in *Sprawl City,* 39.

60. Benfield et al., *Once There Were Greenfields,* 124–25.

61. Orfield, *Metropolitics,* 67.

62. Jane Gross, "Poor Without Cars Find Trek to Work Is Now a Job," *New York Times,* November 18, 1997, 1.

63. Evelyn Nieves, "Many in Silicon Valley Cannot Afford Housing, Even at $50,000 a Year," *New York Times,* February 20, 2000, 16.

64. M. David Lee, speech given at "How We Live: A Civic Initiative for a Livable New England," September 9, 2000.

65. Garreau, *Edge City,* 147–50.

66. Ibid.; and also Jesse McKInnon and Karen Humes, *The Black Population in the United States: March 1999,* (Washington, D.C.: U.S. Census Bureau, 2000), 2, 4.

67. Joel Kotkin, "A Revival of Older Suburbs As Ethnic Businesses Take Hold," *New York Times,* February 27, 2000, business section, 7.

68. Garreau, *Edge City,* 146.

69. Charles Jaret, Elizabeth P. Rudman, and Kurt Phillips, "The Legacy of Residential Segregation," in Bullard, Johnson, and Torres, *Sprawl City,* 116, 122.

70. Lewis Mumford Center/John Logan et al., *Ethnic Diversity Grows,* 1, http://mumford1.dyndns.org/cen2000/WholePop/WPreport/page1.html.

71. Powell, "Addressing Regional Dilemmas for Minority Communities," in Katz, ed., *Reflections on Regionalism,* 218–20. See also John A. Powell, "Race and Space, What Really Drives Metropolitan Growth," *Bookings Review,* vol. 16, no. 4 (fall 1998): 20 and following. See also Jaret, Rudman, and Phillips, "The Legacy of Residential Segregation," 116.

72. "Cities and Suburbs: A Harvard Magazine Roundtable, *Harvard Magazine,* vol. 102, no. 3 (January-February 2000): 60.

73. Lamison-White, *U.S. Census Bureau Statistical Brief, Poverty Areas,* vi–vii.

74. Benfield et al., *Once There Were Greenfields,* 126–27.

75. William H. Lucy and David L. Phillips, *Confronting Suburban Decline: Strategic Planning for Metropolitan Renewal* (Washington, D.C.: Island Press, 2000), 166.

76. Ibid., 166 and following.

77. Ronald D. Utt, "The Relationship of Cities and Suburbs," in Jane S. Shaw and Ronald D. Utt, eds., *A Guide to Smart Growth: Shattering Myths, Providing Solutions* (Washington, D.C.: Heritage Foundation, 2000), 78 and following.

78. Eric Schmitt, "Most Cities in U.S. Expanded Rapidly Over Last Decade," *New York Times,* May 7, 2001.

79. David Rusk, *Cities Without Suburbs* (Washington, D.C.: Woodrow Wilson Center, 1995), 9 and following. See also p. 53.

80. Samuel R. Staley, *The Sprawling of America: In Defense of the Dynamic City,* Policy Study No. 251 (Los Angeles: Reason Public Policy Institute, 1999), 33 and following.

81. Ibid., 33.

82. Ibid., 37.

Chapter 9: Aesthetics and Community

1. Kenneth T. Jackson, *Crabgrass Frontier: The Suburbanization of the United States* (New York: Oxford University Press, 1985), 239–40.

2. James Howard Kunstler, *The Geography of Nowhere: The Rise and Decline of America's Manmade Landscape* (New York: Simon & Schuster, 1993), 121.

3. Randal O'Toole, *The Vanishing Automobile and Other Urban Myths: How Smart Growth Will Harm American Cities* (Brandon, Oreg.: Thoreau Institute, 2001), 68–70.

4. Leo Marx, *The Machine in the Garden: Technology and the Pastoral Ideal in America* (New York: Oxford University Press, 1964), 3.

5. Kunstler, *The Geography of Nowhere,* 220.

6. As quoted by Michael Pollan in "Town Building Is No Mickey Mouse Operation," *New York Times Magazine,* December 14, 1997, 62.

7. Jane Holtz Kay, *Asphalt Nation: How the Automobile Took Over America and How We Can Take It Back* (New York: Crown, 1997).

8. See, for example, Richard Lacayo with Wendy Cole, Dan Cray, Daniel Levy, Todd Murphy, and Timothy Roche, "The Brawl Over Sprawl," *Time,* March 22, 1999, 45; Todd S. Purdum, "Suburban 'Sprawl' Takes Its Place on the Political Landscape," *New York Times,* February 6, 1999; and John G. Mitchell, "Urban Sprawl," *National Geographic,* July 2000, 48.

9. John Rather, "First Mass Housing Suburb," *New York Times,* November 15, 1998; Herbert Muschamp, "Becoming Unstuck on the Suburbs," *New York Times,* October 19, 1997; and David M. Halbfinger, "New Buyers Renew Levittown, Now 50," *New York Times,* September 28, 1997.

10. Paul Goldberger, "L.I. Over 25 Years: Realizing a Dream; Crossing the Island, A Slice of America," *New York Times,* May 5, 1996.

11. James Howard Kunstler, *Home from Nowhere: Remaking Our Everyday World for the Twenty-First Century* (New York: Simon & Schuster, 1996), 22.

12. Herbert Gans, *The Levittowners: Life and Politics in a New Suburban Community* (New York: Pantheon, 1967), 220.

13. Gans, *The Levittowners,* 186.

14. William Whyte, *City: Rediscovering the Center* (New York: Doubleday, 1988) as cited in Jay Wickersham, *The State of Our Environment* (Boston: Commonwealth of Massachusetts, Executive Office of Environmental Affairs, 2000), 28.

15. Study of Chesterfield, New Jersey, by Professor Anton Nelessen of Rutgers University as reported in Randall Arendt, *Rural by Design: Maintaining Small Town Character* (Chicago: American Planning Association, 1994), 28–29.

16. Study by Jack Nasar and David Julian using psychological tools for assessing community cohesion developed by Thomas Glynn to evaluate a variety of neighborhoods in northwestern Columbus, Ohio. Cited in F. Kaid Benfield, Matthew D. Raimi, and Donald D. T. Chen, *Once There Were Greenfields: How Urban Sprawl Is Undermining American's Environment, Economy, and Social Fabric* (Washington, D.C.: Natural Resources Defense Council, 1999), 128–29.

17. Robert D. Putnam, *Bowling Alone: The Collapse and Revival of American Community* (New York: Simon & Schuster, 2000), 19.

18. Ibid., 45.

19. Ibid., 61, 99, 100.

20. Ibid., 215, 283.

21. Ibid., 205.

22. Ibid., 206.

23. Ibid., 209.

24. William Whyte, *The Organization Man* (New York: Doubleday, 1956), 287, as cited in Putnam, *Bowling Alone,* 209.

25. Putnam, *Bowling Alone,* 209–11.

Chapter 10: Growth Management and Smart Growth

1. For a more detailed description of early growth management history, see Douglas Porter, *Managing Growth in America's Communities* (Washington, D.C.: Island Press, 1997), 31–33.

2. Ibid., 8–9, 10–13.

3. Ibid., 33–42.

4. U.S. Census Bureau, *National Population Projections, I. Summary Files,* www.census.gov/population/projections/nation/summary/np-t1.txt.

5. Anthony Downs, "What Does Smart Growth Really Mean?" *Planning,* vol. 67, no. 4 (April 2001): 20.

6. National Association of Industrial and Office Properties/Anthony Downs, *Growing to Greatness: A Growth Management Manual* (Herndon, Va.: 1999), p. 4

7. See Steven Hayward, "The Suburbanization of America," in Jane S. Shaw and Ronald D. Utt, eds., *A Guide to Smart Growth: Shattering Myths, Providing Solutions* (Washington, D.C.: Heritage Foundation, 2000), 3; and Downs, "What Does Smart Growth Really Mean?," 20.

8. David Brollier, *How Smart Growth Can Stop Sprawl* (Washington, D.C.: Sprawl Watch Clearinghouse, Essential Books, 1998), 2.

9. Natural Resources Defense Council, *Paving Paradise: Sprawl and the Environment,* www.nrdc.org/cities/smartgrowth/rpave.asp.

10. David O'Neill, *Smart Growth, Myth and Fact* (Washington, D.C.: Urban Land Institute, 1999), 5.

11. As quoted in O'Neill, *Smart Growth, Myth and Fact,* 4.

12. National Association of Industrial and Office Properties—official definition posted on their Web site: www.naiop.org/legislate/growth/index. html (as of November 2000).

13. National Association of Home Builders (NAHB), *Smart Growth: Building Batter Places to Live, Work and Play* (Washington, D.C.: NAHB, 1999), 5.

14. *Encarta World English Dictionary,* North American Edition, http://dictionary.msn.com.

15. Ann Eberhart Goode, Elizabeth Collaton, and Charles Bartsch, *Smart Growth* (Washington, D.C.: Northeast-Mideast Institute, 1999), as posted on the Smart Growth Network Web site: www.smart growth.org/information/aboutsg.html.

16. Sierra Club/Eric Parfrey, *What Is Smart Growth?,* 1999, www.sierraclub.org.

17. Downs, "What Does Smart Growth Really Mean?," 20.

Chapter 11: Preserving Open Space

1. Smart Growth America, *Smart Growth America: Making Smart Growth Happen* (Washington, D.C.: Smart Growth America, 2000), 3.

2. Ibid., 3.

3. As reported in *LandVote 2000* on the Trust for Public Land Web site: www.tpl.org/tier3_cdl. cfm?content_item_id=847&folder_id=586.

4. National Association of Realtors, *Voter Survey on Open Space,* National Association of Realtors Web site: http://nar.realtor.com/gov/home.htm. See also Belden, Russonello, and Stewart, *National Survey on Growth and Land Development, September 2000, for Smart Growth America,* www.smartgrowthamerica.com/poll.pdf. See also Richard Lacayo with Wendy Cole, Dan Cray, Daniel Levy, Todd Murphy, and Timothy Roche, "The Brawl Over Sprawl," *Time,* March 22, 1999, 44.

5. Sheila Peck, *Planning for Biodiversity: Issues and Examples* (Washington, D.C.: Island Press, 1998), 30.

6. Ibid., 30–31.

7. Ibid., 84–88, 104–5.

8. See the Long Island Pine Barrens Society Web site: www.pinebarrens.org/index.html.

9. National Association of Realtors, *Voter Survey on Open Space,* http://nar.realtor.com/gov/home.htm.

10. Elizabeth Brabec, "The Economics of Preserving Open Space," in Randall Arendt with Elizabeth A. Brabec, Harry L. Dodson, Christine Reid, and Robert D. Yaro, *Rural by Design: Maintaining Small Town Character* (Chicago: American Planning Association, 1994), 280–88.

11. Brabec, *The Economics of Preserving Open Space,* 283.

12. Ibid., 284.

13. Ibid., 286–87.

14. Ibid., 285–86.

15. Tom Daniels, State University of New York at Albany, *Planning, Zoning and Land Preservation for Growth Management: A Comparison of Neighboring Communities,* paper presented at the Association of Collegiate Schools of Planning Conference, Chicago, 1999.

16. For example, in Farmcolony in Stannardsville, Virginia, and South Meadow Concord, Massachusetts, the Home Owners Association leases the land to a farmer. Many other similar developments go the land trust route. See Randall Arendt et al., *Rural by Design,* 301.

17. Arendt et al., *Rural by Design,* 259–61.

18. Ibid., 293.

19. See Douglas Porter, *Managing Growth in America's Communities* (Washington, D.C.: Island Press, 1997), 111–14; and Timothy Beatley and Kristy Manning, *The Ecology of Place: Planning for Environment, Economy and Community* (Washington, D.C.: Island Press, 1997), 49–50.

20. See Porter, *Managing Growth in America's Communities,* 113; and Beatley and Manning, *The Ecology of Place,* 49. See also the Long Island Pine Barrens Society Web site: www.pinebarrens.org.

21. Porter, *Managing Growth in America's Communities,* 101. See also the Land Trust Alliance Web site: www.lta.org/aboutlta/index.html.

22. See, for example, the Commonwealth of Massachusetts General Laws Chapters 61 and 61A, www.state.ma.us/legis/laws/mgl/index.htm.

23. U.S. Department of Agriculture, Natural Resources Conservation Service, *Summary Report, 1997 National Resources Inventory* (Washington, D.C.: U.S. Department of Agriculture, 2000), table 1, www.nhq.nrcs.usda.gov/NRI/1997/summary_report/original/table1.html.

24. National Association of Realtors, *Realtors Release Survey on Growth and Sprawl,* press release, October 30, 2000, http://nar.realtor.com.

25. "What is Private Lands Conservation and What Are Its Benefits?" remarks of Jean Hocker, president, Land Trust Alliance, at Private Lands, Public Benefits: A Policy Summit on Working Lands Conservation, National Governors Association, March 16, 2001, www.lta.org/newsroom/nga_march_2001.htm.

26. Ed Goldstein and Evan Johnson, *Nature by the Numbers: 50 Little Known-Facts from the Nature Conservancy Archives,* http://nature.org/aboutus/resources/#Top.

27. Anthony Flint, "Build-Minded Owner Snubs Land-Buy Bid," *Boston Globe,* June 30, 2001.

28. Interview with Pat Sherman, Concord, NH architect and member of local planning task force and interview with David Dixon, planning con-

sultant to Concord, NH held on November 14, 2000

29. Interview with Pat Sherman held on November 14, 2000 and E-mail interview with Rhett Lamb, Planning Director for Keene, NH held on November 15, 2000.

30. This and other data on Boulder from Peter Pollock, "Controlling Sprawl in Boulder: Benefits and Pitfalls," *Land Lines,* Lincoln Institute of Land Policy, January 1998. See also Porter, *Managing Growth in America's Communities,* 102.

31. Tom Daniels, *Planning, Zoning and Land Preservation for Growth Management: A Comparison of Neighboring Counties,* paper presented at the Association of Collegiate Schools of Planning Conference, Chicago, October 23, 1999, http://w.albany.edu/gp/Faculty_Staff/tdaniels/planning_zoning.html.

32. Lancaster County, Pennsylvania, Web site: www.co.lancaster.pa.us/Agpresrv.htm.

33. Samuel R. Staley et al, *Urban-Growth Boundaries, Smart Growth and Housing Affordability* (Los Angeles: Reason Public Policy Institute, 1999), 1.

34. Pollock, "Controlling Sprawl in Boulder."

Chapter 12: Changing Development Patterns

1. Lewis Mumford, *The City in History: Its Origins, Its Transformations, Its Prospects* (New York: Harcourt, Brace and World, Inc., 1961), 515–16.

2. Peter Calthorpe and William Fulton, *The Regional City* (Washington, D.C.: Island Press, 2001), 280.

3. Congress for the New Urbanism, *New Urbanism Basics,* March 14, 2001, www.cnu.org/about/index.cfm.

4. Congress for the New Urbanism, *New Urbanism Basics.*

5. Peter Calthorpe, *The Next American Metropolis: Ecology, Community and the American Dream* (New York: Princeton Architectural Press, 1993), 56–57.

6. Ibid., 71.

7. See the Orenco Station Web site at www.orencostation.com/home.htm.

8. See Calthorpe, *The Next American Metropolis;* Calthorpe and Fulton, *The Regional City;* and Peter Katz, *The New Urbanism* (New York: McGraw-Hill, 1994) for examples. A notable exception is Atlantic Center, which is planned for Brooklyn, New York. See Calthorpe, *The Next American Metropolis,* 136.

9. Michael Bernick and Robert Cervero, *Transit Villages in the 21st Century* (New York: 1997), 84

10. Ibid., 5.

11. Ibid., 303; and Alan E. Pisarski, *Commuting in America II: The Second National Report on Commuting Patterns and Trends* (Landsdowne, Va.: Eno Transportation Foundation, 1996), 63.

12. Peter Newman and Jeffrey Kenworthy, *Sustainability and Cities: Overcoming Automobile Dependence* (Washington, D.C.: Island Press, 1999), 174–76, 217–23.

13. Bernick and Cervero, *Transit Villages in the 21st Century,* 189–99.

14. Ibid., 228.

15. Ibid.

16. Skidmore, Owings and Merrill, *Planning for Transit-Friendly Land Use: A Handbook for New Jersey Communities* (Newark, N.J.: New Jersey Transit, 1994).

17. Eric Schmitt, "Whites in Minority in Largest Cities, the Census Shows," *New York Times,* April 30, 2001.

18. See chapters 2 and 3 of this book.

19. As described in Richard Moe and Carter Wilkie, *Changing Places: Rebuilding Community in the Age of Sprawl* (New York: Henry Holt, 1997), 184.

20. Moe and Wilkie, *Changing Places,* 190.

21. James Brooke, "Denver Stands Out in Trend Toward Living in Downtown," *New York Times,* December 29, 1998.

22. John Eckberg, "More People Calling Cincinnati's Downtown Home," *New York Times,* July 30, 2000.

23. Eckberg, "More People Calling Cincinnati's Downtown Home."

24. National Trust for Historic Preservation, *National Main Street Center,* http://mainstreet.org.

25. Information on Chippewa Falls from Moe and Wilkie, *Changing Places,* 156–66.

26. Moe and Wilkie, *Changing Places,* 168–69.

27. Information on Franklin, Tennessee, from Moe and Wilkie, *Changing Places,* 166–72.

28. U.S. Environmental Protection Agency (EPA), "Fact Sheet: Clinton Administration Expands Brownfields," www.epa.gov/swerosps/bf/html-doc/wh0513_3.htm.

29. U.S. Environmental Protection Agency Administrator Christie Whitman in an April 20, 2001, press release: www.epa.gov/swerosps/bf/html-doc/pr010420.htm.

30. U.S. Environmental Protection Agency, Office of Solid Waste and Emergency Response, *Innovative Solutions and Private Investment Bring Prosperity to Oregon Mills,* March 22, 2001, www.epa.gov/swerosps/bf/html-doc/ss_orgml.htm.

31. U.S. Environmental Protection Agency, Office of Solid Waste and Emergency Response, *From Slag to Riches,* March 22, 2001, www.epa.gov/swerosps/bf/html-doc/ss_pitts.htm.

32. Information on Telecom City from U.S. Environ-

mental Protection Agency, Office of Solid Waste and Emergency Response (OSWER), *Region 1 Brownfields Pilots: Brownfields Cleanup Revolving Loan Fund Pilots*—EPA Region 1, www.epa.gov/swerosps/bf/reg1rlf.htm; Larissa Brown, David Dixon, and Oliver Gillham, *How We Live: A Civic Initiative for a Livable New England, Regional Charrette Briefing Book* (Boston: Boston Society of Architects, 2001), 56, and the Telecom City Web site: www.telcomcity.com.

33. Brown et al., *How We Live,* 51.

34. Information on Assembly Square from Brown et al., *How We Live,* 50–53; Interviews with Jeffery R. Levine , director of long-range planning, from the Mystic View Task Force Web site: www.theville.com/mysticview; and from the City of Somerville.

35. See Calthorpe and Fulton, *The Regional City,* 223.

36. Ibid., 230–31.

37. See the Congress for the New Urbanism Web site, at www.cnu.org, and the Dover, Kohl and Partners Web site, at www.doverkohl.com/redevelop.html.

38. See Calthorpe and Fulton, *The Regional City,* 226.

39. Anthony Flint, "In Weymouth, Plans for a New 'Village,'" *Boston Globe,* August 20, 2001.

40. Telecom City Web site: www.telcomcity.com.

41. Carey Goldberg, "Massachusetts City Plans to Destroy Public Housing," *New York Times,* April 2, 2001.

42. See Douglas Porter, *Managing Growth in America's Communities* (Washington, D.C.: Island Press, 1997), 182–84. For Cambridge, see *City of Cambridge Zoning Ordinance,* Section 15.000, Cambridgeport Revitalization Development District, www.ci.cambridge.ma.us/~CDD/commplan/zoning/zord/zo_article15_cprdd.pdf.

43. U.S. Census Bureau, *Census 2000 PHC-T-5, Ranking Tables for Incorporated Places of 100,000 or More: 1990 and 2000,* www.census.gov/population/www/cen2000/phc-t5.html.

44. Randal O'Toole, *The Vanishing Automobile and Other Urban Myths: How Smart Growth Will Harm American Cities* (Brandon, Oreg.: Thoreau Institute, 2001), 9–16.

45. National Association of Realtors, *Realtors Release Survey on Growth and Sprawl,* press release, October 30, 2000, http://nar.realtor.com.

46. See Bernick and Cervero, *Transit Villages in the 21st Century,* 282–84; and Calthorpe, *The Next American Metropolis,* 136.

47. Peter Whoriskey, "Is It Smart growth or a Dumb Idea? Plan to Increase Population Density in Some Fairfax Areas Fuels a Debate," *Washington Post,* January 14, 2001.

48. Porter, *Managing Growth in America's Communities,* 39–40.

Chapter 13: Viable Public Transportation

1. See *Encarta World English Dictionary* and *The Encarta Encyclopedia* at www.encarta.msn.com and the Encarta 98 Encyclopedia.

2. Robert T. Dunphy et al., *Moving Beyond Gridlock: Traffic and Development* (Washington, D.C.: Urban Land Institute, 1997), 19–25.

3. Commonwealth of Massachusetts, Executive Office of Transportation and Construction, *Massachusetts Transportation Facts, 1998* (Boston: Commonwealth of Massachusetts, 1998), 15, and Alan E. Pisarski, *Commuting in America II: The Second National Report on Commuting Patterns and Trends* (Lansdowne, Va.: Eno Transportation Foundation, 1996), 61.

4. Information on Hop Shuttle from Surface Transportation Policy Project, *Five Years of Progress: 110 Communities Where ISTEA Is Making a Difference,* www.transact.org/Reports/5yrs/INDEX.HTM. Ridership and auto trip diversion: 4,300 trips divided by 1.09—the average vehicle occupancy rate in 1990 from Pisarski, *Commuting in America II,* 61. 2000 ridership from e-mail interview with Nataly Handlos, transportation planner, Go Boulder, September 24, 2001.

5. Surface Transportation Policy Project, *Five Years of Progress..*

6. Dunphy et al., *Moving Beyond Gridlock,* 125–41.

7. Ibid.

8. San Diego Association of Governments, San Diego Trolley Inc., *Fact Sheet, Mid-Coast Light Rail Transit Extension and Mission Valley East-San Diego Trolley Project,* www.sandag.org.

9. Leon Williams, chairman, Metropolitan Transit Development Board, *State of Public Transportation Address,* January 11, 2001. See also Dunphy et al., *Moving Beyond Gridlock,* 133.

10. Fare box recovery for the nation's thirty largest transit agencies was slightly more than 40 percent in 1994. U.S. Department of Transportation, Federal Transit Administration, *1994 National Transit Database—Transit Profiles—The Thirty Largest Agencies,* www.fta.dot.gov/library/reference/sec15/profiles94/top30/app/app.html. See also Pisarski, *Commuting in America II,* 64. See also Williams, *State of Public Transportation Address.*

11. U.S. Census Bureau, *Journey to Work and Place of Work—1990 Census,* www.census.gov/population/www/socdemo/journey.html. By contrast, the transit figure for the state of Massachusetts is about 8 percent. See Commonwealth of Massachusetts Executive Office of Transportation and Construction, *Massachusetts Transportation Facts, 1998,* 6.

12. U.S. Census Bureau, *Journey to Work and Place of*

Work—*1990 Census.* See also Pisarski, *Commuting in America II,* 63–64.

13. Average for Boston and nine adjacent communities. In the city of Boston alone, the transit mode share reaches more than 30 percent. Telephone interview with William Kuttner, Boston Central Transportation Planning Staff, May 30, 2001. See also U.S. Census Bureau, *Journey to Work and Place of Work*—1990 Census, and Stephen Falbel, Central Transportation Planning Staff, *The Demographics of Commuting in Greater Boston* (Boston: Boston Metropolitan Planning Organization, 1998), fig. 18.

14. Commonwealth of Massachusetts, Executive Office of Transportation and Construction, *Massachusetts Transportation Facts, 1998,* 39.

15. Massachusetts Bay Transportation Authority, "Envisioning the Urban Ring," *The Urban Ring,* (winter 2000/2001); and telephone interview with William Kuttner, May 30, 2001.

16. Adelaide Metro Web site, *Programs and Guides—The Adelaide O-Bahn,* www.adelaidemetro.com.au/guides/obahn.html.

17. A number of manufacturers are now coming out with low-level boarding buses that also eliminate steps and achieve many of the same benefits of the high-level systems without having to build platforms and ramps.

18. Dunphy et al., *Moving Beyond Gridlock,* 60, 95. See also Pisarski, *Commuting in America II,* 65.

19. Dunphy et al., *Moving Beyond Gridlock,* 6–9; and Pisarski, *Commuting in America II,* 64.

20. New York Metropolitan Transportation Council et al., *Travel in the New York–New Jersey Metropolitan Area: A Summary of Results from the 1997/98 Regional Travel-Household Interview Survey* (New York: New York Metropolitan Council, 2000), 2, and Pisarski, *Commuting in America II,* 49.

21. Stephen Falbel, Central Transportation Planning Staff, *Suburban Public Transportation* (Boston: Boston Metropolitan Planning Organization, 1998), 35.

22. Information compiled from the U.S. Department of Transportation (DOT), Federal Transit Administration, *National Transit Summaries and Trends, 1998* (Washington, D.C.: DOT, 1998), 13, 26, 33; Barbara McCann, "Driven to Spend: The Impact of Sprawl on Household Transportation Expenses," Surface Transportation Policy Project/Center for Neighborhood Expenses, *Progress,* vol. 11, no. 1 (2001), 3; and U.S. Department of Transportation (DOT), Federal Highway Administration, *Highway Statistics 1999* (Washington, D.C.: DOT, 2000), table MV-1.

23. Dunphy et al., *Moving Beyond Gridlock,* 65.

24. U.S. Census Bureau, *Journey to Work and Place of Work—1990 Census.*

25. Ibid. See also Pisarski, *Commuting in America II,* 49, 84.

26. Pisarski, *Commuting in America II,* 74.

27. U.S. Department of Transportation (DOT), *1995 Nationwide Personal Transportation Survey* (Washington, D.C.: DOT, 1995), 11.

28. Falbel, *Suburban Public Transportation,* ii.

Chapter 14: Regionalism

1. Robert Yaro, "Growing and Governing Smart: A Case Study of the New York Region," in Bruce Katz, ed., *Reflections on Regionalism* (Washington, D.C.: Brookings Institution Press, 2000), 48.

2. Kenneth T. Jackson, *Crabgrass Frontier: The Suburbanization of the United States* (New York: Oxford University Press, 1985), 139–40.

3. Ibid., 139. See also David Rusk, *Cities Without Suburbs* (Washington, D.C.: Woodrow Wilson Center, 1995).

4. Jackson, *Crabgrass Frontier,* 139.

5. Rusk, *Cities Without Suburbs,* 12–14.

6. Ibid., 27–42.

7. Ibid., 15.

8. At the beginning of a three-day charrette on sprawl held in the Boston area, 240 participants were asked to split into ten self-selected teams to come up with ideas for changing ten categories of "regional systems," including housing, transportation, infrastructure, education, governance, fiscal structure, economic development, and other regionally shared elements. At the end of the first half-day, each team presented its recommendations on sheets of newsprint. The sheets were then pinned up along a wall of the central working space for the duration of the charrette, and all participants were asked to rank the one recommendation they thought was most important by placing a green dot next to the selected item. On the last day of the charrette, the single recommendation with the greatest number of green dots was "coordinate transportation and land use." As the moderator commented: "an idea that's been around for at least fifty years."

9. David Firestone, "Choking on Growth: A Special Report—In Atlanta, Suburban Comforts Thwart Plans to Limit Sprawl," *New York Times,* November 21, 1999. See also the Georgia Regional Transportation Authority Web site: www.grta.org.

10. Myron Orfield, *Metropolitics: A Regional Agenda for Community and Stability* (Washington, D.C.: Brookings Institution, 1997), 84–85.

11. Ibid., 85.

12. Peter Grant, "The Sprawl Debate Has Only Just

Begun," *Wall Street Journal,* November 8, 2000. This information was confirmed in an interview held on November 17, 2000, with Robert Stacey, director of planning for Portland from 1989 to 1993 and executive director of policy and planning for Tri-Met from 1993 to 2000. He is currently on the staff of Congressman Earl Blumenauer of Oregon.

13. Interview with Robert Stacey.

14. Ibid.

15. Richard Moe and Carter Wilkie, *Changing Places: Rebuilding Community in the Age of Sprawl* (New York: Henry Holt, 1997), 219; and interview with Robert Stacey.

16. Additional information on Portland's UGB based on interview with Robert Stacey.

17. Interview with Robert Stacey; and Robert T. Dunphy et al., *Moving Beyond Gridlock: Traffic and Development* (Washington, D.C.: Urban Land Institute, 1997), 48. See also Metro Web site: www.multnomah.lib.or.us/metro.

18. William H. Lucy and David L. Phillips, *Confronting Suburban Decline: Strategic Planning for Metropolitan Renewal* (Washington, D.C.: Island Press, 2000), 250.

19. Ibid., 251.

20. Dunphy et al., *Moving Beyond Gridlock,* 48.

21. Lucy and Phillips, *Confronting Suburban Decline,* 251; and Dunphy et al., *Moving Beyond Gridlock,* 48–49.

22. Lucy and Phillips, *Confronting Suburban Decline,* 250.

23. Ibid., 251.

24. National Association of Realtors (NAR), *Metropolitan Area Prices, First Quarter 2001,* NAR Web site, www.onerealtorplace.com/Research.nsf/Pages/MetroPrice?OpenDocument. See also National Association of Realtors (NAR), *Existing Single-Family Home Sales,* NAR Web site, www.onerealtorplace.com/Research.nsf/Pages/EHSdata?OpenDocument.

25. National Association of Realtors, Metropolitan Area Prices, First Quarter 2001. See also National Association of Realtors, Existing Single-Family Home Sales.

26. Lucy and Phillips, *Confronting Suburban Decline,* 251.

27. Moe and Wilkie, *Changing Places,* 227.

28. Ibid., 226.

29. National Association of Realtors, *Metropolitan Area Prices, First Quarter 2001.* The *Boston Globe* estimated that home prices were increasing at a 24 percent rate at midyear. See Paul E. Kandarian, "Housing Prices Up, Listings Down," *Boston Globe,* August 27, 2000.

30. National Association of Realtors, *Metropolitan Area Prices, First Quarter 2001.*

31. Ibid.

32. Lucy and Phillips, *Confronting Suburban Decline,* 251.

33. Ibid., 252.

34. Moe and Wilkie, *Changing Places,* 223; and interview with Robert Stacey.

35. Dunphy et al., *Moving Beyond Gridlock,* 49; and interview with Robert Stacey.

36. Moe and Wilkie, *Changing Places,* 231; and interview with Robert Stacey.

37. Data from Moe and Wilkie, *Changing Places,* 227; Dunphy et al., *Moving Beyond Gridlock,* 42; and interview with Robert Stacey.

38. Alan E. Pisarski, *Commuting in America II: The Second National Report on Commuting Patterns and Trends* (Lansdowne, Va.: Eno Transportation Foundation, 1996), 64. Additional information from interview with Robert Stacey.

39. Dunphy et al, *Moving Beyond Gridlock,* 49.

40. Jim Robbins, "Oregon: Two Sides of the Anti-sprawl Line," *New York Times,* April 22, 2001.

41. Orfield, *Metropolitics,* 175–76.

42. Ibid., 13, 99–103, 175–76, 189–90; and Lucy and Phillips, *Confronting Suburban Decline,* 247.

43. Lucy and Phillips, *Confronting Suburban Decline,* 247.

44. Orfield, *Metropolitics,* 87; and Lucy and Phillips, *Confronting Suburban Decline,* 247.

45. Orfield, *Metropolitics,* 87.

46. Lucy and Phillips, *Confronting Suburban Decline,* 248.

47. Orfield, *Metropolitics,* 189–96. See also Lucy and Phillips, *Confronting Suburban Decline,* 248.

48. Orfield, *Metropolitics,* 105–7, 113–22. See also Lucy and Phillips, *Confronting Suburban Decline,* 248–49.

49. U.S. Census Bureau, *State and Metropolitan Area Data Book* (Washington, D.C.: U.S. Census Bureau, 1998), 2; U.S. Census Bureau, *Census 2000 PHC-T-2, Ranking Tables for States: 1990 and 2000, Table 1, States Ranked by Population,* http://blue.census.gov/population/cen2000/phc-t2/tab01.pdf; and U.S. Census Bureau, *Census 2000 PHC-T-3, Ranking Tables for Metropolitan Areas, Table 2, Metropolitan Areas in Alphabetic Sort, 1990 and 2000 Population,* http://blue.census.gov/population/cen2000/phc-t3/tab02.pdf.

50. Maryland Office of Planning, *Smart Growth in Maryland,* www.op.state.md.us/smartgrowth/smartwhat.htm.

51. Maryland Office of Planning, *Smart Growth: Designating Priority Funding Areas* (Baltimore: Maryland Office of Planning, 1997), 9, www.mdp.state.md.us/INFO/download/pfa.pdf.

52. Maryland Office of Planning, *Priority Funding Areas, Summary of Criteria for County PFA Designations,* www.op.state.md.us/smartgrowth/pfachart.htm.

53. Maryland Office of Planning, *Priority Funding*

Areas, www.op.state.md.us/smartgrowth/smartpfa. htm.

54. Maryland Office of Planning, *Smart Growth 2001,* www.op.state.md.us/smartgrowth/smart2001.htm.

55. Maryland Office of Planning, *2001 Maryland General Assembly: Summary of Planning Legislation,* www.op.state.md.us/info/leg2001_home.htm.

56. Jackson, *Crabgrass Frontier,* 234–35.

57. All data from U.S. Census Bureau, *State and Metropolitan Area Data Book* (Washington, D.C.: U.S. Census Bureau, 1998), 2; U.S. Census Bureau, *Census 2000 PHC-T-2, Ranking Tables for States: 1990 and 2000, Table 1, States Ranked by Population;* and U.S. Census Bureau, *Census 2000 PHC-T-3, Ranking Tables for Metropolitan Areas, Table 2, Metropolitan Areas in Alphabetic Sort, 1990 and 2000 Population.*

58. Georgia Regional Transportation Authority (GRTA), *What Is GRTA?—Background,* www.grta. org/grta/background.html.

59. Ibid.

60. David Firestone, "Suburban Comforts Thwart Atlanta's Plans to Limit Sprawl," *New York Times,* November 21, 1999. See also Dunphy et al., *Moving Beyond Gridlock,* 6–7.

61. Firestone, "Suburban Comforts Thwart Atlanta's Plans to Limit Sprawl."

62. U.S. Census Bureau, *Travel to Work Characteristics for the 50 Largest Metropolitan Areas by Population in the United States: 1990 Census,* www.census.gov/ population/socdemo/journey/msa50.txt. See also Pisarski, *Commuting in America II,* 64.

63. Georgia Regional Transportation Authority (GRTA), *What Is GRTA?—Background.*

64. Ibid.

65. Christine Kreyling, "Hug That Transit Station," *Planning,* vol. 67, no. 1 (January 2001), 6–7.

66. Yaro, "Growing and Governing Smart," 53–60.

67. See the RPA's Web site: www.rpa.org.

68. Yaro, "Growing and Governing Smart," 56.

69. Ibid., 58. See also the RPA's Web site, "Centers," www.rpa.org/centers/index.html.

70. Yaro, "Growing and Governing Smart," 55.

Chapter 15: Thinking about the Future

1. For example, see Lincoln Institute of Land Policy, *The New Spatial Order? Technology and Urban Development: 2001 Annual Roundtable* (Cambridge, Mass.: LILP, 2001), 4 and following.

2. Reuters, "Trading Floor's Final Day at Pacific Stock Exchange," *New York Times,* May 26, 2001.

3. Mark Landler, "Hi I'm in Bangalore (But I Can't Say So)," *New York Times,* March 21, 2001.

4. Andrew Gillespie in Lincoln Institute of Land Policy, *The New Spatial Order?,* 8.

5. Robert Atkinson in Lincoln Institute of Land Policy, *The New Spatial Order?,* 4.

6. Ibid., 38.

7. Ibid., 4.

8. U.S. Census Bureau: *Working at Home: 1990— Table 1. All Workers and Workers and Workers Who Worked at Home,* www.census.gov/population/ www/socdemo/workathome/wkhtab1.html.

9. Kimberly Blanton, "Good Job, Great View: Putnam Makes Inroads in Growing Telecommuting Movement with Recruitment of Workers in Maine and Vermont," *Boston Globe,* October 16, 2000.

10. Jonathan Glazer, "Telecommuting's Big Experiment," *New York Times,* May 9, 2001.

11. Blanton, "Good Job, Great View."

12. International Telework Association and Council (ITAC), Telework America 2000, ITAC Web site: www.telecommute.org.

13. U.S. Commerce Department, "Retail E-Commerce Sales in First Quarter 2001," *U.S. Commerce Department News,* May 16, 2001, www.census. gov/mrts/www/current.html.

14. Thomas Horan and Mitchell Moss in Lincoln Institute of Land Policy, *The New Spatial Order?,* 18–20.

15. Thomas Horan in Lincoln Institute of Land Policy, *The New Spatial Order?,* 20.

16. Ibid., 24.

17. Joel Kotkin, *The New Geography: How the Digital Revolution Is Reshaping the American Landscape* (New York: Random House, 2000), 61.

18. Thomas A. Horan, *Digital Places: Building Our City of Bits* (Washington, D.C.: Urban Land Institute, 2000), 53.

19. Ibid., 61–62.

20. Robert Atkinson, Thomas Horan, and Mitchell Moss in Lincoln Institute of Land Policy, *The New Spatial Order?,* 4, 9, 11.

21. U.S. Census Bureau, *HH-1, Households by Type: 1940 to Present,* www.census.gov/population/ socdemo/"hh-fam/.

22. U.S. Census Bureau, *HH-4, Households by Size: 1960 to Present,* www.census.gov/population/ socdemo/hh-fam/.

23. Robert Putnam, *Bowling Alone: The Collapse and Revival of American Community* (New York: Simon & Schuster, 2000), 283–84, 357.

24. Horan, *Digital Places,* 63.

25. Randal O'Toole, *The Vanishing Automobile and Other Urban Myths: How Smart Growth Will Harm American Cities* (Brandon, Oreg.: Thoreau Institute, 2001), 25.

26. E. M. Forster, *The Machine Stops and Other Stories: Reprinting of Stories Published in 1911 and 1928,* ed. Rod Mengham (London: Andre Deutsch, 1997), 87.

27. Kotkin, *The New Geography,* 64.

28. Ibid., 7.

29. Caesar McDowell in Lincoln Institute of Land Policy, *The New Spatial Order?*, 35.

30. Elizabeth Burns in Lincoln Institute of Land Policy, *The New Spatial Order?*, 34.

31. National Association of Home Builders (NAHB), *The Next Decade for Housing* (Washington, D.C.: NAHB, 2001), 2, 3, 9. www.nahb.com/facts/nextdecadeforecast.pdf.

32. U.S. Census Bureau, *Census 2000 Housing Units*, http://quickfacts.census.gov/hunits.

33. National Association of Home Builders, *The Next Decade for Housing*, 3.

34. National Association of Home Builders, *The Next Decade for Housing*, 13.

35. Simon Romero, "São Paulo Journal; Rich Brazilians Rise Above Rush-Hour Jams," *New York Times*, February 15, 2000.

36. National Association of Home Builders, *The Next Decade for Housing*, 3, 13.

37. Patrick Simmons and Robert Lang, "The Urban Turnaround: A Decade by Decade Report Card on Postwar Population Change in Older Industrial Cities," *Fannie Mae Foundation Census Note 01* (Washington, D.C.: Fannie Mae Foundation, 2001); and various articles, including Robert Sharoff, "Office Buildings Become Lofts in St. Louis," *New York Times*, June 24, 2001. See also following note.

38. See Morris Newman, "Apartments for Downtown Los Angeles," New York Times, June 4, 2000; Kathryn Hayes Tucker, "Saying Goodbye to the 'Burbs," *New York Times*, March 5, 2000; and John Eckberg, "More People Calling Cincinnati's Downtown Home," *New York Times*, July 30, 2000.

39. Francis Clines, "Blacks Rise as Power in Washington Suburb," *New York Times*, July 1, 2001.

40. Ibid.

Chapter 16: Conclusion

1. According to the National Association of Realtors Web site, November 9, 2000, http://nar.realtor.com/home.htm.

2. Katharine Seelye and Andrew Revkin, "Panel Tells Bush Global Warming Is Getting Worse," *New York Times*, June 7, 2001.

3. Surface Transportation Policy Project, *Changing Direction: Federal Transportation Spending in the 1990's* (Washington, D.C.: Surface Transportation Policy Project, 2001), 13, www.transact.org/Reports/Cd/tea21color.pdf.

4. Eric Schmitt, "Cities and Their Suburbs Are Seen Growing as Units," *New York Times*, July 10, 2001.

Bibliography

Books

Arendt, Randall, with Elizabeth A. Brabec, Harry L. Dodson, Christine Reid, and Robert D. Yaro. *Rural by Design: Maintaining Small Town Character.* Chicago: American Planning Association, 1994.

Avin, Uri. P. *A Review of the Cost of Providing Government Services to Alternative Residential Patterns.* Columbia, Md.: LDR International, 1993.

Bacon, Edmund N. *Design of Cities.* Rev. ed. New York: Penguin Books, 1974.

Barnett, Jonathan. *The Fractured Metropolis.* New York: Harper Collins, 1995.

Barrett, Paul J. *The Automobile in Urban Transport.* Philadelphia: Temple University Press, 1983.

Beatley, Timothy, and Kristy Manning. *The Ecology of Place: Planning for Environment, Economy and Community.* Washington, D.C.: Island Press, 1997.

Bel Geddes, Norman. *Magic Motorways.* New York: Random House, 1940.

Benfield, F. Kaid, Matthew D. Raimi, and Donald D. T. Chen. *Once There Were Greenfields: How Urban Sprawl Is Undermining America's Environment, Economy, and Social Fabric.* Washington, D.C.: Natural Resources Defense Council, 1999.

Bernick, Michael, and Robert Cervero. *Transit Villages for the 21st Century.* New York: McGraw-Hill, 1997.

Boesiger, Willy, ed. *Le Corbusier.* New York: Praeger, 1972.

Bollier, David. *How Smart Growth Can Stop Sprawl.* Washington, D.C.: Sprawl Watch Clearinghouse, Essential Books, 1998.

Bullard, Robert, Glenn S. Johnson, and Angel Torres. *Sprawl City: Race, Politics, and Planning in Atlanta.* Washington, D.C.: Island Press, 2000.

Calthorpe, Peter. *The Next American Metropolis: Ecology, Community and the American Dream.* New York: Princeton Architectural Press, 1993.

Calthorpe, Peter, and William Fulton. *The Regional City.* Washington, D.C.: Island Press, 2001.

Caro, Robert A. *The Power Broker: Robert Moses and the Fall of New York.* New York: Knopf, 1974.

Copi, Irving M. *Introduction to Logic.* New York: Macmillan, 1968.

Creese, Walter L. *The Legacy of Raymond Unwin.* Cambridge, Mass.: MIT Press, 1967.

Dear, Michael J. *The Postmodern Urban Condition.* Malden, Mass.: Blackwell Publishers, 2000.

De Chiara, Joseph, and Lee E. Koppelman. *Site Planning Standards.* New York: McGraw-Hill, 1978.

De Long, David G., ed. *Frank Lloyd Wright and the Living City.* Milan: Skira Editore S.p.A., 1998.

De Tocqueville, Alexis. *Democracy in America.* Vols. I and 2. Trans. Henry Reeve. New York: Bantam Books, 2000.

Diehl, Lorraine B. *The Late, Great Pennsylvania Station.* New York: Four Walls Eight Windows, 1985.

Douglas, George H. *All Aboard: The Railroad in American Life.* New York: Paragon House, 1992.

Downing, Andrew Jackson. *Cottage Residences.* Reprint. New York: Dover, 1981.

Downs, Anthony. *Stuck in Traffic.* Washington, D.C.: Brookings Institution and Lincoln Institute of Land Policy, 1992.

———. *New Visions for Metropolitan America.* Washington, D.C.: Brookings Institution, and Lincoln Institute of Land Policy, 1994.

Duany, Andres, Elizabeth Plater-Zyberk, and Jeff Speck. *Suburban Nation: The Rise of Sprawl and the Decline of the American Dream.* New York: North Point Press, 2000.

Drexler, Arthur. *The Drawings of Frank Lloyd Wright.* New York: Horizon Press, 1962.

Dunphy, Robert T. *Moving Beyond Gridlock: Traffic and Development.* Washington, D.C.: Urban Land Institute, 1997.

Eno Transportation Foundation. *Transportation in America.* 13th ed. Lansdowne, Va.: Eno Transportation Foundation, 1995.

Fischel, William A. *The Economics of Zoning Laws and a Property Rights Approach to American Land Use Controls.* Baltimore: Johns Hopkins University Press, 1985.

Fishman, Robert. *Bourgeois Utopias: The Rise and Fall of Suburbia.* New York: Basic Books, 1987.

Flink, James J. *The Automobile Age.* Rev. ed. Cambridge, Mass.: MIT Press, 1999.

Forster, E. M. *The Machine Stops and Other Stories: Reprinting of Stories Published in 1911 and 1928.* Ed. Rod Mengham. London: Andre Deutsch, 1997.

Froner, Eric, and John A. Garraty, eds. *The Reader's Companion to American History.* Boston: Houghton, Mifflin, 1991.

Gans, Herbert. *The Levittowners: Life and Politics in a New Suburban Community.* New York: Pantheon Books, 1967.

Garreau, Joel. *Edge City: Life on the New Frontier.* New York: Doubleday, 1991.

Geddes, Patrick. *Cities in Evolution.* London: Williams & Norgate, 1915.

Geisler, Charles, and Gail Daneker. *Property and Values: Alternatives to Public and Private Ownership.* Washington, D.C.: Island Press, 2000.

Goddard, Stephen B. *Getting There: The Epic Struggle Between Road and Rail in the Twentieth Century.* New York: Basic Books, 1994.

Gordon, Peter, and Harry W. Richardson. *The Case for Suburban Development.* Los Angeles: Lusk Center Research Institute, 1996.

Gottman, Jean. *Megalopolis: The Urbanized Northeastern Seaboard of the United States.* New York: The Twentieth Century Fund, 1961.

Handlin, David P. *American Architecture.* New York: Thames & Hudson, 1985.

Harrison, Helen A. *Dawn of a New Day: The New York World's Fair, 1939/40.* New York: New York University Press, 1980.

Hayden, Dolores. *Redesigning the American Dream.* New York: Norton, 1984.

Hegemann, Werner, and Elbert Peets. *The American Vitruvius.* Ed. Alan J. Plattus. Reprint. Princeton, N.J.: Princeton Architectural Press, 1988.

Hitchcock, Henry-Russell, and Phillip Johnson. *The International Style.* New York: Norton, 1932.

Hoke, John Ray, Jr., ed. *Ramsey/Sleeper: Architectural Graphic Standards.* 9th ed. Somerset, N.J.: Wiley, 1994.

Horan, Thomas A. *Digital Places: Building Our City of Bits.* Washington, D.C.: Urban Land Institute, 2000.

Howard, Ebenezer, Sr. *Garden Cities of Tomorrow.* London: Faber & Faber, Ltd., 1946.

Huxtable, Ada Louise. *Will They Ever Finish Bruckner Boulevard?* New York: Collier Books, 1972.

Jackson, Kenneth T. *Crabgrass Frontier: The Suburbanization of the United States.* New York: Oxford University Press, 1985.

Jacobs, Jane. *The Death and Life of Great American Cities.* New York: Vintage Books, 1961.

Jordan, Robert Furneaux. *Le Corbusier.* New York: Lawrence Hill, 1972.

Katz, Bruce, ed. *Reflections on Regionalism.* Washington, D.C.: Brookings Institution Press, 2000.

Katz, Peter. *The New Urbanism.* New York: McGraw-Hill, 1994.

Kay, Jane Holtz. *Asphalt Nation: How the Automobile Took Over America and How We Can Take It Back.* New York: Crown, 1997.

————. *Lost Boston.* Boston: Houghton Mifflin, 1999.

Kostof, Spiro. *America by Design.* New York: Oxford University Press, 1987.

Kotkin, Joel. *The New Geography: How the Digital Revolution Is Reshaping the American Landscape.* New York: Random House, 2000.

Krueckeberg, Donald A., ed. *Introduction to Planning History in the United States.* New Brunswick, N.J.: Center for Urban Policy Research, Rutgers University, 1983.

Kunstler, James Howard. *The Geography of Nowhere: The Rise and Decline of America's Manmade Landscape.* New York: Simon & Schuster, 1993.

————. *Home from Nowhere: Remaking Our Everyday World for the 21st Century.* New York: Simon & Schuster, 1996.

Le Corbusier, Frederic Etchells, introduction. *The City of Tomorrow and Its Planning.* New York: Payson & Clarke, 1929.

Le Corbusier and Pierre Jeanneret. *Oeuvre Complète 1910–1929* (Publiée par W. Boesiger et O. Stonorov). Zurich, Switzerland: Les Éditions d'Architecture (Artemis), 1964. Onzième édition, 1984.

————. *Oeuvre Complète 1929–1934* (Publiée par W. Boesiger). Zurich, Switzerland: Éditions H. Girsberger, 1935.

Lucy, William H., and David L. Phillips. *Confronting Suburban Decline: Strategic Planning for Metropolitan Renewal.* Washington, D.C.: Island Press, 2000.

Lynch, Kevin. *The Image of the City.* Cambridge, Mass.: MIT Press, 1988.

MacKenzie, James J., Roger C. Dower, and Donald Chen. *The Going Rate: What It Really Costs to Drive.* Washington, D.C.: World Resources Institute, 1992.

Marx, Leo. *The Machine in the Garden: Technology and the Pastoral Ideal in America.* New York: Oxford University Press, 1964.

Mason, Philip P. *A History of American Roads.* Chicago: Rand McNally, 1967.

McShane, Clay. *Down the Asphalt Path: The Automobile and the American City.* New York: Columbia University Press, 1994.

Moe, Richard, and Carter Wilkie. *Changing Places: Rebuilding Community in the Age of Sprawl.* New York: Henry Holt, 1997.

Moore, Terry, and Paul Thorsnes. *The Transportation/Land Use Connection: A Framework for Practical Policy.* Chicago: American Planning Association, 1994.

Mumford, Lewis. *The City in History: Its Origins, Its Transformations, Its Prospects.* New York: Harcourt, Brace and World, Inc., 1961.

————. *The Highway and the City.* New York: Mentor Books, New American Library, 1963.

Newman, Peter, and Jeffrey Kenworthy. *Cities and Automobile Dependence.* Aldershot Hants, U.K.: Avebury Technical, 1991.

————. *Sustainability and Cities: Overcoming Automobile Dependence.* Washington, D.C.: Island Press, 1999.

Orfield, Myron. *Metropolitics: A Regional Agenda for Community and Stability.* Washington, D.C.: Brookings Institution, 1997.

O'Toole, Randal. *The Vanishing Automobile and Other Urban Myths: How Smart Growth Will Harm American Cities.* Brandon, Or.: Thoreau Institute, 2001.

Papdaki, Stamo, ed. *Le Corbusier, Architect, Painter, Writer.* New York: Macmillan, 1948.

Peck, Sheila. *Planning for Biodiversity: Issues and Examples.* Washington, D.C.: Island Press, 1998.

Pevsner, Nikolaus. *An Outline of European Architecture.* Harmondsworth, U.K.: Pelican Books, 1966.

Pisarski, Alan E. *Commuting in America II: The Second National Report on Commuting Patterns and Trends.* Lansdowne, Va.: Eno Transportation Foundation, 1996.

Porter, Douglas. *Managing Growth in America's Communities.* Washington, D.C.: Island Press, 1997.

Pushkarev, Boris S., and Jeffrey M. Zupan. *Public Transportation and Land Use Policy.* Bloomington: Indiana University Press, 1977.

Putnam, Robert D. *Bowling Alone: The Collapse and Revival of American Community.* New York: Simon & Schuster, 2000.

Rusk, David. *Cities Without Suburbs.* Washington, D.C.: Woodrow Wilson Center, 1995.

Rybczynski, Witold. *City Life.* New York: Simon & Schuster, 1995.

Safdie, Moshe, with Wendy Kohn. *The City After the Automobile: An Architect's Vision.* New York: Harper-Collins, 1997.

Schaeffer, K. H., and Elliott Sclar. *Access for All: Transportation and Urban Growth.* New York: Penguin Books, 1975.

Schaffer, Daniel, ed. *Two Centuries of American Planning.* Baltimore: Johns Hopkins University Press, 1988.

Scott, Mel. *American City Planning Since 1890.* Berkeley: University of California Press, 1969.

Scully, Vincent. *American Architecture and Urbanism.* New York: Henry Holt, 1988.

Serenyi, Peter, ed. *Le Corbusier in Perspective.* Englewood Cliffs, N.J.: Prentice-Hall, 1975.

Shaw, Jane S., and Ronald D. Utt, eds. *A Guide to Smart Growth: Shattering Myths, Providing Solutions.* Washington, D.C.: Heritage Foundation, 2000.

Small, Kenneth A. *Urban Sprawl: A Non-Diagnosis of Real Problems.* Cambridge, Mass.: Lincoln Institute of Land Policy, 2000.

Stern, Robert A. M. *Pride of Place.* Boston: Houghton Mifflin, 1986.

Stein, Clarence S. *Toward New Towns for America.* Liverpool: University Press of Liverpool, 1951.

Stilgoe, John. *Metropolitan Corridor: Railroads and the American Scene.* New Haven, Conn.: Yale University Press, 1983.

————. *Borderland: Origins of the American Suburb.* New Haven, Conn.: Yale University Press, 1988.

Vance, James E., Jr. *Capturing the Horizon: The Historical Geography of Transportation Since the Sixteenth Century.* 2nd ed. Baltimore: Johns Hopkins University Press, 1990.

Venturi, Robert, Denise Scott-Brown, and Stephen Izenour. *Learning from Las Vegas.* Cambridge, Mass.: MIT Press, 1977.

Warner, Sam Bass. *Streetcar Suburbs: The Process of Growth in Boston 1870–1900.* Cambridge, Mass.: Harvard University Press and MIT Press, 1962.

Warner, Sam Bass. *The Urban Wilderness: A History of the American City.* New York: Harper & Row, 1972.

Whyte, William H., Jr. *The Organization Man.* New York: Doubleday, 1956.

Whyte, William H., Jr., ed. *The Exploding Metropolis.* Berkeley: University of California Press, 1993.

Wright, Frank Lloyd. *The Living City.* New York: Horizon, 1958.

————. *Modern Architecture Being the Kahn Lectures for 1930.* Princeton, N.J.: Princeton University Press, 1931.

Yaro, Robert D., and Tony Hiss, *A Region at Risk: The Third Regional Plan for the New York–New Jersey–Connecticut Metropolitan Area.* Washington, D.C.: Island Press, 1996.

Articles

Adams, Charles F., et. al. "Flight from Blight and Metropolitan Suburbanization Revisited." *Urban Affairs Review,* vol. 31, no. 4, 1996.

Barry, Dan, and Al Baker, "Getting the Message from 'Eco-Terrorists.'" *New York Times,* January 8, 2001.

Belluck, Pam. "Chicago Reverses 50 Years of Declining Population." *New York Times,* March 15, 2001.

Black, J. Thomas. "The Economics of Sprawl." *Urban Land,* vol. 53, no. 3, 1996.

Blanton, Kimberly. "Good Job, Great View: Putnam Makes Inroads in Growing Telecommuting Movement with Recruitment of Workers in Maine and Vermont." *Boston Globe,* October 16, 2000.

Brooke, James. "Denver Stands Out in Trend Toward Living in Downtown." *New York Times,* December 29, 1998.

Bushnell, Davis. "Tri-Town Pushes Tech Center Off Runway." *Boston Globe,* February 25, 2001.

Cada, Chryss. "For Colorado Gridlock, Rocky Roads Ahead." *Boston Globe,* May 6, 2001.

Campbell, Colin J., and Jean H. Laherrere. "The End of Cheap Oil." *Scientific American,* March 1998.

Chen, David. "Outer Suburbs Outpace City in Population Growth." *New York Times,* March 16, 2001.

"Cities and Suburbs: A Harvard Magazine Roundtable." *Harvard Magazine,* vol. 102, no. 3, January-February 2000.

Clines, Francis. "Blacks Rise as Power in Washington Suburb." *New York Times,* July 1, 2001.

Constantine, James. "Design by Democracy." *Land Development,* vol. 5, no. 1, 1992.

Conte, Christopher. "The Boys of Sprawl." *Governing,* May 2000.

Downs, Anthony. "The Big Picture: How America's Cities are Growing." *Brookings Review,* vol. 16, no. 4, fall 1998.

————. "What Does Smart Growth Really Mean?" *Planning,* vol. 67, no. 4, April 2001.

Easterbrook, Gregg. "Suburban Myth: The Case for Sprawl." *New Republic,* March 15, 1999.

Ebbert, Stephanie. "For Second Time in Two Decades, A City on the Rise." *Boston Globe,* March 22, 2001.

Eckberg, John. "More People Calling Cincinnati's Downtown Home." *New York Times,* July 30, 2000.

Ellis, Virginia. "California Toll Road Projects Lose Momentum." *Los Angeles Times,* February 8, 2000.

El Nasser, Haya. " A Comprehensive Look at Sprawl in America." *USA Today,* February 22, 2001.

Ewing, Reid. "Characteristics, Causes and Effects of Sprawl." *Environmental and Urban Issues,* vol. 21, no. 2, 1994.

———. "Beyond Density, Mode Choice and Single Purpose Trips." *Transportation Quarterly,* vol. 49, no. 4, 1995.

———. "Is Los Angeles–Style Sprawl Desirable?" *Journal of the American Planning Association,* vol. 63, no.1, 1997.

Ewing, Reid, Mary Beth DeAnna, and Shi-Chiang Li. "Land Use Impacts on Trip Generation Rates." *Transportation Research Record,* no. 1518, 1996.

Fernandez, Bob. "Home, Population Data Show Flight to Suburbia." *Philadelphia Inquirer,* June 15, 2000.

Firestone, David. "Choking on Growth: A Special Report—In Atlanta, Suburban Comforts Thwart Plans to Limit Sprawl." *New York Times,* November 21, 1999.

———. "Booming Atlanta Saps Water As Drought Wilts Georgia." *New York Times,* June 15, 2000.

———. "The New-Look Suburbs: Denser or More Far-Flung." *New York Times,* April 17, 2001.

Flint, Anthony. "Build-Minded Owner Snubs Land-Buy Bid." *Boston Globe,* June 30, 2001.

Glater, Jonathan. "Telecommuting's Big Experiment." *New York Times,* May 9, 2001.

Goldberg, Carey. "Massachusetts City Plans To Destroy Public Housing." *New York Times,* April 2, 2001.

Goldberger, Paul. "L.I. Over 25 Years: Realizing a Dream; Crossing the Island, A Slice of America." *New York Times,* May 5, 1996.

Gordon, Peter, and Harry W. Richardson. "Beyond Polycentricity—The Dispersed Metropolis." *Journal of the American Planning Association,* vol. 62, no. 3, 1996.

———. "Are Compact Cities a Desirable Planning Goal?" *Journal of the American Planning Association,* vol. 63, no. 1, 1997.

Grant, Peter. "The Sprawl Debate Has Only Just Begun." *Wall Street Journal,* November 8, 2000.

Grether, David M., and Peter Mieszkowski. "The Effects of Nonresidential Land Uses on the Prices of Adjacent Housing." *Journal of Urban Economics,* vol. 8, no. 1, 1980.

Gross, Jane. "Poor Without Cars Find Trek to Work Is Now a Job." *New York Times,* November 18, 1997.

Halbfinger, David M. "New Buyers Renew Levittown, Now 50." *New York Times,* September 28, 1997.

———. "Schundler Wins G.O.P. Primary in New Jersey Governor's Race." *New York Times,* June 27, 2001.

Harvey, Robert O., and W.A.V. Clark. "The Nature and Economics of Urban Sprawl." *Land Economics,* vol. 41, no. 1, 1965.

Heikkila, Eric J., and Richard B. Peiser. "Urban Sprawl, Density and Accessibility." *Papers in Regional Science,* vol. 71, no. 2, 1992.

Higgins, Richard. "H$_2$0 Aplenty, But . . ." *Boston Sunday Globe,* May 14, 2000.

Hill, Edward W., Harold L. Wolman, and Coit C. Ford. "Can Suburbs Survive Without Their Cities?" *Urban Affairs Review,* vol. 31, no. 2, 1995.

Holmes, Steven. "Immigration Is Fueling Cities' Strong Growth, Data Show." *New York Times,* January 1, 1998.

Howe, Peter J. "EPA Takes on Sprawl in Region." *Boston Globe,* February 2, 1999.

Janofsky, Michael. "Phoenix Counts Its Many Challenges." *New York Times,* April 11, 2001.

Kahn, Joseph. "Cheney Promotes Increasing Supply as Energy Policy." *New York Times,* May 1, 2001.

Kandarian, Paul E. "Housing Prices Up, Listings Down." *Boston Globe,* August 27, 2000.

Katz, Bruce, and Scott Bernstein, "The New Metropolitan Agenda: Connecting Cities and Suburbs." *Brookings Review,* vol. 16, no. 4, fall 1998.

Katz, Bruce, and Jennifer Bradley. "Divided We Sprawl." *Atlantic Monthly,* vol. 284, no. 6, December 1999.

Kilgannon, Corey. "Road Warriors with Laptops." *New York Times,* August 15, 2000.

Kotkin, Joel. "A Revival of Older Suburbs As Ethnic Businesses Take Hold." *New York Times,* February 27, 2000.

Kranish, Michael. "Cheney Faces Decision on Wyoming Drilling." *Boston Globe,* May 6, 2001.

Kreyling, Christine. "Hug That Transit Station." *Planning,* vol. 67, no. 1, January 2001.

Lacayo, Richard, with Wendy Cole, Dan Cray, Daniel Levy, Todd Murphy, and Timothy Roche. "The Brawl Over Sprawl." *Time,* March 22, 1999.

Lambert, Bruce. "40 Percent in New York City Are Foreign Born, Study Finds." *New York Times,* July 24, 2000.

Landler, Mark. "Hi I'm in Bangalore (But I Can't Say So)." *New York Times,* March 21, 2001.

Longman, Phillip J. "Who Pays for Sprawl: Hidden Subsidies Fuel the Growth of the Suburban Fringe." *U.S. New and World Report,* April 27, 1998.

Lopez, Rigoberto A., Adesoji O. Adelaja, and Margaret S. Andrews. "The Effects of Suburbanization on Agriculture." *American Journal of Agricultural Economics,* vol. 70, no. 2, 1988.

McCann, Barbara. "Driven to Spend: The Impact of Sprawl on Household Transportation Expenses." Surface Transportation Policy Project/Center for Neighborhood Expenses. *Progress* vol. 11, no. 1, 2001.

McCann, Barbara, Roy Kienitz, and Bianca DeLille/

Surface Transportation Policy Project. *Changing Direction: Federal Transportation Spending in the 1990's.* Washington, D.C.: Surface Transportation Policy Project, 2000.

McKinley, James, Jr. "New York Votes to Ban Phones held by Drivers." *New York Times,* June 26, 2001.

Mitchell, John G. "Urban Sprawl." *National Geographic,* vol. 200, no. 1, July 2000.

Moss, Mitchell, L. "Telecommunications, World Cities and Urban Policy." *Urban Studies,* vol. 24, no. 6, 1987.

Muschamp, Herbert. "Becoming Unstuck on the Suburbs." *New York Times,* October 19, 1997.

———. "Critic's Notebook: Fireworks or Fallbacks for a New River City." *New York Times,* March 5, 2001.

Nelson, Arthur C. "Preserving Prime Farmland in the Face of Urbanization." *Journal of the American Planning Association,* vol. 58, no. 4, 1992.

Nieves, Evelyn. "Many in Silicon Valley Cannot Afford Housing, Even at $50,000 a Year." *New York Times,* February 20, 2000.

Newman, Morris. "Apartments for Downtown Los Angeles." *New York Times,* June 4, 2000.

Noss, Reed F., Edward T. LaRoe III, and J. Michael Scott. "Endangered Ecosystems of the United States: A Preliminary Assessment of Loss and Degradation." Article available at the USGS Web site: http://biology.usgs.gov/pubs/ecosys.htm

Oppel, Richard A., Jr. "Efforts to Restrict Sprawl Find New Resistance from Advocates for Affordable Housing." *New York Times,* December 26, 2000.

Ottensmann, John R. "Urban Sprawl, Land Values and the Density of Development." *Land Economics,* vol. 53, no. 4, 1977.

Pivo, Gary. "The Net of Mixed Beads—Suburban Office Development in Six Metropolitan Regions." *Journal of the American Planning Association,* vol. 56, no. 4, 1990.

Pollan, Michael. "Town Building Is No Mickey Mouse Operation." *New York Times Magazine,* December 14, 1997.

———. "The Triumph of Burbopolis." *New York Times Magazine,* April 9, 2000.

Pollock, Peter. "Controlling Sprawl in Boulder: Benefits and Pitfalls." *Land Lines,* Lincoln Institute of Land Policy, January 1998.

Powell, John A. "Race and Space: What Really Drives Metropolitan Growth." *Brookings Review,* vol. 16, no. 4, fall 1998.

Purdum, Todd S. "Suburban Sprawl Takes Its Place on the Political Landscape." *New York Times,* February 6, 1999.

———. "Shift in the Mix Alters the Face of California." *New York Times,* July 4, 2000.

Rather, John. "First Mass Housing Suburb." *New York Times,* November 15, 1998.

Retsinas, Nicholas. "Before We Take On Sprawl, Let's Understand What We're Fighting." *Boston Globe,* January 29, 2000.

Reuters, "Trading Floor's Final Day at Pacific Stock Exchange." *New York Times,* May 26, 2001.

Revkin, Andrew C. "Tiny Bits of Soot Tied to Illnesses." *New York Times,* April 21, 2001.

Robbins, Jim. "Oregon: Two Sides of the Antisprawl Line." *New York Times,* April 22, 2001.

Rodriguez, Cindy. "City, State Take on New Cast." *Boston Globe,* March 22, 2001.

Romero, Simon. "São Paulo Journal; Rich Brazilians Rise Above Rush-Hour Jams." *New York Times,* February 15, 2000.

Ruckelshaus, William D. *Scientific American,* September 1989.

Russell, James S. "Privatized Lives." *Harvard Design Magazine,* vol. 12, no. 3, 2000.

Sachs, Susan. "New York City Tops 8 Million for First Time." *New York Times,* March 16, 2000.

Schmitt, Eric. "Analysis of the Census Finds Segregation Along with Diversity." *New York Times,* April 4, 2001.

———. "Whites in Minority in Largest Cities, the Census Shows." *New York Times,* April 30, 2001.

———. "Most Cities in U.S. Expanded Rapidly over Last Decade." *New York Times,* May 7, 2001.

———. "Cities and Their Suburbs Are Seen Growing as Units." *New York Times,* July 10, 2001.

Scott, Janny. "Hispanics and Asians Fuel New Jersey's Population Growth, Countryside Yields to Suburban Sprawl." *New York Times,* March 9, 2001.

Seelye, Katherine, and Andrew Revkin. "Panel Tells Bush Global Warming Is Getting Worse." *New York Times,* June 7, 2001.

Sharoff, Robert. "Office Buildings Become Lofts in St. Louis." *New York Times,* June 24, 2001.

Stern, Robert A. M., and John Montague Massengale. "The Anglo-American Suburb." *Architectural Design,* vol. 51, no. 10, November 1981.

Tucker, Kathryn Hayes. "Saying Goodbye to the 'Burbs." *New York Times,* March 5, 2000.

Uchitelle, Louis. "Rebuilt City Starts to Feel the Effects of the Slowdown." *New York Times,* April 9, 2001.

Whoriskey, Peter. "Is it Smart Growth or a Dumb Idea? Plan to Increase Population Density in Some Fairfax Areas Fuels a Debate." *Washington Post,* January 14, 2001.

Wright, Frank Lloyd. "The New Frontier: Broadacre City." *Taliesin,* vol. 1, no. 1, 1940.

Yardley, Jim. "For Texas Now, Water, Not Oil, Is Liquid Gold." *New York Times,* April 16, 2001.

Government Publications (Federal, State, and Local)

Beimborn, Edward, and Harvey Rabinowitz. *Guidelines for Transit Sensitive Suburban Land Use Design.* Washington D.C.: U.S. Department of Transportation, 1991.

Burchell, Robert, William Dolphin, and Catherine Galley. *The Costs and Benefits of Alternative Growth Patterns: The Impact Assessment of the New Jersey State Plan*. Trenton: New Jersey Office of State Planning, 2000.

Centers for Disease Control and Prevention (CDC)/Lawrence Frank, Peter Engleke, Thomas Schmid, and Richard Killingsworth. *How Land Use and Transportation Systems Affect Public Health: A Literature Review of the Relationship Between Physical Activity and Built Form*. Atlanta: CDC, 2001.

City of New York, Department of Finance. *Annual Report on the New York City Property Tax: Fiscal Year 2000*. New York: City of New York, 2000.

Commonwealth of Massachusetts, Executive Office of Transportation and Construction. *Massachusetts Transportation Facts, 1998*. Boston: Commonwealth of Massachusetts, 1998.

Dahl, Thomas E. *Status and Trends of Wetlands in the Coterminous United States 1986 to 1997*. Washington, D.C.: U.S. Fish and Wildlife Service, 2000.

Dalaker, Joseph. *Current Population Reports, Series P60-207, Poverty in the United States: 1998*. Washington, D.C.: U.S. Census Bureau, 1999.

Duhart, Detis P., et al. *Urban, Suburban and Rural Victimization, 1993–98*. Washington, D.C.: U.S. Department of Justice, Bureau of Justice Statistics, 2000.

Gibson, Campbell. *Population of the 100 Largest Cities and Other Urban Places in the United States: 1790 to 1990*. Washington, D.C.: U.S. Census Bureau, 1998.

Gibson, Campbell, and Emily Lennon. *Historical Census Statistics on the Foreign Born Population of the United States, 1850–1990*. Washington, D.C.: U.S. Census Bureau, 1999.

Gillham, Oliver, with Paul J. McGinley and Nina Primm. *South Norwalk Revitalization Program*. Norwalk, Conn.: Norwalk Redevelopment Agency, 1980.

Lamison-White, Leatha. *U.S Census Bureau Statistical Brief, Poverty Areas*. Washington, D.C.: U.S. Census Bureau, 2000.

Lippmann, Laura, et al. *Urban Schools: The Challenge of Location and Poverty*. Washington, D.C.: National Center for Education Statistics, 1995.

Liu, Limingk, et al. *Boston's Population—2000*. Boston: Boston Redevelopment Authority, 2001.

New York Metropolitan Transportation Council et al. *Travel in the New York–New Jersey Metropolitan Area: A Summary of Results from the 1997/98 Regional Travel-Household Interview Survey*. New York: New York Metropolitan Transportation Council, 2000.

Project for Public Spaces Inc. *TCRP Report 22: The Role of Transit in Creating Livable Metropolitan Communities*. Washington, D.C.: Transit Cooperative Research Program, Federal Transit Administration, Transportation Research Board, 1997.

Real Estate Research Corporation. *The Costs of Sprawl, Detailed Cost Analysis*. Washington, D.C.: U.S. Government Printing Office, 1974.

Skidmore, Owings and Merrill. *Planning for Transit-Friendly Land Use: A Handbook for New Jersey Communties*. Newark: New Jersey Transit, 1994.

U.S. Census Bureau. *1996 Cooperative Population Estimates*. Washington, D.C. : U.S. Census Bureau, 1996.

———. *1997 Economic Census*. Washington, D.C.: U.S. Census Bureau, 2000.

———. *Population Change and Distribution: Census 2000 Brief*. Washington, D.C.: U.S. Census Bureau, 2001.

U.S. Department of Agriculture, Natural Resources Conservation Service. *A Geography of Hope*. Washington, D.C.: U.S. Department of Agriculture, 1997.

U.S. Department of Commerce. *U.S. Industry and Trade Outlook 2000*. Washington, D.C.: U.S. Department of Commerce, 2000.

U.S. Department of Energy (DOE), Energy Information Administration. *Annual Energy Outlook 2000*. Washington, D.C.: DOE, 1999.

U.S. Department of Energy (DOE), Energy Information Administration. *Buildings and Energy in the 1980's*. Washington, D.C.: DOE.

U.S. Department of Housing and Urban Development (HUD), Office of Policy Development and Research. *Issue Brief No. III—Homeownership: Progress and Work Remaining*. Washington, D.C.: HUD, 2000.

U.S. Department of Transportation (DOT). *Urban Transportation Planning in the United States: An Historical Overview*. Washington, D.C.: DOT, 1992.

U.S. Department of Transportation (DOT), Bureau of Transportation Statistics. *1995 Nationwide Personal Transportation Survey*. Washington, D.C.: DOT, 1995.

———. *Transportation Statistics Annual Report 1995*. Washington, DC: DOT, 1995

———. *Transportation Statistics Annual Report 1996*. Washington, DC: DOT, 1996

———. *Transportation Statistics Annual Report 1997*. Washington, DC: DOT, 1997.

———. *Transportation Statistics Annual Report 1998*. Washington, DC: DOT, 1998

———. *Transportation Statistics Annual Report 1999*. Washington, D.C.: DOT, 1999.

———. *National Transportation Statistics 2000*. Washington, DC: DOT, 2001

U.S. Department of Transportation (DOT), Federal Highway Administration. *Highway Statistics to 1995, Funding for all Highways, All Units of Government, 1921–1995*. Washington, D.C.: DOT, 1995.

———. *Highway Statistics Summary to 1995*. Washington, D.C.: DOT, 1996.

———. *Highway Trust Fund Primer*. Washington, D.C.: DOT, 1998.

———. *Highway Statistics 1999.* Washington, D.C.: DOT, 2000.

U.S. Department of Transportation (DOT), Federal Transit Administration. *National Transit Summaries and Trends, 1998.* Washington, D.C.: DOT, 1998.

U.S. Environmental Protection Agency (EPA), Office of Transportation and Air Quality. *Air Toxics from Motor Vehicles.* Fact Sheet OMS-2, EPA-400-F-92-004. Washington, D.C.: EPA, August 1994.

U.S. Environmental Protection Agency (EPA), Office of Wastewater Management/Tetra Tech, Inc. with Andrew Stoddard and Associates. *Progress in Water Quality: An Evaluation of the National Investment in Municipal Wastewater Treatment.* Washington, D.C.: EPA, 2000.

———. *National Water Quality Inventory: 1998 Report to Congress.* Washington, D.C.: EPA, 1998.

U.S. Environmental Protection Agency (EPA). *The Quality of Our Nation's Water: 1994.* Washington, D.C.: EPA, 1994.

———. *The Quality of Our Nation's Water: 1996.* Washington, D.C.: EPA, 1996.

———. *Water Pollution Control: 25 Years of Progress and Challenges for the New Millennium.* Washington, D.C.: EPA, 1998.

———. *Latest Findings on National Air Quality: 1999 Status and Trends.* Washington, D.C.: EPA, 2000.

Wickersham, Jay. *The State of Our Environment.* Boston, Mass.: Commonwealth of Massachusetts, Executive Office of Environmental Affairs, 2000.

Wilbur Smith and Associates. *Patterns of Car Ownership, Trip Generation and Trip Sharing in Urbanized Areas.* Washington, D.C.: U.S. Department of Transportation, 1968.

Other Reports and Papers (Various Sources)

American Farmland Trust (AFT). *Fact Sheet: Cost of Community Services Studies.* Washington, D.C.: AFT, 2000.

Brookings Institution. *Racial Change in the Nation's Largest Cities: Evidence from the 2000 Census.* Washington, D.C.: Brookings Institution, 2001.

Brown, Larissa, David Dixon, and Oliver Gillham. *How We Live: A Civic Initiative for a Livable New England, Regional Charrette Briefing Book.* Boston: Boston Society of Architects, 2001.

Burrington, Stephen H. *Road Kill: How Solo Driving Runs Down the Economy.* Boston: Conservation Law Foundation, 1994.

Chen, Donald. *Greetings from Smart Growth America.* Washington, D.C.: Smart Growth America, 2000.

Council of American Building Officials (CABO). *One and Two Family Dwelling Code.* Falls Church, Va.: CABO, 1989.

Daniels, Tom. *Planning, Zoning and Land Preservation for Growth Management: A Comparison of Neighboring Communities.* Paper presented at the Association of Collegiate Schools of Planning Conference, Chicago, Illinois, 1999.

Davis, Judy, ed. "Consequences of the Development of the Interstate Highway System for Transit." *Research Results Digest* (Transit Cooperative Research Program of the National Transportation Research Board), no. 21, August 1997.

Falbel, Stephen. *Suburban Public Transportation.* Boston: Boston Metropolitan Planning Organization, 1998.

Falbel, Stephen, Central Transportation Planning Staff. *The Demographics of Commuting in Greater Boston.* Boston: Boston Metropolitan Planning Organization, 1998.

Gillham, Oliver, Allegra Calder, and Nancy Goodman. *Our Sprawling Region: A Point of View.* Boston: Boston Society of Architects, 2000.

Glaeser, Edward, and Jesse Shapiro. "City Growth and the 2000 Census: Which Places Grew and Why." *The Brookings Institution Survey Series: Census 2000.* Washington, D.C.: Brookings Institution, 2001.

Greene, Kenneth. *Defending Automobility: A Critical Examination of the Environmental and Social Costs of Auto Use.* Reason Public Policy Institute Policy (RPPI) Study No. 198. Los Angeles: RPPI, 1995.

Lewis Mumford Center for Comparative Urban and Regional Research at the State University of New York (SUNY) at Albany. *Ethnic Diversity Grows, Neighborhood Integration Is at a Standstill.* Albany: SUNY, 2001.

Lincoln Institute of Land Policy (LILP). *Metropolitan Development Patterns 2000 Annual Roundtable.* Cambridge, Mass.: LILP, 2000.

Lincoln Institute of Land Policy (LILP). *The New Spatial Order? Technology and Urban Development: 2001 Annual Roundtable.* Cambridge, Mass.: LILP, 2001.

Linneman, Peter D., and Anita A. Summers. *Patterns and Processes of Employment and Population Decentralization in the U.S.* Working Paper #106. Philadelphia: University of Pennsylvania, Wharton Real Estate Center, 1991.

National Association of Home Builders (NAHB). *Smart Growth: Building Better Places to Live, Work and Play.* Washington, D.C.: NAHB, 1999.

———. *NAHB's Smart Growth Report.* Washington, D.C.: NAHB, 2000.

———. *The Next Decade for Housing.* Washington, D.C.: NAHB, 2001.

National Association of Industrial and Office Properties (NAIOP) with Anthony Downs. *Growing to Greatness: A Growth Management Manual.* Herndon, Va.: NAIOP, 1999.

O'Neill, David. *Smart Growth, Myth and Fact.* Washington, D.C.: Urban Land Institute, 1999.

Office of Technology Assessment. *The Technological Reshaping of Metropolitan America.* Washington, D.C.: Congress of the United States, 1995.

Sierra Club. *Smart Choices or Sprawling Growth: A Fifty State Survey of Development.* Washington, D.C.: Sierra Club, 2000.

Simmons, Patrick A., and Robert E. Lang. *Fannie Mae Census Note 01, The Urban Turnaround: A Decade by Decade Report Card on Postwar Population Change in Older Industrial Cities.* Washington, D.C.: Fannie Mae Foundation, 2001.

Smart Growth America. *Smart Growth America: Making Smart Growth Happen.* Washington, D.C.: Smart Growth America, 2000.

Sohmer, Rebecca, and Robert Lang. *Downtown Rebound.* Washington, D.C.: Fannie Mae Foundation and Brookings Institution, 2001.

Sorenson, Ann A., Richard P. Greene, and Karen Russ. *Farming on the Edge.* DeKalb, Ill.: American Farmland Trust, 1997.

Staley, Samuel R. *The Sprawling of America: In Defense of the Dynamic City.* Policy Study No. 251. Los Angeles: Reason Public Policy Institute, 1999.

Staley, Samuel R., et al. *Urban-Growth Boundaries, Smart Growth and Housing Affordability.* Los Angeles: Reason Public Policy Institute, 1999.

Texas Transportation Institute (TTI). *2001 Urban Mobility Report.* College Station: TTI, 2001.

Texas Transportation Institute (TTI)/David Schrank and Tim Lomax. *1999 Urban Mobility Study: Information for Urban America.* College Station: TTI, 1999.

Urban Land Institute. *ULI on the Future: Smart Growth.* Washington, D.C.: Urban Land Institute, 1998.

Web Sites

Adelaide Metro, Programs and Guides—The Adelaide O-Bahn: www.adelaidemetro.com.au/guides/obahn.html

American War Library. *Vietnam War Casualties by Branch of Service:* http://members.aol.com/WarLibrary/vwc0.htm

Association of American Railroads. *Railroads: A Historical Perspective:* www.aar.org/.

Boston Metropolitan Area Planning Council: www.mapc.org

Brookings Institution: www.brook.edu/

Center for Watershed Protection. *The Impacts of Urbanization:* www.cwp.org/

Center for Watershed Protection. *Better Site Design, Eight Tools for Watershed Protection and Impacts of Urbanization:* www.cwp.org/

Central Artery/Tunnel: www.bigdig.com/

City of Cambridge Zoning Ordinance, Section 15.000, Cambridgeport Revitalization Development District: www.ci.cambridge.ma.us/~CDD/commplan/zoning/zord/zo_article15_cprdd.pdf

Commonwealth of Massachusetts, General Laws Chapters 61 and 61A: www.state.ma.us/legis/laws/mgl/index.htm

Congress for the New Urbanism. *About the Congress for the New Urbanism:* www.cnu.org/aboutcnu/index.cfm

Dover, Kohl and Partners: www.doverkohl.com

Electronic Toll Collection and Traffic Management: www.ettm.com/

Fannie Mae Foundation: www.fanniemaefoundation.org

Federal Highway Administration: www.fhwa.dot.gov/

Georgia Regional Transportation Authority: www.grta.org

International Telework Association and Council, Telework America 2000,: www.telecommute.org

Lancaster County, Pennsylvania: www.co.lancaster.pa.us/

Land Trust Alliance: www.lta.org/

Lewis Mumford Center for Comparative Urban and Regional Research at the State University of New York at Albany: www.albany.edu/mumford/census/

Long Island Pine Barrens Society: www.pinebarrens.org/index.html

Maryland Office of Planning. *2001 Maryland General Assembly: Summary of Planning Legislation:* www.op.state.md.us/info/leg2001_home.htm

Maryland Office of Planning. *Priority Funding Areas:* www.op.state.md.us/smartgrowth/smartpfa.htm

Maryland Office of Planning. *Priority Funding Areas, Summary of Criteria for County PFA Designations:* www.op.state.md.us/smartgrowth/pfachart.htm

Maryland Office of Planning. *Smart Growth 2001:* www.op.state.md.us/smartgrowth/smart2001.htm

Maryland Office of Planning. *Smart Growth: Designating Priority Funding Areas:* www.mdp.state.md.us/INFO/download/pfa.pdf

Maryland Office of Planning. *Smart Growth in Maryland:* www.op.state.md.us/smartgrowth/smartwhat.htm

Mystic View Task Force: www.the-ville.com/mysticview/

National Association of Home Builders (NAHB): www.nahb.com/

National Association of Industrial and Office Properties (NAIOP): www.naiop.org/

National Association of Realtors: www.onerealtorplace.com/

National Association of Realtors. *Existing Single-Family Home Sales:* www.onerealtorplace.com/Research.nsf/Pages/EHSdata?OpenDocument

National Association of Realtors. *Metropolitan Area Prices, First Quarter 2001:* www.onerealtorplace.com/Research.nsf/Pages/MetroPrice?OpenDocument.

National Association of Realtors. *Voter Survey on Open Space:* http://nar.realtor.com/gov/home.htm

National Center for Education Statistics (NCES): http://nces.ed.gov/

National Governors Association. *A Policy Summit on Working Lands Conservation,* March 16, 2001: www.lta.org/newsroom/nga_march_2001.htm

National Trust for Historic Preservation: www.nation-altrust.org/

National Trust for Historic Preservation, National Main Street Center: http://mainstreet.org/

National Trust for Historic Preservation, Rural Heritage Program: www.ruralheritage.org/

National Wilderness Institute. *State by State Government Land Ownership:* www.nwi.org/

National Wildlife Federation: www.nwf.org/smart-growth/wildlife.html

Natural Resources Defense Council: www.nrdc.org/

Natural Resources Defense Council. *Paving Paradise: Sprawl and the Environment:* www.nrdc.org/cities/smartgrowth/rpave.asp

Nature Conservancy Archives. Ed Goldstein and Evan Johnson. *Nature by the Numbers: 50 Little Known Facts:* http://nature.org/aboutus/resources/#Top

Orenco Station: www.orencostation.com/home.htm

Portland Metro: www.multnomah.lib.or.us/metro

Reason Public Policy Institute: www.rppi.org/

Regional Plan Association (RPA): www.rpa.org/

San Diego Association of Governments (SANDAG), San Diego Trolley, Inc. *Fact Sheet, Mid-Coast Light Rail Transit Extension and Mission Valley East-San Diego Trolley Project:* www.sandag.org

Sierra Club: www.sierraclub.org/sprawl

Smart Growth America: www.smartgrowthamerica.com/

Smart Growth America/Belden, Russonello and Stewart. *National Survey on Growth and Land Development,* September 2000: www.smartgrowthamerica.com/poll.pdf.

Smart Growth Network: www.smartgrowth.org/

South Coast Air Quality Management District: www.aqmd.gov/

State University of New York at Albany. www.albany.edu/

Surface Transportation Policy Project: www.transact.org/

Surface Transportation Policy Project. *Changing Direction: Federal Transportation Spending in the 1990's,* Washington, D.C.: Surface Transportation Policy Project, 2001: www.transact.org/Reports/Cd/tea21color.pdf

———. *Five Years of Progress: 110 Communities Where ISTEA Is Making a Difference:* www.transact.org/Reports/5yrs/INDEX.HTM.

Telecom City: www.telcomcity.com/

Texas Transportation Institute (TTI): http://tti.tamu.edu/

———. *2001 Urban Mobility Study,* "How Much More Road Construction Would Be Needed?" and "How Should We Address the Mobility Problem?" at TTI's 2001 Mobility Study Web site:http://tti.tamu.edu/research/operations/mobility.stm and

http://mobility.tamu.edu/research/operations/mobility.stm

Transportation Cooperative Research Program: http://nationalacademies.org/trb/

Transportation Cooperative Research Program (TCRP)/Kittelson and Associates, Inc, Texas Transportation Institute, Transport Consulting Ltd. *Transit Capacity and Quality of Service Manual* TCRP Web Document no. 6, 1999: http://nationalacademies.org/trb/publications/tcrp/tcrp_webdoc_6-a.pdf

Transportation Research Board (TRB): http://nationalacademies.org/trb/

Truckline Information Center: www.truckline.com/infocenter/

Trust for Public Land. *LandVote 2000:* www.tpl.org/tier3_cdl.cfm?content_item_id=847&folder_id=586

U.S. Census Bureau: www.census.gov/

U.S. Census Bureau. *About Metropolitan Areas:* www.census.gov/population/www/estimates/about-metro.html

U.S. Census Bureau. *Black Population in the United States: March, 1999 (Update): Detailed Tables and Documentation for P20-530 (PPL-130):*www.census.gov/population/www/socdemo/race/black99tabs.html

———. *Census 2000 Housing Units:* http://quickfacts.census.gov/hunits/

———. *Census 2000 PHC-T-1, Population by Race and Hispanic or Latino Origin for the United States: 1990 and 2000:* www.census.gov/population/cen2000

———. *Census 2000 PHC-T-2, Ranking Tables for States: 1990 and 2000, Table 1, States Ranked by Population:* http://blue.census.gov/population/cen2000/phc-t2/tab01.pdf

———. *Census 2000 PHC-T-3, Ranking Tables for Metropolitan Areas, Table 2, Metropolitan Areas in Alphabetic Sort, 1990 and 2000 Population:*

———. *Census 2000 PHC-T-5, Ranking Tables for Incorporated Places of 100,000 or More: 1990 and 2000:* www.census.gov/population/cen2000/phc-t5/tab01.pdf; http://blue.census.gov/population/cen2000/phc-t3/tab02.pdf

———. *Density Using Land Area for States, Counties Metropolitan Areas and Counties:* www.census.gov/population/www/censusdata/density.html

———. *Estimates of the Population of Metropolitan Areas:* www.census.gov/population/estimates/metro-city/ma96-08.txt.

———. *Historical Census of Housing Tables: Homeownership:* www.census.gov/hhes/www/housing/census/historic/owner.html

———. *HH-4, Households by Size: 1960 to Present:* www.census.gov/population/socdemo/hh-fam/

———. *HH-1, Households by Type: 1940 to Present:* www.census.gov/population/socdemo/hh-fam/

———. *Housing Vacancy Survey: First Quarter 2001, Table 5, Home Ownership Rates for the United States: 1965 to 2001:* www.census.gov/hhes/www/housing/hvs/q101tab5.html

———. *Journey to Work and Place of Work—1990 Census:*www.census.gov/population/www/socdemo/journey.html

———. *March 1996 Current Population Survey: Income 1995-Table A: Comparison of Summary Measures of Income by Selected Characteristics: 1994 and 1995:* www.census.gov/hhes/income/income95/in95sum.html.

———. *National Population Projections, I. Summary Files:*www.census.gov/population/projections/nation/summary/np-t1.txt

———. *Population by Race and Hispanic or Latino Origin for the United States, Regions, Divisions, States, Puerto Rico and Places of 100,000 or More Population:* www.census.gov/population/cen2000/phc-t6/tab02.pdf

———. *Profiles of General Demographic Characteristics 2000:* www.census.gov/PressRelease/www/2001/2khus.pdf

———. *Selected Historical Census Data: Urban and Rural Definitions and Data:* www.census.gov/population/www/censusdata/ur-def.html

———. *Statistical Abstract of the United States, 2000:* www.census.gov/prod/2001pubs/statab/sec06.pdf.

———. *Table 22: Population of the 100 Largest Urban Places, 1990:* www.census.gov/population/documentation/twps0027/tab22.txt.

———. *Travel to Work Characteristics for the 50 Largest Metropolitan Areas by Population in the United States: 1990 Census:*www.census.gov/population/socdemo/journey/msa50.txt

———. *Urban and Rural Definitions:* www.census.gov/population/censusdata/urdef.txt

———. *Working at Home: 1990—Table 1. All Workers Who Worked at Home:* www.census.gov/population/www/socdemo/workathome/wkhtab1.html

U.S. Department of Agriculture, Natural Resources Conservation Service (NRCS). *Land Capability by Class, by State, 1992:* www.nhq.nrcs.usda.gov/cgi-bin/kmusser/mapgif.pl?mapid=2771

———. *Land Ownership, 1992:* www.nhq.nrcs.usda.gov/cgi-bin/kmusser/mapgif.pl?mapid=2788

———. *State Rankings by Acreage and Rate of Non-Federal Land Developed:* www.nhq.nrcs.usda.gov/CCS/devtable.html

———. *Summary Report, 1997 National Resources Inventory:* www.nhq.nrcs.usda.gov/NRI/1997/summary_report/original/table1.html

U.S. Department of Commerce. "Retail E-Commerce Sales in First Quarter 2001." *U.S. Commerce Department News,* May 16, 2001: www.census.gov/mrts/www/current.html

U.S. Department of Commerce News/Robert R. Callis and Linda B. Cavanaugh. *Housing Vacancies and Homeownership Second Quarter 2000:* www.census.gov/hhes/www/housing/hvs/

U.S. Department of Energy, Energy Information Administration. *Measuring Energy Efficiency in the United States' Economy: A Beginning:* www.eia.doe.gov/emeu/efficiency/ee_report_html.htm

U.S. Department of Transportation, Federal Transit Administration. *1994 National Transit Database—Transit Profiles—The Thirty Largest Agencies:* www.fta.dot.gov/library/reference/sec15/profiles94/top30/app/app.html

———. *Characteristics of Urban Transportation Systems—Revised Edition September, 1992,* chaps. 2 and 4: www.fta.dot.gov/library/reference/CUTS/

U.S. Department of Transportation, Federal Transportation Administration. *National Transit Summaries and Trends, 1998:* www.ntdprogram.com/NTD/NTST.nsf/NTST/1998/$File/98NTST.pdf

U.S. Environmental Protection Agency (EPA). Administrator Christine Whitman in an April 20, 2001, press release: www.epa.gov/swerosps/bf/html-doc/pr010420.htm

———. "Fact Sheet: Clinton Administration Expands Brownfields": www.epa.gov/swerosps/bf/html-doc/wh0513_3.htm

U.S. Environmental Protection Agency (EPA), History Office. *Taking to the Air:* www.epa.gov/history/publications/formative5.htm

U.S. Environmental Protection Agency (EPA), New England. "The State of the New England Environment": www.epa.gov/region01/ra/sprawl/speech_19990202.html

U.S. Environmental Protection Agency (EPA), Office of Solid Waste and Emergency Response. *From Slag to Riches:* www.epa.gov/swerosps/bf/html-doc/ss_pitts.htm

———. *Innovative Solutions and Private Investment Bring Prosperity to Oregon Mills:* www.epa.gov/swerosps/bf/html-doc/ss_orgml.htm

———). *Region 1 Brownfields Pilots: Brownfields Cleanup Revolving Loan Fund Pilots—EPA Region 1:* www.epa.gov/swerosps/bf/reg1rlf.htm

———. *Water Pollution Control: 25 Years of Progress and Challenges for the New Millennium:* www.epa.gov/owm/25prog.pdf

U.S. Environmental Protection Agency (EPA), Office of Water. *The Quality of Our Nation's Waters: A Summary of the National Water Quality Inventory: 1998 Report to Congress, 2000:* www.epa.gov/305b/98report/98brochure.pdf

U.S. Environmental Protection Agency (EPA), Office of Wetlands, Oceans and Watersheds (OWOW). *Nonpoint Source Pollution: The Nation's Largest Water*

Quality Problem, EPA841–F–96–004A: www.epa.gov/ OWOW/NPS/facts/point1.htm

U.S. Environmental Protection Agency (EPA), Region One. *Opening Remarks, Smart Growth Strategies for* *New England Conference,* February 2, 1999, John DeVillars: www.epa.gov/region01

Weingraf, Richard F. *The Federal Highway Administration at 100:* www.tfhrc.gov/pubrds/fall93/p93au1.htm.

Index

Above, sprawl viewed from, xiii
Accessibility, 7, 10–11
Accidents, traffic, 118–20
Acetaldehyde, 121
Acquisition and open-space preservation, land, 171–72
Aesthetics:
    community, suburbanization and the loss of, 148–51
    cultural landscape
        aging gracefully, 146–47
        city, the, 145
        historic districts, future, 147
        image and reality, 145–46
        metropolis, imageless, 146
        pastoral image, 144
        suburban beautiful, 147–48
        village, the, 144–45
    minority, inflammatory rhetoric of disenchanted, 71
    overview, 143–44
    pro-development groups, 79
    summary, chapter, 151
Affordable housing, xv, 27–28, 59, 75, 196
African Americans, 62, 77, 133–35, 137, 250
Agricultural damage and global warming, 114
Agricultural runoff, 115
Agricultural zoning, 168–69
Agriculture, United States Department of (USDA), 84–86, 88
Air, sprawl viewed from the, xiii
Air pollution:
    automobiles, 76, 113–16, 121
    Clean Air Act of 1970, 52
    counterarguments, 114–15
    emissions, sprawl and, 113–14
    future trends, 252–53
    manufacturing, origins of sprawl and desertion of, 40
    overview, 113
    population densities/growth, 77–78, 114
    summary, chapter, 121–22
    toxic pollutants, 121
Airports, 12, 164, 206
Air transportation, 12–13
Alabama, 187, 196
Albuquerque (NM), 173
American Cancer Society, 121
American Farmland Trust (AFT), 75, 78, 88–89, 123
American Graffiti, 5
American Trucking Association, 34
Anaheim (CA), 196
Annexation, expansion and, 211–12
Annual Mobility Report, 96
Anti-city label, 47
Aquifers, 161

Architectural Graphic Standards, 249
Architectural styles, 37, 41–42, 55–56, 143
Arctic National Wildlife Refuge, 107
Ardmore (PA), 38
"Are Compact Cities a Desirable Planning Goal?" (Gordon & Richardson), 128
Arendt, Randall, 168
Arizona, xv, 65, 181, 252
Arlington (MA), 28
Army Corps of Engineers, 166
Artists and revitalization movements, 57
Asian Americans, 61, 62, 137, 139
Atkinson, Robert, 240
Atlanta (GA):
    fastest-spreading human settlement in history, 83
    future trends, 249
    regionalism, 213, 228–31
    segregation, suburban diversity and, 137
    single-use zoning, 43
    transit, mass, 208
    water demand, 117
Atlantic Monthly, 19–20
Atomic bombs, 35
AT&T, 40
Audubon Society, 171–72
Australia, 70, 207–8
Automobiles:
    air pollution, 76, 113–16, 121
    Clean Air Act of 1970, 52
    dominance, pattern of, 11–13
    energy issues, 63–64, 110–11
    first modern suburbs, 29–30
    hybrid cars, 252
    inactivity and public health, 118
    land made cheap by, 70
    mobility, 70–71
    smart cars, 101
    social divides created by sprawl, cars/mortgages and, 133–36
    subsidies, hidden, 127–30
    technology, 110
    toxic air pollutants, 121
    transit, barrier to mass, 208–9
    see also Highways; roads and automobiles under Origins of sprawl; Traffic; Trucks/trucking

Baby boomers, 61
Baltimore (MD), 48, 49, 53
Banks, 17
Bauhaus, 41
Bay Area Rapid Transit system (BART), 202
Beacon Hill, 17
Beavers, 90
Bel Geddes, Norman, 33
Benzene, 121
Bernick, Michael, 184, 185

Bethesda (MD), 198
Bicycles, 12, 51
Birmingham (AL), 187, 196
Boomers, baby, 61
Boone, Daniel, 83
Boston Globe, xv, 61, 241
Boston (MA):
    Central Artery/Tunnel project, 48–49, 94, 96,
        207
    condominiums, 57, 59–60, 130, 250
    Consolidated Metropolitan Statistical Area, 18
    contextualism in architectural design, 56
    elastic cities, 146
    energy issues, population densities/growth and,
        109
    expansion and annexation, 211, 212
    future trends, 250, 253, 255
    gentrification, 196
    greyfield sites, 194–95
    high-occupancy vehicle lanes, 101
    highways, protesting the, 48–49
    historic preservation, 55
    housing, 219
    immigration, 62
    older cities, resurgent, 57–59, 61
    open space preservation, 164, 176
    population densities/growth, 41, 109, 198
    push factors, 196
    regionalism, 255
    renewal, urban, 44, 45
    reversible lanes, 97
    revitalizing older downtowns/inner-ring sub-
        urbs, 187, 188
    shock of the new, 44
    single-use zoning, 43
    streetcar suburbs, 29
    technology and cyberspace, 243
    transit, mass, 202, 204–7, 253
    water quality/pollution, 53
Boulder (CO):
    future trends, 247
    growth management, 64, 155, 156
    habitat preservation, 162
    open-space preservation, 164, 173–74, 176, 247
    transit, mass, 202
Bowes, David, xv
*Bowling Alone: The Collapse and Revival of American
    Community* (Putnam), 77, 150, 244
Brabec, Elizabeth, 163–64
Bradley, Jennifer, 19–20
Bridgeport (CT), 40, 196
Britain, 70, 180
British Airways, 239
British Columbia (Canada), 49, 184
Broadacre City, 30–31, 89
Brockton Area Transit Authority (BAT), 201–2
Bronx (NY), 28
Brookings Institution, 62, 75, 157
Brookline (MA), 27, 211
Brooklyn (NY), 28, 135, 198
Brownfield sites, 190–93, 226, 228, 250
Bruntland Commission, 80
Buffalo (NY), 196
Building codes, 15–17

Building industries, 65
Burchell, Robert, 123
Burns, Elizabeth, 246
Burton, Mike, 221
Buses, 202, 206, 207–8
    see also Transit, mass
Bush, George, 107
Butadiene, 121
Butterfly, Monarch, 162
Bypass roads, 97

California:
    congestion pricing, 99
    corporate Diaspora, 40
    employment expansion, 137
    farmland, 88–89
    future trends, 246
    gentrification, 196
    greyfield sites, 193–94
    growth management, 155
    habitat preservation, 162
    highway capacity, increasing, 97
    housing, 219, 246
    immigration, 61
    parkways, 32
    taxes, 76, 131
    technology and cyberspace, 243
    transit, mass, 202–4
    transit villages, 186
    water demand, 117
    see also Los Angeles (CA); San Francisco
        (CA)
Calthorpe, Peter, 124, 180, 181, 183–84
Calthorpe Associates, 124
Calvert County (MD), 169
Cambridge (MA), 117, 196, 198
Camden (NJ), 40, 196
Campbell, Colin, 107–8
Canada, 49, 70, 114, 184–86
Cancer, 121
Cape Cod (MA), 171, 172
Carbon dioxide emissions, 113–14
Carbon monoxide emissions, 114
Caro, Robert, 48
Cascade Policy Institute, xv
Cato Institute, xv
Celebration (FL), 180, 182
Census Bureau, U.S., 22, 79, 139, 244
Centers for Disease Control (CDC), 76, 118
Central Artery/Tunnel project, 48–49, 94, 96, 207
Central Park, 27
Cervero, Robert, 184, 185
Changing Places (Moe & Wilkie), 189
Charles River, 44, 45, 49, 53, 187
Charleston (SC), 57
Charter for the New Urbanism, The, 181
Chattanooga (TN), 193, 194
Chestnut Hill (MA), 27
Chevy Chase (D.C), 28
Chicago (IL):
    Consolidated Metropolitan Statistical Area, 18
    employment expansion, 137
    energy issues, population densities/growth and,
        109

expansion and annexation, 212
first modern suburbs, 30
immigration, 62
landscape, the vanishing, 83–84
metropolitan areas, 22
older cities, resurgent, 57
railroad suburbs, 27
segregation, 79
single-use zoning, 43
streetcar suburbs, 28
World Columbian Exposition (1893), 26
Chippewa Falls (WI), 189–90
Cincinnati (OH), 57–58, 188, 249
Cinema business, 15
Cities:
aesthetics, 145
Broadacre City, 30–31, 89
City Beautiful Movement, 26
Consolidated Metropolitan Statistical Area, 18,
187
elastic, 139–41, 146, 211–12
expansion and annexation, 211–12
future trends, 249–50
garden, 179–80
industrial revolution, 25–26
infrastructure costs, 126
manufacturing, origins of sprawl and desertion
of, 39
metropolitan regions more important than,
19–20
mixing of uses, 7
origins of sprawl and interstate highway system,
35
redlining, 37
see also core cities and suburbanization under
Origins of sprawl; older cities, resurgent
under Reactions and countertrends; revitalizing older downtowns/inner-ring suburbs
under Development patterns; Social divides
and sprawl
Cities Without Suburbs (Rusk), 139, 211
City in History, The (Mumford), 25
Civic engagement, 77, 150
Cleveland (OH), 28, 139, 184, 212
Clustering, 10, 12, 14, 167–68
Cold War, 35
Colonial revival architecture, 37
Colorado:
anti-sprawl initiative, defeat of, xv, 65
historic preservation, 55
older cities, resurgent, 57
revitalizing older downtowns/inner-ring sub-
urbs, 187
traffic, 103
see also Boulder (CO)
Colorado River, 117
Columbia (MD), 180
Columbia Regional Association of Governments
(CRAG), 217
Columbus (OH), 139, 149–50
Commerce Department, U.S., 242
Commercial strip development, 5, 131–32
Community, suburbanization and the loss of, 77, 79,
148–51, 243–45

Community needs, open space fulfilling, 162–63
Commuting, 11
Compact communities, 159, 249
see also compact/mixed-use developments under
Development patterns
Computers, 14
Concord (NH), 173
Condominiums, 57, 59–60, 130, 250
Congestion, traffic, 75–76, 99–100, 105, 208–9, 248
Congress for the New Urbanism (CNU), 181
Congressional Office of Technology Assessment,
240
Connecticut:
high-occupancy vehicle lanes, 101
manufacturing, origins of sprawl and desertion
of, 40
population densities/growth, 140, 196
revitalizing older downtowns/inner-ring sub-
urbs, 188–89
shock of the new, 44
transit, mass, 201
water quality/pollution, 53
Conservation Law Foundation, 128
Conservative policy institutions, xv, 75
see also Heritage Foundation; Reason Public Pol-
icy Institute
Consolidated Metropolitan Statistical Area (CMSA),
18, 187
Construction, innovations in wood, 27–28
Constructivists, 41
Contextualism in architectural design, 55–56
Cooperatives, 59–60
Corporate Diaspora, 40–41, 132
Costs, see Economic issues/costs
Cox, Wendell, 95
Crabgrass Frontier (Jackson), 9, 64, 134, 211
Crime, 59, 63
Cropland, 88
Cross-Bronx Expressway, 48
Cultural landscape, see under Aesthetics
Curituba, 208
Cuyahoga River, 53
Cyberspace, see technology and cyberspace under
Future trends
Cyclical issue, sprawl as a, 80

Dallas (TX), 60, 137, 249
Dayton (OH), 164
Death and Life of Great American Cities, The (Jacobs),
26, 47, 48
Debate, outlining sprawl:
anti-sprawl groups, 74
charges against sprawl, 75–77
clouded issues, xv–xvi
defense of sprawl, 69–71
future trends, 256–57
overview, 67
parties to the debate, 72–74
pro-development groups, 74–75, 77–79
untangling the sprawl brawl, 79–81
why is there any debate?, 71–75
see also Reactions and countertrends
Deconcentration, increasing choice and increasing,
245–46

Deer, 90
Deerfield (IL), 202
Defense, development of interstate highways system and national, 35
Dell Computer, 239
Densities, population, *see* Population densities/growth
Denver (CO), 55, 103, 187
Depression, The Great, 36, 232
Desertion, a persistent pattern of, 142
Detroit (MI):
    elastic cities, 146
    employment expansion, 137
    growing cities and expanding boundaries, 139
    manufacturing, origins of sprawl and desertion of, 40
    metropolitan area, 22
    population densities/growth, 62, 140, 212
Development patterns:
    compact/mixed-use developments
        Ebenezer Howard's garden cities, 179–80
        New Urbanism, 180–84
        regional and local implications, 186
        summary, chapter, 186
        traditional neighborhood developments, 181–82
        transit-oriented developments, 182–84
        transit villages, 184–86
    inefficient growth patterns, 130–31
    overview, 179
    population densities/growth, 196–99
    pro-development groups, xv, 69, 74–75, 77–79
        see also Heritage Foundation; Reason Public Policy Institute
    revitalizing older downtowns/inner-ring suburbs
        brownfield sites, 190–93
        city districts, 187–88
        downtown and Main Street, 187
        economic transition, the strains of, 195
        gentrification, 195–96
        greyfield sites, 193–95
        overview, 186–87
        push factors, 196–97
        small cities, 188–89
        village main streets, 189–90
    summary, chapter, 199
    tax revenues, chasing commercial, 131–32
    see also Growth management; Open-space preservation; Reactions and countertrends
Dickens, Charles, 26
Digital Places: Building Our City of Bits (Horan), 242
Digital Places (Mitchell), 13–14
Digital TV, 15
Distracted drivers, 103
District of Columbia (D.C.):
    expansion and annexation, 212
    immigration, 60
    older cities, resurgent, 58, 60
    population densities/growth, 197
    social divides created by sprawl, cars/mortgages and, 135
    streetcar suburbs, 28
    transit, mass, 202
    transit villages, 185

water quality/pollution, 53
Do-nothing approach, traffic and, 102–4
Double decking highways, 96
Downs, Anthony, 129–30, 157
Downtown, revitalizing, 187
    see also older cities, resurgent *under* Reactions and countertrends; revitalizing older downtowns/inner-ring suburbs *under* Development patterns
Downzoning, 166–67
Drinking water, 117–18, 162
Duany, Andres, 16–17, 147, 181, 182
Dunphy, Robert, 50

Earth Liberation Front, xv
Easterbrook, Gregg, 72
Eastern Seaboard, metropolitan areas linked together along the, 22
Economic issues/costs:
    aesthetics, 148
    congestion pricing, 99–100, 105
    development patterns, inefficient, 130–31
    growth management, 159
    highways, 35–36, 94, 96, 98, 105
    housing, 218–20
    income, median, 18
    infrastructure costs, 123–26
    land, 10
    on-line shopping, 242–43
    open space preservation, 163–64
    overview, 123
    postwar suburban expansion, financing the, 36–37
    poverty, 76–77, 132–33, 136, 138–39
    priority funding areas, 225
    pro-development groups, 79
    redlining the cities, 37
    regionalism, 225
    revitalizing older downtowns/inner-ring suburbs, 195
    subsidies, hidden, 126–30
    summary, chapter, 142
    traffic, 93
    transit, mass, 127, 130, 209
    transportation modes, 11
    vested interests and suburbanization, 251
    see also Taxes
"Economics of Preserving Open Space, The" (Brabec), 163
Economies of scale, 14
Eden, quest for a new, 27
Edgartown (MA), 197
Edge City: Life on the New Frontier (Garreau), 18, 64
Edge habitats, 91
Edina (MN), 38
Eisenhower, Dwight D., 35
Elastic cities, 139–41, 146, 211–12
Electricity, 14
Electric streetcars/subway trains and first modern suburbs, 28–29
Electronic telecommunications, 13–15
Elmwood Park (IL), 30
El Niño events, 252

Embarcadero Freeway, 48, 49
Employer programs and managing roadway demand, 99
Employment and revitalizing older downtowns/inner-ring suburbs, 195
Employment expansion, 137
Energy, U.S. Department of (DOE), 76, 106, 252
Energy issues:
　density/sprawl and energy consumption, 108–10
　efficiency of cars and transit, relative energy, 110–11
　gasoline, vehicles consuming billions of gallons of, 105
　misuse of resources, 252
　1970's, 63–64
　oil is left, how much, 107–8
　pro-development groups, 78
　summary, chapter, 111
　transportation energy consumption, increase in, 75
　vehicle technology, 110
Entertainment centers, home, 15
Environmental issues:
　anti-sprawl groups, 74
　Clean Air Act of 1970, 52
　Clean Water Act of 1972, 53
　Earth Liberation Front, xv
　Endangered Species Act of 1973, 53
　environmental impact statements, 49–50
　future trends, 254–55
　green space, common-use, 163
　industrial revolution, 26
　legislation, 54
　manufacturing, origins of sprawl and desertion of, 40
　oil/gas, looking for new sources of, 107
　open-space preservation, 161–62, 169–70
　transit and environmental impact statements, mass, 49–50
Environmental Protection Agency (EPA):
　air pollution, 114
　brownfield sites, 190–91
　Clean Water Act of 1970, 52
　defining sprawl, 4
　growth management, 157
　landscape, the vanishing, 83
　pro-development groups, 78
　toxic air pollutants, 121
　wetlands, 90
Envison (UT), 124
Ethnicity, see Race/ethnicity
Europeans arrival and the concept of individual land ownership, 9
Everglades, Florida, 162
Ewing, Reid, 4, 16
Expansion and annexation, 211–12

Fairfax County (VA), 198
Fairlawn (NJ), 29–30
Fannie Mae Foundation, 41, 62, 249
Farming on the Edge, 89
Farmland, 78, 88–89, 114–15, 168–69
Federal Highway Administration, 99
Federal Housing Administration (FHA), 36–37,

134–36
Finance, see Economic issues/costs
Fish and Wildlife Service, U.S. (FWS), 90
Floor area ratio (FAR), 5–7
Florida:
　aesthetics, 147
　future trends, 255
　growth management, 64, 156
　habitat preservation, 162
　immigration, 60
　infrastructure costs, 123
　New Urbanism, 180, 181
　older cities, resurgent, 60
　open space preservation, 161
　regionalism, 255
　traditional neighborhood developments, 182
　water resources protection, 162
Ford, Henry, 31
Forest Hills (NY), 27
Forestland, 89, 91, 161, 162
Formaldehyde, 121
Forster, E. M., 245
Fossil fuels, policy of increasing supply of, 107
　see also Energy issues
Fragmentation, habitat, 90–91
Framingham (MA), 38
France, 31, 70, 207
Franklin (TN), 189, 190
Freight shipping, 12
Fulton, William, 124, 180
Future trends:
　air pollution, 252–53
　change, prospects for, 239
　debate, outlining the sprawl, 256–57
　environmental issues, 254–55
　growth priorities, changing, 254–56
　guesses, educated
　　cities and infill development, 249–50
　　compact communities, 249
　　congestion, battling, 248
　　open space, 247–48
　　social divisions, 250
　　suburbanization, continuing, 246–47
　open space, 247–48, 254
　overview, 237
　regionalism, 255
　social divides and sprawl, 253–54
　summary, chapter, 250
　technology and cyberspace
　　deconcentration, increasing choice and increasing, 245–46
　　expansion, limitless, 239–42
　　isolation and community of place, 243–45
　　overview, 239
　　shopping, on-line, 242–43
　　telecommuting, 240–42
　transit, mass, 253
　water pollution, 253

G. H. Palmer Associates, 249
Gaithersburg (MD), 173
Gans, Herbert, 149, 150
Garden cities, 179–80
Garden Cities of Tomorrow (Howard), 179

Garden City (NY), 27
Garment industry, 39
Garreau, Joel, 18, 90, 247
Gary (IN), 196
Gasoline, vehicles consuming billions of gallons of, 76, 105
Gasoline taxes, 50, 98
Geddes, Patrick, 20
Geese, 90
General Electric, 239
General Foods, 40
General Motors (GM), 33–34
Genetic code of sprawl, 15–16
Gentrification, 195–96
Geography of Nowhere, The (Kunstler), 64, 71, 143, 144
Geological Survey, U.S., 107
Georges Bank, 107
Georgetown (D.C.), 197
Georgia Regional Transportation Authority (GRTA), 213, 229–30
    see also Atlanta (GA)
Germany, 41, 70, 207
Gillespie, Andrew, 239–40
Glendening, Parris, 76, 158
Goldberger, Paul, 147
Golf courses, 163
Gordon, Peter, 78, 124, 125, 128
Grand Teton National Park, 107
Great Lakes, 107
Greenhouse gases, 113–14, 252
GreenPrint Program, 226–28, 247
Green space, common-use, 163
Greyfield sites, 193–95, 250
Grosse Pointe (IL), 30
Growing to Greatness, 102, 103
Growth management:
    future trends, 254–56
    Maryland, 155–56, 173, 225
    Oregon, 64, 217–20
    published works, 64
    regionalism, 213–14, 225
    smart growth, xiv–xv, 155–60, 255
    see also Development patterns; Open space preservation; Reactions and countertrends
Guide to Smart Growth, A (Shaw), 89–90
Gulf of California, 117
Gulf of Mexico, 117
Gulf Oil, 40

Habitat for Humanity, xv, 75
Habitat preservation:
    edge habitats, 91
    fragmentation, habitat, 90–91
    Guide to Smart Growth, A, 89–90
    national priority, becoming a, 54
    open space preservation, 161–62
    pro-development groups, 77–78
    summary, chapter, 91
Harrington, Paul, 61
Hartford (CT), 101
Harvard Design Magazine (Russell), 13
Harvard University, xv, 121, 137
Hawaii, 162
Hayward, Steven, 77, 80, 85, 157

Health, sprawl development and public, 78, 118–22
Hempstead (NY), 38
Heritage Foundation, xv
    air pollution, 78, 114, 115
    costs, exaggerated, 79
    defining sprawl, 4
    free-market solutions, 74
    habitat, animal, 78
    landscape, the vanishing, 84, 85
    traffic, 93, 95
Highland Park Village (TX), 38
High-occupancy vehicle lanes (HOVs), 100–101, 249
Highways:
    aesthetics, 143
    cities, reaching into, 43
    clustering, reduction of, 12
    economic issues/costs, 35–36, 94, 96, 98, 105
    expanding, 94
    Federal-Aid Highway Act of 1966, 49
    Federal Highway Act of 1970, 50
    Federal Highway Act of 1973, 50
    Highway Trust Fund, 50
    induced demand, 64
    industry moving out of central cities, 39
    network of roads uniting suburbia, 12–13
    smart roads, 101–2
    subsidies, hidden, 127–30
    see also highways, protesting the under Reactions and countertrends; roads and automobiles under Origins of sprawl; Traffic
Hispanic Americans, 61, 62, 137, 139
Historic preservation, 54–56, 64, 74, 147, 188
Home Depot, 191, 193
Horan, Thomas, 242–44
Horizontal zoning, 16–17
Hoteling, 241
Housing:
    affordable, xv, 27–28, 59, 75, 196
    American Dream, 9
    anti-sprawl positions and housing advocates, 75–77
    architectural styles, 37, 41–42
    Boston (MA), 219
    building codes, 15–17
    California, 219, 246
    colonial revival architecture, 37
    Fair Housing Act of 1968, 136
    Federal Housing Administration, 36–37
    future trends, 246–47, 249, 250
    gentrification, 195–96
    innovations, construction, 27–28, 37
    landowners, a nation of, 70
    legislation, postwar, 42–43
    loft condominiums, rehabilitated, 57
    mass-produced, 37–38
    mortgages, home, 17, 59, 77, 130, 135–36
    National Housing Act of 1934, 36
    older cities, resurgent, 59–60
    Portland (OR), 218–20
    public, 136
    redlining the cities, 37
    San Francisco (CA), 220
    single-family detached housing, 18
    single-use development, 7
    social divides created by sprawl, cars/mortgages

and, 133–36
taxes and mortgages, 130
Housing and Urban Development, U.S. Department of (HUD), 190
Houston (TX):
    aesthetics, 145
    growth management, 173
    immigration, 60
    older cities, resurgent, 60
    population densities/growth, 212
    segregation, suburban diversity and, 137
    zoning, 17
Howard, Ebenezer, 172, 179–80
How Land Use and Transportation Systems Impact Public Health, 118
Hudson River, 53
Huxtable, Louise, 54
Hybrid cars, 252
Hyde Park (IL), 28

IBM, 40
IKEA, 191, 193
Illinois:
    aesthetics, 150
    first modern suburbs, 30
    New Urbanism, 181
    transit, mass, 202
    see also Chicago (IL)
Image/reality, aesthetics and, 145–46
Immigration, 60–63
Inactivity patterns and public health, 118
Income, median, 18
Indiana, 196
Induced demand, 64, 93
Industrial revolution, 25–26
Industry, origins of sprawl and desertion of, 39–40
Information economy, 39
Infrastructure costs, 123–27, 131
Injuries, traffic, 118–20
Insurance companies, 17
International Telework Association and Council, 242
Internet, the, 15
    see also technology and cyberspace under Future trends
Intolerability, traffic and level of, 103
Ipswich River, 117
Isle of Wright County (VA), 168
"Is Los Angeles Style Sprawl Desirable?" (Ewing), 125
Isolation, technology/cyberspace and, 243–45

Jackson, Kenneth T., 9, 28, 37, 64, 134, 135, 143, 211
Jacobs, Jane, 26, 41, 47, 48
James Duncan and Associates, 123
Japan, 70
Jeanneret, Charles-Edouard, 41
Job growth, 18–19
Jones Falls Expressway, 49

Kansas City, 30, 38, 83
Katz, Bruce, 19–20, 132
Kay, Jane H., 71, 129
Keene (NH), 173
Kentlands (MD), 147, 173, 181, 182
Kentucky, 217

Kenworthy, Jeffrey, 107, 108–9
Kotkin, Joel, 61, 243, 245–46
Kunstler, James H., xiv, 64, 71, 77, 143, 144, 148

Ladd, Helen, 124
Laherrere, Jean, 107
Lake Erie, 53
Lancaster County (PA), 164, 175
Land:
    acquisition and open-space preservation, 171–72
    conservation, 159
    landowners, a nation of, 70
    ownership/use as essential ingredients of suburbanization, 8–11
    policy institutions, 74
    regionalism, 213–14, 220–21
    transit, mass, 209–10
    trusts, 171
Land Conservation and Development Commission (LCDC), 217
Landscape, the vanishing:
    American Farmland Trust, 75
    character of rural communities, radically altering, 77
    farmland, 88–89
    National Resources Defense Council, 75
    open space next door, 85–88
        see also Open-space preservation
    rate at which nation's land supply is being consumed, 83–85
    summary, chapter, 91
Las Vegas (NV), 139
Leapfrog development, 4–5
Learning from Las Vegas (Venturi & Brown), 5
Le Corbusier, 41, 43
Lee, M. David, 137
Legislation:
    Clean Air Act of 1970, 52
    Clean Air Act of 1990, 50
    Clean Water Act of 1972, 52, 53, 115, 166
    Endangered Species Act of 1973, 52, 53
    Energy Policy Act of 1992, 50
    Fair Housing Act of 1968, 136
    Federal-Aid Highway Act of 1966, 49
    Federal Highway Act of 1962, 49
    Federal Highway Act of 1970, 50
    Federal Highway Act of 1973, 50
    Federal Roadway Acts of 1916/1921, 33
    G.I. Bill, 37
    Housing Act of 1937, 42
    Housing Act of 1949, 43
    Intermodal Surface Transportation Act (ISTEA) of 1991, 50, 51–52, 202, 214, 253, 254
    Interstate Highway Act of 1956, 35, 43
    National Environmental Policy Act (NEPA) of 1970, 50, 52
    National Historic Preservation Act of 1966, 55
    National Housing Act of 1934, 36
    National Mass Transportation Assistance Act of 1974, 50
    National Transportation Act of 1966, 55
    Surface Transportation Act of 1982, 50
    Transportation Equity Act for the 21st Century (TEA-21) of 1998, 50, 51–52, 214, 253, 254

Legislation (*continued*):
    Urban Mass Transit Act of 1964, 49, 51
    Urban Mass Transit Assistance Act of 1970, 50
Levittown (NY), 38, 41, 147, 149
Lexington (KY), 217
Liberal/liberal–center policy organizations, 62,
    74–75, 77, 157
Lincoln Institute of Land Policy, 239–40, 243, 246
Lincoln Tunnel, 101
"Little Boxes," 47
Living City, The (Wright), 30
Llewellyn Park (NJ), 27
Loan program, Veteran's Administration's, 37
Loans, Federal Housing Administration's, 134–36
Local public transportation initiatives, 101–2
Local trips, 11–12
Loft condominiums, rehabilitated, 57
Logan Airport, 164, 206
Lomax, Tom, 97
Long-distance travel, 12
Long Island Expressway, 146
Long Island (NY), 32–33, 38, 173
Long Island Pine Barrens, 162, 166, 169
Los Angeles (CA):
    aesthetics, 145
    first modern suburbs, 30
    immigration, 60
    metropolitan region, 19, 22
    older cities, resurgent, 60
    segregation, suburban diversity and, 137
    single-use zoning, 43
    streetcar suburbs, 28
    transit villages, 186
    transportation demand management, 99
Louisiana, 49
Low-density development, 5–7
Lowell (MA), 25, 53, 55, 195
LTV Steel Corporation, 191
Lucy, William H., 139, 223

Machine in the Garden, The (Marx), 144
"Machine Stops, The" (Forster), 245
Magic motorways, 33–34
Maine, 114, 168
Malaise, suburban, 251–52
Malden River, 191
Mall of America (MN), 39
Malls, shopping, xiii, 9, 38–39
Manufacturing, origins of sprawl and desertion of,
    39–40
Marx, Leo, 144
Maryland:
    aesthetics, 147
    anti-sprawl positions, 74
    future trends, 247, 250, 255
    garden cities, 180
    gentrification, 196
    growth management, 64, 155–56, 173, 225
    highways, protesting the, 48, 49
    infrastructure costs, 127, 131
    New Urbanism, 181
    open-space preservation, 169, 247
    population densities/growth, 198
    regionalism, 224–28, 255

    social divides and sprawl, 250
    traditional neighborhood developments, 182
    transfer of development rights, 169
    transit villages, 185
    water quality/pollution, 53
Maryland–National Capital Park and Planning Com-
    mission (M-NCPPC), 155–56
Massachusetts:
    brownfield sites, 191–93
    congestion pricing, 99
    drinking water, 117
    gentrification, 196
    growth management, 64
    habitat preservation, 91
    historic preservation, 55
    industrial revolution, 25
    land acquisition, 171–72
    open-space preservation, 164, 166, 170–72
    population densities/growth, 196–98
    railroad suburbs, 27
    revitalizing older downtowns/inner-ring sub-
        urbs, 195
    shopping malls/centers, 38
    streetcar suburbs, 28
    taxes, 76, 131, 170–71
    transit, mass, 201–2
    water quality/pollution, 53
    zoning, 17
    see also Boston (MA)
Massachusetts Institute of Technology (MIT), 246
Mass transit, *see* Railroads/rail transit systems; Transit,
    mass
Mayors, United States Conference of, 255
McDonald's, 40
McDowell, Caesar, 246
McKim, Meade, and White, 54
Medford (MA), 28
Metropolitan Atlanta Rapid Transit Authority
    (MARTA), 229–30
Metropolitan planning organizations (MPOs), 49,
    214
Metropolitan regions, 19–22
    see also Regionalism
*Metropolitics: A Regional Agenda for Community and
    Stability* (Orfield), 126, 214, 223
Miami (FL), 60
Michigan, see Detroit (MI)
Middle class, communities draining the cities of
    their, 41, 141–42, 196–97
Minneapolis/St. Paul, 187, 222–24
Minnesota, 38–39, 137
Minorities, *see* Race/ethnicity
Mississippi River, 53
Missouri, *see* St. Louis (MO)
Mitchell, William J., 13–14
Mobility, 70–71
Mobility Report, 97
Model T, 31–32
Modes, transportation, 11–12
Moe, Richard, 38, 189, 190
Monarch butterfly, 162
Montgomery County (MD), 64, 155, 156, 169, 185
Moore, Terry, 10, 93, 98, 99, 104–5, 128–29
Mortgages, home, 17, 59, 77, 130, 135–36

Moses, Robert, 32–33, 48, 232
Mountainview (CA), 193–94
Movie houses, suburban, 15
Mumford, Lewis, 22, 40, 41, 47–48, 71, 179–80, 212
Muschamp, Herbert, 56
Mystic Valley Development Commission (MVDC), 191, 195, 250

Nantucket (MA), 17, 197
Nassau County (NY), 30
National Academy of Sciences, 252
National Association of Home Builders (NAHB):
    compact communities, 249
    future trends, 246–47, 249
    growth management, 157–58
    landscape, the vanishing, 84
    pro-development groups, xv, 69, 75, 78, 79
    transit-oriented developments, 184
National Association of Industrial and Office Proper-
    ties (NAIOP), 75, 102, 157–58
National Association of Realtors (NAR), xv, 75, 161, 163, 252
National Brownfield Partnership, 190
National Center for Education Statistics, 63
National Geographic, 83, 146
National Park Service, 195
National Register of Historic Places, 55, 188
National Resources Defense Council (NRDC), 64
    defining sprawl, 4
    energy issues, population densities/growth and, 108
    farmland, 88
    growth management, 157, 158
    landscape, vanishing, 75, 83–84
    literature produced by, 74
National Resources Inventory, *84*
National Trust for Historic Preservation, 4, 64, 74, 190
National Wildlife Federation, 75
Native Americans, 9
Nature Conservancy, 171–72
Nevada, 139
New Bedford (MA), 196
Newburyport (MA), 188
New Deal, The, 232
New England:
    energy issues, 107
    forestland, 91
    open space preservation, 163, 164
    revitalizing older downtowns/inner-ring sub-
        urbs, 188
    transit, mass, 208
    see also individual states
*New Geography, The: How the Digital Revolution Is
    Reshaping the American Landscape* (Kotkin), 61, 243, 246
New Hampshire, 173, 194
New Jersey:
    aesthetics, 149, 150
    anti-sprawl positions, 74
    congestion pricing, 99
    first modern suburbs, 29–30
    future trends, 253, 255
    garden cities, 180
    growth management, 64
    infrastructure costs, 123, 127, 131

manufacturing, origins of sprawl and desertion
    of, 40
open-space preservation, 169
Pine Barrens, 169
population densities/growth, 196
railroad suburbs, 27
regionalism, 255
transfer of development rights, 169
transit, mass, 253
transit villages, 186
*New Jersey State Development and Redevelopment Plan,
    2001,* 126
Newman, Peter, 107, 108–9
New Mexico, 173
New Orleans (LA), 49
New Republic, 72
New Urbanism, 16, 64–65, 180–84
New Urbanism (Katz), 181
New York:
    aesthetics, 145, 149
    brownfield sites, 190–91
    condominiums, 59
    Consolidated Metropolitan Statistical Area, 18
    contextualism in architectural design, 56
    drinking water, 117
    Earth Liberation Front, xv
    elastic cities, 146
    energy issues, population densities/growth and, 109
    expansion and annexation, 211, 212
    first modern suburbs, 30
    future trends, 249, 253, 255
    gentrification, 196
    growth management, 155, 173
    high-occupancy vehicle lanes, 101
    highways, protesting the, 48
    historic preservation, 54–55
    housing, mass-produced, 38
    immigration, 60, 61
    industrial revolution, 25
    land, high cost of, 10
    land acquisition, 171
    metropolitan areas, 22
    older cities, resurgent, 57–61
    open-space preservation, 164, 166, 167, 169, 171, 176
    parkways, 32–33
    population densities/growth, 196, 198
    railroad suburbs, 27, 183
    regionalism, 231–34, 255
    renewal, urban, 44, 45
    revitalizing older downtowns/inner-ring sub-
        urbs, 187
    segregation, 79
    segregation, suburban diversity and, 137
    shock of the new, 44
    shopping malls/centers, 38
    single-use zoning, 43
    social divides created by sprawl, cars/mortgages
        and, 135
    streetcar suburbs, 28
    technology and cyberspace, 243
    transfer of development rights, 169
    transit, mass, 202, 208, 253

New York (*continued*):
  transit villages, 184
  water quality/pollution, 53, 162
  Worlds Fair in 1939, 33
  zoning, 26
New York Times:
  aesthetics, 146–47
  contextualism in architectural design, 56
  defining sprawl, 19
  growing cities and expanding boundaries, 139
  historic preservation, 54
  landscape, the vanishing, 83
  older cities, resurgent, 61
  quality of life issue, sprawl as a, 80
  regionalism and land value, 221
  technology and cyberspace, 239
  telecommuting, 241
New Zealand, 70
Next American Metropolis, The (Calthorpe), 181, 183
1970's and energy crisis, 63–64
Nonpoint source pollution, 115–17
Northbrook (IL), 202
Northeastern University, 61
Northeast Midwest Institute, 158
Northern and Southern State Parkway systems,
  32–33
North/South Rail Link, 207
Norwalk (CT), 196, 201
Norwalk River, 53
Norway, 70

Oakbrook (IL), 40
Oak Grove (OR), 197, 198
Oak Park (IL), 27
O-Bahn, 207–8
Office development, 132
Ohio:
  aesthetics, 149–50
  employment expansion, 137
  future trends, 249
  growing cities and expanding boundaries, 139
  older cities, resurgent, 57–58
  open-space preservation, 164
  population densities/growth, 212
  revitalizing older downtowns/inner-ring sub-
    urbs, 188
  streetcar suburbs, 28
  transit villages, 184
  water quality/pollution, 53
Oil, 76, 78, 105–8, 252
  see also Energy issues
Olmsted, Frederick L., 27, 164
1000 Friends of Oregon, 184
On-line shopping, 242–43
  see also technology and cyberspace *under* Future
    trends
Open space preservation:
  community needs, 162–63
  conservation programs, 164–66
    see also regulatory controls *below*
  downside of, 175–76
  economic benefits, 163–64
  environmental considerations, 161–62
  future trends, 247–48, 254

  growth boundaries, 172–75
  lack of public open space, 7–8
  national priority, becoming a, 53–54
  next door, people worried about open space,
    85–88
  regulatory controls
    agricultural zoning, 168–69
    clustering, 167–68
    downzoning, 166–67
    environmental restrictions, 169–70
    federal/state/local, 166
    land acquisition, 171–72
    tax incentives, 170–71
    transfer of development rights, 169
    zoning, 168–69
  summary, chapter, 176–77
  see also Development patterns; Growth manage-
    ment; Reactions and countertrends
Opinion polls, xiv–xv, 79–80, 85, 163
Oregon:
  anti-sprawl positions, 74
  farmland, 169
  growth management, 64, 217–20
  Measure 7, xv
  open space preservation, 164, 169, 170–71
  taxes, 170–71
  see also Portland (OR)
Orfield, Myron, 126, 132, 214, 254
Organization for Economic Cooperation and Development (OECD), 105
Organization Man, The (Whyte), 47, 150
Origins of sprawl:
  core cities and suburbanization
    expressways, urban, 43
    middle class, draining the cities of the, 41
    moving the suburbs downtown, 43–44
    renewal, urban, 41–45
    shock of the new, 44–45
    vision for America's cities, a new, 42
    Voisin Plan for renewal of Paris, 42
  first modern suburbs
    Broadacre City, 30–31
    motor age, suburbs for the, 29–30
    railroads, 27
    streetcar suburbs, 28–29
    wood construction, revolution in, 27–28
  industrial cities, 25–26
  overview, 25
  postwar suburban expansion
    final pattern, the, 41
    financing the suburban boom, 36–37
    housing, mass-produced, 37–38
    manufacturing moves out, 39–40
    redlining the cities, 37
    shopping centers, 38–39
  reforms, 26–27
  roads and automobiles
    defense, development of interstate highways
      system and national, 35
    highways, national, 33
    Interstate Highway Act of 1956, 35
    magic motorways, 33–34
    overview, 31
    parkways, 32–33

Road Gang, 34
rutted roads, 32
triumph of the automobile, 35–36
trucks, 34
summary, chapter, 45–46
O'Toole, Randal, 78, 79, 95–96, 124–25, 143, 197, 245
Owls, 162

Pacific Research Institute for Public Policy, 157
Pacific Stock Exchange, 239
Panhandle-Golden Gate Freeway, 48
Paris, 42, 43
Paris RER system, 207
Parking areas, 13
Parking fees and managing roadway demand, 99, 105
Parks, 163
Parkways, 32–33
  see also Highways
Particulate matter, 121
Pastoral image, 144
Peck, Sheila, 90–91
Pedestrian projects, 51
Peiser, Richard, 124
Penn Station, 54–55
Pennsylvania:
  air pollution, 40
  brownfield sites, 191
  historic preservation, 55
  older cities, resurgent, 57
  open-space preservation, 163, 164, 175
  population densities/growth, 140
  shopping malls/centers, 38
  see also Philadelphia (PA)
Petaluma (CA), 155
Petroconsultants, 107
Petroleum, 76, 78, 105–8, 252
Philadelphia (PA):
  elastic cities, 146
  expansion and annexation, 211
  first modern suburbs, 30
  growing cities and expanding boundaries, 139
  historic preservation, 55
  manufacturing, origins of sprawl and desertion of, 39
  metropolitan areas, 22
  population densities/growth, 61–62, 140
  railroad suburbs, 27
Phillips, David L., 139, 223
Pinelands Development Credit Bank, 169
Pittsburgh (PA), 40, 55, 57, 140, 191
Planning, 130
index1:Planning for Biodiversity (Peck), 90
Plater-Zyberk, Elizabeth, 181
Politics and smart growth, 159
Pollan, Michael, 19
Polls, public opinion, xiv–xv, 79–80, 85, 163
Pollution, see Air pollution; Water quality/pollution
Population densities/growth:
  air pollution, 78, 114
  center city vs. suburbs, 18–19, 41
  debate, outlining the sprawl, 79
  development patterns, 196–99
  elastic cities, 139–41, 211–12

energy issues, 108–10
farmland, 88
floor area ratio, 5–7
future trends, 249
growing cities and expanding boundaries, 139–41
landscape, the vanishing, 84
metro areas, top ten, 116
older cities, resurgent, 57, 61–62
open space next door, 85
Portland (OR), 220
push factors, 196
traffic, 93, 94
urban growth boundaries, 220
zoning, 15–16
Portland (OR):
  development patterns, 197
  future trends, 253
  growth management, 156
  highways, protesting the, 48–49
  historic preservation, 55
  open-space preservation, 172
  regionalism
    evolving process, 221–22
    housing costs, 218–20
    land use and transportation, coordination of, 213
    Metro, 217
    overview, 215, 217
    results, 220–21
    transit, mass, 213–14, 220
  shock of the new, 45
  transit, mass, 253
  transit-oriented developments, 183–84
  transit villages, 186
Ports, 12
Portsmouth (NH), 194
Post Properties, 249
Potomac River, 53
Poverty, 77, 132–33, 136, 138–39
Power Broker, The (Caro), 32, 48
Prairie dog, black-tailed, 162
President's Council on Sustainable Development, 81
Pricing measures and managing roadway demand, 98–99
  see also Economic issues/costs
Prince George County (MD), 155, 250
Priority funding areas (PFAs), 225
Pro-development groups, xv, 69, 75, 77–79
  see also Heritage Foundation; Reason Public Policy Institute
Progressive Policy Institute, 240
Property taxes, 76
Providence (RI), 53, 55, 57, 196
Public health, affects of sprawl on, 77, 118–22
Public housing, 136
Public open space, lack of, 7–8
Public transportation, see Railroads/rail transit systems; Transit, mass
Published works on burgeoning suburban sprawl, 64
Purdum, Todd, 80
Push factors, 79, 141–42, 196–97
Putnam, Robert, 77, 150–51, 244
Putnam Investments, 241

Quality of life issue, sprawl as a, 80
Queens (NY), 190–91

Race/ethnicity:
    elastic cities, 212
    future trends, 250
    immigration, 61–63
    minorities moving to suburbs, increasing number
        of, 79
    segregation, suburban diversity and, 137–38
    social divides and sprawl, 79, 133–39
Racial Change in the Nation's Largest Cities, 62
Radburn (NJ), 29–30, 180
Radio, 15
Railroads/rail transit systems:
    Brockton Area Transit Authority, 201–2
    first modern suburbs, 27, 183
    long-distance trips no longer made using, 12
    passengers moved per hour, 104
    roadway network dwarfing, 12–13
    transit villages, 184–86
Ramapo (NY), 155
Reactions and countertrends:
    City Beautiful Movement, 26
    community attempts at controlling sprawl, 64
    Dickens, Charles, 26
    Eden, quest for a new, 27
    environment, cleaning up the, 52–54
    growth management, 64
    highways, protesting the
        accomplishments, antihighway, 50–52
        Cross-Bronx Expressway, 48
        environmental impact statements, mass transit
            and, 49–50
        fighting for survival, 48–49
        Intermodal Surface Transportation Act of
            1991 and Transportation Equity Act of
            1998, 50
        results, getting, 49
    historic preservation movement, 54–56
    Mumford, Lewis, 47–48
    New Urbanism, 64–65
    older cities, resurgent
        analyzing the trends, 61–63
        homeownership options, changing, 59–60
        immigration, 60–61
        overview, 57
        resources and improving environments,
            unique, 58–59
        revitalization movements, 57–58
    published works on burgeoning suburban sprawl, 64
    real estate and building industry organizations,
        65
    recessions, national, 63–65
    Riis, Jacob, 26
    smart growth, xiv–xv
    summary, chapter, 65–66
    zoning, early, 26
    see also Debate, outlining the sprawl
Reagan, Ronald, 50
Real estate industry/markets, 9–10, 65, 75
Real Estate Research Corporation, 123
Reason Foundation, xiv
Reason Public Policy Institute (RPPI), xv

air pollution, 78, 114, 115
    defining sprawl, 4
    energy issues, 78
    free market solutions, 74
    landscape, the vanishing, 84
    open space next door, 85
    population densities/growth, 85
    push factors, 79
    traffic, 93
Recessions, national, xv, 63–65
Recording media, 15
Redlining the cities, 37
Regional City, The (Fulton & Calthorpe), 124, 180, 181
Regionalism:
    case studies
        Atlanta (GA), 228–31
        Maryland, 224–28
        Minneapolis/St. Paul, 222–24
        New York, 231–34
        overview, 215
        Portland (OR), 215, 217–22
        sample regional programs, 216
    contemporary, 212–13
    expansion and annexation, 211–12
    future trends, 255
    growth control, 213–14, 225
    land use, coordination of transportation and, 213–14
    opposition to, 160
    recurrent, 212
    summary, chapter, 234–35
    tax base sharing, 214–15
    transit, mass, 202
Regional Planning Association of America (RPAA), 212
Registration fees and managing roadway demand, 99
Regulations/standards governing development in
    communities, 15–17
    see also regulatory controls *under* Open space
        preservation; Zoning
"Relationship of Cities and Suburbs, The" (Utt), 139
Renewal, urban, 41–45
    see also older cities, resurgent *under* Reactions
        and countertrends; revitalizing older down-
        towns/inner-ring suburbs *under* Develop-
        ment patterns
Resources and improving environments, unique,
    58–59
Reston (VA), 180
Retsinas, Nicholas, xv–xvi
Reversible lanes and increasing roadway capacity, 97
Revitalization movements, 57–58, 126, 255
    see also older cities, resurgent *under* Reactions
        and countertrends; revitalizing older down-
        towns/inner-ring suburbs *under* Develop-
        ment patterns
Reynolds, Malvina, 47
Rhode Island, 53, 55, 57, 196
Ribbon patterns of new construction, 28–29
Richardson, Harry, 78, 124, 125, 128
Riis, Jacob, 26
Rio Grande, The, 117
Riparian systems, 161
    see also Wetlands
Riverside (IL), 27
Road Gang, 34

Roads, Federal Bureau of, 33
Roadways, *see* Highways; roads and automobiles *under* Origins of sprawl; Traffic
Rockville (MD), 196
Roosevelt, Franklin D., 36
Runoff pollution, 115
Rural by Design (Arendt), 168
Rural Legacy Program, 224–25, 247
Rush hour, 99–100, 103
Rusk, David, 211–12
Russell, James S., 13
Russia, 41
Rutgers University, 149
Rutted roads, 32

Salem (OR), 164
Salt Lake City (UT), 124
San Antonio (TX), 53, 212
San Diego (CA), 186, 202–4
San Francisco (CA):
    condominiums, 59
    future trends, 249
    gentrification, 196
    highways, protesting the, 48, 49
    housing, 59, 220
    immigration, 60
    metropolitan regions, 19, 22
    older cities, resurgent, 57–60
    population densities/growth, 198
    shock of the new, 45
    streetcar suburbs, 28
    transit, mass, 202
    transit villages, 185, 186
San Jose (CA), 137
Sargent, Francis, 49
S-Bahn systems, 207
Scale, economies of, 14
School desegregation, 136
Schools, urban, 62–63
Scientific American, 107
Sears, 38
Seaside (FL), 147, 180, 181
Seattle-Tacoma metropolitan area, 22
Seattle (WA), 164, 187
Seeger, Pete, 47
Segregation, 79, 132–33, 136–38, 212
Self-interest fueling anti-sprawl debate, 71–72
Service industry/sector, 14, 39, 59
Settlement patterns and sprawl development, 136–37
Shaker Heights (OH), 28
Shaw, Jane, 89–91
Shopping, on-line, 242–43
Shopping malls/centers, xiii, 9, 38–39
Shuttle Bug Reverse Commute Project, 202
Sierra Club, 60, 64, 74, 78, 157–58
Silicon Valley (CA), 40
Silver Spring (MD), 198
Single-family detached housing, 18, 63–64
Single-occupant vehicles (SOVs), 99
Single-use development/zoning, 7, 43
Small-town America, 144–45
Smart cars, 101
Smart growth, xiv–xv, 155–60, 255
Smart Growth America, 93, 161

Smart roads, 101–2
Smokestack industries, 59
Social capital, 150
Social divides and sprawl:
    desertion, a persistent pattern of, 142
    future trends, 250, 253–54
    gentrification, 195–96
    growing cities and expanding boundaries, 139–41
    liberal policy institutions, 77
    mortgages, cars and, 133–36
    poverty, 132–33, 138–39
    pro-development groups, 77
    public housing, 136
    push factors, 141–42
    school desegregation, 136
    segregation, 132–33, 137–38
    settlement patterns, the resulting, 136–37
    streetcar exodus, 133
    summary, chapter, 142
    technology and cyberspace, 246
Social interaction, see Community, suburbanization and the loss of
Somerville (MA), 191, 195
South Berwick (ME), 168
South Carolina, 57
South Norwalk (CT), 188–89
Species extinctions and global warming, 114
Sprawl, what is it:
    alternatives to the pattern of suburbanization, 153
        see also individual subject headings
    characteristics and indicators of sprawl
        accessibility, poor, 7
        commercial strip development, 5
        leapfrog development, 4–5
        overview, 3–4
        population densities/growth, 5–7
        public open space, lack of, 7–8
        sample characterizations, 4
        single-use development, 7
    defining sprawl, xiii, 3, 4, 8, 19
    essential ingredients of suburbanization
        land ownership and use, 8–11
        regulations and standards, 15–17
        telecommunications technology, 13–15
        transportation patterns, 11–13
    fighting sprawl, see Debate, outlining the sprawl; Reactions and countertrends; Growth management; Open space preservation; Development patterns
    limitless city, the
        defining suburbs, 17–19
        metropolitan, beyond, 20–22
        metropolitan nation, 19–20
        suburbs, beyond, 18–19
    negative perception of sprawl, xv
    overview, xiii–xiv, 1
    positive things suburbanization has brought nation, 252
    summary, chapter, 22–23
    see also Origins of sprawl; individual subject headings
St. Louis (MO):
    Federal Housing Administration, 135
    future trends, 249

St. Louis (MO) (*continued*):
    growing cities and expanding boundaries, 139
    population densities/growth, 84, 196
    transit, mass, 208
Staley, Samuel, 77, 93, 99, 141
Stanford (CT), 44
State governments and anti-sprawl positions, 74
State University of New York, 137–38
Stern, Robert, 146
Storm runoff, 161
Streetcar suburbs, 28–29, 133
Streetcar Suburbs (Warner, Jr.), 29
Strip development, commercial, 5, 131–32
Subsidies, hidden, 126–30
Suburbanization, 17–19
    see also Sprawl, what is it; *individual subject head-ings*
Suburban Nation (Duany, Plater-Zyberk & Speck),
    16, 147, 181, 182
Sugar maple, 114
Sulfur compounds, 121
Surface Transportation Policy Project (STPP), 17, 127
Sustainability, 80–81
Sustainability and Cities (Newman & Kenworthy),
    107, 108–9
Switzerland, 70
Syracuse (NY), 196

Taxes:
    commercial tax revenues, chasing, 131–32
    gasoline, 50, 98
    growth patterns, inefficient, 131
    Maryland, 226
    Minneapolis/St. Paul, 223
    mortgage, home, 130
    new tax dollars, continuous chase for, 76
    older cities, resurgent, 59, 60
    open space preservation, 164, 170–71
    regionalism, 214–15, 223, 226
    revolts caused by residential property, 75
    roadway demand, managing, 98
Technological Reshaping of Metropolitan America, The, 240
Technology:
    automobiles, 110
    housing, 27–28, 37
    telecommunications, 13–15
    traffic, 101–2
    transit, mass, 207–8
    see also technology and cyberspace *under* Future
        trends
Telecom City project, 191–93, 195
Telecommunications technology, 13–15
Telecommuting, 15, 240–42
Telephones, 14–15, 239–40
Television, 15
Tennessee, 189, 190, 193, 194
Texaco, 40
Texas:
    future trends, 249
    segregation, suburban diversity and, 137
    shopping malls/centers, 38
    single-use zoning, 43
    water demand, 117
    water quality/pollution, 53
    see also Houston (TX)
Texas Transportation Institute (TTI), 76, 93
Textile industry, 39
Thoreau Institute, 77
Thorsnes, Paul, 10, 93, 98, 99, 104–5, 128–29
Time, 146
Time/CNN polls, xiv, 79, 85
Toll roads, 99
Toluene, 121
Toward New Towns for America (Stein), 180
Toxic air pollutants, 121
Traditional neighborhood developments (TNDs),
    181–82
Traffic:
    capacity, creating more roadway, 95–97
    congestion, 75, 99–100, 105, 208–9, 248
    demand, managing
        congestion pricing, 99–100
        employer programs, 99
        high-occupancy vehicle lanes, 100–101
        overview, 97–99
        pricing measures, 98–99
    do-nothing approach, 102–4
    future trends, 248
    induced demand, 93
    injuries and fatalities, 118–20
    oil consumption, 75
    pro-development groups, 77–78
    suburban or urban problem, 93–94
    surveys ranking traffic as a major problem, 93
    technology, high, 101–2
    transit solutions, 104–5
    trends, continuing, 94–95
Transferable development rights (TDRs), 164, 169
Transit, mass:
    anti-sprawl groups, 74
    Atlanta (GA), 208, 228–31
    barriers to, 208–9
    energy efficiency of cars and, 110–11
    environmental impact statements, 49–50
    funding for, 127, 130
    future trends, 253
    growth management, 159
    importance of, 201
    Intermodal Surface Transportation Act (ISTEA)
        of 1991, 50, 51–52
    land-use connection, 209–10
    local initiatives, 101–2
    metropolitan initiatives
        Boston (MA), 204–7
        North/South Rail Link, 207
        overview, 202–3
        San Diego, 203–4
        Urban Ring, The, 206
    National Mass Transportation Assistance Act of
        1974, 50
    Portland (OR), 220
    regionalism, 213–14, 220
    summary, chapter, 210
    Surface Transportation Act of 1982, 50
    technology, innovative, 207–8
    as a traffic solution, 104–5
    transit-oriented developments, 182–84
    Transportation Equity Act for the 21st Century

of 1998, 50, 51–52
Urban Mass Transit Act of 1964, 51
Urban Mass Transit Assistance Act of 1970, 50
see also Railroads/rail transit systems
Transit-oriented developments (TODs), 182–84, 204, 255
Transit villages, 184–86, 255
Transit Villages in the 21st Century (Bernick & Cervero), 184
Transportation, U.S. Department of (DOT), 12, 15, 55, 105, 184
Transportation demand management (TDM), 99
Transportation improvement program (TIP), 49
Transportation/Land Use Connection, The (Thorsnes & Moore), 10, 93, 98, 128–29
Transportation patterns, 11–13
see also Automobiles; Highways; Railroads/rail transit systems; Traffic; Transit, mass
Trucks/trucking:
    air pollution, 114, 121
    defense, development of interstate highways system and national, 35
    freight shipping, 12
    industry moving out of central cities, 39
    injuries and fatalities, 119
    origins of sprawl, 34
    toxic air pollutants, 121
Trust for Public Land, 171–72
Tunneling and increasing roadway capacity, 96

United Kingdom, 70, 180
United Nations, 80, 252
University of Pittsburgh Medical Center, 40
University of Virginia, 139
Urban growth boundaries (UGBs), 172–76, 213, 217–20
Urban Land Institute, 50, 74, 84, 157
Urban renewal, *see* Cities; older cities, resurgent *under* Reactions and countertrends; revitalizing older downtowns/inner-ring suburbs *under* Development patterns
Urban Ring, The, 206
Urban sprawl, *see* Sprawl, what is it; *individual subject headings*
U.S. News and World Report, 126, 129
Utah, 124
Utt, Ronald, 79, 139

Vancouver (British Columbia), 49, 184
Vanishing Automobile and Other Urban Myths, The (O'Toole), 95, 104, 124–25, 197, 245
Vaux, Calvert, 27
VCRs, 15
Vehicle miles/hours traveled, 7, 93–95, 114
Vested interests and suburbanization, 251
Veteran's Administration (VA), 37
Village ideal, the, 144–45
Village main streets and revitalizing older downtowns/inner-ring suburbs, 189–90
Virginia:
    garden cities, 180
    open space preservation, 168
    population densities/growth, 197, 198
    shopping malls/centers, 38
    transit villages, 185
Voisin Plan for renewal of Paris, 42, 43

Volatile organic compounds (VOCs), 114
Voting rights and land ownership, 9

Walden (Thoreau), 27
Walking, 25
Wall Street Journal, xv
Warming, global, 113–14
Warner, Sam B., Jr., 29
Washington, 22, 162, 164, 187
Washington-Baltimore Consolidated Metropolitan Statistical Area (CMSA), 224–25
Water quality/pollution:
    Centers for Disease Control, 76
    Clean Water Act of 1972, 53
    drinking water, 117–18
    future trends, 253
    habitat preservation, 161, 162
    leading sources of water quality impairment, 117
    nonpoint source pollution, 115–17
    overview, 115
    regulatory controls, 166
    suburban contribution, 116–17
    summary, chapter, 121
Watersheds, 90
Watertown (MA), 28
Water transportation, 12–13
Webster's New World Dictionary, 18
Wetlands:
    Centers for Disease Control, 76
    habitat, animal, 90
    legislation protecting, 88, 162
    regulatory controls, 169–70
    storm runoff, 161
Whites, non-Hispanic, 61–63, 77, 133, 134, 250
Whyte, William, 47, 149, 150
Wilkie, Carter, 38, 189, 190
Willamette River, 53
Williamsburg (VA), 197
Wisconsin, 189–90
Wood construction, revolution in, 27–28
Woonasquatucket River, 53
Worcester (MA), 164
World Columbian Exposition in Chicago (1893), 26
World War I/II, 35
Wright, Frank L., 30–31, 41, 89

Xerox, 40
Xylene, 121

Yaro, Robert, 19, 61
Yellowstone National Park, 107
Young urban professionals, 61, 63
Zoning:
    agricultural, 168–69
    downzoning, 166–67
    early, 26
    horizontal, 16–17
    Houston (TX), 17
    open space preservation, 166–69
    population density and land use regulated by, 15–16
    Portland (OR), 217
    single-use, 43
    Voisin Plan for renewal of Paris, 43